Edited by two leading analysts of postcommunist politics, this book brings together distinguished specialists on the former Soviet republics of Central Asia and the Caucasus. Chapters on Armenia, Azerbaijan, Georgia, Kazakstan, Kyrgyzstan, Tajikistan, Turkmenistan, and Uzbekistan provide a systematic analysis of elite politics, factionalism, party and interest group formation, and social and ethnic groupings. Karen Dawisha and Bruce Parrott provide theoretical and comparative chapters on postcommunist political development. This book will provide students and scholars with detailed analysis by leading authorities, plus the latest research data on recent political trends in each country.

Democratization and Authoritarianism in
Postcommunist Societies: 4

*Conflict, cleavage, and change in
Central Asia and the Caucasus*

Editors

Karen Dawisha
University of Maryland at College Park

Bruce Parrott
*The Paul H. Nitze School of Advanced International Studies
The Johns Hopkins University*

These four volumes, edited by two well-known analysts of
postcommunist politics, bring together distinguished specialists to
provide specially commissioned up-to-date essays on the
postcommunist countries of Eastern Europe and the former Soviet
Union. Each contributor analyzes both progress made toward
democratization, and the underlying social, economic, and cultural
factors that have shaped political change. All chapters contain
information on the emergence of political parties, elections,
institutional reform, and socioeconomic trends. Each volume also
contains chapters by the editors juxtaposing the overall trends in
these countries with comparable transitions and processes of
democratization elsewhere.

1. *The consolidation of democracy in East–Central Europe*
2. *Politics, power, and the struggle for democracy in South-East
   Europe*
3. *Democratic changes and authoritarian reactions in Russia,
   Ukraine, Belarus, and Moldova*
4. *Conflict, cleavage, and change in Central Asia and the
   Caucasus*

Conflict, cleavage, and change in Central Asia and the Caucasus

edited by

Karen Dawisha

University of Maryland at College Park

and

Bruce Parrott

The Paul H. Nitze School of Advanced International Studies
The Johns Hopkins University

CAMBRIDGE
UNIVERSITY PRESS

PUBLISHED BY THE PRESS SYNDICATE OF THE UNIVERSITY OF CAMBRIDGE
The Pitt Building, Trumpington Street, Cambridge CB2 1RP, United Kingdom

CAMBRIDGE UNIVERSITY PRESS
The Edinburgh Building, Cambridge, CB2 2RU, United Kingdom
40 West 20th Street, New York, NY 10011-4211, USA
10 Stamford Road, Oakleigh, Melbourne 3166, Australia

First published 1997

Printed in the United Kingdom by Bell & Bain Ltd, Glasgow

Typeset in 10/12 pt, CG Times

A catalogue record for this book is available from the British Library

Library of Congress Cataloguing in Publication data

ISBN 0 521 59246 1 hardback
ISBN 0 521 59731 5 paperback

FR

To Adeed, Nadia and Emile,
with love
K.D.

To Lydia,
who loves horses and books
B.P.

Contents

Tables

Contributors

AUDREY L. ALTSTADT is Associate Professor of History at the University of Massachusetts-Amherst. She is the author of *The Azerbaijani Turks: Power and Identity under Russian Rule* (1992), and more than two dozen articles on Azerbaijan and Central Asia published in edited volumes and in such journals as *Studies in Comparative Communism, Central Asian Survey* (Oxford, London), *Yeni Forum* (Ankara), and others. She has lectured in Tokyo as a guest of the Foreign Ministry of Japan and Tokyo University and in Baku as a guest of the Azerbaijan Ministry of Culture. Professor Altstadt received her doctorate in history from the University of Chicago. She conducted research on the history and culture of Azerbaijan during sixteen months in Baku as an IREX exchange fellow during the 1980s.

MURIEL ATKIN is Associate Professor of History at George Washington University. She is the author of *The Subtlest Battle: Islam in Soviet Tajikistan* (1989), and *Russia and Iran, 1780-1828* (1980), as well as numerous articles on contemporary Tajikistan. She received her Ph.D. in history from Yale University.

KAREN DAWISHA is Professor of Government and Director of the Center for the Study of Postcommunist Societies at the University of Maryland at College Park. She graduated with degrees in Russian and politics from the University of Lancaster in England and received her Ph.D. from the London School of Economics. She has served as an advisor to the British House of Commons Foreign Affairs Committee and was a member of the policy planning staff of the US State Department. Her publications include *Russia and the New States of Eurasia: The Politics of Upheaval* (with Bruce Parrott, 1994), *Eastern Europe, Gorbachev and Reform: The Great Challenge* (1989, 2d ed., 1990), *The Kremlin and the Prague Spring* (1984), *The Soviet Union in the Middle East: Politics and Perspectives* (1982), *Soviet-East European*

Dilemmas: Coercion, Competition, and Consent (1981), and *Soviet Foreign Policy Toward Egypt* (1979).

NORA DUDWICK is Research Associate at the Institute for European, Russian and Eurasian Studies, George Washington University and a consulting cultural anthropologist for the World Bank. Her recent publications include "The Cultural Construction of Political Violence in Armenia and Azerbaijan," *Problems of Post-Communism*, "Armenian-Azerbaijani Relations and Karabagh: History, Memory, and Politics," *Armenian Review*, "Out of the Kitchen, Into the Cross-fire," in *Post-Soviet Women: From Central Asia to the Baltic*, (1997), "Nagorno-Karabagh and the Politics of Sovereignty," in *Transcaucasia, Nationalism and Social Change: Essays on the History of Armenia, Azerbaijan and Georgia* (1996), and "Independent Armenia: Paradise Lost?" in *New Politics, New States: Building the Post-Soviet Nations* (1996). She is currently completing a manuscript on the changing discourse of memory and identity in Armenia between 1988 and 1991. She received her Ph.D. in anthropology from the University of Pennsylvania.

WILLIAM FIERMAN is Associate Professor in the Department of Central Eurasian Studies and Director-Designate of the Inner Asian and Uralic National Resource Center at Indiana University. His publications include "Policy Toward Islam in Uzbekistan in the Gorbachev Era," *Nationalities Papers* (Spring 1994), *Language Planning and National Development: The Uzbek Experience* (1991), and *Soviet Central Asia: The Failed Transformation* (1991). He received his Ph.D. from Harvard University.

EUGENE HUSKEY is Professor of Political Science and Director of Russian Studies at Stetson University in Florida. He has written extensively on Soviet and post-Soviet law, Russian executive politics in transition, and the politics of national identity and state formation in Kyrgyzstan. Among his works on Kyrgyzstan are studies of elections, language policy, economic reform, and ethnic conflict. His publications include *Russian Lawyers and the Soviet State* (Princeton, 1986 and Russian edition, Russian Academy of Science, 1992), *Executive Power and Soviet Politics* (M. E. Sharpe, 1992), and over twenty articles or book chapters. He is currently completing a book on the Russian presidency. He received his Ph.D. from the London School of Economics.

MICHAEL OCHS has been a professional staff advisor on the Commission on Security and Cooperation in Europe, US Congress, since 1987. He observed Turkmenistan's 1991 referendum on independence, and its 1994 parliamentary election, and again traveled to Ashgabat in December 1995. From September to November 1995, he was OSCE co-cordinator of the OSCE/UN Joint Electoral Observation Mission for Azerbaijan's parliamentary election. He received his Ph.D. in Russian history from Harvard University.

MARTHA BRILL OLCOTT is Professor of Political Science at Colgate University and a senior associate at the Carnegie Endowment for International Peace. She is the author of *The New States of Central Asia* (1996) and *The Kazakhs* (2d ed., 1995). She received her Ph.D. from the University of Chicago.

BRUCE PARROTT is Professor and Director of Russian Area and East European Studies at the Paul H. Nitze School of Advanced International Studies of The Johns Hopkins University. He is author of *Russia and the New States of Eurasia: The Politics of Upheaval* (with Karen Dawisha, 1994), *The Soviet Union and Ballistic Missile Defense* (1987), and *Politics and Technology in the Soviet Union* (1983); and editor of *The End of Empire? The Transformation of the USSR in Comparative Perspective* (with Karen Dawisha, 1996), *State-Building and Military Power in Russia and the New States of Eurasia* (1995), *The Dynamics of Soviet Defense Policy* (1990), and *Trade, Technology, and Soviet–American Relations* (1985). He received his Ph.D. in political science from Columbia University.

DARRELL SLIDER is Professor of International Studies at the University of South Florida in Tampa. He is author of *The Politics of Transition: Shaping a Post-Soviet Future* (with Stephen White and Graeme Gill, 1993). His publications on Georgia include "Georgia," in *Armenia, Azerbaijan, and Georgia: Country Studies* (1995), "The Politics of Georgia's Independence," *Problems of Communism*, November/December 1991, and "Crisis and Response in Soviet Nationality Policy: The Case of Abkhazia," *Central Asian Survey* 4, no. 4 (1985). He received his Ph.D. in political science from Yale University.

Preface

This study of democratization in Central Asia and the Caucasus is one of four books produced by the Project on Democratization and Political Participation in Postcommunist Societies. The project has been sponsored jointly by the School of Advanced International Studies of The Johns Hopkins University and the University of Maryland at College Park. It draws on the talents of scholars from a wide array of other universities and research institutions.

As codirectors of the project, we are grateful for material support furnished by two organizations. Principal funding for the project has been provided by the United States Department of State as part of its external research program. In addition, the intellectual planning of the project was aided at a crucial juncture by a grant from the Joint Committee on Eastern Europe of the American Council of Learned Societies. However, none of the views or conclusions contained in the book should be interpreted as representing the official opinion or policy of the Department of State or of the Joint Committee.

The three other volumes in the series deal with the countries of East-Central Europe, the countries of South-East Europe, and Russia, Ukraine, Belarus, and Moldova. Any student of contemporary international affairs knows that the delineation of "Europe" and its constituent regions frequently generates intellectual controversy about which countries belong to Europe or to "the West." We adopted our quadripartite grouping of countries to facilitate the management of a large research project and to produce books that match the curricular structure of many college and university courses devoted to the countries of the postcommunist world. Neither the grouping nor the names were chosen with any intention of suggesting that some countries are necessarily more "advanced" or "backward" politically than others. Most of the regional groups exhibit considerable internal political diversity among the member countries, and the comparative judgments presented in the volumes are based on the findings of the individual country-studies, not on preconceptions about one or another region.

In the course of this project we have received assistance from many individuals and incurred many personal obligations. We wish to thank John Parker and Susan Nelson of the Department of State for proposing the general idea of the project to us, for making helpful suggestions about how it could be carried out, and for encouraging the project participants to draw whatever conclusions the evidence supports. We are grateful to Jason arker of the ACLS Joint Committee on Eastern Europe for his assistance. We also wish to thank several scholars who helped us sort out the basic issues in an initial planning workshop: Nancy Bermeo, Valerie Bunce, Ted Robert Gurr, Joan Nelson, and Robert Putnam. Herbert Kitschelt was likewise very helpful in this regard.

We are deeply indebted to the country-study writers for the high level of effort that they invested in writing their chapters, for their active participation in the project workshops, and for undertaking more extensive revisions than are customary in collective enterprises of this kind. We also are grateful to the four authors who served as coordinators of the workshops: Sharon Wolchik, Vladimir Tismaneanu, Ilya Prizel, and Muriel Atkin. We benefited from their advice during the organizational stage of the project, and we profited from the written comments that they made on the draft chapters presented at the project workshops.

We wish to express our special thanks to Griffin Hathaway, the Executive Director of the project, who performed a nearly endless series of administrative and intellectual tasks with exemplary efficiency; to Florence Rotz, staff person of the SAIS Russian Area and East European Studies program, who managed the production and revision of several versions of the chapters with admirable calmness and consummate skill; and to Steve Guenther, who helped organize the logistics of the workshops. Not least, we are grateful to Murray Feshbach for generously providing demographic data for a number of the country-studies.

Finally, we express our thanks to Michael Holdsworth of Cambridge University Press for his willingness to take on this large publishing project and see it through to the end. Bruce Parrott also thanks Gordon Livingston, without whose help he could not have completed his portion of the project.

K. D.
B. P.

1 Perspectives on postcommunist democratization

Bruce Parrott

Of all the elements of the international wave of democratization that began some two decades ago, the transformation of communist political systems, once thought impervious to liberalization, is the most dramatic.[1] Since 1989, more than two dozen countries within the former Soviet bloc have officially disavowed Marxist–Leninist ideology and have dismantled, in varying degrees, the apparatus of communist dictatorship and socialist economic planning. In many cases this transformation has led to a reinvention of politics, in the sense of genuine public debate about the purposes of society and the state, and has produced significant progress toward the establishment of a liberal–democratic order.[2]

This extraordinary turn of events has evoked a surge of scholarly research and writing from specialists on the former communist countries and other social scientists. Analysts have probed the causes of the demise of communism in Eastern Europe and the former Soviet Union.[3] They have examined the communist legacies inherited by the East European and Soviet successor states and have constructed parallel narratives of early postcommunist developments in regional groupings of these states.[4] They also have produced detailed studies of recent trends in individual countries.[5] Extensive analysis and debate have likewise been devoted to the political and institutional aspects of market reform.[6]

To date, however, scholars have devoted relatively little effort to systematic cross-country comparisons of political change in the postcommunist states. With some notable exceptions, Western thinking about attempts to democratize these polities has generally been based on the experience of the countries of North America, Western and Southern Europe, and Latin America.[7] Among scholars and laypersons alike, there has been an unconscious tendency to view postcommunist political developments through interpretive lenses derived from the experiences of countries that have not undergone the historical transformations and traumas associated with

1

communism. Yet the relevance of the paradigms of democratization (and failed democratization) derived from these countries is far from self-evident. Just as some economists have challenged the applicability of models drawn from noncommunist societies to the dilemmas of economic reform in postcommunist states, some political scientists have questioned whether paradigms of democratization drawn from noncommunist countries are relevant to the study of postcommunist political change.[8] This is an issue of central importance both for social theory and for the day-to-day policies of Western governments and nongovernmental organizations.

An adequate understanding of this exceptionally complex theoretical issue, however, requires a better understanding of the nature of the political changes occurring inside the postcommunist countries themselves. Because the communist era saddled these countries with many similar political and socioeconomic dilemmas, it is logical to examine them for similar processes of political change. A strong case can be made that communist countries passed through a distinctive set of profound political and socioeconomic alterations that makes comparisons among postcommunist patterns of political development especially fruitful. On the other hand, these societies also have been shaped by dissimilar processes - witness the contrast between the Czech Republic and Turkmenistan, which today have little in common besides the fact that they were once called communist - and analysts cannot assume that they are destined to follow identical political trajectories. Controlled comparisons among postcommunist countries can help us identify the causes of the varying national outcomes that have begun to crystallize roughly a half-decade after the demise of communism.

Some valuable comparative work on postcommunist political development has already been done.[9] But the immense forces that have been unleashed and the profound questions that they raise demand much fuller exploration. Only a sustained research effort by the broad community of scholars can provide a surer baseline for evaluating recent trends and the prospects for democracy in particular postcommunist states. This long-term effort must address many aspects of each country's political life – its constitutional arrangements, the objectives of its leaders, public attitudes toward politics, ethnonational sentiments, the interplay of politics and economics, and the effects of international influences, to name only a few – and juxtapose them with comparable phenomena in other postcommunist states.

Although the project that produced this book touches on a number of these themes, the central goal has been to trace changes and continuities in elite and mass political participation in each of the postcommunist countries of Eastern Europe and the former Soviet Union.[10] By examining the major political actors and the means through which they exercise power, the project has sought to assess the extent of democratization in each country and the strength of countervailing authoritarian tendencies. In particular, we have examined the degree to which postcommunist political arrangements have fostered or inhibited an expansion of popular political participation through the introduction of competitive elections and the formation of competitive political parties. Where feasible, we also have offered preliminary assessments of the strength and orientation of the network of groups and institutions sometimes known as "civil society" – or, more generally, as political society.[11] The writers of the country-studies have necessarily approached these topics from various angles, depending on the particulars of the country being analyzed. In each instance, however, the writer has sought to clarify whether formative influences and political choices have propelled the country's postcommunist politics in a democratic or an authoritarian direction, and how durable the new constellation of power appears to be.

This approach has both intellectual advantages and limitations. The contributors to the project have harbored no illusions that we could treat all the relevant issues in the necessary depth. Separate volumes could easily have been written on particular facets of the overall comparisons we have undertaken. The value of our enterprise is that it presents a comprehensive set of carefully researched case-studies based on a common research agenda and on close interaction among the country-study writers and editors. The project provides a useful picture of each country's political development up to the mid–1990s, along with a sense of the national trends that may prevail during the next few years. In addition, it lays the groundwork for delineating and explaining alternative paths of democratic and nondemocratic change in postcommunist societies. Today, less than a decade since communist regimes began to fall, the challenge of charting these paths remains daunting. In the words of one scholar, "it is a peculiarity of political scientists that we spend much of our time explaining events that have not finished happening."[12] Identifying and explaining patterns of postcommunist political development will become easier as additional events and a longer historical perspective make those patterns more distinct; but it is not too early to begin the task.

The remainder of this chapter situates the country-studies in a general intellectual framework and highlights some of the principal themes they address. First it examines the meaning of key concepts, such as democracy and democratic transition, and sketches the types of regimes that may emerge from the wreckage of communism. Next the chapter explores the impact of the international environment and of national historical legacies on the evolution of postcommunist regimes. It then turns to a discussion of elections, party systems, and their role in the success or failure of democratization. Finally, the chapter surveys the potential effects of political culture and the intermediate groups that constitute a country's political society. In treating each theme, I draw on the chapters included in this book and the companion volumes.[13]

Democracy and the alternatives

Because the general notion of democracy has been interpreted in many different ways, it is essential to begin by discussing some of these variations and their implications for the study of postcommunist countries. After all, during their heyday Marxist–Leninist regimes claimed to be quintessentially democratic and ridiculed the "bourgeois" democracies found in other parts of the world. More to the point, proponents of liberal democracy have long disagreed among themselves about which institutional arrangements constitute the essence of a democratic system. Equally significant, some admirers of the advanced industrial democracies prefer to call such systems "polyarchies" and to treat democracy as a set of normative standards against which all political systems must be measured, in order not to gloss over the serious defects of contemporary liberal polities.[14]

For the purposes of this project, we have adopted a less stringent criterion for classifying a country as democratic. According to this standard, democracy is a political system in which the formal and actual leaders of the government are chosen within regular intervals through elections based on a comprehensive adult franchise with equally weighted voting, multiple candidacies, secret balloting, and other procedures, such as freedom of the press and assembly, that ensure real opportunities for electoral competition. Among the various attributes of democracy, competitive elections are the feature that is most easily identifiable and most widely recognized around the world. Competitive elections are arguably a precondition for the other political benefits that a democratic system may confer on its citizens, and they are a valuable yardstick for analyzing and distinguishing among postcommunist countries. One fundamental question is why some countries, such as Poland, have introduced fully competitive elections, while others, such as Uzbekistan, have not. Another question is why some postcommunist countries have continued to choose their governmental leaders through free elections, whereas other countries that initially introduced such elections, such as Armenia and Albania, have recently fallen victim to large-scale electoral fraud.

Although useful, our minimalist definition of democracy also involves potential pitfalls. Because it does not stipulate all the individual liberties that most Western observers consider an essential element of genuine democracy, it groups together the majoritarian and constitutionalist/libertarian traditions of democratic governance.[15] Under certain conditions, a competitively elected government is capable of behaving in a despotic fashion toward large numbers of its citizens or inhabitants, especially when those persons belong to a distinct ethnic or religious minority.[16] The behavior of the Croatian government toward many ethnic Serbian inhabitants of Croatia is a graphic example. Other postcommunist governments, such as those of Estonia and Latvia, have faced major dilemmas posed by the presence of sizable minorities, but they have dealt with these issues in a more humane though sometimes controversial manner. Confronted with ethnic mixes that pose less obvious risks to the state, still other governments have accorded full rights to citizens of minority extraction; Bulgaria is a case in point. In a fully functioning constitutional democracy, the rights of citizens and inhabitants are legally specified and protected by the government, no matter how sweeping a mandate it has received at the polls.

Another caveat concerns the application of the criterion of competitive elections. The project's case-studies show that in several countries postcommunist elections have been considerably more competitive than the typical stage-managed charades of the communist era, yet have not been entirely free by strict democratic standards. In the long run, however, this movement from communist-style to semidemocratic elections may constitute an important step in the process of liberalization and may lead, despite powerful resistance, to voting procedures that are fully democratic. One strand of the scholarly literature emphasizes that democracy is sometimes the unintended consequence of political struggles among antagonists who did not initially seek to create it. The political import of semi-competitive elections thus depends on whether they mark a national step forward from completely rigged elections or a regression from elections that were genuinely democratic. Semi-competitive elections in Turkmenistan would be a sign of dramatic democratic progress, whereas similar elections in the Czech Republic would not.

Care is also required in applying the notion of democratic transitions. Due to the astonishing cascade of events that brought about the collapse of communism and a Western victory in the Cold War, virtually all postcommunist leaders proclaimed their commitment to democratization – sometimes sincerely, sometimes not – and a considerable number of outside observers assumed that democracy would be the natural result of communism's demise. However, when thinking about the evolution of the postcommunist states it is important to maintain the distinction between transitions from communism and transitions to democracy. It may be true that liberal democracy has become the prevailing model of modern politics in much of the world.[17] But both historical experience and a priori reasoning suggest that a spectrum of possible postcommunist outcomes still exists. This spectrum includes variants of democracy, variants of authoritarianism, and some hybrids in between.

The consolidation of democracy is another important idea that warrants careful handling. To say that democracy has been consolidated in a country suggests, at a minimum, that the introduction of fully competitive elections has been completed and that the new political system has become stable. In this discussion, consolidation denotes the condition of a political system in which all major political actors and social groups expect that government leaders will be chosen through competitive elections and regard representative institutions and procedures as their main channel for pressing claims on the state.[18] A few scholarly critics have challenged the idea of consolidation, arguing that some democracies have demonstrated considerable staying-power without ever satisfying certain commonly accepted criteria of consolidation.[19] Nevertheless, the concept remains useful for differentiating democratic systems that have achieved internal stability from systems that have not, and for making probabilistic assessments of a particular democracy's political prospects. It calls attention to internal factors, such as fundamental divisions over national identity, constitutional structure, and criteria of citizenship, that can destroy a democratic polity. Because all systems are subject to political decay, consolidation does not guarantee that a democracy will survive, but does improve its chances. Although democratic consolidation typically required a long time in earlier eras, the contemporary ascendancy of liberal-democratic norms in many parts of the globe may accelerate the process. Since the 1970s the consolidation of new democratic systems has occurred quite quickly in some noncommunist countries, though not in others.[20]

Whether any of the postcommunist states have achieved democratic consolidation is a complex issue. A case can be made that the Czech Republic, Poland, and Lithuania have reached this political watershed, even though controversy persists over the shape of the Polish constitution. But most postcommunist states have not reached it. Some, such as Latvia and Estonia, have established representative institutions and political structures that work quite smoothly, but have not yet admitted large ethnic minorities to citizenship. Others, such as Russia, have made impressive progress in introducing competitive elections, but contain particular political parties and social groups whose loyalty to democratic principles remains highly questionable. Still others, such as Uzbekistan and Belarus, are plainly developing along authoritarian lines.

The spectrum of possible postcommunist outcomes includes such variants of democracy as parliamentary rule and presidential government. Each of these forms of government has been adopted by some postcommunist countries, and each has champions who argue that it is the least susceptible to political breakdown.[21] In addition, the spectrum of potential outcomes includes hybrid systems similar to the "delegative democracy" identified by students of comparative politics.[22] In a delegative democracy, the president is chosen through competitive elections. Once in office, however, he rules in the name of the whole nation, usually on the pretence that he transcends the petty concerns of particular parties and interest groups. Unconstrained by the legislature or the courts, the president governs without significant checks on his power, save for the constitutional requirement that regular presidential elections be held and the de facto power held by other officials, and he often seeks to change the constitution so as to prolong his time in power.[23] Several postcommunist countries, particularly some former Soviet republics, have concentrated governmental power in an executive president with the authority to issue decrees having the force of law. Depending on the future course of events, this hybrid arrangement has the potential to become either a constitutional democracy or a clear-cut form of authoritarianism.

The main potential forms of postcommunist authoritarianism are personal dictatorships, one-party states, and military regimes. The socioeconomic turmoil following the collapse of communism may make it hard to build stable versions of any of these types of authoritarianism, but oscillations among them may still preclude successful democratization. In countries where a substantial part of the population has already undergone sociopolitical mobilization, the lack of a well developed party structure makes a personal dictatorship vulnerable to sharp shifts in the public mood and to unbridled power-struggles when the dictator is incapacitated or dies.[24] Nonetheless, a few postcommunist countries are likely to come under the sway of such dictatorships. Contemporary Belarus fits this model, and Turkmenistan bears a significant resemblance to it.

Generally speaking, authoritarian states built around a single ruling party are more stable than personal dictatorships. A ramified party organization helps harness mass political participation to the leaders' objectives, reduces elite conflict, and smooths the process of succession. For postcommunist leaders set on following this path, the challenge is to create a party mechanism that can actually control mass participation and the behavior of any quasi-democratic governmental institutions that already have been set up. This stratagem is often more difficult to apply than it might seem. Once the old communist mechanisms of control have been weakened, building a stable new ruling party is a problematic undertaking, as developments in Kazakstan indicate. Success depends both on the top leader's willingness to assign high priority to building such a party and on the party's capacity to contain new socioeconomic forces within its structure. Absent these two conditions, leaders with a dictatorial bent may move toward a system of personal rule, eliminating quasi-democratic institutions and processes, such as elections, that they cannot effectively control.

As of the mid–1990s, direct military rule seemed the least likely postcommunist authoritarian outcome. Historically, one-party states have proven less susceptible to military coups than have other forms of authoritarianism.[25] Ruling communist parties exercised especially close civilian control over their military professionals, and this heritage of subordination appears to have shaped military behavior in most postcommunist countries. The rare episodes in which the armed forces have intervened collectively to affect the selection of national leaders have usually been precipitated by "demand pull" from feuding politicians eager to defeat their rivals rather than by any military desire to rule.[26] That said, it should be noted that irregular military forces and militias have played a sizable role in the politics of some postcommunist countries, especially those parts of the former Soviet Union and the former Yugoslavia that have become embroiled in warfare. In a number of countries the parlous economic and social condition of the regular military has facilitated transfers of weapons and personnel to irregular military forces. Although irregular forces have caused a change of government leadership in only a few cases, such as Georgia and Azerbaijan, they frequently have had a strong effect on the political balance inside their "host" states, whether those states are nominally democratic or authoritarian in character.[27]

The international environment and national historical legacies

The dynamics of postcommunist political change have been shaped by several major variables. One of the most important is the international environment, which includes geopolitical, institutional-normative, and cultural elements. Historically, the overall effects of the international environment on attempts to promote democratization have ranged from highly beneficial to extremely harmful.[28] By historical standards, the contemporary international setting has been relatively favorable to the creation and consolidation of new democracies, although there have been important regional variations in this respect. The generally propitious international environment has been shaped by a number of factors: the heightened Western commitment to human rights as a major aspect of interstate relations; the gradual absorption of liberal ideas into once-autarkic societies made increasingly permeable by competitive pressures from an open global economy; the decision of the Soviet leadership not to shore up communist regimes in Eastern Europe with military threats or intervention; the "gravitational pull" exerted by highly prosperous Western democracies and by multilateral institutions prepared to assist postcommunist liberalization; and the intensifying bandwagon effects exerted by leading exemplars of reform, such as Poland, on other former communist countries that initially dragged their feet.[29]

International conditions have not favored all postcommunist efforts at democratization in equal measure. The effects of the international setting have varied sharply by region and by the form of outside influence in question. For the most part, the Western powers have refused to intervene with decisive military force to suppress the savage ethnic violence that has undermined the chances for democratization in parts of the former Yugoslavia and the Transcaucasus.[30] In contrast to the situation after World War II, when the geostrategic interests of the Western Allies required the imposition of democratic institutions on the defeated Axis powers, the West has had no compelling strategic reason to impose liberal-democratic arrangements on such countries as Serbia.[31] Perhaps as significant, the West's political and economic impact on most European postcommunist states has exceeded its influence on the postcommunist states of the Transcaucasus and Central Asia. The scale of such influence is not determined solely by the receiving state's location or culture; witness the isolation of Belarus from the countries to its west. But the large cluster of established European democracies and the prospect of close political and economic ties with them have had a much stronger effect in Eastern Europe than in other postcommunist regions. In Eastern Europe, a desire to be admitted to NATO and the European Union has tempered the political conduct even of lagging states such as Romania.

Several factors account for this variation in Western influence: the greater physical and cultural distance between the West and most of the non-European postcommunist states; the lower level of Western strategic interest in these countries, coupled with a tendency to manifest less concern about their internal liberalization than about their potential as sources of energy and raw materials; the countries' greater vulnerability to pressures from a Russia preoccupied with ensuring the stability of its southern flank; and the substantial limits on the West's diplomatic leverage in Asia, where booming economies have emboldened some authoritarian regimes, such as China, to defy Western human-rights standards.[32]

In addition to being influenced by the international environment, the direction of postcommunist political development has been shaped by whether struggles over political change taken place within the arena of a firmly established nation-state. In a handful of postcommunist countries, politics has unfolded within the boundaries and administrative framework of the old communist state. In most cases, however, the struggle over democratization has coincided with efforts to create the political scaffolding of a new state on a portion of the territory of the old communist regime. Due to the breakup of Czechoslovakia, Yugoslavia, and the Soviet Union, twenty-two of the twenty-seven postcommunist states are new sovereign entities. This is one of the main features that distinguishes postcommunist efforts to build democracy from comparable processes in Latin America and Southern Europe.[33]

The break-up of states severely complicates efforts to achieve democratization. The process frequently triggers incendiary controversies over the national identity of the new states, contested borders, and rival groups' competing claims to be the only indigenous inhabitants of their new country. In cases as diverse as Croatia, Azerbaijan, Georgia, Moldova, and

Russia, national declarations of independence from a larger communist regime have coincided with simultaneous attempts by local minorities to declare their own independence from the newly established states. Such centrifugal processes, which cannot be resolved by appealing to the principle of national self-determination, increase the probability of violent communal conflict and the emergence of ultranationalist sentiments harmful to democratization.[34] The conflicts between Serbia and Croatia and between Armenia and Azerbaijan provide examples. The collapse of an established state also accelerates the disintegration of the government bureaucracies that must function smoothly to ensure the administrative effectiveness of democratic institutions. This, in turn, may undermine the popular appeal of democracy as a political system.[35]

The creation of new states from old does not always preclude democratic development, however. The Czech Republic and Slovakia, Russia and the Baltic states, and the former Yugoslav republic of Slovenia are cases in point. Democratization is liable to fail when efforts to dismantle the old state interact with the mobilization of large internal ethnic "diasporas" and the emergence of ultranationalism in internal ethnic "homelands" to ignite large-scale violence. Democratization stands a greater chance of success when internal ethnic diasporas are small or are willing to be incorporated into successor states outside their "homeland," and when nationalist movements in the ethnic homelands are moderate rather than extremist.[36] In new, ethnically divided states, the political impact of ethnic differences depends on the actions both of the dominant group and of ethnic minorities and outside parties, as the contrasting internal political dynamics of Croatia and Estonia demonstrate.

Whether linked to the collapse of an established state or not, manifestations of nationalism and efforts to democratize can affect each other in very different ways. Careful observers have distinguished between two types of nationalism: inclusionary "civic" nationalism, which is compatible with the observance of individual rights, and exclusionary ethnic nationalism, which tends to subordinate such rights to the collectivist claims of the nation.[37] Rarely if ever do these two types of nationalism exist in pure form, but the weighting of the two tendencies in citizens' attitudes varies enormously from one country to another.[38] For example, Ukraine might be placed close to the "civic" end of the spectrum, Latvia nearer the middle, and Serbia near the "ethnic" end.[39] Before the final third of the nineteenth century, when European nationhood became closely linked to ethnicity, nationalism was commonly understood to be a concomitant of democracy, and in postcommunist cases such as Poland, this connection can still be seen.[40] A modicum of nationalism is indispensable for the creation and cohesion of a modern state; without it many citizens will lack an incentive to participate actively in democratic politics, as the case of Belarus demonstrates. On the other hand, exclusionary nationalism can lead to the effective disenfranchisement of substantial segments of the population – witness the behavior of the Serbian and Croatian governments toward minorities within their borders – and undergird dictatorial practices.

In addition to examining the historical roots of national identity in each country, analysts of postcommunist political change must examine other effects of the country's precommunist political legacy. Studies of democratization in states lacking a communist past have shown that countries which have had a prior experience of democracy, even if the experience has been unsuccessful, have a better chance of democratizing successfully on their second attempt.[41] Prior democratic experience may promote current democratization in several ways. If fairly recent, it may provide "human capital" – that is, persons with a first-hand understanding of democratic institutions and practices who can help launch and maintain the new political arrangements. Even if historically remote, previous experience may provide instructive lessons in the design of democratic institutions matched to the particular features of the country in question. Finally, previous experience may help legitimize new democratic institutions by protecting them against the xenophobic charge that they are an alien cultural import.

By comparison with many democratizing countries that were never communist, the postcommunist countries have little prior democratic experience on which to draw, as Valerie Bunce has forcefully argued. This disadvantage is clearest with respect to human capital. Measured against Latin America and Southern Europe, where authoritarian and democratic rule frequently alternated with one another in the past, "Eastern Europe has no such democratic tradition. The so-called democratic experiments of the interwar period lasted less than a decade and are best understood, in any case, as authoritarian politics in democratic guise." Lacking "the 'feel' for democracy that Latin America and Southern Europe enjoyed," postcommunist states face special political obstacles.[42]

These obstacles are not insurmountable, however. Even if short-lived, a nation's previous attempts to build democracy can give reformers not only potential models for contemporary governmental arrangements but also lessons about constitutional flaws that have contributed to past democratic failures. Political learning of this kind has occurred, for example, in Estonia and Latvia. More broadly, national memories or even myths of a democratic past may facilitate popular acceptance of democratic political structures.[43] This sort of process has occurred in both the Czech Republic and Poland. Citizens of Slovakia, by contrast, tend to regard interwar Czechoslovakian history as a period of alien domination by the Czechs rather than as an integral part of their own national past, and countries such as Ukraine effectively lack any modern experience of independent statehood. But even in nations such as these, a strong popular aversion to decades of communist oppression may compensate for the absence of a "usable" democratic past. Due to the exceptional severity of most communist regimes, this kind of negative learning may be considerably stronger in postcommunist countries than in noncommunist countries that aspire to democratize.

Like the effects of the precommunist legacy, the effects of communist rule on the prospects for democratic political participation warrant careful scrutiny in each country. Exactly what constitutes political participation, it should be said, is a matter of some disagreement among Western scholars. Defining the concept narrowly, specialists on the "classic" democracies have tended to concentrate on citizen involvement in such activities as voting and contacting government officials, and have frequently excluded citizen involvement in such "unconventional" activities as peaceful protests and demonstrations.[44] This narrower definition may stem from an understandable concern, sharpened by the history of Fascism and Communism, that authoritarian elites bearing the standard of "direct democracy" can manipulate mass movements to destroy the institutions of representative democracy.[45] By contrast, scholars interested in comparative political development have tended to define participation more broadly and have sometimes classified nearly all politically motivated activities, including political violence, under this rubric.[46] Analysts also have differed over the importance of the distinction between voluntary and compulsory participation. Specialists on established democracies have generally treated the contrast between these two forms of political involvement as a key difference between democratic and non-democratic systems, whereas some students of political development have minimized its significance.[47]

Voluntary participation and compulsory participation can each be found in both authoritarian and democratic polities. However, the relative proportions of these types of participation differ dramatically in authoritarian and democratic systems and help explain the qualitative differences between the two.[48] Main-line communist regimes systematically excluded most kinds of voluntary participation – particularly competitive elections for high government office and the freedom to form independent associations – and introduced novel forms of compulsory mass participation directed from above. Mandatory participation reached its zenith in the stage of full-fledged totalitarianism. Communist totalitarianism rested on the discovery that under certain conditions the expansion of mass education and the creation of new social organizations could be joined with mass coercion to multiply rather than diminish the power of the state.[49]

The totalitarian approach to political participation was linked with a radical stance toward society. In the Stalin era, Marxist–Leninist regimes sought to create a political system that not only compelled every citizen to endorse a common sociopolitical program but excluded the very notion of a pluralist society with autonomous interests distinct from those of the ruling elite.[50] In essence, these regimes sought to obliterate the dividing-line between state and society. Although they never completely succeeded, some of them came quite close. For most of the twentieth century, communist systems remained the most stable form of dictatorship – a form so stable that their transformation into liberal polities was said by some observers to be impossible.[51]

The erosion of communism did, of course, pave the way for the expansion of autonomous political participation by citizens and groups acting outside the control of the political elite. To begin with, not all national societies went through so shattering a totalitarian experience as did the nations of the USSR, and this lent them greater political resilience. Poland, where the Catholic Church retained a substantial measure of autonomy and agriculture was never fully collectivized, is probably the best example. Moreover, although communist regimes went to unprecedented lengths to instill the official ideology, their simultaneous drive to transform the economy and raise educational levels gradually expanded the social groups whose members later found those ideological claims implausible or absurd. For example, during the early stages of Stalin's industrialization drive, citizen support for the Soviet regime was directly correlated with an individual's youth and level of education – no doubt partly because education served as an important vehicle of upward social mobility. During the next four or five decades, the stratum of persons with higher education grew dramatically, but at some point support for the regime became inversely correlated with youth and level of education.[52] In many communist countries a small group of citizens became the nucleus of a nascent civil society – that is, in the broadest sense, a society whose members insisted on a separation between state and society and on the moral primacy of societal interests – which ultimately contributed to the downfall of the political regime.[53]

Although communist regimes have generally pursued similar social and economic policies, the effects of communist rule have varied among countries and have contributed to different national patterns of postcommunist political change. At each stage in the transition from communism, the course of events has been shaped by the strength of the ruling elite vis-à-vis the political opposition, as well as by the relative strength within each camp of hard-line groups hostile to compromise and groups favoring compromise for the sake of peaceful change.[54] The overall disposition of the ruling communist elite for or against reform has thus had an important effect on the political development of individual countries. The dynamics of change have also been affected by the presence or absence of a vigorous dissent movement, which has sometimes exerted an indirect but powerful long-term influence on both elite and mass attitudes toward democratization. The influence of a generation of liberal Soviet dissenters on the policies of Mikhail Gorbachev contrasts strikingly with the absence of reformist currents among the intellectuals and communist party leaders of Belarus during the same period. In addition, disparate levels of social development and varying mass political cultures have affected the political evolution of individual countries. A case can be made, for instance, that Central Asia's comparatively low levels of urbanization and education have impeded efforts to democratize the states of the region. In such countries as Kyrgyzstan, these low levels have made it difficult to subordinate particularistic loyalties and local ties to a countrywide sense of political engagement and civic responsibility.

Ruling elites and opposition leaders have typically crafted their stances toward democratization with an eye to the shifting national constellation of political forces, and each group's successes and failures have been strongly influenced by its capacity to generate political power. In struggles over the postcommunist order, new forms of democratic participation, ranging from peaceful mass demonstrations to competitive elections, have frequently been pitted against antidemocratic forms of political action, ranging from attacks by hired thugs to mob violence or all-out civil war, as in Tajikistan and Georgia. Intermediate types of political action, such as organized boycotts of elections and general strikes, have been resorted to by both advocates and opponents of democracy. In cases where hostile camps of similar strength have confronted one other, the outcome has depended not only on elite objectives and tactics, but on the content of mass attitudes and the level of mass mobilization in behalf of democratic reforms.[55]

The impact of violence on struggles over the postcommunist order is complex. The prevalence of nonviolent and noncoercive forms of politics improves the chances for a democratic outcome but does not guarantee it. Under certain conditions, dictators and authoritarian parties may be voted into office and then roll back a political system's democratic features, as the example of Belarus shows. In authoritarian systems, many forms of voluntary participation regarded as normal in democratic systems are illegal, and "unconventional" forms of participation such as mass demonstrations and strikes may be indispensable for launching and sustaining the process of democratization. In these circumstances, eyeball-to-eyeball confrontations and the implicit threat of violent escalation may be a spur to reform.[56] Nor does limited violence necessarily eliminate the possibility of further democratic change; instead it may sharpen leaders' and citizens' awareness of the high risks of further violence, as it arguably did in the clash between Russian president Boris Yeltsin and his parliamentary opponents in the fall of 1993. The example of Georgia suggests that even civil war may not completely block a state's subsequent movement in a democratic direction.[57]

Nevertheless, the threshold between nonviolent and violent political action remains extremely important. Violence makes the political stakes a matter of life or death. It deepens grievances among the losers, intensifies fears of liberalization among the winners, and reduces the chances for political compromise. Often it creates armed camps that are prepared to resort to force and have a vested interest in the continued use of force to decide political conflicts, as in the countries of the Transcaucasus. Even if it sweeps away old communist structures, it may make noncommunist dictatorship more likely. Paradoxically, it also may extend the political life of established elites that are tied to the military or the security police but manage to shift the blame for past misdeeds onto the shoulders of a few fellow culprits – as the first phase of Romania's postcommunist development illustrates. The absence of violence does not guarantee a democratic outcome, but it improves the chances for substantial progress in this direction; witness the contrast between Georgia's first violence-laden years of postcommunist politics and Bulgaria's relatively peaceful transition to democracy.

Elections, parties, and political development

The introduction of competitive elections as a means of selecting a country's governmental leaders is a watershed in the transition to democracy. Because electoral rules can decisively affect the prospects for the survival of particular parties – and sometimes for the survival of an entire country – they generally become an object of intense struggle.[58] In transitions from communism, this struggle has been shaped both by the attitudes of established communist elites and by the power at the disposal of the proponents of full-fledged democratization. In a large number of cases, a combination of ideological erosion within the elite and vigorous public pressure for reform have led the elite to accept electoral procedures that are genuinely democratic by Western standards. In some instances the elite has accepted a major expansion of democratic participation partly because of doubts about the strength or reliability of the instruments of coercion needed to block it. Some major turning-points in the history of the "classic" democracies of North America and Western Europe were shaped by a similar calculus of power.[59] In contrast to most of the classic cases, however, the introduction of competitive elections at the close of the communist era generally entailed an extremely rapid expansion of voluntary political participation.[60]

Numerous postcommunist countries, of course, have experienced only a partial liberalization of electoral rules and conditions; a handful have experienced none at all. In Uzbekistan and Kazakstan, for example, where popular pressure for democratization was relatively weak, established elites managed to exert a large measure of influence over the quasi-competitive elections introduced near the close of the communist era, and thereby kept enough control over national politics to avoid comprehensive democratic reforms.[61] In lands such as Belarus, the postcommunist manipulation of electoral rules was initially more oblique, but led within a few years to flagrant violations of democratic electoral practices. Another graphic illustration of this trend is the refusal of the Serbian and Croatian regimes to recognize the victories of opposition parties in national rounds of urban elections conducted in 1995 and 1996.

In those transitions from communism in which the balance of political forces has favored the introduction of genuinely democratic elections, the choice of possible electoral systems has been wider than in most noncommunist countries. By comparison with cases of democratization in Latin America, far fewer preauthoritarian political parties have survived in the former communist states; this has reduced pressures to return to preauthoritarian electoral rules and has increased the scope for political maneuver in framing new rules.[62] Communist successor parties and nascent noncommunist parties have often altered their stance on the specifics of electoral reform according to apparent shifts in their chances under one or another electoral dispensation. However, by the mid–1990s it became clear that many of the postcommunist regimes that have introduced genuinely competitive elections have adopted rules for legislative elections that show certain broad similarities. These rules, which commonly distribute some or all legislative seats on the basis of proportional representation, have been tacitly designed to reduce the risk of extra-constitutional clashes by ensuring that all major groups will be represented in the legislature.[63]

Competitive elections have given rise to a host of postcommunist parties.[64] But just how these parties have affected the development of democracy remains an open question. Western observers have long debated the positive and negative consequences of parties for democracy and democratic values.[65] Political parties often fail to perform some functions deemed essential by democratic theorists, and in many established democracies the political salience of parties has diminished in recent decades.[66] Nonetheless, every contemporary political system that satisfies either the minimalist or a more rigorous definition of democracy has political parties. This fact indicates that the political mechanisms which enable citizens to replace governmental leaders through competitive elections cannot function effectively in the absence of parties. In this sense, parties are indispensable for the survival of democratic systems.

Party-formation in postcommunist countries has been subject to some influences that are distinctive and others that are common to postcommunist and noncommunist countries alike. As noted above, the industrial and social policies of communist regimes created many of the socioeconomic conditions – especially vastly expanded education and urbanization – that facilitate the emergence of voluntary associations and political parties. On the other hand, after seizing power communist regimes typically destroyed all noncommunist parties – with the occasional exception of one or two small "satellite" parties. Moreover, the high level of mandatory participation in communist party activities reportedly imbued the public in many countries with a distrust of parties of any kind. Also, the turbulence of postcommunist socioeconomic upheavals has hampered the efforts of voters to assess their short- and long-term interests and to pick a party that will represent those interests.[67]

Postcommunist party-formation thus appears to face an unusual array of structural obstacles. Unlike many post-authoritarian transitions in Latin America and other parts of the Third World, there are virtually no shadow-parties, independent trade unions, or other societal organizations that have roots in the pre-authoritarian period and that can quickly be reactivated to fight new elections.[68] This suggests that the rate at which postcommunist parties crystallize into reasonably stable institutions might be closer to the rates of party-formation during the nineteenth century than to the rates in other new democracies near the end of the twentieth.[69] Preliminary results of studies currently under way suggest that in several cases, postcommunist levels of electoral volatility – that is, the aggregate shift of voters among parties from one national election to the next – are unusually high by comparison with democratizing countries that lack a communist past.[70]

Other considerations, however, point in the opposite direction. Techniques of party-formation may be learned from abroad by ambitious political leaders and activists who have a large stake in party development. In addition, the proportional-representation features of the electoral systems hammered out in many postcommunist countries facilitate the formation of new parties. The sudden expansion of the scope of participation in meaningful elections also must be taken into account. In the nineteenth century, the step-by-step expansion of the franchise in most countries provided an incentive to create programmatic parties that appealed to the interests of each newly enfranchised segment of the population. By contrast, the simultaneous admission of all social strata and economic groups into postcommunist electoral systems has created an incentive to establish catch-all parties that appeal to many different constituencies.[71] Hence the low level of programmatic coherence in many postcommunist parties should not necessarily be equated with institutional weakness. Finally, the postcommunist states show major differences in the rate at which reasonably stable parties and competitive party systems are taking shape. For instance, parties in the Czech Republic and Poland appear to be fairly well institutionalized and to have established partisan attachments with a significant proportion of the citizenry. In Russia and Ukraine, by contrast, the level of party identification remains very low.[72]

In evaluating the relationship between party systems and democratization, it is important to remember that parties and party systems are overlapping but distinct concepts.[73] As used here, party system denotes all a country's politically significant parties – that is, those parties, small as well as large, whose behavior has a major impact on national politics – and the dominant characteristics of those parties taken as a constellation of political actors. Although the classification of party systems is a notoriously tricky matter, some of the relevant criteria are the number of significant parties, the strength of parties' linkages to particular social groups, the ideological range separating major parties on any given issue, and whether the strongest parties are situated near the extremes of the political spectrum or clustered near the center. Among polities lacking meaningful party competition, Giovanni Sartori has distinguished strictly one-party systems from systems dominated by a hegemonic party that permits but may not be challenged by "satellite" parties. Among polities with meaningful party competition, he has differentiated polarized multiparty systems, moderate multiparty systems, two-party systems, and systems characterized by one dominant party that is open to real electoral challenge. Sartori also has emphasized the importance of whether a particular party system promotes centripetal or centrifugal forms of competition among the parties.[74]

Scholars disagree about the effects of different types of party systems and electoral arrangements on democracy. In particular, these disagreements center on the effects of multiparty systems versus two-party systems and of proportional-representation versus winner-take-all electoral arrangements.[75] However, scholars generally agree that systems having a large number of significant parties with weak ties to a volatile electorate are harmful to democracy. They also agree that democracies with relatively strong extremist parties are vulnerable to authoritarian takeovers. Such anti-system parties may function under democratic conditions for an extended period without giving up their authoritarian orientation. This point is illustrated by the communist parties of Western Europe after World War II: most retained an anti-system orientation for many years, whereas socialist parties tended to undergo a gradual change of political ethos.[76] The largest anti-system parties, in France and Italy, appear to have been sustained by the political orientations of party activists and intellectuals, national levels of personal dissatisfaction among ordinary citizens that were unusually high by international standards, and the polarizing effects of the Cold War.[77]

Writing in 1990, Samuel Huntington observed that the international wave of democratization that began in the mid–1970s was characterized by a "virtual absence of major antidemocratic movements" that posed "an explicit authoritarian alternative" to new democratic regimes.[78] It is important to ascertain whether the same can be said of the postcommunist parties and political movements that have arisen since Huntington wrote these words. In a number of countries, such as Hungary and Lithuania, communist successor-parties have shed their hostility toward liberal democracy and accepted alternations in control of the government as the normal state of affairs. In cases such as Russia and Belarus, however, the main successor-party has not clearly disavowed its past authoritarian ethos.

As a rule, the postcommunist evolution of a party's goals and strategy depends on both elite and mass attitudes. Some observers have suggested that substantial rates of continuity between communist-era and postcommunist elites give members of the old guard a personal stake in the emerging democratic and economic system and reduce the incentive to try to restore authoritarianism. According to this analysis, extremely low or extremely high rates of elite continuity invite an antidemocratic backlash or a smothering of democratic reforms.[79] By themselves, quantitative measures of elite turnover cannot explain democratization's victories and defeats. But they may explain a great deal when combined with an analysis of elite values and the institutional structures through which elite members strive to advance their interests.[80] Taken together, these factors can help identify the point at which personal attitudes and the national political context "tip" old elites into acceptance of democratic political arrangements and practices.

Broadly speaking, the likely causes of moderating change among communist successor parties include the erosion of authoritarian ideas through the discrediting of Marxism–Leninism and generational turnover among top party leaders; a sense of "democratic inevitability" produced by shifts in the balance of organized political forces inside the country and by the seeming international triumph of liberal democracy; and widespread opportunities for personal enrichment through privatization and insider dealing.[81] In Hungary, for example, the path of political reform has been smoothed by elite opportunities for personal gain. Conversely, the factors that have facilitated the persistence of anti-democratic orientations in some successor parties include low leadership turnover; an exodus of moderate and liberal members who joined the party purely to advance their professional careers; the weakness of popular pressures for political liberalization; and a centripetal pattern of inter-party competition caused in part by deepening socioeconomic cleavages.

New anti-system parties based on ethnicity can also disrupt the process of democratization. The apparent explosion in the worldwide incidence of ethnic conflicts in the 1990s is largely a product of the increased public salience accorded such conflicts due to the end of the Cold War.[82] Still, extremist parties do pose a special danger to societies in which deep ethnic cleavages override or coincide with other socioeconomic divisions. Under these conditions, as Donald Horowitz has shown, the ethnicization of political parties and party competition for immobile blocs of ethnic supporters can lead to polarizing elections that preclude democratic alternations of government and pave the way for violence and an authoritarian seizure of power.[83] Whether postcommunist ethnic cleavages are as deep and unmitigated as the Third-World cleavages analyzed by Horowitz is a matter for careful consideration. In such countries or regions as Bosnia Herzegovina and the Transcaucasus, they often are. But in other countries, such as Kazakstan and the Baltic states, they appear to be more susceptible to political management and more compatible with democratization. Occasionally, ethnic cleavages are deeper among national elites than among ordinary citizens, and the competition to mobilize voters for electoral campaigns actually serves to reduce ethnic polarization, as in Moldova.

Anti-system parties that promote antidemocratic goals through nonviolent means should be differentiated from parties that are closely linked with paramilitary forces and are prepared to initiate large-scale violence. Although parties of both types constitute threats to democratization, the latter are probably a greater threat than the former. Nonviolent anti-system parties may gradually be coopted into the status of semi-loyal or even loyal supporters of a democratic system.[84] By contrast, parties predisposed to violence may trigger cycles of political conflict that spiral out of control. They also may precipitate military intervention in politics, either by design or as a result of the violent civil clashes that they set in motion, as some radical parties did in Latin America during the 1970s. To date, most postcommunist antidemocratic parties appear to fall in the nonviolent category. But there have been exceptions, as in Tajikistan, and under the stresses of prolonged social and economic turmoil, this broad pattern might change.[85]

A country's party system, it should be emphasized, can undercut democracy even in the absence of significant antidemocratic parties. One threat to the survival of democratic government is a widespread public perception that it is incapable of dealing with the numerous political and socioeconomic problems bequeathed by the collapse of communism. Such a perception may be fostered by feuding parliaments and inertial cabinets that seem unable to solve critical problems, or by frequent changes in governing coalitions that give the appearance of failing even to address the problems. Some types of multiparty systems are especially conducive to frequent changes of government; to the degree that they contribute to the formation of ineffectual coalition governments, they may erode the legitimacy of the whole democratic enterprise.

Such debilitating party systems may be less common than one might suppose, however. Certain types of coalition governments may last nearly as long as single-party ones, and turnover in the partisan make-up of governing coalitions does not always result in sharp changes of policy.[86] Much depends on the political longevity of individual cabinet ministers – which may considerably exceed the duration of a particular government coalition – and on the degree of public consensus or division over policy questions. Some postcommunist countries, such as Poland, Lithuania, and Hungary, have experienced several changes in the governing coalition but still have sustained quite consistent macroeconomic and social policies for several years. Moreover, a democratic government may experience several failures of performance in the economic and social realms without necessarily undermining the popular legitimacy of democratic institutions, as we shall see below.

Some postcommunist countries, of course, have remained in the grip of a single monopolistic party, or a hegemonic one. Sartori has distinguished totalitarian and authoritarian one-party systems from "one-party pragmatic systems" that have low levels of ideological intensity and are based primarily on political expediency.[87] This characterization bears a close resemblance to Turkmenistan and might become applicable to a few other postcommunist countries. The question is whether such parties have become effective instruments of authoritarian rule or have encountered serious challenges from other political forces. In addition, it is important to determine whether the satellite parties tolerated by hegemonic rulers have acquired real political influence or have become even more marginal since the cresting of pro-democratic symbolism and gestures immediately after the fall of communism. The experience of Kazakstan suggests that the role of these parties depends in part on whether elite factions seek to develop them as a means of defending their interests against attacks from other elite groups.

The effects of political culture and political society

As already noted, the political development of any postcommunist country is strongly influenced by the attitudes and strategies of elites and the character of the parties and other institutions through which they vie for power. Equally important to long-term postcommunist outcomes are the initial condition and subsequent evolution of the country's political culture and political society. Broadly speaking, a country's political culture reflects the inhabitants' basic attitudes toward such matters as the trustworthiness of their fellow citizens, the legitimacy of others citizens' rights and interests, the fashion in which conflicting interests ought to be reconciled, the ability of citizens to influence government policies, and the legitimacy of existing political institutions. A civic political culture embodies high levels of interpersonal trust, a readiness to deal with political conflict through compromise rather than coercion or violence, and acceptance of the legitimacy of democratic institutions.[88] It stands to reason that political culture affects whether citizens choose to support moderate or extreme political movements and parties, and whether they choose to engage in democratic or anti-democratic forms of political participation.[89]

Empirical evidence suggests that a country's political culture is neither fixed once and for all, nor completely malleable. It changes in response to new historical events and personal experiences, but with a considerable lag, and primarily through the generational turnover of citizens.[90] This makes political culture an important determinant of the way that political institutions evolve and operate. Over time political institutions and major sociopolitical events exert a reciprocal influence on the content of the country's political culture. But in any given period, the content of the political culture shapes the perceptions and actions of the political elite and the mass public.

A country's political culture and its political society are closely intertwined. The notion of political society is often defined broadly to include political parties, but here it is used to denote those nonparty, nongovernmental groups and associations that participate, directly or indirectly, in shaping a country's political life. The nature of these groups and associations varies widely according to the type of political society in question.[91] Civic associations, commercial enterprises, extended clans, and criminal organizations are examples of such groups. As some of these examples suggest, a political society may include a sizable number of organizational components but still not embody the values of a civic culture. In a statistical sense, social structure and the content of political culture are related; witness the widely accepted proposition that the rise of the middle class is a source of liberal democracy, and the more controversial notion that the working class is the main social basis of authoritarianism.[92] Analytically, however, social structure and political culture are distinct, and the relationship between them may vary from one country to the next. Taken in the aggregate, a country's political society generally reflects its prevailing political culture and significantly affects the operation of its governmental institutions.[93]

Civil society is a form of political society based on a dense network of nongovernmental associations and groups established for the autonomous pursuit of diverse socioeconomic interests and prepared to rebuff state efforts to seize control of these activities.[94] The components of a civil society may include such elements as independent media, religious confessions, charitable organizations, business lobbies, professional associations, labor unions, universities, and non-institutionalized movements for various social causes. The existence of a civil society depends not only on the presence of large numbers of associations and organized groups but on the spirit in which they act. The divergent fashions in which political thinkers have depicted civil society reflect the reality that relations among societal groups inevitably entail conflict as well as cooperation.[95] A society is civil only if its constituent groups demonstrate a substantial measure of self-restraint rooted in a recognition of the legitimacy of the interests of other groups – a recognition often reinforced by the existence of overlapping group memberships – and a commitment to forgo violence as means of deciding social conflicts. Because in the aggregate the structures of a civil society embody a civic culture, such a society is conducive to the consolidation of democratic governmental institutions. Under a democratic dispensation, the relationship of civil society to the state involves a large measure of cooperation as well as conflict.[96]

The application of the concepts of political culture and civil society to countries during their communist phase entails several difficulties. Until the late communist era, systematic survey data on citizens' political attitudes were generally unavailable for most communist countries; this created a risk that analysts would erroneously attempt to infer the characteristics of mass political culture from the history and structure of the regime rather than from the empirically measured values of the population.[97] Confusion also has arisen from the attribution of several disparate meanings to the concept of civil society: these range from the notion of small oppositional movements under communist regimes to the notion of the macrostructure of entire societies in noncommunist or postcommunist states.[98] Certainly the *idea* of a civil society with values and interests superior to those of the party–state apparatus was ardently embraced by many dissidents and played an important role in delegitimizing the quasi-totalitarian pretensions of a number of communist regimes. But how widely this idea was held by ordinary citizens in most countries is difficult to establish. During the communist era the notion of civil society was plainly not embodied in a ramified network of independent social organizations and associations, although elements of such a network began to crystallize during the late communist era in Poland.[99]

In addition, it is important to inquire whether all the activists who tenaciously championed the concept of civil society as a source of resistance to communism have been capable of making a postcommunist transition to tolerance and cooperation with groups whose central values and concerns differ from their own. Put differently, not all dissidents and anticommunist groups were liberals. Adamant opposition to communist rule was not necessarily equivalent to support for democracy or for compromise among conflicting societal groups, as the examples of Georgia's Zviad Gamsakhurdia and Croatia's Franjo Tudjman show. Nor do all autonomous social institutions find the transition from communism to liberal democracy easy; witness the controversies in Poland over the efforts of the Roman Catholic hierarchy to influence legislation on abortion and the curriculum of public schools.

Applying the concepts of political culture and civil society to postcommunist countries has proved easier but still entails some complexities. In many countries a wealth of survey data on popular attitudes and behavior has now become available. However, scholars have tended to disagree about the implications of political culture for postcommunist democratization.[100] Those who believe that it constitutes a serious obstacle have generally argued that the political culture which existed before the end of communism has considerable staying-power. The sources of this inertia may include enduring precommunist traditions of dictatorship and ultranationalism, as well as authoritarian attitudes absorbed by citizens from Marxist–Leninist propaganda and frequent contact with the party–state apparatus. According to this view, the content of mass political culture increases the possibility of a reversion to some form of authoritarian rule – or to its preservation in countries where the political hold of the old elite has never been broken.

Other scholars have taken a different approach that stresses the compatibility of postcommunist political culture with democratization in many countries. Research along these lines has revealed that major West European democracies and some East European countries show broad if incomplete similarities in political culture – and that some East European citizens exhibit greater acceptance of the rights of ethnic minorities than do most West Europeans.[101] Analysts of this school have often stressed the depth of the ideological erosion that occurred during the final decades of communist rule. Arguing that postcommunist political culture is more prodemocratic than Marxist–Leninist propaganda would lead one to expect, they have suggested that memories of the violence and repression experienced under communism have strengthened citizens' attachment to attitudes of tolerance and non-violence conducive to democratization.[102] Adherents of this school of thought also maintain that intergenerational turnover strongly favors democratization because younger citizens are more enthusiastic about a transition to democratic politics and market economies, partly because they can adapt more easily and have longer time-horizons in which to enjoy the personal benefits of reform.

Closely related to such issues is the question whether a particular country's postcommunist political society bears any resemblance to a civil society in the social-structural sense. Mapping the organizational density and value orientations of a whole society is an enormous intellectual task that scholars have only begun to attempt. Nonetheless, several things seem clear. Without key components of civil society, governmental structures that are formally democratic cannot be expected to operate in a fashion that is substantively democratic. This is particularly true of independent media, which serve not only as direct advocates for societal interests but as important channels through which the members of societal groups communicate with one another and voice demands on the government. In Poland, for instance, independent print and broadcast media have played a major part in the democratic process. In Serbia, by contrast, government manipulation of the media has been so extensive that opportunities for fair electoral competition at the national level have virtually been eliminated.

The character of political society varies sharply among postcommunist countries. Networks of nongovernmental organizations and voluntary associations are growing far more rapidly in states such as Poland and the Czech Republic than in states such as Belarus and Uzbekistan. But even in countries where this growth has been relatively rapid, the infrastructure of civil society has not yet approached the density and durability of such social networks in long-established democracies; in many countries the heavy dependence of the non-profit sector on funding from the state or foreign sources makes it particularly vulnerable.[103] Moreover, processes occurring after the collapse of communism may profoundly alter a country's political society and political culture – and not necessarily in a direction favorable to democracy. Of particular consequence are economic stabilization and liberalization, the privatization of state property, and changes in the levels of legality and public order.

Economic stabilization and liberalization hold out the promise of a long-term improvement in living standards, but at the cost of bruising economic hardships in the short run. When communism first collapsed, outside observers tended to adopt the pessimistic view that democratization and market reform were basically incompatible.[104] This outlook appears to have been shaped by a tendency to analyze the political behavior of economic groups schematically and to view the issue through the lens of a few dramatic but unrepresentative cases such as Chile.[105] With time it has become clear that the relationship between postcommunist democratization and economic reform varies from one phase to another and from one country to another. Economic elites and members of the working class are not monolithic blocs and do not pursue static goals. Moreover, the goals of more narrowly defined economic groups, including labor unions, encompass interests that are broadly political as well as strictly economic.[106] The citizens of many postcommunist countries do regard economic prosperity as a central feature of liberal democracy, but they seem prepared to endure material hardships so long as they believe that economic circumstances will ultimately improve.[107] On the other hand, the severe hardships inflicted on many persons by economic reform may ultimately sharpen disillusionment with democracy – especially if these hardships are accompanied by rapidly increasing disparities of income and extensive corruption.[108]

The effects of privatization on the prospects for democratization also are likely to vary. A wide distribution of private property has long been regarded by many political theorists as an essential check on the authoritarian tendencies that may arise even in popularly elected governments. In addition to this putative benefit, the privatization of state property may facilitate democratization by offering members of the old elite a means of personal aggrandizement more lucrative and far less risky than attempting to reinstate an authoritarian order. However, the insider dealings that help neutralize the former elite as a source of collective opposition also may give rise to mass sentiments that equate democracy with social injustice and rampant corruption. This is especially likely to occur if elite corruption and an equivocal elite attitude toward economic reform produce a protracted depression of popular living standards. Although national understandings of corruption and conflict of interest vary substantially from country to country, the process of economic transformation has made postcommunist countries susceptible to corruption on an unusually large scale.[109] Under these conditions, threats to democracy may come not so much from political and economic elites as from newly enfranchised citizens embittered by the emergence of a plutocracy. In Russia and several East Europe states, public disapproval of the privatization of state economic enterprises has grown substantially since 1991.[110] For most voters, political patience has thus far outweighed economic dissatisfaction, but a long-term economic downturn and an appearance of unchecked social injustice might alter their outlook.

This is one reason that changes in the level of legality and public order are significant. Economic liberalization may lead toward a civil society sustained by the growth of socioeconomic groups with a vested interest in further democratic change, predictable commercial laws, and vigorous civic associations. But the legacy of the totalitarian state may favor elements of an "uncivil" society rather than a civil one. Unless augmented by the growth of smaller civic associations, quasi-corporatist labor and industrial organizations like those in Slovakia and the Czech Republic may become the sort of large, impersonal entities that some Western political theorists view as endangering rather than embodying a civil society.[111] Similarly, deregulation of economic life in the absence of an adequate legal structure and a trustworthy state bureaucracy may lead to the domination of economic activity by predatory business and criminal groups indifferent or hostile to democracy, especially a democracy which blocks some highly profitable activities through effective laws and institutions.[112] At its worst, deregulation of this sort could generate not only citizen disillusionment with the elected leaders who set the process in motion, but also a widespread reaction against basic democratic values.

Perhaps the most fundamental question is whether most citizens in each country believe that democratization and economic reform are essential or that realistic alternatives exist. Comparing the initial phases of dual transitions – that is, the simultaneous liberalization of national political and economic systems – in selected countries of Latin America and Eastern Europe sheds light on this question. One striking difference between the two sets of countries is that elites and citizens were much more strongly convinced of the necessity for fundamental economic change in Eastern Europe than in Latin America.[113] This conviction, in turn, apparently has given greater impetus to the postcommunist drive for liberalization and has reduced the potential for a powerful political backlash against economic reforms. Evidence from some cases, such as Russia, shows that despite economic turmoil and dissatisfaction, public support for democratic political practices has grown substantially since 1991.[114]

In other words, the "deep beliefs" of the citizens of postcommunist countries – their most strongly held attitudes and values, as opposed to transient opinions about day-to-day politics – may be of decisive importance. In Western countries, disillusionment and cynicism about particular leaders and governmental institutions coexist with a continuing commitment to democratic principles.[115] The project's case studies suggest that similar split-level outlooks exist among the citizens of a number of postcommunist countries. The fact that significant proportions of citizens believe that their new governments are unresponsive or corrupt may be taken as a loss of faith in democracy. But it also may be interpreted quite differently – as an accurate assessment of current political realities, and as the social foundation for further efforts to achieve a full-fledged democratic order.

NOTES

I am grateful to Joan Nelson, Valerie Bunce, and Karen Dawisha for helpful comments on an earlier version of this chapter.

1   For a penetrating analysis of the global process of democratization, see Samuel Huntington, *The Third Wave: Democratization in the Late Twentieth Century* (Norman, OK: University of Oklahoma Press, 1991). For shifting Western views of communist systems, including the assertion that they could never be liberalized, see Abbott Gleason, *Totalitarianism: The Inner History of the Cold War* (New York: Oxford University Press, 1995), pp. 198–209.
2   The notion of the reinvention of politics is borrowed from Vladimir Tismaneanu, *Reinventing Politics: Eastern Europe from Stalin to Havel* (New York: Free Press, 1992).
3   See, among many possible examples, J. F. Brown, *Surge to Freedom: The End of Communist Rule in Eastern Europe* (Durham, NC: Duke University Press, 1991); Gale Stokes, *The Walls Came Tumbling Down: The Collapse of Communism in Eastern Europe* (New York: Oxford University Press, 1993); Sabrina Petra Ramet, *Social Currents in Eastern Europe: The Sources and Consequences of the Great Transformation*, 2d ed. (Durham, NC: Duke University Press, 1995); Tismaneanu, *Reinventing Politics*; Brendan Kiernan, *The End of Soviet Politics: Elections, Legislatures, and the Demise of the Communist Party* (Boulder, CO: Westview Press, 1993); Archie Brown, *The Gorbachev Factor* (Oxford: Oxford University Press, 1996); John Dunlop, *The Rise of Russia and*

the Fall of the Soviet Empire (Princeton: Princeton University Press, 1993); and M. Stephen Fish, *Democracy from Scratch: Opposition and Regime in the New Russian Revolution* (Princeton: Princeton University Press, 1995).

4   For example, *The Social Legacy of Communism*, ed. James R. Millar and Sharon L. Wolchik (Washington, DC and Cambridge: Woodrow Wilson Center Press and Cambridge University Press, 1994); *The Legacies of Communism in Eastern Europe*, ed. Zoltan Barany and Ivan Volgyes (Baltimore: Johns Hopkins University Press, 1995); J. F. Brown, *Hopes and Shadows: Eastern Europe after Communism* (Durham, NC: Duke University Press, 1994); Karen Dawisha and Bruce Parrott, *Russia and the New States of Eurasia: The Politics of Upheaval* (New York: Cambridge University Press, 1994); *New States, New Politics: Building the Post-Soviet Nations*, ed. Ian Bremmer and Ray Taras, 2d ed. (New York: Cambridge University Press, 1996); Anatol Lieven, *The Baltic Revolution: Estonia, Latvia, Lithuania and the Path to Independence*, 2d ed. (New Haven: Yale University Press, 1994); and *Central Asia and the Caucasus after the Soviet Union: Domestic and International Dynamics*, ed. Mohiaddin Mesbahi (Gainesville: University Press of Florida, 1994).

5   See, for instance, *Transition to Democracy in Poland*, ed. Richard F. Starr (New York: St. Martin's, 1993); Raymond Taras, *Consolidating Democracy in Poland* (Boulder, CO: Westview Press, 1995); Rudolf Tőkés, *Negotiated Revolution: Economic Reforms, Social Change, and Political Succession in Hungary, 1957–1990* (Cambridge: Cambridge University Press, 1996); Lenard J. Cohen, *Broken Bonds: Yugoslavia's Disintegration and Balkan Politics in Transition*, 2d ed. (Boulder, CO: Westview, 1995); Sabrina Petra Ramet, *Balkan Babel*, 2d ed. (Boulder, CO: Westview, 1996); Susan Woodward, *Balkan Tragedy: Chaos and Dissolution after the Cold War* (Washington, DC: Brookings Institution, 1995); Richard Sakwa, *Russian Politics and Society* (New York: Routledge, 1993); *Elections and Political Order in Russia*, ed. Peter Lentini (New York and Budapest: Central European University Press, 1995); *The New Russia: Troubled Transformation*, ed. Gail W. Lapidus (Boulder, CO: Westview Press, 1995); Stephen White, Richard Rose, and Ian McAllister, *How Russia Votes* (Chatham, NJ: Chatham House Publishers, 1997); *Independent Ukraine in the Contemporary World*, ed. Sharon Wolchik (Prague: Central European University Press, forthcoming); and Alexander Motyl, *Dilemmas of Independence: Ukraine after Totalitarianism* (New York: Council on Foreign Relations, 1993).

6   For example, Anders Åslund, *Post-Communist Economic Revolutions: How Big a Bang?* (Washington, DC: Center for Strategic and International Studies, 1992); Adam Przeworski, *Democracy and the Market: Political and Economic Reforms in Eastern Europe and Latin America* (Cambridge: Cambridge University Press, 1991); *A Precarious Balance: Democracy and Economic Reforms in Eastern Europe*, ed. Joan Nelson (Washington, DC: Overseas Development Council, 1994); Joan Nelson et al., *Intricate Links: Democratization and Market Reforms in Latin America and Eastern Europe* (Washington, DC: Overseas Development Council, 1994); *The Privatization Process in Central Europe*, ed. Roman Frydman et al. (Budapest and New York: Central European University Press, 1993); *The Privatization Process in Russia, Ukraine, and the Baltic States*, ed. Roman Frydman et al. (Budapest and New York: Central European University Press, 1993); Roman Frydman et al., *Corporate Governance in Central Europe*

and Russia, 2 vols. (Budapest and New York: Central European University Press, 1996); *Banking Reform in Central Europe and the Former Soviet Union*, ed. Jacek Rostowski (Budapest and New York: Central European University Press, 1995); Max Ernst et al., *Transforming the Core: Restructuring Industrial Enterprises in Russia and Central Europe* (Boulder, CO: Westview, 1996); and Anders Åslund, *How Russia Became a Market Economy* (Washington, DC: Brookings Institution, 1995).

7   Although the fullest coverage of democratization in the Third World has been devoted to Latin America, in the past few years more attention has been paid to democratization in other Third-World countries. See, for instance, *Politics in Developing Countries; Comparing Experiences with Democracy*, ed. Larry Diamond, Juan J. Linz, and Seymour Martin Lipset (Boulder, CO: Lynne Rienner, 1990).

8   For differing views on this question, see Kenneth Jowitt, *The New World Disorder: The Leninist Extinction* (Berkeley: University of California Press, 1992), pp. 284–305; Sarah Meiklejohn Terry, "Thinking about Post-Communist Transitions: How Different Are They?" *Slavic Review* 52, no. 2 (Summer 1993), 333–37; Philippe C. Schmitter and Terry Lynn Karl, "The Conceptual Travels of Transitologists and Consolidologists: How Far to the East Should They Attempt to Go?" *Slavic Review* 53, no. 1 (Spring 1994), 173–85; Valerie Bunce, "Should Transitologists Be Grounded?" *Slavic Review* 54, no. 1 (Spring 1995), 111–117; idem., "Comparing East and South," *Journal of Democracy* 6, no. 3 (July 1995), 87–100. See also Beverly Crawford and Arend Lijphart, "Explaining Political and Economic Change in Post-Communist Eastern Europe: Old Legacies, New Institutions, Hegemonic Norms, and International Pressures," *Comparative Political Studies* 28, no. 2 (July 1995), 171–99. The most comprehensive empirical examination of this issue is Juan J. Linz and Alfred Stepan, *Problems of Democratic Transition and Consolidation: Southern Europe, South America, and Post-Communist Europe* (Baltimore: Johns Hopkins University Press, 1996), which appeared just as this book was going to press.

9   *Developments in East European Politics*, ed. Stephen White, Judy Batt and Paul G. Lewis (Durham, NC: Duke University Press, 1993); *Developments in Russian and Post-Soviet Politics*, ed. Stephen White, Alex Pravda, and Zvi Gitelman (Durham, NC: Duke University Press, 1994); *The New Democracies in Eastern Europe: Party Systems and Political Cleavages*, 2d ed., ed. Sten Berglund and Jan Ake Dellenbrant (Brookfield, VT: Edward Elgar, 1994); *Party Formation in East-Central Europe*, ed. Gordon Wightman (Aldershot: Edward Elgar, 1995); *Public Opinion and Regime Change: The New Politics of Post-Soviet Societies*, ed. Arthur H. Miller et al. (Boulder, CO: Westview Press, 1993); *Political Culture and Civil Society in Russia and the New States of Eurasia*, ed. Vladimir Tismaneanu (Armonk, NY: M. E. Sharpe, 1995); Richard Rose, *What Is Europe?* (New York: HarperCollins, 1996); *Social Justice and Political Change: Public Opinion in Capitalist and Post-Communist States*, ed. James R. Kluegel, David S. Mason, and Bernd Wegener (New York: Aldine de Gruyter, 1995); *Stabilising Fragile Democracies: Comparing New Party Systems in Southern and Eastern Europe*, ed. G. Pridham and P. G. Lewis (London: Routledge, 1996).

10   As noted in the Preface, the term "Eastern Europe" is employed for the sake of conciseness; in this book it does not presuppose political or cultural uniformity among the countries that it encompasses.

11   The distinction between civil society and other forms of political society is discussed below.

12   Barbara Geddes, "Challenging the Conventional Wisdom," *Journal of Democracy* 5, no. 4 (October 1994), 117.

13   *The Consolidation of Democracy in East-Central Europe*, ed. Karen Dawisha and Bruce Parrott (New York: Cambridge University Press, 1997); *Politics, Power, and the Struggle for Democracy in South-East Europe*, ed. idem (New York: Cambridge University Press, 1997); and *Democratic changes and authoritarian reactions in Russia, Ukraine, Belarus, and Moldova*, ed. idem (New York: Cambridge University Press, 1997).

14   See especially Robert Dahl, *Polyarchy: Participation and Opposition* (New Haven: Yale University Press, 1971), and Dahl, *Democracy and Its Critics* (New Haven: Yale University Press, 1989).

15   I am obliged to Sabrina Ramet for bringing this important point to my attention.

16   It is worth noting that such cases have not been confined to postcommunist democracies but have occurred in other democracies as well. India and Turkey, for example, have harshly suppressed some ethnic minorities among their citizens. (Samuel Huntington, "Democracy for the Long Haul," *Journal of Democracy* 7, no. 2 [April 1996], 10.)

17   Ghia Nodia, "How Different Are Postcommunist Transitions?" *Journal of Democracy* 7, no. 4 (October 1996), 15–17, 22–24.

18   This definition is derived from Joan Nelson, "How Market Reforms and Democratic Consolidation Affect Each Other," in Nelson et al., *Intricate Links*, pp. 5–6. For a similar but stricter definition designed to take direct account of military threats to democracy, see Juan J. Linz, "Transitions to Democracy," *Washington Quarterly*, 13 (1990), 156. For a more complex definition that deals also with the social and economic realms, see Juan J. Linz and Alfred Stepan, "Toward Consolidated Democracies," *Journal of Democracy* 7, no. 2 (April 1996), 34–51.

19   Guillermo O'Donnell, "Illusions about Consolidation," *Journal of Democracy* 7, no. 2 (April 1996), 38 and passim. Cf. Richard Guenther et al., "O'Donnell's 'Illusions': A Rejoinder," ibid. 7, no. 4 (October 1996), 151–59.

20   For example, a team of scholars has argued that consolidation was achieved within five years of the first democratic elections in Spain and within seven years of such elections in Greece. About a decade after the elections, elite and public acceptance of the superiority of democracy over all other forms of government in these two countries matched the average level in the countries of the European Union. By contrast, in Brazil, where the process of electoral democratization began at about the same time as in Spain, the level of elite and public acceptance of democracy remained far lower. Guenther et al., "O'Donnell's 'Illusions,'" 155-56.

21   For a sample of the Western debates over which form of democracy is more stable, see the chapters in Part II of *The Global Resurgence of Democracy*, ed. Larry Diamond and Marc F. Plattner (Baltimore: Johns Hopkins University Press, 1993).

22 Eugene Huskey discusses the applicability of this concept to Kyrgyzstan in his chapter in *Conflict, Cleavage, and Change*.

23 Guillermo O'Donnell, "Delegative Democracy," *Journal of Democracy* 5, no. 1 (1994), 59–60, 67.

24 Cf. Huntington, *Political Order in Changing Societies*, p. 177 f.

25 Huntington, *The Third Wave*, pp. 231–32.

26 On the other hand, the breakdown of communism has frequently been accompanied by a blurring of the line between civilian and military affairs and by the participation of some military men, as individuals, in civilian politics. See *State Building and Military Power in Russia and the New States of Eurasia*, ed. Bruce Parrott (Armonk, NY: M. E. Sharpe, 1995), esp. chs. 2, 8, and 13. Cf. Cohen, *Broken Bonds*, pp. 85–88, 183–88, 227–33, and Woodward, *Balkan Tragedy*, pp. 166–69, 255–62.

27 Charles Fairbanks, Jr., "The Postcommunist Wars," *Journal of Democracy* 6, no. 4 (October 1995), 18–34.

28 Assessing the character of the international environment leaves considerable room for disagreement among observers, especially where ideological and cultural currents are concerned. For example, Samuel Huntington has asserted that Marxist–Leninist regimes, Nazi Germany, and the advanced capitalist democracies shared some ultimate political values because they were all parts of the same Western civilization. In my view these three Western traditions were divided at least as fundamentally as are liberal democratic thought and the authoritarian strands of non-Western cultural traditions. See Huntington, "The Clash of Civilizations?" *Foreign Affairs* 72, no. 3 (Summer 1993), 23, 44, plus the reply from Fouad Ajami in ibid., 72, no.4 (September–October 1993), 2–9.

29 Huntington, *The Third Wave*, pp. 86–100; see also the chapters by Geoffrey Pridham, Laurence Whitehead, John Pinder, and Margot Light in *Building Democracy? The International Dimension of Democratisation in Eastern Europe*, ed. Geoffrey Pridham et al. (New York: St. Martin's Press, 1994), pp. 7–59, 119–68; and Nodia, "How Different are Postcommunist Transitions?" 15–16, 20–23.

30 Richard Ullman, "The Wars in Yugoslavia and the International System after the Cold War," and Richard Sobel, "U.S. and European Attitudes toward Intervention in the Former Yugoslavia: *Mourir pour la Bosnie?*" in *The World and Yugoslavia's Wars*, ed. Richard H. Ullman (New York: Council on Foreign Relations, 1996), pp. 9–41, 145–81.

31 During the critical early phases of the Yugoslav civil war, NATO's member-states were preoccupied with managing the consequences of the unification of Germany, other major European-security problems thrown up by the collapse of the Soviet bloc, and the Persian Gulf War. See Ullman, "The Wars in Yugoslavia and the International System after the Cold War," Stanley Hoffman, "Yugoslavia: Implications for Europe and for European Institutions," and David C. Gombert, "The United States and Yugoslavia's Wars," in *The World and Yugoslavia's Wars*, pp. 14–15, 24–31, 36, 102–18, 122–30, 136–37.

32 Samuel Huntington, *The Clash of Civilizations and the Remaking of World Order* (New York: Simon and Schuster, 1996), pp. 192–98.

33 Bunce, "Comparing East and South," 91.

34 In such instances, democratic theory provides no reliable means of determining which proposed outcome is preferable. This, in turn, often spurs the advocates of each proposed outcome to argue their case in still more vehement and uncompromising terms. See Dahl, *Democracy and Its Critics*, pp. 32–33.

35 Linz and Stepan, "Toward Consolidated Democracies," 20–21; Jacek Kochanowicz, "Reforming Weak States and Deficient Bureaucracies," in *Intricate Links*, pp. 195–96.

36 For a fuller treatment of this question, see my "Analyzing the Transformation of the Soviet Union in Comparative Perspective," in *The End of Empire? The Transformation of the USSR in Comparative Perspective*, ed. Karen Dawisha and Bruce Parrott (Armonk, NY: M. E. Sharpe, 1996), pp. 13–14, 16–20.

37 Liah Greenfeld, *Nationalism: Five Roads to Modernity* (Cambridge: Harvard University Press, 1992), pp. 8–12. Cf. John Breuilly, *Nationalism and the State*, 2d ed. (Chicago: University of Chicago Press, 1993), pp. 404–24.

38 For a penetrating discussion of this issue, see Rogers Brubaker, *Citizenship and Nationhood in France and Germany* (Cambridge: Harvard University Press, 1992).

39 One set of opinion surveys suggests considerable variation in the levels of acceptance or hostility expressed by members of several East European nations toward other ethnic groups. The levels of hostility expressed by Serbs in 1992 appear to be unusually high, although this contrast may be due partly to the fact that Serbia was at war when the survey was conducted. Mary E. McIntosh and Martha Abele MacIver, *Transition to What? Publics Confront Change in Eastern Europe*, Occasional Paper No. 38, Woodrow Wilson International Center for Scholars, Washington, DC, 1993, pp. 15–17.

40 On these linkages in the nineteenth century, see E. J. Hobsbawm, *Nations and Nationalism since 1780: Programme, Myth, Reality*, paperback ed. (New York: Cambridge University Press, 1990), ch. 1.

41 Huntington, *The Third Wave*, p. 44.

42 Bunce, "Comparing East and South," 89. Bunce grants that interwar Czechoslovakia constitutes a partial exception to this generalization.

43 Note, too, that democratic experience is a matter not simply of kind but of degree; hence scholars may apply different chronological and substantive standards to assess whether a country has had prior national experience with democracy.

44 See, for example, Sidney Verba, Norman H. Nie, and Jae-on Kim, *Participation and Political Equality: A Seven-Nation Comparison* (Chicago: The University of Chicago Press, 1978).

45 For an analogous trend in historians' treatment of American populism, see Peter Novick, *That Noble Dream: The "Objectivity Question" and the American Historical Profession* (New York: Cambridge University Press, 1988), pp. 337–41.

46 See, for example, Samuel Huntington, *Political Order in Changing Societies* (New Haven: Yale University Press, 1968), chs. 1, 3; and Samuel Huntington and Joan Nelson, *No Easy Choice: Political Participation in Developing Countries* (Cambridge: Harvard University Press, 1976), p. 13.

47 In his classic study of political development, Huntington adopts a definition that conflates voluntary and compulsory forms of political participation and attaches little explanatory significance to the differences between the two. (*Political Order in Changing Societies*, chs. 1, 3; cf. Theodore H. Friedgut, *Political Participation in the USSR* [Princeton: Princeton University Press, 1979], ch. 5.) In a later book he and Joan Nelson do emphasize the distinction by differentiating "autonomous" from "mobilized" participation. (Huntington and Nelson, *No Easy Choice*, pp. 7–15.) In *The Third Wave*, Huntington sometimes employs the narrower definition favored by students of liberal democracy. For example, he states that one-party systems, among which he includes communist regimes, have "suppressed both competition and participation" (p. 111).

48 Huntington and Nelson, *No Easy Choice*, pp. 7–15.

49 In Russia, for example, the tsarist regime long feared the expansion of mass education as a threat to its legitimacy. The Soviet regime quickly recognized that the expansion of mass education would allow it to indoctrinate individuals during a stage of social and personal development when their capacities for abstract thought were weakly developed, making them highly susceptible to manipulation from above.

50 Gregory Grossman, "The USSR – A Solidary Society: A Philosophical Issue in Communist Economic Reform," in *Essays in Socialism and Planning in Honor of Carl Landauer*, ed. Gregory Grossman (Englewood Cliffs, NJ: Prentice Hall, 1970); Robert F. Miller, "Civil Society in Communist Systems: An Introduction," in *The Developments of Civil Society in Communist Systems*, ed. Robert F. Miller (New York: Allen and Unwin, 1992), p. 5.

51 Huntington, *Political Order in Changing Societies*, emphasizes the stability of communist dictatorships. See also Gleason, *Totalitarianism*, pp. 198–209.

52 Brian D. Silver, "Political Beliefs and the Soviet Citizen," and Donna Bahry, "Politics, Generations, and Change in the USSR," in *Politics, Work, and Daily Life in the USSR: A Survey of Former Soviet Citizens*, ed. James Millar (New York: Cambridge University Press, 1987), pp. 116–121; Donna Bahry, "Society Transformed? Rethinking the Social Roots of Perestroika," *Slavic Review* 52, no. 3 (Fall 1993), 514–17.

53 Miller, "Civil Society in Communist Systems: An Introduction," pp. 6–11; Moshe Lewin, *The Gorbachev Phenomenon* (Berkeley, CA: University of California Press, 1988). The concept of civil society as a separate sphere of social life superior to the state first emerged in the late eighteenth and early nineteenth centuries. See John Keane, "Introduction," and idem., "Despotism and Democracy," in *Civil Society and the State*, ed. John Keane (New York: Verso, 1988), pp. 22–25, 35–71.

54 For a general discussion of these factors, see Huntington, *The Third Wave*, ch. 3, and Guillermo O'Donnell and Philippe C. Schmitter, *Transitions from Authoritarian Rule: Tentative Conclusions about Uncertain Democracies*, paperback ed. (Baltimore: Johns Hopkins University Press, 1986), pp. 61–64.

55 For an illuminating analysis of this general issue based on noncommunist cases, see Sidney Tarrow, "Mass Mobilization and Regime Change: Pacts, Reform, and Popular Power in Italy (1918–1922) and Spain (1975–1978)," in *The Politics of Democratic Consolidation: Southern Europe in Comparative Perspective*, ed.

Richard Gunther et al. (Baltimore, MD: Johns Hopkins University Press, 1996), pp. 204–30.

56 For example, in the spring of 1991 the radical reform forces led by Boris Yeltsin staged a peaceful mass demonstration in Moscow, and Soviet miners launched a damaging strike that included demands for political reform and the resignation of President Mikhail Gorbachev. The sequence of events suggests that these public demonstrations of support for Yeltsin helped persuade Gorbachev to abandon his temporary reliance on conservative political forces and grant large concessions to the advocates of further reform. Brown, *The Gorbachev Factor*, pp. 283–88; Jonathan Aves, "The Russian Labour Movement, 1989–91: The Mirage of a Russian Solidarność," in Jeffrey Hosking et al., *The Road to Post-Communism: Independent Political Movements in the Soviet Union, 1985–1991*, paperback ed. (New York: St. Martin's Press, 1992), pp. 151–52.

57 In addition to the chapter by Darrell Slider in *Conflict, Cleavage, and Change*, see Jonathan Aves, *Georgia: From Chaos to Stability?* (London: Royal Institute of International Affairs, 1996).

58 In conditions of acute political tension, certain electoral rules can heighten the probability of civil war; and different electoral rules can lead to a legitimate victory of right–wing, centrist, or left–wing parties under the same distribution of popular votes. See Rein Taagepera and Matthew S. Shugart, *Seats & Votes: The Effects & Determinants of Electoral Systems* (New Haven: Yale University Press, 1989), ch. 1.

59 For example, the weakness of the US government's coercive capacities played a major role in the Federalists' reluctant decision to accept the creation of the Democratic–Republican party in the 1790s, when parties were still generally regarded as illegitimate factions harmful to democratic government. (Martin Shefter, *Political Parties and the State: The American Historical Experience*, paperback ed. [Princeton: Princeton University Press, 1994], pp. 9–10; James R. Sharp, *American Politics in the Early Republic: The New Nation in Crisis* [New Haven: Yale University Press, 1993], pp. 208–25).

60 One noteworthy historical exception is revolutionary France. For a concise historical description of the complex struggles over the scope and forms of electoral participation in several European countries, see Stein Rokkan, "Elections: Electoral Systems," *International Encyclopedia of the Social Sciences*, vol. 5 (London: Macmillan and the Free Press, 1968), pp. 7–13.

61 White et al., *How Russia Votes*, pp. 29–34; Dawisha and Parrott, *Russia and the New States of Eurasia*, pp. 148–53.

62 Barbara Geddes, "A Comparative Perspective on the Leninist Legacy in Eastern Europe," *Comparative Political Studies* 28, no. 2 (July 1995), 261–65.

63 Krzysztof Jasiewicz, "Sources of Representation," in *Developments in East European Politics*, pp. 137–46. Most of these new electoral systems also have established a minimum-vote threshold for party representation, meant to avoid a paralyzing proliferation of splinter parties in the legislature.

64 In this discussion a political party is defined as an organization that (a) is identified by an official label (b) seeks to place its representatives in government office or to change the governmental system and (c) employs methods that include mobilizing citizens and participating in free elections if the state allows such elections. This definition encompasses both political organizations that

pursue or exercise power solely through democratic methods and organizations that pursue or exercise power largely through non-democratic means. On the other hand, it excludes single-issue interest groups whose avowed purpose is not to place their representatives in government office. It also excludes organizations that pursue power solely through violent means.

65 For a brief historical account of American distrust of the impact of parties on democracy, see Alan Ware, *Citizens, Parties, and the State: A Reappraisal* (Princeton: Princeton University Press, 1987), ch. 1.

66 A list of important democratic functions includes (a) mobilizing a large proportion of the citizenry to participate in politics (b) ensuring the representation of all social groups (c) allowing citizens to select individual governmental leaders directly (d) promoting the optimal aggregation of social interests (e) ensuring that government officials fulfill their electoral promises and (f) punishing the originators of failed governmental policies. Note that not all these functions can be fulfilled simultaneously. For example, (b) and (c) are at odds, as are (b) and (d). (Ware, *Citizens, Parties, and the State*, pp. 23–29, 150–241; G. Bingham Powell, Jr., *Contemporary Democracies: Participation, Stability, and Violence*, paperback ed. [Cambridge: Harvard University Press, 1982], pp. 73–78.) The causes of party decline are attributable to such factors as media-based political campaigns, the "surrogate" effects of public opinion surveys, the displacement of some party activities by narrowly-focused interest groups, and a tendency for more citizens to regard themselves as political independents unwilling to vote automatically for any party's slate of candidates. (Robert D. Putnam, "Troubled Democracies: Trends in Citizenship in the Trilateral World," paper prepared for the planning workshop of the Project on Democratization and Political Participation in Postcommunist Societies, Washington, DC, April 1995; and Thomas Poguntke, "Explorations into a Minefield: Anti-Party Sentiment," *European Journal of Political Research* 29, no. 3 (April 1996), 319–44.)

67 Valerie Bunce, "Uncertainty in the Transition: Post-Communism in Hungary," *East European Politics and Societies* 7, no. 2 (Spring 1993), 240–75.

68 Nelson, "Introduction," in *A Precarious Balance*, pp. 4–5; Robert H. Dix, "Democratization and the Institutionalization of Latin American Political Parties," *Comparative Political Studies* 24, no. 4 (January 1992), 488–511.

69 In nineteenth-century democracies, most political parties crystallized and expanded gradually, as the suffrage was widened and as socioeconomic changes made more citizens susceptible to political mobilization. In England, for example, Liberal and Conservative elites took at least 20 years to build party structures capable of exploiting the widening of the suffrage that occurred in mid-century. Ware, *Citizens, Parties, and the State*, pp. 22–23.

70 Conference on Political Parties and Democracy, sponsored by the International Forum for Democratic Studies, National Endowment for Democracy, November 18–19, 1996, Washington, DC.

71 Geddes, "A Comparative Perspective," 253–57.

72 See the chapters by Andrew Michta and David Olson in *The Consolidation of Democracy in East-Central Europe*; the chapters by Michael Urban and Ilya Prizel in *Democratic changes and authoritarian reactions in Russia, Ukraine, Belarus, and Moldova*; Dawisha and Parrott, *Russia and the New States of Eurasia*, p. 131; and White et al., *How Russia Votes*, p. 135.

73 The pioneering scholarly writings on parties focused solely on individual parties rather than on party systems, and a tendency to blur the distinction has persisted in some more recent scholarly analyses. (Harry Eckstein, "Parties, Political: Party Systems," *International Encyclopedia of the Social Sciences*, vol. 11, pp. 436–53.) One weakness of Huntington's seminal treatise on political development is that it assigns great weight to parties but tends to conflate parties with party systems. See Huntington, *Political Order in Changing Societies*, ch. 7.

74 Giovanni Sartori, *Parties and Party Systems: A Framework for Analysis* (New York: Cambridge University Press, 1976); Powell, *Contemporary Democracies*, pp. 74–80. For a discussion of the problems of classifying party systems, particularly by numerical criteria alone, see Eckstein, "Party Systems."

75 See especially Powell, *Contemporary Democracies*, pp. 74–80.

76 Sartori, *Parties and Party Systems*, pp. 132–42.

77 For the correlation between levels of personal dissatisfaction and the strength of extreme parties of the Left or Right in these two countries, see Ronald Inglehart, *Culture Shift in Advanced Industrial Society*, paperback ed. (Princeton: Princeton University Press), pp. 36–40.

78 Huntington, *The Third Wave*, p. 263.

79 John Higley et al., "The Persistence of Postcommunist Elites," *Journal of Democracy* 7, no. 2 (April 1996), 133–47; Michael Burton and John Higley, "Elite Settlements," *American Sociological Review* 52 (June 1987), 295–307.

80 For a critique of past elite studies and comparative survey data showing unusually deep attitudinal cleavages within the Soviet/Russian political elite during both the Gorbachev and Yeltsin eras, see David Lane, "Transition under Eltsin: The Nomenklatura and Political Elite Circulation," forthcoming in *Political Studies*.

81 For data showing that the political attitudes of former communist party members and individuals who never belonged to the communist party are quite similar in Bulgaria, Romania, and several countries of East–Central Europe, see the table in Rose, *What Is Europe?*, p. 142. (The table pools the national data sets, so that no conclusions for individual countries can be drawn from it.)

82 According to a careful study, in the past decade the number of ethnic conflicts has grown at approximately the same rate as in the 1960s and 1970s. See Ted Robert Gurr and Barbara Harff, *Ethnic Conflict in World Politics* (Boulder, CO: Westview, 1994), pp. 11, 13.

83 Horowitz, *Ethnic Groups in Conflict*, Part Three.

84 Juan Linz, *The Breakdown of Democratic Regimes: Crisis, Breakdown, & Reequilibration* (Baltimore: Johns Hopkins University Press, 1978), ch. 2.

85 For a general discussion of the connection between political parties and terrorism, see Leonard Weinberg, "Turning to Terror: The Conditions under Which Political Parties Turn to Terrorist Activities," *Comparative Politics* 23, no. 4 (July 1991), 423–38.

86 Arend Lijphart, *Democracies: Patterns of Majoritarian and Consensus Government in Twenty-One Countries*, paperback ed. (New Haven: Yale University Press, 1984), ch. 7; Powell, *Contemporary Democracies*, ch. 7.

87 Sartori, *Parties and Party Systems*, pp. 221–25.

88 My interpretation of these concepts, which have sparked vigorous scholarly debate, is derived from such works as Gabriel Almond and Sidney Verba, *The Civic Culture: Political Attitudes and Democracy in Five Nations*, paperback ed.

(Boston: Little, Brown and Co., 1965), and Inglehart, *Culture Shift in Advanced Industrial Societies*. Most of the controversial issues are well covered in *The Civic Culture Revisited*, ed. Gabriel Almond and Sidney Verba (Newbury Park, CA: Sage Publications, 1980). For reasons of space, my discussion omits several important distinctions, such as the existence of national political subcultures and differences between elite and mass political cultures.

89 However, scholars have disagreed about the particular cultural dispositions that actually support democracy. See especially Edward Muller and Mitchell Seligson, "Civic Culture and Democracy: The Question of Causal Relationships," *American Political Science Review* 88, no. 3 (September 1994), 635–52. Naturally, an important role is also played by non-cultural factors, such as the behavior of the state and major changes in citizens' socioeconomic circumstances.

90 Inglehart, *Culture Shift*, chs. 1–3. For evidence of dramatic increase in the democratic elements of German political culture and a decline In the civic elements of British and US political culture during the three decades following World War II, see the chapters by David Conradt, Dennis Kavanagh, and Alan Abramowitz in *The Civic Culture Revisited*.

91 For a discussion that relates civil society to other forms of political society, see Ernest Gellner, *Conditions of Liberty: Civil Society and Its Rivals* (New York: Allen Lane/The Penguin Press, 1994).

92 Seymour Martin Lipset, *Political Man: The Social Bases of Politics* (New York: Anchor Books, 1963), ch. 4.

93 Robert Putnam, *Making Democracy Work: Civic Traditions in Modern Italy* (Princeton: Princeton University Press, 1993). Cf. Sidney Tarrow, "Making Social Science Work Across Space and Time: A Critical Reflection on Robert Putnam's *Making Democracy Work*," *American Political Science Review* 90, no. 2 (June 1996), 389–98.

94 This paragraph is based on Dawisha and Parrott, *Russia and the New States of Eurasia*, pp. 123–25. For a nuanced discussion of the historical evolution of the concept of civil society, see Keane, "Despotism and Democracy," pp. 35–72.

95 For an exposition of these theoretical differences, which have centered especially on whether commercial organizations based on private property belong to civil society or undermine it, see Keane, "Introduction," pp. 13–14, and "Despotism and Democracy," esp. pp. 62–66. On the connection between civil society and relations within the family, see Carol Pateman, "The Fraternal Social Contract," pp. 101–28 in the same volume.

96 Larry Diamond, "Rethinking Civil Society: Toward Democratic Consolidation," *Journal of Democracy* 5, no. 3 (July 1994), 4–17.

97 For a discussion of this and other problems of analyzing political culture in the USSR and Russia, see Frederick J. Fleron, Jr., "Post-Soviet Political Culture in Russia: An Assessment of Recent Empirical Investigations," *Europe–Asia Studies* 48, no. 2 (March 1996), 225–60.

98 In keeping with prevailing usage before about 1800, the concept of civil society has sometimes been construed even more broadly to include both democratic governmental institutions and social structures conducive to democracy. However, this definition prevents analysis of the interactions between government and society that may fundamentally change the political system.

99 "Under whatever name – 'parallel *polis*,' 'independent culture,' or 'independent society' – the idea of civil society remained largely restricted to narrow circles of independent intellectuals in every East and Central European country save one. The exception . . . was Poland." Aleksander Smolar, "From Opposition to Atomization," *Journal of Democracy* 7, no. 1 (January 1996), 26.

100 Of necessity, this short excursus oversimplifies the analytical issues and omits discussion of the empirical variations among countries. For a general discussion of scholarly tendencies to explain postcommunist political development in terms of either "communist legacies" or "liberal institutional" determinants, see Crawford and Lijphart, "Explaining Political and Economic Change in Post-Communist Eastern Europe."

101 McIntosh and MacIver, *Transition to What? Publics Confront Change in Eastern Europe*, esp. pp. 6, 14.

102 For an insightful juxtaposition of survey data gathered from displaced Soviet citizens after World War II and data collected from Soviet emigrants during the late Brezhnev period, see Bahry, "Society Transformed? Rethinking the Social Roots of Perestroika." The data suggest that in the late Stalin years up to 50 percent of Soviet citizens may have favored a relaxation of intellectual controls, and that by the late Brezhnev period this percentage may have increased substantially (ibid., p. 539). On the role of authoritarian violence in strengthening the appeal of democracy, see Giuseppe di Palma, *To Craft Democracies: An Essay on Democratic Transitions*, paperback ed. (Berkeley: University of California Press, 1990), pp. 19–23, 150–51.

103 For a survey of the voluntary sector in advanced industrial democracies, see *Between States and Markets: The Voluntary Sector in Comparative Perspective*, ed. Robert Wuthnow (Princeton: Princeton University Press, 1991).

104 Geddes, "Challenging the Conventional Wisdom," 104; Jose Maria Maravali, "The Myth of the Authoritarian Advantage," *Journal of Democracy* 5, no. 4 (October 1994), 17–31; Joan Nelson, "Labor and Business Roles in Dual Transitions: Building Blocks or Stumbling Blocks?" in *Intricate Links*, p. 147. This issue was, of course, the subject of vigorous public debate in the West.

105 Geddes, "Challenging the Conventional Wisdom," 109–111.

106 In Eastern Europe, for example, labor unions have played a role in dislodging some government coalitions from power and have pressed governments to adopt their policy preferences. However, anti-democratic union violence and general strikes have been unusual and have tended to occur in countries, such as Romania, whose party systems have been least capable of representing workers' interests. Nelson, "Labor and Business Roles in Dual Transitions," pp. 154–63.

107 Linz and Stepan, "Toward Consolidated Democracies." For example, in Russia's 1996 presidential run-off, Boris Yeltsin won the votes of more than two-thirds of the persons who believed the government would solve the economy's problems in 10 years or less. By contrast, Genadii Zyuganov, the communist party candidate, won the support of 70 percent of those who thought the government would never be able to solve these problems. (*New Russia Barometer VI: After the Presidential Election*, Centre for the Study of Public Policy, University of Strathclyde, Glasgow, 1996, p. 13.) Considerable evidence also suggests that many categories of workers, though hard-hit by economic reform, have devised unofficial sources of income that are not reflected in

gloomy official estimates of declining output. See Daniel Kaufman and Aleksander Kaliberda, "Integrating the Unofficial Economy into the Dynamics of Post-Socialist Economies: A Framework of Analysis and Evidence," in *Economic Transition in Russia and the New States of Eurasia*, ed. Bartlomiej Kaminski (Armonk, NY: M. E. Sharpe, 1996), pp. 81–120.

108 In Russia and several democracies of Eastern Europe, public opinion has shifted since 1991 toward more support for government involvement in the economy, although acceptance of economic inequalities has simultaneously grown in most of the same countries. A recent survey of several postcommunist countries found that the only one in which public attitudes have moved toward greater support for egalitarianism is Russia. (James Kluegel and David S. Mason, "Social Justice in Transition? Attitudinal Change in Russia and East-Central Europe," paper presented at the annual convention of the American Association for the Advancement of Slavic Studies, Boston, November 1996.) In the early 1990s, measurable economic inequalities in postcommunist countries generally remained smaller or no larger than than those in Western democracies. (Branko Milanovic, "Poverty and Inequality in Transition Economies: What Has Actually Happened," in *Economic Transition in Russia and the New States of Eurasia*, pp. 180–81.)

109 For a discussion of national variations in the understanding of corruption, see Michael Johnston, "Historical Conflict and the Rise of Standards," in *The Global Resurgence of Democracy*, pp. 193–205.

110 Kluegel and Mason, "Justice Perceptions in Russia and Eastern Europe, 1991–1995"; Richard Dobson, "Is Russia Turning the Corner? Changing Russian Public Opinion, 1991–1996," *Research Report*, Office of Research and Media Reaction, US Information Agency, September 1996, pp. 11–13.

111 Miller, "Civil Society in Communist Systems," p. 9; Keane, "Despotism and Democracy," pp. 64–66.

112 Richard Rose, "Toward a Civil Economy," *Journal of Democracy* 3, no. 2 (1992), 13–25, and Kochanowicz, "Reforming Weak States and Deficient Bureaucracies," pp. 195–204, 214–22. The fullest account of the criminalization of economic activities in Russia is Stephen Handelman, *Comrade Criminal* (New Haven: Yale University Press, 1995).

113 Nelson, "How Market Reforms and Democratic Consolidation Affect Each Other," pp. 11–13.

114 Dobson, "Is Russia Turning the Corner?" pp. 8–9.

115 For example, surveys of citizens in the European Community's member-countries show that the average percentage of respondents saying they were "very satisfied" or "fairly satisfied" with the way democracy works ranged between 66 and 41 percent in 1985–1993. Leonardo Morlino and Jose R. Montero, "Legitimacy and Democracy in Southern Europe," in *The Politics of Democratic Consolidation: Southern Europe in Comparative Perspective*, p. 239.

2 Democratization and political participation: research concepts and methodologies

Karen Dawisha

The primary objectives of the Project on Democratization and Political Participation have been to gauge the prospects for democratization in Eastern Europe and the former Soviet Union by systematically examining and comparing trends in the organized political activities of society in each country and to contribute to the theoretical discussion about the determinants of these trends. This chapter has several objectives. It begins with an discussion of how the concepts of democracy, democratization, and democratic consolidation are defined and operationalized in this project. Three sections then follow in which the research questions which have guided the project are discussed (the questions themselves are presented in the Appendix), along with propositions and hypotheses derived from the existing literature on democratization. The sections substantively address three disparate parts of the democratization process: two sections on inputs to the process, namely factors influencing the formation of political groups and parties, and the political evolution of society, and one section on outcomes, namely the factors affecting the possible emergence of party systems in postcommunist states.

Conceptualizing democracy and democratization

What is meant by democracy, and how is the process of democratization understood in this project? In line with recent research,[1] a procedural or minimalist conception of democracy was employed. Democracy is defined as a political system in which the formal and actual leaders of the government are chosen through regular elections based on multiple candidacies and secret balloting, with the right of all adult citizens to vote. It is assumed that leaders chosen via free and fair elections, using universal adult suffrage, will be induced to modify their behavior to be more responsive to popular wishes and demands than leaders in authoritarian states.

There remains, however, the crucial task of making the transition from the conceptual level to the empirical-observational level. Even if the features of the conception can be elaborated, how does one determine their presence or their absence over time, within individual countries or across the postcommunist world? Simply put, how does one know when the level of democracy is high, or when it is low or non-existent? Over the past thirty years or so, there have been numerous attempts at objectively measuring democracies.[2] Some of the more recent efforts such as those of Kenneth Bollen have, arguably, resulted in more finely calibrated instruments.[3] These measures are most useful as indicators of the extent to which democracy exists in a country at a specific time. In and of themselves, they are not useful for explaining democratic change. As noted recently, "with these scores, one can only estimate the extent to which democracy has advanced or regressed in that given country over a very long period of time or compare the country with others similarly scored."[4] Indeed most analysts who draw up such indicators would be the first to recognize that their contribution has been in measuring democracy, not explaining its underlying dynamics.

Civil liberties and political rights can be viewed as two distinct conceptual dimensions of democracy. The dimension of political rights can be, more or less, directly observed. The degree to which adult suffrage is universal, elections are fairly conducted, and all persons are eligible for public office can be directly observed through objective analysis of electoral laws and practices. The degree to which leaders freely compete for votes can be ascertained in a similar manner. An analysis of political rights allows one to draw conclusions about the level of democracy, since it can reasonably be hypothesized that the higher the number of rights universally enjoyed by the population, the greater will be the level of democratization.

Democracy is also dependent upon the provision of civil liberties, specifically: (1) freedom to form and join organizations; (2) freedom of expression; and (3) access to multiple and competing sources of information. Empirical data can be garnered to support a judgment about the extent to which the three components of civil liberties exist. It is assumed that the more the number and level of civil liberties enjoyed by a country's population, the greater will be the level of democratization. Thus, political rights and civil liberties serve as indicators of democracy and both must be present in order for a country to be classified as democratic. Through the assignment of numerical values to the empirical properties representing political rights and civil liberties, according to consistent rules, one could draw up a representation of the level of democracy existing within a country at any given time.

Such a measure, however, would not necessarily allow one to conclude that any given democracy was likely to be both stable and durable. Indeed, the free and unfettered exercise of political rights and liberties has been seen on occasions as negatively affecting the durability of democracies, sometimes obliging leaders and populations to accept various trade-offs which would limit the degree of representation of societal groups in return for sustaining democratic institutions over time. A good example is the tendency of democracies to introduce measures which effectively limit the number of parties that can be represented in the legislature to those which gain above a certain percentage threshold of the popular vote, so as to lessen the impact of minority opinion and of groups at the left and right of the political spectrum and magnify the influence of majoritarian views and centrist groups. Such measures, while in fact denying some voters the right to have their votes have an equal impact upon outcomes, are justified by reference to the universal interests of all voters in ensuring the long-term durability of democratic institutions.

Equally, democracies vary in their protection of civil liberties such as freedom of speech and assembly. Many established democracies curtail the rights of groups which have in the past shown their intent to overthrow the democratically elected order. These actions, too, are justified by reference to the right of the state to limit the liberties of some in the short term in order to ensure the liberty of all in the long-term.

Finally, one must distinguish between democracy and democratization. To a certain extent, all states, even those that call themselves, and are recognized by others as, democratic are still evolving, either towards or away from more democracy. The perennial debates in even the most stable democracies about justice, liberty, equity, rights, and governability reflect this continuing concern. But more problematic is drawing the line between an authoritarian polity which is breaking down and a democratic entity which is emerging. When can one say that the process of democratization actually begins? For the purposes of this project, democratization is said to begin when the first set of free and fair elections for national-level office takes place. This first set of elections must be accompanied in short order by the granting of civil liberties and political rights and the establishment of both state institutions that operate according to the rule of law and intermediate organizations that mediate between the citizen and the state. If these events do not take place, then it is likely that the process of democratization will not be fully consolidated.

Measuring democratic consolidation

Unlike the numerous efforts to measure democracy systematically, relatively few attempts have been made to measure democratic consolidation. Central to this notion is acceptance that not all states that start out on the road to democracy will complete the transition. Some will fall back into authoritarianism, others might regress into civil war, others will maintain a low equilibrium democracy for decades, verging constantly on the brink of collapse.[5] And all transitions will differ, combining as they do on the one hand individual historical legacies, leaders, socioeconomic foundations and international interactions and on the other hand the policies pursued by elites and their varied impact on individual societies at any given time.

A consolidated democracy is one in which most major social groups expect that government leaders will be chosen through competitive elections and regard representative institutions and procedures as their main channel for processing claims on the state. One way of measuring consolidation is to apply a "two-turnover test," in which a democracy "may be viewed as consolidated if the party or group that takes power in the initial election at the time of the transition loses a subsequent election and turns over power to those election winners, and if those election winners then peacefully turn over power to winners of a later election.[6] Thus, for example, when communism fell, a first round of elections was held. Typically two to four years later, a second round was held: if the group in power since the fall of communism was displaced, this would count as the first turnover. Only after this group or party was displaced by a second round of elections could one then speak of a country having passed the 'two turn-over test.' Of the postcommunist states, only postcommunist Lithuania had by the end of 1996 passed such a test: the Lithuanian Democratic Labor Party, the renamed Communist Party, took power from the conservative Sajudis led by Vytautas Landsbergis in 1992, and then surrendered it back to Landsbergis' party (the renamed Homeland Union) when they lost parliamentary elections in November 1996. However, such a test has been criticized on the grounds that it would fail to classify either interwar Eastern Europe or postwar Italy or Japan as democracies. Moreover, if used alone, it does not provide levels of calibration and gradation adequate for the comparative scope of the project. Also while a determination could be made if a democracy were consolidated or not using a two-turnover test, it would not be possible to answer the questions "why?" or "why not?" using the test.

In measuring democratic consolidation over time within a given country or across nations, it may prove more theoretically informative to treat it as a continuum, rather than a two-step process. There are at least four distinct conceptual aspects of democratic consolidation, each of which could be observed by various measures: the two-turnover test, low public support for anti-system parties or groups, high public commitment to the fundamental values and procedural norms of democratic politics, and elite consensus about the desirability of institutionizing and legitimizing democratic norms and values.[7]

An index could be constructed by combining the latter three indicators if the criteria for the two-turnover test are not met. This would serve at least three purposes. First, several variables relating to democratic consolidation could be represented by a single score, thereby reducing the complexity of the data and facilitating comparison. Second, such an index could provide a quantitative measure of democratic consolidation amenable to statistical manipulation. Finally, because it measures several properties, the index is inherently more reliable than a measure based on a single factor.

Clearly, democratic consolidation is still a goal in almost all of the postcommunist countries, yet significant strides have been made. Autonomous societal action has largely replaced communist dictatorship in most countries; and the notions of choice, competition, and tolerance are increasingly salient. As emphasized in the working definition of democracy, elections should be based on multiple candidacies that ensure real opportunities for electoral competition. Informal alliances rapidly evolved into political parties in the wake of the communist collapse: these parties are gradually becoming rooted and stable. The following section examines some of the factors influencing the formation of political groups and parties across the countries under investigation. In each of the following sections, the research questions (as presented in the Appendix) which were given to the authors are used as the basis for deriving hypotheses and propositions, and a consideration is made of the range of results which might be expected from the various hypotheses. This section is followed by sections on the political evolution of society and on the emergence of political parties and party systems.

Factors influencing the formation of parties

Authors were presented with a number of questions, listed in the Appendix, which addressed the factors influential in forming the political groups and parties, considered as a cornerstone in any country's move toward democracy. The comparative literature is deeply divided over the relative influence of historical, ethnic, social, cultural, institutional, and economic factors in determining the success of a country's move toward democracy. This section was intended to elicit the panel's responses to these various issues.

In the literature on transitions, it is generally assumed that those countries which have to establish a national identity before going on to build the institutions of the state and inculcate civic virtues in the populace will face the greatest challenge.[8] In doing so they will have to replace other national identities which may command popular support if the new state was carved out of old ones and strive to surpass and mobilize the other nested identities of family, clan, region, and ethnicity in the service of a new civic minded-ness.

Authors were asked to elaborate the key elements of the precommunist historical legacy of each country. They were additionally asked to focus on any precommunist experience of democracy, and whether elements of the postcommunist polity, such as particular government structures, intermediary associations, and political parties have been modeled on precommunist patterns.

The literature would appear to support three interrelated hypotheses: polities with a strong, unified national identity based on a precommunist legacy of independence will be able to make the most rapid and peaceful transition to sovereign independence; those polities with a precommunist tradition of exclusivist nationalism will have more difficulty in making the transition to democracy; and those polities with a precommunist tradition of competitive multiparty systems are most likely to be successful in establishing stable multiparty democracies.

It could reasonably be assumed that those countries which are being "reborn" after a period of communist suppression would have an enormous advantage over states being established for the first time. One would expect a shorter time in putting basic institutions in place, in passing a constitution and other basic laws, and in regularizing state-society relations on the basis of a national accord. States coming into existence for the first time are not able to operate on the basis of historical trust or on a shared remembrance of the role the state played in the past in forging a partnership between state and society to nourish and sustain the nation. On the contrary, given the role of the state in the communist period in suppressing both nation and society (although to be sure the nation was often harnessed to the needs of the state during times of crisis in all the communist states and was symbiotically allied to the state in Yugoslavia, Hungary, and Romania in particular), any state without a precommunist legacy of trust might reasonably be expected to falter in the project of legitimization.

There are, however, two related dilemmas: first, countries that are resurrecting states which, in the precommunist era, had an authoritarian character may have more difficulty overcoming the burden of this legacy than countries that are creating state institutions anew. Secondly, while a regeneration of a previous national identity is expected to facilitate the process of state-building, if the national identity was exclusivist, then its renaissance might promote state-building but impede democratization. This tendency is underscored by Beverly Crawford and Arendt Lijphart, who address the problem that unlike in France or England, where nationalism had its origins in the Enlightenment, in Eastern Europe and the former Soviet Union, it had its roots "in the Russian and German tradition of *Volk*, blood, *narod*, and race as the basis for membership in the nation."[9] To be sure, the distinctions between the historical origins of the national identities of the Germans and Russians on the one hand and the British and the French on the other are clear. Yet this view does not account sufficiently for the fact that even in England, the process of transforming narrow English identity centered in the Home Counties into a greater United Kingdom entailed the forcible suppression of independent national aspirations in Wales and Scotland, as we;; asa lengthy and continuing struggle with Northern Ireland. And despite this, democratization proceeded apace in Great Britain, suggesting that the connections between a state's formative national identity and the identity which underpins its institutions is not fixed for all time.

It is also posited in the transitions literature that those states with precommunist traditions of multiparty elections and capitalist development are more likely to be able to reestablish these institutions. There are two reasons: one is that to the extent that a state had already adopted a multiparty system and/or capitalism in the past, protracted and often divisive national debates on paths of development could be avoided. Additionally many of the actual laws governing political and economic life can be resuscitated with only minor amendments. Of course, given the number of ultra-nationalist parties that inhabited the landscape of interwar Eastern Europe, the resuscitation of these parties has not necessarily promoted simultaneous liberalization.

Postcommunist states have had to sift through, resurrect, and overcome elements not only of their precommunist heritage, but also of their communist past. Authors were asked to identify key elements of the legacy of the communist era. In addition, they were asked to speculate on how the political and social evolution of each country in the late communist era (e.g., the emergence or nonemergence of a significant dissent movement) affected the postcommunist formation of societal interest groups and parties.

Prevalent in the field are two core assumptions that require some systematic elaboration: first, the assumption that the more and the longer a country was subjected to the antidemocratic and totalitarian features of Stalinism, the less likely will be the chances of democracy succeeding, and secondly, if there is a prior history of democracy and civil society, and a communist legacy of reform and openness, then the chances of a successful transition to democracy will be greater and the speed of transition will be quicker.

The literature on the legacy of the communist era is vast, growing, and divided. Most would agree that communism left a "poisonous residue"[10] on virtually all aspects of society, but whether that residue can easily be washed away is open to controversy. Those who subscribe to the view that the legacy of communism will be significant and abiding look at its effect in several areas.[11] Politically, the fact that there essentially were no public politics in the communist era is presumed to have left a deep legacy: there were no self-governing institutions, no interest groups or rival parties operating independent of the state, and no competing sources of information. At the same time, Soviet systems were characterized by a single elite which, while capable of being split into factions, did not regularly or routinely circulate into and out of power. These elites, it was assumed by some, would resist the construction of new institutions which would limit the reach of their authority.[12] Some would see these features as a significant barrier to the emergence of democracy and civil society.[13] Other authors also assume that the Soviet-era largely succeeded in one of its aims, namely to destroy the pre-Leninist past, thus robbing these societies of their ability to resurrect precommunist identities, parties, and institutions.[14]

Soviet-style systems, in addition, were command economies controlled from the center, without private ownership of the means of production or market relations. As the sector ideologically most suited to the Stalinist world view and economically most capable of thriving under command conditions, the military-industrial complex grew to become not only the dominant sector of the economy but also the only sector which functioned more or less according to plan. The performance of this sector in most communist countries (most notably the USSR, Yugoslavia, and the Slovak sector of Czechoslovakia) not only gave central planning whatever credibility it enjoyed but also was designed to form the protective outer shell for the entire system, leading analysts inside and outside the country to attribute far more capability to the economy and the system as a whole than ultimately it possessed.[15] This sector bequeathed to the successor states industries which could produce high quality goods but which required both continued subsidies and a Cold War-style mission concomitant with its size and orientation. Additionally, it is believed by some that sectors of the military-industrial complex in Russia, in support of like-minded groups within the Ministry of Interior, the revamped KGB, and the Ministry of Defense, have been a major buttress of a strong but not necessarily democratic or non-imperial state.[16]

Underneath this strong outer shell resided the light industrial and consumer sectors of the economy which were denied funds, resources, initiative, and personnel – virtually everything except planning targets; and after de-Stalinization ended the use of terror to force compliance, these could be met only by bribery, corruption, distortion, and the formation of informal and illegal production networks. The fact that such a high percentage of total state economic interactions took place outside the plan meant that whatever performance the economy achieved was bought at the expense of the integrity of the planning mechanism of the state and the trust, loyalty, and ultimately the compliance of the population. These socioeconomic and political failures weakened central control, but also left a legacy of cynicism and disrespect for the state, to say nothing of the vast array of informal economic networks which fell out of the state and beyond the law when the regimes collapsed.[17] In *New World Disorder*, Ken Jowitt predicted that the combined legacy of bureaucracy, corruption, and interpersonal distrust would hinder the implementation of democratic reforms, although it is unclear from his analysis whether and why this legacy might vary across countries and whether and why it might be relatively transient.[18]

The great difficulty of establishing political and economic institutions from the bottom up cannot be overstated: Samuel Huntington found that twenty-three of the twenty-nine countries that democratized during the so-called "third wave" (between 1974 and 1990) had previous democratic experience. Equally, those that had not democratized by 1990 had no democratic past. So while states are not condemned necessarily to relive their past, clearly the results of Huntington's study would support the thesis that all other factors being equal, previous democratic experience greatly facilitates the transition to democracy.[19]

The hypotheses generated in the remainder of the section are designed to address not the legacy of the precommunist or communist era, but the nature of the transition and the actual social situation inherited by the first postcommunist leaders. In particular, questions focus on the possibility of overcoming the Leninist legacy through what Crawford and Lijphart call "the imperatives of liberalization." As they state, this approach "suggests that new institutions can be crafted and new international pressures can be brought to bear that shut out the negative influences of the past."[20] Even those authors like Samuel Huntington who favor a strong political cultural argument are supportive of the view that the success of one country or region in introducing democratic reforms can have a snowballing effect in encouraging democratization elsewhere. The economic, political, and cultural policies pursued by actors in the external environment also are seen as extremely consequential for stimulating and supporting movement toward liberalization, particularly in an era when communication is global and international norms favor human rights and democracy.[21]

From this discussion and the literature on transition, it is possible to generate a number of propositions and hypotheses: the following are among the most salient. In those countries whose transition was non-violent and pacted between the elites and the opposition, a party system is most likely to be quickly established.[22] In those countries whose transition was non-violent and pacted between different groups of elites, the ruling party or group will be most able to maintain their elite status, if not their monopoly.[23] In those countries where the new elites moved most quickly to impose rapid liberalization, privatization, and democratization, extremist opposition parties will be less likely to gain a foothold amongst the populace.[24] In those transitions marked by violence, the elites are most likely to attempt to preempt the emergence of independent associations and parties.[25]

Another crucial aspect of transition is the assertion of civilian control over violent coercion in society. Many theorists, most notably Robert Dahl, have underlined the civilian control of the military as a crucial requirement for successful democratization,[26] leading one to suppose that it should be possible to demonstrate the validity of the following propositions: the greater the popular support for democracy as opposed to other political systems or of democratic values as opposed to other political ends (for example, stability, social justice, and so forth), the lower the levels of military intervention in domestic politics;[27] the greater the participation of the citizenry in electoral politics, the lower the levels of military intervention in politics;[28] and the greater the tradition of civilian control of the military within a country, the less will be the tendency of the military to intervene in politics.[29]

Also of concern is the need to analyze the impact on democratization of the political balances among the transitional groups, since much has been made by Adam Przeworski, Mancur Olson, and others of the likelihood that transitional elites would attempt to shape new institutions to maximize their interests. Thus it could be hypothesized that the more that the transition is coopted by hard-liners on the ruling side and radical factions amongst the opponents, the greater will be the prospect for failure of talks to produce a workable and democratic electoral system.[30] And conversely, the more evenly balanced the power amongst diverse elite groups at the time of transition, the more will be the tendency to design electoral legislation which does not favor any particular electoral constituency.[31]

Social and ethnic cleavages suppressed under communism are likely to emerge in the transition and are often intensified by economic changes and political and personal uncertainty. The challenge facing authors is both to identify these cleavages and to analyze the extent to which they have shaped the formation of parties and other political groups. The literature suggests the following relationships exist between social and ethnic cleavages and the prospects for democratization: the more that societies are characterized by spatial distances between mutually reinforcing and exclusivist ethnic, social, economic, and religious groups, the greater will be the tendency for parties to be formed reflecting these divisions;[32] the larger the size of ethnic minorities as a proportion of the total population, the greater is the probability that democratization using majoritarian formulas will fail to contain communal violence if it breaks out;[33] as long as no group has a monopoly over control of resources, then social divisions and unequal access to those resources can be mitigated within a democratic regime;[34] and to the extent that parties and associations promote and facilitate social mobility and civic awareness, then their aggregative function will assist democratization.

The pattern and pace of postcommunist economic change is another independent variable seen as having an impact on democratic outcomes, affecting the emergence of political parties, and increasing the stakes of winning and losing in the political arena. On the whole, it is accepted that the pattern and pace of economic change is a function of the political will of the ruling elites, but that both elites and social groups interact to maximize their access to resources. Thus, political elites will structure economic reforms to maximize their political and economic interests, while setting the pace of change in order to minimize the chances of systematic and widespread social unrest.[35]

Among the greatest challenges to successful democratization is the existence of violent conflict either inside the country or with other states. Indeed, it would appear that the greater the level of violent conflict within a society, the more democratic institutions will be undermined.[36] But its actual impact, upon observation, is diverse, depending on the level and direction of conflict, elite reaction, state capacity to terminate, suppress, resolve, or withstand the violence, and the impact of the violence on the attitude of core social groups toward the process of democratization. Violence may weaken existing institutions in an emerging democracy, but it can also increase pressure toward the adoption of changed institutional arrangements which maintain democracy, ranging from the introduction of nonmajoritarian consociational arrangements to widen the representation of marginalized and alienated minorities[37] to the adoption of corporatist forms of democracy in which large interest-based groups mediate between the state and the citizenry, to a certain degree suppressing citizens' direct involvement in policy making and aggregating overlapping and pluralistic intermediate groups into larger and more monopolistic associations.[38]

The political evolution of society

Central to the questions in this section is the assumption that citizens' attitudes matter. Gabriel Almond and Sidney Verba's theory of civic culture[39] postulates that the viability of democratic institutions is significantly affected by attitudes such as belief in one's ability to influence political decisions, feelings of positive affect for the political system, and the belief that fellow citizens are trustworthy. Challenges to political culture theory have taken place primarily on two levels and have emerged from two intellectual camps.

One challenge emerged in the 1960s and lasted throughout the 1970s as radical scholars polemicized against political culture theory. These scholars, many of them Marxist or neo-Marxist, argued that the dominant political culture in any society was a necessary reflection of the relationships between the ruling and subordinate classes. As Almond later wrote, political culture theory, in particular, "was challenged on the grounds that political and social attitudes were reflections of class and/or ethnic status or else were the 'false consciousness' implanted by such institutions as schools, universities and media."[40]

Also in the 1960s another challenge to political culture theory emerged with the ascension of rational choice models, which asserted that all individuals and institutions in a political system – whether ordinary members of society or politicians or parties, coalitions, intermediate organizations, and governmental institutions comprised of or representing those individuals – would act efficiently to maximize interests, often defined in economic terms.[41] By the late 1960s models based on rational choice and game theoretic approaches had become a dominant mode of social analysis. This emergence of "rational choice," "public choice," and "positive political theory" challenged the very premise of political culture theory. From within this perspective, examining political culture amounted to little more than a superfluous exercise. It was widely held that sufficient explanatory power could be generated by assuming self-interested, short-run rationality. Contributing to the ascension of this mode of analysis, especially within comparative political science, were the availability of economic data and the lack of sufficient cross-national data on political attitudes.

This paucity of aggregate data or large-N studies that would allow researchers to go beyond individual country or region case-studies and draw broader conclusions about factors outside the economic realm hampered efforts by those interested in political culture to reach generalizable conclusions. However, by 1988, Ronald Inglehart[42] had compiled data on attitudes of the general public for a sample of countries large enough to permit multivariate statistical analysis of the relative influence of mass political attitudes as compared with macro-socioeconomic variables on democratization. The accumulation of cross-national data on attitudes of the general public combined with the collapse of Marxism as an alternative explanatory system and the reorientation of some public choice theorists toward a "new institutionalism" has led to a resurgence of interest in political culture as an explanatory variable.

It is now more generally accepted that democracy requires a supportive culture, even if it is agreed that this culture can be strongly shaped both by transient and short-term factors including economic performance and by more underlying variables, including the institutional setting in which this culture is set. Democratic institutions both promote and are promoted by a democratic political culture. In a democracy, popular support for the creation of an independent civil society embodying intermediate groups and associations which feed into the political process and aggregate different societal interests is also required. Because freedom of speech, media, religion, assembly and the right to form independent groups and opposition parties were all suppressed in the communist era, the norms associated with a civic culture cannot be expected to emerge overnight. The legacy of mistrust must first be overcome in order for a previously atomized society to establish the basic level of tolerance and civic responsibility required to sustain even the most basic levels of freedom.[43] Even then, clearly, underlying cultural factors independent of the communist legacy could accelerate or impede the emergence of the kind of civil society associated with liberal democracy.[44]

When examining the emergence of political associations in early transitional societies, authors were asked to collect data on the types of political associations or actors that have become most prominent in each country's political life, that is, political parties, state sector managerial lobbies, trade unions, business organizations, professional associations, religious organizations, clans, paramilitary units, criminal groups, and so forth. In addition, data was collected on how the public perception of political parties and what they claim to represent has affected citizens' attitudes to the political system. Authors were asked to comment on the relative importance of parties as vehicles for new elites intent on accumulating political power and wealth, as opposed to alternative vehicles, such as associations, informal groupings, and the like.

The assumptions in the comparative politics literature that underlie the section on the emergence of political parties are several, including: the higher the level of citizen distrust of political institutions, the greater will be the difficulty of establishing a viable party system; parties will gain preeminence as intermediary institutions only if elections are regular, free, and fair; and the holding of regular, and free and fair elections will increase civic trust over time.[45]

Also central to an understanding of the evolution of societies in transition is the extent to which attempted marketization and privatization have affected the political strength and behavior of various economic groups in society. Operating at the level of abstraction, one could envision distinct responses from economic groups along a continuum ranging from strategies of intransigent resistance to reforms which directly (and in the short-term, negatively) impact their respective economic interests to strategies of ready accommodation with the reforms based on the assumption that these individuals are, or could easily become, aware of the long-term benefits of marketization and privatization which are readily observable throughout the West. With this continuum in mind, authors were asked to analyze the extent to which attempted marketization and privatization have affected the political strength and behavior of business and managerial groups, agricultural groups, and organized industrial labor. Authors were asked to gather information on whether these groups had formed or formally affiliated themselves with political parties and what role they had assumed in the financing of elections and the control of the media.

Monitoring of the emergence of new economic strata in transitional polities is important because of the assumptions about the relationship between marketization and democratization which underpin the literature. The transition to democracy has previously been thought to occur as a result of a long period of capitalist development in which previously subordinate classes – the middle class, most notably, but also the urban working class and small and medium-sized farming interests – evolved an economic interest in the promotion of democracy as a way of balancing class power. Thus, a strong middle class allied with commercial and industrial elites in the private sector is generally seen as a necessary but not sufficient condition for successful democratization.[46] Economic winners are thought to support democracy to the extent they feel it legitimizes and sustains their dominant economic position, whereas economic losers are seen as supporting democracy to the extent they feel the existence of democratic state autonomous of dominant economic classes erodes economic inequality.[47]

This obviously raises the question of whether an economy which liberalizes before the rule of law is in place can prevent the rise of organized criminal activity which in turn can disrupt, impede, and even capture the process of democratization itself. Authors were asked to analyze the political impact of organized criminal groups in the respective countries under review and to discuss the extent to which associations or political parties have become linked with organized crime. In general, it can be assumed that the emergence of organized crime will not be welcomed by the population, and authors were asked to gather data on how the public perception of the role of organized crime has affected citizens' attitudes toward the political system. But studies done in economic theory suggest that to the extent that organized crime provides stability and economic security and benefits, the population will be more likely to acquiesce in its existence.[48] And further, it is postulated that the existence of widespread random criminality will predispose the population to allow organized crime to establish rules and norms over geographic regions.[49] The public's predisposition to prefer organized criminal activity to large-scale inchoate activity does not necessarily translate into greater support for democracy, however, and indeed one could suppose that the existence of connections between elected officials and organized crime would erode public confidence in democracy and increase public support for a "strong hand" to end corruption, even if democracy is put on hold for a time.[50]

The redistribution of wealth, the emergence of political parties tied to diverse societal interests, the struggle to control marketization – all have an impact on citizen attitudes toward the democratic process. The collapse of communism has allowed researchers to conduct public opinion surveys and collect data on the changes over time in the level of public support for democratization. Many of these countries have had declines in economic performance which have matched or even exceeded rates seen in the West during the Great Depression, a depression in which democracy endured the test in most of Western Europe and North America, but was wiped out in Germany, Austria, and Italy by the rise of fascism. Based on past trends, it can obviously be expected that the impact of poor economic performance can and will erode support for government leaders, but it is not clear that such performance will necessarily also diminish popular support for democracy as a whole; and authors were asked to collect data on this where it exists.[51]

Surveys also exist which measure a number of factors – such as attitudes toward specific institutions, levels of tolerance in the society, the likelihood of participation in elections, and membership in political parties and intermediary associations – as among different sectors of the society: specifically, authors were asked to gather data which surveyed attitudes by various groups. As with other democratic countries, one would expect attitudes toward democratization to vary across generations, ethnic identification, region, class, and gender.[52]

Popular attitudes are in constant interaction with a free media, which both reflects those attitudes and helps to shape them. What is at stake in postcommunist countries is the establishment of a media which is a channel for the expression of a range of societal interests independent of the preferences of the government. And while the media in all countries are subject to some regulation, what is vital to examine is whether control of the media has affected the conduct of elections and other forms of political participation. It can generally be assumed that the greater the independence and pluralism of the media from the outset of the democratization process, the greater will be the level of civic trust and civic involvement.

Political parties and the party system

With the political evolution of society and increases both in levels of tolerance and in civic involvement, it is assumed in a democracy that a system which promotes parties' sustained competition and pluralism over time will enhance the possibility that political parties will develop and become rooted. Clearly, the comparative literature supports the proposition that a strong civil society is a necessary but not sufficient condition for a strong party system, and it is difficult to find examples where party systems have been established in states with weak civic cultures.[53] Authors were presented with a number of questions addressing the actual emergence of party systems in postcommunist states. They were asked to assess the strength and durability of political parties and the impact of electoral laws, electoral competition, and the type of government on the development of a party system. Particular attention was paid to the renamed communist parties and extremist anti-democratic parties and social movements. Finally, the effect of the party system on the strength of government itself was studied.

Literature in the field traditionally has been divided over the prerequisites for the creation of a strong party system between those who assess the strength of political parties by reference to their intrinsic qualities (internal structure, leadership, platform) and those who emphasize their strength in terms of their ability to perform effectively as a channel for, and reinforcement of, citizens' interests. The former view minimizes the relationship between civil society and political parties; the latter sees that relationship as intrinsic to, and the *raison d'etre* for, a party system. Thus, the former would see a strong party system existing without civic engagement as unproblematic for democracy: the latter would see such a situation as inimicable to the very aims of democracy.

Authors were also asked to comment on the type of electoral system introduced in the postcommunist states and the results. Electoral laws provide the method for the conversion of votes into the selection of leaders for electoral office. There are two major types of electoral systems – majoritarian and proportional representation (or PR). Plurality and majority systems reflect a majoritarian philosophy – the candidate who garners the largest number of votes wins. These formulas can be used to elect both individual leaders, as with presidential elections, and multimember bodies, as with parliaments and legislatures. The PR model, which can be used only for multimember bodies, provides proportional allocation of seats according to the percentage of votes parties received. These differences in electoral systems have an impact on party evolution, with parties in majoritarian systems tending to move toward the center of the political spectrum (median voter theorem), and parties in PR systems likely to be more diverse and more extreme in their approach.[54] The desire to favor majoritarian rule while not disenfranchising minorities has also produced a large number of mixed systems, including in the postcommunist states. Mixed systems typically utilize a version of PR to elect the legislature, and one of several majoritarian formulas to select the chief executive, thereby balancing the benefit of governability produced by majoritarian results with the value of representativeness exhibited by PR formulas.[55]

The strength and structure of the party system is also affected by the structure of government, especially whether the system is parliamentary or presidential. Studying the failures of presidential regimes in Latin America, Juan Linz has concluded that parliamentarism imparts greater flexibility to the political process, promotes consensus-building, and reconciles the interests of multiple political parties. Presidentialism, by focusing on the election of a single individual to an all-powerful post, diminishes the influence of the party system. Political parties tend to be less cohesive in presidential than in parliamentary systems. Presidential systems foster the creation of a two-party or two-bloc system.[56] It has also been shown that presidentialism favors the emergence of two large parties and reduces their distinctiveness and internal cohesion. Party discipline is stronger in parliamentary systems where the prime minister or chancellor belongs to the legislative branch and depends on disciplined and cohesive parties for the survival of government. It is possible for presidential systems to maintain a strong party system and better represent minorities by encouraging federalism and separation of powers, but one cannot ignore findings which point to the tendency of presidentialism to overrepresent the majority, thereby increasing the chance that an alienated and mobilized minority might drop out of party life and pursue political objectives by other, often violent, means.[57]

The attitudes and activities of extremist and communist parties and movements are central to an analysis of the future stability and cohesiveness of party systems in postcommunist countries. The impact of all these parties will depend on their leadership, the institutional and legal setting, constituency, and organization. But postcommunist regimes are challenged to build consensus at the center at the same time they are trying to overcome the institutional and bureaucratic inheritance of a one-party system which still has many well-organized adherents at the political extreme. Trying to construct an electoral and legal system which favors a shift to the center while these groups remain powerful is, therefore, a significant and indeed unprecedented challenge.

Turning to parties of the left and the right, authors were asked to examine the extent to which the renamed communist parties have actually changed (a) their attitudes toward liberal democracy (b) their political leadership, and (c) the interests that they represent as a result of their experience in the emerging democracies. On the other side of the political spectrum, anti-democratic parties and social movements based on clericalism, fascistic traditions, or radical nationalism have arisen in some countries, and authors were asked to determine, among other things, the number and importance of such parties, their willingness to endorse political violence, and their links with paramilitary forces. The literature is split between those who maintain that when electoral systems provide the possibility of coming to power by legal means, the tendency of communist and extremist parties to support the overthrow of the current elected government will subside and those who assert that extremist parties become most destructive to the democratic process when they win elections. These two views are reconciled by the notion that extremist groups will become less extreme through participation in the democratic process, that they will lose their authoritarian and anti-democratic impulse and cease to be a threat to the democratic order. This assumption works best when there is a strong and stable center, fairly good economic conditions, and low levels of social mobilization. However, as the example of Weimar Germany demonstrated, both the Nazis and the Communists won seats in the legislature; and the violent fighting between them paralysed the body in the face of Hitler's rise to power. Concern about the possibility of a repeat of the Weimar example has been widespread in postcommunist countries, most notably Russia, with many analysts concerned about the growth of extremist groups. It is assumed that such groups have the best chance of coming to power without a significant moderation of their political platform when poverty is on the rise, when elected officials are perceived as unable or unwilling to take steps to ameliorate the situation, and when the electoral system is so structured in favor of a pure PR formula as to give parties little incentive to moderate their stand.[58]

Authors were asked to assess the strength of the countries' political parties and party system, including whether emerging party systems are characterized only by the creation of ephemeral parties, or by more stable parties, as indicated by patterns of leadership, electoral results, and survey data. Studies have shown that the more a party exhibits a stable constituency, a consistent party platform, and internal consensus, the greater its durability over time.[59] In looking at parties, authors were also asked to speculate on how the structure and durability of political parties has been affected by any laws on campaign finance and by the timing of elections – including regional versus countrywide elections. Additionally, the literature suggests many propositions which deserve analysis in light of results from postcommunist elections: that the number of coalitions amongst parties will be lower in countries with a proportional representation system than in a majoritarian electoral system; that parties representing women and minorities will fare better in proportional representation systems than in majoritarian systems; that voter turnout will be less among women and minorities in majoritarian systems; that majoritarian systems produce moderate parties, weak in ideological and social class definition, whereas proportional representation systems encourage parties defined along class, ethnic, and regional lines, including extreme right-wing and left-wing parties. All of these propositions can be tested in the new environment provided by postcommunist transitions. Elsewhere, it has been shown that even in a mixed presidential/parliamentary system with proportional representation used for the legislative elections, the large parties which are favored in a winner-take-all presidential election continue to be favored in elections to the legislature, particularly if they are held at the same time, thereby reducing the bias of proportional representation toward greater inclusion of minorities, regional elites, and women.[60]

The party system as it has emerged in postcommunist countries has sometimes facilitated and sometimes obstructed the creation of governments able to formulate and carry through reasonably coherent policies. And conversely the capacity of postcommunist regimes to formulate and implement policies has affected citizen support of democratization and marketization processes. This interaction and essential circularity makes the identification and isolation of variables responsible for shaping the process of democratization difficult. Yet the reasons for undertaking the attempt go beyond the normal intellectual curiosity of academe: never before have so many countries which cover such a large percentage of the world's surface started at the same time along the path of transition from one single kind of regime to another; never before have populations embarking upon a democratic path been so educated, urban, and mobile; and never before has the international system been so clear and unequivocal (if not unanimous) in its support for democracy and marketization as the dominant paradigm. This unique opportunity essentially to control for so many variables makes it all the more likely that observers will be able to judge whether differential strategies for democratic development will also have predictable outcomes. Democracy may be the "only game in town" but as with any game there can be winners and losers, and the winners will be those countries where social, economic, and institutional engineering has received the most attention by elites, parties, and citizens alike.

NOTES

For their generous and insightful comments on an earlier draft of the chapter, the author wishes to thank Valerie Bunce, Joan Nelson, Bruce Parrott, Darya Pushkina, Melissa Rosser, and DelGreco Wilson.

1 *Politics in Developing Countries: Comparing Experiences with Democracy*, ed. Larry Diamond, Juan Linz, and Seymour M. Lipset (Boulder, CO: Lynne Rienner, 1990); *Elites and Democratic Consolidation in Latin America and Southern Europe*, ed. John Higley and Richard Gunther (Cambridge: Cambridge University Press, 1992); Samuel Huntington, *The Third Wave: Democratization in the Late Twentieth Century* (Norman, OK: University of Oklahoma Press, 1992); Stephanie Lawson, "Conceptual Issues in the Comparative Study of Regime Change and Democratization," *Comparative Politics* 25 (January 1993), 88–92; Scott Mainwaring, "Transition to Democracy and Democratic Consolidation: Theoretical and Comparative Issues," in *Issues in Democratic Consolidation*, ed. Scott Mainwaring, Guillermo O'Donnell, and J. Samuel Valenzuela (Notre Dame, IN: University of Notre Dame Press, 1992).

2 Among the more pioneering works are Daniel Lerner, *The Passing of Traditional Society* (Glencoe, NY: Free Press, 1958); Seymour M. Lipset, "The Social Requisites of Democracy," *American Political Science Review* 53 (1959), 69–105; James P. Coleman, "Conclusion: The Political Systems of the Developing Areas," in *The Politics of Developing Areas*, ed. Gabriel A. Almond and J. S. Coleman (Princeton: Princeton University Press, 1960); Phillips Cutright, "National Political Development: Its Measures and Analysis," *American Sociological Review* 28 (1963), 253–64; *On Measuring Democracy*, ed. Alex Inkeles (New Brunswick, NJ: Transaction Publisher, 1991); and Arthur S. Banks and R. B. Textor, *A Cross Polity Survey* (Cambridge, MA: MIT Press, 1963).

3 For example, see Kenneth Bollen, "Issues in the Comparative Measurement of Political Democracy," *American Sociological Review* 45 (1980), 370–90; Kenneth Bollen, "Political Democracy: Validity and Method Factors in Cross-National Measures," *American Journal of Political Science* 37 (November 1993), 1207–30; Raymond D. Gastil and Freedom House, *Freedom in the World* (New York: Freedom House, annual); and Ted Robert Gurr, et al., Polity I, II and III data sets, Inter-University Consortium for Political and Social Research.

4 Doh Chull Shin, "On the Third Wave of Democratization," *World Politics* 47 (October 1994), 148.

5 See Valerie Bunce, "It's the Economy, Stupid . . . Or Is It?" Paper presented for the Workshop on Economic Transformation, Institutional Change and Social Sector Reform, National Academy of Sciences/National Research Council, Task Force on Economies in Transition, Washington, DC, September 19-20, 1996.

6 Huntington, *The Third Wave*, 266–67.

7 Peter McDonough, Samuel Barnes, and Antonio Lopez Pina, "The Growth of Democratic Legitimacy in Spain," *American Political Science Review* 80, no. 3 (September 1986), 735–60. While focusing on the prerequisites and indicators of democratic legitimacy they nevertheless are concerned with consolidation more broadly. Also see *Transitions from Authoritarian Rule: Prospects for Democracy*, ed. Guillermo O'Donnell, Philippe C. Schmitter, and Laurence Whitehead (Baltimore, MD: Johns Hopkins University Press, 1986).

8 For a classic statement of this view and the corollary that factors other than a country's level of economic development were crucial to the explanation of why some countries embarked upon democratization and others did not, see Dankwart Rustow, "Transitions to Democracy," *Comparative Politics* 2 (April 1970), 337–63.

9 Beverly Crawford and Arend Lijphart, "Explaining Political and Economic Change in Post-Communist Eastern Europe: Old Legacies, New Institutions, Hegemonic Norms, and International Pressures," *Comparative Political Studies* 28, no. 2 (1995), 187.

10 Tina Rosenberg, "Overcoming the Legacies of Dictatorship," *Foreign Affairs* 74, no. 3 (May–June 1995), 134.

11 There are many articles and books in the literature, but one which approaches the subject thematically is *The Legacies of Communism in Eastern Europe*, ed. Ivan Volgyes (Baltimore, MD: Johns Hopkins University Press, 1995).

12 The best case is made by Ken Jowitt, *New World Disorder: The Leninist Extinction* (Berkeley, CA: University of California Press, 1992).

13 See Jacques Rupnik, *The Other Europe: The Rise and Fall of Communism in East Central Europe* (London: Pantheon, 1989); Roy Medvedev, *Let History Judge: The Origins and Consequences of Stalinism* (Oxford: Oxford University Press, 1989); Jeffrey Goldfarb, *After the Fall: The Pursuit of Democracy in Central Europe* (New York: Basic Books, 1992); Timothy Garton Ash, *The Uses of Adversity: Essays on the Fate of Central Europe* (New York: Vintage Books, 1989); Milovan Djilas, *The New Class: An Analysis of the Communist System* (New York: Praeger, 1957); and Vladimir Tismaneanu, *Reinventing Politics: Eastern Europe from Stalin to Havel* (New York: The Free Press, 1992).

14 Richard Rose in doing cross-national surveys found support for the hypothesis that "if the common historical experience of Sovietization has had a decisive influence, generational differences in attitudes should be similar from one former Communist country to another." "Generational Effects on Attitudes to Communist Regimes: A Comparative Analysis," *Post-Soviet Affairs* 11, no. 1 (January–March 1995), 37. Also see Ellen Comisso, "Legacies of the Past or New Institutions?" *Comparative Political Studies* 28, no. 2 (July 1995), 200–38; and Barbara Geddes, "A Comparative Perspective on the Leninist Legacy in Eastern Europe," ibid., 239–74. Both maintain that the Soviet era destroyed popular support for pre-Leninist parties and traditions in most countries.

15 See, for example, Anders Åslund, *Gorbachev's Struggle for Economic Reform* (Ithaca, NY: Cornell University Press, 1989); and Ed A. Hewett, *Reforming the Soviet Economy* (Washington, DC: Brookings Institution Press, 1988).

16 The varied political views and splits within the military/security services are discussed in Karen Dawisha and Bruce Parrott, *Russia and the New States of Eurasia* (Cambridge: Cambridge University Press, 1993), ch. 6. Although she is dealing only with the security service, the role and political attitudes of this service are discussed by Amy Knight, *Spies without Cloaks* (Princeton, NJ: Princeton University Press, 1996).

17 Janos Kornai, *The Socialist System: The Political Economy of Communism* (Princeton, NJ: Princeton University Press, 1992). See also Peter Wiles, *The Political Economy of Communism* (Cambridge, MA: Harvard University Press, 1962).

18 Jowitt, *New World Disorder*. Also see Sten Berglund and Jan Dellenbrant, "Prospects for the New Democracies in Eastern Europe," in *The New Democracies in Eastern Europe*, ed. Sten Berglund and Jan Dellenbrant (Brookfield, VT: Edward Elgar Publishing Company, 1991).

19 Huntington, *The Third Wave*, pp. 40–6; also see Valerie Bunce and Maria Csanadi, "Uncertainty in the Transition: Post-Communism in Hungary," *East European Politics and Societies* 7 (Spring 1993), 240–75.

20 Crawford and Lijphart, "Explaining Political and Economic Change," p. 172.

21 Huntington, *The Third Wave*, pp. 85–108.

22 For a consideration of the impact of previous regime type on transition success and of transition type on prospects for consolidation, see Juan J. Linz and Alfred Stepan, *Problems of Democratic Transition and Consolidation: Southern Europe, South America, and Post-Communist Europe* (Baltimore, MD: Johns Hopkins University Press, 1996), ch. 4.

23 For a discussion of pacted transitions, see Arend Lijphart, *Democracy in Plural Societies: A Comparative Perspective* (New Haven: Yale University Press, 1977); and in the Arab world, see *Democracy without Democrats? The Renewal of Politics in the Muslim World*, ed. Ghassan Salame (New York: I. B. Taurus, 1994).

24 This hypothesis is drawn from Joan Nelson, "How Market Reforms and Democratic Consolidation Affect Each Other," in *Intricate Links*, ed. Joan Nelson (New Brunswick, NJ: Transaction Publishers, 1994).

25 See Alfred Stepan, "Paths toward Redemocratization: Theoretical and Comparative Considerations," in *Transitions from Authoritarian Rule*, ed. O'Donnell, Schmitter, and Whitehead, pp. 79–81.

26 Robert A. Dahl, *Democracy and Its Critics* (New Haven: Yale University Press, 1989).

27 The idea that a state's movement toward democracy is conditioned by its ability to exercise civilian control of violent coercion is most fully developed by Dahl in *Democracy and Its Critics*.

28 See, for example, Jendayi Frazer, "Conceptualizing Civil–Military Relations during Democratic Transition," in *Africa Today*, Quarters 1 & 2 (1995), 39–48; Philippe Schmitter, "Dangers and Dilemmas of Democracy," *Journal of Democracy* 5, no. 2 (April 1994); and *Civil–Military Relations in the Soviet and Yugoslav Successor States*, ed. Constantine Danopoulos and Daniel Zirker (Boulder, CO: Westview, 1996).

29 S. E. Finer, *The Man on Horseback: The Role of the Military in Politics*, 2d ed. (Boulder, CO: Westview Press, 1988); and Morris Janowitz, *The Military in the Political Development of New Nations* (Chicago: University of Chicago Press, 1964).

30 This proposition is derived from Adam Przeworski, *Democracy and the Market: Political and Economic Reforms in Eastern Europe and Latin America* (Cambridge: Cambridge University Press, 1991). It largely coalesces with the view promoted by rational choice theorists such as Douglass C. North, *Institutions, Institutional Change, and Economic Performance* (Cambridge: Cambridge University Press, 1990); Anthony Downs, *An Economic Theory of Democracy* (New York: Harper and Row, 1957); and Mancur Olson, "Dictatorship, Democracy, and Development," *American Political Science Review* 87 (September 1993), 567–76.

31 G. Bingham Powell, Jr., *Contemporary Democracies: Participation, Stability and Violence* (Cambridge, MA: Harvard University Press, 1982); Larry Diamond and Marc F. Plattner, *The Global Resurgence of Democracy* (Baltimore, MD: Johns Hopkins University Press, 1993).

32 See, for example, Phillippe C. Schmitter, "The Consolidation of Democracy and Representation of Social Groups," *American Behavioral Scientist* 35 (March–June 1992), 422–49.

33 See Ted Robert Gurr, *Minorities at Risk: A Global View of Ethnopolitical Conflict* (Washington, DC: US Institute of Peace, 1993). Also Linz and Stepan, *Problems of Democratic Transition and Consolidation: Southern Europe, South America and Post-Communist Europe*.

34 This problematic relationship between capitalism and democracy is most fully explored in Przeworski, *Democracy and the Market*.

35 The debate over whether shock therapy or gradualism is the best policy is extensive and is well analyzed in *The Postcommunist Economic Transformation: Essays in Honor of Gregory Grossman*, ed. Robert W. Campbell (Boulder, CO: Westview Press, 1994); and in articles by Anders Åslund and Bela Kadar in *Overcoming the Transformation Crisis: Lessons for the Successor States of the Soviet Union* (Tubingen, 1993). Public choice literature has contributed most to a discussion of rational calculations in polities which are already established, not in those being formed, so its contribution has been more limited, but is discussed in Dennis Mueller, "Public Choice: A Survey," in *The Public Choice Approach to Politics*, ed. Dennis Mueller (Brookfield, VT: Edward Elgar, 1993), pp. 447–89.

36 Donald L. Horowitz, *Ethnic Groups in Conflict* (Berkeley, CA: University of California Press, 1985); Juan Linz, *The Breakdown of Democratic Regimes: Crisis, Breakdown, and Reequilibration* (Baltimore, MD: Johns Hopkins University Press, 1978).

37 See especially Arendt Lijphart, "Consociational Democracy," *World Politics* 21 (January 1969), 207–25.

38 Charles Tilly, *Coercion, Capital, and European States*, rev. ed. (Oxford: Blackwell, 1992); Harry Eckstein, ed., *Internal War: Problems and Approaches* (Glencoe, IL: Free Press, 1963); and *Organizing Interests in Western Europe: Pluralism, Corporatism, and the Transformation of Politics*, ed. Suzanne Berger (Cambridge University Press, 1981).

39 Gabriel Almond and Sidney Verba, *The Civic Culture: Political Attitudes and Democracy in Five Nations* (Princeton: Princeton University Press, 1963).

40 Gabriel Almond, "Foreword: The Return to Political Culture," in *Political Culture and Democracy in Developing Countries*, ed. Larry Diamond, ix–xii. Among the more important critiques lodged against mainstream comparative politics during this era were the following: Mark Kesselman, "Order or Movement? The Literature of Political Development as Ideology," *World Politics* 26, no. 1 (1973); Fernando H. Cardoso and Enzo Faleto, *Dependency and Development in Latin America* (Berkeley: University of California Press, 1979); and André Gunder Frank, *Latin America: Underdevelopment or Revolution* (New York: Monthly Review Press, 1969).

41 Among the seminal works are Downs, *Economic Theory of Democracy*, and William Riker, *The Theory of Political Coalitions* (New Haven: Yale University Press, 1962).

42 Ronald Inglehart, "The Renaissance of Political Culture," *American Political Science Review* 82, no. 4 (December 1988), 1203–30; and idem., *Culture Shift in Advanced Industrial Society* (Princeton: Princeton University Press, 1990).

43 This requirement is explored most fully by Ernest Gellner, *Conditions of Liberty: Civil Society and Its Rivals* (New York: Allen Lane, The Penguin Press, 1994).

44 The debate about this possibility was begun by the publication of Samuel P. Huntington, "The Clash of Civilizations," *Foreign Affairs* 72 (Summer 1993), 22–49.

45 See Seymour M. Lipset, "The Social Requisites of Democracy Revisited," *American Sociological Review* 59 (February 1994), 1–22; Inglehart, "The Renaissance of Political Culture"; and Inglehart, *Culture Shift in Advanced Industrial Society*; Almond and Verba, *The Civic Culture*. The dilemma of how

to build trust in societies where the state had systematically gone about its destruction is deftly argued in Richard Rose, "Postcommunism and the Problem of Trust," in Diamond and Plattner, *The Global Resurgence of Democracy*, 2d ed., pp. 251–63.

46 Barrington Moore, *Social Origins of Dictatorship and Democracy* (Boston: Beacon Press, 1966); and Charles Lindblom, *Politics and Markets: The World's Political-Economic Systems* (New York: Basic Books, 1977). They were among the first to assert the connection between a strong bourgeoisie and democracy. This view has been challenged only rarely, including by Dietrich Reuschemeyer, Evelyne Huber Stephens, and John D. Stephens in *Capitalist Development and Democracy* (Chicago, IL: University of Chicago Press, 1993) who argued that it was the working class that had proved over time to have been the greatest supporter of democracy.

47 Mancur Olson, "Dictatorship, Democracy, and Development," *American Political Science Review* 87, no. 3 (September 1993), 567–76; Rueschemeyer, Stephens, and Stephens, *Capitalist Development and Democracy*; and Edward N. Muller, "Democracy, Economic Development and Income Inequality," *American Sociological Review* 53 (1988), 50–68.

48 Louise Shelley, "The Internalization of Crime: The Changing Relationship Between Crime and Development," in *Essays on Crime and Development*, ed. Ugljesa Zvekic (Rome: UN Interregional Crime and Justice Research Institute, 1990); J. S. Nye, "Corruption and Political Development: A Cost-benefit Analysis," *American Political Science Review* 61, no. 2 (1967), 417–27.

49 This is a central tenet of Olson, "Dictatorship, Democracy and Development."

50 James Walston, *The Mafia and Clientism* (London: Routledge, 1988); Rensselaer W. Lee III, *The White Labyrinth* (New Brunswick, NJ: Transaction Publishers, 1989).

51 Studies done in six Central European countries suggest that respondents continue to have a very positive perception of the political benefits of democracy even as they hold a very negative perception of the economic benefits of marketization. See Richard Rose and Christian Haerpfer, "New Democracies Barometer III: Learning from What is Happening," *Studies in Public Policy* 230 (1994), questions 26,35,36,39,40,42, as presented in Linz and Stepan, *Problems in Democratic Transition and Consolidation*, 443.

52 The first attempt to see democracy as strongly affected by culture was Almond and Verba, *The Civic Culture*. Page and Shapiro have argued that irrespective of cleavages within public opinion, overall the public in aggregate is able to make rational and informed judgments (Benjamin Page and Robert Shapiro, *The Rational Public: Fifty Years of Trends in Americans' Policy Preferences* [Chicago: University of Chicago Press, 1992]). One of the first attempts to gauge public opinion and attitudinal shifts in the Soviet Union was Ada W. Finitfer and Ellen Mickiewicz, "Redefining the Political System of the USSR: Mass Support for Political Change," *American Political Science Review* 86 (1992), 857–74. More recently, a wide array of authors have examined changes in public opinion and political culture in postcommunist states: see, for example, James L. Gibson, "The Resilience of Mass Support for Democratic Institutions and Processes in the Nascent Russian and Ukrainian Democracies," and Jeffrey W. Hahn, "Changes in Contemporary Political Culture," in *Political Culture and Civil Society in*

Russia and the New States of Eurasia, ed. Vladimir Tismaneanu (Armonk, NY: M. E. Sharpe, 1995).

53 In *Making Democracy Work: Civic Traditions in Modern Italy* (Princeton, NJ: Princeton University Press, 1993), Robert Putnam argues that a strong party system can operate within a weak civic culture; also see Robert Putnam, "Troubled Democracies," paper prepared for the University of Maryland/Johns Hopkins University Workshop on Democratization and Political Participation in Postcommunist Societies, US Department of State, May 1995; and Robert Putnam, "Bowling Alone: America's Declining Social Capital," in Diamond and Plattner, *The Global Resurgence of Democracy*, 2d ed., pp. 290–307.

54 Connections between electoral laws and political parties are the subject of many works, of which some of the best are Arend Lijphart, *Democracies* (New Haven, CN: Yale University Press, 1984); Arend Lijphart, *Electoral Systems and Party Systems: A Study of Twenty-seven Democracies, 1945–1990* (Oxford: Oxford University Press, 1994); Richard S. Katz, *A Theory of Parties and Electoral Systems* (Baltimore, MD: Johns Hopkins University Press, 1980); and *Electoral Laws and Their Political Consequences*, ed. Bernard Grofman and Arend Lijphart (New York: Agathon Press, Inc., 1986). Also see Part II of Dennis Mueller, *The Public Choice Approach to Politics* (Brookfield, VT: Edward Elgar, 1993).

55 On the effects of different varieties of electoral systems, see Douglas W. Rae, *The Political Consequences of Electoral Laws*, 2d ed. (New Haven: Yale University Press, 1971); and Rein Taagapera and Matthew Soberg Shugart, *Seats and Votes: The Effects and Determinants of Electoral Systems* (New Haven: Yale University Press, 1989).

56 See Juan Linz and Arturo Valenzuela, *The Failure of Presidential Democracy* (Baltimore, MD: Johns Hopkins University Press, 1994), for an argument in support of this hypothesis. By contrast, see Donald Horowitz, *A Democratic South Africa? Constitutional Engineering in a Divided Society* (Berkeley: University of California Press, 1991), who finds no necessary link, and W. H. Riker, who theorizes that all party systems converge to two coalitions of equal size (*The Theory of Political Coalitions* [New Haven, CN: Yale University Press, 1962]).

57 Juan Linz, "Presidential or Parliamentary Democracy: Does it Make a Difference?" in Linz and Valenzuela, *The Failure of Presidential Democracy: Comparative Perspectives*, 3–91; and Arend Lijphart, "Democracy in Plural Societies: A Comparative Exploration," in *The Failure of Presidential Democracy*, 91–105. Also see Vladimir Tismaneanu, *Fantasies of Salvation: Post-Communist Political Mythologies* (Princeton, NJ: Princeton University Press, forthcoming).

58 Quentin L. Quade examines the impact of an unmodified proportional representation system on the potential for takeover by extremist groups in "PR and Democratic Statecraft," in Diamond and Plattner, *The Global Resurgence of Democracy*, 2d ed., pp. 181–7. The case for the likely rise in extremist politics was first and most forcefully made in Jowitt, *The New World Disorder*.

59 Giovanni Sartori, *Parties and Party Systems* (Cambridge: Cambridge University Press, 1976), 6; and Lijphart, *Democracies;* in opposition to Robert Michels (*Political Parties* [Glencoe, IL: The Free Press, 1958]) who dismissed the need for constituency support, focusing instead on the centrality of elites and their ability to instill beliefs in the masses. On the need for a party to show internal consensus, see Katz, *A Theory of Parties and Electoral Systems*.

60 The seminal work on the relationship between party and electoral systems is Maurice Duverger, *Political Parties: Their Organization and Activity in the Modern State* (New York: Wiley, 1954); see also Douglas J. Amy, *Real Choices/New Voices: The Case for Proportional Representation in the United States* (New York: Columbia University Press, 1993); and Michel L. Balinski and H. Peyton Young, *Fair Representation: Meeting the Ideal of One Man, One Vote* (New Haven, CN: Yale University Press, 1982).

The Caucasus

3 Political transformations in postcommunist Armenia: images and realities

Nora Dudwick

Introduction

Themes and argument of the chapter

Since 1991, Armenia has become recognized as an independent republic, complete with a popularly elected president and parliament, its own army, and the signs and symbols of independent statehood. It has become a member of international organizations and a signatory to international treaties and covenants. Nevertheless, I argue in this paper that it is not yet possible to speak of or predict with any certainty the pace or direction of democratic development in Armenia. Janus-like, Armenia presents one face to foreign observers, another to its own citizens. While the foreign community follows with attention the course of electoral politics, party formation and activity, parliamentary process, and the emergence of a plethora of nongovernmental organizations (NGOs), for its own citizens, life in Armenia has become a disturbing mixture of chaos and authoritarianism.

Until 1995, Armenia maintained the image of a democratic republic which largely respected the civil rights of its citizens. It was among the first Soviet republics whose population mobilized around a national and democratic agenda, the only republic to organize a referendum on independence according to Soviet law, and the only Transcaucasian republic continuously ruled since independence by a democratically elected president. Armenian leaders frequently contrasted their republic to Georgia and Azerbaijan, unstable Transcaucasian neighbors racked by coups, ethnic conflict, and civil unrest.

A historical legacy of statelessness and subordination, and after 1991, severe economic crisis and war, have left many Armenians too busy struggling to survive to maintain active political engagement. Regions damaged by the 1988 earthquake remain largely unrestored, industry runs at a fraction of its capacity because of severe energy shortages, and the undeclared war with Azerbaijan has taken a serious toll of government resources. Hundreds of thousands of Armenians have resorted to the time-honored Armenian solution to economic crisis and war; they have emigrated to Russia and the West, in search of work. Even this large-scale emigration of the work-force has failed to resolve unemployment and underemployment.

As a result, Armenian society has become sharply stratified, with a small political and economic elite at the top, and a large newly impoverished mass forming the base. This social and economic stratification has been accompanied, as well, by the emergence of new patron–client relationships which are dominated by well-placed government officials and enterprise directors able to use their positions to take advantage of privatization, in the context of an amorphous legal framework and a general tolerance for nepotism and corruption. What local people refer to metaphorically as "mafias" function as the social and political skeleton of the new Armenian polity. I would argue that these patron–client groups constitute a strong barrier to democratization, because they use political pressure and coercion to sharply restrict access to positions of political power and economic influence. Awareness of these groups' growing power contributes to the cynicism and alienation of Armenians, who feel increasingly ineffective as citizens.

Civil society in Armenia thus remains fragmented and enfeebled. The majority of organizations which fill its space have been created by members of the social and political elite, and remain top-heavy, with few members. For some organizations, their very *raison d'être* appears to derive from the financial support they receive from international NGOs and funding agencies. Through large infusions of humanitarian assistance and credits, these organizations have indirectly allowed the government to ignore the fact it continues to lose large sums through the corruption of its own agencies and officials.

The 1994 suspension of the largest opposition party, the Dashnaktsutiun (Armenian Revolutionary Federation, or ARF), the closure of over a dozen newspapers and journals, and the government's continued monopoly of television have restricted access to information and curtailed informed public debate. These factors, together with the government's overt manipulation of the July 1995 parliamentary elections and constitutional referendum, have made it clear that democratization, party-based politics, and civic engagement which the international community is trying to encourage in Armenia, are terms which do not accurately capture the flavor of political life. Rather, an authoritarian Armenia is rising out of the ashes of the Soviet Union. Western democracy-building organizations and international funding agencies which ignore these trends face the danger of legitimizing them by their involvement.

A word about sources

The following analysis draws on my own observations of and research on Armenian society and politics from 1987 to 1995, and extensive informal discussion with present and former government officials; political activists and party representatives; journalists; representatives of local and international NGOs; officials from international organizations and funding agencies; American officials; Armenian diaspora organizations; ordinary citizens; and finally, my own observations and experiences as an election monitor in July 1995 under the aegis of the joint United Nations/Organization for Security and Cooperation in Europe monitoring operation. Many people spoke to me with the expectation – or explicit request – for confidentiality. I hope that any insight their opinions and remarks add to the argument below outweigh the lack of explicit attribution.

Many of the people I interviewed alleged to serious corruption and wrongdoing on the part of government officials and leaders. I have no way of confirming or disconfirming such allegations and rumors. Nevertheless, I have repeated many of their allegations in this chapter because their prevalence demonstrates the general discontent and public cynicism which characterize the political atmosphere in contemporary Armenia, in the same way many respondents' desire for anonymity attests to their fear of speaking openly on certain topics. As scholars of politics and society well understand, whether or not beliefs, convictions, or fears are based on fact, they nevertheless exercise a profound influence on the behavior and expectations of citizens.

Because my principle intention in this paper has been to convey the attitudes of ordinary people, along with something of the political and moral atmosphere, I have not concentrated on the political party elite. Many people spoke to me with the expectation – or explicit request – for confidentiality. I hope that any insight their opinions and remarks add to the argument below outweigh the lack of explicit attribution.

Structure of the chapter

Armenians' attitudes to the present are deeply rooted in perceptions of the past. The discussion therefore begins with Armenian society under imperial Ottoman and Russian rule, the ruptures and continuities which characterized national life during the Soviet era, and the beginning of the dissent movement. The second section describes the mass mobilization that began in 1988 and led to independence. The third section sketches out the economic and social situation prevailing in the newly independent Armenia, the emerging formal and informal institutions of political life, and examines the

July 1995 parliamentary elections and constitutional referendum. The final section evaluates the state of the new free-market economy and society and Armenia's relations to its most important neighbor, Russia.

Armenia: imperial and Soviet legacies

Armenians in the Ottoman and Russian empires

Many of the patterns of thinking and behavior which today guide and limit the development of political institutions in Armenia date to the pre-Soviet period, when the majority of Armenians lived as an ethnoreligious minority in the Ottoman Empire and as a largely urban population in cities of the Russian Empire. In Constantinople or Smyrna, Armenians were indispensable for their expertise and wealth as industrialists, merchants, bankers, and craftsmen. But it was through their prestige and control over the Ottoman economy rather than through political office that they exerted political power in the empire.[1]

In the countryside, Armenian village life was largely autonomous, built around patriarchal extended families of up to fifty members. Authority was wielded by a village headman who generally came from one of the more prosperous and respected families in the village, a pattern that continued in different guises right through the Soviet period.

Armenians often attribute what they characterize as their "national failings" to their centuries of statelessness in these empires, where they kept their heads low and adapted to the prevailing political climate. A host of proverbs attest to an ethos of self-protective passivity, disengagement, even resignation and surrender. Contemporary Armenians refer to this self-image in contemporary tales, jokes, and proverbs about their reputation as clever, sly merchants as an adaptive mechanism which helped them cope with their vulnerability as an encapsulated minority in Islamic empires.

In the eighteenth and nineteenth centuries, a nationalist awakening began in the Armenian diaspora. During the second half of the nineteenth century, Armenians founded several parties, including the ARF, the Hnchak ("bell") Party, and the Ramgavar ("democratic") Party, which combined demands for political liberalization with national autonomy. Despite terrorist actions and the formation of a limited self-defense force, organized by Armenian political parties (today the ARF takes credit for most of the self-defense), massacres in the last decades of the nineteenth century and beginning of the twentieth century, followed by mass slaughter in 1915–18, completely shattered the Turkish Armenian community. Survivors regrouped either in diaspora communities throughout the Middle East, in Europe and the Americas, or crossed the border into Russian Armenia.

Table 3.1 *Demographic and educational trends in Armenia*

	Year				
	1940	1959	1970	1979	1987
Total population	375,000	882,000	1,482,000	1,993,000	2,324,000
% urban	28	50	59	66	68
% rural	72	50	41	36	32
Age distribution (%)				(1979)	(1989)
15–24				23.5	16.9
25–49				30.0	33.5
50–59				7.6	10.0
Over 60				7.9	9.3

Students in institutes of higher education

(1940–41)	(1960–61)	(1970–71)	(1980/81)
11,100	20,200	54,400	58,100
(1985/86)	(1986/87)	(1990–91)	(1991–92)
54,800	54,600	68,800	66,100
(1992–93)	(1993–94)	(1994–95)	
58,000	46,500	36,500	

Sources: US Department of Commerce, *Statistical Abstracts of the United States*; Paul S. Shoup, *The East European and Soviet Data Handbook*; UNESCO, *Statistical Yearbooks*; United Nations, *Demographic Yearbooks*; *Narodnoe khoziaistvo SSSR za 70 let* (Moscow: Finansy i Statistika, 1987), pp. 378, 548; *Statisticheskii ekzhegodnik: Sodruzhestva Nezavisimykh Gosudarstv v 1994 godu* (Moscow: Mezhgosudarsvennyi Statisticheskii Komitet Sodruzhestva Nezavisimykh Gosudarstv, 1995), p. 148.

Today, these diaspora communities are linked by their shared memory of the destruction of their community and loss of their homeland, and a deep interest in the republic of Armenia as the only surviving piece of the remembered homeland. The turn-of-the-century political parties which fought for Armenian liberation continued to exist in the diaspora, and have now returned to independent Armenia, drawing on historical prestige and diaspora funding.

After Sovietization, and especially after World War II, the industrial transformation of Armenia became an important basis for regime legitimation for Armenians, who saw it as a kind of national resurrection.[2] The ecological costs of industrializing this arid, energy- and resource-poor mountainous region did not become a serious ecological or political concern until the end of the 1970s.

New social and political patterns, however, were deeply influenced by older indigenous traditions of authority.[3] Rural life continued under the control of officials from prominent local families. Today, many of these nomenklatura families play important roles in their communities as part of the new ruling party. Urban areas developed their own informal structures outside the official bodies and structures. Poor urban neighborhoods had their own feared and respected chief, who dispensed favors and "regulated" local life. Given perennial deficits of goods and services, the extended kinship network remained the most effective source of information and access to goods. The pervasive shortages encouraged a sense of competition and mutual distrust, further increasing the importance of the family as a dependable and trustworthy safety net. The privileges enjoyed by members of the Communist Party encouraged people to make use of contacts and connections in the government hierarchy. The importance of these connections reinforced the patron–client hierarchies characteristic of pre-Soviet Armenian life.

The state's attempt to dominate its citizens' private lives increased the public-private split which for different reasons characterizes both Middle Eastern and Soviet societies such as Armenia. As elsewhere in the former Soviet Union, social life became highly fragmented. Helping one's own relatives was a moral (and reciprocal) obligation. But years of obligatory "volunteer work" contributed to the judgment that anyone who works for the good of an abstract community is naive and easily exploited. Today, impersonal relations in Armenia remain notable for the distrust, even hostility, which accompanies them; people and organizations tend to view each other in terms of potential competitors rather than collaborators.

The hierarchical structure of pre-Soviet and Soviet Armenian society deeply influenced political culture. Both in imperial Russia and the Soviet Union, ordinary citizens have often exonerated the tsar or the first secretary for abuses during their rule, in the belief they were ignorant of the behavior of their underlings. It may be this same mentality which gave rise to a complaint by a former government employee that people frequently appealed directly to the office of the president for help resolving individual problems, "as if it is the president's job to see why a particular person doesn't have telephone service!"

Today, despite the glib references to "democracy," many participants in and observers of the political scene in Armenia question whether Armenians actually understand the meaning of democracy in all its historical and cultural specificity. A former Communist Party member who served in the previous parliament flatly asserted that Armenians do not understand the concept of "democracy": "People only theoretically support democracy, but in fact it

Table 3.2 *Public opinion data on the most serious problems facing Armenia (N=1,000)*

	Most serious (%)	Next most serious (%)	Total
Security issues			
Ending Karabagh war; peace	48	20	68
Ending blockade	4	7	11
Strengthening defense, army	1	1	2
Strengthening independence	1	1	2
Economic/social issues			
Overcoming economic crisis; economic recovery	15	21	36
Social problems	6	10	16
Survival, starvation	5	5	10
Energy crisis, nuclear power	4	6	10
Unemployment problem	1	3	4
Everyday life problems	1	3	4
Other (crime, ecology, health, earthquake, privatization, land reform)	2	5	7
Political issues			
Government's resignation	3	3	6
Internal political problems generally	2	3	5
Establishing/improving democracy	–	1	1
Other (political course changes, establish law and order, strengthen legislative rule)	1	3	4

Note: The questions were: "What do you feel is the *single most serious problem* facing Armenia today? And what do you think is the *next most serious problem?*"
Source: *USIA Opinion Analysis*, USIA Office of Research and Media Reaction, Washington, DC, November 17, 1994.

often turns out that [what] they want is for the issues to be resolved by others and in a particular way . . . they consider the leader with a strong hand as just, even if that isn't the case. Even if he does more for himself and his family, this is accepted on the whole as a normal phenomenon." In his own view, "what is most important is that people living in this state feel that they have order and justice."

A poll written by the USIA Office of Research and administered by Yerevan State University between August 16 and September 6, 1994, resulted in a surprisingly similar conclusion – not a single respondent considered the establishment or improvement of democracy was the "single most serious problem facing Armenia today," and only one respondent considered it the "next most serious problem."

Dissent in Armenia

Armenia and the other FSU republics lacked the pre-World War II tradition of civic development which took place in some Central and East European countries. In Armenia, radical dissent was inextricably linked to irredentism. It arose among a small group of people born toward the end of the Stalin era into working-class or lower-middle-class families, most of whom had roots in Turkish Armenia. They instrumentalized human rights issues to serve "Hai Dat" (literally, "the Armenian Cause," or Armenian irredenta). Their activities received little support either in Armenia or in the diaspora.[4] For despite the fiercely anti-Turkish and irredentist sentiments of many diaspora Armenians, the majority hesitated to challenge the Soviet Union, which they saw as the only guarantor of Armenia's physical survival, and which allowed Armenia at least formal "national" and cultural self-expression. To this day, an irredentist agenda and a concept of "group [ethnic] rights" distinguishes the Armenian conception of human rights.

Some contemporary Armenian politicians began their political careers as members of these small irredentist and independence oriented organizations. Paruir Hairikian, still active in Armenian political life, was one of the first political figures to call for independence. He was a member of the National Unification Party (NUP), formed in 1966. The NUP called for an independent Armenia to include the "lost lands" in Turkey and Nakhichevan (an autonomous republic under Azerbaijani jurisdiction), despite the fact that almost no Armenian still resided there, and Nagorno-Karabagh (an autonomous oblast in Azerbaijan), of which the Armenian population, by 1987, was 75 percent.[5] When its leaders were arrested in 1968, Hairikian took over leadership until his own arrest a year later. Following his arrest, he was to serve a total of seventeen years in Soviet prisons for anti-Soviet activity. Today, his personal history contributes to his charisma as a leader of a radical political party.

The first mass outbreak of national feeling occurred on April 24, 1965, when public officials, representatives of the Armenian Gregorian church, and diaspora representatives met in Yerevan's Opera Theater to commemorate the fiftieth anniversary of the genocide. An estimated 100,000 people gathered in front of the Opera and marched in the streets, demanding Soviet support for the return of Armenian lands in Turkey. Many of the student-age participants, including Vazgen Manukian and Levon Ter-Petrossian, later activists in the Karabagh movement and leaders in the first independent government, spent several days in jail.

In 1977, a small group of Armenian dissidents, including several members of the NUP, founded the Armenian Helsinki Watch group to monitor civil rights violations and the "anti-nationality policies" of Moscow and Yerevan. By 1978, the organization had been crushed. Sporadic arrests and trials for dissemination of underground literature urging independence continued into the early 1980s.

During the same period, a small "reform" movement started in the Armenian Komsomol, as Ashot Manucharian (a future Karabagh Committee member) and a small university cohort, later among the first Karabagh movement activists, attempted to "democratize" Komsomol organizational life. In the eighties, concern over chemical and nuclear pollution resulted in formation of an ecology "initiative group." Its weekly lectures became the only public forum for discussing not just ecological but other political and social issues. In September 1987 and February 1988, Karabagh activists used ecology rallies to announce demonstrations in support of the Armenians in Karabagh, which soon displaced ecology as the unifying symbol and movement.

The Karabagh movement

The mass mobilization of 1988

For the most part, Armenians were content for their republic to remain part of the Soviet Union, which they considered their strongest guarantee against Turkish aggression. Much of the Armenian elite spoke Russian and were imbued with Russian culture, despite the lip-service they gave to the importance and significance of Armenian language and culture. By the 1970s, many educated Armenians preferred to send their children to Russian-language schools, and often to Moscow or Leningrad, for university education. Once known as the "loyal millet" in the Ottoman Empire, Armenia became the "loyal millet" of the Soviet Union.[6]

Despite these differentiations, Armenians were linked together in an abstract but emotionally significant imagined community based on shared language, religion, cultural traditions and history, and on their memory of shared suffering in 1915. The acquisition of national symbols and institutions as a Soviet republic further consolidated this identity, as did the high degree of ethnic homogeneity in Armenia – in 1964, Armenians made up 88 percent of the population; in 1987, because of higher fertility than Slavic nationalities, and the migration from other republics,[7] Armenians constituted 93 percent of the population. Today, given the continuous outmigration of minorities, this figure is probably higher.[8]

Despite grievances about everything from pollution to corruption, nationalism played an important role as a unifying ideology, when Gorbachev's reforms, under the banner of "perestroika" and "glasnost" encouraged popular expectations among Armenian citizens that they could exert some control over the shape of political, economic, and social life. Nationalism therefore became the rallying point in 1988, when Armenians demonstrated to support the Armenian majority living in Nagorno-Karabagh, where the oblast soviet had unanimously voted to request that Armenia and Azerbaijan approve the region's unification with Armenia.[9]

The fate of Nagorno-Karabagh dominated political discourse and public life. Interest and peer pressure drew most urban residents to frequent public "mitings" (rallies) at Yerevan's Opera Square. People who claimed indifference to politics became vitally involved in the unfolding political drama. For most of 1988, Armenians were united in a festival of good feeling and activity,[10] directed at what they believed would be a successful drive to recreate part of "historic Armenia." Armenians rhapsodized that they had rediscovered the community thought to be destroyed by modern industrial and urban Soviet life.

The framework for a grassroots political movement was laid in February 1988, when a movement activist called for people to form workplace committees to serve as conduits of information to the population. Nationalist and reformist goals often collided. The main goal of the nationalist wing was the unification of Nagorno-Karabagh with Armenia, rather than political or social reform. The nationalists opposed public criticism of corrupt Armenian officials, since they viewed the conflict as a national liberation struggle. Reformists argued that democratization was a prerequisite to a peaceful, democratic resolution, that corrupt officials would only act as obstacles. This tension, between the goal of building an Armenian national state, and of building an open and democratic society, still creates contradictions in contemporary Armenian political life. Armenian irredentism, and the need to guarantee Armenia's physical security, has at times threatened the civil rights of dissenting or critical Armenian citizens. The gang-pressing of Armenian youth into the new Armenian army in 1993 and 1994, scandalizing Armenian citizens as well as the international community, is one example.

As a result of such ideological disputes, workplace committees became sites of struggle. Aided by Gorbachevian reforms such as the establishment of the new Councils of Workers' Collectives which gave workers authority, among other things, to choose enterprise directors, and the reduction of sanctions on speech, many Armenians challenged the restrictions they encountered in daily life. As a scientist active in his workplace committee told me in 1991, it was essential to democratize the workplaces, for as long as people lacked control as workers, how could they "bring something up on the square?" He added, "this spirit of democracy was so intoxicating! Democracy – anything was possible! And why not? We also want to live like white people!"

People who had previously tried to democratize Communist Party organizations or address human rights violations or Armenia's ecological problems, used the movement to pursue social and political reforms. Both nationalists and reformers pursued their political aims through a wide array of political strategies such as demonstrations, strikes, and electoral campaigns.

By summer 1988, a number of informal groups came together to form an umbrella group, the Hayots Hamazgayin Sharzhum (Armenian National Movement, or ANM). The first *ad hoc* "Orgkomitet" (organizing committee) solidified into the "Karabagh Committee,"[11] consisting of intellectuals in their thirties and forties, mainly non-party, without direct connections to government. In 1989, the ANM held its first congress and elected board members.

By 1990, the movement had catalyzed the formation of new cultural, social and political organizations and publications, some only tangentially related to the issue of Nagorno-Karabagh. Most such groups simply appeared, fissioned, and vanished. Yet they provided participants with their first experience of autonomous and voluntary participation in public life. Many of the people who came to prominence in 1988 are now in government or active in the opposition.

"Street democracy"

Between 1988 and 1990, Armenians frequently took to the streets to make their wishes known to the authorities, sometimes physically forcing their deputies into parliament for a critical vote. When the 19th Conference of the Communist Party of the Soviet Union (CPSU), held in Moscow in June 1988, failed to support Armenian demands, Armenians successfully pressured their parliament to support Nagorno-Karabagh's unification with Armenia. The authorities also acceded to popular will during the 1988 by-elections held to fill vacancies in parliament. Voters wrote-in the names of two candidates, Khachik Stamboltsian, a devout Christian and ecology activist, and Ashot Manucharian, a member of the Karabagh Committee. When the Central Electoral Committee invalidated the election results, mass demonstrations forced them to re-run the elections and validate their new victories.

Such demonstrations, which detractors contemptuously labelled "street democracy," were the means by which activists and hundreds of thousands of supporters pressured the authorities. Many Armenians found the experience of such confrontations liberating. They felt that their very presence at such demonstrations was a form of participation in democratic process. At demonstrations, movement leaders encouraged this form of participation by soliciting the crowd's approval for their course of action. The tradition of *mitings* continues to this day. These *mitings* serve as informal barometers which measure public concern or support for issues and individuals.

In December 1988 and January 1989, Stamboltsian, Manucharian, and the rest of the Karabagh Committee were arrested, and remained in Moscow prisons until May 31, 1989. Their imprisonment was the catalyst for a new wave of social and political activity in Armenia, and their release became an important campaign issue during the spring 1989 elections for the Congress of Peoples' Deputies.

Although most seats had multiple candidates, they had all been put forth by the Communist Party, and the government press allowed no genuine debate. According to a survey of Yerevan inhabitants, only 6 percent considered the elections democratic, and 30 percent, partly democratic. Fearing a complete Communist Party victory, Armenian activists urged the electorate to boycott the election. Their appeal succeeded in producing a surprisingly low turnout, relative to Soviet standards of the time, 72 percent nation-wide and 53.2 percent in Yerevan. Communist Party functionaries won thirty-six seats. During run-off elections in four districts where the boycott produced less than the necessary 50 percent turnout, the incarceration of the Committee members became most salient issue. The victorious campaign to place "movement candidates" in these four districts drew in many men and women who had never before taken an active role in political or public life. (Levon Ter-Petrossian won by 72 percent.) This election marked the shift of power from the Communist Party to the ANM.[12]

When Karabagh Committee members were released, they immediately resumed political activity, their stature having increased to that of national martyrs as a result of their six months in Moscow prisons. Their release marked the gradual and relatively peaceful transfer of real power in the republic from the Communist authorities to the Karabagh Committee. In August 1989, the ANM successfully fielded candidates, including the current president, Levon Ter-Petrossian, in five run-off elections to the Armenian parliament. The communist leadership began to cooperate more actively with the ANM leadership, and the First Secretary of the Armenian Communist Party, Suren Harutiunian, and his prime minister, Vladimir Markariants, addressed the ANM's founding congress in November 1989. By the end of 1989, the communist authorities' inability to respond adequately to further anti-Armenian violence in Azerbaijan resulted in the creation of voluntary armed "self-defense detachments" in Armenia.

War, blockade, and the earthquake destruction[13] shaped political debate and policy. During this period, activists focused on parliament as the most effective instrument for pursuing nationalist goals. A total of 1,511 candidates

Table 3.3 *Parliamentary elections in Armenia, 1990*

Party	Seats
Armenian National Movement (Hayots hamazgayin sharzhum)	52
Ramgavar-Azatakan Party	14
Armenian Revolutionary Federation (Hai Dashnaktsutiun)	12
National Democratic Union (Azgayain zhoghorvrdakan miutiun)	9
Constitutional Rights Union (Sahmandrakan iravunk)	1
Union for National Self-Determination (Azgayain inkhnoroshum miavorum)	1
Christian Democratic Union (Khristonea-demokratakan miutiun)	1
Republican Party (Hanrapetakan kusakstutiun)	1
Total seats in parliament	260

Note: Remaining seats were filled by independents, or left vacant.
Source: *Nations in Transit: Civil Society, Democracy and Markets in East Central Europe and the Newly Independent States* (New York: Freedom House, 1995), p. 21.

competed for 259 seats (including 13 in Nagorno-Karabagh). The ANM fielded candidates on a platform calling for democratic reform, attention to ecological issues, economic privatization, and the unification of Nagorno-Karabagh with Armenia.

One third of the candidates were nominated by residents' meetings, a higher proportion than anywhere else in the Soviet Union with the exception of Estonia. Yet voters were apathetic, and most campaigns were run "in an individual and idiosyncratic manner." There was only a 60.2 percent turnout, and only ninety-nine candidates managed to garner more than the required 50 percent of the registered votes on the first round, and it took four more rounds, over six months, to fill all but fifteen seats of parliament. The ANM emerged as the strongest political force in multiparty elections to the Armenian parliament, winning 193 seats, or 35 percent, to the communists' 129 seats.[14] Of the ANM candidates, 73 percent were Communist Party members. Indeed, many members of the present government were once communists. Perhaps one of the reasons Armenia never experienced a serious backlash against its communist rulers was because many individual communists were quick to express support for the irredentist agenda, which united a far broader range of political groups than did the explicitly reformist and anti-communist groupings.

Independent Armenia

The economic and social context

Soon after its inception, the nationalist movement resulted in interethnic violence, resulting in the mass deportation of Armenians from Azerbaijan and Azerbaijanis from Armenia in November and December 1988. Azerbaijan organized a rail blockade of Nagorno-Karabagh and Armenia, which failed to crush Armenian activism, but seriously disrupted reconstruction of the earthquake region and created siege conditions for Armenians.

The failure of Soviet authorities to halt the ethnic violence and end the blockade removed Armenians' incentive to cling to the Soviet state. After their September 1991 referendum on independence, in which 95 percent of the electorate participated, and 94 percent voted "yes," Armenians jubilantly greeted their new status. Independence, however, had not been the initial goal of the nationalist movement, so it is not surprising that after the August 1991 putsch and the collapse of the Soviet Union, Armenia was among the first republics to join the Commonwealth of Independent States and to sign the 1992 Collective Security Treaty.

By 1993, economic life in Armenia had hit rock-bottom. The Soviet collapse fragmented intrastate economic and trade relationships; Armenia had closed the Metsamor Nuclear Power Station after the earthquake; the unremitting Azerbaijani and Turkish blockade reduced energy and other supplies; civil unrest in Georgia, and frequent explosions of the gas pipeline where it went through the Azerbaijani-populated Georgian district of Marneuli[15] frequently interrupted the supply of natural gas from Turkmenistan. Beginning in the winter of 1991, the Armenian population found itself surviving without heat, without gas, and with only a few hours (if any) electricity a day. Deprived of energy, most Armenian industries ceased to function. Ruble inflation, followed by conversion to the Armenian dram on November 22, 1993, led to further inflation and then to a sharp drop in real incomes.

Between 1988 and 1990, the conflict between Armenians and Azerbaijanis turned into war on Armenia's border and in Nagorno-Karabagh itself. Azerbaijan's daily bombardment of Nagorno-Karabagh's capital, Stepanakert, with deadly Grad missiles and their attacks on border towns such as Kapan and Goris, resulted in thousands of military and civilian casualties and mass property destruction. Eroding living standards and unemployment forced hundreds of thousands of Armenians from the republic for Russia or the West. A January 1996 UNDP study estimated that 667,000 Armenians have left the republic. Of this number, 229,000 came from Yerevan, which means that if the country as a whole has lost 18 percent of its population, Yerevan

Table 3.4 *Indicators of economic trends in Armenia since 1989*

	1989	1990	1991	1992	1993	1994	1995[a]
GDP	14.2	-7.4	-10.8	-52.4	-14.8	5.4	6.5
Industrial output	-8.0	-7.5	-7.7	-48.2	n.a.	n.a.	n.a.
Rate of inflation	4.8	10.3	100	825	3,732	5,273	175
Rate of unemployment	n.a.	n.a.	4	19	26	n.a.	n.a.
GNP per capita	n.a.	n.a.	n.a.	n.a.	n.a.	2,170	n.a.
% Workforce in private activity[b]	11.8	15.2	29.0	37.1	n.a.	n.a.	n.a.
% GDP from private sector	8.1	11.7	24.2	36.7	n.a.	n.a.	n.a.

Notes: GDP – % change over previous year; industrial output – % change over previous year; rate of inflation – % change in end-year retail/consumer prices; rate of unemployment – % of labor force as of end of year; GNP per capita – in US dollars at PPP exchange rates. [a]Estimate. [b]Non-state sector.

Sources: European Bank for Reconstruction and Development, *Transition Report 1995: Economic Transition in Eastern Europe and the Former Soviet Union* (London: EBRD, 1995); European Bank for Reconstruction and Development, *Transition Report Update, April 1996: Assessing Progress in Economies in Transition* (London: EBRD, 1996); The World Bank, *Statistical Handbook 1993: States of the Former USSR* (Washington, DC: The World Bank, 1994); The World Bank, *Statistical Handbook 1994: States of the Former USSR* (Washington, DC: The World Bank, 1995).

has lost nearly one in four residents.[16] Those who leave fall into several overlapping categories, including people who are already bicultural and bilingual; those with education and skills in demand outside Armenia; and those who simply have relatives abroad willing to help them emigrate. Although it would be impossible, with the data at hand, to accurately characterize the emigrants, what is clear is that this exodus greatly disturbs many Armenians. Those remaining feel abandoned in their time of need by better-connected, more cosmopolitan, and presumably less patriotic fellow citizens, and this abandonment has increased the defensive mentality of a people who feel themselves to be under siege.

In these conditions, pressured by their own population not to make concessions on Nagorno-Karabagh, but to alleviate the economic crisis, Armenia's postcommunist leadership struggled to rebuild state and government. In the summer of 1990, having been chosen chairman of parliament, Levon Ter-Petrossian was forced to respond to the increasing public disorder caused by the proliferation of armed groupings, which had originally formed around the slogan of defending Armenia and Karabagh. His successful ultimatum to these groups to disarm reasserted the primacy of government, restored a measure of quiet to the internal affairs of the republic, and enhanced his credibility as a statesman. In 1991, the year of transition, the government consisted of the parliament which had been elected before independence in 1990, and a president, popularly elected by 83 percent of the voters (70 percent of the electorate actually voted) after independence. In addition to President Levon Ter-Petrossian, members of the ANM soon found places in national or city government. Many members of the former administration joined the ANM, while the former political elite went into business (former First Secretary Karen Demirjian, for example, now heads a factory), or into academic life.

The emerging party system

In the years following independence, founding members of the ANM defected to form splinter parties.[17] The diaspora parties established themselves on Armenian soil, several splinters of the ARF and Ramgavar parties emerged,[18] and quasi-fascist parties such as Tseghakron ("race religion"), or Zharang ("heritage"), organized by former Karabagh activist Igor Muradian, appeared. As of October 1995, forty-nine "public-political organizations" – as parties have been termed since the perestroika era, when "informal" organizations with political aims were first allowed to officially exist – had registered with the Armenian Ministry of Justice. They hardly function as parties in the Western understanding of the term, however, nor do they have much appeal for most voters. In effect, their activities simply mask the real political structure which is emerging in Armenia, that of hierarchical networks of relatives, friends, and acquaintances loyal to charismatic or powerful individuals.

A huge gap exists today between these political parties and the majority of citizens. According to polls and interviews, Armenian voters view most political actors with suspicion and cynicism. According to a sociological poll carried out in July 1995, 62 percent of the population did not trust government, 54 percent did not trust the president – and 42 percent did not trust anyone.[19] While citizens of western countries also express distrust of public officials, this distrust is usually in the context of a general confidence in the fundamental stability of their polity. So soon after the destruction of the powerful Soviet state, there is hardly a basis yet for this kind of confidence in Armenia.

Shortly after the election, I conducted informal interviews about attitudes toward political parties among graduate students at the American University of Armenia, an English-language university funded by a diaspora organization under the aegis of the Regents of the University of California, and an important training ground for Armenia's future elite. The students were almost without exception cynical and distrustful of party politics. The following response was typical: "their [the parties'] real goal is high position, which provides power and money." Another told me, "Dishonest acts and falsehood can be noticed at every step. Bribes play a great role. Falsehood has penetrated all spheres – culture and education, media, politics, economy."

Conversations with Armenian citizens reveal that such cynicism is also the result of the trajectory followed by the ANM, which led Armenia to independence. Once the repository of popular hopes, the ANM has lost credibility in proportion to its monopolization of power and reputation for rampant corruption. Although its leadership still prefer to term it a "movement," it is functionally the largest and most influential party in Armenia. After independence, membership swelled as individuals interested in obtaining positions in the new government joined en masse.

Since 1991, personal conflicts and ideological differences over handling of the conflict in Nagorno-Karabagh and increasing government corruption caused prominent ANM activists such as Vazgen Manukian, David Vartanian, Ashot Manucharian, Khachik Stamboltsian, Shavarsh Kocharian, and others to form the National Democratic Union (NDU), the Scientific-Industrial Civic Union (SICU), and the National Progress Party (NPP), all of which oppose the ANM.

Most platforms do not differ very substantially. They support to a greater or lesser degree privatization and conversion to a free market economy, normalization of relations with Turkey (with differences as to preconditions), economic support for Nagorno-Karabagh (with disagreements about whether to recognize its independence), and the importance of maintaining a "special relationship" with Russia. One point of strong difference was the president's draft of the constitution, which opposition parties such as the NDU, the SICU, and the NPP, strongly opposed, primarily because they felt it concentrated too much power in the office of the presidency.

Rather than representing particular constituencies, most Armenian parties appeal to the entire Armenian nation. Many claim to present a "national ideology" which revolves around defense of the Armenian "nation" (ethnic Armenians), which they see as threatened from the east by "Turks" (a term referring to citizens of Turkey and Azerbaijan), and from the west by too sudden and severe an assault on Armenian traditions. The importance of the "national" issue is suggested by the frequency of the term "nation" in the names of parties – National Progress, National Republic, Christian National Self-Determination Union, and so forth. The parties' appeal to morality and their focus on personalities is exemplified by a recent statement of Paruir Hairikian, who heads the CNSDU, that "our president is the embodiment of

Table 3.5 *Data on public confidence in Armenian political parties, 1992–94 (in percent)*

	Great deal	Fair amount	Sub-total	Not much	None at all	Sub-total	DK/ NA[a]	Total 9/94[b]	At least fair 9/93[c]	At least fair 6/92[d]
Armenian National Movement	7	17	24	22	53	75	2	101	22	14
Ramgavar-Azatskan	1	6	7	30	46	76	18	101	15	9
Dashnak Party	8	21	29	26	39	65	7	101	32	43
National Self-Determination Assn.	2	8	10	20	61	81	8	99	12	n.a.
National Democratic Union	3	8	11	24	46	70	19	100	9	n.a.
Communist Party	13	21	34	22	37	59	8	101	39	n.a.
Democratic Party	2	9	11	24	46	70	20	101	12	n.a.
Christian Democratic Party	3	8	11	21	46	67	23	101	n.a.	n.a.

Notes: Question: "[Now] please tell me how much confidence you have in the following Armenian political parties or movements. First, do you have a great deal of confidence, a fair amount of confidence, not very much confidence, or no confidence at all in . . .?" "And what about . . .?" Questioners cited the parties listed in the table. [a] "Don't know" or no answer. [b] n = 1,000. [c] n = 1,031. [d] n = 1,000.

Source: USIA Opinion Analysis, USIA Office of Research and Media Reaction, Washington, DC, November 17, 1994.

evil. Whatever he does for the people, he does not out of kindness, but because he needs to stay in power."[20]

Except for the ANM and the Communist Party, each of which claim membership in the tens of thousands, and the ARF, which claims membership in the thousands, most parties have a very small base ranging from several dozen to several hundred members.[21] Some parties have established a national network. The Ramgavars, for example, have forty-five clubs in town and district centers throughout Armenia, and the CNSDU and NDU claim members in the countryside. Many parties are reluctant to recruit on a mass scale, but prefer to screen their memberships for fear the "wrong people" may join. They consciously limit membership to close and "trusted" associates.[22]

The SICU, chaired by Suren Zolian, advised by Ashot Manucharian, with its moderate and reformist ideology, refuses the label of "party," describing itself as a public-political organization which accepts individuals who are members of political parties. Its leaders think of it as an organization for elites, and have aimed at attracting people viewed as morally and intellectually outstanding. Although the SICU initially recruited industrialists and enterprise directors, arrests of several directors on various charges resulted in most of them dropping their membership, at least officially.

The parties fall into several major categories, each with different claims to credibility. The communists, for example, can appeal to their practical experience in running the government. It is likely their lingering popularity (they won six seats in the 1995 parliamentary elections) was due not to their economic and political platform, but to the fact that a sorely beleaguered population associated them with political and social order and predictability, a functioning economy, and a guaranteed minimum standard of living. Several communist splinter parties also exist, but failed to attract members or votes.

Diaspora parties form another important category. The ARF in particular, and to a lesser extent, the Ramgavar and Hnchak parties, base claims to legitimacy on their historic role in the nineteenth and twentieth century Armenian liberation struggle in the Ottoman Empire. Organizational experience, advisors, and funds from the diaspora abroad have enabled these parties to set up offices and publish newspapers. The ARF also claims moral authority for the active financial and military role members have played in the armed struggle in Nagorno-Karabagh, where it has a strong representation in the government. A number of volunteer detachments which guarded Armenia's borders or fought in Nagorno-Karabagh were ARF members. As a result, many Armenians view the ARF as the most patriotic of the political parties, even if they do not support its socialist platform. In 1994, opinion polls showed the ARF to be, after the communists, the most popular opposition party.

Since 1994, the ARF's symbolic capital, if not its actual political influence, has been enhanced by the war the government declared on it. On December 28, 1994, shortly after the shocking assassination of former Karabagh Committee member Hambartsum Galstian, President Ter-Petrossian accused the party of harboring a secret cell, "Dro," whose members engaged in terrorism, sabotage, and narcotics trafficking with the knowledge of the ARF's Central Committee. The president also implicated Dro in the assassination of Hambartsum Galstian. Dro's alleged aim was the destabilization of the republic so that the ARF could come to power. The government charged twenty ARF members with political terrorism, drug trafficking, and murder. In January 1995, the Supreme Court formally suspended the activities of the ARF for six months (the suspension to end just after parliamentary elections). The government also closed a dozen newspapers, journals, and magazines either funded by the ARF, or whose editorial boards included ARF members. In many cases, closures were accompanied by raids on editorial offices and seizure of office equipment.

In a speech on May 18, 1995, President Ter-Petrossian broadened his attack on the opposition. He claimed the opposition media "was filled with curses, slander, fabrication," and announced that "the Armenian Revolutionary Federation is not a political party, but rather a terrorist, fascist organization." He also accused members of the NDU, which had implicated the ANM in the murder of Hambartsum Galstian, with "experiencing the most severe case of moral decay."[23]

The ARF does have a history of terrorism, and highly-placed American officials as well as some opposition activists believe in the truth of at least some of the charges against Dro. Most opposition parties avoided taking a stance as to the guilt or innocence of those charged. But they protested the government's move to close down the party as a whole in response to the alleged crimes of individual members. The president, however, argued that although Article 7 of the Law on Civil and Political Organizations stipulates that only the Supreme Court can suspend the activities of a public political organization, Article 8 on the Law on the President of the Republic of Armenia allows the president to undertake measures necessary to secure the security of citizens. In response to a petition from the Ministry of Justice which followed the president's decree, the Supreme Court ultimately upheld the six-month's suspension (which as of 1996, had been extended another year), without references to the charges against Dro, but rather on the grounds that the party violated a decree banning participation of foreign nationals in Armenian political parties.[24]

The government's attack on the ARF had the unintended effect of enhancing the party's reputation. Of the respondents in a July 1995 poll, 24 percent declared that they would have voted for the ARF if it had appeared on the party lists.[25] Many people interpreted the closure of the party and opposition papers as the government's first step in securing its own victory in the upcoming parliamentary elections.

The other opposition parties, including the NDU, headed by Vazgen Manukian, former prime minister and former minister of defense, portrayed themselves as carrying on ideals the ANM has forgotten or betrayed. The opposition accuses the ANM and the government of downplaying Armenian demands that Turkey acknowledge the 1915 genocide for the sake of establishing diplomatic relations, of abandoning Nagorno-Karabagh, of failing to stem the brain drain, of allowing science and education to deteriorate, and of indifference to the population's economic misery.

Except for the ANM and the diaspora parties, funding remains a problem. Parties are forced to rely on individual sponsors rather than dues. Likewise, a journalist who has extensively covered the development of political parties alleged off the record that the 1994 arson of the large children's department store in central Yerevan, and the arrest of Armen Mardirosian, a founder of the successful Aragast enterprise, were part of a government campaign to eliminate the sources of income of wealthy sponsors who supported opposition parties such as the NDU or the SICU. It is difficult to confirm or disconfirm such allegations, but I repeat them here to convey the atmosphere of suspicion and cynicism that infects the Armenian political scene.

Again with the exception of the ARF and the Communist Party, both of which have a long history and an established "face," most Armenian parties are built around a few well-known or charismatic individuals. It would be more apt to characterize them as informal groups of friends and like-minded individuals than as organizations. An Armenian colleague compared them to "tusovkas," the Russian youth phenomenon of the informal group of friends who frequently gather to talk, smoke, and drink coffee. As such, they remain small, unstable, and prone to fission when leaders have a falling-out.

Emerging patron–client networks

Although parties remain a primary topic of interest for the few activists who participate in them and for foreign democracy-building organizations, they largely function, intentionally or unintentionally, as a façade for the real structure of power in today's Armenia, or what Armenians refer to as "mafias." These groupings consist of clusters of relationships based on networks of relatives, friends, colleagues, acquaintances, and neighbors, hierarchically bound together through the ongoing exchange of favors and obligations. Such relations characterized Armenian society under communist rule, although not to the degree present in some other republics of the FSU. In Soviet Armenia, top party and government officials were also related directly or indirectly by ties of kinship, friendship, and mutual obligations. But the hegemony these patron–client relations enjoyed was limited by their members' fear of Moscow. In egregious cases of injustice, individuals could and did appeal to authorities in Moscow, and sometimes Moscow intervened in their favor.

When the Karabagh movement precipitated the end of communist rule in Armenia, it dislodged powerholders and disrupted many of these networks. Since 1991, the new powerholders have become entrenched. Today, the ruling elite consists of what many people I interviewed referred to as competing teams, clustered around key figures such as President Levon Ter-Petrossian, his eldest brother Telman, Prime Minister Hrant Bagratian, Minister of the Interior Vano Siradeghian and Defense Minister Vazgen Sarkissian. These men in particular are seen as nodes in a system which some people consider more ruthless and self-serving than the previous communist regime.

Despite the apparent bankruptcy of the state budget, there are enormous sums to be made during this period of rapid and unpredictable change. Well-placed people are scrambling to secure their access to this wealth by buying and selling of state holdings which are being privatized, asserting control over natural resources, and establishing trade and production monopolies. Given the confusing hodge-podge of Soviet-era and post-independence laws and the fact that Armenia no longer has to answer to Moscow, new authorities can demand with impunity whatever bribes or payments the market will bear. As a twenty-four year old graduate student at the American University of Armenia wrote in response to a question I posed on the role of democracy in Armenia, "Money dictates the relations among members of society. If you have enough money you are heard, considered, and respected. In Armenia, money rules everywhere – from hospitals to high posts of government. This is our 'democracy.'"

Who, exactly, are the individuals who head these powerful groupings? We can begin by scrutinizing the Ter-Petrossian family. Telman Petrossian, Levon Ter-Petrossian's eldest brother, is widely described as one of the most powerful men in Armenia. A former member of the Central Committee of the Armenian Communist Party once attacked for his corruption by perestroika-minded Armenian politicians such as Haik Kotanjian, Telman was and is director of Hrazdanmash, a large industrial enterprise near Yerevan. At one time, he was also deputy chairman of the government Commission on Privatization and Denationalization, which formed to oversee privatization of factories and many services, including hotels. Many Armenians consider

Telman Ter-Petrossian the man who controls Armenian industry. Suspicions and rumors have also circled around Petros Ter-Petrossian, the second eldest brother, who headed the commission charged with privatizing unfinished construction and building equipment.[26]

Vano Siradeghian, a writer and former member of the Karabagh Committee, and today the minister of the interior, is today considered another center of personal power. Because police, tax inspectors, and customs authorities who are part of this ministry regulate trade and transportation in and out of Armenia, they are well placed to demand and receive payments, a percentage of which is widely believed to travel up the ministerial hierarchy to the top. Observers link the unsolved murders of Avtandil Kandelian, the powerful director of the Armenian railway, and of Hambartsum Galstian (at the time of his death a strong critic of the government, but who had already left politics for business) to competition to control trade and transportation routes.

The Ministry of Defense is thought to be the center of yet another powerful group aggrandizing power and money, since the army and military police have access to large illicit profits through their control of borders. Moreover, individuals in the army hierarchy "earn" large sums of money each time a draftee pays the local military authorities – reportedly US $500 to $1,500 – for an exemption.

Such groupings, often formed around people who come from the same district or village or who are kin, can exercise considerable control and influence over government political and economic policies.[27] In this light, the 1995 parliamentary elections can be just as easily interpreted as competition between patron–client networks and the powerful individuals who lead them, as between political parties. Many people cynically dismiss parliament as a façade for this competition for wealth and personal power. When I asked them what motivated individuals to run for parliament, I was surprised that one of the most frequent responses was, "they just want parliamentary immunity from prosecution for their economic crimes."

The 1995 Armenian elections

Government manipulation

The international community views elections as an important avenue and measure of political participation and democratization. The Armenian government therefore went to considerable pains to make the elections appear free and fair. Anticipating that the elections would enhance the republic's democratic image, it invited hundreds of individuals and organizations to Armenia as election observers.[28]

To the government's dismay, international organizations such as the Organization for Security and Cooperation in Europe and the European Parliament, as well as Washington-based organizations such as the International Foundation for Electoral Systems and the National Democratic Institute, which had participated in election training and monitoring, concluded that the elections had not been conducted fairly. They noted that the government had frequently acted illegally and arbitrarily to ensure the success of its candidates and guarantee its control of parliament.[29] Overall, the government did what it could, legally or illegally, to guarantee its control of parliament, although it is likely the government would have retained control, albeit not so completely, if elections had been fairly conducted. The Armenian government is not monolithic, and the races also revealed a number of rifts between different groupings or clans within the government. After the election, a member of the Central Election Committee (CEC) referred to the arrest of well-known underworld figures as the part of the infighting between Minister of the Interior Vano Siradeghian and the particular government figures these underworld figures had supported in the election. Thus, as far as the electorate was concerned, electoral races were largely about personalities rather than platforms.

The constitutional referendum

The election consisted of two parts, a parliamentary election for representatives to the National Assembly, to be chosen for five-year terms, and a referendum on the government draft of the proposed constitution. Months after the election, the conduct and results of both votes remain in dispute. The draft constitution itself emerged out of considerable controversy. Although the opposition had produced a variant, the government decided to offer the electorate its own draft. The opposition criticized the constitution on the grounds that it dangerously concentrated power in the presidency, weakened the independence of the judiciary, and reduced the autonomy of local government. Polls conducted shortly before the referendum indicated that most citizens did not understand the constitution very well. A poll carried out by the Armenian State Television and Radio Ministry reported that 51 percent of respondents did not have an opinion because they lacked information, and only 32 percent planned to vote for it.[30]

Taking advantage of its virtual monopoly of television and radio, the government conducted a campaign which largely misrepresented the issue as whether to have a constitution rather than which version to adopt. The campaign for the constitution culminated in a strong and – according to the

Table 3.6 *Constitutional referendum in Armenia, 1995*

	Popular vote	% of electorate	% of actual voters
Yes	828,370	37	68
No	349,721	16	28
Invalid votes	39,440	2	3

Notes: eligible voters: 2,189,804; voter turnout: 1,217,531 (56% of eligible voters).
Source: Linda Edgeworth and Scott R. Lansell, *Technical Assistance to Armenia: July 5, 1995 National Assembly Elections and Constitutional Referendum* (Washington, DC: International Foundation for Electoral Systems, 1995), Appendix 17, "Result Summary of the Constitutional Referendum and Parliamentary Elections in Armenia."

watchers I interviewed – convincing television appearance by President Ter-Petrossian the day before the election, in which he warned that failure to vote "yes" on the government's draft constitution would expose Armenia to the danger of civil war and loss of its international reputation as a democratic country. According to CEC figures, the constitution passed by a margin of 68 percent to 27 percent (37.8 percent of eligible voters). Given the strong sentiment in Yerevan against the constitution and the fact that the CEC never published precinct-level voting figures, either for candidates or the referendum, many opposition sympathizers suspected the CEC of fabricating the results.

The new constitution will have important effects on the construction of a democratic society. It provides for a National Assemby to be elected for four-year terms, and is the only government body which can pass laws, although some decisions by regional and local executive committees, as well as government decisions and presidential decrees, will also have the effect of law. The constitution also replaces thirty-nine administrative districts with ten large districts, of which Yerevan will be a single large district. The governor, or *marzpet*, of each of the new districts will be appointed by the central government, who can also remove locally elected officials based on findings by the regional governor. The only local self-government will be village councils representing several hundred people. This highly centralized structure may facilitate even stronger vertical patron–client relations, effectively discouraging local community political participation. The constitution provides for a weak legislature, "what some observers have called the strongest presidency among the Helsinki nations,"[31] and a judiciary system which lacks adequate independence.[32] Article 55, for example, allows the president to dissolve parliament after minimal consultation with the president of the National Assembly and the prime minister, appoint the prime minister and government, appoint or dismiss the chief prosecutor, and appoint or dismiss members and the president of the constitutional court (based on a finding of the Court). Thus, "at almost every layer of the judicial system, the appointees owe their jobs" to the president,[33] a fact which creates serious fears for the independence of the judiciary.

Finally, the Constitution guarantees a broad array of civil rights and freedoms. However, Articles 44, 45, and 55, and Section 14 define in dangerously vague terms the conditions under which the government can rescind fundamental rights and restrict fundamental civil liberties, in the view of some experts thereby offering loopholes which could allow the government to abuse opposition and seriously undermine democracy.[34]

Parliamentary elections

Popular cynicism about the referendum and constitution was matched by the public attitude to the parliamentary election. Voters were to choose 190 deputies, 150 from a slate of candidates from the 150 districts, and 40 nationwide from party lists, according to which parties receiving more than 5 percent of the votes won a proportional number of seats. The law governing elections was passed on April 13, 1995, less than three months before the election, a period insufficient to address the vagueness and inconsistency of many points. Elections were to be regulated by the CEC, district (DEC), and precinct (PEC) electoral committees.

Given the role of powerful personalities now vying for power and control in government, many electoral races were essentially contests between "sponsors" of individual candidates. The ANM, through the domineering pro-ANM chairman of the CEC, Robert Amirian, was able to determine the membership and chairmanship of district level committees, control the registration of parties and candidates, and in many cases annul undesirable results. As a result of CEC rulings, 129 out of 150 DEC chairpersons were representatives of the Hanrapetutiun ("republic") Bloc, consisting of the ANM and five affiliated parties,[35] and more than 1,600 representatives of opposition parties were removed or excluded from DECs and PECs.[36] The DECs registered only 1,473 of the approximately 2,300 candidates who applied for registration, and two blocs and eleven parties of the three blocs and nineteen parties which had applied. According to an Armenian journalist, the level of rejection was larger than it had been during the previous election, held under Communist Party rule.[37] Disqualified candidates were almost invariably from opposition parties or running as independents. The single court empowered to hear appeals failed to reinstate a single candidate or party. In one case, it postponed the appeal until after election day because the CEC lawyer had a death in his family.

A special CEC ruling allowed voting to occur at military installations, which allowed army authorities to pressure recruits to vote for government candidates and for the constitution. In one case, this was accomplished by threatening to send recruits to the front-line if the government measures did not pass. An international election observer even reported seeing soldiers presenting their completed ballots to their officer for inspection before depositing them in the ballot box.

Each bloc could rely on certain votes, beginning with the family members and relatives of the candidates, and including the network of dependents. Especially in rural areas, single-district candidates could count on their home villages, as well as on those groups of people who were dependent on them for employment or favors.

A brief description of the election for the representative from the northern city of Vanadzor (formerly Stepanavan) should provide a flavor of the elections.[38] The race took place between two former friends – Mayor Aram Babajanian, and Head Doctor Misha Bablumian, director of the German Red Cross Hospital – whose candidacy had turned them into bitter enemies. Dr. Bablumian headed the local ANM committee. Babajanian, previously a member of the Ramgavar Party, ran as an independent. Each candidate controlled blocs of voters to whom they were linked by clientalistic and kinship relations. As mayor, Babajanian controlled the police and city government employees, while the doctor was supported by hospital employees, the population of his natal village, and the army installation in Vanadzor.

Mayor Babajanian won the election by 500 votes, but the CEC cancelled the results amidst a spectacular exchange of accusations on both sides. The doctor's supporters accused the mayor's supporters of kidnapping members of the DEC and stealing ballot boxes. They also accused the mayor of calling on his brother, who occupied an important position in the Zvartnots International Airport police department, and on the local police to intimidate voters, even preventing them from entering the polling places. The mayor accused the doctor and the ANM of trying to falsify the vote of the military installation in Vanadzor by packing the PEC with relatives of the military commander.

Although Babajanian won the re-run on July 29, his supporters claimed the army installation (whose votes would have been enough to swing a close election) had initially tried to claim twice as many voters as during the first election. In return, the head of the DEC, a supporter of the doctor, claimed that the mayor had physically threatened his life, and had personally typed out a new protocol which gave lower figures for the army installation. The CEC ratified the results of the second election, however, possibly fearing municipal insurrection in Vanadzor if the contest were repeated.

In some districts, the nature of the electoral races revealed splits within the ANM. In District 22, the government candidate lost to a candidate thought to be sponsored by Vano Siradeghian, who although he was officially an ANM member, was seen as striving to increase his personal power base. In District 16, according to a journalist for the Noyan Tapan news agency, Vazgen Sarkissian had family members of a popular independent, Araik Sarkissian (not a relative), arrested, to force him to withdraw his candidacy in favor of the minister of defense's childhood friend, David Zadoyan, former minister in charge of bread production.

The new parliament consists of several large blocs, formed around the ANM (sixty-five seats) and the remaining five parties which make up the Hanrapetutiun Bloc (twenty-one seats); Shamiram (eight seats); and the Reform Bloc of thirty-one of the deputies who won as independents. Of the opposition parties, the Communists won seven seats, the NDU five seats, the CNSDU three seats, the Ramgavar Party one seat, and the ARF one seat. In terms of real affiliations, however, the parliament can be interpreted as groupings based on loyalty to one or another of the figures striving for power and wealth in Armenia. The Reform Bloc, for example, is headed by Telman Ter-Petrossian's deputy at Hrazdanmash; Shamiram, formed only two months before the election, is a women's party many of whose members were related by marriage or friendship to the political elite, although many people considered it the particular creation of Vano Siradeghian. The ANM bloc also includes individuals thought to be sponsored by Vano Siradeghian, Vazgen Sarkissian, Telman Ter-Petrossian, and others. Some have speculated that the forty enterprise and business directors who won seats in parliament could form a "faction" with voting power. According to a member of the parliamentary apparatus interviewed in October 1995, this may be unlikely in the short term, as long as the state sector remains powerful. In the future, it is possible these entrepreneurs will recognize their common interests and start to lobby for them.

Despite the fact that government now controls parliament, it lost some international credibility for its obvious manipulation of the election, although there do not seem to be any serious repercussions from this loss. Approximately 55 percent of Armenia's 2.2 million voters participated in the election, although 35 percent of the ballots cast for parties were declared invalid (many voters crossed off all the parties as a show of general dissatisfaction). The results of the election seriously demoralized the electorate. Opposition parties were shocked at their poor showing, and intellectuals sympathetic to the opposition felt that the population's political will had been completely ignored by the government's obvious manipulation. The impact of the election has been to further polarize government and opposition to the point where they can no longer work together constructively.

Table 3.7 *National Assembly elections in Armenia, 1995*

Party/bloc	No. votes[a]	% votes[a]	No. seats[b]	% seats[b]
Hanrapetutiun bloc	329,300	42.7	119	62.6
Armenian National Movement			(65)	
Liberal Democratic Party			(6)	
Republican Party			(4)	
Christian Democratic Party			(3)	
Union of Intellectuals			(3)	
Social-Democratic Hnchak Party			(2)	
Others			(36)	
Shamiram	130,252	16.9	8	4.2
Communist Party	93,353	12.1	7	3.7
National Democratic Union	57,996	7.5	5	2.6
Union of Self-Determination	42,987	5.6	3	1.6
Ramgavar-Azatakan Party	19,437	2.5	1	.5
Armenian Revolutionary Federation				
"Dashaktsutiun"	n.a.	2.0	1	.5
Independents	n.a.	n.a.	45	23.7
Vacant seats			1	.5
Parties failing to win seats				
Will and Dashnaktsutiun	15,424	2.0		
Armenian Democratic Party	13,784	1.8		
Armenian Agrarian Democratic Party	12,143	1.6		
Mission (Arakelutiun)	10,428	1.3		
Armenian Scientific–Industrial				
Civic Union	9,940	1.3		
National State	8,397	1.1		
People's Party	6,706	0.9		
Total	771,830		190	

Notes: Eligible voters: 2,178,699; voter turnout: 1,195,283; total ballots cast: 1,183,573 (54.9% of eligible voters); invalid ballots: 411,743 (35% of ballots cast). Percentages may not add to 100 due to rounding. [a]Total from first round, July 5, 1995. [b]Includes seats filled through party-list and direct elections.

Sources: *Hayastani Hanrapetutiun*, July 12, 1995; Edgeworth and Lansell, *Technical Assistance to Armenia*, Appendix 17; Azbarez-on-Line, Armenia–Karabakh News, July 12, 1995. Keesings Historisch Archief and IFES Armenia on http://www.universal.nl/users/derksen/election/home.htm.

As an Armenian journalist commented after a sharp attack in the government paper, *Respublika Armeniia*, on a conference organized by opposition parties on foreign policy, "They've completely defeated the opposition, now they don't even want to allow them to do anything." An opposition politician commented that given Armenian political culture, parties always speak very badly of each other even if they share platforms. But after the election all the parties hated the government so intensely, he felt they would like to see it make catastrophic mistakes just to discredit itself.

Civil society in Armenia

Given weak Armenian political parties, an increasingly authoritarian government, and the strengthening mafia-like patron–client networks, we must ask if non-governmental organizations have the potential to provide an outlet and route for citizens to influence the shape of state and society. In recent years, such organizations have burgeoned in Armenia. As of October 1995, almost 900 charities, religious groups, sports clubs, cultural organizations, issue-oriented and civic organizations had registered with the Ministry of Justice. In theory, such organizations constitute an important component of civil society.[39] But in Armenia, most of them are short-lived and diffuse, led by one or two members of the political or economic elite (or their wives), with a small and fluid membership. At best, they are clusters of friends and acquaintances interested in pursuing a common goal; rarely are they organizations in the usual sense of having an impersonal structure, an accepted set of procedures, and a fairly stable membership. The groups frequently split over competition between leaders or changes in their mission. Similar organizations tend to compete for resources – often computers and other equipment donated by western organizations and charities – rather than collaborate or share resources.

Other reasons for failure include the general economic context. Organizations have few resources; most people can only pay very nominal dues. Many organizations are unable to effectively inform the public about their existence, purpose, and activities, since they cannot afford radio time, newspaper advertisements, or the printing of brochures. The endemic distrust so common in postcommunist regimes facilitates the continuing atomization and fragmentation of social and civic life. Distrust, combined with harsh economic conditions and competition for funding, sponsors, equipment, and so forth, discourages the sharing of resources or even information.[40]

The Church, as an autonomous, wealthy institution in Armenian society, has the potential to play an important role in the construction of a civil society. Given the president's open support for the selection of Garegin I, the new Catholicos (head of the church), who was elected in Spring 1995 to replace the recently deceased Vazgen I, many Armenians view him as a government spokesman. This view is buttressed by the Church's stated support for the government, and its indifferent response to attacks carried out by armed detachments linked to the Ministry of Defense on members of minority religions. Church and government appear to be working together to affirm the Church's monopoly on Armenian religious life, as part of the government's nation and state-building project.

Opposition attempts to use the Church as a counterweight to the government have thus far proved unsuccessful. In October 1995, twelve well-known and respected intellectuals (including the head of the Armenian Encyclopedia and members of the Academy of Science) wrote to Garegin I asking him to mediate between the ARF and the president to ease the growing social tension caused by the crackdown on the party. The Catholicos is said to have raised the matter with the president, who was said to have replied that the matter was in the courts and out of his hands. According to a journalist who closely followed the election of the Catholicos, the latter was compromised by the nature of his election, and is no longer independent enough to oppose the government.

Civil society faces another serious obstacle in Armenia, and that is the ongoing war with Azerbaijan. Despite the cease fire, which began in the summer of 1994, the conflicting parties have yet to come to any consensus about the shape of a final settlement. Although Armenia was never officially involved in the war, it openly supported the aims of the Karabagh Armenians and unofficially provided not just humanitarian but also military support. Especially during the hottest period of the conflict, the war also subdued the opposition, in the interests of a united front, and encroached on civil rights – drafting men into the army became a potent form of intimidation.

The war has increased Armenian nationalism and the sense of being a nation under siege. Two sorts of nationalist discourses have emerged from the dual processes of constructing a nation-state and carrying out a war. The first asserts and maintains the symbolic boundaries of the nation by accentuating national differences. The second, more militant nationalism, calls for the defense of the Armenian nation – seen as threatened by its Azerbaijani and Turkish neighbors – through the reincorporation of "historic territories." When it suits their purposes, officials and politicians use these nationalist discourses to quell opposition and criticism of human rights violations in the name of a "united front." Until the undeclared war with Azerbaijan over the status of Nagorno-Karabagh is decisively resolved, nationalism will remain a potent force for quelling independent, anti-government activities.

Creating a free-market economy

In 1991, Armenia was the first republic to privatize land, thereby creating a class of small rural landowners. Land distribution was carried out relatively equitably, livestock distribution less so. By 1996, over 80 percent of agriculture had been privatized. But because subsidies on seed, fodder, fertilizer, and fuel were simultaneously cut, most farmers were barely succeeding in eking out a subsistence on the land. For the most part, barter has replaced a cash economy in the countryside.[41]

In towns and cities, privatization proceeded more slowly. Because parliamentary deputies are allowed to simultaneously hold nongovernment positions, they have frequently acted as lobbyists for economic interests related to their outside employment. This gives them ample opportunities for what in the United States would be considered serious conflicts of interest. Small enterprises have been privatized, and large enterprises are now being privatized through a system of vouchers. Many of the small enterprises which sprang up in 1989–91, however, have already disappeared. Bank failure, harsh tax policies, and high bribes drove many to the relatively more hospitable business climate of Russia.

Since 1988, Armenian society has assumed the shape of a sharp pyramid. At the top are members of the old and new nomenklatura who have managed to profit in the postcommunist free-for-all. A small emerging middle class incudes people who earn a living servicing the growing international community of embassies, international organizations, and international NGOs as office managers, translators, technical assistants, cooks, drivers, and maids, and a new commercial class of traders who import cheap consumer items from the Middle East, Persian Gulf, China, and East Europe, for resale in Armenia. They also provide a meager income to hired salespeople who resell the goods at street markets. Teachers, researchers, professors, doctors, engineers, architects, writers, artists, and civil servants who have not been able to adapt to the new economic demands form a large impoverished class. Those with relatives or connections abroad have emigrated to Russia or the west; others manage to keep their families alive by working simultaneously at three or four jobs.

Most people consequently have little time or energy for political participation. A former communist who served in the previous parliament explained, "People didn't become active with the declaration of independence . . . during the last election, there was again great political activity, but this was, so to speak, a one-act event. People are only active now in terms of searching for work and money . . . if people had normal work and with that, normal salaries, they would start to become interested in something and would gradually show initiative." A former dissident, Georgi Khomizuri, now a human rights activist, warns that

Everyone . . . remembers very well, that when we had a dictatorship, every citizen was guaranteed some sort of minimum . . . For the majority of the population, dictatorship is of course bad, but on the other hand, everyone is guaranteed something, while now no one is guaranteed anything – they are driven from work, they receive assistance of 540 drams [$1.30] on which they could die . . . That is, there are grounds for a return to dictatorship.

The economic crisis has also eroded the communication infrastructure, thereby affecting the ability of the population to remain informed about or even discuss public affairs. Lack of electricity has reduced access to television and radio, especially in rural regions. Few newspapers reach small towns or villages, and the urban population no longer buys papers on an everyday basis. A recent poll indicated that only 3 percent of the population reads a paper on a regular basis. Non-existent street lighting, expensive transportation, and for many people, lack of free time, prevent the frequent socializing that characterized Soviet Armenian society. The telephone system, always bad in Armenia, has become abysmal. In most villages, one cannot even telephone the nearest town. As a result, people are unable to remain informed about what the government is doing. As one man put it, each family now sits alone in the dark, rather than meeting with others to evaluate and discuss these issues. As a result, "public opinion" cannot develop.

The educational system, an essential aspect of creating a literate, informed citizenry, has suffered a sharp decline since independence. Claiming insolvency, the government has ceased to repair or maintain schools, or subsidize textbooks or school supplies. Protesting terrible working conditions and salaries which barely cover daily transportation to work, up to 20 percent of Armenian teachers nationwide[42] have left their jobs.

Higher education has been effectively privatized. Bribes required for university entrance are now higher than tuition fees to the new "private universities." Fewer Armenians now have the possibility of attending the first-rate universities of Russia. The decline in the quality of and access to education means that Armenia will not be able to maintain the well-educated and well-trained labor force which constitutes one of the republic's few resources. Given the current brain-drain of scientists, scholars, and cultural figures to other republics, the Middle East, Europe, and North America, the diminished cadre may reduce the benefits of privatization and slow Armenia's entrance into the world market.

Armenia and Russia

Finally, most Armenians are aware that their country is still not completely independent of Russian influence. Many Armenians fear that lack of resolution of the war in Karabagh provides an ongoing basis for Russia to intervene in internal policy. They express skepticism that Armenia can maintain its *de facto*, if not *de jure*, independence. Russian and Armenian troops now jointly defend Armenian borders; the Armenian dram responds to the ups and downs in the Russian ruble. Finally, Armenia depends economically on open Russian borders, for without the remittances from Armenians working in Russia, the Armenian economy would be in a shambles and the population could probably not have survived the past few years. Hence, Armenia must continue to reckon with the vestiges of empire and Russian influence in its internal and foreign policies.

Conclusions

The combined impact of economic crisis and decline, war and nationalism, corruption and authoritarianism raise doubts whether it is useful to search for "democracy," "political participation," and "civil society" in Armenia. Developments there suggest that these may be models that cannot be transferred so easily from the established Western democracies to the decolonializing Soviet successor states.

Certainly, independent Armenia has acquired the attributes of a modern, electoral democracy – it has a new constitution, a new parliament, over four dozen registered political parties, and a non-communist president who will run for re-election in September 1996. Economically, Armenia has won the praise of international lending agencies for bringing inflation under control, abolishing subsidies, and progress in privatizing land and production. At least formally, Armenia is transforming itself into a Western-style democracy.

Yet the underlying structure of the new polity is inconsistent with this democratic facade. Whether one refers to this underlying structure as a network of clans, mafias, or cliques, the fact remains that individuals who have used their government positions to aggrandize enormous wealth exercise the greatest share of political power in the fledgling state structure. Ordinary Armenians, who began to speak of themselves as "citizens" rather than "subjects" for the first time in 1988, now feel more impotent than ever. As one former activist, now busy trying to support his three children, told me, "At least under the communists I knew where I should go to make a complaint. Now I could be shot in the street, and the police wouldn't even pay attention!" Many Armenians still expect change to come from the top; the little civic initiative that timidly emerged in 1988 has dissipated, and the lesson the electorate has learned from recent elections is that their votes do not mean much.

In conclusion, I note the following disturbing trends: (1) the increasing power of vertical, clientalistic relationships are displacing the horizontal ties fundamental to civil society, even despite the "Potemkin village" of "civic organizations," largely controlled by Westernized elites; (2) the sharp economic stratification of Armenian society carries the danger that in one generation, Armenia will no longer have the educated, skilled labor force essential to a prosperous economy; (3) economic distress, political authoritarianism, social anomie, and increasing nationalism are encouraging an emigration which can lead to the homogenization and provincialization of Armenian society; and (4) the curtailing of press freedoms and the potential limitation of judicial independence and civil rights[43] in the interests of preserving "national harmony" and "stability" are moving the government in an increasingly authoritarian direction.

The situation in Armenia is too fluid to predict with any certainty how the economic and political situation may alter over the next five or ten years. Much depends on developments in Russia, Armenia's relations with all its neighbors, and the policies of international political and economic organizations involved in Armenia. Finally, it depends on the Armenian people themselves whether democracy, now just a word, becomes reality in their country.

Epilogue: the Armenian presidential election of 1996

On September 22, 1996, Armenians again went to the polls, re-electing Levon Ter-Petrossian as president. Levon Ter-Petrossian's victory in Armenia occurred in the context of voter apathy, and allegations by opposition politicians, journalists, and international observers of vote manipulation. Serious violations of election law,[44] according to the OSCE final report, gave cause for a "lack of confidence in the integrity of the overall election process."[45]

The leading opposition candidate, Vazgen Manukian, won 41.29 percent of the vote after four other opposition candidates withdrew their candidacy and formed a "National Accord" to support Manukian. Interestingly, Manukian won a majority of votes in the capital, where the electorate is usually more well-informed, prosperous, and pro-reform. Ter-Petrossian had reason to fear Manukian might win a run-off vote, especially since the other presidential candidates, Sergey Badalian and Ashot Manucharian, promised to throw their support to him in a run-off.

When the CEC released preliminary figures, Manukian and other opposition politicians entered the parliament building to negotiate with CEC members; shortly afterwards, hundreds of their followers forced their way into the building after them, assaulting the speaker of the National Assembly, Babken Ararktsian, and Deputy Speaker Ara Sahakian. As police quelled the crowed, participants and onlookers were beaten and dozens detained. The following day, in a 150 to 0 vote (with two abstentions), the National Assembly stripped eight of the opposition deputies who had been involved in the demonstrations of their immunity, and physically assaulting some, and detaining all of them except Manukian, who was not present. Ter-Petrossian announced a state of emergency and banned public demonstrations, while

Table 3.8 *Presidential elections in Armenia, 1996*

Candidate	Party	Votes	% of votes
Levon Ter-Petrossian	ANM	646,888	51.75
Vazgen Manukian	National Accord	516,129	41.29
Sergey Badalian	Communist Party	79,347	6.34
Ashot Manucharian	SICU	7,529	.60

Notes: number of eligible voters: 2,210,189; voter turnout: 1,333,204 (60.32%); invalid ballots: all candidates eliminated – 10,012, voided – 48,681, forged – 2,442.
Source: CEC figures, reported by Noyan Tapan in Azbarez-on-Line, September 30, 1996.

Table 3.9 *Votes cast in Yerevan, Armenian presidential elections, 1996*

Candidate	Votes
Vazgen Manukian	209,322
Levon Ter Petrossian	154,125
All others	60,660
Total votes in Yerevan	424,107

Source: CEC figures, reported by Noyan Tapan in Azbarez-on-Line, September 30, 1996.

army troops patrolled Yerevan, security forces closed offices of opposition political parties, in some cases beating those present as foreign journalists looked on.[46]

The conduct and rhetoric of the election suggest that political culture in Armenia remains a matter of personalities rather than institutions. The two leading candidates were not radically opposed regarding the importance of free-market reforms, developing production, and foreign policy. Manukian, however, promised to resolve the Karabagh conflict, and addressed the economic distress of the population by promising to fight the clan structures impeding economic recovery and raise wages tenfold. Ter-Petrossian emphasized stability as the prerequisite for deepening reforms necessary for improving the population's standard of living.

The highly ideologized and moralistic campaign language, however, revealed that the contenders perceived their candidacies as a mission on which depended the very fate of the Armenian nation. As election day approached, Ter-Petrossian warned the electorate that Manukian's victory would lead to civil war and bloodshed.[47] After the election, each side accused the other in apocalyptic language of behaving as "traitors to the nation"[48] or as "state criminals,"[49] the opposition labelled the president's electoral victory a coup d'état, while the minister of the interior compared the post-election violence to an "attempted putsch,"[50] and Ter-Petrossian characterized it as a "fascist" coup by "mentally ill people."[51]

The victory of an incumbent during the painful political and economic transition that characterized post-socialist societies distinguishes Armenia from Eastern Europe, as well as from Lithuania, Ukraine, and Moldova, where incumbents peacefully relinquished power, and suggests that for now, personalities rather than institutions continue to rule Armenian politics.[52]

Acronyms

ANM	Armenian National Movement (Hayots hamazgayin sharzhum)
ARF	Armenian Revolutionary Federation (Hai Dashnaktsutiun)
CEC	Central Electoral Commission
CNSDU	Christian National Self-Determination Union
CPSU	Communist Party of the Soviet Union
DEC	District Electoral Committee
FSU	Former Soviet Union
NDU	National Democratic Union
NPP	National Progress Party (Azgayin arajendats kusaktsutiun)
NUP	National Unification Party (Azgayin miutiun kusaktsutiun)
PEC	Precinct Electoral Committee
SICU	Scientific–Industrial Civic Union (Gita-ardiunaberakan ev kaghakatsiakan miutiun)

NOTES

Research for this chapter was completed as part of a project funded by the Harry Frank Guggenheim Foundation, and written while I was a research associate at the Institute for European, Russian, and Eurasian Studies at George Washington University. I would like to thank both institutions for their generous support. I would also like to thank the many individuals in Armenia who helped me with this project. I am grateful to Karen Dawisha and Bruce Parrott for inviting me to participate in the project on political participation and democratization in postcommunist societies. The writing of this paper has had both positive and negative consequences for me. Without my prior knowledge or permission, copies of the first draft, "Mirage of Democracy," were circulated in Azerbaijan and Armenia, and parts of it were reprinted in Azerbaijani and Armenian newspapers. On June 29, 1996, the Armenian Embassy in Washington, DC refused to grant me a visa for a work-related trip to Armenia. Such an act is to be regretted, because it will encourage self-censorship on the part of scholars working on contemporary Armenian topics.

1   Vartan H. Artinian, "The Role of the Amiras in the Ottoman Empire," *The Armenian Review* 34 (June 1981), 192.

2   Claire Mouradian, *De Staline á Gorbatchev: Histoire d'une république sovietique* (Paris: Editions Ramsay, 1990).

3   See Mary Kilbourne Matossian, *The Impact of Soviet Policies in Armenia* (Leiden: E. J. Brill, 1962).

4   Mouradian, *De Staline á Gorbatchev*.

5   Despite a short-lived war with Georgia in 1918 over disputed border regions, Armenia's relations with Georgia, with which it shares a similar religion and a similar history of victimization at the hands of Arab, Persian, and Turkic forces, have never provoked the same kind of widespread irredentist passions. The Dashnaktsutiun, however, still supports Armenian claims to districts along the Georgian–Armenian border and Black Sea coast, and is rumored to have supplied arms to their Armenian populations.

6   Ronald Suny, *Armenia in the Twentieth Century* (Chico, CA: Scholars Press, 1983).

7   Ronald Suny, *Looking Toward Ararat: Armenia in Modern History* (Bloomington: Indiana University Press, 1993), p. 185.

8   See Nora Dudwick, "Armenia: The Nation Awakens," in *Nations and Politics in the Soviet Successor States*, ed. Ian Bremmer and Raymond Taras (New York: Cambridge University Press, 1993).

9   The following discussion of the Karabagh movement is based, except where noted, on the research I carried out for my dissertation, "Memory, Identity and Politics in Armenia," University of Pennsylvania, 1994.

10 See the essay by Levon Abramian, "Archaic Ritual and Theater: From the Ceremonial Glade to Theater Square," *Soviet Anthropology & Archeology* 29, no. 2 (1990), 45-69.

11 When its members were arrested, the Karabagh Committee consisted of Babken Ararktsian, Hambartsum Galstian, Samvel Gevorkian, Rafael Ghazarian, Samson Ghazarian, Ashot Manucharian, Vazgen Manukian, Vano Siradeghian, Levon Ter-Petrossian, and David Vardanian.

12 Peter Rutland, "Democracy and Nationalism in Armenia," *Europe/Asia Studies* 46 (1994), 849.

13 On December 7, 1988, a powerful earthquake destroyed two cities, as well as towns and villages, in northern Armenia, killing 25,000 people, making homeless 500,000 more, and destroying over one-third of Armenia's industrial capacity. Despite Gorbachev's vow that Armenia would be rebuilt in two years, war, blockade, and state collapse soon halted reconstruction. Much of this region remains in a ravaged state.

14 Rutland, "Democracy and Nationalism," p. 852.

15 Although Armenians assume that the Azerbaijani population has been responsible for most of the explosions, some Armenians suspect that the Armenian "fuel mafia" may have played a part, deliberately reducing supplies of cheap fuel in order to keep prices high.

16 *Golos Armenii*, 17 February 1996.

17 The following section draws on my own experience as an election monitor, and on "Report on Armenia's Parliamentary Election and Constitutional Referendum," CSCE, August 1995; "A Report on the Constitutional Referendum and the

National Assembly Elections in the Republic of Armenia on July 5 and July 29,"
by Vote Armenia (An Independent Local Election Observer Organization); and
Linda Edgeworth and Scott R. Lansell, *Technical Assistance to Armenia: July 5,
1995 National Assembly Elections and Constitutional Referendum* (Washington
DC: International Foundation for Electoral Systems, 1995).

18 Some people suspect the ANM and its security apparatus of playing a role in the
creation of the pro-government ARF and Ramgavar splinter parties. Whether or
not the ANM was involved, such rumors indicate the deep suspicion with which
Armenians view the ANM, and their propensity to see conspiracy at every step.

19 Armen Akopian, "Takie vybory iskliuchaiut formirovanie pravovogo
gosudarstva," *Golos Armenii*, 14 October 1995.

20 From an interview published in *Golos Armenii*, 31 January 1995, as translated in
the on-line "Daily News Report from Armenia," Armenian Assembly of
Armenia.

21 These numbers are from a detailed party directory compiled by David Petrosian.

22 I would like to thank David Petrosian for providing many of the details in this
section.

23 Translated in *Azbarez on Line*, Armenia–Karabakh News, 19 May 1995.

24 Edgeworth and Lansell, *Technical Assistance to Armenia*, pp. 31–33.

25 Akopian, "Takie vybory iskliuchaiut formirovanie pravovogo gosudarstva."

26 This commission had responsibility for privatizing the millions of dollars' worth
of construction materials and equipment Armenia received after the earthquake,
and the many buildings left unfinished when the Soviet Union fragmented and
workers from other republics returned home. Several years ago, a parliamentary
investigation prompted by Khachik Stamboltsian into the illegal sale of this
equipment to Central Asia was allegedly quashed by the president because of his
brother's involvement.

27 Sometimes the relationship between policy and practice is direct and public, as
in a recent case which incensed Armenian car-owners. According to an official
order of the Ministry of the Interior, all cars on the road (approximately 50,000)
must carry a special kind of fire extinguisher. According to respondents, this fire
extinguisher was imported for $0.75 apiece into Armenia from Dubai by a
company, SAF, headed by the son of the minister of the interior. The fire
extinguishers were purchased at $13.00 each by "Garzo" Sukiasian, a well-known
entrepreneur who runs casinos, shops, and a large wholesale market (and happens
to be godfather to the minister's son), and sold to the public for $18–20. These
transactions allegedly resulted in considerable profits for the friends and relatives
of the author of the decree.

28 Except where noted, the following account is based on my own experiences and
observations as an election monitor under the aegis of the joint UN/OSCE
mission.

29 Edgeworth and Lansell, *Technical Assistance to Armenia; Armenia 1995:
Democracy and Human Rights* (Oxford: The British Helsinki Human Rights
Group, 1995).

30 Edgeworth and Lansell, *Technical Assistance to Armenia*, p. 14.

31 *Nations in Transit: Civil Society, Democracy and Markets in East Central Europe
and the Newly Independent States* (New York: Freedom House, 1995) p. 23.

32 Except where noted, the following discussion is based on Edgeworth and Lansell, *Technical Assistance to Armenia*.

33 Edgeworth and Lansell, *Technical Assistance to Armenia*, p. 16.

34 Article 44 reads, "The fundamental human and civil rights and freedoms established in Articles 23–27 of the Constitution can be limited only by law if it is necessary for the protection of state and societal security, social order, the health and mores of society, and the rights and freedoms and honor and good reputation of others." Cited in Edgeworth and Lansell, *Technical Assistance to Armenia,* p. 18.

35 The Republic Bloc consisted of the Republican Party, the Christian Democratic Union, the Hnchak Party, the Liberal Democratic Party (an offshoot of the Ramgavars), and the Union of Intelligentsia.

36 See the report by Vote Armenia.

37 Edgeworth and Lansell, *Technical Assistance to Armenia*, p. 49.

38 The following account is based on interviews I carried out, along with another election monitor, after the election.

39 See, for example, Larry Diamond's definition of civil society "as the realm of organized social life that is voluntary, self-generating (largely) self-supporting, autonomous from the state, and bound by a legal order or set of shared rules," in "Toward Democratic Consolidation," *Journal of Democracy* 5, no. 3 (July 1994), 5.

40 See Richard Rose, "Postcommunism and the Problem of Trust," ibid., 18–30, on the distrust for public institutions as a widespread phenomenon in post-Soviet life.

41 For a detailed description of current living standards in Armenia, see Nora Dudwick, "A Qualitative Assessment of the Living Standards of the Armenian Population, October 1994 to March 1995," Poverty Assessment Working Paper No. 1, The World Bank.

42 The labor union asserts that 20 percent of the 60,000 teaching positions nationally are now vacant; the Ministry of Education claims 10 percent. Neither figure takes into account that many vacancies have been filled by unqualified or retired persons.

43 For the conditions under which the constitution allows the limitation of civil rights, see n.34 above.

44 The OSCE Observer Mission noted a discrepancy of 22,013 votes between the number of people who had voted and the number of voter coupons registered in the official results. They also expressed concern over 21,128 missing ballots that had not been accounted for. These inaccuracies were of particular concern since Ter-Petrossian surpassed the 50 percent margin required by Armenian law to avoid a run-off by 21,941 votes.

45 "Final Post-Election Statement: Armenian Presidential Elections," OSCE Office for Democratic Institutions and Human Rights, 22 September 1996.

46 Lawrence Sheets, "Armenian Government Detains Opponents in Crackdown," Reuters New Service, 30 September 1996.

47 Noyan Tapan, 19 September 1996.

48 Arshak Sadoyan, an opposition deputy, at a September 25, 1996 demonstration, cited by Armenpress, 15 October 1996.

49 Babken Araktsian, September 25, 1996, cited by Armenpress, 15 October 1996.

50 Vano Siradeghian, cited by Selina Williams, "Tanks Roll as Armenia Poll Protest MPs Are Arrested," *The Daily Telegraph*, 27 September 1996.
51 Lawrence Sheets, "Elections, Crackdown Dull Armenian Leader's Image," Reuters, reprinted in Azbarez-On-Line, 1 October 1996.
52 Despite international reservations concerning the 1995 elections, and now the harsh OSCE evaluation of the presidential elections, the Armenian government does not appear to have suffered any consequences from the conduct of the election or its excessive reaction to the post-election disturbances. Armenian citizens have thereby received yet another lesson in how broadly some of the international community – not least the United States government, which cautiously reprimanded the opposition for its violence – is willing to interpret "democratization" and "construction of civil society."

4   Azerbaijan's struggle toward democracy

Audrey L. Altstadt

Azerbaijan, in the eastern Caucasus, was brought under Russian rule early in the nineteenth century and under Bolshevik control in 1920. Prized for the rich oil deposits around its capital, Baku, the Azerbaijan Soviet Socialist Republic was used thereafter as an economic colony of Russia, providing not only petroleum products but also Caspian Sea caviar, carpets, and silks for foreign export. Brutal political and cultural control, characterized by extensive attempts at russification, was imposed in the first decades of Soviet rule. In many respects Azerbaijan has yet to recover. Since the Brezhnev era, Azerbaijan has experienced a gradual weakening of Soviet control coupled with a tentative, uneven democratization. The republic's fitful journey toward political democracy, advanced with free elections in June 1992, was set back since a coup of June 1993 which unseated the elected president and paved the way for the return of a charismatic former communist leader who, to the end of 1996, still holds the presidency.

The deterioration of totalitarian control in Azerbaijan, a necessary prelude to later efforts to establish democracy, began in the cultural, not the political, realm. The process began in the 1970s, and an understanding of the nature of this process is essential to a clear analysis of the subsequent political events in Azerbaijan. Cultural changes were pioneered by and, in turn, facilitated the emergence of a democratically inclined intellectual elite. This group was soon thrust into the political arena by the force of events that were beyond its control. Weakening of state and communist party control as well as demands of the neighboring republic of Armenia for the surrender of territory led the Azeri cultural-intellectual elite to draw on the example of an earlier generation of intellectuals who had shifted their energies from the cultural realm in order to found and lead a short-lived republic in the wake of the Bolshevik Revolution. Mindful of this brief but vibrant democratic experience, the Azeri elite of the 1980s and 1990s struggled to establish democratic institutions and to create a civil society in postcommunist

Azerbaijan. These efforts were stalled by war, repression from Moscow, internal divisions, and by remnants of the Soviet legacy that had long shaped their lives. The outcome of the struggle has not, by the mid-1990s, been determined.

Factors influencing the formation of political groups

Precommunist legacies

Legacies of precommunist political and intellectual life in Azerbaijan provide keys to the understanding of today's situation. First, the development in the Baku area of a modern oil industry led to a dramatic transformation of the city itself. Non-natives came to outnumber the Azeris (see table 4.1). Russians, mostly peasants, came from the central provinces to become oil workers; a smaller number came from the imperial capitals as bureaucrats and law enforcement officials. Armenians arrived from neighboring provinces as well as Iran and Turkey, adding to the existing Armenian community of merchants and craftsmen. Europeans invested in and also managed local firms. Technical change was characterized by the creation of an industrial infrastructure with banks, a machine-building industry, and modern technology. As a result of contact with Europeans, even those Azeris who did not have Western education were exposed to such practices as free enterprise, individual initiative, and other contemporary European values that led them to expect higher standards of living and greater political participation. This legacy, provided a basis for political participation when the tsarist regime permitted it in 1905 and later, when secular elites founded a republic in Azerbaijan in 1918. After the repressions of Soviet rule and destruction of much of the historical record from this period, the present-day population had to be reminded of this democratic legacy in the cultural movement of the 1970s (described below). Most Azeris, however, have remained more conscious of the natural wealth of their republic, especially oil, than entrepreneurial or democratic precedents. With the Soviet collapse, the people awaited rediscovery of the oil by Western investors.

One aspect of the legacy of development was its localized character. The economic modernization of Baku created a gulf between the city with its multinational population and modern technology and the countryside which remained more traditional in all respects. While Baku and other cities slowly grew more secular, the village held on to religious practice. When tsarist Russia opened the door to political organization in 1905, urban groups held meetings and formed parties, but the peasantry continued its usual forms of protest such as illegally cutting timber. The legacy of this urban–rural gap, though diminished, remains today. Political activities, including party

Table 4.1 *Ethnic composition of Baku, 1897, 1903, 1913*

Nationality	1897	1903	1913
Azeris	40,148	44,257	45,962
Russians	37,399	56,955	76,288
Armenians	19,060	26,151	41,680
Georgians	971	n.a.	4,073
Jews	2,341	n.a.	9,690
Iranian citizens[a]	9,426	11,132	25,096
Total[b]	111,904	155,876	214,672

Notes: [a]Based on language data elsewhere in this census, these seem to be primarily Iranian Azeri, but precise numbers are not provided. [b]Includes groups not in table.
Sources: *Naselenie imperii po perepisi 28-go ianvaria 1897 goda po uezdam* (St. Petersburg: I. A. Iakovlev, 1897); *Perepis' naseleniia gor. Baku, 1903* (Baku: Kaspii, 1905); *Perepis' naseleniia gor. Baku, 1913* (Baku: Kaspii, 1916).

formation, tend to be greater in cities than in rural areas. Voting practices, too, as described below, differ.

A second major legacy was a movement for reformist Islam manifested by such phenomena as a rejection of sectarian animosities (especially between Sunni and Shi'i Muslims), the campaign to end veiling of women and polygamy, and the *Jadid* Method in schools (this "New Method" included replacing memorization of the alphabet with phonetics and broadening of curricula to include secular subjects such as arithmetic). Satirical journals supported the modernists and attacked veiling, polygamy, arranged marriages and unquestioning reverence for mullahs (prayer leaders).[1] A number of prominent writers, poets, and community leaders attempted to foster the beginnings of a national consciousness; some strove to demonstrate that Islam could be compatible with democracy in such aspects as its provision that leaders "consult" with the community in making important decisions. This, argued the modernists, provided the foundation for constitutional government.[2] These arguments were crucial in convincing some Azeris, at least among the more educated, that adopting such "Western" practices as democracy did not require forsaking their own traditions and did not, therefore, constitute a betrayal of native culture and values. (Along these lines, nineteenth century Azeri playwright Mirza Fath Ali Akhundzade [Akhundov] proposed replacing the Arabic script, despite its religious associations, with a Latin alphabet, a movement which gained support until Latin script was officially adopted in the 1920s.)

Third, from the 1880s onward, the educated Azeri elite attempted to gain the right for wider political participation, especially in the Baku City Council, and the campaign to get the *zemstvo*, an organ of rural self-government, extended to the Caucasus. Although the zemstvo was never established in the Caucasus, the Azeris did succeed, after 1908, in increasing their representation in the City Council. Imperial law restricted the number of non-Christians in a City Council to less than half, but in 1908 the Baku Azeri (constituting about 80 percent of the electors), voted in a bare majority of Azeri council members. The Viceroy tacitly accepted this violation of the law, and the Azeri thus succeeded in exercising their *de facto* power.[3]

The Azeri secular elite had been educated in Russian universities since the annexation of Caucasia early in the nineteenth century. By the last quarter of that century, some attended one of the few Westernized Ottoman universities, or European universities, particularly in Paris. At that time, even Russian institutions were far more Western than they would become under Soviet rule. As a result, such educated Azeris understood the Enlightenment and democracy without a Russian filter. These social and cultural leaders voiced political ideas that can be described as "anti-colonial" (the satirical journal *Molla Nasreddin* lampooned European states and their treatment of Asia), pro-constitution, and even democratic. The Azeris favored constitutions for Turkey, Iran and, later for their own young republic. Their program is fairly well known in the extant literature on pre-revolutionary Azerbaijan.[4]

A nation's elite alone, however enlightened, is never sufficient to establish democracy. Essential to the process was the emergence in the last two decades of the existence of imperial Russian Empire of a stratum of Azeri bureaucrats, accountants, journalists and other skilled professionals. These professionals were concentrated in Baku, but many Azeri men (and women in a few fields such as education and music) played a significant role in local administration and commerce outside Baku, throughout the imperial provinces that would later constitute the Republic of Azerbaijan.[5] In this way, a native middle-level professional-bureaucratic stratum was created to take up posts in the new republic of 1918. The republican government made Azeri (then called "Turkish") the official language of government.

Building on these pre-war trends within the Azeri community itself, the Republic of Azerbaijan was founded in May 1918. The constitution declared that sovereignty rested with the people, that "all citizens were guaranteed full civil and political rights regardless of their nationality, religion, social position or sex." The constitution separated religion from the state, and extended suffrage to females.[6] Elections were held on this basis and Azerbaijan's first Parliament was elected in winter 1918–19. Occupation by British troops, from November 1918 until August 1919, prevented the republican government from exercising full sovereignty, but did provide a friendly atmosphere for multiparty politics. In addition to the main national party, the Musavat, dozens of other political parties and groups representing national and religious minorities – including Russian, Armenian, Georgian, Jewish, and Estonian national committees – set up offices in Baku and campaigned for parliamentary representation. The climate of tolerance also paved the way for the revitalization of a communist party which, in April 1920, facilitated the fall of the republic.[7]

Democratization and the evolution of national consciousness, both evolving since the nineteenth century, were cut short by the Bolshevik occupation of Azerbaijan in the spring and summer of 1920 and the purges that followed intermittently until the late 1930s. The old elites were driven into exile, imprisoned or killed; some were hounded to their deaths. The revival of the memory of these people and their ideas was one of the first stages of the break-down of Soviet power in Azerbaijan.

The Soviet regime's destruction of this elite was thorough. The estimated 12,000 deaths in a population of 2 million from the "permanent purge" of the interwar period[8] is suggestive of the extent of destruction but by no means tells the whole story. The killing of both elites and the middle level professionals and bureaucrats was not enough to ensure communist party control over Azerbaijan. The Soviet regime felt compelled to defile their reputations, denouncing them as anti-popular servants of "British interests" or "khan-mullah circles." Furthermore, the party smashed institutions created or reshaped according to the ideals of the pre-revolutionary modernist forces – the state structure, political groups, cultural associations, and the education system at all levels, including Baku University where the language of instruction at its founding in 1919 was Azeri, but became Russian by 1925. Nor were these measures enough for the Stalin-era appetite for control. By the 1930s, a campaign was launched to finish the blood purges and institutional transformation, and now also to obliterate the very memory of the ideals and political actions of the republican era. Privately held book and manuscript collections were impounded; those in libraries or archives were placed under restrictive controls. Part of this effort entailed a decisive measure to cut off future generations from their own past – a change of alphabet from the Latin script, favored by modernists, adopted in the 1920s and now used in the Turkish Republic where many Azeri émigrés wrote anti-Soviet materials, to Cyrillic script, imposed abruptly on the eve of World War II. The change of alphabet that cut links to the past, was one attack on culture that Azerbaijan's neighbors, Armenia and Georgia, were spared. As a result of this vigorous and successful campaign, no structures or associations and few records or memories of the precommunist era survived to the end of the Soviet Union.

Legacies of communist rule

Many communist legacies lingered in Azerbaijan as the Soviet regime came to its end – the strength of the communist party, the power of the KGB (staffed at the top largely from Moscow), cultural directives from the USSR Academy of Sciences, and economic planning with its job security and price ceilings. These were the various instruments of control by which the Soviet regime imposed and maintained control in its empire. Each one left a mark on the political, social, economic, and intellectual life of the country. The non-Russians were left with a legacy of russification – the use of Russian language in official life, the technical professions, and as the language of "inter-ethnic communication;" the primacy of Russian history and historical figures in education and culture and the claim to the "progressive impact" of Russian rule;[9] the rhetoric of the Russian "elder brother," and so forth. Few questioned the use of Russian writers or revolutionaries as the yardsticks by which to measure talent, dedication, and even inclination to democracy among non-Russians.[10]

Together, these elements of communist policy produced the single most enduring legacy, a mentality of control. This led the populace as a whole to expect to be controlled by the authorities and, in turn, led the Azeris to expect that their republic would be controlled by "the center." Until late in the communist era, the intellectual and the "ordinary citizen" alike believed that Moscow would put down protest in Azerbaijan with armed force. At the same time, they believed that only a strong leader could help Azerbaijan hold its own within the Soviet hierarchy of republics in which those with traditionally Muslim populations were even lesser "lesser brothers" than other non-Russian republics. Inconsistent policies of the Gorbachev period had some impact on this mentality of control, but that issue belongs to the story of "transition" from soviet rule which follows.

The post-Soviet belief in the power of oil wealth led the population to pin its hopes for the future on oil development and the lure of that wealth for foreign investors. In an odd way, this expectation, too, was a legacy of communism, specifically of Leninism. Even as the founder of the Soviet state was slowly vilified, the Azeris remained prisoners of his belief that capitalists, in pursuit of their own financial gain, would invest in a country that strove to destroy the capitalist system. In Lenin's words, capitalists will "sell us the rope that we'll hang them with." Though the Azeris did not see themselves as "communist enemies" of capitalism, they certainly expected Western investors to race for a piece of oil wealth to Azerbaijan's great – even disproportionate – gain. Azeri thinking, like that of most Soviets, had failed to keep up with the sophisticated cost-benefit calculations of Western businessmen who consider legal protection of property, stability of political climate and skill of work force as well as dollars to be earned. Relying on their Leninist images of capitalist greed, successive governments dragged their feet on an oil deal and nearly lost their chance for an agreement.

Two groups seemed to challenge the mentality of control, but in different ways. The educated elite in the University, Academy of Sciences, and writers' and artists' unions sought to clarify national history and regain at least some degree of autonomy for their republic. At the other end of the social and intellectual spectrum, black marketeers strove to circumvent controls and manipulate the system for private gain. Both groups reflected the gradual transition from totalitarian control.

Transition from communist control: early steps

Azerbaijan's transition from communist control was exceedingly complex. Some processes reflected the breakdown of the Soviet system without necessarily leading to democracy. The growth of the black market is a prime example. Black market activity, especially from the 1960s onward, revealed the weaknesses of the Soviet system, particularly in supplying consumer goods. Union-wide tolerance for this "second economy" reflected the regime's realization of the inadequacies of its command economy. Though the "second economy" pervaded the USSR, black marketeers were often associated with the Caucasus from which many did, indeed, transport fresh produce, flowers and other goods to Russian cities. The nationalities of the Caucasus exhibited an entrepreneurship which the Russians disdained and which within the Soviet system was officially banned. Elsewhere, many of these economic activities might merely be "private initiative."

Azerbaijan's role in the second economy of the USSR was greater than the republic's size might suggest, and Azerbaijan had an active internal black market. Among the most lucrative illegal activities was flower and fruit growing and selling. State-subsidized gas was siphoned from legitimate enterprises or homes and used to heat make-shift hothouses to grow fruit and flowing plants all year. Subsidized airfare enabled black marketeers to fly cheaply to Moscow and Leningrad to sell their wares. The profits could then be used, in part, to pay bribes to cargo handlers at various airports.

Azeris within Azerbaijan often engaged in classic "middle man activity," which did not require the effort or know-how that the flower-sellers needed to cultivate and transport their goods. Young men with little capital could and did "go into business" by buying "imported" clothing and electronics often from Polish tourists (young Poles went to Baku specifically to sell their clothes, wrist watches, and other goods). These items were then sold to Azeris, who seemed to be perpetually "hanging out" at Baku subway stations. Since the subway stops with the most vigorous mercantile operations were located near precinct police stations, hefty bribes surely were paid to law enforcement authorities to permit this activity to go on unimpeded. The system of growing or buying, selling and bribery reflected the decay of the entire Soviet economic system and disregard of its values.[11]

More significant resistance to the system came from other quarters, primarily from the Azeri artistic and intellectual elite who were pursuing specifically national goals and a gradual movement toward de-colonization and democratization. From the 1970s, this elite – professors and researchers, writers and artists – began systematically to circumvent and subvert official directives meant to govern their intellectual and artistic work. (Sporadic efforts along these lines had accompanied local de-Stalinization from the mid-1950s to the early 1960s, but the work of that period was limited primarily to "rehabilitations" of people and artistic works vilified in the 1930s.)[12] This challenge to party guidelines was carried out in the native language, especially in the realm of literature, strengthening the nationalist flavor of the earliest dissent. It was this segment of the population that revived the memory of the last pre-revolutionary generation and the republic of 1918–20. Poets and novelists seem to have taken the lead with "homeland poetry" (poetry being a particularly popular and powerful art form) that praised nature ("crystal waters," sacred mountains, and the like) and the language and history of Azerbaijan. Novelists produced historical novels with national themes and accurate historical narratives. A key vehicle for this literature was the Azeri-language literary journal of the writers' Union, *Azerbaijan*.[13] The early stage of this process, including the appearance of "homeland poetry," took place while Heydar Aliyev was communist party first secretary. Aliyev enjoyed associating with artists, musicians and literati, and paid attention to their work in his ideological statements.[14] Despite his much publicized "internationalist" rhetoric on arts and education (including his own public use of Russian and repetition of "elder brother" slogans from Moscow), Aliyev was surely aware of this national awakening in the arts and seemingly did nothing to stop it. Thus even while acting as a Brezhnev sycophant, for which he is well known, he was not without some sense of appreciation for his native culture.[15] This is noteworthy in considering his return to power as a "national savior" in 1993.

As Azeri literature experienced a revitalization, Azeri historians, too, deviated from prescribed topics. Making use of the apparent latitude afforded the journal *Azerbaijan* and, perhaps, the daring of its editor, novelist Ekrem Eylisli, Azeri historians supplied short articles under the rubric "Unopened Pages." This series described, in cautious terms, key figures of the republican period who had been vilified throughout Soviet rule. Most controversial among these was the leader of the first republic's Musavat Party, Mehmed Emin Rasulzade. These articles, or versions of them, were often picked up by wider circulation Azeri-language newspapers so that they reached a larger audience than did literary journals.[16] The pinnacle of historians' defiance of Soviet guidelines was reached with a reinterpretation of what had been called the "voluntary unification" of Azerbaijan to Bolshevik Russia. Historian Nasib Nasibzade described the combination of communist party intimidation and military pressure – directed by Lenin in order to get control of Baku's oil – that led to the invasion of Azerbaijan by the Red Army in spring 1920 and subsequent "sovietization." Nasibzade's work, first serialized in a Baku newspaper, then published as a monograph in 1989, was the most fully documented and detailed indictment of the forcible Bolshevik take-over of the Azerbaijan Republic.[17] Thus, as this movement accelerated from "recovery of history" to denunciation of Soviet rule over Azerbaijan, it was not only elite circles that were affected, but any Azeri (for other nationalities rarely knew the language of the republic)[18] who read the fiction, poetry, and histories, or who saw the plays, operas, paintings, and puppet shows produced by this nationally conscious minority. Even casual newspaper readers became aware of key issues and the changing climate.

Transition from communist control: steamroller from without

Against this background of gradual but increasing national awakening, events outside Azerbaijan exerted their own impact on the republic. The first, whose effect was delayed and muted, was Gorbachev's rhetoric of glasnost; the second and far more important was the Armenian demand for transfer of the Nagorno-Karabagh Autonomous Region (NKAR) from Azerbaijani to Armenian jurisdiction. Although Gorbachev came to power in 1985, the Azerbaijan communist party organs did not reflect the verbiage or practice of "openness" until mid-1986, and then only with regard to cultural matters. The continuity of party leadership inside the republic (all Aliyev appointees) perhaps explains the reluctance to follow Gorbachev's lead. It was not unlikely that his "thaw" would be as short-lived as Khrushchev's, so party members played it safe. Side by side with the few articles on "Our Cultural Heritage" were orthodox pieces on "fraternal friendship" of Soviet peoples. This bifurcation, which first appeared during 1986–87 in the communist party journal *Azerbaijan Kommunisti* may have reflected some disagreement within the republican party concerning an appropriate posture toward the national awakening displayed in other publications. It is not clear whether there was a real "split" in the party at this time, but some party members would later support opposition political groups.

More significant for Azerbaijan and the region was the reemergence in 1987–88 of a long-standing dispute over the region of Nagorno-Karabagh.[19]

The territory is in the western, mountainous ("nagorno-" in Russian) portion of the large region of Karabagh. It had been presumed by both Armenians and Azeris to be part of their historical patrimony and was openly disputed during their republican periods, 1918 to 1920-21 (Armenia was not sovietized until 1921). The Bolshevik resolution to the clash was part of a broader territorial settlement involving two other disputed regions, Zangezur, which lies to the southwest of Karabagh, and Nakhjivan, located southwest of Zangezur. As a result largely of Bolshevik strategic needs and pressure from the Turkish nationalist (Kemalist) movement in Asia Minor, Lenin's government agreed to recognize Nakhjivan (with its overwhelmingly Azeri population) as a non-contiguous part of Azerbaijan,[20] but to separate it (and thus Turkish republican forces and influence) from the rest of Azerbaijan by awarding Zangezur to Armenia (the region forms a "panhandle" that gives Armenia a border with Iran). Nagorno-Karabagh, with its predominantly Armenian population, was left inside Azerbaijan, but was to have some form of autonomy. That autonomy, cultural and political, was realized by the creation in 1924 of the Nagorno-Karabagh Autonomous Region, run by an ethnically Armenian communist organization but funded from Baku. An Armenian campaign intended to achieve the transfer of the NKAR began in summer 1987 at the same time Aliyev was forced by Gorbachev to leave his Moscow post on the Central Committee and go into early retirement. The conflict remained a low level one from 1988 to early 1992, when it was characterized by deportations or flight of Azeris from Armenia and Armenians from Azerbaijan (sometimes into the NKAR) and a series of localized armed clashes. The destruction of the Azeri town of Khojaly, which lies between the NKAR and Armenia, by Armenian and Russian forces in early 1992 transformed the conflict into a major war, according to US journalist Thomas Goltz, who was on the scene. He estimated 1,000 Azeris killed.[21] It was this event that would bring down Azerbaijan's government and set in motion a chain of events that would, later that year, bring the opposition Popular Front to power.

The war continued to see-saw with millions of refugees, deployment of Russian forces (always called renegades or deserters by the Russian military command and Moscow's diplomats), and land lost and won. Efforts at negotiation by various groups and individuals produced no results because the combatants continued to believe they could gain more by fighting than talking. A cease-fire was achieved in May 1994, after a decisive Armenian victory that included their occupation of approximately 20 percent of Azerbaijan's territory. The former NKAR was thus effectively annexed to Armenia. A political settlement, however, remains elusive.

The first reactions to the early Armenian campaign (the "Karabagh movement") in 1987, one confined to the printed word and popularly circulated petitions, came not from the state or party of Azerbaijan, but from the same stratum of Azeri society that had so cautiously pursued the cultural-historical revival – the intellectuals at the University and Academy of Sciences. A young researcher at the Academy circulated a manuscript refuting historical claims to Karabagh advanced by Armenian writer Zori Balayan; that researcher was Isa Gambar(ov), later co-founder of the Azerbaijan Popular Front.[22] University historian Suleiman Aliyarov co-authored with poet Bahtiyar Vahabzade an "Open Letter" refuting an array of Armenian claims to Nagorno-Karabagh in the February 1988 issue of *Azerbaijan*.[23] Later that year in the University and Academy of Sciences, the formation of a popular front was first discussed, and historical preservation groups, which preceded the creation of the popular front here as in many republics, were first formed.

Clearly, the dispute over Nagorno-Karabagh did not create national consciousness among the Azeri elite, but did act as the catalyst which accelerated the emergence of Azerbaijan's national movement in the late 1980s. It led those who had been active in the cultural-intellectual realm to move into politics, perhaps before they were really ready, that is, before they had determined for themselves the nature of their national identity and a national agenda. They remained a potential leadership group with a clear set of grievances, but without a specific plan of action for the future. The problem would not become apparent until this opposition came to power in 1992. For the time being, the dispute over Nagorno-Karabagh did succeed in clarifying for the Azeris the substance of their discontent with Moscow's rule. The particulars were voiced during an unprecedented two-week demonstration in November–December 1988.

In their anger and frustration at official inactivity, thousands of Azeris, not merely an educated elite, gathered in front of the government building on Lenin Square (renamed by them "Freedom Square") to state their complaints and demands. No representatives of Azerbaijan's government or party apparatus appeared during the demonstration. The absence of the authorities combined with popular anger allowed many people to overcome, at least for a time, the "control mentality" of decades of Soviet rule. The agenda of speakers gave way to an "open microphone" policy when anyone in the crowd could come forward and speak. Although environmental and economic issues were raised, the main focus of attention was on the NKAR and the lack of official response to the Armenian movement. Speaker after speaker sounded the same themes: Moscow should have rebuffed Armenian demands for territorial change and arrested Armenian militants; press coverage concerning the dispute and the history of the region itself was biased because it came from Erevan or Armenian sources in Moscow and treated Azeris as villains in a drama of economic and cultural deprivation of Nagorno-

Karabagh; Moscow was taking sides with the Christian Armenians against them, as Muslims, even though the dispute had nothing to do with religion.

On the night of December 4, after unrest had spread to other cities of the republic, tanks and police dispersed demonstrators remaining on the Square and jailed identifiable leaders. Strikes and demonstrations throughout Azerbaijan followed. In Moscow, *Izvestiia* issued a "call to reason" for such "extremism" as that in Baku threatened the program of perestroika. "There is democracy for you, there is openness," concluded the writer.[24]

Only the release of leaders of the "Freedom Square" demonstration the following spring permitted the formation of the Azerbaijan Popular Front in July 1989. The leaders were from the University and Academy of Sciences, and its first president was a man once jailed for nationalist tendencies, Abulfez Aliyev, who later took the name Elchibey. The Front's early program bore the marks of its founders' broad liberal commitments. Its goals included democratization of society with full civil and human rights for all citizens, local control over elections, achieving "political, economic and cultural sovereignty for Azerbaijan within the USSR," returning all land to peasants and granting them "full freedom" in agricultural policy, ending "barbaric exploitation of natural resources," and ensuring equal treatment for all nationalities.[25] In short, despite the stated willingness to remain within the USSR, the Popular Front's program was nothing less than a call to dismantle the Soviet system. The continuing fight over the status of the NKAR and the presence of tens of thousands of Azeri refugees made the Karabagh issue the most pressing item of business for the Popular Front (and the small, often short-lived groups that formed thereafter).

Communist officials in Azerbaijan would not permit the Popular Front to register until forced by railway workers' action. In the late Soviet and early post-Soviet periods, labor organizations for the most part maintained a low profile and were not involved in politics. The railroad workers' strike in late summer and fall 1989 was one of few exceptions. Railroad workers had stopped running trains across Armenian Zangezur to reach Nakhjivan because of bombings on that line and rocks thrown and shots fired at the trains themselves as they passed through Armenia.[26] Security had been the primary demand when the strike began. But as the stoppage continued, workers added official recognition of the Popular Front to their demands. Largely because of this the government allowed the Popular Front to register on October 5. Rail service resumed, despite continued attacks.

Despite the apparent success of the Popular Front, the pressure of developments around Nagorno-Karabagh prevented the Front from working out a *modus vivendi* with the communist party.[27] Instead, events of late November raised the stakes in the conflict when Armenian residents of the NKAR capital Stepanakert (Khankendi in Azeri) formed "self-defense groups," but the Baku government rejected a Popular Front appeal to establish a national army. On November 20, Gorbachev restored the power of the NKAR's old Armenian-dominated soviet (it had been suspended in favor of a special commission appointed by Moscow and headed by Arkadii Volskii). On December 1, the Supreme Soviet of Armenia declared the annexation of the NKAR, and demonstrations broke out in several Azeri cities against the Baku regime for its inaction. Early in January, the Popular Front organized a Military Defense Council under the direction of the young historian Etibar Mamedov and mathematician Rahim Gaziyev. Prominent Azeri communists now openly criticized the republic's communist party and its inaction in the face of Armenian initiatives in the NKAR.

On the weekend of January 13–14, 1990, bloody ethnic conflict erupted in Baku. Dozens of Armenians were killed. The Popular Front was blamed for instigating these attacks, but armed groups were seen (by local and Moscow reporters) ignoring the efforts of well-known Front figures to disperse them. The republic's own internal affairs minister ignored appeals of Popular Front leaders to use troops to quell the violence. Kazakh writer Almaz Estekov, then visiting Baku, was told by a local commander of Soviet Internal Affairs forces that the communist party first secretary, A. Vezirov, had instructed him not to intervene in "national conflicts."[28]

The night the violence ended, Evgenii Primakov, then chairman of the USSR Supreme Soviet's Council of the Union, arrived in Baku. The Supreme Soviet decided, despite the presence of – but failure to deploy – thousands of troops already in Baku, to dispatch eleven thousand (additional) troops. The justification was not protection of national minorities in Azerbaijan but, in official words, that Moscow faced in Baku "attempts at armed overthrow of Soviet power."[29] Using this pretext, coupled with subsequent references by Gorbachev to "Islamic fundamentalism," Soviet troops moved into Baku the weekend *after* the unrest had occurred. The action began just after midnight on January 20, 1990. By 6 am, the army had control over the undefended city. Tanks rolled over private cars and ambulances, crushing their passengers. Soviet soldiers opened fire on apartment buildings and shot civilians on the streets, including doctors and nurses who were helping the wounded. Outright fatalities were at least 120: the newspaper *Seher* published the names and birth dates of 120 dead ranging in age from 14 to 70; an independent investigation by the Russian military group *Shchit*, conducted the following summer, confirmed 120 civilian dead and hundreds more wounded.[30] The Popular Front was clearly a main target of this action. Its offices were immediately occupied and sealed. Files were seized and the phone was cut off. Forty-three Popular Front leaders were arrested with other "extremists." A State of Emergency was imposed, permitting press censorship, curfew, and the continued presence of soldiers and tanks on the streets of Baku. First

Secretary Vezirov was sacked and replaced by Ayaz Mutalibov. Newspapers throughout Azerbaijan vented their outrage against Gorbachev and Soviet rule; Nakhjivan even declared its independence until a "helicopter full of [Soviet] generals" persuaded the local leaders there to "see reason."[31]

Despite the weakening of Soviet power as a whole during 1990–91, the unusual brutality of Moscow's actions in Azerbaijan strengthened central control over that republic. No Western protest was raised – in contrast to close US and European attention to far lesser levels of intimidation in the Baltic states – an omission that did not go unnoticed in Azerbaijan. Moreover, Moscow found a firm supporter in Ayaz Mutalibov. As the republican party strove to regain some fragment of credibility, Mutalibov leveled the necessary criticism, but never of a serious nature, against Moscow. He steered the party's new platform (prepared for the presidential elections in May 1990) toward a cross between Soviet rhetoric and Popular Front ideas.[32] When elections were held, Mutalibov permitted no opponent to run against him for the presidency. He supported Gorbachev during the August 1991 coup and after the fall of the USSR. When Russia moved to reestablish a semblance of its hegemony in the so-called Commonwealth of Independent States, Mutalibov conducted himself as if Azerbaijan were a member, despite the refusal of the republic's Supreme Soviet to join. Because of Mutalibov, therefore, the "postcommunist" era for Azerbaijan cannot be said to coincide with the end of CPSU or the disintegration of the USSR. The real postcommunist era began in spring 1992 with the overthrow of Mutalibov and, shortly thereafter, of his successor, Yakub Mamedov.

Mutalibov and his relationship with the Popular Front in the late Soviet period led to the creation of the first major political party in Azerbaijan. Etibar Mamedov and Rahim Gaziyev, both former leaders of the Popular Front's Military Defense Council who had been jailed during most of 1990 at Lefortovo prison in Moscow, broke with the Popular Front during summer 1991. Mamedov prepared to form his own party; Gaziyev declared his intention to remain unaffiliated, saying he had belonged to one party in his life (CPSU) and that had been enough. Mamedov charged the Front in summer 1991 with accommodating the powers that be. The Front, he said, "operates within the framework established for" Baku by Moscow. These "guidelines" included a limitation on criticism permitted to the Popular Front's newspaper *Azadlıg* (for example, Mutalibov was not to be a target) which its editor accepted. The Baku government, in turn, used the existence of an opposition group as evidence of its own political tolerance. Mamedov further argued that being in the Soviet empire had led to the republic's pollution, economic dependence, suppression of religion, inability to defend its territory (that is, Nagorno-Karabagh), and other problems. The Popular Front, as an umbrella group for individuals with various grievances, lacked

the necessary unifying ideal to achieve the single most important goal –
national independence. Without complete independence, reforms would be
mere "ornamentation," he said. Therefore, Mamedov advocated the creation
of a party around the goal of "national independence."[33] He soon founded
the Azerbaijan National Independence Party (ANIP, Azerbayjan Milli Istiklal
Partiyasi).

Mamedov's action revealed a generational difference among those in
opposition. The younger generation of scholars and writers, who now moved
into politics, was free of memories of the midnight knock on the door that
lingered in the minds of those who remembered Stalinism. Those in their 60s
made the first daring moves, such as the "Open Letter" by Aliyarov and
Vahabzade (his earlier poetry on linguistic and historical topics nearly landed
him in jail in the Brezhnev era). Those in their 30s and 40s came to act with
greater daring in pushing the bounds of the permissible. Historian Nasibzade,
for example, was the first to denounce the 1920 "Bolshevik take-over" of
Azerbaijan. Leyla Yunusova, historian and co-founder of a social democratic,
then a national democratic party was known for her outspoken criticism of
all political opponents from communists to the Popular Front. Isa Gambar,
increasingly the power behind Elchibey's throne in the Popular Front and,
later, in government itself, put his own safety at risk when a 1993 coup
unseated Elchibey and brought back the republic's most powerful former
leader, Heydar Aliyev.

Elections: from fixed to fair and back

Since the disintegration of the USSR, Azerbaijan has had only one genuinely
competitive election, the presidential election of June 1992. Parliamentary
elections, on the other hand, did not take place between fall 1990, when the
last communist-era Supreme Soviet was elected, and November 1995. Thus
the old Supreme Soviet remained in power through a succession of governments. The 1990 elections were characterized by intimidation, including the
jailing of several Popular Front candidates, the murder of two others, and
unabashed stuffing of ballot boxes in at least some districts in Baku, as
witnessed by observers from the US Embassy-Moscow and the US Commission for Security and Cooperation in Europe (CSCE). Results were no
surprise: in a body of 350 members, 300 were former communists and, after
run-offs, about 30 were opposition candidates from the Popular Front and
other non-communist groups who together formed a Democratic Bloc
("Dembloc").[34] They remained as a bloc in the Supreme Soviet (popularly
called, later officially renamed, "parliament").

To contend in these elections, the Popular Front had formulated a new
program, the basis for the Dembloc and the later Elchibey government. It

began with a statement that the parliament should declare the entire sovietization of Azerbaijan an illegal act carried out by an occupying Red Army. It went on to call for full civil liberties, the creation of a market economy, territorial integrity (including the dissolution of the NKAR as an inappropriate soviet political administrative device), environmental protection, full cultural rights for all national groups, and freeing the state and legal systems from party and other ideological influence.[35]

The full "parliament" of 1990 did not sit throughout its term of office. During 1991, Mutalibov was forced to acquiesce in the formation, by fifty members of the Supreme Soviet, of a smaller body, the National Council (*Milli Shura*) comprising half former communists and half Dembloc and non-party deputies. This National Council sat in nearly continuous session, supplanting the prorogued Supreme Soviet, and actively debated all the important issues of the republic. Prominent Dembloc figures gained national prominence and political experience in this forum. In contrast to the always-delayed parliamentary elections, presidential elections were held with surprising frequency, annually from 1990 to 1993.

As in May 1990, so in September 1991, Mutalibov ran for president without permitting opponents to register. His ability to remain in power, however, ultimately depended on the course of the war over Nagorno-Karabagh. Under pressure from his increasingly vocal critics, Mutalibov had set presidential elections for June 7, 1992. As a result of the loss of the Karabagh town of Khojaly and the massacre there in February 1992 of over a thousand Azeri, Mutalibov was abruptly forced to resign on March 6.[36] As provided in the republic's constitution (the Soviet-era one was still in force) the Speaker of the Supreme Soviet, Yakub Mamedov, became acting president.

A Mutalibov crony, Yakub Mamedov had been director of the republic's Medical Institute and was known as "Dollar" Mamedov allegedly for preferring bribes in that currency. He continued Mutalibov's policies, but accepted into his government three opposition members. Thus Rahim Gaziyev, mathematician from the Academy of Sciences and former Popular Front activist, was appointed defense minister. A few months earlier, Gaziyev had been in the historic Karabagh capital Shusha when that city came under Armenian assault; he was credited with organizing the defense of that city. The circumstances of the episode are utterly unclear with Gaziyev's supporters and opponents telling nearly opposite stories. Nonetheless, his reputation was made, and on its strength, he became minister of defense in a temporary coalition government led by a thoroughly disreputable communist party hack. Gaziyev told the parliament at the time of his appointment that a national army had to be formed and, despite calls of "here, here," by those assembled,[37] such action was not taken.

As candidates registered for the upcoming presidential election, Mamedov's unpopularity became apparent.[38] Most candidates were from opposition groups, and Popular Front leader Abulfez Elchibey was widely regarded as the likely winner. Loss of power by the former communists appeared imminent. Carefully orchestrated pro-Mutalibov demonstrations began in Baku early in May. The war in Karabagh was going badly for Azerbaijan. Mamedov continued to negotiate with the Erevan government with Iranian mediation. On May 8, Mamedov and Armenian President Levon Ter-Petrossian signed a cease-fire agreement in Tehran. On the following day, Armenian forces overran the last Azeri city in mountainous Karabagh, Shusha. In a tumultuous session of the parliament on Thursday, May 14, in which many former communists took part, Mamedov was roundly criticized and removed as president. He merely returned to his post as Speaker. With the tiny religious Repentance Party chanting outside (for both the glory of God and the return of Mutalibov), the former communist leader and president appeared in the parliamentary chamber. Mutalibov's supporters gathered around him; they did not constitute a quorum. Nonetheless, those present voted to rescind his March resignation and reinstate him as president. Mutalibov took the podium and accepted "their decision." He cancelled elections, banned activities of all political Opposition groups, declared a State of Emergency in Baku, and imposed a curfew. He declared he was "ready to be a dictator" if that were needed to save the country "from disaster." The path to salvation, he said, meant "making peace" with Russia by joining the CIS.

Mutalibov's restoration probably had more to do with the likely outcome of presidential elections than the loss of Shusha. Popular anger, the habit of public protest, and scrutiny by reporters and new embassies in Baku made it impossible simply to cancel elections. The fall of Shusha provided a pretext for Mutalibov supporters to clamor for his return as a "strong man," which generally Mutalibov was not. The Popular Front forces were not prepared to accept what they called a "state coup."

Popular Front leaders met in long sessions to work out a strategy all the while fearing that locally stationed troops, under Mutalibov's orders, would attack their headquarters. Elchibey issued a blunt ultimatum to "Citizen Mutalibov" to vacate the presidential palace by the next afternoon. In defiance of the curfew, tens of thousands of Popular Front supporters demonstrated late into the night. The next day, pro-Front forces led by Iskender Hamidov, a career police officer with his own devoted following, made a feint toward the presidential palace, but sent an armored column – put together somehow by Hamidov during the night – against the undefended parliament building, a structure uphill from the presidential palace. The surprised Mutalibov defenders fled rather than wage an uphill street battle against tanks and men with automatic weapons.[39] The Popular Front leadership announced it had taken control of the presidential palace and the Parliament building. Mutalibov fled. He turned up later in Moscow where he has resided ever since. After days of waiting and parliamentary maneuvering, the politically astute Isa Gambar, Popular Front co-leader, became Speaker of the parliament and thus, until the June elections, acting president of the republic. Noting the Popular Front had not simply seized power when it had the chance, Gambar confirmed the importance of the rule of law. He affirmed that presidential elections would be held on June 7. As for police colonel Iskender Hamidov, known both derisively and admiringly as a "firecracker" in the Popular Front,[40] he was soon appointed minister of internal affairs.

The presidential elections of June 1992 were observed by embassy staffs present in Baku (including the US embassy), CSCE representatives and an array of foreign journalists. Observers visited many polling places in and near Baku, in the republic's second largest city, Ganje, and a few smaller towns throughout the republic. Observers saw voting "irregularities," most of which seemed not to be intended to unfairly influence the election, but more as a reflection of the popular understanding of democracy. One person, one–ballot voting predominated in cities, but in villages, it was common for the head of the household to cast ballots for all family members. This was accomplished by presenting each family member's passport – whether four or twenty – and receiving and signing for the corresponding number of ballots. Locally-based poll watchers had permitted this procedure, obviously regarding it as legitimate and probably standard. When pressed, they explained that this was "democratic," in the sense that each person got a vote and a choice. They did not regard as important the notion that the mechanical act of voting need be exercised by each individual. Foreign observers, though some were more distressed than others by this procedure, agreed that these irregularities were random rather than organized and seemed to favor no particular candidate. Elchibey was elected with about 60 percent (his nearest opponent got 30 percent) of the vote.[41] He was to remain in power only a year.

Until 1993, no military officers had interfered with politics in Azerbaijan. The Soviet Army had assigned Azeris (as it did Central Asians) to construction rather than combat battalions, so there were few combat-trained Azeris to call home or mobilize. Nor had Azeris been readily accepted into officer training. Despite nominal independence, the republic had no national army, and Mutalibov had avoided recruiting one arguing that Azerbaijan could best defend its territory (that is, Nagorno-Karabagh) within the confines of the CIS forces. Shortly after the disintegration of the USSR and because of losses at the front, individuals without military training had begun to assume roles in the nascent, ill-equipped and barely trained army of Azerbaijan.[42] Among the most prominent was Rahim Gaziyev.

Despite the successful offensives of summer 1992, fall and winter brought only Armenian victories. On February 8, 1993, the Elchibey government removed Rahim Gaziyev from his post as defense minister and dismissed Surat Huseinov, commander of forces on the northern front. Huseinov, a man in his thirties, had managed a wool factory in Soviet times, a position that allowed a great deal of "on the side" sales and the accumulation of considerable wealth. After using his own money to attract armed supporters, Huseinov had become *de facto* commander of the northern front arbitrarily taking the rank of colonel. He had no military training nor, for that matter, battle field success. He did, however, develop a close working relationship with Gaziyev and the local Russian commander of former Soviet forces (the 104th Airborne Division) in Ganje. He also reportedly accepted into his forces deserters from other units and escaped criminals.[43] Once removed from his command, Huseinov withdrew his forces from the line, opening the door to a successful Armenian offensive (Kelbejer, between the NKAR and Armenia, fell in March) while castigating Elchibey for unsuccessful prosecution of the war. Huseinov and his men took refuge on the Russians' Ganje base until the Russians withdrew in May.

The Russian garrison outside Ganje departed on May 24 or 25, 1993, making Azerbaijan the first of the former Soviet republics to be rid of former Soviet troops. Huseinov's mutiny began on June 4. He started with accusations against the government, even taking hostage a few deputy ministers who were in Ganje. Huseinov's spokesmen claimed they had been attacked by government forces and that seventy people, including women and children, had been killed – but foreign journalists could find no evidence of more than four military burials (nor could they find bodies in local hospitals or morgues) in the indicated time period. From Baku, Elchibey stated he did not wish to shed the blood of his fellow countrymen, and offered to negotiate. Huseinov began his march on Baku within a week, along the main rail line into the capital. This self-styled colonel, who had never conducted a successful military operation, suddenly emerged with a coherent plan, heavy equipment (which bore Russian rather than Azerbaijan government markings)[44] and apparently airborne troops. It is impossible to believe that he was not aided by the recently departed Russian garrison that had turned over its equipment to him rather than a representative of the government, as the withdrawal agreement had specified. For its part, the Azerbaijani army withdrew as the rebel troops advanced. Elchibey's subsequent declaration that the government would "defend itself," was followed by no such action.

By mid-June, Surat Huseinov was outside Baku demanding the resignation of Elchibey, Isa Gambar, the State Secretary and eventually the entire government. Elchibey continued to drift through the crisis. He refused to call his supporters into the streets because he said he did not want to turn Baku into "another Tbilisi," then sunk in bloody and protracted street fighting among factions. Into this chaos came the republic's most charismatic, perhaps its only real, "strong man" – former Communist Party leader Heydar Aliyev. Career KGB general-turned-democrat Aliyev flew to Baku to meet with Elchibey, at the president's own request and the urging of the Turkish government, whose representatives had urged Elchibey to make use of this elder stateman's wisdom and advice.[45] On June 13, Isa Gambar's resignation from the post of Speaker of the National Assembly became known. After a few days' respite, Aliyev was made a member of the Assembly by a "special vote" whose legality was highly questionable. He was then elected to Gambar's vacated post as speaker, the man first in line to the presidency. On June 17, Elchibey was on his way to his own family home, in the remote mountains of Nakhjivan, leaving Aliyev as acting president, according to the republic's constitution. Aliyev had insinuated himself back into power but seems not to have had any part in the Ganje coup. He merely walked through the door which Surat Huseinov had opened. It is more likely that Russia's candidate, Mutalibov, was to be the beneficiary of the coup, but Aliyev acted too quickly for the conspirators. Aliyev displayed disdain for Surat Huseinov when he finally reached Baku. But the "colonel" had fire power. Aliyev moved cleverly to destroy the upstart, giving him "a long and oily rope with which to hang himself,"[46] in other words, power and obligations to solve problems he could not handle. Aliyev appointed Huseinov prime minister on June 30.

Though Aliyev had come to power behind the flimsiest fig leaf of legitimacy, he was quick to validate that move. In late August, Aliyev held a referendum of confidence on Elchibey. The results were decisive; a vast majority of the people voted "no confidence" in the elected president. By early October, Aliyev organized presidential elections in which two unknowns were permitted to run against him. Aliyev thus was "elected" president not only, as in the old days with absurdly high voter turn out and near-unanimity, but apparently needing to assert his greater popularity, with a hair's breadth more votes than Mutalibov had arranged for his 1991 election. Aliyev officially got 98.8 percent of the vote with an alleged 96 percent voter turnout, compared to 98 percent majority claimed by Mutalibov, with 92 percent of those eligible voting![47]

It was Aliyev, finally, who arranged parliamentary elections. A new electoral law, the first of the postcommunist era, was passed on August 12, 1995.[48] It provides for election of a 125-seat unicameral parliament to serve a five-year term. One hundred representatives are elected by majority vote from electoral districts; the other twenty-five are selected from political party lists on a country-wide proportional basis. Whether running with or without party affiliation, a candidate must collect 2,000 valid signatures from her/his respective district, and parties need 50,000 signatures to participate in proportional elections. The law does not specify procedures for validating (or excluding) signature lists.

The law creates needless obstacles, including a requirement that for elections to be valid, at least 50 percent of the registered voters must participate and, for a candidate to win in a district, s/he must receive at least 50 percent of votes cast. The Central Election Commission (CEC), "a neutral body" without representatives from political parties, oversees elections. Similarly, District-level Election Commissions (DECs), whose chairs are appointed by the CEC, could not belong to parties. On Precinct Election Commissions (PECs), however, which have direct contact with voters, 20 percent of the members represent candidates, 30 percent are members of political parties, and the remaining half represent "state enterprises and entities." The law is silent on the permissibility of the presence of police or executive branch officials in polling stations.

International observers noted a wide variety of serious irregularities in the 1995 elections. It seemed that Aliyev and his supporters strove to eliminate as many opponents as possible during the pre-election registration period. Four parties were denied registration, including the Yeni Musavat party,[49] whose leader, Isa Gambar, is perhaps the biggest thorn in Aliyev's side. Government handwriting experts declared invalid so many signatures on the lists of these parties (5,233 of 53,000 in the case of Musavat) that they were denied the right to participate. Furthermore, the signatures were invalidated without comparison to original signatures and despite affirmations by many of those whose signatures that were questioned.[50] About 60 percent of individual candidates were similarly disqualified. US-based observers noted that one of the inconsistencies in election practice was that signatures on these lists were routinely disqualified if the head of the family signed for all members, but at the polling stations, the same practice was usually permitted at the time of voting.[51] By election day, therefore, only eight parties remained. Five of these are regarded as "pro-government," including Aliyev's Yeni (New) Azerbaijan Party.[52]

Campaigning began officially on October 20, and all candidates were assured time on national (state-run) television. Opposition candidates, including Elchibey in his first television appearance since his departure from Baku in 1993, criticized Aliyev and his policies. A number of the more outspoken candidates had their spots cut and censored. Candidates also used major newspapers which generally circulate only in Baku. (Party-affiliated candidates presumably used party newspapers, also rarely available outside Baku.) In local meetings with voters, "there were generally no debates, no platforms were presented and only a few pre-arranged questions were asked."[53]

On election day itself, the "traditional" bloc voting (by heads of families for all family members) was tolerated. Although the CSCE called this "the most consequential irregularity,"[54] its report did not clarify how this was measured or in what sense it was significant. Observers noted obvious ballot box stuffing in many precincts, although in a few they were prevented from observing the counting procedures at all. Observers from political parties were sometimes excluded. Not surprisingly, OSCE/UN observers regarded these elections as neither free nor fair. The results looked more like the old Soviet-era (or post-Soviet Aliyev period) results with impossibly large voter turn-out and approval of government candidates and positions, including approval of the proposed constitution (described below): the CEC reported that 86 percent of the electorate took part in the constitutional referendum and 91.9 favored the constitution (75 percent approval was necessary for ratification); 79.5 percent of the electorate had voted for the twenty-five national representatives to parliament and only three parties received more than the minimum 8 percent for representation – Aliyev's Yeni Azerbaijan won nineteen seats and the parties of the Popular Front and National Independence won three each; of individual candidates running, seventy-one were elected outright, twenty districts had to have run-offs, and in eight districts, elections were cancelled entirely for either low voter turn-out (four districts) or violations of the electoral law (four districts).[55] Run-offs were held on November 26; new elections (requiring new candidates), for February 4, 1996. Run-offs produced parliamentary representatives in thirteen districts, turn-out was inadequate in five others and results were invalidated in two others for electoral law violations.[56] The elections also produced a new constitution whose language is unmistakably democratic.

The 1995 constitution

Until this document was approved in the November 1995 referendum, Azerbaijan had continued to operate under the 1978 Azerbaijan SSR constitution, the so-called Brezhnev constitution. The new constitution reflects both the stated desire of most political leaders in Azerbaijan to carry out democratization and also sensitivities to various issues that linger from the Soviet era.

The 1995 Constitution comprises 199 Articles divided into 13 chapters including a statement that sovereignty rests in the people (ch. 1), a description of state structure and basic principles (e.g. unitary, secular state, ch. 2), and the distribution of power among the three branches of government – legislative, executive, and judicial (chs. 6 and 13, 7, 8, respectively); an articulation of human and civil rights (chs. 3, 4, 5); provisions for constitutional amendment (chs. 11, 12) and subnational administration (ch. 10); and preservation of a Soviet creation, the Autonomous Republic of Nakhjivan (ch. 9).

The division of powers seems inspired by the Western, specifically US, example. The legislature, however, is unicameral, with 125 members elected for five years (Arts. 90, 91). Deputies enjoy immunity from prosecution.

The articles on human and civil rights reveal not only the Western traditions, but the Soviet-era failures to honor such rights. Thus the constitution contains individual articles guaranteeing rights of personal inviolability, inviolability of dwelling place, rights to live, work, strike, marry, rest, to guard one's health, to get an education, to use one's native language, and a host of others. Among legal rights are the presumption of innocence (Art. 71), the right to defend oneself in court, to have legal assistance, and to appeal (Arts. 68, 69, 73); not to be compelled to testify against a relative (Art. 74) or to be deprived of property without a court decision (Art. 78). Lacking is specific language on "due process of law," but the right to appeal would seem to provide some safety net in this regard. Foreigners enjoy the same legal rights as citizens, perhaps an item meant to assure the many foreign investors of the security of their business endeavors.

Duties of citizenship are also spelled out, including loyalty to and defense of the homeland (Arts. 83, 85); payment of taxes "and other obligations" on time (Art. 82); respect for national symbols including the flag (Art. 84) and for national and historical monuments (Art. 86).

It remains an open question whether this constitution will be enforced under the Aliyev administration. It is, however, in place, and has been widely publicized. Because democratic verbiage has become the necessary language of political discourse in all post-Soviet states and thanks to international scrutiny by political and economic circles, political leaders in Azerbaijan would surely find it more difficult to ignore the provisions of a constitution than did their Soviet predecessors. Furthermore, this constitution provides the political opposition with a weapon for legal protest and action.

The democratic experiment that failed

The failure of the Elchibey government which had been led, one might argue, by some of Azerbaijan's "best and brightest" was a source of considerable disillusionment to many Azeris. A frank analysis of Elchibey's year in power reveals two reasons for the failure of his government – the weaknesses and errors of his ministers and his own leadership, and the successes of his government's enemies.

When Elchibey came to power, he faced three major problems – the war in Nagorno-Karabagh (with loss of land and creation of refugees), inflation and related economic problems (including slow progress on an oil deal with foreign investors), and the remnants of Russian-Soviet control and influence of the old order. The most immediately pressing problem was unrest around Baku. Gunfire could be heard at night, and a state of emergency and curfew remained in effect. Soldiers patrolled the streets of the capital. Despite the warm weather, people did not stroll outside in the evening, as is customary, and women avoided wearing jewelry for fear of robbery, even in the daytime.

The election of Elchibey was accompanied by considerable optimism, especially in the capital.[57] At his inauguration, Popular Front members looked on with tears of relief, joy, and perhaps a little disbelief, streaming down their faces. Yet the prevalence of the old control mentality was expressed by individuals at all levels of society – the "great man" had now come to power and he was expected almost by magic to solve the republic's problems and establish peace, genuine independence, democracy and prosperity. Few shared the notion that resolution of Azerbaijan's complex difficulties would require prolonged effort by all segments of society. Even Elchibey's appointees were not equally prepared for the hard work. Although some worked virtually round the clock, others settled in to enjoy the tea-toting secretaries and big offices where they listened to their own voices resound as they "consulted" with foreign visitors.

Among those who got promptly to work was the indefatigable Iskender Hamidov. His police from the Ministry of Internal Affairs staged raids on illegal operations in and around Baku, seizing smuggled goods (including caviar and guns) from basements throughout the capital and stopping private cars and taxis to uncover illegal weapons that had crossed the northern border from Russian Daghestan. By summer's end, quiet was restored in Baku, and people resumed their evening strolls. Hamidov's actions, it should be noted, were not without violations of individual privacy and human rights, but as US journalist Thomas Goltz pointed out, only half joking, people were glad it was the police banging down their doors, not "mafia gangs or kidnappers."[58] In those early days, Hamidov was tremendously popular both for his actions against crime and for successes at the front. These results perhaps encouraged unrealistic expectations that other difficulties could be quashed equally quickly.

Elchibey's government launched successful offensives in Nagorno-Karabagh using a large cache of weapons they (and other former Soviet republics) had just received from the former Soviet armed forces. These weapons, when the transfers were completed, would include 200 battle tanks, GRAD missile launchers, 100 combat aircraft.[59] On at least one evacuated base north of Baku, however, most of the equipment left to Azerbaijan was not in working condition,[60] so it is unclear how much of this weaponry genuinely aided Azerbaijan's war effort. It was enough, apparently, to launch the successful summer offensives.

In political terms, the Popular Front, like all opposition forces, had equated protection of Nagorno-Karabagh with the principle of "territorial integrity." This demand, like the creation of democratic government, was regarded as perfectly compatible with the full sovereignty that opposition programs demanded. The most coherent statement of policy concerning Karabagh was articulated by the Popular Front, whose guidelines became state policy with Elchibey's election: (1) Peaceful means for the resolution of the conflict should be pursued; (2) The Azerbaijan republic will not surrender or accept reduction of its sovereignty over the former NKAR, on the principles of territorial integrity and the inviolability of borders; (3) Azerbaijan is committed to defense of human rights, and demands that Azeri as well as Armenian victims be considered by international human rights organizations; (4) Azerbaijan is prepared to ensure cultural, but not political, autonomy for Armenian and other minorities;[61] (5) As preconditions to negotiations, (a) Armenian forces must leave Azerbaijani territory, and (b) the Armenian Supreme Soviet must rescind laws which interfere in Azerbaijan's internal affairs (referring to legislation of December 1989 annexing the former NKAR and making the members of its regional soviet deputies in the Armenian Supreme Soviet); and (6) Azerbaijan considers its own independence and military strength to be its ultimate guarantee of security and an equitable resolution of this conflict.

On this basis, Elchibey's government pursued negotiations sponsored by the so-called Minsk Group of the CSCE, then headed by an experienced diplomat Mario Rafaelli. The Minsk Group comprised representatives from eleven CSCE states including the United States, Russia, Turkey, and European states. The talks dragged on during 1992–93 partly because of a failure to agree on the status of Karabagh Armenian representatives who demanded to be recognized as a separate party to negotiations; Azerbaijan refused this because it would have implied autonomy for Nagorno-Karabagh, the key point at issue. Azerbaijan insisted that both Armenians and Azeris of the former NKAR be represented within Azerbaijan's delegation. Nonetheless, a modus vivendi appeared to be on the horizon by spring 1993. A successful cease-fire under CSCE auspices would have undercut the Russian demand to be recognized as the sole peacekeeper in former Soviet republics.

In a second problem area, the economy, Elchibey's government failed to bring inflation under control. By November, however, it had taken the important step of issuing a national currency, the manat. Initially, the manat and the ruble were to circulate simultaneously, but the manat would displace the ruble at some unspecified future time. Presidential advisers indicated that the timetable for what was essentially leaving the "ruble zone" had to remain confidential. By the next spring, the decision had been taken to switch over solely to the manat during summer 1993. Had this taken place, Azerbaijan would have left the ruble zone.

To support the transition to the free market, the parliament, now led by the new president's Popular Front lieutenant Isa Gambar, passed legislation to strengthen the private sector.[62] More important to most Azeris was the prospect of foreign investment and the influx of hard currency. During this year, Elchibey's government negotiated a beneficial oil contract with a consortium of Western oil companies that was to be signed in London in June 1993. Had this been accomplished, Azerbaijan's oil would have competed with Russia's on international markets rather than being, as it had for over a century, a supplementary supply for Russian needs.

Finally, concerning Russian relations, Elchibey moved decisively to cut ties with the CIS. With the momentum of the Popular Front's victories, a parliamentary vote on CIS membership was defeated in late summer 1992. Despite being called "anti-Russian," Elchibey stated that he wished to maintain good relations with Russia, and he signed a bi-lateral agreement with Russia on the heels of parliament's rejection of CIS membership. Elchibey thereby strove to place relations with Russia into a broader context while rejecting the Russian dominance implicit in the CIS. His government planned to dismantle the old communist system domestically, including the remnants of the KGB and the old Supreme Soviet, the planned economy and its "shadow" the black market. They lacked the personnel to replace the old bureaucracy wholesale, but the problem was compounded by the attitude of some members of government, suggested in word or deed, that they could afford to take their time. One of the worst mistakes made in this regard was the failure to hold parliamentary elections. Some government advisers suggested it would be best to ride the wave of Elchibey's victory to parliamentary elections by fall, but others seemed almost complacent, arguing "more time" was needed for the various parties to prepare. As a result, the Soviet-era "parliament" was still in power when Surat Huseinov marched on Baku and demanded Elchibey's resignation.

More serious errors involved the behavior of some key government ministers. The one who got the greatest notoriety, indeed infamy, in Western human rights circles, was Iskender Hamidov. During fall 1992, Hamidov read an article in a Baku newspaper that, he said, constituted a personal insult to his family. He went promptly to the newspaper office and beat the responsible journalist. A similar incident in spring 1993 would lead to his dismissal from office. Although Hamidov's behavior was certainly a violation of the democratic principles for which his government stood, it should be noted that, in contrast to Soviet-era (or other totalitarian) ministers, he did not use the power of his office to retaliate for what he regarded as a personal insult. Unlike his many predecessors, he "settled" the issue with his fists; the journalist and his editor did not just disappear, the newspaper was not shut down. Hamidov believed, and stated precisely this,[63] that despite being a government minister he could – and in this case did – act as a private individual. He spoke out also as a private individual, declaring in one instance that he had tactical nuclear bombs he planned to drop on Erevan. Less flamboyant but just as loose-lipped were a few other ministers who interpreted "democracy" to mean they could expound their own versions of state policy or openly dissent from that of the government. In the final analysis, Elchibey bore responsibility for the actions of all his appointees, and his failure to rein them in contributed to a loss of public confidence in him. Thus, Elchibey's weaknesses were these – his failure to act decisively in some areas, for example, overseeing his cabinet and holding parliamentary elections, while moving too slowly in those where he was making tangible progress, e.g. securing an oil contract and a cease-fire.

Elchibey's enemies were making no such mistakes. Russia was clearly threatened by his successes – or impending successes in the cease-fire, oil contract, and currency reform – and a significant Russian role in Surat Huseinov's coup can hardly be doubted. The commander of the Russian base at Ganje certainly had cultivated his relationships with the self-proclaimed colonel and the defense minister, and these proved useful once both men were removed from their posts. But inciting Iskender Hamidov to a final, fatal outburst was perhaps the decisive calculated step to remove Elchibey's most able defender. A well-aimed newspaper article by a leader of the tiny, but overtly pro-Russian, social democratic party concerning Hamidov's lineage (it was suggested he was a Kurd not an Azeri) led Hamidov to a physical attack on the writer and, in turn, to Hamidov's dismissal. Given the strength of the armed forces loyal to Hamidov (see below) and his willingness and ability to use them, removing him from power would have been essential to overthrowing Elchibey. Indeed, Surat Huseinov's coup began shortly after Hamidov was dismissed.

Elchibey's successor, Heydar Aliyev, had been accumulating power in his native Nakhjivan (also Elchibey's home) since 1990, when he was elected chair of that autonomous republic's soviet. He played on his personal power and prestige at home and abroad. In 1992–93, he negotiated significant aid packages for Nakhjivan from Iran, Turkey (his personal relationship with then-prime minister Suleyman Demirel appeared to be a friendship of equals), and even the US. Aliyev became a satrap at home and retained his reputation as a forceful and effective leader. Thus when Elchibey appeared unequal to the challenge of Surat Huseinov's coup, which he could neither quell nor defeat, the populace, with few exceptions, gladly turned to someone whose leadership was beyond question – Heydar Aliyev. This manifestation of the "control mentality" is no surprise; it was apparent by late 1992. After only six months in power, Isa Gambar admitted frankly that "the people are tired of mass politics."[64]

Contrary to expectation, however, was that Aliyev's return did not mean a restoration of Russian dominance or even, in simple terms, the "old order." Aliyev did throw a sop to Russia in his prompt acceptance of CIS membership, but he never permitted the return of Russian troops to Azerbaijani soil. He is an authoritarian ruler, but in the popular mind his forcefulness is equated with "law and order." Furthermore, many were disillusioned with Popular Front failures in the war and the economy and were therefore no longer interested in mobilizing to save Elchibey or to defend Popular Front leaders. When Isa Gambar accused Aliyev of usurping power on the floor of parliament in August 1993, Aliyev had him stripped of parliamentary immunity and arrested. Vocal protest from the diplomatic community, not the local population, led several weeks later to his release. Subsequent arrests of Iskender Hamidov, former Foreign Minister Tofik Gasimov, other members of the opposition and even journalists, have elicited no greater public displeasure. Those few demonstrations of discontent, mostly by opposition groups or parties rather than unaffiliated citizens, have been suppressed with vigor. As opinion polls suggest (below), the desire for security has come to outweigh interest in democracy or, at least, has become identified with it.

The economy

The most obvious economic changes in Azerbaijan since 1990 have been the availability of foreign goods and inflation. The ordinary consumer who formerly went from store to store to find the one kind of cheese or sausage in town, fresh bread, "generic" rice and cans cryptically labeled "fish," now routinely passes shops selling pizza, imported German beer, a host of products from Turkey, and other items that most had never seen before. But these items, as well as the old products, come at a high price. During the first half of 1992, Baku residents reported[65] such dramatic increases as a 50 percent rise in the price of women's shoes (produced locally) and 10–20 percent weekly increases in the price of chicken at the city markets. The problem was compounded by black marketeers' price gouging. The behavior had not changed from Soviet times, but now there were more goods to sell.

Table 4.2 *Indicators of economic trends in Azerbaijan since 1989*

	1989	1990	1991	1992	1993	1994	1995[a]
GDP	-4.4	-11.7	-0.7	-22.6	-23.1	-21.2	-17
Industrial output	0.7	-6.3	4.8	-23.8	-7.0	-22.7	n.a.
Rate of inflation	n.a.	7.8	106	616	1,130	1,664	412
GNP per capita	n.a.	n.a.	n.a.	n.a.	n.a.	1,720	n.a.

Notes: GDP – % change over previous year; industrial output – % change over previous year; rate of inflation – % change in end-year retail/consumer prices; GNP per capita – in US dollars at PPP exchange rates. [a]Estimate.

Sources: European Bank for Reconstruction and Development, *Transition Report 1995: Economic Transition in Eastern Europe and the Former Soviet Union* (London: EBRD, 1995); European Bank for Reconstruction and Development, *Transition Report Update, April 1996: Assessing Progress in Economies in Transition* (London: EBRD, 1996);   The World Bank, *Statistical Handbook 1993: States of the Former USSR* (Washington, DC: The World Bank, 1994); The World Bank, *Statistical Handbook 1995: States of the Former USSR* (Washington, DC: The World Bank, 1996).

Formal statistics, too – despite their many flaws – confirm this trend during the first half of the 1990s. Average annual consumer prices, from official sources and reported by the European Bank for Reconstruction and Development (EBRD) (table 4.2), show growing price increases from 1990 to 1994 with a projected drop for 1995.[66]

These levels of inflation had led the Azeri population to believe, in keeping with Soviet propaganda since the era of Lenin, that a free market economy and competition lead to unbridled exploitation of the many by the few rather than to the benefit of the consumer. Furthermore, since democracy was equated in the popular mind with prosperity, disillusionment with political promises and leaders set in as prices rose. Elchibey was ousted before his reform plans took effect. Under Aliyev, the manat continued to circulate with the ruble. The value of the manat against the ruble (and dollar) fell and inflation continued, though both processes have slowed in 1995. Since May 1994, the official exchange rate for the manat has been set weekly, based on a "weighted average" of exchange rates by commercial banks authorized to deal in foreign exchange. The EBRD further noted, "Both current and capital account convertibility is heavily restricted."[67]

Other aspects of Azerbaijan's economy are more difficult to measure than inflation; the distortions in official statistics render tidy columns of figures virtually worthless. It is these figures that the EBRD, the World Bank and other financial institutions use in their publications and (one hopes limited) analyses for former Soviet republics just as they do in analyses of Switzerland or Japan. The EBRD spells out clearly some of the pitfalls with this procedure – the existence of "hidden activities" (hidden, that is, from state authorities) that may account for 10 to 25 percent (!) of Gross Domestic Product (GDP) of the country's economy; the faulty official estimates of "non-material services" which were not counted under the Soviet system; the extent and value of the new private sector; distortions introduced by high inflation rates, and others.[68]

More useful than statistics are reports of laws and procedures. The EBRD notes a variety of laws that affect, at least in theory, economic practices in Azerbaijan. These include Azerbaijan's nationalization of "all former Soviet property" in November 1991; a series of measures ending price controls during 1992 and 1993, leaving only bread and oil "as the main goods under price controls" (though these too were relaxed in 1994–95); an anti-monopoly law of 1993; imposition of wage ceilings since May 1994; a state decree of June 1994 requiring state-owned enterprises to bank with the state sector.[69] But the report fails to follow up on the success of these and other measures as governments had been formed and overthrown since 1992.

Azerbaijan's wealth is, nonetheless, undisputable. The Soviet state had used the republic as an economic colony from which Moscow extracted Caspian Sea caviar and carpets for direct export to East Germany and western countries. Steel from Azerbaijan was used to manufacture cars in Georgia. The Soviet central planning agency (Gosplan) mandated extensive grape and cotton cultivation for supplying other Soviet republics. Pesticides, chemical fertilizers and growth stimulants were used lavishly on the cotton crop (as in Central Asia) and grapes, a policy which led by the 1980s to extensive environmental damage and increased health risks. Ironically, Communist Party boss Heydar Aliyev had boasted to CPSU congresses of increased use of chemicals.[70]

The most important money-making component of Azerbaijan's economy is its oil industry and the foreign investment it has drawn. The lure of oil reserves has brought conquerors and investors to the Caspian shore for centuries, especially since the "oil rush" of the 1870s when drilled wells were first sunk and gushers became common place.[71] Discouraged by depletion of the on-shore reserves early in the twentieth century, then driven out by the Bolshevik take-over of 1920, foreign investors returned to the Baku scene only after the collapse of the USSR. They found an out-dated industrial infrastructure and operations that paid no attention to environmental or workers' health.

Virtually all Azeris share the belief that foreign investment in oil will yield a financial bonanza and make everyone rich. Having been cut off, however, from the global financial milieu for seven decades, even the most astute in Azerbaijan's political world have unrealistic notions about dealing with oil companies, the criteria by which oil executives make investment decisions, the nature of modern investing and the speed with which a return on investment can be felt, and the legal and ethical rules by which reputable companies operate.

Not until Elchibey had been in power for nearly a year was an agreement prepared between Azerbaijan's state oil company, SOCAR, and a consortium of western companies (in June 1993, these included British Petroleum, Norway's Statoil, Amoco, Pennzoil, Unocal, McDermott, Aberdeen-based Ramco, and Turkish Petroleum Company). Involved are oil reserves estimated at 17.5 billion barrels (equivalent to North Sea reserves) in the southern Caspian,[72] $9 billion for development, $2 billion for pipelines, and projected profits of $118 billion.[73]

When Heydar Aliyev took power, his government stated publicly it wanted to "review" the agreement. Aliyev assured the company representatives privately that the deal would go through. After three months of "intense talks" a new agreement was worked out in October 1993 the terms of which were even more advantageous to Azerbaijan than those of the previous deal. According to oil officials and the British Ambassador in Baku, Thomas Young, the oil companies were to increase their "signature bonus" to Azerbaijan from $300 million to $500 million and increase their share of project costs from 70 to 75 percent; Azerbaijan's share of profits grew to 80 percent. Aliyev's negotiators, for unknown reasons, dragged out talks despite the terms. Aliyev delayed signing the agreement until September 1994.[74] Finally, with the agreement in place, a "no profit/no loss" operating company called Azerbaijan International Operating Company (AIOC) could be created to carry out the terms of the agreement. AIOC is headed by British Petroleum executive Terry Adams, a man with experience in Iranian oil operations and as head of a similar consortium in Abu Dhabi. AIOC comprises half SOCAR/Azerbaijani government representatives and half consortium members. All decisions must be unanimous. Adams anticipates "early oil" from the combined offshore fields of up to 80,000 barrels per day. Production would be boosted after thirty months, by which time the controversial pipeline issue would hopefully be resolved, to 300,000 barrels per day.[75]

Both the production and pipeline questions have brought Azerbaijan's neighbors into the oil picture. First and most vocal, Russia challenged Azerbaijan's right even to negotiate oil extraction issues. With Aliyev in power, however, Russia's Lukoil was cut into Azerbaijan's profits and Russian attentions shifted to the pipeline. Russia demands a "northern route" for the pipeline, through Grozny (Chechnya) and terminating at the Black Sea port of Novorossiisk. Turkey objects to this or any route that will increase oil tanker traffic through the ecologically sensitive Bosphorus. Nonetheless, this route was approved in fall 1995 for "early oil." To further accommodate the transport of early oil, the United States approved in May 1995, an oil swap with Iran. This arrangement will allow Azerbaijan to sell a certain (still unspecified) amount of oil to Iran; Iran will then substitute an equivalent amount of its own oil for loading onto tankers at southern ports.[76] Still favored for the later oil is a route across either Georgia, Armenia (in the belief that this economic interest will provide an incentive to maintain peace for warring parties), or even Iran, connecting to existing pipelines that cross Turkey to the Mediterranean port of Ceyhan.

Main beneficiaries of the influx of wealth are those connected in some way with foreign business, primarily those in government or formerly state-owned enterprises. The "business process" in Azerbaijan is characterized by rampant bribe-taking and petty charges – foreign businessmen are sometimes needlessly delayed so that hotels can charge extra nights' fees of $150/night for roach-infested rooms. Other corruption is more serious and on a larger and more organized scale. Foreign oil men realize that those responsible for negotiating on Azerbaijan's behalf are those who got rich from the flaws in the old system. For example, diesel fuel refined in Baku and sold at the old Soviet price of $2/ton could be sold for $150/ton on the international spot market. Locals wanted to sustain the old networks that permitted them to siphon off this diesel, and know that efficient foreign companies would plug the holes. These acts were connected to other economic activities:

Some of the loot . . . returned to the national economy in a Ronald Reaganesque 'trickle-down' manner: well connected folks went into import/export business. This provided jobs (and assumed the loyalties) for hundreds of people, ranging from travelers to Istanbul and Dubai to purchase textiles and electronics to clerks in the newly opened kiosks around town filled with everything from Snickers bars to VCRs . . . It was all for today with nothing for tomorrow.[77]

Azeri society and the evolution of political attitudes

Cleavages in society

Society in Azerbaijan is characterized by various social and ethnic cleavages not all of which are characterized by unrest. The educated elite is distinct from the rest of society by virtue of its greater awareness of social, political and economic problems and by its role in politics. The urban–rural cleavages are by no means unique to Azerbaijan and, in contrast to the situation earlier in this century, no longer coincide with ethnic differences. The Azeri are a decisive majority both in the republic as whole (80 percent in 1989) and in the cities, including Baku, where their numbers had shrunk at the beginning

Table 4.3 *Demographic trends in Azerbaijan since the 1950s*

	1950s	1970s	1980s
Percentage of population	(1951)	(1979)	(1989)
Rural	55.0	47.4	45.8
Urban	45.0	52.6	54.2
Average annual rates of	(1951–61)	(1971–79)	(1990–99)[a]
population growth (%)	3.2	1.7	1.3
Age distribution (%)		(1979)	(1989)
15–24		23.8	19.7
25–49		26.7	30.6
50–59		6.5	9.1
Over 60		7.6	7.8

Note: [a]Estimate.
Sources: US Department of Commerce, *Statistical Abstracts of the United States*; Paul S. Shoup, *The East European and Soviet Data Handbook*; UNESCO, *Statistical Yearbooks*; United Nations, *Demographic Yearbooks*.

of this century, to about 40 percent, equal with the Russians. A more thorny division is regionalism (*yerbazlik*). In the Soviet political environment, important political and economic figures tended to surround themselves with long-time friends from their home regions. Heydar Aliyev, as communist and, now, nationalist, leader, was notorious for appointing fellow Nakhjivanis and excluding others, especially those from Ganje, the traditional rivals. (Ironically, Elchibey is a Nakhjivani without such a regional support base.) National consciousness, though apparently growing, is not yet so widely embraced as to overcome regional loyalties.

Ethnic conflict is far more obvious. Veiled but mutual hostility existed between the Azeris and Russians since the conquest of the early nineteenth century; it persisted in many circles in the Soviet period. Azeris may perceive Russians as crude and smug. The Russians seem to have believed the regime's "elder brother" rhetoric (and the "civilizing mission that preceded in imperial times); even Russians in the lowliest socio-economic positions considered themselves more "civilized" than the Azeri. Nonetheless, many Azeri who were educated in Russian-language schools, and some in Russia itself, feel no such enmity and sometimes regarded their fellow Azeris as "backward." Russians, however, rarely accepted Azeris as equals, however russified they might be. Tensions between the two groups came out into the open at times over language issues (Russians rarely learn the language of any republic, even if they are the second or third generation to be born there), and then decisively with the struggle over Karabagh when Russians, in Russia at least, tended to support Armenians.

Other national minorities in Azerbaijan include two small ethnic groups that came to public attention after 1990: the Talysh, an Iranian-speaking people in the south of the republic, and the Lezghi, a Daghestani group in the north. Relations between both groups and the Azeris had been painted in such consistently rosy terms that it is difficult to judge the degree and nature of discontent that may have existed. Some Talysh suggested they resented being submerged in the Azeris' Turkic culture. This is a complaint of many small minorities in national republics and stems from Soviet policy. The regime failed to give adequate guarantees of cultural rights for those groups that were not granted autonomous territory (which would have conferred such rights); and, second, it provided only two options for school children in national republics, education in the republic's language (in this case Azeri) or Russian. As for the Azeris, some in Baku, in the 1980s at least, believed that Talysh were occasionally favored over them for positions of authority – in 1980, the Baku police chief was Talysh – either to sow enmity or to divide police authorities from locals. As for the Lezghis, their position would have been similar, but misgivings were not openly expressed. Thus when Talysh and Lezghi national movements emerged in 1991–92, Azeris suspected that unrest had been stirred up by Russia, as was the case of Abkhazian separatism in Georgia when that republic attempted to assert its independence from Moscow.

The large Armenian minority has constituted a stable and sizeable community in Baku and other areas of the Caucasus before the Russian conquest of the early nineteenth century. With the rise of Armenian and Azeri national movements at the turn of this century, bloody clashes occurred throughout the Caucasus region and continued as the two peoples founded their republics in 1918. Under Soviet rule peace was imposed though issues were not resolved to either side's satisfaction. When the Karabagh conflict broke into the open in 1988, many Azeris expressed surprise at the enmity the Armenians harbored toward them. Even refugees from Shusha, after it was overrun in spring 1992, expressed the belief that their former Armenian neighbors has been blameless in the conflict. The Azeris said that they would be prepared to return and live among the Armenians again, believing that Armenians from Armenia or abroad were at fault.[78] Other Azeris were less forgiving, and expressed profound disdain for the Armenians, stating that distrust between themselves and the Armenians would last for the foreseeable future. Many Baku Armenians abandoned the city during the early years of the Karabagh conflict and especially during January 1990, when the authorities failed to stop organized attacks on the Armenian quarter. It is impossible to know, until the next census, how many Armenians remain in Azerbaijan.

The worst unrest in Azerbaijan of the late Soviet and post-Soviet period was linked to Armenian-Azeri relations in the form of the war in Nagorno-Karabagh. The Armenian demand for direct political control of this territory is a continuation of the dispute from the late nineteenth-early twentieth century period when, as in European nationalism, possession of patrimonial land became a fundamental part of national values. At the root of the conflict is the belief by both peoples that this land is their own historic patrimony. This war, however, is hardly felt in Baku. Fighting was so remote that the people outside the war zone were long optimistic about victory and the creation of a democratic order in the aftermath of Russian (for this was increasingly the Azeri view of communist rule) domination. In this mood, the Popular Front and other political groups grew.

In contrast, other types of unrest, especially the Soviet army's invasion of January 1990, the overthrow of Mutalibov in 1992 and, of course, Surat Huseinov's coup of June 1993 produced repercussions elsewhere in the republic. These were political acts and, despite Russian involvement, cannot be considered a result of social "cleavages" in Azerbaijan.

Opinion surveys

Several USIA-sponsored surveys taken in summer 1994 in urban areas of Azerbaijan have produced suggestive results if used with due caution. A few caveats are in order in analyzing survey results. First, the results reflect only the views of the urban population (accounting for just over 54 percent of the republic's population according to the 1989 census), which has far greater exposure than the rural population to political activities and debate, republican and international media, and to foreign communities and products. The urban population, compared to the rural, is less aware of national and religious traditions. Second, the survey was actually conducted by what USIA identified as a "Baku-based research firm." Although the nationality of the questioner and the language in which questions were posed would be highly relevant, they are not indicated in the "Opinion Research Memoranda" that provide results. The adults questioned can be expected to exercise some caution in dealing with strangers asking questions, as Soviet census takers and foreign anthropologists discovered long ago.[79] Finally, views of major issues, including the meaning of democracy and Islam, have been powerfully shaped by the Soviet-era experience, not by the fundamental works of the systems themselves – translations of John Locke's *Social Contract* or the Federalist papers have been no more readily available in Azerbaijan than the Koran.

One of the USIA surveys strove to measure Azeri attitudes on "democratic principles."[80] One thousand adults were asked to rate several attributes of a democratic society as "essential," "important," "not very important," or "not at all important." ("Don't know" was also an option.) The one item that most people thought "essential" (84 percent) to democratic society was "a government that provides for the basic material needs of citizens," an idea that may reflect some modern "welfare states," but is hardly a trait that is a fundamental part of political democracy. The more important principles of free elections and the right to criticize government were deemed "essential" by fewer people – 78 and 55 percent, respectively. It is, of course, noteworthy that a majority of those interviewed did recognize these as "essential" principles of democracy. Furthermore, because 73 percent agreed (41 percent "completely" and 32 percent "somewhat") that "voting is a means to influence government," one may conclude that the groundwork for building democracy does exist in the (urban) popular mind.

On the other hand, the survey revealed significant support for censorship of "dangerous ideas." Eighty-one percent agreed (56 percent "completely") that the government should exercise such censorship. Before writing this off as a vestige of the Soviet-era mentality of control, one might look for the prevalence of such views among US citizens. (One is reminded of those Americans who, when given an unmarked copy of the US Constitution's Bill of Rights declared it "too radical.")

By the same token, Azeris are not necessarily familiar with Islamic tradition and law (Shari'a). On top of a secularizing trend among Azeri elites in the late pre-Soviet era, the population was subjected to more than six decades of anti-religious propaganda and a ban on the teaching of Islam and disseminating religious literature. These efforts by the Soviet state, despite the persistence of nominal (or cultural) adherence to Islam among a majority of the population, were remarkably successful. Field work in the early 1980s revealed that Baku Azeris often thought the Novruz holiday (pre-Christian "Iranian New Year," marking the start of spring) was an Islamic holiday. More surprising, a senior Azeri student in the Mir-i Arab medresse (theological school) in Bukhara claimed that the Shi'a–Sunni split came "late in Islamic history" and was never very important.[81] So the finding that 44 percent of the urbanites interviewed agreed (23 percent strongly) that "Shari'a laws should be the laws of the country" requires clarification – did those questioned understand the provisions of Shari'a; was this response a cultural statement, a protest against Russian law, Soviet law or Russian influence (an Azeri artist confessed in 1981 that he put crescent moons in his paintings because "it drives the Russians crazy"[82]); was the favoring of Shari'a merely a way of registering discontent with secular society and the spread of perceived immoral behavior? Without knowing the meaning of the phrase "Shari'a laws" to the respondents, it is not possible to draw entirely reliable conclusions about this response.

Similar caveats must accompany the examination of results of a separate survey concerning perceptions of Islam.[83] A majority of urban respondents agreed that "the teachings of Islam should play a larger role" in Azerbaijan. The survey does not indicate whether those interviewed were asked which teachings they had in mind – prohibitions against theft, for example, or stoning of adulterers. The underlying assumptions of the respondents would make a great difference in the meaning of their answers. Neither enlightened nor helpful is the comment, presumably by USIA personnel, that "the Muslim heritage . . . may even come into conflict with democratic values."[84] The nature of the impact of "the Muslim heritage" will depend at least in part on the aspects of that heritage that Azeris embrace in social, political, cultural, or other spheres. One aspect of "the Muslim heritage" in Azerbaijan is a trend that argues that Islam and democracy are compatible.[85] Furthermore, Azeri communist party members under Soviet rule could say that it was possible to be a Muslim and a communist;[86] why should it not now be possible to be a Muslim and a democrat?

With the relaxation of controls on the media, broadcasting and newspapers have shaped public opinion. Before Elchibey's presidency and since his ouster, the media have been largely controlled by the government. This control is tightest on broadcast media, especially television. Until the fall of Mutalibov the old Soviet controls were in place. After his fall, television became more open, especially for candidates who registered for presidential elections. On the eve of 1992 elections, debates among candidates were televised. Etibar Mamedov hosted a call-in show for those wishing to know more about his positions. Since 1992, Turkish television is broadcast to Baku several hours each day, and young people quickly master the difference in the two closely related languages. Under Elchibey these trends continued. Aliyev imposed censorship, and used television as his own vehicle. Broadcasts of parliamentary sessions alternated with lengthy press conferences in which Aliyev freely answered some questions and criticized journalists for asking others.

Relatively less controlled were the printed media. Newspapers proliferated in greater numbers than political parties. Every professional or interest group seemingly had its own weekly or bi-weekly newspaper (only the state could afford dailies): the Union of Jurists, various refugee aid societies, assorted branches of the Popular Front, theater groups, Afghanistan veterans, regions of the republic and all the major parties, including the former communists (at least into 1991).[87] Thus a wide range of issues was aired and some papers even began to carry ads, print horoscopes and offer health advice. In response to Aliyev's imposition of censorship, most political newspapers have simply left blank spots for every sentence cut by censors. Nonetheless, what remains is sometimes critical of the government, if only indirectly, and the existence of the tell-tale blank spots serves as a constant reminder of censorship and the ability of the papers to protest, at least to that extent.

Political parties and the party system

Political parties after the fall of the USSR

Parties and similar groups are the most common forms of political association in Azerbaijan. It is fairly obvious that more than forty political groups and parties exist because of personalities rather than forty distinct visions for Azerbaijan's future. The political scene in the republic is characterized by the seeming inability of many individuals to subordinate themselves to a party led by someone else. Membership in and electoral support for particular parties are often a matter of the popularity of its key figure whether he is nominal leader (Gambar of Musavat and Etibar Mamedov of ANIP) or not (Hamidov of Bozkurt). The most successful leaders are in some sense charismatic; most are highly educated. If both these traits are not present, charisma is certainly the more important.

It is presently difficult to assess the strength of Azerbaijan's party system since the return of Aliyev has meant a *de facto* return to one-man rule. Integral to the party system is the notion of a "loyal opposition" which is not being nurtured in the present environment. (The term has been used by Etibar Mamedov to mean "non-critical" or "cooperative" opposition rather than indicating the opposing parties' loyalty to a democratic system.) Toleration for opposition and criticism remains low. The main parties can be grouped as opposition and pro-government, that is, pro-Aliyev. The leading opposition parties include the following.[88]

The Party of the Azerbaijan Popular Front, an umbrella group since its founding in 1989, registered as a party in 1995 in order to contend in the fall elections. It claims to have more than 81,000 members. Of 93 people who collected signatures to run for parliament, the petitions of only 23 were approved. Elchibey, in self-imposed exile, remains the head of the party.

The Yeni (New) Musavat was founded by Isa Gambar, co-leader of the Popular Front, as a "friendly" rival to the Front. Although some Western sources suggest that the Musavat existed before 1992 and cooperated only temporarily during Elchibey's presidency, at the time when Gambar became parliamentary speaker the Musavat party did not yet exist. It was probably founded in 1992 or 1993. The party was denied certification in 1995 – perhaps because of Aliyev's intense dislike of Gambar, who has sharply criticized him – and was therefore unable to run for nation-wide representation. Had the party been certified, Gambar would have been the first candidate on the proportional list and would, thereby, have been returned to parliament. Of eighty-three members who tried to run individually, only ten were certified as candidates.

The Bozkurt ("Grey Wolf") group was formed and published a newspaper by 1992, but the precise date of its creation is unclear. It was registered as a party in 1994. The Bozkurt movement in Azerbaijan, including a significant armed force, is led by Iskender Hamidov. The armed force is bound to him by personal loyalty and has fought in Karabagh. Hamidov does not formally head the Bozkurt party. The name Bozkurt refers to the ancient totem of the Turkic peoples of Central Asia and is the same as that of an ultra-nationalist party in Turkey. Although Hamidov has denied subordination to Turkey's Bozkurt,[89] Baku's Bozkurt newspaper has included biographical information about and excerpts from the writings of the leader of the Turkish Bozkurt, Alparslan Turkeş. At the same time, this material and other articles in the newspaper are almost entirely dedicated to pre-modern Turkic history and culture rather than current politics or ideology. The newspaper reflects a relatively weak understanding of the Turkish Bozkurts' program. Azeri Bozkurt rhetoric is decidedly nationalist, anti-communist, pro-Turkish and unfriendly to Russian or other external domination over Azerbaijan. Hamidov himself was jailed by Aliyev in 1994 (for alleged involvement in an anti-Aliyev coup attempt) where he still remained in late 1996. The Bozkurts did not attempt to participate in the 1995 elections.

The Azerbaijan National Independence Party (ANIP) was founded in 1991 by former Popular Front member Etibar Mamedov. His posture as a critic of the status quo has changed significantly since 1991. He negotiated with Aliyev in July 1993 for a cabinet post, but was finally snubbed by Aliyev who rejected his bid for a share of power. Despite his lingering anger and embarrassment at being openly rebuffed by Aliyev at that time, Mamedov calls his party a "loyal" (meaning "friendly") opposition. Of seventy-eight members who wished to run for parliament, only twenty-nine were certified as candidates.

The Azerbaijan Communist Party was registered in spring 1994, and claimed in 1995 to have 64,000 members. It was prevented from participating in parliamentary elections when 5,000 of the 53,000 signatures on its petition lists were declared invalid. Of twenty-four individuals trying to run for seats, two were certified to run in electoral districts.

Several parties are clearly pro-government, that is, pro-Aliyev. Yeni (New) Azerbaijan is Aliyev's own party, founded by him in 1993. It claims to have over 100,000 members. The various branches are said to "actively promote the president."[90] Of ninety members who planned to run for parliament, sixty were certified.

The Azerbaijan Democratic Proprietors' Party seems to be the only party claiming to represent business interests. It claims 27,000 members, and of thirty members who collected signature to run for parliament, nine, including party leader Mahmud Mamedov, were certified as candidates.

The Ana Vatan (Motherland) Party was founded in 1990, but officially registered in August 1992. Initially supporting the Popular Front government of Elchibey, it now supports Aliyev. It is led by Fazil Agamali. Three of eighteen members were certified to run for parliament in November 1995.

Other pro-government parties include the small Social Democratic Party (founded 1989), the Alliance for Azerbaijan (founded 1994 and registered 1995), the Azerbaijan Democratic Independence Party (split from ANIP in 1993), and the National Statehood Party (founded 1994), led by the highly suspect personality Neimat Panahov. Panahov first got a name for himself in 1988 on Freedom Square as a "worker-democrat" who was celebrated by the Russian-language Baku daily *Bakinskii rabochii*. He later engaged in extensive foreign travel (the source of his funds was unknown), waffled on various issues and later "consulted" with the Aliyev government. He is now identified as "minister of national fisheries." As for religious parties, there have not been more than four or five small Islamic parties since 1989, including the pro-Mutalibov Repentance Party, whose few leaders are now in prison. None of the parties noted here can be considered "major." All use the language of democracy, if only as the new rhetoric of politics, but not all parties' behavior is consistent with democratic principles.

Conclusion

Azerbaijan's pro-democracy forces have tried, since late Soviet times, to build a democratic civil society on fragmentary historical foundations. In their favor was a brief but clear-cut legacy of the founders of the first republic (1918–20). Operating against their efforts was a far longer legacy of Russian colonialism and Soviet totalitarianism. Continued Russian pressures, overt and covert, as well as an on-going war and rampant corruption in and out of government, have bolstered the forces militating against democracy or even domestic peace. The pro-democracy forces have also been handicapped by individual weaknesses and lack of a unified political vision of their own goals and a program to achieve them. Political action was thrust upon them before they had formulated such plans.

The movement toward democracy, slow though it had been before and during the Elchibey government, has been stopped cold by the return of Heydar Aliyev and his authoritarian rule, replete with intolerance of political opposition and criticism, both of which are still equated with disloyalty. Because of Aliyev's iron fisted rule, one might be tempted to welcome the post-Aliyev era. In the absence of an equally strong leader to succeed him in the current climate, his death or retirement would be more likely to lead to greater unrest than to the further development of civil society. In the long run, it will take extremely skilled and patient leadership to provide the sort of broadly based political education needed for a lasting democratic foundation. In the short run, Azerbaijan would benefit greatly from the enforcement of laws that currently exist in order to create a climate of legality and public confidence in the rule of law. This is a vital step in a long and arduous process, and will require courageous individuals, perhaps those not currently involved in political life, to begin to lay this foundation for civil society. The task is not more daunting than the beginning of the cultural movement of the 1970s, which was begun by a handful of men and women prepared to take risks to achieve goals in which they believed.

NOTES

1 By the early twentieth century, Azerbaijan had lost most of its *ulema*, or Islamic scholars. State restrictions forced Islamic scholars and judges into a system of training and licensing that genuine religious figures tended to shun. Records of the Ecclesiastical Boards of Transcaucasia showed that most posts were vacant. For detail, see Audrey L. Altstadt, *The Azerbaijani Turks: Power and Identity Under Russian Rule* (Stanford: Hoover Institution Press, 1992), pp. 57–62.
2 A series of newspaper essays along these lines was written by prominent journalist and activist Ahmet Agaev (later Agaoglu) for the newspaper *Baku*, 8 December 1905 and 17 September 1906. This trend is discussed in Altstadt, *The Azerbaijani Turks,* chapter 4, especially pp. 68–73.
3 In Baku, Azeris constituted over 80 percent of the eligible electors, but Muslims were prevented from holding more than one-half (and from 1892 to 1900, one-third) the seats in the City Council. In the 1908 election, they won over 50 percent of the seats and simply held them. See Altstadt, *The Azerbaijani Turks*, pp. 24–6.
4 In English, see Altstadt, *The Azerbaijani Turks* and Tadeusz Swietochowski, *Russian Azerbaijan, 1905–1920: The Shaping of National Identity in a Muslim Community* (Cambridge and New York: Cambridge University Press, 1985).
5 *Pervaia vseobshchaia perepis' naseleniia rossiisskoi imperii, 1897 g.*, volumes 61 and 63, for Baku and Elizavetpol *gubernii* (provinces), respectively, provide data on employment and nationality; these data are discussed in Altstadt, *The Azerbaijani Turks*, pp. 28–33.
6 Nasib Nasibzade, *Azärbayjan demokratik respublikası* (Baku, 1989), pp. 43–4; an English translation of some passages is in Swietochowski, *Russian Azerbaijan*, p. 129.
7 On the history of the republic and its fall, see Altstadt, *The Azerbaijani Turks*, chapters 6–7; Nasibzade, *Azärbayjan;* and Swietochowski, *Russian Azerbaijan*, chapters 6–7.

8 Zbigniew Brzezinski, *The Permanent Purge: Politics in Soviet Totalitarianism* (Cambridge: Harvard University Press, 1956), Appendix B.

9 This pattern is documented by Lowell Tillett, *The Great Friendship* (Chapel Hill: University of North Carolina Press, 1969).

10 This campaign, apparent in the contemporary Azerbaijani press, is one element of what I have called "Culture Wars," and is the topic of a monograph in progress on Soviet cultural repressions in Azerbaijan during the interwar period.

11 Harder to uncover was information about more dangerous commodities, such as drugs. Ilya Zemstov, in his exposé about the Azerbaijan communist party, *Partiia ili Mafia?* (Paris: Les Editeurs Reunis, 1976), alleges widespread use of dangerous drugs, but is not so forthcoming about their origins. Zemstov states that his sources are CP archives, but cites none in this brief book.

12 This is detailed in Altstadt, *The Azerbaijani Turks*, pp. 169–76.

13 Discussed in ibid., pp. 185–91.

14 For example, for Aliyev's views on arts and literature, see "Milli azadlıg häräkäti vä antikommunizmä garshı mübarizä mäsäläläri," *Azärbayjan kommunisti*, no. 12 (1971) (this reports Aliyev's speech in the Azeri-language organ of the Azerbaijan Communist Party Central Committee), and, citing his remarks to writers on "internationalization" in literature, Gasım Gasımzadä, "Garshılıglı ädäbi tä'sir problemi," *Azärbayjan*, no. 1 (1980).

15 For a full development of this argument, see Altstadt, *The Azerbaijani Turks*, pp. 185–91.

16 Initially such items appeared in *Odlar Yurdu*, which was published for export to Azeris in Europe, Turkey and Iran (in Cyrillic, Latin, and Arab script) and only after 1989 in papers more readily available in Baku. Readers of major Russian-language dailies such as *Bakinskii rabochii* would have been unaware of this movement.

17 Because Nasibzade, *Azärbayjan demokratik respublikası* was published in 1989, it can be assumed that the research was conducted in the previous one or more years. Nasibzade became a Popular Front member and later, under President Elchibey, was named Azerbaijan's ambassador to Iran.

18 Both the 1970 and 1979 censuses show that fewer than 10 percent of non-Azeri living, even born, in Azerbaijan knew the language of that republic.

19 The following summary is detailed in two companion articles which I wrote during 1993–94. The articles trace the use of documentary evidence by both sides and the maze of events, including warfare and negotiation efforts to 1994–95. See Altstadt, *"O Patria Mia*: National Conflict in Mountainous Karabagh," in *Ethnic Nationalism and Regional Conflict in the Former Soviet Union and Yugoslavia*, ed. W. Raymond Duncan and G. Paul Holman, Jr. (Boulder, CO: Westview Press, 1994), and "Ethnic Conflict in Nagorno-Karabagh," in *Ethnic Conflict in the Post-Soviet World*, ed. L. Drobizheva et. al. (Boulder, CO: Westview Press, 1996).

20 Stated in the Treaty of Kars (1921) between Moscow and Kemalist forces. The present Turkish Republic treats this as a precedent for its "special interest" in Nakhjivan.

21 The point is made – and Goltz's experience in Khojaly, vividly recounted – in his book, *Azerbaijan: Requiem for a Would-Be Republic* (Istanbul: Isis Press, 1994), chapter 7.

22 The manuscript, "Starye pesni i novye legendy," was provided to me several years into the conflict; I do not know whether it was ever published. Gambarov dropped the "-ov" from his name in 1993.

23 An English translation appeared in *Journal of the Institute of Muslim Minority Affairs* (London) 9, no. 2 (July 1988).

24 Mikhail Shatrov, "Prizyvaiu k razumu i vole," *Izvestiia*, 28 November 1988. Details of the demonstration itself can be found in Altstadt, *The Azerbaijani Turks*, pp. 200–4.

25 A full English-language translation appeared in *Caucasus and Central Asian Chronicle* (London) 8, no. 4 (August 1989).

26 Georgii Rozhnov, an *Ogonek* correspondent who rode one of the first trains once service was resumed, wrote about this strike and the dangers of passing through Armenian Zangezur. His article, "Doroga bez kontsa," was refused, he wrote, by Moscow newspapers, but later appeared in the Russian-language Baku newspaper *Vyshka*, 11 February 1990.

27 The following is summarized from Altstadt, *The Azerbaijani Turks*, chapter 12.

28 Estekov described his experiences once he had safely arrived in Riga: "Politicheskaia otsenka sobytii v Baku," *Turkestan* (supplement to *Obozrevatel'*), no. 1 (January–February 1990).

29 Reported by *RFE/RL Daily Report*, 15 and 16 January 1990, on the basis of Radio Moscow news broadcasts.

30 The *Shchit* report appeared in *Moskovskie novosti*, 12 August 1990, and was reprinted in *Bakinskii rabochii*, 17 August 1990.

31 *RFE/RL Daily Report*, 12 March 1990. Moscow had imposed a news blackout on information from Azerbaijan for at least a week after the January invasion.

32 The program appeared in *Bakinskii rabochii*, 10 May 1990.

33 Mamedov articulated these ideas in "Birleshdiriji khätt – milli-azadlıg khätt olmalıdır," *Aydınlıg*, 2 August 1991; a full translation is found in *Central Asian Reader*, ed. H. B. Paksoy (Armonk, NY: M. E. Sharpe, 1994), pp. 191–200.

34 "Parliamentary Elections in Azerbaijan," the CSCE report by observers, was published on 25 October 1990.

35 *Azadlıg*, 8 September 1990.

36 The story of Mutalibov's fall is told in gripping detail in Goltz, *Requiem*, chapter 8.

37 Ibid., pp. 194–5.

38 The following account has been pieced together from various native and foreign participants or eye witnesses and the Baku press. A vivid account is found in Goltz, *Requiem*.

39 Although most of this narrative was reported by *RFE/RL Daily Reports*, the details of the attack by Hamidov's troops were provided by Goltz, a witness to the events, in *Requiem*, chapter 10.

40 Goltz, *Requiem*, pp. 314–15.

41 The CSCE report was able to provide only estimates because official results were delayed until after the departure of the Commission observer; they did, however, conform to numerous "exit polls" conducted by Western diplomats and reporters. Among the concrete early returns from Baku districts: 79 percent turnout with 55.1 percent for Elchibey and 29 percent for his nearest rival, Nizami Sulei-

manov, called by reporters an "Aliyev stalking horse" who openly said he was prepared to summon Aliyev to Baku.

42 Among the poignant pieces of evidence of the lack of training of the so-called army was the very high rate of death from "friendly fire," documented by Goltz, *Requiem*, chapter 13.

43 These charges were levelled by Isa Gambar once he began to mutiny.

44 This according to Goltz, *Requiem*, pp. 411–12, one of the first to arrive in Ganje when news of the mutiny began to spread. Goltz also paints a damning picture of the inarticulate Huseinov, prompted constantly by Soviet-era stooges to give answers in his first "press conference" in Ganje.

45 Goltz, *Requiem*, documents the Turkish involvement, but detail on that aspect of this complex saga is beyond the scope of this chapter.

46 The phrase is from Goltz, *Requiem*, p. 445.

47 This pattern was noticed by the chargé d'affaires of the Turkish Embassy, Mehmet Ali Bayar, and reported by Goltz, *Requiem*, p. 476.

48 The follow summary is taken from *Report on Azerbaijan's November 1995 Parliamentary Election* (Washington, DC: Commission on Security and Cooperation in Europe, 1996), pp. 8–9.

49 The others were smaller parties – the Umid (Hope) Party, the Party of People's Democracy and the recently (in 1994) revived Communist Party. Information and description of the abortive appeals for reconsideration are in *Report on Parliamentary Elections in Azerbaijan, November 12, 1995*, by the OSCE (Organization for Security and Cooperation in Europe) Parliamentary Assembly. These delegates were from various European states; the Commission on Security and Cooperation in Europe (the Helsinki Commission) is the US-based counterpart, attached to Congress.

50 *Report on Azerbaijan's November 1995 Parliamentary Election*, pp. 11–12.

51 Ibid., p. 15.

52 *Compendium of Statements from Political Parties on the Constitutional Referendum and Parliamentary Elections of November 12, 1995: Republic of Azerbaijan*, report by the National Democratic Institute for International Affairs (December 1995), Appendix B, briefly describes and categorizes major parties.

53 *Report on Azerbaijan's November 1995 Parliamentary Election*, pp. 13–14.

54 Ibid., p. 15.

55 These are the figures given in ibid., p. 17, although there are reportedly only 100 districts.

56 Ibid., p. 17. The reports cited here were produced in December or January 1996; no reports were available, at the time of writing, on the February 1996 repeat elections.

57 I arrived in Baku late in May 1992 and remained until mid-June. The following section, therefore, includes references to personal observations and experiences.

58 Goltz, *Requiem*, p. 315.

59 The agreement had been signed in mid-May in Tashkent, Uzbekistan. Each former Soviet republic would receive weapons in exchange for assuming a portion of the USSR's collective debt.

60 A Baku television special shown in early June followed Defense Minister Rahim Gaziyev on a tour of the base in question and his confrontation with the Russian officers in command there. Even types of equipment for non-military use,

including medical supplies and sinks, were broken and scattered in the run-down buildings. Many of the aircraft could not be flown.

61 The law guaranteeing cultural autonomy was passed under the Elchibey government on September 16, 1992 and published in *Bakinskii rabochii*, 19 September 1992.

62 Shirin O. Entezari and A. Rothschild-Seidel, "Azerbaijan: Laws Concerning Privatization and Foreign Investment," *Caspian Crossroads*, no. 3 (1995), 13. This is a publication of the Washington-based US–Azerbaijan Council.

63 Private interview, November 1992.

64 Private conversation in November 1992.

65 In interviews with this writer.

66 European Bank for Reconstruction and Development, *Transition Report 1995: Economic Transition in Eastern European and the Former Soviet Union* (London: EBRD, 1995).

67 Ibid., p. 35.

68 Ibid., pp. 178–84.

69 Ibid., p. 35.

70 For details and sources, see Altstadt, *The Azerbaijani Turks*, pp. 182–3, 208.

71 There is an extensive literature on the imperial era oil industry, ranging from contemporaneous accounts to later scholarly descriptions and analyses. Among the best of the latter is John McKay, "Entrepreneurship and the Emergence of the Russian Petroleum Industry, 1813–1881," in *Research in Economic History: A Research Annual*, ed. Paul Uselding, Vol. 8 (Greenwich CT: Greenwood Press, 1983).

72 Estimate given by Terry Adams, President of the Azerbaijan International Operating Company (identified in text, below), in "Historical Beginnings: The AIOC – Azerbaijan International Operating Company," *Azerbaijan International* 3, no. 2 (Summer 1995), 36. This magazine is published with the cooperation of the Azerbaijan Embassy in the United States and funded, at least in part, by oil companies investing in Azerbaijan's oil.

73 James M. Dorsey, "Oil Pursuit Proves Slippery in Azerbaijan," *Washington Times*, 25 April 1994.

74 Ibid.

75 "Historical Beginnings: The AIOC," 33–4, 37.

76 Reported by *Monitor* 1, no. 18 (24 May 1995). This is an electronic publication of The Jamestown Foundation.

77 Goltz, *Requiem*, pp. 334–5; quotation from p. 335.

78 Interviews in refugee camps by this writer, June 1992.

79 This was true of the case of Uzbekistan, in which "knowledge of Russian" language jumped astronomically from one census to another; and of Nazif Shahrani's comments on the "who/what are you?" question in Central Asia.

80 *USIA Opinion Research Memorandum*, M–150–94 (24 June 1994) (Washington, DC: USIA Office of Research, 1994).

81 To this researcher.

82 Personal conversation with this researcher.

83 *USIA Opinion Research Memorandum*, M–153–94 (24 June 1994).

84 Ibid., p. 1.

85 Such was the topic of a newspaper series by a leading Baku political reformer, Ahmet Agaev (later Agaoglu) in 1908.
86 This researcher's field work of 1984–85.
87 A list as of fall 1991 is given in Altstadt, *The Azerbaijani Turks*, pp. 227–30.
88 These summaries are drawn in part from lists compiled by the Helsinki Commission and the National Democratic Institute.
89 Private interview, November 1992.
90 *Pre-Election Report: The November 1995 Parliamentary Elections, Republic of Azerbaijan*, compiled and published by the National Democratic Institute for International Affairs (31 October 1995), p. 14.

5   Democratization in Georgia

Darrell Slider

Of those republics that actively sought independence from the Soviet Union, Georgia has had perhaps the most difficult transition. The republic has experienced high levels of political instability and violence, ethnic conflict, and economic disruption. Despite the problems, however, there is reason to be hopeful that some progress in the direction of democratization has taken place and that the political violence and economic difficulties experienced by Georgia in the period from 1990 to 1995 will not prove to be permanent features of Georgian political life. The series of elections that have been held since 1990, as well as the interaction of deputies in parliament, has led to an increasingly well-defined structure of political parties and movements. The elections themselves have been judged by international observers as relatively free and fair, itself a major accomplishment when compared to the experience of other former Soviet republics in the Caucasus and Central Asia.

A brief overview of the recent political history of Georgia would include: the election to power of a political movement led by the Georgian nationalist dissident, Zviad Gamsakhurdia, in the October 1990 parliamentary elections and his subsequent (May 1991) election as president; the outbreak of fighting in the autonomous region (oblast) of South Ossetia resulting in the effective loss of control by Tbilisi over that region by the end of 1990; the overthrow of Gamsakhurdia at the beginning of 1992 by a military coup; the return in March 1992 of the former Georgian communist party leader and Soviet Foreign Minister Eduard Shevardnadze to serve as head of the State Council that was formed by the coup leaders; Shevardnadze's election as head of government and the election of a new parliament in October 1992; the outbreak of fighting in the autonomous republic of Abkhazia in August 1992 which led to *de facto* independence for that region from Georgian control in September 1993; a civil war in Western Georgia where supporters of Gamsakhurdia briefly seized power; the violent suppression of this rebellion in late 1993 and the death of Gamsakhurdia at the end of 1993; the assassination of Giorgi Tchanturia, the leader of one of the most popular political parties in December 1994; the attempted assassination of Eduard Shevardnadze in August 1995; and the parliamentary and presidential elections held in November 1995 under a new republic constitution adopted in August 1995.

Georgia's uneven progress in state-building and democratization occurred simultaneously with a struggle over the republic's role in the Soviet Union and – after the breakup of the USSR – the relationship between Georgia and Russia and the CIS. Gamsakhurdia followed a course designed to break almost all ties between Georgia and the Soviet Union.[1] The Soviet leadership took advantage of the ethnic divisions in Georgia to attempt to change Georgian policies – tacitly threatening to break up the country if it left the Soviet (and later Russian) orbit. Prior to the loss of Abkhazia, Shevardnadze had largely continued Gamsakhurdia's policy and refused to join the Commonwealth of Independent States (CIS). In October 1993, Shevardnadze yielded to Russian pressure for Georgia to allow Russia to play a peacekeeping role in Abkhazia and for Georgia to join the CIS. In return, Russia helped defend Georgia's borders and strategic objects and promised to guarantee the territorial integrity of the Georgian state.

This chapter will begin with an overview of the Soviet period and its implications for the democratization process, followed by a discussion of the rise of independent political movements and parties that began in the late Soviet period. Next, it will explore the pattern of violence that has marred Georgian politics, followed by a discussion of the ethnic conflicts that threaten to split Georgia into its component parts. The role of elections and the character of Georgia's political institutions will then be discussed, along with a review of the economic problems facing the country.

Background

Well before Georgia was forcibly incorporated into the USSR in 1921, its independent existence was constrained by virtue of its location on the one of the "fault lines" between Orthodox Christianity and the Islamic world. The region was frequently divided or controlled by powerful neighbors. Georgians, despite considerable regional conflicts and differentiation, developed bonds of common identity over the centuries through their ancient written language and literature (especially Shota Rustaveli's epic poem *Knight in the Panther Skin*, written around the year 1200) and the unifying force of the Georgian Orthodox Church. Georgia's rulers sought protection from the Persian and Turkish threats in 1801 by signing a pact with tsarist Russia, but eventually Georgia was incorporated into the Russian empire.

The collapse of the tsarist regime in 1917 led to the election of an independent Social Democratic (Menshevik) government in March 1918, a period that was frequently invoked in the 1990s as Georgia moved once again toward independence. The Social Democrats in the Georgian parliament chose Noe Zhordania as the republic's first president and adopted a democratic constitution. Georgia's independence was recognized by the leading European powers, and in May 1920 Lenin signed a treaty with the Georgian government. In February 1921, however, the Red Army invaded, and Georgia was incorporated into the new Soviet empire. As a legal formality a treaty was signed in May 1921 between the newly established Georgian Soviet Socialist Republic and the Russian Soviet Republic.[2] In the years that followed, Georgia was brought under control by the reestablishment of a Georgian Bolshevik party and the repression of the Social Democrats – particularly after an attempted revolt in 1924.[3]

The period of Soviet rule was marked by repeated efforts to suppress expressions of Georgian nationalism. In an attempt to submerge nationalist tendencies in the Caucasus generally, the republics of the region were placed from 1922 to 1926 under the Transcaucasus regional committee (*Zakkraikom*) of the party headed by the Georgian Bolshevik Sergo Orjonikidze. Orjonikidze's harsh treatment of Georgian communist leaders, supported by Stalin, brought a rebuke from Lenin.[4] Georgians widely held the belief that the republic suffered disproportionately under Stalin and Beria because of fears of Georgian separatism. Lavrentii Beria, another Georgian who later gained prominence as head of the Soviet secret police, was the brutal party leader in Georgia until 1938. Kandid Charkviani, Beria's replacement as Georgian party first secretary, was removed from his post in December 1951 at the same time that Mingrelians in the leadership were accused – probably falsely – of plotting for independence. (Mingrelians are a Georgian minority, to which Beria also belonged, in Western Georgia and Abkhazia.) As a result of this purge, many thousands of Georgians and Mingrelians were arrested and sent into exile.

Fear of Georgian nationalism also was apparent in post-Stalinist policies toward the republic. In March 1956, protests against Khrushchev's de-Stalinization campaign quickly turned into an expression of Georgian nationalism, and the Soviet regime responded brutally with tanks and troops on the streets of Tbilisi. It is estimated that hundreds were killed in the ensuing mêleé. In 1972, Vasily Mzhavanadze, who had been named Georgian party first secretary in September 1953 was removed at the behest of Moscow as a result of rampant corruption in the republic and Mzhavanadze's efforts to protect his cronies. Eduard Shevardnadze, the minister of the interior who had investigated much of the corruption and reported it to Moscow, was named first secretary. Shevardnadze developed a reputation as one of the most innovative republic-level leaders in the USSR. During his rule, Georgia was the site of a number of policy experiments.[5] In his public speeches Shevardnadze was much more frank in his treatment of problems facing the republic than were other regional (or national) party leaders of the time.[6] Shevardnadze held the post until Gorbachev appointed him Soviet foreign minister in 1985.

Jumber Patiashvili was selected to succeed Shevardnadze.[7] If Gorbachev anticipated that Patiashvili would continue Shevardnadze's policies and implement reforms in Georgia, he was mistaken. Most of the experiments of the Shevardnadze period atrophied under Patiashvili's leadership, and no new policy innovations were undertaken. Patiashvili set out to remove officials who had been close to Shevardnadze in several key posts, though it would have been impossible to remove the large number of Shevardnadze appointees at the middle echelon of power without doing serious damage to the party apparatus. One of Shevardnadze's closest aides – and the man rumored to have been Shevardnadze's choice to succeed him – was the party secretary for personnel matters, Suliko Khabeishvili. Patiashvili arranged for Khabeishvili to be arrested and imprisoned on corruption charges.[8]

Fragmented pluralism: the rise of new political movements and parties

Shevardnadze's approach as communist party leader toward Georgian nationalism and dissent was marked by a willingness to meet with dissident leaders, to explain and defend his (and Soviet) policies in front of demonstrators and other hostile audiences, and to seek compromise solutions. In 1978, on instruction from Moscow the draft Georgian constitution included a new provision elevating Russian to a status equal to Georgian as a state language of Georgia. University students took to the streets in protest. Shevardnadze met with the protesters and had the political skills required to rescind the disputed provision without drawing the wrath of Moscow. Despite these intimations of liberalism, however, dissidents and Georgian nationalists were closely monitored by the police throughout the Shevardnadze years. Organizers of the 1978 language protest, for example, were quietly arrested and imprisoned in the months that followed the demonstrations.

The two best-known Georgian human rights activists in the 1970s were Zviad Gamsakhurdia and Merab Kostava, boyhood friends trained in philology and musicology respectively, who were founders of the Tbilisi branch of the Helsinki group. Both had been subjected to intensive KGB monitoring, and were imprisoned on several occasions for anti-Soviet activities. Kostava, who was an extremely popular opposition leader, died in an automobile accident in October 1989. Gamsakhurdia was the son of a famous Georgian writer, Konstantin Gamsakhurdia, and his dissent was based on what he considered the erosion of traditional Georgian culture and threats to Georgian cultural landmarks.[9] Perhaps because of his prominent ancestry, when Gamsakhurdia was released from prison Shevardnadze approved his appointment to a post at a prestigious institute of literature in Tbilisi.

Shevardnadze's successor, Jumber Patiashvili, handled dissent in a way that was much more in line with the conventional behavior of Soviet regional party officials. He considered nationalist and informal groups to be dangerous "opposition" forces. A major controversy erupted over a large-scale project to build a new Transcaucasian railroad to connect Orjonikidze and Tbilisi. The railroad was planned to parallel the Georgian Military Highway, crossing some of the most beautiful parts of the republic and threatening both the ecology and historic landmarks along the way.[10] Patiashvili championed the project, and in a televised speech he called opponents of the project "enemies of the people" – a phrase used in the 1930s to label the targets of Stalin's terror. Patiashvili created obstacles to the creation of a Georgian Popular Front, forcing progressive and opposition leaders to organize underground and adopt confrontational strategies that only confirmed Patiashvili's opinion of their intentions.

The 1989 elections to the newly constituted USSR Congress of People's Deputies did little to stimulate political movements, nor did they push forward a group of reformist deputies who could take advantage of the political reforms in Moscow to establish a political reputation in Georgia. Unlike the elections in many urban areas of the European USSR, the March 1989 elections in Georgia were highly controlled by communist party officials and thus were far from democratic. Attempts to run effective opposition candidates were largely blocked at the nomination stage. As in the prereform past, the elections were stage-managed to produce results set by the republic communist party leadership. The officially sponsored candidates, including Patiashvili himself, ran unopposed in forty-three of seventy-five races.[11]

There were only a few exceptions to the prevailing pattern, but they were later to prove significant in that they foreshadowed the rise of independent candidates and ad hoc political movements organized around electoral campaigns. Genuine competition occurred only where there was active public pressure – including demonstrations – which forced the regime to pit their favored candidates against popular, non-party figures. All three competitive races were in Tbilisi, and the campaigns were initially organized by scientists, primarily physicists.[12] Several later joined together to form a new organization that later became a political party, Democratic Choice for Georgia (DCG, DASi in Georgian). The expertise acquired by DCG on issues connected with electoral procedures was widely acknowledged by virtually all political forces in Georgia, and it played a leading role in drafting the electoral laws used for the 1990, 1991, and 1992 elections.

Opposition political movements began to flourish in Georgia in 1989 and 1990, particularly in the aftermath of the early morning events of April 9, 1989, when Soviet troops were used to break up a peaceful demonstrators in front of the government building. The origins of the order to send in troops has never been explained fully, but the result was that twenty Georgians, mostly women and children, were killed in the attack.[13] The military authorities and the central press attempted to blame the demonstrators themselves, and opposition leaders were arrested. It would be difficult to exaggerate the impact of these events – made worse by the subsequent attempted cover-up by Soviet authorities – on Georgian politics. Public opinion was inflamed, and what was afterwards referred to as the "April tragedy" fundamentally radicalized political life in the republic. The authorities in Moscow at first tried to assuage public opinion by several steps. In the immediate aftermath of the events the Politburo sent Shevardnadze, who had not had a major role in Georgian affairs since he moved to Moscow in 1985, to Georgia to try to restore calm. He engineered the removal of Patiashvili as well as Zurab Chkheidze, the prime minister. Named as Patiashvili's successor was the newly named head of the Georgian KGB, Givi Gumbaridze, widely rumored to be a distant relative of Shevardnadze.

These steps did little to restore public confidence, and opposition groups had overwhelming support for a confrontational, separatist agenda. Many competing groups emerged in the course of 1989 and 1990. Partly as a result of the conspiratorial nature of opposition activity prior to 1989, opposition groups tended to be small, tightly knit units organized around prominent individuals. Soon their number exceeded 100. In this atmosphere of renewed nationalist fervor, the greatest authority was accorded to prominent dissidents from the past, and no one had better credentials than Zviad Gamsakhurdia. Gamsakhurdia headed the Helsinki Union, the successor to the Helsinki group from the 1970s, along with the Society of St. Ilia the Righteous. These later became the two most important components of the bloc of parties known as the Round Table, created in April 1990. Other groups that joined in the Round Table/Free Georgia coalition included a group that split from the Popular Front – the Popular Front/Radical Union – and the Union of Georgian Traditionalists, a party that split from the Monarchist party.

The range of programatic differences of the various political movements extended from the Monarchists, who sought the restoration of the Georgian royal family now residing in Spain, to a Georgian Green party, to a group that called itself the "Stalin" party.[14] The Rustaveli Society, led by Akaki Bakradze, was a broad-based social and cultural organization that also registered as a political party. The Social Democratic Party laid claim to the legacy of the party that led Georgia in the independence period from 1918–21. By the time the election campaign was underway, virtually all parties, including the Communist Party, agreed on the need for independence; they differed mainly in the pace of the proposed separation and in the concept of what was meant by independence.

The Popular Front, formed in June 1989, was a very different structure from the popular fronts that emerged in the Baltic states, Moldova, Belarus, and Ukraine. The Georgian Popular Front was neither very popular nor was it a front representing a range of political movements. Led by the mercurial Nodar Natadze, a philosopher and linguist, the front began as an attempt to forge alliances among opposition movements on the Baltic model. However, personal ambitions and ideological differences could not be bridged, and no major political movements were willing to submerge themselves within an umbrella organization.

The opposition was able to come together long enough to force the regime to cancel the elections to the republic Supreme Soviet that were supposed to take place in March 1990. Five days prior to the elections the Supreme Soviet bowed to pressure and rescheduled the elections until the fall. The election decision was the result of intense negotiations between Communist Party first secretary Givi Gumbaridze and opposition leaders.

Two of the best-known radical groups, the National Democratic Party of Georgia led by Gia Tchanturia and the Party for the National Independence of Georgia headed by Irakli Tsereteli, continued to oppose all "official" institutions including any manifestation of a Supreme Soviet. In early 1990 they urged the selection of a completely new representative body, the National Congress, and to boycott the elections. The justification for this decision was that to participate under existing conditions would be inherently unfair and would only serve to legitimize a continuation of what they described as the "colonial status" of Georgia within the Soviet system. Most other political groups, however, including more moderate political organizations such as the Rustaveli Society and the Popular Front as well as Gamsakhurdia's organizations, did not participate in the National Congress elections and concentrated instead on gaining control of the Supreme Soviet (see below). The elections, with a turnout that was probably below the minimum set by the organizers, created a body that was dominated by Tsereteli and Tchanturia.

The nationalist political opposition to the communist regime and Soviet institutions often relied on nonconventional methods to confront the authorities. Political strikes in key industries, often personally instigated by Gamsakhurdia, put pressure on the Georgian leadership that forced them to make concessions on many issues. The opposition also made use of unauthorized mass demonstrations, often in the main squares or thoroughfares of Tbilisi, sometimes accompanied by hunger strikes and vigils by the leaders of various movements.

After Gamsakhurdia's election, the political opposition continued its war of words with the new leader, with each side accusing the other of KGB ties and betraying true Georgian interests. The National Congress refused to recognize the legitimacy of the elections its component parties had boycotted, and they applied many of same tactics – street demonstrations and rallies, hunger strikes, etc., that they had used against Soviet rule. The leader of the National Democratic Party, Gia Tchanturia, was arrested in the latter stages of Gamsakhurdia's rule and imprisoned, accused of seeking help from Moscow to overthrow the government.

Meanwhile, there were significant changes in the Georgian Communist Party which affected its role. The now humbled party resumed its suspended congress in December 1990, and immediately removed Gumbaridze from the top post. A new central committee and bureau were chosen, and Avtandil Margiani, who had only five months earlier been chosen party leader of the Gardabani raion, was elected first secretary. The party finally took the step of breaking with Moscow, agreeing to adopt its own platform and rules. Gamsakhurdia had earlier insisted on this step as a prerequisite for the continued legal operation of the party in Georgia. Despite these changes, Gamsakhurdia's visceral hatred of the communist party eventually led him to ban the party and deprive its deputies of their seats in the aftermath of the August 1991 coup attempt in Moscow. In fact, the communist party had already largely collapsed and was unable to make the shift from ruling to opposition party.

After police used force to break up an opposition demonstration in September 1991, several of Gamsakhurdia's top supporters in the Round Table, distanced themselves by joining the parliamentary opposition. These included the Merab Kostava Society, led by Vazha Adamia, and a group of parliamentarians led by Tedo Paatashvili that organized a new party, "Charter–91." These groups, along with another former component of the Round Table coalition, the Union of Georgian Traditionalists (a monarchist party headed by the speaker of the Supreme Soviet under Gamsakhurdia, Akaki Asatiani), became well-known political parties in the post-Gamsakhurdia environment that often embraced nationalist positions but were willing to work within the new framework.

Once Gamsakhurdia had been driven from power, his remaining supporters (often referred to as "Zviadists") became the most vocal opponents of the new regime, which they considered illegal and illegitimate. Their organizations and leaders were openly suppressed by the new leadership, sometimes brutally. In this context, any participation in the 1992 elections was out of the question. Several groups of Gamsakhurdia loyalists did participate, however, in the 1995 elections. (see below)

The loss of Abkhazia in 1994 and the renewal of close ties with Russia led to the formation of a more or less stable, radical opposition to Shevardnadze and his government. The parties that formed the radical opposition had little in common other than maximalist demands. The National Independence Party, led by Irakli Tsereteli, again shifted into the camp of radical opposition to Shevardnadze after his decision to enter the CIS. The group organized numerous street demonstrations against the regime, including some in alliance with supporters of Gamsakhurdia who were formerly their bitter enemies. A party that formerly was a part of the Round Table coalition, the Merab Kostava Society (led by Vazha Adamia) also joined the radical opposition.

Various groups that tried to present themselves as the successors to the Communist Party emerged after the 1992 elections. They differed from groups that used this label in other republics in their open allegiance to Stalin, a position that appealed especially to the older generation of Georgians. In September 1994, several groups including the Communist Workers' Party, the Union of Communists, and the Stalin Society merged to form the United Communist Party. It was the only political group in Georgia calling for the restoration of the Soviet Union.[15] There was also a separate Communist Party and a Stalin Party among the left opposition.[16]

In June 1994, three liberal reformist parties with representatives in parliament decided to merge into a new opposition group called the United Republican Party. It included the Republicans (Vakhtang Dzabiradze), Charter–91 (Tedo Paatashvili), and the Popular Front (Nodar Natadze).[17] The party worked for limitations on Shevardnadze's powers and complained about the lack of genuine economic reform. Another moderate opposition group that in the past had largely supported Shevardnadze's policies was the Union of Georgian Traditionalists. The party, which also had a monarchist agenda, was led by the speaker of the Gamsakhurdia-era Supreme Soviet, Akaki Asatiani.

Shevardnadze abandoned his attempt to remain above partisan politics in August 1993 with the creation of a new political organization, the Union of Citizens of Georgia. Shevardnadze became the chairman of the party in November, while the secretary general and effective leader of the party was Zurab Zhvania, founder of the Georgian Green Party. The party, while not officially registered as a faction in the parliament, had over sixty deputies and was the largest voting bloc. Made up of the more reformist supporters of Shevardnadze as well as leading communist-era intellectuals and cultural figures, the Union held its first congress in March 1994. No party other than the Greens, however, was willing to give up its independent existence to join the movement. In public opinion polls, the party immediately became the most popular in Georgia.

The development of other elements of civil society, such as trade unions, business organizations, have proceeded more slowly than the organization of political parties, and little is known about their possible contribution to opportunities for citizen participation in politics.

Political violence

Beginning in 1990, political violence escalated in Georgia to a level not seen in most other post-Soviet states. Much that characterizes this aspect of Georgian political life is, for understandable reasons, unknown. A series of still unexplained bombings and other attacks on candidates, their homes, and party offices provided a justification for an increasingly dangerous development in Georgian politics: leading opposition groups including Gamsakhurdia's Round Table, the National Democratic Party, and the National Independence Party and other movements created armed formations of "bodyguards" or security guards to defend themselves.

One possible explanation for the level of political violence lies in the role that clans and criminal mafias have played in Georgia dating back to the Soviet period. The rapid political change that engulfed Georgia beginning in 1990 threatened a loss of political/economic power for these organizations which were interconnected with political leaders and administrators at various levels. As a result, some of these groups attempted to retain influence in local and national politics through money, intimidation, and ultimately violence. This led to a general escalation of the levels of violence as groups under attack sought the support of other groups to defend themselves, through financial or quasi-military backing.

One armed formation, the Mkhedrioni (which means "horsemen" in Georgian), entered the scene in 1990 as a political force under the leadership of Jaba Ioseliani. The Mkhedrioni became one of the largest armed groups with a membership of from 3,000 to 5,000 men. Ioseliani, a former art historian who had spent time in prison for theft, allied himself with various political movements and leaders over time, but it is clear that the organization and its members survived on such activities as drug smuggling, robberies, offering "protection" to businesses, and using roadblocks manned by armed men to collect tribute from drivers. One clue to possible links between the Mkhedrioni and Soviet-era structures was the reported role of Guram Mgeladze in its formation. Mgeladze, formerly chairman of the Georgian agricultural ministry, Gosagroprom, was widely viewed in Georgia as one of the leaders of the informal "party-economic mafia."

Under Gamsakhurdia, efforts to root out "mafia" influence were part of the motivation behind efforts to dismantle communist and Soviet-era institutions, particularly in the KGB, military, and police. Among Gamsakhurdia's first conflicts with Gorbachev was a dispute over designating a candidate to take over the Georgian KGB. Gamsakhurdia also attempted to create a new military structure in Georgia that would be independent of Soviet control. The Soviet military draft was effectively ended on Georgian territory in 1990–91 (only 10 percent of eligible draftees responded to the fall call-up in Georgia, the lowest percentage of all the republics) and Gamsakhurdia introduced a "national guard" to be composed of men of draft age.[18] Tengiz Kitovani, a friend of Gamsakhurdia and a former sculptor with no military background, was ultimately named commander of the national guard. Gamsakhurdia undertook a number of steps against illegal armed formations attached to opposition groups, in particular the Mkhedrioni. Several raids were conducted against Mkhedrioni bases, and eventually Ioseliani was arrested and held without trial in a cell at the Georgian KGB headquarters.

The violent struggle between contending groups was brought into the open during the ouster of Gamsakhurdia at the end of 1991. Various "business circles" and others poured money to one side or the other. In the ensuing period large quantities of weapons were purchased – presumably from Soviet military units stationed in Georgia – including heavy artillery, tanks, armored personnel carriers, and helicopters. Gamsakhurdia's actions at the time of the August 1991 coup in Moscow set these events in motion. Apparently fearing that a victory by Soviet hardliners would be followed by an attack on Georgia, Gamsakhurdia ordered the National Guard to turn in its weapons and subordinate itself to the interior ministry. Kitovani refused to obey the order and left Tbilisi with most of his troops for a safe encampment. The opposition to Gamsakhurdia joined in an uneasy coalition with the former prime minister Tengiz Sigua and Kitovani and became increasingly bold in their attacks on Gamsakhurdia; they demanded that he resign from the presidency and call new parliamentary elections. Under circumstances which remain in dispute by the parties involved, opposition rallies were dispersed by force in September and December 1991, and the result was ultimately open warfare. On January 6, after withering gunfire and bomb attacks virtually destroyed the parliament building and the center of Tbilisi, Gamsakhurdia and his entourage fled the country.

The Military Council that replaced Gamsakhurdia, far from renouncing violence, depended on it to strengthen its hold on power. Two of its key members, Jaba Ioseliani and Tengiz Kitovani, derived virtually all their status from their connections to military or quasi-military units. The two men, and their respective organizations, were fierce rivals – a factor that further increased the overall level of violence. Shevardnadze, once he had returned to lead the new government, also depended on the two men and their armed formations. Ioseliani had been instrumental in engineering Shevardnadze's return, and they reportedly developed a close relationship.[19] The Mkhedrioni and National Guard, along with the Tbilisi city police, acted to intimidate the opposition, and made forays to Western Georgia when Gamsakhurdia's followers staged a revolt centered in Zugdidi.[20] Shevardnadze's government was either unable or unwilling to curb these forces. Both forces served as an undisciplined and brutal substitute for the non-existent Georgian army.[21]

Repeated human rights abuses and rising crime in Georgia focused attention repeatedly on the problem of the role of armed groups in Georgian politics. A wide array of centrist parties, convened at the initiative of the Georgian Greens, in late July 1992 called for the return of the National Guard and Mkhedrioni to their barracks outside of the major cities. Even if their leaders wanted to restrain their supporters, neither group had sufficient internal discipline to carry out any significant demobilization and disarmament. It was only in 1995 that Kitovani and Ioseliani were removed as major players in Georgian politics. In the aftermath of the 1992 elections, Kitovani was forced out of his post as minister of defense – though a protege was named as his replacement, and he retained much of his power – partly, according to widespread rumors in Tbilisi, through his control over the Georgian "energy mafia." Kitovani and Sigua later joined in opposing Shevardnadze, particularly on his Abkhaz policy, and in the fall of 1994 they organized the National Liberation Front to push for a military solution in Abkhazia. In January 1995, both men were behind a quixotic attempt to retake Abkhazia: busloads of around 700 lightly armed followers departed Tbilisi in the direction of Abkhazia only to be stopped en route by Georgian police. As a result of this incident, Kitovani was arrested and imprisoned.

Jaba Ioseliani remained close to Shevardnadze until 1995. When a state of emergency was declared in Georgia in fall 1993 to cope with the Zviadist uprising in Western Georgia, Ioseliani was named to head the Provisional Committee of the State of Emergency. Ioseliani was also chosen to conduct negotiations on Abkhazia and South Ossetia. But the activities of Ioseliani's Mkhedrioni were a constant irritant. Shevardnadze repeatedly ordered the Mkhedrioni to turn in their arms, but without effect. In September 1993, in an attempt to coopt and mollify the organization, Mkhedrioni personnel were given official status as the Georgian Rescue Corps. In August 1995, a car bomb came within seconds of killing Shevardnadze, who was on his way to the ceremonial signing of the new Georgian constitution. Investigators tied the bombing to several Mkhedrioni-linked officials from the Security Ministry, and the head of the Rescue Corps was also implicated. An arrest warrant was issued for Ioseliani, and it was put into effect as soon as the

November 1995 election results made it clear that he would no longer enjoy parliamentary immunity.

The attempt on Shevardnadze was preceded by other political violence, much of which was later attributed to the Mkhedrioni and the Security Ministry. One of the most popular political leaders and head of the National Democratic Party, Giorgi Tchanturia, was assassinated in December 1994 by unknown assailants.[22] NDP deputies had, for the most part, supported Shevardnadze in parliament, though Tchanturia was openly critical of Ioseliani and the Security Ministry. In October 1993, government ministers from the NDP resigned to protest the decision to enter the CIS. Party leaders were also involved in commercial dealings, and a number of its members had received patronage posts as customs officials – an activity notorious for its opportunities to extort bribes. Thus, as with so much of the political violence in Georgia, it is nearly impossible to separate political violence from the struggle for economic power.

Ethnic conflict

According to the 1989 census, the total population of Georgia was 5.4 million. Relatively few Georgians lived outside the republic, and in 1989 Georgians made up 70.1 percent of the population. The largest ethnic minorities were Armenians (8.1 percent), followed by Russians (6.3 percent), and Azeris (5.7 percent). In eastern and southern Georgia, in areas such as Marneuli, Bolnisi and Dmanisi, Azeris made up a local majority. Armenians formed a majority of the population in Akhalkalaki and Ninotsminda (formerly Bogdanovka) in the south.[23] In the period since 1989, the most likely change in the totals would be the decline in the number of Russians living in Georgia as a result of emigration.

The most serious ethnic disputes in recent years arose from concentrated populations of other, less numerous nationalities. Three ethnic territories were given special status in the form of so-called "autonomous" administrative units within the republic: the Abkhaz Autonomous Republic, the South Ossetian Autonomous Oblast (Province), and the Ajarian Autonomous Republic. The most anomalous of these is the latter, since there is no clearly defined group of Ajars; they consider themselves ethnically Georgian in spite of the forced conversion to Islam of many of their ancestors when the region was under Turkish occupation.[24] In Abkhazia, the borders were drawn to include not only Abkhaz who were native to the region, but areas with a large native Georgian (Mingrelian) population as well. This, along with the in-migration of Georgians in the Soviet period, left the Abkhaz a small minority (17.8 percent), while Georgians comprised 45.7 percent of the population. There were small areas, such as the Gudauta district, where the

Table 5.1 *Ethnic composition of Georgia (in percentages)*

Nationality	1937	1959	1979	1989
Georgians	59.0	64.3	68.8	70.1
Armenians	11.7	11.0	9.0	8.1
Russians	8.2	10.1	7.4	6.3
Azeri	5.3	3.8	5.1	5.7
Ossetians	4.3	3.5	3.2	3.0
Greeks	2.6	1.8	1.9	1.8
Abkhaz	1.6	1.5	1.7	1.8
Others	7.3	4.0	2.9	3.2

Sources: Vestnik statistiki, no. 10 (1980), 67 and no. 7 (1990), 78; *Zaria vostoka*, March 23, 1990.

Abkhaz formed the largest ethnic group. In the South Ossetia autonomous region the total population in 1989 was less than 100,000 – and Georgians were a minority (29 percent), including in the cities of Java and in the capital city, Tskhinvali. Ossetians comprised 66.2 percent of the South Ossetian region, while an equal number of Ossetians lived in Georgia outside of South Ossetia and were mostly integrated into Georgian society.

The "autonomies" had their origins both in the 1921 constitution of independent Georgia and in Soviet policy which created in Georgia more autonomous units than in any other republic besides Russia. Georgian communist leaders, particularly Beria, sometimes had as their purpose the wiping out of the cultural identity of the Abkhaz and others. Later Soviet-era policies, however, gave considerable autonomy to Abkhazia and South Ossetia – particularly in the area of personnel policy. Many Georgians blamed Shevardnadze personally for recent manifestations of the "Abkhaz problem." In 1978, while Shevardnadze was party first secretary, Abkhaz literary and political figures launched a protest over cultural, linguistic, political and economic conditions in the region, and they demanded the right to secede from Georgia. Shevardnadze, under pressure from Moscow, diffused the crisis by a number of concessions, including an affirmative action program that increased the role of Abkhaz elites in running "their" region.[25] These actions were especially unsettling to the local Georgian population, who made up the largest ethnic group in Abkhazia, and who felt that their rights were threatened by the privileges granted to the Abkhaz.

Thus, the situation in 1990 was that the party and state apparatus as well as most of the local economy in Abkhazia and South Ossetia were firmly under the control of the Abkhaz and Ossetians, respectively. Ossetians comprised 78 percent of the state apparatus and 61 percent of the party apparatus in their region; Abkhaz made up 67 percent of government ministers and 71 percent of obkom department heads.[26]

Both Abkhazian and South Ossetian elites, acting in anticipation of an independent and more nationalistic Georgia, began to push for secession. Unlike most ethnic minorities nested within Soviet republics, local elites in both regions began to undertake these steps prior to the republic parliamentary elections. Both groups organized boycotts on their territories of the 1990 elections. Both Abkhaz and Ossetians also actively lobbied for Soviet/Russian interference – up to and including annexation of their regions to Russia. Elites in both regions sought to retain their status through expressions of fealty to Moscow and by maintaining direct institutional links through the KGB, the Komsomol, the CPSU, and, in Abkhazia, through ties with Soviet military forces stationed on their territory.

Gamsakhurdia's activities as a dissident were closely linked to issues of ethnicity and gave cause for concern by all of Georgia's ethnic minorities.[27] He frequently led protests in support of Georgians perceived to be suffering discrimination because they lived in areas (Abkhazia, South Ossetia, Marneuli) where local non-Georgian elites were dominant. The preservation and enhancement of Georgian culture – including language, the Georgian Orthodox religion, and historical monuments (many of which are located in Abkhazia and South Ossetia) – were also an important focus of his activities. Thus, his victory was naturally perceived as threat by non-Georgians living in the republic who had their own languages, religions, economic interests, and claims to land. One threat, for example, was that Georgian citizenship would be granted only to Georgians or to non-Georgians who could prove they were descendants of pre-1801 inhabitants of Georgian territory.[28] Gamsakhurdia's campaign cry of "Georgia for Georgians" was interpreted by some as heralding repression of minorities, though Gamsakhurdia claimed that the slogan was directed against Soviet domination of the republic under the communists. In fact, Gamsakhurdia frequently sought to reassure minorities that existing political-administrative arrangements would not be changed without the agreement of the groups involved, and that the cultural autonomy of all ethnic groups would be respected.[29]

Once in power, Gamsakhurdia did not push an extreme nationalist agenda – perhaps out of awareness that Georgian disunity would impede the process of gaining independence from the Soviet Union. For example, Gamsakhurdia's parliament adopted a liberal law on citizenship in July 1991 that granted it to almost all residents of the republic. The law defined citizens as persons "living permanently in the Republic of Georgia on the day this law takes effect, who are permanently employed or have a legal source of income on the territory of the Republic of Georgia, or any immovable property in the Republic of Georgia, and who declares a desire to take the citizenship of the

Republic of Georgia and sign an oath-declaration of loyalty to the Republic of Georgia."[30] Relatively few non-Georgians – only the most recent and poorest of illegal immigrants or refugees – were denied citizenship.[31] Another of Gamsakhurdia's actions that caused ethnic resentment was the appointment of Georgian prefects to serve as local administrators in non-Georgian areas. Here, too, Gamsakhurdia showed a willingness to compromise on many of these appointments, and he withdrew initial appointments in several regions that protested, including in Abkhazia and in Armenian areas. In the most important Azeri region, Marneuli, however, he appointed a Georgian and refused to bow to pressure. Disturbances in Marneuli led Gamsakhurdia to declare a state of emergency in the region in November 1991.

South Ossetia was the first region to separate de facto from Georgia, and the regime's response was harsh and unyielding. Even before Georgia became independent, a goal of the South Ossetian leadership was to secede from Georgia and unite with North Ossetia, a republic within the Russian Federation. Interethnic violence erupted in the South Ossetian Autonomous Oblast while the communists were still in power in Georgia. In August 1990 the oblast soviet adopted a declaration of sovereignty and soon thereafter designated the region a "Soviet Republic."[32] The Georgian government immediately overturned these steps as unconstitutional, a position that was supported at the time in Moscow. When Gamsakhurdia was elected, South Ossetia's leaders continued to adopt a confrontational stance. After successfully boycotting the Georgian Supreme Soviet elections, Ossetian nationalists organized elections for their own newly formed "Supreme Soviet" in December 1990. Shortly afterward, Gamsakhurdia's parliament declared the results of the balloting invalid and escalated the conflict by voting unanimously to abolish South Ossetia as an autonomous oblast.[33] When several Georgians were killed in a machine-gun attack in Tskhinvali the next day, Tbilisi attempted to impose direct rule on the region, and the result was war. After months of fighting, an agreement was brokered with the help of Russia which at least temporarily left South Ossetia outside of Georgian control.

The Abkhaz events also had their immediate origins in events that occurred before Gamsakhurdia came to power, and the denouement of Abkhaz separation from Georgia came after Gamsakhurdia was gone. In March 1989, Abkhaz leaders, including the party first secretary Boris Adleiba, signed an appeal to Moscow calling for the right to self-determination. Most of the document was an account of accumulated past grievances which the Abkhaz claimed had placed them "on the edge of ethnic catastrophe."[34] In July 1989, an attempt by Georgians to transform the Georgian sector of Abkhaz State University into an affiliate of Tbilisi University led to violence that killed eighteen and led to Adleiba's dismissal. A session of the

Abkhaz parliament was held on August 25, 1990 which proclaimed Abkhazia a "Soviet Socialist Republic" with full state power on its territory. To protect the status of the Abkhaz people, one provision guaranteed the Abkhaz "institutional representation" in the Abkhaz Supreme Soviet. The declaration also proclaimed "the right of each citizen to keep USSR citizenship."[35] The Georgian leadership (at that time still communist) ruled that procedural rules had been violated and invalidated the decisions adopted.

In talks with the newly elected Gamsakhurdia government, the Abkhaz demanded guaranteed representation of not less than 50 percent of the seats in the Abkhaz Supreme Soviet. The Abkhaz leaders objected to democratic elections because their small share (less than 18 percent) of the population would surely lead to a radical shift of power away from the Abkhaz to Georgians living in Abkhazia. Rather than force a confrontation, Gamsakhurdia agreed to a compromise on the formation of the Abkhaz parliament that gave greater representation to predominantly Abkhaz districts: of sixty-five seats, twenty-eight were reserved for the Abkhaz, twenty-six for Georgians, and eleven for other nationalities.[36] Conflicts between Georgians and Abkhaz deputies continued after the parliament was in place, however, especially over appointments to Abkhaz government posts.

It was under Shevardnadze that relations between the Abkhaz and Georgian leadership deteriorated into war and de facto separation from Georgia. A Georgian military expedition was sent to Sukhumi in August 1992, with the purpose of finding and freeing the Georgian interior minister and other hostages taken earlier in the month by supporters of Gamsakhurdia and believed to be in Abkhazia. Abkhaz authorities reacted violently to this transgression of their self-proclaimed sovereignty. After being fired upon by Abkhaz militias, Georgian forces led by Tegiz Kitovani seized the Abkhaz capital of Sukhumi and the parliament building. The Abkhaz government fled to safer ground in Gudauta. Over the next year, largely as a result of assistance to the Abkhaz from Russian military stationed in Abkhazia as well as from Chechens and other North Caucasian peoples, the badly outnumbered Abkhaz (to reiterate, they made up only 1.8 percent of the population of Georgia) succeeded in driving the Georgian military out of Abkhazia in September 1993. They were followed by a massive exodus of over 200,000 Georgian refugees, encouraged by the Abkhaz who practiced a brutal form of "ethnic cleansing" in the region. An estimated 20,000 civilians were killed. The loss of Abkhazia was a personal blow to Shevardnadze, and at great risk he had gone to Sukhumi during the last days of the fighting in an effort to inspire his forces.

Shevardnadze's accommodation with Russia brought Russian peace-keeping forces to the border between western Georgia and Abkhazia where they were supposed to prevent further attacks on the Georgian population of

Gali and begin to facilitate the return of refugees. Few Georgians had been allowed to return by the end of 1995, however.[37] Russian-sponsored negotiations between the two sides also failed to yield a solution, as Georgia insisted that Abkhazia was part of Georgia, and the Abkhaz leadership rejected any federal relationship with Georgia.

Georgian popular attitudes toward ethnic minorities living within the republic indicate a relatively uncompromising view that will make conflict resolution more difficult. Given the lack of good data from earlier periods, it is impossible to say whether this is a continuation of past attitudes that may have contributed to ethnic tension or whether the most recent conflicts have caused Georgians to become more rigid in their attitudes. In a January 1993 poll, 52 percent of urban residents disagreed with the statement "the rights of ethnic minorities are so important that the majority should be limited in what it can do."[38] Specific objects of Georgian hostility were the Abkhaz and Ossetins. Three of four Georgians had negative views of these groups, and two of three Georgians rejected a compromise that would give South Ossetia significant autonomy while remaining within Georgia. Georgian attitudes to other ethnic groups were most positive toward Jews (85 percent positive) and Russians (about two-thirds positive), while they were split more evenly on Azeris and Armenians. On the other hand, in the abstract, Georgians support minority rights. In a May 1994 poll, 62 percent of Georgians considered preservation of the rights of minorities to be an essential attribute of a democratic society.[39]

Georgia's third autonomous region, Ajaria, has been one of the most stable. Although Gamsakhurdia proposed a referendum on the continuation of special status for Ajaria, none was held. Like the leaders of Abkhazia and South Ossetia, Ajaria's elite had a clear interest in retaining autonomy, but it followed a radically different strategy. Aslan Abashidze, who emerged as the autocratic local leader under Gamsakhurdia, followed a course of cooperating with whomever was in power in Tbilisi while negotiating significant local control over the region's economy and political life.[40]

Political institutions in Georgia have not proved a suitable forum for the resolution of ethnic conflict. The leaders of Abkhazia and South Ossetia successfully organized boycotts of every Georgian election starting with the 1990 elections. The more numerous Armenian, Russian, and Azeri minorities were also underrepresented in parliament, largely because national political parties were overwhelmingly Georgian in their ethnic make-up.

Parliamentary elections

The 1990 elections

The drafting of the election law took place in June/July 1990. Two commissions, one comprising members of the Supreme Soviet and the other dominated by members of opposition groups prepared drafts for the elections to be held in October 1990. A measure of the power and stature of the opposition was that the election law adopted in August largely corresponded to the draft that the opposition had prepared. An electoral scheme was adopted that combined single-member districts and majority balloting with republic-wide proportional representation based on voting by party lists. A compromise figure of 250 deputies was adopted; half were to be elected according to each system. Nominations for the single-member districts would come mostly from political parties. As an "occupation army" Soviet military forces in Georgia were not allowed to vote in the election, a violation of the Soviet constitution that was not seriously challenged by Moscow. A provision in the election law that forbade candidates from having dual party affiliations proved to be an important factor in the decline of the communist party and in stimulating the first truly multiparty elections in Soviet history. As a result of this provision, the Georgian elections were the first in which the majority of candidates were not members of the communist party.

Twenty-nine parties initially passed through the registration process and were approved by the Central Electoral Commission. Unlike electoral commissions in other republics, which were often hand-picked by the communist party leadership, the Georgian commission comprised representatives of all political parties that were registered for the elections as well as one representative each for Abkhazia, Ajaria, South Ossetia, Tbilisi University, and the trade unions.[41] A number of parties were denied permission to register, while several others refused to take part in "Soviet" elections, preferring instead to establish an alternative parliament, the National Congress. Among the parties denied registration was the Stalin Party; many of its candidates had not resigned from the communist party by the deadline set by the electoral commission, thus bringing the number of candidates on their list below the minimum required by law (125). By election day eleven parties or blocs of parties remained. Efforts to create a unified anti-communist opposition broke down, mostly because of personal ambitions of individual party leaders and the leaders of their regional affiliates who wanted to be on the ballot.

With the exception of the communist party, the Round Table was by far the best organized, with strong affiliates in most areas in the republic and many enterprises. Zviad Gamsakhurdia was a tireless campaigner, often travelling to distant parts of Georgia in one day. He attracted huge crowds, frequently at rallies held at sports arenas. The Round Table also benefited from the reverse impact of a wild attack on Gamsakhurdia by one of the leaders of the National Congress, Irakli Tsereteli, televised on election eve just as viewers were tuning in for the final five-minute appeals by the parties participating in the election.

The communists had a number of advantages in the campaign, including access to materials or services needed to mount an effective campaign such as transport, fuel, paper, printing facilities and telephone connections to remote areas of the republic. Nevertheless, the communists seemed inert in much of the campaign. Few posters were displayed, though the party-controlled media was used to publicize communist candidates. The party leader Givi Gumbaridze made several last-minute attempts to appeal to voters, including the first ever visit by a party leader to the headquarters of the patriarch of the Georgian Orthodox Church. The communists fielded a strong slate of candidates. The party list was not made up simply of apparatchiks seeking to avoid defeat in the single member districts; the party attempted to garner support in the elections by including in its list a number of progressive intellectuals.

The most surprising outcome of the voting was that of the eleven political parties or blocs that participated in the campaign, only two got enough votes – 4 percent was the threshold – to be allocated seats from the proportional voting. These were the Round Table bloc, which received 54 percent of the vote across the republic, and the Georgian Communist Party, which succeeded in obtaining 30 percent. As a result, the Round Table received eighty-one seats from their party list compared to the Communist Party's forty-four. The Round Table was also successful in the single mandate districts; by the end of the second round it emerged from the election with well over the majority needed to control the new parliament – 155 of the 250 seats contested. Just over 16 percent of the vote was "wasted" – in other words, votes given to parties that did not meet the 4 percent barrier that were not reflected in the distribution of seats by party list.

The scale of the victory by the Round Table was unexpected, even to its own leaders. Once it became clear, negotiations with other opposition parties began immediately. The Round Table sought ways to bring candidates from other parties into the parliament, even withdrawing their candidates from run-off contests in which the second candidate was not from the communist party.[42] Most of the candidates of the Popular Front won in the second round because of Round Table withdrawals.

Table 5.2 *Parliamentary elections in Georgia, 1990*

Party/bloc	% vote	Seats won[a]	% seats
1. Round Table – Free Georgia[b]	54.0	81+ 74	62
2. Communist Party	29.6	44+ 20	26
below 4% threshold:			
3. Concord, Peace, Rebirth bloc[b]	3.4	0	0
4. Freedom bloc[b]	3.1	0	0
5. Rustaveli Society	2.3	0+ 1	< 1
6. Liberation and Economic Rebirth bloc[b]	1.5	0+ 1	< 1
7. Popular Front	1.9	0+ 12	5
8. Democratic Georgia[b]	1.7	0+ 4	2
9. Social Democratic Party	1.4	0	0
10. Popular Party	0.7	0	0
11. Union of Workers of the Land	0.4	0	0
Independent candidates	n.a.	0+ 9	4

Notes: Registered voters: 3,444,002; voter turnout: 2,406,742 (69.88%). [a]The number of seats won from the party list voting is given first, and then the number of seats from the single-member districts. [b]Coalition members: *Roundtable-Free Georgia bloc* – Helsinki Union, Saint Ilia the Righteous Society, Merab Kostava Society, Union of Georgian Traditionalists, Popular Front–Radical Union, National-Christian Party, National-Liberal Union; *Concord, Peace, Rebirth bloc* – Union for National Concord and Rebirth, Peace and Freedom (Afghans); *Freedom bloc* – Republican-Federal Party, Democratic Choice for Georgia (DASI), Liberal-Democratic National Party, Party of Georgian "Greens," Association for National Concord, Christian-Democratic Union; *Liberation and Economic Rebirth bloc* – Constitutional-Democratic Party, Progressive-Democratic Party, Labor Party; *Democratic Georgia bloc* – Ilia Chavchavadze Society, Republican Party, Union of Free Democrats, Ivan Javakhishvili Society, Archil Jorjadze Society, Democratic Popular Front, Georgian Demographic Society.

Sources: *Zaria vostoka*, November 3, 1990, November 9, 1990, and November 14, 1992.

Support for the Round Table and Communist Party was not uniform across the republic. The Round Table won large majorities in large and medium-sized cities. Gamsakhurdia won his own race in a Tbilisi district with over 70 percent of the vote. In the proportional voting by party list, the Round Table won by a landslide in most Tbilisi districts. Communists ran strongest in the southern part of the republic, particularly in Ajaria and areas with large Armenian and Azeri populations. The Round Table and Gamsakhurdia caused apprehension among non-Georgians, and the traditional communist power structure was still in place – particularly in rural areas. Communist candidates won in all the rural districts in the Ajarian Autonomous Republic, including the isolated border district where party leader Gumbaridze ran. The communists also ran strongly in districts bordering

Armenian and Azerbaijan, and in several rural districts around Gori. One of the few urban areas won by the communists was Gagra, where there was a large non-Georgian population. After the first round of voting was completed and it became clear that the communist party would no longer be the ruling party, its support declined still further. Communist candidates won only three seats in second-round voting for single-member districts, even though they had candidates in over forty races.[43]

The 1992 elections

The lack of legitimacy was a problem recognized by the post-Gamsakhurdia leadership, and in particular the two leaders not linked directly to the military forces who ousted Gamsakhurdia – Shevardnadze and Tengiz Sigua. Almost immediately after the new government was constituted, work began on drafting a new law on elections. The lack of effective political control over many regions led the leadership to abandon the idea of quick elections, and in May it was announced that the elections would take place only in October.

In the period immediately after the seizure of power the new leadership's greatest fear was that Gamsakhurdia might return to power – if not by force, then through new elections. As a result, in March 1992 the State Council adopted an electoral system, the single transferable vote, that would virtually guarantee representation by small parties and make it difficult for a party list headed by one prominent figure to take the lion's share of seats.[44] No minimum threshold was adopted for the 1992 elections, in order to permit the presence of as many parties as possible.

A major question was whether Gamsakhurdia's supporters, and even Gamsakhurdia himself, would be permitted to participate in the elections through the Round Table or in some other form. Shevardnadze ruled out Gamsakhurdia's return when he indicated in an interview with *Der Spiegel* that "everyone who has not committed a crime against the people may run."[45] Gamsakhurdia was officially accused of stealing over 40 million rubles from the republic's budget and it was reported that another 4 billion rubles that had been given to various organizations, cooperatives, and joint ventures could not be accounted for. Gamsakhurdia was also accused of taking hostages and employing torture during the events of December/January. Gamsakhurdia's supporters, claiming harassment and rejecting the legitimacy of new elections, for the most part boycotted the elections.

Another question that arose was whether the Georgian Communist Party, forcibly disbanded by Gamsakhurdia in the aftermath of the failed August coup in Moscow, would be allowed to regroup (its parliamentary deputies were also deprived of their seats). Under the Military Council, the deputy justice minister indicated that the sanctions against the CP would remain in effect for one full year – thus upholding Gamsakhurdia's actions and the Law on Political Associations passed by his parliament.[46]

The registration of political parties, which had been suspended by Gamsakhurdia in 1991, resumed and by mid-1992 over 40 parties had been registered. Among the newest of these parties was the Democratic Union, a group comprised mostly of former communists and officials. The party was headed by one of the recent leaders of the Georgian Communist Party, Avtandil Margiani. The Democratic Union claimed a broad mass following and set up affiliates in most regions of the country. The Democratic Union and other parties tried to claim Shevardnadze as their own, but at the time he refused to associate himself with any political party or movement, preferring to maintain his status as an independent. Shevardnadze's obvious popularity led ten parties to meet at the beginning of August to discuss joining together in a large "Democratic Bloc" that would have been headed by Shevardnadze and Sigua. Disputes about which parties would get how many places on the ballot effectively ended the idea of a broad coalition, however.[47]

In a move that shocked the reformist parties in the State Council, Shevardnadze initially decided to join the "Peace Bloc," a coalition dominated by the Democratic Union. Later, the Peace Bloc would use this temporary connection with Shevardnadze to argue that it was, in essence, the "Shevardnadze Party." Other parties represented in the State Council, worried about their electoral chances without Shevardnadze on their candidate list, acted to reverse Shevardnadze's decision and voted to make one last change in the election law. A new elected post was created explicitly for Shevardnadze, that of chairman of the parliament. The post was established in an amendment to the law on elections, and it was specified that the chairman could not belong to any political party. The law required that 5,000 signatures be gathered to nominate any candidate for this post and that, to win, a candidate had to receive at least one-third of the votes cast. No other candidate chose to challenge Shevardnadze for the post, and he won easily.

In debates over the 1992 election law it was clear that the parties represented in the State Council wanted to create a system that would provide the best chance for their parties to win seats in the new parliament. As the date of the elections approached, fears about the return of Gamsakhurdia abated, and many parties in the State Council began to push for a revision in the election law that would simplify the process and give parties greater control over the results. After long debates and a succession of draft laws, the State Council approved the new law on August 1.[48] They dropped the single-transferable vote system and returned to a system closer to that used in October 1990: a combination of single-member districts and proportional voting by party lists. There were several major differences, however. In order to give parties with regional strengths a chance at gaining representation, the

Table 5.3 *Parliamentary elections in Georgia, 1992*

Party/bloc	First place votes	% of votes	Seats won[a]	% seats
1. Peace bloc	528,328	20.38	29+6	16
2. October 11 bloc	277,496	10.71	18+1	9
3. National Democratic Party	211,938	8.18	12+2	6
4. Unity bloc	190,844	7.36	14+1	7
5. Democratic Party	162,014	6.25	10+0	4
6. Union of Traditionalists	127,923	4.94	7+1	4
7. Greens	113,028	4.36	11+0	5
8. Charter 91	111,148	4.29	9+1	4
9. Chavchavadze Society	69,306	2.67	7+0	3
10. Merab Kostava Society	65,381	2.52	5+2	3
11. National Independent Party	62,198	2.40	4+0	2
12. Socialist Workers' Party	54,364	2.10	4+0	2
13. Union of National Agreement	49,595	1.91	4+1	2
14. Social Democratic Party	23,819	0.92	2+0	1
15. People's Friendship & Justice Party	23,489	0.91	2+0	1
16. Union of Social Justice	22,160	0.85	2+0	1
17. Union of God's Children	19,732	0.76	2+0	1
18. Assoc. of Mountain Peoples	19,675	0.76	1+0	<1
19. Farmers' Union	19,565	0.75	2+0	1
20. Constitutional Demo. Party	19,156	0.74	1+0	<1
21. Nat. Integrity/Mountain bloc	16,088	0.62	1+0	<1
22. Motherland's Revival	15,847	0.61	1+0	<1
23. Radical Monarchists' Union	15,814	0.61	1+0	<1
24. State/Nation Integrity Party	10,846	0.42	1+0	<1
25. Nat. Front/Radical Union	9,895	0.38	0	0
26. Demographic Society	9,495	0.37	0	0
27. Physical Labor Party	8,976	0.35	0	0
28. National Party	8,535	0.33	0	0
29. S. Khimshiashvili Society	6,721	0.26	0	0
30. Restoration of Justice Union	6,490	0.25	0	0
31. St. Ilia the Righteous Society	6,428	0.25	0	0
32. National Radical Party	5,816	0.22	0	0
33. National Legal Party	3,838	0.15	0	0
34. Christian-Liberal Party	1,683	0.06	0	0
35. United Georgia Movement	1,545	0.06	0	0
36. Association of Sworn Georglans	1,483	0.06	0	0
Independent candidates	n.a.	n.a.	0+60	26
Total elected	n.a.	n.a.	150+75	100

Notes: Registered voters: 3,466,677; voter turnout in party-list vote: 2,592,117 (74.77%). Registered voters in districts where single-member voting occurred: 2,942,987; voter turnout in single-member districts: 2,254,830 (76.62%). [a]The number of seats won from the party-list voting (determined by first-, second-, and third-place votes) is given first, then the seats from the single-member districts.
Source: Georgian Central Election Commission.

separate party lists were submitted for each of ten historical regions of Georgia. Seats were allocated according to the relative population of these regions. Unlike the 1990 elections, there was no national tally for each party, and there was no minimum threshold set for representation in parliament. Voters were allowed to chose three parties in the proportional voting, with ranked and weighted votes.[49] The total number of seats to be awarded from the party list system was 150. The second part of the election was the election of "independent" deputies from eighty-four single-member districts that corresponded to the administrative divisions of the republic.[50]

The elections took place as scheduled on October 11, 1992 in most regions of the country. Elections were postponed indefinitely in nine of the eighty-four administrative districts (in Western Georgia, Abkhazia and South Ossetia). All told, these districts represented 9.1 percent of the total number of registered voters in Georgia. Forty-seven parties registered to participate in the 1992 election, some of which joined coalitions. The Central Election Commission, in contrast to the 1990 elections, did not refuse to register any parties that submitted applications.

The Peace Bloc won the largest number of votes of any party or bloc, and obtained thirty-five seats. In addition to the Democratic Union, the bloc comprised six parties, including the Union for the Revival of Ajaria led by that region's leader Aslan Abashidze. Ultimately the coalition did not hold together as a parliamentary faction. The Democratic Union dominated the coalition and decisions made about the electoral lists. According to one of the co-chairmen of the party, the Democratic Union was responsible for filling 70 percent of the places on the party lists.[51] The second most important electoral bloc was named after the date of the elections, the "October 11 Bloc." This bloc was made up of moderate reformers who were leaders of the Republican Party, Democratic Choice for Georgia (DCG), the Georgian Popular Front, and the Christian-Democratic Union. Its members typically had academic backgrounds with few or no connections to the communist party. There was a significant generational difference between the leaders of these two blocs. The median age of leading members of the Democratic Union (those appearing in the top 100 spots on the Peace Bloc ticket) was fifty-two. Most were at the mid-career level in 1985 when Shevardnadze left for Moscow. The median age of the top fifty candidates from the October 11 Bloc, by contrast, was only thirty-seven.

Among the parties that ran alone, it was Gia Tchanturia's National Democratic Party that won the most seats – fifteen. It had one of the strongest national organizations of any party, with affiliates in many regions and strong internal party discipline. It also was the party with the youngest candidates, on average. The Democratic Party also was among the winners. It was a relatively unknown party that apparently benefited over confusion between itself and the Democratic Union (which ran under the Peace Bloc), and from the fact that it was first on the ballot. Its leaders were not well known at the time of the election. Three parties made up of former supporters of Gamsakhurdia who broke with him in the closing months of 1991 did well in the elections. Charter–91, was composed mostly of young intellectuals, engineers, economists, and entrepreneurs. The monarchist Union of Georgian Traditionalists, was headed by former chairman of the parliament, Akaki Asatiani. The All-Georgian Merab Kostava Society, headed by Vazha Adamia, was a nationalist party that had played a direct military role in the conflicts in South Ossetia and Abkhazia.

Local races in the seventy-five single-member districts did not provide for runoff elections, and it was possible for candidates to win with a very small percentage of the total votes. Among those who chose to run in local races were a number of prominent former communist officials, none of whom had been members of the State Council and none of whom had a party affiliation. The biggest surprise was the reemergence of ex-Georgian leader Jumber Patiashvili, who had disappeared in disgrace after the Soviet military intervention of April 9, 1989. At least eight other former communist officials were also elected to single-member district seats, including Zhiuli Shartava (former head of the Georgian communist party's Organizational-Party Work Department) elected with 90 percent of the vote from Rustavi (he was later brutally executed by Abkhaz forces during the storming of Sukhumi) and Teimuraz Shashiashvili (former first secretary of the Kutaisi city party committee – 81 percent from Kutaisi). All three members of the Military Council (Sigua, Kitovani, and Ioseliani) who, with the addition of Shevardnadze, had made up the presidium of the State Council, won election to the parliament as independent deputies.

The 1995 elections

Elections were held in November 1995, both for the newly resurrected post of presidency (see below) and for a new parliament. There were several significant changes in the electoral system compared to 1992. Though the number of deputies chosen by each system remained the same (150 from party list and then one of each of 85 single-member districts), the complicated system of tabulating the proportional voting by regions was replaced by a national district with each voter limited to a single choice. More significant for the final outcome was the introduction of a 5 percent threshold. The purpose, of course, was to encourage parties to form coalitions and blocs. Despite this, an even larger number of parties and blocs registered – fifty-three as opposed to thirty-five in 1992.

An encouraging development in the 1995 elections was the participation of nearly the complete spectrum of political parties and movements. On the downside, a number of movements that were doctrinally indistinguishable ran as separate entities. Also, it was apparent that the registration process set up too few barriers to gaining a place on the ballot, thus allowing groups with only a few thousand supporters to clutter the ballot. The legal requirement for a place on the party list ballot was 50,000 signatures, with no restrictions on where these signatures could be collected. There was evidently significant fraud. If, in fact, all parties that were on the ballot had legitimately collected this number of signatures, the total number would have exceed the number of voters who actually came to the polls in November. In single-member districts, 1,000 signatures were required, but in correction to the procedures used in 1992 a run-off for the top two candidates was instituted if no one received over 50 percent.

Following a pattern set by previous elections, the result of the elections was that several of the most significant political forces were now excluded from parliament. This time the exclusion came about not because of boycotts or prohibitions, but because of the fragmented nature of Georgia's emerging party system and the 5 percent barrier. As a result, at least for the seats chosen by party list, parliament represented the views of a minority of the population – less than 39 percent of the electorate voted for the three parties that surpassed the 5 percent barrier.

The party that received a plurality of votes (almost 24 percent) was Shevardnadze's Union of Georgian Citizens. While this far surpassed all other parties, this nonetheless represented only about one-third the number of votes cast for Shevardnadze in the presidential race held concurrently (see below). The party that came in second, with almost 8 percent was the National Democratic Party, the only opposition party to win seats in the party list voting. The party was led by Irina Sarishvili-Tchanturia, the widow of the party's founder, Gia Tchanturia, who was assassinated in late 1994. The last party to exceed the 5 percent barrier was the All Georgian Revival Union (winning almost 7 percent), a conservative bloc dominated by the Ajarian leader Aslan Abashidze.

Among those political movements that contested the elections but were left largely unrepresented in parliament were: (1) communist parties, the combined support for which (the United Communists, the Stalin Communist Party, and the Communist Party of Georgia) was just under 9 percent; (2) supporters of the late Zviad Gamsakhurdia who together gained over 5 percent and who were returning to legal politics for the first time since the coup that ousted him (these groups included "21st Century/Konstantin Gamsakhurdia/United Georgia" which received over 4 percent of the vote, and "Way of Zviad/Voice of the Nation");

Table 5.4 *Parliamentary elections in Georgia, 1995*

Party/bloc	Votes	% vote	Seats won[a]		% seats
1. Union of Georgian Citizens	504,586	23.71	90+	21	48
2. National-Democratic Party	169,218	7.97	31+	5	16
3. All Georgian Revival Union	145,626	6.84	25+	7	14
below 5% threshold:					
4. Bloc "United Communist Party of Georgia and Social Democrats"	95,506	4.49		0	0
5. Union of Georgian Traditionalists	89,752	4.22	0+	2	<1
6. Bloc "21st Century/Konstantin Gamsakhurdia Society/United Georgia"	88,405	4.15		0	0
7. Socialist Party	80,747	3.79	0+	3	1
8. Bloc "Union of Georgian Reformers/National Agreement"	61,424	2.89	0+	1	<1
9. Merab Kostava Society	49,829	2.34		0	0
10. Stalin Communist Party	46,174	2.17		0	0
11. Political Union "Tanadgoma"	45,747	2.15	0+	3	1
12. Abkhazia – My Home	44,191	2.08		0	0
13. Communist Party of Georgia	44,117	2.07	0+	1	<1
14. Party of Peace & Freedom (Afghans)	43,017	2.02		0	0
15. National-Independence Party of Georgia	39,788	1.87		0	0
16. Democratic Party	37,643	1.77		0	0
17. United Republican Party	35,051	1.65	0+	1	<1
18. Bloc "For Life"	32,534	1.53		0	0
19. Bloc "Progress"	29,189	1.37	0+	4	2
20. Bloc "Way of Zviad"/Voice of the Nation	25,213	1.18		0	0
21. Social Justice Union of Georgia	22,190	1.04		0	0
22. Union of Women's Protection	20,384	0.96		0	0
23. State Legal Unity	19,675	0.92		0	0
24. Party of Social Protection of Citizens	15,898	0.75		0	0
25. Ilia Chavchavadze Society	15,510	0.73		0	0
26. Political Movement "Future of Georgia"	15,316	0.72		0	0
27. New Georgia	14,030	0.66		0	0
28. Union of God's Children	13,661	0.64		0	0
29. Union "Georgian Women for Elections"	12,865	0.60		0	0
30. Organization "Lemi"	8,722	0.41		0	0
31. Bloc "Christian Democrats/ European Choice"	8,607	0.40		0	0

Table 5.4 (cont.)   *Parliamentary elections in Georgia, 1995*

Party/bloc	Votes	% vote	Seats won[a]	% seats
32. Motherland Party	8,561	0.40	0	0
33. Party of Liberty	8,188	0.38	0	0
34. Agrarian Union	7,420	0.35	0	0
35. Family Revival Union	7,141	0.34	0	0
36. Liberal-Conservative Party	7,123	0.33	0	0
37. Organization "Trade Unions for Elections"	6,969	0.33	0	0
38. Bloc "Economic Revival/ 'Yellows'"	6,564	0.31	0	0
39. Peoples' Friendship and Justice	6,412	0.30	0	0
40. Agrarian Party	6,095	0.29	0	0
41. National Integrity & Social Equality Party	5,999	0.28	0	0
42. Christian-Democratic Party	5,854	0.28	0	0
43. Organization "Mamuli"	5,729	0.27	0	0
44. Progressive Party	5,673	0.27	0	0
45. League of Economic & Social Progress/Bourgeois-Democratic Party	5,611	0.26	0	0
46. Liberal-Democratic National Party	5,515	0.26	0	0
47. All Georgian Clans' Union	4,791	0.23	0	0
48. League of Intellectuals	4,746	0.22	0	0
49. National "Democratic Choice for Georgia"	4,523	0.21	0	0
50. Movement "Motherland, Language, Faith"	4,339	0.20	0	0
51. Society "Elections"	3,825	0.18	0	0
52. State/Nation Integrity Party	3,807	0.18	0	0
53. Conservative (Monarchist) Party	3,743	0.18	0	0
Independent candidates	n.a.	n.a.	0+ 38	16
Total elected	n.a.	n.a.	146+ 87	100

Notes: Registered voters: 3,121,075; voter turnout: 2,127,946 (68.18%). [a]Number of seats from party-list voting is given first, and then seats from single-member districts.
Source: Georgian Central Election Commission.

(3) moderate oppositionists such as those who united under the former speaker of Gamsakhurdia's parliament Akaki Asatiani in the Union of Georgian Traditionalists (which won over 4 percent of the vote), as well as the liberal party made up of some of the most outspoken young reformers in the previous parliament, and the United Republicans (who received under 2 percent, a major reversal from the share won by the October 11 Bloc and

Charter–91 in the 1992 elections); 4) several of the most vocal nationalist parties and their leaders, including Irakli Tsereteli's National Independence Party (less than 2 percent) and the Merab Kostava Society (under 3 percent).

Georgia's political institutions

In the process of creating new state structures, Georgia has shifted from a brief period of a predominately parliamentary system after the 1990 elections to a presidential system. Opposition political forces have been weak or nearly non-existent in all of Georgia's parliaments beginning with the 1990 parliament. The lack of an effective opposition in the parliament and the links between the parliamentary majority and the leader (both Gamsakhurdia after 1990 and Shevardnadze after 1992 and especially after the 1995 elections), led to the creation of an unusually strong executive. The government, formally approved by the parliament, in fact represented persons who were usually hand-picked by the chief executive.

The new Supreme Soviet met on November 14, 1990 and quickly approved Zviad Gamsakhurdia as its chairman. He ran unopposed and was elected by a vote of 232 to 5. Communists elected to the parliament met and decided not to act as an opposition fraction, but instead voted with the Round Table on almost every issue. Many of the deputies who had been elected on the communist list were often public figures (including intellectuals and members of the cultural elite) who had no real loyalty to the party as such or careerists whose interest in the party depended on its being in power. As a result, votes in the newly elected Supreme Soviet were nearly always unanimous, or close to it. Gamsakhurdia's personal influence over the parliament was enhanced by the fact that most of the Round Table deputies had no background in politics and were elected solely because they were associated with Gamsakhurdia. The result was a majority that was easily manipulated by Gamsakhurdia.

Prior to the elections, Gamsakhurdia's opponents accused him of seeking to replace one dictatorship with another. Gamsakhurdia's personality was in part the source of this hostility: he was intolerant of those who disagreed with him and had a tendency to see conspiracies behind any setbacks. Gamsakhurdia, for instance, was quick to label opponents as "KGB agents." The low level of political debate in Georgia was characterized by many such charges and countercharges, including similar ones directed by opposition leaders such as Tchanturia and Tsereteli against Gamsakhurdia. The leaders of the opposition National Congress accused Gamsakhurdia of himself being a KGB collaborator who secretly intended to prolong Soviet rule in Georgia.

Despite this, Gamsakhurdia's early appointments gave hope that he was willing to open a dialogue with opposition forces. While most of the people chosen to head standing committees of the Supreme Soviet and key government ministries were from the various parties making up the Round Table coalition, there was also an important role for representatives of other parties, including communist deputies. In spite of his strong anti-communist beliefs, Gamsakhurdia did not undertake a purge of communists but rather expressed a willingness to work with those who supported his goals for Georgia. The head of the parliamentary commission for overseeing industry, transportation, construction, energy, and communications was a leading reform communist and former first deputy chairman of Gosplan, Bakur Gulua.[52] The important Commission on Legislation and Observing Legality to a great extent replicated the informal parliamentary commission that drafted the law on elections, and it included three Round Table and three communist deputies.[53]

Gamsakhurdia's most significant appointment after the 1990 election was that of a new prime minister. Rather than choosing an ally, Gamsakhurdia picked an outsider, Tengiz Sigua, who was one of the leaders of the Rustaveli Society and director of the Georgian Academy of Science's Institute for Metallurgy. Sigua had distinguished himself as an effective and impartial administrator as deputy chairman of the Central Election Commission in the period before and after the elections. His selection as prime minister was widely supported by the other parties that participated in the election.

Early in his rule, and following the lead of Gorbachev at the national level, Gamsakhurdia sought enhanced powers through the creation of a republic presidency. The new office gave Gamsakhurdia the right to veto parliamentary decisions, and to declare martial law or presidential rule.[54] In a contrast with Gorbachev, whose popularity was waning by 1991, Gamsakhurdia chose to legitimize his new status through an election. In what was the first competitive presidential election in a Soviet republic, held in May 1991, Gamsakhurdia won an overwhelming victory.[55] The effect of this victory, however, was to make Gamsakhurdia less open to compromise with his opponents and reluctant to consult even with his allies.

Gamsakhurdia often remarked that he modelled his rule on that of French president Charles DeGaulle. One institution taken directly from the French experience was the prefecture. In January 1991, Gamsakhurdia dissolved all local soviets and replaced them with a system of powerless assemblies (*sakrebulebi* in Georgian). Real power at the local level was in the hands of prefects appointed by Gamsakhurdia himself, many of whom moved into the offices of the former raikom party first secretary and operated in a similar fashion. In this way, Gamsakhurdia was able to exercise personal control over local officials, though in some regions he was forced to accept candidates from among the local elites. Gamsakhurdia's policies and personnel decisions became increasingly erratic in the months that followed

Table 5.5 *Presidential elections in Georgia, 1991*

Candidate	Votes	% vote
Zviad Gamsakhurdia	2,565,362	86.41
Valerian Advadze	240,243	8.09
Jemal Mikeladze	51,717	1.74
Nodar Natadze	36,266	1.22
Irakli Shengelaia	26,886	0.91
Tamaz Kvachantiradze	8,553	0.29

Notes: Registered voters: 3,604,810; voter turnout: 2,978,247 (82.62%).
Source: *Svobodnaia Gruziia*, July 2, 1991.

the May 1991 presidential elections, while his attitude toward the opposition became more strident. The dilemma of finding appropriate personnel to help in the transition was common to all former Soviet republics. In Georgia under Gamsakhurdia, however, there was the additional factor of an extreme anticommunist prejudice that led Gamsakhurdia to reject most potential nominees for top posts because of past links to the communist system. Gamsakhurdia valued loyalty more than competence, but frequently his new appointments proved to be an embarrassment. A number of scandals and inappropriate appointments alienated allies who deserted or distanced themselves from Gamsakhurdia. Intense conflicts between Gamsakhurdia and his prime minister over control over appointments and government policy led Tegiz Sigua to resign in August 1991.

After Gamsakhurdia was ousted, political power was in the hands of an uneasy coalition of the former prime minister Sigua, the National Guard chief Kitovani, and the Mkhedrioni leader Ioseliani. After overthrowing the constitutionally elected president, they desperately needed to take steps to increase their legitimacy. It is unlikely that this fragile coalition would have held together had Eduard Shevardnadze not agreed to return to Georgia. He arrived on March 7, 1992, ostensibly to create a new Foundation for Georgian Revival and Democracy. Three days later, Shevardnadze met with the newly formed State Council and agreed to serve as chairman of its presidium along with the three leaders of the Military Council. All four were given the power of veto over any State Council decision.[56]

Public opinion polls conducted in February 1992 (in Tbilisi) and April 1992 (in various regions of Georgia) showed increasing support for the new government. In February, 56 percent supported (and 36 percent opposed) the idea of Shevardnadze's return; by April, 72 percent supported (while only 16

Table 5.6 *Election of the Chairman of Parliament in Georgia, 1992*

Candidate	Votes	% vote
Eduard Shevardnadze	2,472,345	96.01

Notes: Registered voters: 3,471,866; voter turnout: 2,575,197 (74.17%).
Source: Georgian Central Election Commission

percent opposed) his new role. When asked in April to choose between the new State Council and Gamsakhurdia, 55 percent supported the state council while Gamsakhurdia was supported by 14 percent; approximately 24 percent supported no one. Similarly, when asked to name which political leaders they supported, 71 percent named Shevardnadze, while only 11 percent supported Gamsakhurdia.[57]

Initially the State Council was a kind of pseudo-parliament that consisted of parties that had opposed Gamsakhurdia along with representatives of several non-Georgian nationalities and the Georgian intelligentsia. The statute that created the council gave it the right to admit new members by a two-thirds vote, and by May 1992 the State Council included representatives of over thirty parties and twenty social movements.[58] There was considerable continuity between the State Council and the parliament elected in October 1992: fifty-four members of the State Council out of a total membership of ninety-two (including the three members of the presidium besides Shevardnadze) were elected to parliament. The lack of dominant coalitions and the large number of parties resulted in a parliament that was deeply fragmented. No party or bloc of parties could approach a majority of votes on their own, and the level of absenteeism among deputies often meant that the body lacked a quorum. This left the process of forging a working majority to Shevardnadze, who at least at the time of the elections, was in a good position to take advantage of his overwhelming electoral mandate to this end. In the first sessions of the new parliament in early November, Shevardnadze became the de facto head of both legislative and executive power and was given the new title "head of government."

Even with the relatively fractious parliament elected in 1992, Shevardnadze was able to prevail on issues that were crucial to his rule (though sometimes this entailed threatening to resign if he did not get his way). There was a large group of deputies, including most of those elected in the Peace Bloc (though the organization itself did not survive after the elections), that consistently supported Shevardnadze. In the immediate aftermath of the 1992 elections, virtually no group was prepared to label itself as the "opposition" to the popular Shevardnadze.

While initially Shevardnadze tried to maintain continuity and appointed Tengiz Sigua as prime minister, Shevardnadze gradually consolidated his own power base with his own appointments. Sigua resigned in August 1993 after parliament refused to pass the budget he recommended and in the face of criticism of his economic policy. Shevardnadze chose as his replacement Otar Patsatsia, a little-known administrator from western Georgia. Patsatsia was no reformer; for example, he proposed an extremely conservative notion of "privatization" that would allow the state to retain control of 65 percent of industrial output.[59] Beneath the prime minister, and supervising the work of ministries, were five to six deputy prime ministers. For these posts, Shevardnadze often turned to former communist officials of his own generation with whom he had worked in the 1970s–early 1980s and who had experience in administering regions or branches of the economy.

Shevardnadze won the 1995 presidential election handily in the first round, with over 74 percent of the vote. This time Shevardnadze was opposed by five candidates, including three leaders of various communist factions. His leading opponent, Jumber Patiashvili, Georgia's communist party leader from 1985 to 1989, received about 19 percent.

The parliament elected in November 1995, almost to the same degree as Gamsakhurdia's 1990 parliament, was overwhelmingly composed of deputies loyal to the president. The number of seats won by Shevardnadze's Union of Citizens of Georgia (111) gave it close to a majority in the new parliament, and the addition of other pro-Shevardnadze legislators easily gave him effective control over its decisions. Zurab Zhvania, a close associate of Shevardnadze and head of the Georgian Greens, was elected speaker of the new parliament. Given that the post of president was already enhanced in the new Georgian constitution, Shevardnadze enjoyed a combination of democratic legitimacy and dominance over political institutions that was unmatched in any of the other former Soviet republics.

The Georgian mass media frequently came into conflict with political authorities, and part of the struggle for power was reflected in a fight for control over the media. In 1989 and 1990 a number of Georgian newspapers were founded by various other parties and social movements, while the communists retained control over a substantial publishing base. After the elections, Gamsakhurdia made sustained efforts to gain control over the media, though with only partial success. The communist party was stripped of most of its media holdings and publishing houses, and Gamsakhurdia loyalists replaced the editorial staff of several leading newspapers that were now officially subordinate to the parliament. Many who worked in the Georgian press were opponents of Gamsakhurdia, and there was an intense

Table 5.7 *Presidential elections in Georgia, 1995*

Candidate	Votes	% vote
Eduard Shevardnadze	1,589,909	74.32
Jumber Patiashvili	414,303	19.37
Akaki Bakradze	31,350	1.47
Panteleimon Giorgadze	10,697	0.50
Kartlos Garibashvili	10,023	0.47
Roin Liparteliani	7,948	0.37

Notes: Registered voters: 3,106,557; voter turnout: 2,139,369 (68.87%).
Source: Georgian Central Election Commission.

struggle for control of television in the fall of 1991. After Shevardnadze's return, newspapers and television were largely supportive of the new political order. Several pro-Gamsakhurdia publications were periodically closed, and others "voluntarily" suspended after repeated harassment of its editors, staff, and their families.

Economic context

Georgia's transition has occurred against a backdrop of worsening economic conditions – a massive decline in output, shortages of fuel and electricity, unemployment, hyperinflation, and one of the lowest reported per capita incomes in the former Soviet republics (see table 5.8). In 1994, for example, Georgia experienced the largest drop in industrial production and the highest average retail price increases of all former Soviet republics.[60]

Under Soviet rule, Georgia, along with the Baltic republics of Estonia and Latvia, was one of the richest republics measured in terms of per capita consumption and real income. Inaccurate statistics make absolute comparisons with other newly independent states difficult, but the relative decline in the economic well-being of Georgia in the post-Soviet period is almost certainly greater than that experienced by any other former Soviet republic. At the same time, the relatively high rural population in Georgia (over 44 percent in 1989, as shown in table 5.9) undoubtedly distorts the actual impact of these economic changes on living standards, since much private food production is missed in the official statistics. There was a direct connection between the success of separatist movements in Abkhazia and South Ossetia and the economic crisis that faced Georgia. Major transportation and communication links with Russia were severed for long periods as a result of the conflicts in these two regions. Another ethnic conflict outside of Georgia,

Table 5.8 *Indicators of economic trends in Georgia since 1989*

	1989	1990	1991	1992	1993	1994	1995[a]
GDP	-4.8	-12.4	-13.8	-40.3	-39	-35	-5
Industrial output	-6.9	-29.9	-24.4	-43.3	-21	-40	n.a.
Rate of inflation	n.a.	3.3	79	887	3,126	18,922	160
Rate of unemployment	n.a.	n.a.	n.a.	5.4	8.4	n.a.	n.a.
GNP per capita	n.a.	n.a.	n.a.	n.a.	n.a.	1,160	n.a.
% Workforce in private activity[b]	20.5	24.5	24.9	30.7	34.3	36.3	n.a.
% GDP from private sector[b]	17.6	28.1	27.3	49.0	56.9	60.0	n.a.

Notes: GDP – % change over previous year; industrial output – % change over previous year; rate of inflation – % change in end-year retail/consumer prices; rate of unemployment, annual average; GNP per capita – in US dollars at PPP exchange rates. [a]Estimate. [b]Including cooperatives.

Sources: European Bank for Reconstruction and Development, *Transition Report 1995: Economic Transition in Eastern Europe and the Former Soviet Union, 1995* (London: EBRD, 1995); European Bank for Reconstruction and Development, *Transition Report Update, April 1996: Assessing Progress in Economies in Transition* (London: EBRD, 1996).

between Azerbaijan and Armenia, spilled over into Georgia in the form of sabotage of the pipelines carrying Azeri oil to Georgia and the transportation links providing supplies to Armenia. Political unrest combined with ethnic conflict was used as a justification for not proceeding to implement economic reforms, though the basic outline of necessary market reforms had long been accepted in principle.

The level of commitment to the development of market institutions was not great, either by Zviad Gamsakhurdia or Eduard Shevardnadze. Gamsakhurdia knew little about economics and depended on advisors who also had little economic expertise. In several of his writings and interviews, Gamsakhurdia expressed hostility toward capitalism, and he considered the values of a capitalist society alien to Georgia.[61] Shevardnadze, even though he had sponsored reforms in Georgia under communism that tacitly rejected the command economy in favor of market principles and decentralization, nonetheless gave mixed signals on the role of the state in regulating economic activity. The natural inclination of the former communist officials chosen by Shevardnadze for top economic posts was to resist radical economic reforms and to push for a return to centralized economic management. Particularly influential among Shevardnadze's deputy prime ministers was Avtandil Margiani, a former Communist Party leader who represented the interests of

Table 5.9 *Demographic trends in Georgia since the 1950s*

	1950s	1970s	1980s
Percentage of population	(1959)	(1979)	(1989)
Rural	57.6	49.0	44.6
Urban	42.4	51.0	55.4
Average annual rates of			(1980–90)
population growth (%)	n.a.	n.a.	0.87
Age distribution (%)		(1971)	(1990)
15–24	n.a.	18.1	15.4
25–49	n.a.	32.7	33.4
50–59	n.a.	20.6	12.0
Over 60	n.a.	12.5	14.4
Levels of education (%)	(1959)[a]	(1979)[a]	(1989)[b]
Primary (4–8 years)	n.a.	n.a.	n.a.
Secondary	31.5	63.8	70.2
Postsecondary	3.8	13.6	17.5

Notes: [a]Indicates attainment of completed education at each level (among persons over 15 years of age). [b]Data are for persons over 25 years of age and include completed or partial education at each level.
Sources: *Zaria vostoka*, 23 March 1990; *Gruzinskaia SSR: Kultura* (Tbilisi, 1971).

the heads of state enterprises at the top levels of government. At the same time, Shevardnadze often gave lip service to the need for reform, and appointed one or two advocates of economic reform. A pattern developed of reform proponents resigning in protest when their policies were subverted by the other ministers or deputy premiers and the National Bank. In the politically charged area of privatization, unresolved conflicts over the division of state property paralyzed the work of the privatization ministry until at least late 1994. A decree introducing a system for privatization through vouchers was issued only in March 1995.[62]

The result of the unwillingness of the Gamsakhurdia and Shevardnadze governments to push through reforms was a devastating economic free-fall. Georgia suffered hyperinflation worse than, and sustained longer than, in any other former Soviet republic. The Georgian "coupon," designed to serve as a temporary currency until conditions would permit the introduction of a new monetary unit, became virtually worthless. By April 1994, the coupon was trading for over one million to the dollar, and it was hardly accepted anywhere in Georgia. Part of the reason is the soft-money policies of the central bank, which frequently yielded to lobbying (and bribery) to extend credits.[63] International Monetary Fund and World Bank-recommended stabilization reforms began to be introduced only in September 1994.[64] With the assistance of the IMF, Georgia introduced a new currency, the lari, in October 1995.

Official statistics showing a high percentage of output and employment in the private sector are misleading for several reasons. With the decline in industrial output, the statistics are influenced by a higher relative share of agricultural output. Even in the Soviet period, Georgia had the highest officially reported level of private agriculture among Soviet republics. In 1982, for example, 46 percent of gross agricultural output came from private plots (compared with 24 percent in Russia), and 55 percent of meat (28 percent in Russia).[65] Secondly, as in Russia, much industrial privatization does not represent a real change in effective ownership and has not resulted in changes in enterprise behavior.

Conclusion

Georgia, like other former Soviet republics, has had since 1989 a series of elections that reflected and subsequently shaped the political landscape of the republic. Taken in isolation, these elections have been free and fair. The broader political context, however, has been marred by a pattern of mutual intolerance and ethnic and political violence that have erupted in open warfare on occasion. The official military and police, both under Gamsakhurdia and Shevardnadze, often played a greater role in exacerbating violence than in curtailing it.

The process of state building and democratization has been complicated by the fact that it is occurring at the same time as a national liberation struggle against the Soviet leadership and post-Soviet Russian interference. Both Soviet and Russian collusion with separatist leaders in South Ossetia and Abkhazia created substantial problems for the Georgian leadership and increased the popularity of extreme nationalist positions. After the Abkhaz victory, however, Russian policy has been more supportive of Shevardnadze and of the need to guarantee Georgia's territorial integrity – particularly after the experience of Chechnya, the leaders of which were key allies of the Abkhaz.

Other types of international influence on the process of Georgian state building have been minor. Georgians abroad represent a very small diaspora. The successor generations to those Georgians who emigrated to the West at the time of the 1921 incorporation of Georgia into the Soviet empire have had little impact on contemporary events. The only semi-diaspora is made up of Georgian Jews who emigrated to Israel in the 1970s and 1980s. Many have retained ties to the republic, and have played some role in expanding foreign trade.

Despite the considerable political/ethnic strife and the economic chaos that accompanied it, Georgia has made some genuine strides toward normalization. In 1995, the economy began recovering with international help. At the same time, political stabilization is enhanced by the overwhelming popular mandate give Eduard Shevardnadze. Much depends on how wisely Shevardnadze uses this mandate to deal with the supremely difficult problems of ethnic conflict resolution and economic reform. Shevardnadze has thus far proven to be a stabilizing factor in Georgian politics; in his absence one could surmise that the process of democratization would have faced insurmountable obstacles and that a total institutional collapse of the country might well have occurred. His international visibility and reputation has also help smoothed the way for Georgia's entry into the international community.

One of the factors contributing to instability in Georgia was the exclusion or self-exclusion of major political forces from the political process starting with the 1990 Supreme Soviet elections. The return to relative political stability in Georgia in 1995 attracted the participation of virtually the entire spectrum of forces. This new inclusiveness represents a foundation on which democratic institutions might be consolidated. The results of the elections, however, as a consequence of the 5 percent barrier, threatened to undermine these fragile achievements. Future stability may depend on the ability of the regime to give a role to political groups that have been deprived of a voice in parliament, but who are well-versed in destabilizing extraparliamentary methods from the recent past – unauthorized street demonstrations, hunger strikes, violence, and the politics of confrontation.

NOTES

1 See Darrell Slider, "The Politics of Georgia's Independence," *Problems of Communism* 40, no. 6 (November–December 1991), 63–79.
2 For Western accounts of the history of modern Georgia, see David Marshall Lang, *A Modern History of Soviet Georgia* (New York: Grove Press, 1962) and Ronald Grigor Suny, *The Making of the Georgian Nation* (Bloomington and Stanford: Indiana University Press and Hoover Institution Press, 1988).
3 Stephen Jones, "The Establishment of Soviet Power in Transcaucasia: The Case of Georgia, 1921–1928," *Soviet Studies* 40, no. 4 (October 1988), 616–39. Jones notes that the Mensheviks were strongest in western Georgia, particularly in Guria, and the revolt was briefly successful there.
4 See the documents published in *Izvestiia TsK KPSS*, no. 9 (September 1990), 147–64. Lenin's policy toward Georgia is treated in some detail in Moshe Lewin, *Lenin's Last Struggle* (New York: Monthly Review Press, 1968).

5 See Darrell Slider, "Regional Aspects of Policy Innovation in the Soviet Union," in *Politics and the Soviet System: Essays in Honour of Frederick C. Barghoorn*, ed. Thomas F. Remington (London: Macmillan Press, 1989), pp. 139–69.

6 For more on Shevardnadze and his policies in Georgia, see Elizabeth Fuller, "A Portrait of Eduard Shevardnadze," *Radio Liberty Research*, no. 219 (3 July 1985).

7 Patiashvili had previously served as central committee secretary for agriculture at a time when Gorbachev held the same position in Moscow. The two men undoubtedly had many close contacts independent of Shevardnadze, and that was perhaps the chief reason Patiashvili was selected as first secretary.

8 Khabeishvili was murdered in 1995, in what was considered a political assassination. He headed the charitable foundation that Shevardnadze had set up on his return to Georgia.

9 Many of Gamsakhurdia's and Kostava's protests and petitions are documented in *Arkhiv samizdata*, compiled by Radio Liberty.

10 For a discussion of events surrounding this project, see Stephen Jones, "The Caucasian Mountain Railway Project: A Victory for *Glasnost*'?" *Central Asian Survey* 8, no. 2 (1989), 47–59.

11 Election results from March 26 were published in *Zaria vostoka*, 2 April 1989.

12 See the interview with one of the leaders of these initiative groups, Revaz Shavishvili, in ibid., 11 October 1990.

13 Gorbachev claims in his memoirs that he knew nothing of the attack in advance, and that the local communist leadership along with the Soviet military were apparently guilty of acting without his or Ryzhkov's knowledge and approval. Mikhail Gorbachev, *Zhizn' i reformy* (Moscow: Novosti, 1995), pp. 514–16.

14 The range of political parties as they existed in 1992, and a description of their origins, are contained in *Parliamentary Elections in Georgia, 11 October 1992: Regulations and Political Parties*, ed. Ghia Nodia (Tbilisi, 1992).

15 *Georgian Chronicle*, nos. 9–10 (September–October 1994).

16 An interview with the head of the Communist Party, Ivane Tsiklauri, appeared in Foreign Broadcast Information Service, *Daily Report: Central Eurasia* (hereafter *FBIS-SOV*), 8 August 1995, 82–4.

17 The new faction had twenty-two members of parliament. *Georgian Chronicle*, no. 6 (June 1994).

18 The call-up figures were reported in *Izvestiia*, 8 January 1991. The resolution creating the national guard was carried in *Zaria vostoka*, 21 December 1990.

19 Ioseliani, in an interview on Russian television, indicated that he "was the initiator of this invitation," and that he had "prepared this matter for a long time," *FBIS-SOV*, 24 March 1992, pp. 77–8.

20 Until his death, Gamsakhurdia maintained that he was the legally elected president of Georgia. Gamsakhurdia had set up a government-in-exile in Chechnya, where he enjoyed the support of the Chechen leader, Jokar Dudayev.

21 On this phenomenon in postcommunist polities with special reference to Georgia, see Charles H. Fairbanks, Jr., "The Postcommunist Wars," *The Journal of Democracy* 6, no. 4 (October 1995), 18–34.

22 Tchanturia's wife, Irina Sarishvili, was wounded in the assassination but survived and became the leader of the NDP.

23 The ethnic breakdown of southern districts for 1979 and 1989 appeared in *Zaria vostoka*, 8 September 1990.

24 Another ethnic group, the Meskhetians, were a Turkish people moved en masse by Stalin to Central Asia. Many Meskhetians have tried, unsuccessfully, to return to Georgia.

25 For more detail on the issues in the Abkhazia dispute and Shevardnadze's policy, see Darrell Slider, "Crisis and Response in Soviet Nationality Policy: The Case of Abkhazia," *Central Asian Survey* 4, no. 4 (1985), 51-68.

26 The South Ossetia statistics were reported by a Georgian commission created by the republic Supreme Soviet before the 1990 elections (see *Zaria vostoka*, 14 December 1990), and the Abkhaz data for 1990 appeared in R. Miminoshvili and G. Pandzhikidze, *Pravda ob Abkhazii* (Tbilisi, 1990), p. 6.

27 A lengthy analysis by Gamsakhurdia of Georgia's ethnic problems written in 1987 appeared in the *samizdat* journal he published, *Vestnik Gruzii*, no. 3 (March 1990), 38–48.

28 Russia annexed Georgia in 1801, a date Georgian nationalists consider the beginning of a policy of giving away traditionally Georgian land to "outsiders."

29 See, for example, Gamsakhurdia's interview in *Izvestiia*, 16 November 1990.

30 The draft was published in *Gruziia spektr*, 1–7 July 1991.

31 To become a citizen in the future, however, one had to reside in Georgia for ten years, speak Georgian (and also the state language of an autonomous republic, if applicable), as well as pass a test on Georgian history and the constitution.

32 The Ossetian declaration of sovereignty was published in *Sovetskaia Osetiia*, 13 August 1990 and 22 September 1990.

33 *Zaria vostoka*, 14 December 1990.

34 A version of the appeal appeared in *Sovetskaia Abkhaziia*, 24 March 1989.

35 Ibid., 28 August 1990.

36 *Svobodnaia Gruziia*, 12 September 1991.

37 See the report by the Open Society Institute, *Forced Migration: Repatriation in Georgia* (New York: Open Society Institute, 1995).

38 Thirty-one percent agreed at least partially with this statement, while 17 percent were undecided or gave no answer. Based on a survey of 826 urban adults commissioned by the USIA Office of Research, *Opinion Research Memorandum* (12 November 1993).

39 May 1994 survey of 1,003 Georgians commissioned by the USIA Office of Research, *Opinion Research Memorandum*, 8 July 1994 and 12 August 1994.

40 During Georgia's parliamentary elections in 1992 and 1995, the most significant violations occurred in Ajaria, where the local leadership actively suppressed opposition candidates and their parties.

41 All parties registered directly by the Central Electoral Commission except the Popular Party of Georgia were represented. *Zaria vostoka*, 7 September 1990.

42 Based on the author's interviews with leaders of the Round Table and other opposition parties in early November 1990.

43 Election results from October 28 were published in *Zaria vostoka*, 9 November 1990. Results from November 11 appeared in the November 14 issue. Vote totals for the proportional voting by district appeared in the Georgian-language newspaper *Shavlego*, no. 2 (February 1991).

44 The single transferable vote system of proportional representation allows voters
    to indicate second choices among the list; a quota is set for each seat, and once
    the seat has been filled the votes exceeding the quota are transferred to the second
    choices indicated by voters for the winning candidate or party.
45 The interview was published in *Der Spiegel*, 13 April 1992, pp. 193–8.
46 *Sakartvelos respublika*, 14 February 1992, in *FBIS-SOV*, 4 March 1992, p. 81.
47 Based on an interview by the author with the film-maker Lana Gogoberidze, a
    member of the State Council and participant in the talks, in May 1992.
48 The law was published in Russian in *Svobodnaia Gruziia*, 15 August 1992.
49 The total points received by all parties were summed and divided by the number
    of seats to be awarded in the district, which yielded a quota for each seat. Any
    party which received this minimum number of points received a seat. All votes
    which did not result in a party's getting a seat were transferred to a national
    compensation pool. The compensation system ultimately was used to allocate over
    half of the total, 79 of the 150 seats.
50 This provision had been inserted at Shevardnadze's urging, in the belief that this
    would interest local voters in electing "their own" deputies and increase the
    turnout.
51 This was disclosed by Margiani during a presentation by Peace Bloc leaders to the
    National Democratic Institute election observation team in October 1992.
52 Gulua, former first secretary of the Poti city party committee, was the initiator
    of an important experiment in local self-management in the late Shevardnadze
    period. Gulua was perhaps the only person to have served in high level positions
    under the communists, Gamsakhurdia, and Shevardnadze. In early 1996 he
    became agriculture minister.
53 The composition of the commission was described by the chairman of the
    commission in *Molodezh Gruzii*, no. 47 (30 November 1990). Missing were
    representatives from the group, Democratic Elections in Georgia, which did not
    win any seats in the parliament.
54 The law was published in *Svobodnaia Gruziia*, 16 April 1991.
55 Gamsakhurdia received over 86 percent of the vote, while his closest competitor,
    the economist Valerian Advadze, received only 8 percent.
56 Report on Russian radio, 12 March 1992 in *FBIS-SOV*, 12 March 1992, p. 72.
57 The results reported above were from a poll conducted between April 16 and
    April 21, 1992, in fifteen regions of Georgia by the Institute of Demography and
    Sociological Research of the Georgian Academy of Sciences. Of 1,477 respon-
    dents, 76 percent were ethnic Georgians. The results were reported to the author
    by the deputy director of the institute, Revaz Gachechiladze.
58 Information presented here on the State Council and its operations comes largely
    from interviews conducted by the author in May 1992 with three of its members:
    Vakhtang Khmaladze, Tedo Paatashvili, and Victor Rtskhiladze.
59 *Georgian Chronicle*, nos. 2–3 (February–March 1994).
60 See the report in *Financial Times*, 6 December 1994.
61 See, for example, Gamsakhurdia's lengthy article from exile in *Nezavisimaia
    gazeta*, 21 May 1992.
62 *Kavkasioni*, 22 March 1995, translated in *FBIS-SOV*, 7 April 1995, pp. 81–3.

63 The former chairman of the Georgian Central Bank, Demur Dvalishvili, committed suicide in the course of an investigation of his activities by the state prosecutor.
64 *Georgian Chronicle*, nos. 9–10 (September–October 1994).
65 *Zaria vostoka*, 4 December 1983, and *Voprosy ekonomiki* no. 11 (November 1983), p. 53.

Central Asia

6 Democratization and the growth of political participation in Kazakstan

Martha Brill Olcott

Kazakstan is an accidental country, a nation that was carved out of a Soviet republic whose boundaries were never intended to be those of an independent state. Independence has shaped the nature of Kazakstan's politics, and not always in ways that are supportive of democratic principles. Although the home of one of the first glasnost-era popular protests, the Almaty riots of 1986, prior to independence Kazakstan did not make the same strides towards democratization that neighboring Kyrgyzstan did. While independent political groups were organized, they lacked real influence on the political process.

Partly this was a reflection of fears that multinational Kazakstan could become an ethnic tinderbox if the republic's nearly equal numbers of Kazaks and Russians were to turn on one another. Democracy was understood by many as synonymous with ethnic empowerment, and there were grounds for concern as the republic's first political groups were almost all organized along ethnic lines.

Yet another reason why those in power were eager to temper the pace of political reform was the vast potential wealth of the republic, and fear that it might elude their control. This was true during the Soviet era, when the battle was between Moscow and the republic elite as to how wealth was to be divided between the center and the periphery. It became even more true after independence, when political control brought with it the right to manage the privatization of the nation's resources.

The leadership in Kazakstan is still one which is largely derived from the former Communist Party nomenklatura, but it is an elite that has been partially transformed. New and old groups have been added to it. Economic reform has helped create a new and partially self-sufficient economic elite. Independence and the demise of the old communist party also helped create new roles for pre-Soviet institutions, the most prominent of which is the largely invisible albeit still powerful clan network. In fact, it remains the only semi-effective institution.

The existence of a large population of Russian or European decent who are automatically excluded from the network has helped to limit the scope of clan-based politics, as Kazakstan's leaders remain mindful of the fact that Kazakstan is a state that has been formed within Russia's shadow. Russia still provides Kazakstan's only real outlet to the outside world, which gives Russia a critical lever to use in relations with its new neighbor. Some of Kazakstan's key resources remain under the management of a Russian elite whose loyalty is in question.

Kazakstan's President Nursultan Nazarbaev also remains acutely aware of Russia's keen interest in the fate of ethnic Russians who live beyond its borders, and Moscow's self-proclaimed right to intervene in their protection. Thus Nazarbaev has made efforts to try to accommodate all political groups. Kazak remained the state language; however, Russian was given a formal legal status as well. Dual citizenship has not been recognized, but promises have been made of the reciprocity of citizenship. The formal borders between the two countries have become more rather than less permeable over time, as President Nazarbaev searches for a formula for integration with Russia that would leave his nation's independence intact.

Pre-Soviet roots of self-government

Many of the dilemmas that Kazakstan currently faces have their roots in Kazak history. The present-day Kazaks formed in the mid-fifteenth century when clan leaders Janibek and Girei broke away from Abul Khair, leader of the Uzbeks, to seek their own territory in the lands of Semirechie, between the Chu and Talas rivers. The first Kazak leader was Khan Kasym (1511–1523), who united the Kazak tribes into one people. Their numbers were augmented in the sixteenth century, when the Nogai Horde and Siberian Khanates broke up, and clans from each joined the Kazaks.

The Kazaks separated into three *zhus*, or Hordes: the Great Horde, which controlled Semirechie and southern Kazakstan; the Middle Horde, which had north-central Kazakstan; and the Lesser Horde, which migrated in western Kazakstan.

The political organization of these nomadic groups was primarily familial and tribal, with major decisions affecting large numbers of Kazaks taken by groups of leaders, meeting in concert for discussion and consultation. To a certain extent, this model of consultations by tribal elders has been adopted into the postcommunist political environment. In 1995, as part of the process of annulling Kazakstan's elected parliament (explained in greater detail below), President Nazarbaev convened an extra-constitutional body he called a "People's Assembly," to ratify his decisions and to extend his presidency;

a similar type of assembly, called the Halk maslahaty, which is openly based upon the pre-conquest "council of elders," is directly mandated in Turkmenistan's constitution, which Nazarbaev appears in this instance to have imitated.

In addition, in May 1993 Nazarbaev convened a meeting of neighboring presidents Karimov and Akaev, delegations from each of Kazakstan's nineteen oblasts and the two administratively independent cities of Leninsk and Almaty, and thousands of local Kazaks at a ceremony outside Shymkent, which was intended to commemorate the meeting in 1726 on that site of three local Kazak leaders, or *bis* – Tole Bi, Kazybek Bi, and Aiteke Bi – who were worried about the threat of invading Jungars, and so wished to unite the disparate Kazak tribes to mount a more effective defense.

This consultative precedent of the nomadic Kazaks in the fifteenth century through to the eighteenth has also been cited as a political model for the republic by A. Kekilbaev, the speaker of the 1994–95 parliament. Although Kekilbaev, whose candidacy as speaker was more or less rammed through parliament, is a close supporter of President Nazarbaev, he nevertheless asserted that the Kazaks have a parliamentary tradition in these councils of *bis*, which they must resurrect and defend. To Kekilbaev, it is the parliament, not the presidency, which embodies the democratization of the people, and leaders must not be permitted to forget to render account for their actions to the people whom they lead.[1]

Traditional nomadic political structures proved inadequate once Russian traders and soldiers began to appear on the northwestern edge of Kazak territory, in the seventeenth century. The Kazak khans at the time were preoccupied with the threat presented by Kalmyk invaders, of Mongol origin, who in the late sixteenth century had begun to move into Kazak territory from the east. Forced westward, in what they call their "Great Retreat" (*Aqtaban shubirindi*), the Kazaks were increasingly caught between the Kalmyks and the Russians. In 1726, Abul-khair, one of the khans of the Lesser Horde, sought Russian protection. Although his intent had been temporary help against the stronger Kalmyks, the Russians assumed permanent control of the Lesser Horde. The Russians conquered the Middle Horde by 1798, while the Great Horde managed to remain independent until the 1820s, when the expanding Kokand Khanate to the south forced the Great Horde khans to choose the protection of the Russians.

The Kazaks began to resist Russian control almost as soon as it was complete. The first mass uprising was led by Khan Kene (Kenisary Kasimov), of the Middle Horde, whose followers fought the Russians for more than a decade (1836–47). Khan Kene is now regarded as a Kazak national hero.

In 1863 Russia elaborated a new imperial policy, announced in the Gorchakov Circular, which asserted the right to annex "troublesome" areas on its borders. This led immediately to Russian conquest of the rest of Central Asia, and creation of two administrative districts, Turkestan and the Steppe district. Most of present-day Kazakstan was in the latter, while parts of the south were in the former. At this time Kazaks lost their last vestiges of rights of self-rule, becoming entirely subject peoples.

Establishment of Russian forts in the early nineteenth century had begun the destruction of the Kazak traditional economy, making nomadism more difficult. The final disruption of nomadism began in the 1890s, when large numbers of Russians were settled on the fertile lands of northern and eastern Kazakstan. Between 1906 and 1912 more than a half-million Russian farms were started as part of the Stolypin reforms, shattering what remained of the Kazak traditional way of life.

In 1917 a group of secular nationalists called the Alash Orda, or the "Horde of Alash" (named for a legendary founder of the Kazak people), attempted to set up an independent Kazak national government, but this lasted for less than two years (1918–20) before surrendering to the Bolsheviks.[2] The political model for this government was essentially democratic, with some overtones of the earlier government by council-of-elders; questions of repatriation of land seized by the tsarist government, for example, were to be adjudicated by such councils.

Although the Alash Orda government made some first steps toward organization of a civil administration, the conditions of civil war and the Red Army's subsequent conquest of Siberia and Central Asia overwhelmed the young state, the last remnants of which collapsed in summer and early fall of 1920. The Kazak Autonomous Soviet Socialist Republic was set up in October 1920, and in 1936 the territory was made a full Soviet republic.

Kazak government in the Soviet era

During the Soviet period Kazakstan saw such demographic changes as the rapid population growth in the sixties, the increase of urban population, and the drastic increase in the level of education (see table 6.1).

From 1964 until 1986 Kazakstan was led by Dinmukhamed Kunaev, an ethnic Kazak who achieved the status of full member of the Politburo (an honor shared by only one other Central Asian leader, Sharif Rashidov of Uzbekistan). Kunaev was a particularly close associate of long-time Soviet leader Leonid Brezhnev, who had first risen to prominence within the party during the Virgin Lands campaigns, when huge tracts of Kazakstan's land were being plowed under and planted to grain. Although the political system was the centralized dictatorship of the Communist Party, conditions in the

Table 6.1 *Demographic trends in Kazakstan*

	1950s	1970s	1980s
Percentage of population	(1959)	(1979)	(1989)
Rural	56.2	46.5	42.9
Urban	43.8	53.5	57.1
Average annual rate of	(1940–60)	(1960–70)	(1970–90)
population growth (%)	2.5	3.9	1.3
Age distribution (%)	(1959)	(1979)	(1989)
15–24	18.2	20.7	16.9
25–49	30.2	30.6	33.3
50–59	7.4	7.6	8.6
Over 60	7.8	8.4	9.1
Levels of education[a] (%)	(1959)	(1979)	(1989)
Primary	63.7	n.a.	n.a.
Secondary[b]	32.1	56.0	73.7
Postsecondary[c]	2.6	7.3	10.2

Notes: [a]For the population ages 10 and above. [b]Includes complete and incomplete secondary education. [c]Includes complete and incomplete postsecondary education.
Sources: US Department of Commerce, *Statistical Abstracts of the United States*; Paul S. Shoup, *The East European and Soviet Data Handbook*; UNESCO, *Statistical Yearbooks*; United Nations, *Demographic Yearbooks*; Goskomstat SSSR, *Demograficheskii ezhegodnik SSSR, 1990*; Goskomstat Kazakstana, *Kazakstan v tsifrakh, 1990*; TsSU SSSR, *Narodnoe khoziaistvo SSSR v 1961 godu*; TsSU SSSR, *Narodnoe khoziaistvo SSSR v 1989 godu*; *Narodnoe khoziaistvo SSSR, 1922-1982*; Goskomstat SSSR, *Itogi Vsesoiuznoi perepisi naseleniia 1979*; TsSU SSSR, *Itogi Vsesoiuznoi perepisi naseleniia: Kazakhstan, 1959*.

Brezhnev era permitted the flourishing of strong local patronage networks, in Kazakstan and elsewhere in the Soviet Union. Although these were far from democratic, they did permit local elites to assume considerable control of at least some parts of their local economies. After nearly a quarter century of Kunaev's rule, the republic had developed a genuine Kazak infrastructure, in which Kazaks held many of the important jobs, especially in party politics, republic government, agriculture and in the cultural networks and educational systems.

However, on December 16, 1986, the new Soviet leader Mikhail Gorbachev forced Kunaev's resignation, replacing him with Gennadi Kolbin, an ethnic Russian who had no previous ties to Kazakhstan. The announcement of Kolbin's appointment caused spontaneous street demonstrations, despite sub-zero temperatures. Alarmed Soviet authorities responded brutally, soaking the demonstrators with high-pressure water cannon and, when that failed to disperse them, using troops to attack the crowds with dogs and sharpened trench shovels. The demonstrators, many of them students, responded by rioting. Although official accounts continue to maintain that only two people died in the two days of disorders which followed, it is generally accepted that more than 200 died in the rioting or were summarily executed soon after; some accounts put casualties at more than 1,000.

In large part Kunaev was ousted because Kazakstan's economy was failing. Although it had the third largest gross domestic product in the USSR (after the RSFSR and Ukraine), labor productivity had dropped to only 88 percent, and per capita income to only 76 percent, of the national norm by 1987. Gorbachev and his reformers saw cronyism, corruption, and native incompetence to be the cause of such failings, the only cure for which was a rational rotation of cadre across the entire Soviet Union, without regard for local sentiment.

What to Gorbachev in Moscow seemed a sensible policy of cadre rotation, however, looked in Almaty like a slap in the face, a statement that Moscow no longer trusted Kazaks even to pretend to run their own affairs. To the non-Russians, including the Kazaks, Gorbachev's actions were particularly threatening because Gorbachev was the most intensely Russo-centric Soviet leader in memory, with no period of service outside of Russia proper. Indeed, there is no evidence that Gorbachev ever fully came to understand the emotive power of nationalism. The economic message which made sense to Gorbachev, that all of the parts of the USSR should contribute to the over-all health of the union economy, looked to the non-Russians, including the Kazaks, like a command that their place in the new scheme of things was to feed Moscow.

Kolbin's inability to master either Kazakstan's economy, which continued to decline, or Kazakstan's complex social and demographic make-up, compounded by Gorbachev's inability to cope with the rising tide of nationalism across the USSR, led within three years to Kolbin's being replaced by Nursultan Nazarbaev, an ethnic Kazak who since 1984 had been chairman of the republic's Council of Ministers. Although he was a strong supporter of economic reform, and had been prominent among those leading the attack on Kunaev, Nazarbaev also had an excellent idea of how much Kazakstan was supplying to Moscow's coffers, and how little the republic was receiving in return, particularly since as chairman of the Council of Ministers he was spending a third of each year traveling about the republic, studying the various industries and enterprises on site.[3]

Quickly proving himself to be a skilled politician, Nazarbaev was able to bridge the gaps between the republic's Kazaks and Russians at a time of increasing nationalism, while also managing to remain personally loyal to

Gorbachev and to his program of reform. His firm support of the major Gorbachev positions in turn helped Nazarbaev gain national and, after 1990, even international visibility. There are many reports that, had the USSR not collapsed, Gorbachev planned to name Nazarbaev to be his deputy and president of the new Union.[4]

From his appointment in 1989 until the collapse of the USSR two years later Nazarbaev supported Gorbachev strongly, but also fought hard to have his republic benefit economically from the resources which it was supplying to the center. Even though his appointment originally came through Moscow, Nazarbaev realized that successful administration required that he develop some kind of popular mandate within the republic. This was no mean feat, since Nazarbaev had to find a way to have Kazakstan become more Kazak without also alienating the republic's large Russian and European populations.

Demography as destiny

While all of the Soviet republics were multiethnic to some degree, in the late Soviet years Kazakstan had the distinction of being the sole republic in which the eponymous nationality was a minority. At the last Soviet census, taken in 1989, Kazaks constituted 39.7 percent of the population, while Russians, ethnic Slavs and other "Russian-speakers" were 50.1 percent.

It is not simply the numbers, however, which make ethnicity in Kazakstan important. In most ways Kazakstan's two major ethnic groups live in different countries. To Russians, Kazakstan is an extension of the Siberian frontier, into which Russia expanded in the eighteenth century, and which Soviet Russia developed and built up, in several waves of settlement. To the Kazaks, this numerical inferiority was the product of deliberate Russian and Soviet policies. Russian imperial policies had caused the deaths and dislocation of large numbers of Kazaks, as well as the in-migration of significant numbers of land-hungry Russian peasants. During collectivization, Stalin's policies and the famines they caused killed as many as 1.5 million Kazaks, and forced many more to emigrate to China. Large numbers of non-Kazak Soviet citizens and a great deal of Russia's industry were relocated to Kazakstan during World War II. Many more non-Kazaks came in the years 1953–65, during the so-called Virgin Lands campaign, which ploughed up huge tracts of Kazak grazing land to plant wheat and other cereal grains, and still more came in the 1960s and 1970s, as part of the further industrialization of the republic. As a consequence, the Russian population of Kazakstan is relatively newly-arrived; 38 percent of the present Russian population was born outside the republic, while the great majority of the remainder are either first- or, at most, second-generation.

Equally important is that neither the Russians nor the Kazaks are uniformly distributed within the republic. Some of this diversity is the legacy of Soviet development patterns, which sited factories, cities, and transportation networks in ways that benefited the all-union economy, rather than the individual republics. Thus, for example, there are virtually no roads or railroads which cross the republic east to west or north to south; transportation links in the north were built to run through Russia, while in the south they pass through Uzbekistan. It was not until many months after Kazakstan became independent that it even became possible to fly directly between cities in the country's extreme east and extreme west, because flight patterns were all routed with Moscow as the hub.

These patterns of development have left marked regional differences, and orientations, within Kazakstan. Communities in the northeast, for example, are inextricably linked with Russia, mining coal for electrical generating plants which are in Siberia, and from which they get their electricity. The population here is heavily Russian, closely integrated with the Siberian cities over the border; during the early days of the Russian republic those Russian cities declared the existence of a "Siberian republic," which they could do again, this time drawing in Kazakstan's Siberian cities as well.

By contrast, further west along the 3,000 mile border with Russia, the communities are more agricultural. Here the dependency is of a different sort. Kazakstan has no silos in the north, and no flour mills; all of these were built in Russia. The far west, near the Volga, is also Russian, but it is more oriented toward Moscow and central Russia. This is also the first territory which the Russians took from the Kazaks, at the end of the seventeenth century, so here is the place with the strongest claim to Russian "ownership." This is also a region where the Cossacks are particularly influential, asserting that they are a distinct ethnic group who have a right to establish their "homeland." Further south, in Mangyshlak, there is abundant oil, but no means to refine it or ship it, since both refineries and pipeline are in Russia. To complicate matters further, existing pipeline runs west, out of the republic, rather than east, to Kazakstan's industrial centers.

In the south, which is ethnically much more Kazak, development follows the same sort of pattern of dependence upon another republic, in this case Uzbekistan. Tashkent was the major hub city along the southern flank of the USSR, so that most road and rail traffic for the southern oblasts lies within Uzbekistan. The imposition of customs and currency laws has made it all but impossible, for example, to maintain the Soviet-era spaceport of Baikonur; although physically on Kazakstan's territory, the Baikonur complex was supplied out of Tashkent, which now means that not even typewriters and air-conditioners can be sent out for repair, to say nothing of more complex equipment. The same integration obtains in the southeast, where the economy of Kyrgyzstan has become heavily dependent upon that of its larger neighbor. Here too, as is true all along the eastern boundary, the proximity to China has created a very different economic and political "microclimate" than is true of the rest of Kazakstan.

Nazarbaev as leader of Kazakstan

Nazarbaev's first step in consolidation of his mandate was to have the legislature, elected in 1990, convert his position to a presidency, as was common practice across the USSR. Both as republic first secretary and then as president Nazarbaev strongly supported Gorbachev, yet at the same time fought with increasing energy to increase the real economic sovereignty of his republic. This was not to be confused with a struggle for political sovereignty; the other theme which Nazarbaev repeated endlessly through these years was his conviction that, whatever the present injustices and stupidities of the Soviet system, the economies of the Soviet republics were too tightly interwoven to permit the republics even to dream about going it alone, as independent entities.

The strength of Nazarbaev's conviction that independence would prove economic suicide for the republics in general and Kazakstan in particular showed in his continued support for Gorbachev even after the attempted coup of August 1991 for example, it was Nazarbaev who presented the hastily reworked version of a new union covenant to the hurriedly assembled USSR legislators in the days that followed the failed coup.

Being a realistic politician, Nazarbaev also spent the last three months of Soviet history increasing his control over the administrative infrastructure of the republic, generally preparing Kazakstan for a far greater degree of autonomy than it had enjoyed during most of its existence. Nationalist sentiment in the republic was strong, but Kazakstan never developed the sort of separatist parties as had grown up in the Baltics and Ukraine. Rather Nazarbaev and even more nationalist leaders all appear to have assumed that Kazakstan would gain sovereignty, but would remain part of some kind of redefined union. Following the example of presidents of other Soviet republics, Nazarbaev sought a public affirmation of his presidency, in an uncontested presidential election held December 1, 1991.

Although he has subsequently attempted to downplay his surprise at the December 8, 1991 agreement among the leaders of the three Slavic republics which ended the Soviet Union, by saying that he was offered the chance to sign that agreement but refused because he had not read the documents and had had no hand in preparing them,[5] Nazarbaev appears in fact to have been stunned by what seemed to him, and most of the rest of the world, an unthinkable turn of events.[6]

Ethnicity and the dynamics of politics

Kazakstan had begun to become politicized, especially about issues involving the republic's deeply split demography, well before the unexpected independence of December 1991 was thrust upon it. Even as he took office Nazarbaev had understood that Kazakstan had to become more explicitly the homeland of the Kazaks, but in such a way that the increased visibility of Kazak culture, language and history would not alienate the republic's large Russian and European population.

One of Nazarbaev's early and important steps in this regard was to sponsor legislation which made Kazak the state language of the republic. Passed in August 1989, the bill took effect on July 1, 1990, and provided for a graduated program for increasing Kazak language instruction in republic schools and for shifting the conduct of local and republic level government business into Kazak. Areas where the Kazaks made up under 50 percent of the population had until the end of 1994 to make this change.[7]

The Russian population, especially those who lived in northern Kazakstan, immediately began to lobby for changing the language legislation. Their agitation intensified in September and October 1990, when the language issue became fused with the debate over sovereignty for Kazakstan, which had become imperative because of Russian's own declaration of sovereignty.

Many of Kazakstan's Russians, especially those who were descendants of the earliest Russian settlers in the region, began to join an informal group, the "Organization for the Autonomy of Eastern Kazakstan," which successfully sponsored candidates for election in local and city soviets in the five northern oblasts. Another organization with a similar program was Edinstvo (Unity).

The Kazaks too began to form nationalist groups, which the Nazarbaev regime found at least as threatening, and perhaps more, as it did the Russian nationalists. The Kazak groups included Zheltoksan (December, after the Alma Ata uprising) and Azat (Freedom), whose programs were more nationalistic than Nazarbaev was prepared to tolerate.[8] From the early days of its existence Azat supported Kazakstan's independence. The party tends to criticize Nazarbaev's policies, considering them pro-Russian.

Zheltoksan was formed to seek amnesty and rehabilitation for all of the participants of the December 1986 uprising in Almaty. Later, its leader, Kozhahmetov, actively campaigned against nuclear disarmament. He argued that nuclear weapons could protect the country from the Russian and the

Chinese threat. He advocated repression of those who did not support the idea of Kazakstan's independence.[9] Zheltoksan was also responsible for organizing numerous protests, hunger strikes, and building takeovers.

The only nationalist group which has been actively suppressed, however, is Alash (named both for the legendary founder of the Kazaks and for the party of the same name which had briefly governed independent Kazakstan in 1918–20). The party supports the idea of pan-Turkism and the creation of the Great Turkestan state. It has a paramilitary structure where subordinates must never question orders from their superiors in the party hierarchy. In October 1991, Alash threatened to start a jihad and resort to terror.[10] Seven senior party leaders were arrested in December 1991, after the group stormed a mosque in Almaty, assaulted Kazakstan's chief mufti, Ratbek Nysanbaev, and announced his resignation.

By contrast, informal organizations that were supportive of regime goals, like Kazak tili, the Kazak language society, or the Nevada-Semipalatinsk Anti-Nuclear movement, enjoyed considerable support. The Nevada-Semipalatinsk movement, headed by long-time Kazakstan Communist Party central committee member and Writer's Union head Olzhas Suleimenov, was quasi-governmental in origin, and came to play a key role in the republic. Indeed, Nevada-Semipalatinsk, the major goal of which was to shut down the nuclear testing facilities in Semipalatinsk, was and remains Kazakstan's only grass-roots organization which had strong appeal across most of the republic's ethnic communities.

After the attempted coup of August 1991, when it was clear that the Communist Party was no longer a viable political entity, Nazarbaev also attempted to stimulate the formation of political parties. The first such attempt was the Socialist Party, which inherited the property and was supposed to inherit the membership of the Kazakstan Communist Party. The first president was the Kazak writer Anuar Alimzhanov, but the membership was predominantly Russian. Nevertheless, the party failed to thrive. In 1994 parliamentary elections, party members were nominated in fifty-five electoral districts. However, they won only twelve seats: eight on party lists and four in single-mandate districts.[11] By the end of 1995, only 7 percent of both Kazaks and Russians had heard about the party.[12]

Nazarbaev's next attempt to create a party was People's Congress, which was registered in October 1991. This was meant to be a loose party of enthusiasts modeled after and largely drawn from Suleimenov's Nevada-Semipalatinsk movement. Indeed, Suleimenov and his fellow Kazak poet, Mukhtar Shakhanov, were the party's first co-chairmen. PCK, as the party is called, proved popular and, very important, appealed both to Kazaks and to Russians. The party was originally strongly supportive of Nazarbaev, but Suleimenov, who has political ambitions of his own, as well as a large new fortune that was reputedly obtained by borrowing from the treasury of Nevada-Semipalatinsk to engage in metals trading, became increasingly critical of the president.

Nazarbaev's third attempt at a national party did not come until after independence; this was the Union of People's Unity for Kazakstan, or UPU, later renamed People's Unity Party, or PUP. It was registered in October 1992, initially under the leadership of Supreme Soviet deputy Serik Abdrakhmanov. He too proved to have personal political ambitions, so the chairmanship of what is now identified as the official government party has changed several times. The Union announced that it would attempt to represent the interests of every citizen of Kazakstan. However, it provided undeniable support for President Nazarbaev. The party program states that "the leader of the Union is not an administrative figure and does not carry any executive-administrative functions in the organization." At the same time, "he, as a carrier of the political strategy of the Union, is nominated as its official candidate for the Presidency." Nazarbaev, who in 1991 promised not to affiliate himself with any political party, in 1993 agreed to become PUP's leader. It is not a coincidence that the leader of the Kostanai oblast party organization insisted that "PUP's people are represented in all key ministries."[13]

When the USSR broke up, the Russians of Kazakstan, who had been part of the overwhelming majority population of the Soviet Union, now found themselves losing a demographic race for dominance with the Kazaks, while the Kazaks now found themselves not only approaching demographic dominance but also in charge of an independent political and geographic entity which bore their name. Even though it was many months, or even years before citizens of the new states came fully to appreciate what independence meant, even at the time of the break-up of the USSR, observers understood intuitively that the republic's multi-ethnicity was an inherent liability which would impair, if not make wholly impossible, the development of a viable, independent state.

To a surprising degree Kazakstan has managed to avoid the consequences of its potentially divisive ethnic diversity for nearly five years of independent existence. Although there have been periodic rumblings of threatened ethnic dissension, of possible separatist movements, and of growing Russian discontent, Kazakstan has managed to fashion and adopt two constitutions, to elect (and then dismiss) a parliament and then elect a new one, and to embark firmly, perhaps irrevocably, upon a path of economic transformation.

Even though the republic's Russians were immediately aware that independence threatened them with second-class citizenship, they did not take what might have seemed the obvious step – one taken by many Russians elsewhere in the new republics – of gravitating back to Russia. Russian emigration from Kazakstan has not been especially dramatic since independence, as it has also been partly offset by an inflow (illegal but real) of Russians from elsewhere in the former USSR, especially Central Asia. The statistics of both the Russian and the Kazakstani governments are contradictory, but they suggest that something on the order of a half-million "Russian-speakers" may have emigrated since independence, while about half that number have moved in, largely from elsewhere in Central Asia.

Since independence there has been a steady exodus of non-Kazaks from Kazakstan, as well as a government-sponsored settlement of "foreign" Kazaks, from within the CIS as well as from Mongolia and China, but demography still leaves the Kazaks a minority within the republic. Kazakstan's official projections suggested that at the beginning of 1995 Kazaks were 44.3 percent of the population, while Russians, Ukrainians, Belarusians and Germans were 45.6 percent.[14] The total population of Kazakstan has dropped by about one percent since independence, but that figure reflects increased adult and infant mortality and decreased birthrates, as well as emigration.[15]

There are a number of reasons why the Russians of Kazakstan have largely stayed in place, not least of which is the expense and difficulty of moving to Russia. Of course, one consequence of that difficulty has been that it is primarily the best and the brightest who have attempted to relocate; 46 percent of the emigrants in the first half of 1994 had higher or specialized education, while 48.5 percent were age sixteen and above.[16] In addition, a full 70.6 percent of the emigrants were from urban environments, suggesting that emigration, even if not yet a flood, is becoming a serious "brain drain."

Also important in encouraging most Russians to remain where they are is the prestige and popularity which President Nazarbaev continued to enjoy, at least through the first two years of independence. While Nazarbaev got the support of most Kazaks because of his ethnic identity, most Russians saw him as figure of prominence from the multi-ethnic Soviet past, who could be counted on to be more sympathetic to their "Russianness" than would any possible successor. Indeed, as someone of great stature during the late Gorbachev years, Nazarbaev enjoyed considerable lingering support from people of all ethnic groups who were seeking elements of continuity in a radically and rapidly changing political environment.

It is also possible to see now that Kazakstan's Russians did not immediately feel themselves to be threatened because the various effects of independence and consequent separation from Russia were slow to make themselves felt. It was not until November 1993 that Kazakstan and Russia began to use separate currencies, and not until the election of the parliament in 1994 that Russians found themselves "represented" by a body which was only 21 percent Russian, and 58 percent Kazak.

The political landscape at present

It is increasingly clear, however, that by 1995 the issue of ethnicity is becoming fully political, to a degree that is potentially destabilizing to the republic. There are a number of political groups in Kazakstan, both Kazak and Russian, which are now beginning to reject multi-ethnicity. The Kazak groups, such as Azat (Freedom), have moved close to demanding that the republic become a virtually mono-ethnic homeland for their people, on the model of neighboring Uzbekistan or Turkmenistan, while the Russian groups, such as Lad (Harmony), are demanding so great a degree of local autonomy for the areas of compact, ethnically-uniform Russian settlements in the republic's north and east, that the result would be virtual secession of the Russian-dominated areas from the Kazak ones. Some groups, such as the Cossacks of the Uralsk area, go even further, to demand outright separatism, either to join with Russia or, farther east, perhaps to link up with an eventual "Siberian republic." Reports that some of these Cossacks are undergoing training across the border in Russia, where the Cossacks have been given the right to bear arms (a right denied them in Kazakstan), further raise the spectre that some of those with separatist sentiments may be arming themselves.

By the beginning of 1995 it was also wholly clear that the Russians of Kazakstan were beginning to take seriously the decision with which they were faced, in having to declare their country of citizenship. The original deadline for that decision, March 15, 1994, had been pushed back a year because of the 1994 parliamentary elections; delay, however, had only sharpened the objections which a majority of the republic's Russians had to being forced to choose between citizenship in Russia or in Kazakstan.

Although there was a wide spectrum of objections which the Russians raised, there were essentially three issues which concerned the majority of the Russian population – what would be the nature of the future Kazakstani state, what language its inhabitants would be required to speak, and who would own most of the property within that state.

As a number of Russian and Kazak deputies to the 1994–95 parliament pointed out, Kazakstan's constitution, adopted in January 1993, was ambiguous on the question of whether or not the state is an ethnically defined entity. Although Article 1 guaranteed citizens of Kazakstan equality of rights and freedoms regardless of race, nationality, sex, language, and a number of other conditions of status, the Preamble of that same document claimed that the right to adopt a constitution springs from the "unshakeability of the Kazak statehood," and declared as its first basis that the republic is a form of statehood "self-determined by the Kazak nation."[17] The constitution, which was adopted by a popular referendum in August 1995, is similarly ambiguous, although it, too, specifically prohibits discrimination based upon ethnicity, native language, place of origin, and a number of other factors which might be considered ethnic.

To Russians, a prospect that Kazaks should enjoy any sort of political priority raised the likelihood that they would inevitably become second-class citizens, or worse, that their children would have second-class futures, because of preferences given to Kazaks.[18] Indeed, several of the Russian deputies in the 1994–95 parliament took the issue of the constitution's wording sufficiently seriously to have persuaded Nazarbaev to appoint, in mid-1994, a joint parliamentary and government commission to undertake a major rewrite of the republic's fundamental law. However, little came of the effort, at least in part because the deputy put in charge of the committee, S. Zimanov, is a Kazak "national-patriotic hawk"[19] who refused to convene the group.[20] Following the dissolution of parliament, a reworked constitution was drafted in a few months, and has been circulated for public consideration.

The other issue which this commission would have addressed was that of the national language, which both the 1993 and the 1995 constitutions stipulate will be Kazak; the 1993 constitution relegates Russian to the nebulous status of the "language of interethnic communication," while the 1995 constitution is much more specific but not much clearer, giving Russian the status of "the social language between peoples" and saying that "in government offices and in offices of local administration Russian is officially used equally with Kazak."[21] In 1990, in the context of the Russian-dominated USSR, when the law making Kazak the state language was first adopted, the issue had not seemed a serious threat to most Russians; by 1995, however, linguistic requirements began to make themselves increasingly felt for entry into universities, for job security, and even for public entertainment (as Russian television, magazines, and newspaper became harder to get. For example, the session of the Karaganda city maslihat even had to file an official complaint denouncing the termination of the ORT and RTV broadcasting in Karaganda).[22] Although the issue is one on which President Nazarbaev has shown considerable flexibility, delaying some deadlines for imposition of "Kazak-only" laws, the Russian population nevertheless finds itself increasingly on the defensive, faced either with having to learn a language which it regards as having no utility or with being cut off forever from the life of the republic.

President Nazarbaev has shown no flexibility, however, on the issue of dual citizenship, which many Russians see as an important guarantee of their future rights; ever since this issue first surfaced, in mid-1993, Nazarbaev and other senior Kazakstani officials have refused even to discuss such a possibility. However, a treaty signed by presidents Yeltsin and Nazarbaev in late January 1995 essentially obviates the problem, permitting citizens of Russia and Kazakstan to own property in either republic, to move freely between them, to sign contracts (including for military service), and, upon request, to exchange one citizenship for the other.[23]

For all the passion which dual citizenship has provoked, it is the third issue, that of economics, which has excited the most substantive objection. As is true elsewhere in the former Soviet Union, since independence Kazakstan has seen an enormous transfer of power and wealth, while also suffering a catastrophic decline in production to a 1994 GNP which by some accounts is only about half that of 1990.[24]

For approximately the first year of independence, the Soviet-era administrators and political authorities enjoyed enormous economic advantages because of their opportunities for "spontaneous privatization" (or theft). This advantage was not universal, but most administrators who had access to stocks of metals or minerals were able to use contacts in Russia and elsewhere to make substantial private fortunes selling these on the world market. This first phase of "spontaneous privatization" predominantly benefited Russians, or the Kazaks who worked closely with them, because it was they whom the Soviet system had put in power. Indeed, at independence, 43 percent of the republic's industry was entirely subordinate to ministries or other organizations in Moscow, 48 percent was under joint central and republic control, and only 6 percent was entirely under republic control.

The introduction and execution of the government's privatization scheme, however, has systematically shifted economic advantage toward the Kazaks. Kazaks control virtually the entire apparatus of republic government, meaning that they have a monopoly on the granting of export licenses and tax concessions, as well as on other important bureaucratic functions. Even more important, though, certain Kazak families have been able to use the voucher system of privatization to secure control of huge portions of the state economy.

Privatization in Kazakstan

The economic situation in Kazakstan resembles those of the other countries in transition: the collapse of industrial production, the decline in GDP, acceleration of the rates of inflation and unemployment. In 1994, GDP fell

Table 6.2 *Indicators of economic trends in Kazakstan since 1989*

	1989	1990	1991	1992	1993	1994	1995[a]
GDP	n.a.	-0.4	-13.0	-13.0	-12.0	-25.0	-8.9
Industrial output	2	-1	-1	-14	-16	-28	-8.0
Rate of inflation	n.a.	n.a.	150	2,567	2,169	1,160	140
Rate of unemployment	n.a.	n.a.	n.a.	0.5	0.6	1.6	2.4
GNP per capita	n.a.	n.a.	n.a.	n.a.	2,830	n.a.	n.a.
% Workforce in private activity	3.3	3.8	4.4	n.a.	n.a.	9.0	n.a.
% GDP from private activity	15.0	7.2	12.2	n.a.	20	20.2	n.a.

Notes: GDP – % change from previous year; industrial output – % change from previous year; rate of inflation – % change in end-year retail/consumer prices; unemployment – percent of labor force, end-year; GNP per capita in US dollars at PPP exchange rates. [a]Estimate.

Sources: European Bank for Reconstruction and Development, *Transition Report 1995: Economic Transition in Eastern Europe and the Former Soviet Union, 1995* (London: EBRD, 1995); European Bank for Reconstruction and Development, *Transition Report Update, April 1996: Assessing Progress in Economies in Transition* (London: EBRD, 1996); CIA, *The World Factbook 1995* (Washington, DC: CIA, 1996); PlanEcon, *Review and Outlook for the Former Soviet Republics* (Washington, DC: PlanEcon, 1995), pp. 129–54; *Financial Times*, November 11, 1994, p. 15; Goskomstat Rossiiskoi Federatsii, *Sotsial'no-ekonomicheskoe polozhenie Rossii, 1995*, p. 513; *Nezavisimaia gazeta*, January 26, 1996, p. 3.

25 percent while industrial production plummeted 28 percent. However, in 1995 Kazakstan made substantial progress towards economic stabilization: GDP declined 8.9 percent and industrial production declined 8 percent (see table 6.2).

The structure of the economy is changing. According to official statistics, more than 20 percent of GDP is now produced by the private sector, which employs more than 9 percent of the work force. This is largely due to the privatization program which began in April 1994. The voucher system of privatization which the Kazaks adopted was similar to the model in the Czech Republic; citizens were issued vouchers, which they could deposit in holding companies, which would then be able to buy up to 20 percent of large companies being privatized. In theory Kazakstan's citizens had a wide choice of funds, since 170 holding companies were eventually registered. In fact, however, just twenty companies were able to accumulate nearly 60 percent of the coupons, and another nineteen companies accumulated more than 20 percent, so that one-quarter of the holding companies came to control more than three-quarters of the privatization vouchers, while half the companies have less than 4 percent among them. One company, Butia-Kapital, received nearly 10 percent of the vouchers, giving it the largest single holding.[25]

While it may not be true, as it is widely rumored to be, that this company is controlled by Nazarbaev's nephew,[26] there is no doubt that the system of privatization has put most of the nation's new wealth into a small group of Kazak hands. There are also a number of complaints that the process of privatization itself is fixed, with the prices for choice properties set artificially low, and the number of bidders strictly controlled. The perception that the privatization process is rigged was further cemented in the public mind by a series of scandals in autumn 1994, which eventually ended in the fall of the Tereshchenko government, and forced former Finance Minister Urkumbaev to face charges of criminal malfeasance.

It must also be said that there is growing public hostility to the entire concept of privatization in Kazakstan, in part because of suspicions about the narrow elite which is benefiting from it, and in part because of the pauperization of huge swaths of society which are not.

Although some Russians have been able to enter the new Kazak commercial structures, they have done so only as junior partners; the great majority of the republic's Russians have felt themselves to be entirely excluded from the new wealth which is being created. The same may also be said of the republic's Kazaks, of course, but with the important difference that Russians find an ethnic explanation for their economic disenfranchisement, while the Kazaks have explanations only of clan, horde, and other "insider" connections.

The 1994 parliament – arena of discontent

An ironic consequence of the process of politicization of ethnicity, however, has been the general increase of political sophistication which the development of democracy has brought to the republic. President Nazarbaev's attempts to create a Western-style democracy with independent executive, legislative, and judicial branches, as mandated by the 1993 constitution, provided a parliamentary forum in which the various ethnic constituencies were free not only to air their own grievances and concerns but also, and more importantly, to engage in strategic coalition-building. The most striking result of this was the emergence in the 1994–95 parliament of coalitions of deputies representing diverse, even antithetical constituencies, who were able to find common ground in their opposition to governmental policies.

Like most of the rest of the new republics, Kazakstan began independence with a legislature and local authorities which had been elected in 1989–90, under Soviet rules. Local elections were held in Kazakstan for aul, rural, raion, city, and oblast councils in late 1989-early 1990. A total of 72,997 seats were contested. At the oblast level, more than half the races (53.4 percent) had registered more than one candidate; at the raion and city level just under half the districts (49.3 percent) had competitive contests. The more local races in the rural areas were conducted in a far less competitive fashion.[27] Though little was written about these elections, the available information suggests that there was a great deal of voter apathy, that nomination meetings were often poorly attended, as were the campaign appearances of the candidates themselves.[28] Voters did not use these local races to vote out political incumbents. When the first round of elections was completed, in all but 9 of the republic's raion and city soviets, the local party first secretary was chosen as council chairman.[29]

In March 1990 elections were held for a legislature in the first multiple-candidate contests to have been held since 1925. As in previous years, deputies for the Supreme Soviet of the republic were chosen for the term of five years both by direct election by the electorate according to territorial districts and by public organizations in the republic. As was true with the 1989–90 local elections, public organizations were also provided with approximately a quarter of the seats, to be chosen "competitively" by their respective memberships. There were 1,229 candidates for 270 districts (4.6 per race) and 544 candidates for 90 mandates chosen by public organizations.

Almost all of the 270 territorial district races were contested, although a handful of senior party officials were allowed to run unopposed. In just under half of the districts (131) candidates won first round victories in balloting in which 83.9 percent of the eligible electorate participated.[30] There were run-off elections held for 251 candidates in 126 districts, in which 74.7 percent of the eligible voters participated. New elections were held in thirteen districts, with 80.9 percent of those eligible participating.

Most of the defeated political incumbents seem to have lost simply because they were highly unpopular figures, not because of any sort of anti-regime protest. In general, the selection of candidates was left to local election commissions and they did not always follow democratic principles. In late January 1990, the electoral commission questioned the performance of local commissions throughout Semipalatinsk oblast, as well as in a series of raions of Kustainai, Uralsk and Chimkent oblast.[31]

In the end, the new legislature was dominated by the senior political elite of the republic, almost all of whom were elected in territorial districts.[32] The legislature was also disproportionately ethnic Kazak, 54.2 percent versus only 28.8 percent Russian, while in the 1989 Supreme Soviet Kazakhs comprised 46.7 percent and Russians 41.8 percent.[33] It was in large part a product of permitting public organizations to be directly represented in the legislature, since Kazakhs made up 49.3 percent of those elected in territorial districts and 69.3 percent of those elected by public organizations, while Russians made up 33.0 percent and 15.9 percent respectively.[34]

The Supreme Soviet was a balky and slow-moving partner for the task of economic and political reform. Although he probably did not have the legal authority to do so, Nazarbaev pressured this parliament into a "voluntary" early dissolution in December 1993, in order to allow the creation of the smaller and what the Kazak leadership hoped would be a more pliant "professional parliament" which was envisioned in the 1993 constitution.

Elections for the new parliament's 177 seats were held in March 1994, following a tightly controlled period of national campaigning (see table 6.3). Requirements that aspiring political parties be both multiethnic and pan-republic in constituency have always kept the number of official parties in Kazakstan rather low, but requirements were further tightened for this election. Campaigning was also sharply restricted, so that voters had difficulty learning the political affiliations, and often even the platforms, of the candidates. Legislative districts were gerrymandered, in the attempt to create Kazak-majority districts wherever this was remotely possible.

The list of candidates was also closely managed. Out of 900 nominated candidates more than 200 were not registered.[35] In addition to the forty deputies who were chosen directly from presidential lists, most of the candidates came from lists put together by the government. Of the deputies who were eventually elected, 70 percent had not held office before,[36] while more than 90 percent of them were senior administrators in state or partially-state organizations.[37]

As a final precaution, the actual voting, which was done by crossing off the names of the people on the ballot against whom one was voting, was so closely stage-managed that those on the scene at the time strongly hinted that European observers sent to Kazakstan by the OSCE were originally reluctant to certify that the process had been fair.

In addition to the previously discussed Lad, PCK, PUP, and the Socialist party, candidates also represented the Confederation of Trade Unions, the Peasants' Union, and a number of small parties and organizations. The Confederation of Trade Unions of the Republic of Kazakstan is a successor of the Soviet-type trade unions. In January 1995, it organized a series of protests all over Kazakstan, involving more than 2 million people. Their demands were social: elimination of wage and pension arrears, slowing down the decline in industrial production and the growth of unemployment, inflation adjustment of wages, and so forth. In March 1995, in his speech to the Confederation's Second Congress, Nazarbaev cautioned the organization against becoming too political and stressed the hopelessness of the standoff

Table 6.3 *Party composition of the Supreme Soviet of Kazakstan following the general election of 1994*

Party/organization	Seats	% of Seats
Union of People's Unity of Kazakstan	33	18.6
Confederation of Trade Unions of the Republic of Kazakstan	11	6.2
People's Congress of Kazakstan	9	5.1
Socialist Party of Kazakstan	8	4.5
Peasants' Union of the Republic of Kazakstan	4	2.2
Social Movement Harmony (Lad)	4	2.2
Organization of Veterans	1	0.6
Union of Youth of Kazakstan	1	0.6
Democratic Committee for Human Rights	1	0.6
Association of Lawyers of Kazakstan	1	0.6
International Public Committee "Aral-Asia-Kazakstan"	1	0.6
Congress of Entrepreneurs of Kazakstan	1	0.6
Deputies of the 12th Supreme Soviet	40	22.6
Independent candidates	62	35.0
Total	177	100.0

Source: CIA, *World FactBook 1995*.

between the government and the trade unions. The Congress adopted a program creating a social safety net for workers and a resolution supporting the government's foreign and domestic policies.[38] The Peasants' Union, formed in February 1991, states in its program that the main purpose of its existence is to facilitate the transition to a market economy in agriculture. The Union does not participate in the country's political debate.

However, political party recognition remained low. According to a 1994 USIA poll, only 32 percent of Kazaks and 10 percent of Russians have heard of Azat, 14 percent of Kazaks and 3 percent of Russians have heard of Alash, and 3 percent of Kazaks and 6 percent of Russians have heard of Lad.[39] According to the report of the Central Election Committee, out of 9,561,534 people eligible to vote, 73.52 percent (7,030,050 people) participated in the election. Among the elected were 106 Kazaks, 49 Russians, 10 Ukrainians, 3 Germans, 3 Jews, 1 Uzbek, 1 Tatar, 1 Ingush, 1 Korean, 1 Pole, and 1 Uigur.[40]

The extraordinary attention which Nazarbaev and his men devoted to the attempt to insure the president a compliant legislature actually netted Nazarbaev a reliable bloc of only about sixty seats, an important bloc to be sure, but far too small to guarantee that the legislature would be a rubber stamp. Instead of compliance, the new parliament began not only to exhibit independence, but also to strengthen and consolidate itself as an institution.

In part the legislators were reflecting a confidence bred by a growing culture of political pluralism which was beginning to develop in the republic after two or three years of independence. By early 1994, Kazakstan had developed an increasingly more independent press; the increasing prominence of the non-governmental press, in particular, made institutional constraints on the development of a multiparty system insufficient to stifle public debate on alternatives to government policy.

This in turn gave the new national legislature a greater sense of institutional empowerment than those who drafted the republic's constitution and orchestrated the first post-Soviet elections had intended for it. As a result the legislature was quick to flex its muscles and test its powers.

Despite some fairly broad threats from the presidential office, to the effect that the new deputies should not be in a hurry to give up their old jobs or apartments,[41] the majority of Kazakstan's first independent parliament quickly organized themselves into so-called "constructive" and "non-constructive" opposition blocs. The former, a left–center opposition bloc called Respublika, brought together such disparate political groups as the Socialists (the legal successor to the banned Communist Party), the Social-Democrats, the new Communist Party, the Russian nationalist party Lad (Harmony), the Kazak nationalist party Azat (Freedom), and even the tiny Tabigat group, Kazakstan's Greens.[42] Soon afterward, a sub-group of Respublika called Legal Development of Kazakstan went so far as to organize a formal "shadow cabinet," with the stated intention of providing alternative viewpoints and programs in competition with those of the government.

At the end of May 1994 the parliament passed a vote of no-confidence in the government of Sergei Tereshchenko, whom Nazarbaev had appointed as prime minister even before independence.[43] In addition to being a long-time close associate of Nazarbaev, Tereshchenko, an ethnic Ukrainian born in Russia, was also an important symbolic figure in the republic, because he speaks fluent Kazak, a skill shared by less than 1 percent of the republic's Slavs.

Since the 1993 Constitution gave the president the right to name the prime minister, subject only to parliamentary confirmation, Nazarbaev was able to ignore the vote for a time, saying that Tereshchenko would remain at his post at least two more years, until the completion of privatization.

However, parliamentary pressure continued to mount. In July the Parliament overrode the presidential veto on two consumer-oriented economic bills,[44] and Respublika fissioned further, spawning a new "non-constructive" opposition, which issued a demand for replacement of both Tereshchenko and

Nazarbaev.[45] Calling itself Otan-Otechestvo ("Fatherland" in both Kazak and Russian), this coalition brought together representatives from: the (largely Russian) Workers' Movement; the Kazak nationalist party, Alash; the new Communist Party, All-Union Communist Bolshevik League, and All-Union Communist Leninist Youth League (all mostly old nomenklatura of both ethnic groups); the Russian nationalist groups Lad and Russian Community; and the Democratic Human Rights Community (Russian and Kazak intellectuals).

In mid-October, following a month-long scandal about the private dealings of Tereshchenko's ministers of economics and interior, Nazarbaev was finally forced to submit to parliamentary objections and accept the resignation of the Tereshchenko government. Although Nazarbaev was notably imperious in the manner in which he appointed the successor government of Akezhan Kazhegeldin, putting the nomination forward in a hastily called special session and permitting no discussion of the candidate, it seemed nevertheless that this conflict between executive and legislative branches had been a perhaps imperfect, but nevertheless real demonstration of the checks and balances which the various parts of government are meant to perform in a functioning democracy.

By late 1994, Kazakstan's legislature increasingly was understanding itself to be the republic's main brake on presidential power. In many ways the best indicator of that transformation was the change in A. Kekilbaev, who had been named Speaker of the new parliament. Kekilbaev, formerly a minor member of the presidential staff, was a compromise candidate who seems to have been chosen largely for his loyalty to Nazarbaev. While that loyalty appears to have remained unchanged, the Speaker became increasingly insistent that government actions and decrees must have a basis in law, which must be properly followed. Kekilbaev also began to insist that normal democratic practice is to have the parliament propose new legislation, rather than the president (as stipulated by the constitution), and he expressed concern about lack of a legal framework for the economic and political transformations which the president was attempting to impose. Kekilbaev was particularly active in resisting Nazarbaev's early attempt to create a bicameral legislature without amending the constitution.

Kekilbaev also began to devote parliamentary resources to educating his deputies, sending legislators to study how other parliaments and legislatures function. Under Kekilbaev's leadership, work in parliament was beginning to move into standing committees and away from the long-winded, unfocused floor debates of past parliaments. As noted above, Kekilbaev had begun to assert that the Kazaks' political tradition is essentially parliamentary, a tradition which the legislators must resurrect and defend.

As may be imagined, this appearance of parliamentary power emboldened the legislators, who found the parliament an increasingly "bully pulpit" from which to air a wide variety of concerns, both public and those which were more self-interested. One of the unforeseen consequences of the election of the professional parliament was that most deputies came to understand that their responsibilities were to their particular group of constituents, which inevitably meant that the parliament began to develop regional and economic blocs, as well as ethnic ones, because of the wide differentiation in the social and ethnic make-up of the republic.

Beginning in the late Soviet period, and accelerating since independence, the economic and ethnic differentiation of Kazakstan has led to a mushrooming of non-governmental organizations in the republic, with more than 2,000 parties, social organizations, movements, and funds now legally registered,[46] across a broad political spectrum. With the exception of the few "presidential" parties, such as the People's Unity Party, the Republican Party, and the entrepreneurial group For Kazakstan's Future, most of these organizations have little or no access to presidential decision-making. For the greatest part of Kazakstan's population the result of privatization and of economic transformation in general has been what one government critic has called "Latin-Americanization" of the republic,[47] or the sharp impoverishment of most of the population, who are made even more bitter at their new poverty by the fantastic enrichment of the tiny favored elite.

An undeniable, if less broadcast, dimension of the deputies' opposition to economic reform has been that privatization is also shifting economic advantage away from the Soviet-era elite, the nomenklatura, to a new elite. To a certain extent the criticisms of the opposition are ethnic, because it was Russians who predominated in the nomenklatura, particularly in productive and management capacities. However, there are also ethnic Kazaks who are now nomenklatura "losers."[48] Indeed, Nazarbaev's creation of a new Kazak economic and political elite has also stimulated long-dormant divisions among the Kazaks themselves.

As noted above, the Kazaks historically had identified themselves with one of three groups of clans and tribes, called *zhus*, or Hordes, each of which had traditional territories. Because the Small Horde controlled western Kazakstan and the Middle Horde migrated to what today is northern and eastern Kazakstan, it was they who came under Russian control first, when colonial policies were relatively benign. The traditional nobility of these hordes managed to retain many of their privileges, and to educate their sons in Russian schools. It was these sons who became the first Kazak nationalists, and so it was *their* sons who were destroyed by Stalin, when the Soviet leader set out to destroy the Kazak intelligentsia.

The Large or Great Horde was dominant in the south, and so did not fall under Russian control until colonialism had grown much harsher. While they often violently opposed this Russian conquest, those from the Great Horde were not strongly attracted to the nationalist movement. In part this may have been because the nationalists were dominated by sons of many of the same aristocratic families that had long dominated in the Steppe. Some Great Horde leaders did join with the socialists, which made them more acceptable to the communists when they came to power. This, combined with the fact that Kazakstan's capital was eventually set in Almaty, which is Great Horde territory, helps explain why it was they who came to dominate Kazak politics in the Soviet era.

Since the collapse of the Communist Party and its patronage networks, and in the absence of any other functional equivalent, clan and, especially, *zhus* membership has come to play an increasingly important role in the economic and political life of the republic, both at the national and oblast level. Naturally this further alienates the republic's Russians, who see clan and *zhus* patronage as yet another way in which they are excluded from economic and political advantages.

At the same time, though, the rising importance of clan puts Great Horders at odds with Small and Middle Horders, since in the event of a Russian secession, the latter would lose most of their land, while the Great Horde lands would remain intact, even if the people themselves would be very much impoverished. In addition, there are even within the Great Horde favored families, which prompts members of those less favored into defensive reaction.

Many members of the former nomenklatura who have now fallen on harder times have extensive training in the various Soviet hierarchies, which they can use with considerable effect in Kazakstan's complex political environment,[49] particularly as the economy continues its precipitous decline. In particular Nazarbaev's insistence on continuing his economic and social policies regardless of public support for them[50] allowed politically skilled but otherwise disempowered deputies to use the Parliament as an arena in which to form anti-presidential coalitions of disparate, even antagonistic groups. As noted, the Respublika bloc was elastic enough to contain both the Russian nationalists and the Kazak nationalists, while Otan-Otechestvo was able to use the widespread desire to return to the political and social structures of a decade ago as a way to forge a coalition of Russians, Kazaks, and even Cossacks.[51]

Inevitably this proliferation of opposition blocs and parties also began to push forward candidates with presidential aspirations of their own. Until April 1995 Nazarbaev was continuing to serve as president based upon his Soviet-era election, in December 1991. That term would have expired by

1996, at the latest, at which time elections would have had to have been called. Continued economic decline and the general disenchantment which followed independence exerted a steady downward pressure on Nazarbaev's popularity, to such an extent that in early 1995 there began for the first time to appear speculation that presidential elections might be held early, and even that Nazarbaev might not stand again.[52]

As Nazarbaev's popularity waned, a number of parliamentarians began to speak openly of their plans to run against Nazarbaev. Potential presidential candidates included: Serik Abdrakhmanov, the first head of *PUP*; Olzhas Suleimenov (who was also trying to take over the Respublika opposition);[53] Serikbolsyn Abdildin, who had been speaker of the 1990–93 parliament and who then became head of the Socialist Party; and Gazziz Aldamzhanov, also of the Socialists, who had made a bid to become speaker of the new parliament, which had ultimately failed but which had succeeded in blocking the candidacy of Nazarbaev's first choice for the job, Kyanysh Sultanov, who was head of PUP.

In sum, in less than a year of operation, Kazakstan's new parliament, which had been so carefully engineered to provide a compliant, unsophisticated accomplice to Nazarbaev's vision of political and economic transformation, had instead proven itself to be an institution both strong enough and independent enough to make Kazakstan's president at least partially dependent upon its deliberations and decisions.

Parliament annulled

On March 6, 1995, the growing assertiveness of the legislature was suddenly curtailed by a totally unexpected assertion of power on the part of the nearly forgotten third branch of Kazakstan's government, the judiciary. Without warning the Constitutional Court, then one of the republic's three supreme courts, rendered a decision upholding the complaints of one Tatiana Kviatkovskaia,[54] a disappointed candidate for the parliament, who in April of the previous year had sued to have the 1994 election in her district annulled, on the grounds that the voting had violated the constitution. Despite the fact that the complaint referred only to one district of Almaty, the case was immediately interpreted as casting doubt on the legitimacy of the entire parliament. Although President Nazarbaev had ten days in which to appeal the court's decision, his response team promptly filed their objection on March 8, a national holiday.

Nazarbaev's appeal of the court's decision had only two elements: an assertion that the question of voting procedures was in the jurisdiction of a general court, not the constitutional court, and a reminder that the court's decision would further complicate socioeconomic reform in the republic.[55] The Constitutional Court reaffirmed its original decision on March 11, at which point Nazarbaev went before parliament, to tell the deputies that they were an improperly assembled body, and so were now to be annulled, as were all the decisions and laws they had passed, including those which had confirmed the government of Prime Minister Kazhegeldin. All perquisites, such as use of state automobiles, offices, and apartments, were immediately revoked. Using powers given him by the previous parliament just before it disbanded, Nazarbaev re-appointed Kazhegeldin and named a new temporary government, and asserted his own imposition of direct presidential rule, pending new parliamentary elections in December 1995.

Legislative response was immediate but ineffectual. One deputy, an ethnic Russian who had earlier put several motions of no-confidence in the government, locked himself in his office and began a hunger strike. He was initially joined by about seventy more deputies, but their numbers evaporated after about a day. Deputy Olzhas Suleimenov attempted to convene an alternative "People's Assembly," but this was forced to meet on the street outside parliament, because Nazarbaev not only had the parliament's power and telephone lines turned off, but also sent in teams of workmen to begin "necessary remodeling" of the building.

Even several months after the closing of Kazakstan's parliament, it is far clearer what Nazarbaev did than why he did so. There has been considerable speculation that Nazarbaev may have orchestrated the parliament's dismissal entirely, particularly as the Constitutional Court has been a notably unproductive organ of power, rendering only eight decisions in its more than two years of existence.[56] There are other aspects of the case which have also struck observers as curious: Marash Nurtazin, an ex-deputy who had brought a similar complaint himself, supported the decree in principal, but declared it invalid in fact, since Article 14 of the republic's legal code imposes a 6-month statute of limitations on such decisions;[57] others were puzzled by Nazarbaev's rapid but strangely insubstantial objection, followed by his swift and apparently well prepared response to the decision, once the court re-affirmed it. Many observers have also found it strange that the court should have announced its decision at the particular moment it did, after having the case on its docket for more than ten months.

One of the reasons that such speculations abound is that the dissolution of parliament spared Nazarbaev a number of political inconveniences. It deprived his potential presidential challengers of their forum and constituencies. Equally important, it obviated the mounting opposition to his course of privatization and economic reform; in late January parliament had put forward its own proposed New Economic Policy, which would have slowed the pace of privatization, overhauled the tax structure, and given pronounced preference to local producers, rather than to foreign investors or trading companies.[58]

The Constitutional Court may have acted entirely on its own initiative. There is little question that the original case had merit; in the 1994 elections there not only were wide discrepancies in the size of the legislative districts, and so in the number of voters which each deputy would represent, but citizens were also asked to vote by crossing out the names of candidates whom they did *not* want to have represent them, which allowed vote-counters to interpret a single ballot as having been cast for many people at once, if a voter had not followed instructions. The result, in many districts, was that more total votes were cast than there were voters.

Perhaps even more importantly, the Constitutional Court was involved in a bureaucratic fight for its own existence. Kazakstan had three "supreme courts" – the Constitutional Court, the State Arbitrage Court (which in fall 1994 had backed the parliament in stopping the further distribution of privatization vouchers),[59] and the Supreme Court – which employ a total of sixty-six judges.[60] Of the three, the Constitutional Court was widely regarded as the most expensive and least effective, as well as the most poorly administered. Arrears for services had become so large that in late November 1994 the court had its telephones cut off and its automobiles revoked for two weeks. In spite of these financial problems, the eleven justices of the court had taken thirty-five trips abroad at state expense since 1993, including two trips to France made by Chief Justice Baimakhanov, and another trip to America on which Baimakhanov and his deputy, Amanzhol Nurmamgambetov, substituted themselves for lesser deputies at the last moment. Nurmagambetov later went to Moscow for a year's legal study, while remaining on the state payroll.[61] Two of the judges, Udartsev and Malinovskii, were the subjects of recall attempts, for actions they had taken against student demonstrators in the aftermath of the December 1986 Alma-Ata riots, when they were, respectively, Dean of the Kazak University Law Faculty and assistant head of that faculty's Party committee.[62] In addition, the court moved extraordinarily slowly, rendering no decisions at all in the first ten months of 1994.[63]

The powers of the Constitutional Court were accordingly under steady attack. In mid–1993 Kazakstan's earlier parliament had taken from the body the right to institute legal proceedings on its own or to question presidential, parliamentary, or presidium decrees,[64] and the speaker, Serikbolsyn Abdildin, attempted unsuccessfully to cut the support staff from forty-five to twenty.[65] In November 1994 the new parliament succeeded in cutting the court's staff, and reduced its available funding.

More substantively, however, there was growing sentiment in the parliament and in some parts of the government to do away with the court entirely, creating instead a single Supreme Court, on the model of that in America. The most vocal advocate of this approach was Minister of Justice Shaikenov, who was also pushing actively for a fundamental revision of the republic's constitution. As long as the president enjoyed full power of judicial appointment, with no public airing of the way in which candidates for top judicial positions were selected, Shaikenov argued, it would be impossible to create a genuine independent judiciary in the republic.[66]

There are also indications that the Constitutional Court itself was deeply divided, with the judges split into various warring factions, over which Chief Justice Baimakhanov had little control. Indeed, Baimakhanov is described as an intellectual but ineffectual man, who long ago had ceded effective administration of the court to his secretary, Igor Rogov.[67]

Who benefits?

Public opinion in Kazakstan appears to have accepted the imposition of presidential rule, at least in part because the issues to which parliament had paid the greatest attention while in session, and immediately after its dissolution, were questions of the members' own emoluments and benefits. According to USIA polls, 67 percent of respondents think that the Constitutional Court was correct in making the ruling, and 85 percent are in favor of holding a referendum on presidential rule.[68] International public opinion has made a few token objections to Nazarbaev's transformation of the republic's presidency (explained below), but otherwise has had no comment on the extra-constitutional transformation of the legislature.

The imposition of presidential rule seems to bring several immediate advantages to Nazarbaev. As is suggested above, politics in the republic was growing messy, with a number of blocs and coalitions beginning to attract considerable public followings, and their leaders to emerge as credible political rivals to Nazarbaev. Perhaps significantly, the one group of parties which has failed to thrive in Kazakstan are those which Nazarbaev himself has founded, in the attempt to create a "presidential party" which might serve as the *functional* successor to the Communist Party, imposing discipline on junior members as it trains them for eventual senior positions. PUP has been marginally more successful than Nazarbaev's first two attempts at parties, in that, unlike the Socialists and the PCK, it remains identified as Nazarbaev's party, but even with considerable government help, PUP failed to produce enough deputies to allow Nazarbaev to control the 1994–95 parliament. Closing parliament not only reduces the viability of Nazarbaev's rivals and their parties, but may also give PUP and its new allies, such as the entrepreneurial party For Kazakstan's Future, an opportunity to develop into stronger entities.

Closing parliament has also obviated that body's growing encroachments on what Nazarbaev views as executive prerogative. While being notably unproductive itself – the body passed only seven laws in its year of existence[69] – Parliament had managed severely to impede the progress of privatization, including stopping entirely the further distribution of vouchers.[70] Further, in addition to having put into circulation its own alternative New Economic Policy, parliament attempted at the end of 1994 to censure the cabinet of ministers for its faulty execution of the state budget (including deep arrears on wages and pensions), and to assume oversight for future dispensation of funds. Parliamentary commissions were also preparing to publish and turn over to the procurator the findings of investigations into the activities of the Economic Transformations Fund which Tereshchenko and his fellow displaced ministers had established after their resignation; this fund, it was asserted, had taken over funds which had been appropriated for other uses (including considerable funds which were diverted to help build Nazarbaev's vast new presidential palace).[71]

The future of democratization in Kazakstan

Permitting the parliament to be annulled was not Nazarbaev's only modification of Kazakstan's political environment. About ten days after the parliament was shut down, on the ancient Central Asian holiday of Navruz, Nazarbaev assembled a "People's Assembly" of his own, a presidential-sponsored "advisory committee" which is not mentioned in the 1993 constitution, but which adopted a resolution for Nazarbaev to remain president, without election, until December 2000.[72] Nazarbaev agreed, but submitted the decision to a national referendum, held on April 29, 1995, which he won overwhelmingly: 91.3 percent of the population turned out to vote, and 95.8 percent of the ballots cast supported extending the presidential rule.[73]

Nazarbaev also scheduled another referendum, for August 1995, which sanctioned the adoption of a new constitution which, among other things, mandated the creation of a bicameral legislature. The referendum on the constitution was held August 30, 1995, with a 91 percent voter turnout, 89.1 percent of whom voted for the adoption of the constitution. The constitution formalized President Nazarbaev's increased power, which was already great under the 1993 constitution. The new basic law continues to define Kazakstan as a unitary state with a presidential form of government. The president is the highest state officer, responsible for naming the government (subject to parliamentary approval) and all other republic officials. He is elected for a term of five years with a maximum of two terms. He has the power to declare states of emergency which put the constitution into abeyance, and is the sponsor of all legislation. He also functions as the guarantor of the constitution and of the proper function of government. Importantly, he has the power to override the decisions and actions of local authorities and councils. The only grounds on which a president can be removed from his position are infirmity and treason, either of which must be proven by a majority of the joint upper and lower houses of the new parliament.

The constitution denies a possibility of dual citizenship, and prohibits the activities in Kazakstan of foreign political organizations and trade unions. It also abolishes the Constitutional Court and institutes in its place the Constitutional Council with six members: two appointed by the president, and two by each chamber of the parliament. The new parliament, elected in December 1995, consists of two houses, a Senate and a Majilis, both operating in continual session. Each of Kazakstan's nineteen oblasts and the city of Almaty, which has oblast status, will have two senators. Rather than being elected directly by the populace, these will be chosen by joint sessions of the oblasts' representative bodies, for terms of four years. An additional seven senators will be appointed directly by the president. In addition, ex-presidents (should there ever be any) will be senators-for-life.

The Majilis has sixty-seven representatives, one from each district drawn to have roughly equal populations. Elections for half the seats will be held every two years. Out of 8,927,701 people eligible to vote, 79.3 percent (7,076,294 people) participated in the December 1995 election. According to the results of the elections, representatives of sixteen parties and organizations, and raion and city maslihats will participate in the work of the first bicameral parliament of Kazakstan.[74] Among the elected are sixty-seven Kazaks, thirty-one Russians, one Uighur, one Korean, two Ukrainians, and one German. Initiative for most legislative actions will come from the president. If parliament passes a law which the president vetoes, a two-thirds vote of both houses is required to override; a similar margin is needed to express no-confidence in a prime minister.

Presidential authority will similarly be strengthened at the local level, even though it is already quite strong. Under the current system Kazakstan is divided into nineteen oblasts (provinces); the city of Almaty also has administrative status equal to that of the oblasts, as did Leninsk, the support city for the Baikonur launch facility; by a 1994 treaty, however, administrative control of Leninsk was passed to Russia. The nineteen oblasts are in turn divided into raions (regions), consisting of a number of settlement points. Each oblast, raion, and, usually, even settlement has its own elective council, called a *maslihat*, which is charged with drawing up a budget and supervising local taxation. Cities have their own local councils as well, and large cities

Table 6.4 *Party representation in the parliament of Kazakstan, December 1995*

Party/organization	Number of deputies nominated[a]
For the Majilis (65 of 67 seats)[a]	
People's Congress of Kazakstan (PCK)	1
Peasant Union	5
Youth Union	3
Lawyers' Union	1
Confederation of Trade Unions of Kazakstan	5
People's Unity Party (PUP)	24
Union of Entrepreneurs	1
Nevada-Semipalatinsk Social Movement	1
Social Fund for the Assistance of Victims of Natural Disasters "Komec"	1
People's Cooperative Party (PCP)	1
Engineering Academy of Kazakstan	3
Club of Creative Workers and School Principals of Aktiubinsk	1
Democratic Party of Kazakstan (DPK)	12
"Revival of Kazakstan" Party	1
Communist Party of Kazakstan (CPK)	2
Independents	14
For the Senate (38 of 47 seats)[b]	
Raion Maslihaty	34
City Maslihaty	2
Independents	2

Notes: [a]The total number of party-nominated candidates elected to the Majilis in December was fifty-one. Several deputies were nominated by more than one party/organization. The results of the run-off elections in Koktetau and Semipalatinsk oblasts were not available at the time of writing. [b]In the Senate, two elected seats and seven presidential appointees were still to be filled. *Source*: *Vesti Kazakstana*, December 30, 1995, p. 2.

are divided into raions, each with its own council. These local legislatures lack the authority to choose the local executive, who has the job of insuring that republic governmental decisions are enforced and that the republic constitution is observed. Oblast and raion heads of administration, known as glavs or hakims, are presidential appointees. The head in turn appoints the members of his staff, who are the department heads of the oblast.

Elections to local councils began in 1994; despite strenuous efforts by the central government to control the results, inevitably the councils which were seated began to represent the interests and demands of the populations which had elected them, and to which they answer. The issues which have been mobilizing local councils vary by region, but the sum effect is that the oblast structures may be beginning to move out from under the authority of the presidentially appointed hakims.[75] The imposition of presidential rule and the closing of the central parliament have obviously strengthened the hands of the hakims, but there has been no fundamental change in the demands of certain oblasts, particularly those in the Russian north, to make the post of hakim elective, rather than appointive. In 1994 Nazarbaev indicated that he would consider making this change, but the 1995 constitution provides instead only that the local maslihats can express no-confidence in the hakims, by a two-thirds vote. As noted, the president also has the power to override or revoke decisions taken by the maslihats, while the hakims will have the power to control budgetary decisions taken by the local councils, suggesting that the power of the local bodies over their immediate administrators is at best only slightly enhanced by the new constitution.

Clearly the effect of the new constitution and the postponement of presidential elections is to concentrate virtually all political power in the republic in the hands of President Nazarbaev and his immediate advisors, which of necessity will delay the further democratization of Kazakstan, if not stop it completely.

Nevertheless, in the short run at least, Kazakstan's retreat from democratization has some immediately identifiable benefits. For one thing, imposition of direct presidential rule is likely to reduce some ethnic tensions within the republic. Indeed, one of the primary justifications which Nazarbaev gave in his speech to the People's Assembly on Navruz for having "acquiesced" in the Constitutional Court's decision was the rising ethnic hostility in the republic, including a general rise in anti-Semitism,[76] which presidential rule would now allow him to suppress.

The ethnic constituency which was probably most important, however, was the Russians, both within the republic and in Russia proper. Stability in Kazakstan is overwhelmingly shaped by developments in Russia, especially as Russia returns to a more re-integrationist mood. Kazakstan's vulnerability to Russian political and economic intervention (to say nothing of military intervention) is so great that it must be assumed that Russian interests, national and ethnic, played a considerable part in Nazarbaev's calculations. The fact that Russia has voiced no objection to his retreat from democracy suggests, at the least, that authorities in Moscow did not find Nazarbaev's retreat from democracy a surprise.

Although Kazakstan has always been mindful of the wishes of its northern neighbor, under Prime Minister Kazhegeldin the two republics have grown even more interdependent economically than they were before. Kozykorpesh Esenberlin, president of the State Property Commission under Prime Minister Tereshchenko, had conducted privatization in a way which favored the large voucher holding companies, which are, as noted, Kazak-dominated; by contrast, his replacement under Kazhegeldin, Sarybai Kalmurzaev, has not only begun to permit privatization auctions to be held for cash (including rubles), as well as vouchers, but has also begun the practice of giving Russia rights of first refusal for large industrial plants, especially those which had been of military significance in the Soviet era. Kalmurzaev also favors raising the stake which investment funds might take in enterprises from one-fifth to one-third.[77] The Kazhegeldin government, unlike the virtually all-Kazak Tereshchenko government, returned the key Finance Ministry to a Russian, Aleksandr Pavlov, and gave the Economics Ministry to Altai Tleuberdin, a Middle Horde Kazak from the Russified north.

It also seems likely that Nazarbaev will use presidential rule to increase the linguistic and cultural rights of the republic's Russians. In addition to having signed the treaty with Russia which all but obviates the issue of dual citizenship, Nazarbaev had the deadline for the citizenship choice moved back again, to December 31, 1995. Since Parliament's annulment there has been some talk of postponing the deadline still further, perhaps until the year 2000, as Russia has done.

Nazarbaev also seems likely to backpedal on the language issue. His Navruz speech to the People's Assembly concluded with the observation that there was no need for adult Russians to have to learn Kazak, but that all Kazaks must learn Russian, because that language would remain a means to get information for a long time yet to come.[78]

Nazarbaev seems to run little immediate risk from his assumption of so much political power. He could face opposition from his own people, if concessions to the republic's Russians grow. Should the constitution be changed again so as to permit two official languages or dual citizenship, the Kazaks will feel themselves to have lost a hard-gained privilege, although it is difficult to predict what form opposition might take, since the Kazaks are seriously divided by clan and family differences, which make some of them share more interests with the Russians than with their ethnic fellows.

The Kazaks also have no institutions that might serve as alternative focuses for political will; despite a wave of mosque-building since independence, Islam is not well established in the republic, and has no network through which it might mobilize disaffected Kazaks. USIA polls provide only minimal guidance as to support for Islam or its likely future role. In a

September 1994 survey only 45 percent of Kazaks felt confident of the Islamic Immamate, while 27 percent were not confident and 28 percent expressed no opinion. For the public as a whole, however, greater confidence was expressed in the Russian Orthodox Church than in the Immamate, by a margin of 47 to 27 percent. Kazaks, though, expressed greater confidence in the Immamate than in the Orthodox church (by 45 percent to 27 percent) while Russians were more confident in the Orthodox church than in the Immamate (by 60 percent to 13 percent).[79]

The Kazak leadership has also tried to keep in check the power of locally elected councils. Should their demands for greater autonomy resume, it might also become necessary to dissolve the local councils, especially in the predominantly Russian north. Although the voting districts were different from those for parliamentary elections, the method of voting (crossing out unwanted candidates) was the same. However, the many concessions that Nazarbaev appears to have made to Russian concerns in his handling of parliament and his appointment of an interim government suggest that he would be unlikely to attempt to rein in the councils of the northern regions, or to be successful if he were to try.

If the northern councils are permitted greater powers, it seems inevitable that the southern, Kazak-dominated councils would also claim them; this would present Nazarbaev with the dilemma of whether to permit this further dilution of his power, or to crack down on the Kazaks for claiming freedoms given to the Russians.

In truth, however, Nazarbaev appears to face very little immediate political opposition. Despite the proliferation of potential candidates, there is virtually no possibility that Nazarbaev could have been unseated, or even seriously challenged, in a contested presidential election. The people of Kazakstan, Russians and local nationalities alike, are generally very conservative, and have a strong respect for authority, which has only been strengthened further by the fears of possible chaos which the civil war in Tajikistan has unleashed, as well as by the discomforts of ballooning crime closer to home.

However, in Kazakstan, just as in the rest of Central Asia, democracy itself, with its requirement that the right to power be periodically submitted to the consent of the governed, has increasingly come to be seen as inherently threatening. President Nazarbaev, like his fellow presidents Karimov, Niiazov, and even Akaev, has come to see the need to submit to election as a weakness.

The use of referendums rather than elections and the attempt to fashion an ever-weaker parliament are both parts of a movement across not just Kazakstan, but the entire region, to treat the present elites as the only ones which can be trusted to govern. It is almost as if, now that they are faced with the realities of how difficult it will be to execute the transition to independence, Nazarbaev and his advisors are falling back on political instincts formed by their careers in the Brezhnev, Andropov, and Chernenko eras. The ideal of reform has taken on a life distinct from that of the society which they are nominally trying to reform, so that the people of Kazakstan, who are supposed to benefit from the reform process, have instead become identified as its enemy.

The gamble which Nazarbaev has undertaken is that imposition of presidential rule will permit him to transform the republic's economy in such a way that opposition will eventually be bought off, by an indisputable and wide-spread improvement of living standards. Certainly the republic has the natural resources and industrial potential to make this a credible wager.

At the same time, however, Kazakstan faces an enormous number of obstacles before it may realize its potential, or even return to the relatively threadbare beginnings from which most citizens have tumbled since independence. With the long Soviet experience still so green in memory, the elites of Kazakstan ought to be acutely aware of the dangers inherent in failing to elaborate a mechanism for regular succession of leadership. Situations change, and people age. If Kazakstan cannot find some way to insure a regular movement of new talent into positions of greater responsibility, then a kind of political fatigue will set in, as leaders continue to make the same sorts of old responses to new and changing problems. If there is no turnover of cadre, then political and economic power in the state will become increasingly dependent upon the health and physical fitness of the present authorities.

Since Nazarbaev is only fifty-five years old and is, as far as we are aware, in good health, Kazakstan is not likely to face an immediate prospect of a catastrophic change of political leadership. However, the ultimate frailty of even the fittest human flesh means that political succession is inevitable. Societies which attempt to freeze or halt the process of political change may enjoy long periods of apparent stability, but they face violent and sudden changes when fate forces the inevitable successions upon them. Societies which permit more groups and people to compete for political control must endure a certain amount of political turmoil on a more-or-less constant basis, but in the end such societies find political transformation more gradual, and changes less wrenching.

The situation in Kazakstan is no exception. The fact that there is no obvious venue for expression of popular dissatisfaction in the republic at present does not mean that there will be none. The republic remains two ethnic entities, each of which tends to see the gains of the other as its own loss, bound within a single border. During the year of its existence, Kazakstan's parliament, for all its balkiness and imperfections, was beginning to emerge as a genuine partner in the process of economic and political transformation. Whatever frustrations that partnership may have given President Nazarbaev, it also offered him an institution, and a number of prominent personalities, with which he could share the public opposition which such radical transformations inevitably produce, especially if the economy continues to deteriorate, as it seems likely to do.[80] By taking upon his office the entire burden of government, Nazarbaev has also given both of Kazakstan's ethnic groups, and all the republic's dissatisfied citizens, something upon which they may focus their opposition – himself.

Political parties or movements and leaders

People's Unity Party (Partiya Narodnoye Edinstvo Kazakstana, formerly Soyuz Narodnoye Edinstvo Kazakstana)
    Kuanysh Sultanov, chairman; Nursultan Nazarbaev, unofficial leader

"Republic" Coordinating Council of Public Associations (Koordinatsionnyi Sovet Obshestvennyih Obyedinenyi Respubliki)
    Serikbolsyn Abdildin, coordinator

People's Congress of Kazakstan (Narodnyi Kongress Kazakstana)
    Olzhas Suleymenov, chairman

Socialist Party of Kazakstan (Sotsialisticheskaya Partiya Kazakstana)
    Yermukhamet Yertyshbaev, Peter Svoik, Gaziz Aldamzhanov

Communist Party of Kazakstan (Kommynisticheskaya Partiya Kazakstana)
    Leonid Korolykov

Freedom Civil Movement of Kazakstan (Grazhdanskoye Dvizhenie Kazakstana Azat)
    Mikhail Isinaliyev

Democratic Party of Kazakstan (Partiya Demokraticheskogo Poryadka)
    Tulegen Zhukeyev

Confederation of Trade Unions of the Republic of Kazakstan (Konfederatsiya Profsoyuzov Respubliki Kazakstan)
    Mukashev, chairman, member of the "Republic" Coordinating Council

Republican People's Slavic Movement – Harmony (Respublikanskoye Obshestvennoe Slavyanskoye Dvizhenie – Lad)
    Aleksandra Dokuchaeva

Democratic Committee for Human Rights (Demokraticheskiy Komitet po Pravam Cheloveka)
Member of the "Republic" Coordinating Council of Public Associations

December National Democratic Party (Natsionalnaya Demokraticheskaya Partiya Zeltosan)
Hasen Kozhahmetov

Revival of Kazakstan Party
Altynshash Dzhaganova

Social Democratic Party of Kazakstan (Sotsial-Democraticheskaya Partiya Kazakstana)
Dos Koshimov

People's Cooperative Party (Narodno-Kooperativnaya Partiya Kazakstana)
Umirzak Sarsenov, chairman

"New Generation" Social Movement (Sotsialynoe Dvizhenie "Novoe Pokolenie")
Bakhtzhan Dospanov, first secretary

Tabigat [Nature] Ecological Party (Ekologicheskaya Partiya Tabigat)
Member of the "Republic" Coordinating Council of Public Associations

Alash National Freedom Party (Partiya Natsionalnoi Svobody Alash)
Aron Atabek and Rashid Nutushev

Society for Assistance to the Cossacks in Semirechye (Obshestvo Podderzhki Kazakov Semerechya)
Nikolay Gunkin

Unity Movement (Dvizheniye Edinstvo)
Yuri Startsev

Republican Party of Kazakstan (Respublikanskaya Partiya Kazakstana)
Sabetkazy Akatayev

Independent Trade Union Center (Birlesu; an association of independent trade union and business associations)
Leonid Solomin, president

(*Sources*: CIA, *The World Factbook 1995*; Foreign Broadcasting Information Service, *Daily Report: Central Eurasia*, various numbers; *Political Handbook of the World: 1995–1996*, ed. Arthur Banks, Alan Day, and Thomas Muller.)

NOTES

1 *Sovety Kazakstana*, 2 November 1994, pp. 1–2, as translated in Foreign Broadcast Information Service, *Daily Report: Central Eurasia* (hereafter FBIS-USR), 15 November 1994, p. 87.
2 For more information on Alash Orda, see Martha Brill Olcott, *The Kazakhs* (Stanford: Hoover Institution Press, 1995).
3 *Ogonek*, no. 26, 1988, p. 11.
4 *Rossiiskie vesti*, 20 October 1992, p. 2, as translated in *FBIS-USR*, 31 October 1992, p. 84. Other rumors say Nazarbaev was slated for a vice-presidency, presumably behind Gorbachev; still others say he was to become prime minister.
5 *Argumenty i fakty*, no. 2, 1993, 2.
6 Interviews by the author, March and May 1992.
7 *Kazakhstanskaia pravda*, 25 August 1989.
8 As late as September 1990, Nazarbaev was complaining of the dysfunctional role played by these organizations. *Kazakstanskaia pravda*, 9 September 1990.
9 *Birlesu*, 14 November 1991.
10 *Kazakstan: Realities and Perspectives of Independence*, ed. Yevgeny Mikhailovich Kozhokin (Moscow: Russian Institute of Strategic Research, 1995), p. 179.
11 Ibid., p. 185.
12 USIA, *Opinion Analysis*, 2 October 1995.
13 Kozhokin, *Kazakstan: Realities and Perspectives*, p. 193.
14 *Panorama*, no. 28, 16 July 1994, p. 1.
15 *Ekspress-K*, 14 October 1994, p. 4.
16 *Panorama*, 5 November 1994, as translated in *FBIS-USR*, 8 November 1994, pp. 43–4.
17 *The Constitution of the Republic of Kazakstan*, as translated by the International Republican Committee.
18 One indication of the present state of "reverse discrimination" is the pattern of admissions to Al Farabi State University, where 79.5 percent of the new students are Kazaks, as opposed to 14.6 percent Russian. *Kazakstanskaia pravda*, 28 June 1994, p. 2.
19 The characterization is from an account of a slander suit brought against Zimanov by deputies Peregrin and Roze, who claimed that Zimanov had accused them of advocating a secessionist autonomous government in Kazakstan's north. *Karavan*, 22 February 1995, pp. 1, 3, as translated in Foreign Broadcast Information Service, *Daily Report: Central Eurasia* (hereafter *FBIS-SOV*), 27 February 1995, p. 70.
20 *Karavan*, 17 February 1995, p. 7.
21 *Konstitutsia Respubliki Kazakstan* (Almaty, 1996).
22 *Ekspress-K*, 3 October 1995, p. 4.
23 *Kazakstanskaia pravda*, 21 January 1995, p. 1, as translated in *FBIS-SOV*, 30 January 1995, pp. 55–8.
24 *Karavan*, 3 March 1995, p. 8.
25 *Kazakstanskaia pravda*, 21 February 1995, p. 2, as translated in *FBIS-SOV*, 16 March 1995, pp. 48–50.
26 It is equally rumored that the founder of Butia began this rumor himself in order to enhance his image.

27 This is based on the report of Kazakstan's election commission, published before the elections. *Kazakhstanskaia pravda*, 6 December 1989.
28 This theme was underscored in the final pre-election coverage. See ibid., 23 December 1989.
29 *Izvestiia*, 24 January 1990.
30 *Pravda*, 27 March 1990.
31 Unpublished report of Kazakstan's republic elections commission of 31 January 1990.
32 87.3 percent of the candidates for deputies' mandates were members of the CPSU.
33 Valerii Tishkov, "Ethnicity and Power in the Republics of the USSR," *Journal of Soviet Nationalities* 1, no. 1 (1990), 50.
34 Ibid., 51.
35 Kozhokin, *Kazakstan: Realities and Perspectives of Independence*, p. 171.
36 *Sovety Kazakstana*, 2 November 1994, pp. 1–2, as translated in *FBIS-USR*, 15 November 1994, p. 87.
37 *Izvestiia*, 12 May 1994, p. 4.
38 Kozhokin, *Kazakstan: Realities and Perspectives*, p. 204.
39 For more information see USIA, *Opinion Analysis*, 2 October 1995.
40 *Vremia*, 19 March, 1994, p.1.
41 *Nezavisimaia gazeta*, 2 April 1994, p. 3.
42 Ibid., p. 3.
43 The vote was 111 for the motion, 28 against, and 38 not voting.
44 The bills defined a minimum consumer budget and a minimum wage. In both instances the parliament objected that the President's figures were far too low. *Panorama*, 30 July 1994, p. 11, as translated in *FBIS-USR*, 9 August 1994, p. 102.
45 Ibid., pp. 101–2.
46 *Nezavisimaia gazeta,* 19 May 1994, p. 3.
47 Ibid., 27 May 1994, p. 1.
48 See for example V. Mukushev, who lost his job as head of TV in Karaganda in 1993 in a loud administrative struggle (*Nezavisimaia gazeta*, 9 February 1993, p. 1); the next year Mukushev attempted to run for parliament but was denied the right to register as a candidate, after which he went on a hunger strike (*Vechernii Bishkek*, 9 March 1994, p. 6).
49 An important case in point is Vitalii Roze, who created the parliamentary "shadow cabinet"; he is an economist trained in Moscow's elite Trade-Union School (*Nezavisimaia gazeta*, 27 May 1994, p. 1).
50 *Ekspress-Khronika*, 18 August 1994, p. 3, as translated in *FBIS-USR*, 29 August 1994, p. 92.
51 *Panorama*, 30 July 1994, p. 11, as translated in *FBIS-USR*, 9 August 1994, p. 101.
52 Nazarbaev was elected on 1 December 1991 under the old constitution, for a five-year term. Under the new constitution he could stand for up to two five-year terms.
53 *Nezavisimaia gazeta*, 2 April 1994, p. 3.

54 This led Olzhas Suleimenov to quip that whereas Yeltsin had required many tanks to shut his parliament (in October 1993), all Nazarbaev had required was one Tan'ka.
55 Almaty TV, 8 March 1995, as translated in *FBIS-SOV*, 9 March 1995, pp. 46–7.
56 *Sovety Kazakstana*, 11 November 1994, p. 2, as translated in *FBIS-USR*, 29 November 1994, pp. 95–8.
57 *Karavan*, 24 May 1995, p. 7, as translated in *FBIS-SOV*, 30 March 1995, pp. 59–60.
58 *Karavan*, 3 March 1995, p. 8.
59 *Kommersant*, 16 September 1994, p. 3, as translated in *FBIS-SOV*, 26 September 1994, pp. 53–4.
60 *Sovety Kazakstana*, 11 November 1994, p. 2, as translated in *FBIS-USR*, 29 November 1994, pp. 95–8.
61 *Ekspress-K*, 1 November 1994, p. 1.
62 *ABV*, 21 January 1994, p. 2.
63 *Ekspress-K*, 1 November 1994, pp. 1, 3.
64 *Izvestiia*, 21 July 1993, p. 1, as translated in *FBIS-SOV*, 22 July 1993, p. 61.
65 *Panorama*, 12 November 1994, p. 5.
66 *Nezavisimaia gazeta*, 24 November 1994, p. 3, as translated in *FBIS-USR*, 20 December 1994, pp. 89–90.
67 *Ekspress-K*, 1 November 1994, pp. 1, 3.
68 USIA, *Opinion Analysis*, 2 October 1995.
69 *Komsomol'skaia pravda*, 15 March 1995, p. 2.
70 *Panorama*, 7 January 1995, p. 2, as translated in *FBIS-SOV*, 17 January 1995, pp. 62–4.
71 *Sovety Kazakstana*, 28 December 1994, p. 1, as translated in *FBIS-SOV*, 5 January 1995, p. 36.
72 Almaty TV, 24 March 1995, as translated in *FBIS-SOV*, 27 March 1995, pp. 68–70.
73 Open Media Research Institute, *Daily Digest*, 2 May 1995.
74 Azat boycotted the December elections since it considered the presidential edict "On Elections," adopted by Nazarbaev in the absence of a parliament in the country, to be an "illegal document." See *FBIS-SOV*, 8 December 1995, p. 55.
75 *Ekspress-K*, 4 November 1994, p. 5, as translated in *FBIS-USR*, 15 November 1994, p. 92.
76 Almaty TV, 24 March 1995, as translated in *FBIS-SOV*, 27 March 1995, pp. 68–70.
77 *Delovoi mir*, 16 December 1994, p. 5, as translated in *FBIS-SOV*, 9 January 1995, pp. 44–6.
78 Almaty TV, 24 March 1995, as translated in *FBIS-SOV*, 27 March 1995, pp. 68–70.
79 USIA, *Opinion Analysis*, 17 February 1995.
80 See, for example, *Izvestiia*, 12 May 1994, p. 4.

7   Kyrgyzstan: the fate of political liberalization

Eugene Huskey

During its first two years of independence, Kyrgyzstan enjoyed a reputation as an oasis of democracy in the harsh political landscape of Central Asia. Under the leadership of Askar Akaev, a progressive scientist whose sources of support lay outside the Communist Party apparatus, the country began to aggressively dismantle the political and economic pillars of Soviet rule.[1] Although political power remained highly concentrated, the state laid the foundations for a civil society by promoting a free press, private political associations, and a market economy. Akaev's reforms quickly attracted the attention and largesse of Western donors, who by the end of 1993 had pledged almost half a billion dollars to assist Kyrgyzstan in its transition toward democracy.[2]

The Kyrgyz political miracle began to fade, however, in the mid-1990s. Faced with an economic crisis, an inefficient and corrupt state bureaucracy, and deep divisions within the country's elites and masses, the political leadership experimented with anti-democratic measures to shore up its authority. In the summer of 1994, President Akaev closed down two opposition-minded newspapers, launched a referendum to create new political institutions – in violation of the existing constitution – and conspired in a successful attempt to shut down parliament several months before its term had expired. In the parliamentary elections that followed in February 1995, fraud, corruption, and public anomie reigned. New criminal elements allied with segments of the old nomenklatura to return a legislature that promised little support for the reformist agenda advanced by the president. The elections appeared to represent a victory for traditional local elites against modern politicians like Akaev who sought to elevate the interests of the state and nation above clan, region, and ethnicity.

The end of the romantic period in Kyrgyzstan's transition from communism poses vital questions about the country's potential for democratization. To assess that potential, we explore below the elements of Kyrgyz history and society that may facilitate or obstruct the rise of democratic politics. How countries build on historical and social legacies depends, of course, on the tactics of leaders. We must also investigate, therefore, the behavior of elites during the breakdown of communist rule and the construction of new political institutions. Within the confines of Kyrgyzstan's heritage and resources, elite choices on questions of political architecture, social mobilization, and the everyday policies of state shaped the direction and pace of the country's political development.

The political and social legacy – pre-1917

Based on its historical legacy alone, few successor states of the USSR would appear as ill-prepared for a democratic transition as Kyrgyzstan. At independence, the country lacked even the fundamental elements of a modern polity, a sense of statehood and nationhood. Like their ethnic kin, the Kazaks, the Kyrgyz were a nomadic people whose traditional political and social relations did not extend beyond the family, the clan, and the tribe.[3] This was true of virtually all Kyrgyz until the 1920s; it remains true of many Kyrgyz even today. The 1,000-year old legend of Manas describes a rare moment when the Kyrgyz were ruled by a single, indigenous leader.

When state institutions existed on the lands of the Kyrgyz in more recent centuries, they came on the heels of foreign conquest. Thus, in the late nineteenth century, Kyrgyzstan was divided between the Russian Empire in the North and the Kokand Kingdom of the Uzbeks in the South. Until the Soviet era, the Kyrgyz lived on the very margins of modern political life.

The Kyrgyz lacked a national as well as a civic consciousness before the Soviet period. Although bound by a common language, traditions, and legend, the Kyrygz – like rural French before the twentieth century – had yet to imagine their membership in a national community. They defined themselves as members of clans – linked directly by blood or marriage – or, in more recent times, as Muslims. Obviously, the absence of a Kyrgyz state impeded the development of a national identity. But an even more fundamental barrier to nation-building was the physical geography of Kyrgyzstan.

Towering, and often impassable, mountains have severely restricted communication and commerce between the ethnic Kyrgyz. Because of limited contacts, the Kyrgyz have developed fierce regional loyalties. Each of the five major valleys – Ferghana, Talas, Chui, Issyk-Kul', and Naryn – has nurtured a distinct Kyrgyz culture, evident in patterns of speech, dress, food, and even, one may argue, in political and social values. These differences are due, in large part, to the scale and sources of exogenous influence on the five valleys. In the Ferghana valley, which embraces the regions of Osh and Jalal-Abad in contemporary Kyrgyzstan, a longstanding Uzbek presence has

Table 7.1 *Regional population in Kyrgyzstan*

Year	Region	Population	% growth	% rural
	Jalal-Abad Oblast			
1990		766,600		70.2
1995		826,800	7.9	73.2
	Issyk-Kul Oblast			
1990		418,100		67.7
1995		425,300	1.7	68.3
	Naryn Oblast			
1990		257,900		79.5
1995		264,200	2.4	78.7
	Osh Oblast			
1990		1,295,000		72.2
1995		1,415,500	8.7	74.8
	Talas Oblast			
1990		197,400		83.6
1995		204,600	3.7	84.7
	Chu Oblast			
1990		797,600		71.8
1995		747,900	- 6.2	76.3
	Bishkek City			
1990		634,600		0.5
1995		592,100	- 6.7	0.5

Source: *Geografiia* (weekly supplement to the newspaper *Pervoe Sentiabria* [Moscow]), December 1995, no. 47, p. 1. My thanks to Alexander Fetisov for supplying this source.

deepened the ties of local Kyrgyz to Islam, while at the same time heightening their fear of domination by the Uzbeks. It is here, as we shall see below, that tensions between ethnic Uzbeks and Kyrgyz exploded into ethnic violence as the Soviet order began to crumble.

Where the Ferghana valley opens up to Uzbekistan, the Chui valley gives onto Kazakstan. However, in the Chui valley, as in parts of neighboring Issyk-Kul', it is the Slavs rather than the Kazaks who have been the dominant foreign influence. The russification of these northern provinces of Kyrgyzstan has affected not only the language and culture of the local Kyrgyz but also their political orientation. Residents of the northern valleys appear more receptive than their southern counterparts to political and social change imported from Europe. For its part, the most isolated and mountainous region of the country, the Naryn valley, has been the least subjected to the movements of non-indigenous peoples and ideas. Even at the end of the twentieth century, 97 percent of the residents in this region were ethnic Kyrgyz.[4] Only now, with the flowering of economic relations with a more prosperous China, are the Kyrgyz of the Naryn being drawn into another cultural orbit like their ethnic kin.

The portrait of the Kyrgyz sketched thus far emphasizes their lack of direct experience with democratic institutions and values. They have had no history of parties, parliaments, elections, or the intermediary institutions associated with a civil society. However, many observers argue that elements of traditional Kyrgyz culture will in fact facilitate the transition toward democracy.[5] Without a powerful aristocracy or a high degree of social stratification, Kyrgyz society seems better prepared than many of its neighbors – or Europeans in earlier centuries – to accept ideas of legal and political equality that serve as the foundation for democratic development. In Kyrgyzstan, there are simply fewer barriers to democracy to be dismantled than in sedentary societies with more complex and hierarchical social structures.[6] This is especially true regarding the involvement of women in public affairs. Although women have by no means been the social equals of men in Kyrgyzstan, they have enjoyed greater social autonomy than women in many other traditional societies. Finally, in spite of their relative isolation, the Kyrgyz have exhibited a tolerance and openness toward other peoples and cultures that may provide useful social capital in a transition to democracy. As Robert Putnam has argued, trust and civility in relations among elites provides the mortar for the construction of democracy.

The political and social legacy – Soviet era

As the communist era came to a close, Kyrgyz nationalists attributed their republic's political and economic backwardness to Russian, and subsequently Soviet, domination. Taking advantage of the more liberal regime of expression and inquiry associated with Gorbachev's policy of glasnost, many Kyrgyz writers indicted Russians for their massacre of the Kyrgyz during the wartime mobilization of 1916, for their exploitation of the local economy – buying cheap wool to ship to mills in European Russia – and for their spoilage of the environment, whether through industrial waste or consumer litter.[7] This literature served both as a rallying point for an emerging Kyrgyz nationalism and as a justification for the creation of an independent state.

But the role of Russia and the Soviet Union in the political and economic development of Kyrgyzstan was, of course, far more nuanced than this literature suggests. Indeed, one may argue that Kyrgyzstan as an independent state, and perhaps even the Kyrgyz as a separate nation, would not have existed at the end of the twentieth century without Imperial Russian and

Soviet rule. The unintended consequences of St. Petersburg and Moscow's control of Kyrgyzstan was the development of the necessary pre-conditions for a modern state and nation. In the words of Kyrgyzstan's most famous son, the novelist, Chingiz Aitmatov, "the Soviet past, with all its difficulties and suffering, prepared us for the surprising opportunity to suddenly receive as a small nation the status of a state and world recognition."[8]

One of the first pre-conditions of statehood is a fixed territory. In late Imperial and early Soviet history, the territory of what is now Kyrgyzstan was divided between two larger administrative regions. But in 1936, a redrawing of the boundaries of Soviet Central Asia brought the overwhelming majority of ethnic Kyrgyz into a single political unit – the Kyrgyz Soviet Socialist Republic. Kyrgyzstan was now one of five nominally sovereign republics in Central Asia, a division of the region designed to stifle pan-Turkic sentiments and facilitate rule from Moscow. The mythology of republican sovereignty aside, the creation of the Kyrgyz republic provided the residents of Kyrgyzstan with many of the symbols and rituals of statehood. These trappings of state would later smooth the transition of Kyrgyzstan from a constituent republic of the USSR to an independent country.

When Kyrgyzstan was absorbed into Imperial Russia at the end of the nineteenth century, it had no formally educated indigenous elite. Building on the growth of literacy among the Kyrgyz in the first years of this century, the Bolsheviks launched an active campaign in the 1920s to create a national intelligentsia, which they hoped would provide reliable communist leaders in the region. However, the first generation of a Soviet Kyrgyz elite fell victim to Stalin's purges in the 1930s.[9] It was replaced by Kyrgyz of more modest class and educational backgrounds. Through the recruitment of sycophantic local leaders and the placement of Slavic overseers in strategic posts in the capital of Frunze (now Bishkek), Moscow retained firm control over this distant republic in ensuing decades. But the very presence over time of ethnic Kyrgyz in the republic's leading posts created the expectation among masses and elites that these jobs "belonged" to indigenous cadres. Kyrgyzstan should be ruled by a Kyrgyz lord, even if he swore fealty to Moscow. The depth of such sentiments was revealed in neighboring Kazakstan in December 1986, when Gorbachev faced a public uprising after replacing the ethnic Kazak party leader with a Russian.

In its own way, Soviet rule also launched the social mobilization of the Kyrgyz population. Strangers to modern politics in the period before 1917, the Kyrgyz became politically active in the Soviet era through elections, party membership, and incessant agitation. To be sure, this was not akin to the democratic revolution that swept across the Atlantic world in the eighteenth and nineteen centuries. Public participation under communism lacked the essential elements of democratic mobilization, such as openness and competitiveness.

Table 7.2 *Ethnic composition of Kyrgyzstan*

	1926		1959		1989	
	no.	%	no.	%	no.	%
Kyrgyz	668,700	66.8	836,800	40.5	2,229,663	52.4
Russians	116,800	11.8	23,600	30.2	916,558	21.5
Uzbeks	106,300	10.6	218,900	10.6	550,096	12.9
Ukrainians	64,200	6.4	137,000	6.6	108,027	2.5
Germans	4,300	0.4	39,900	1.9	101,309	2.4
Tatars	4,900	0.5	56,300	2.7	70,068	1.6
Uighurs	8,200	0.8	13,800	0.7	37,318	0.9
Kazaks	1,700	0.2	20,100	1.0	36,928	0.9
Dungans	6,000	0.6	11,100	0.5	36,779	0.9
Tajiks	7,000	0.7	15,200	0.7	33,518	0.8
Other	13,600	1.4	93,400	4.5	137,491	3.2
Total population	1,001,700		2,066,100		4,257,755	

Source: *Narodnoe khoziaistvo Kirgizskoi SSR* (Frunze, 1982), p. 16; *Vestnik statistiki*, no. 4 (1991), 76–8.

Many patterns of behavior developed in the Soviet period would have to be unlearned in the transition from communism. For example, an old woman voting in the 1989 election asked: "For what purpose are two names entered on the ballot?"[10] But in spite of the perversities of participation in the communist era, the residents of Soviet Kyrgyzstan developed an image of politics as a potential outlet for social demands. This is a necessary, if modest, step on the path toward modern and democratic politics. Those schooled in contemporary Anglo-American democracies, with their mythologies of a social contract bridging the gap between a state of nature and a civil society, can easily forget the long and difficult road to democracy traversed by their own political forebears.

The Soviet legacy in Kyrgyzstan extends beyond political geography and culture to the very ethnic and linguistic makeup of the country. During seventy-four years of communist rule, large numbers of European settlers, primarily Slavs and Germans, migrated to Kyrgyzstan to join an already diverse group of indigenous Central Asian peoples, which included Kyrgyz, Uzbeks, Kazaks, Uighurs, Dungans, and Tajiks (see table 7.2). By the end of the Soviet era, Slavs accounted for almost a quarter of the republic's population, and they formed an overwhelming majority of residents in the capital. The consequences of Russian migration for the political, social, and economic life of Soviet and post-Soviet Kyrgyzstan are difficult to overstate. Questions of housing, employment, language, and education formed part of a dense web of ethnic politics, which tended to elevate group concerns over those of the individual or the nation.

Russian immigration had an especially far-reaching effect on language development. Like all national republics of the former USSR, Kyrgyzstan promoted the use of Russian both as a *lingua franca* and as a tool of assimilation into the new Soviet order. But linguistic russification went much farther in Kyrgyzstan than in other republics because of the toadyism of the Kyrgyz leadership, the density of Russian settlement in the northern regions of the country, and the vulnerability of the Kyrgyz language itself, which acquired written form only at the turn of the twentieth century. By the 1970s, Russian had virtually eliminated Kyrgyz in some areas as a language of public discourse. With Russian as the language of opportunity, many Kyrgyz parents enrolled their children in Russian-language schools as a means of enhancing their life chances. This in turn produced a generation of Kyrgyz youth, living primarily in the Chui valley and Issyk-Kul', who lacked facility in their ancestral tongue.[11]

What did this linguistic and cultural legacy mean for Kyrgyzstan in transition? First, that the revival of the Kyrgyz language would serve as a powerful mobilizing issue for Kyrgyz nationalists. At stake were not just the symbolic victories associated with the renaming of places – Kirgizia, for example, became Kyrgyzstan – but a reshaping of the structure of educational and career opportunities. To reward speakers of Kyrgyz was to punish those without a knowledge of the language, which included all but a handful of Slavs. Predictably, language politics divided the country along ethnic lines, with the two largest minorities, the Russians and Uzbeks, most exercised by the campaign to introduce Kyrgyz linguistic hegemony. But the revival of Kyrgyz also highlighted the divisions within the Kyrgyz community itself.

The varying degrees of linguistic russification among the Kyrgyz exacerbated fundamental intra-ethnic cleavages between North and South,[12] city and country, young and old and Muslim and non-Muslim.[13] When a predominantly russified, urban, and northern Kyrgyz elite gained power during the transition from communist rule, its most vulnerable flank lay exposed not to the Russians and Uzbeks but to Kyrgyz leaders who were willing to outbid them as defenders of ethnic Kyrgyz interests. During the drafting of a new constitution in 1993, these leaders succeeded in securing a provision that disqualified candidates for the presidency who did not

Table 7.3 *Social indicators for Kyrgyzstan (percentage of population)*

	1959	1979	1989	1993
Rural population	66	61	62	63
Agricultural employees	n.a.	n.a.	32	26
Primary or no education	68	n.a.	34	n.a.
Full secondary education	19	n.a.	56	n.a.
Full tertiary education	3	n.a.	9	n.a.
Age 0–19	45	n.a.	47	n.a.
Age 20–29	17	n.a.	18	n.a.
Age 30–39	13	n.a.	13	n.a.
Age 40–49	8	n.a.	7	n.a.
Age 50–59	7	n.a.	7	n.a.
Age 60–69	6	n.a.	5	n.a.
Age 70+	4	n.a.	3	n.a.

Sources: Itogi Vsesoiuznoi perepisi naseleniia 1959 goda. SSSR (svodnyi tom) (Moscow, 1962), pp. 17, 54–5, 82; *Itogi Vsesoiuznoi perepisi naseleniia 1989 goda,* tom I, chast' 1, p. 2, tom II, chast' 1, p. 578, tom VI, chast' 2, pp. 542–3, tom X, p. 106 (East View Publications, 1992–1993); *Kyrgyzskaia Respublika: otchet o chelovecheskom razvitii 1995* (UNDP, May 1995), pp. 12, A–8.

speak Kyrgyz. This measure was not directed against the Russians and Uzbeks, who lacked the demographic base to seek the post, but against russified Kyrgyz such as the northerner Felix Kulov, a close protege of Akaev who was frequently touted as a potential successor to the president.[14]

The effects of Soviet-era migrations were also evident in Kyrgyzstan's economic development. Soviet power brought the material and educational infrastructure associated with industrial societies, but without fully integrating indigenous Central Asians into a modern economy. Newly arrived Russians and other Slavs formed the industrial class while the Kyrgyz worked in state administration, culture and the arts, or in traditional agricultural pursuits, such as shepherding.[15] Such a strong correlation between occupation and ethnicity, as Donald Horowitz has shown, is a common feature of multiethnic societies.[16] However, the case of Kyrgyzstan is unusual in that the titular nationality lacked access to some areas of employment that provided attractive financial, social, and housing benefits. This legacy of ethnic stratification in Soviet economic development has imposed a heavy burden on the transition regime in Kyrgyzstan.

The breakdown of the communist order

Moscow, and not internal political forces, precipitated the transition from communism in Kyrgyzstan. At the end of the 1980s, Kyrgyzstan was ruled by an orthodox and deeply entrenched political elite, which pointed proudly to the continuing quiescence of the population of Kyrgyzstan at a time of open political opposition in European parts of the USSR. Even some progressive Kyrgyz intellectuals, such as Chingiz Aitmatov, remarked on the inappropriateness for Kyrgyzstan of independent social movements found in the West. Alluding to the Asiatic roots of Kyrgyz political culture, Aitmatov warned that Kyrgyzstan was not like the Baltic states. "That's Europe, an advanced society with the achievements of democracy behind it. And who's behind us? China, with its almost feudal dictatorship."[17]

Reluctant to dig their own political graves, the Kyrgyz leadership became vigorous critics of Gorbachev's reform agenda and tacit supporters of his main adversary in the Central Committee, Yegor Ligachev. They also tightened their grip on the republic by mobilizing the local security services against any manifestation of independent political activity. When the republic's first discussion club, Demos, prepared a draft program for a national front in Kyrgyzstan in the fall of 1989, it prompted "a reaction of panic among the authorities and the repression of the [club's] activities."[18] But the leadership was powerless to block centrally mandated reforms, such as the enhancement of titular languages and the holding of competitive elections for newly designed legislative assemblies. It was the latter campaign, to democratize political institutions, that finally opened the way for the growth of social movements in Kyrgyzstan.

Under the scrutiny of central authorities, the population of Kyrgyzstan participated in elections for an all-union parliament in March 1989. Although the elections were not fully democratic, they departed from Soviet electoral rituals in several important respects. First, in thirty-four of the forty-three districts, candidates ran opposed for the first time in the history of Kyrgyzstan. Only in the Osh region was the level of competitiveness disappointing to the advocates of reform. Furthermore, four of the new deputies defeated candidates advanced by the party apparatus, and even some of the party-sanctioned victors, such as Askar Akaev, became open supporters of Gorbachev once in Moscow. Unlike in the past, the first secretary of the Communist Party of Kyrgyzstan, Absamat Masaliev, was unable to lead a united delegation to the all-union parliament in Moscow.[19] A Kyrgyz counter-elite developed in Moscow that would eventually challenge the conservative leadership in Frunze. Finally, the electoral campaign, taken together with the demonstration effect of political activism in other Soviet republics, mobilized new members into the republic's fledgling informal groups.

The elections of 1989 marked a watershed in the political history of Kyrgyzstan. If politics in the republic had previously been an elite game played out against the backdrop of an inert and undemanding society, it was now subject to pressure from below. In the spring of 1989, Kyrgyz youth unable to find housing in Frunze began seizing land on the outskirts of the capital and constructing their own homes. In order to extract concessions from the authorities, such as construction materials and infrastructure improvements, these self-styled "builders" formed the public association Ashar (Mutual Assistance) at the end of June 1989. Ashar's formal charter as a social and economic, rather than a political, association paved the way for its early recognition by the city government.[20] But city and republican officials understood immediately the potential dangers inherent in such a movement. A large settlement of squatters posed a direct physical threat to nearby party and state headquarters. But even more ominously, the demands of Ashar, if unsatisfied, threatened to deepen Kyrgyz resentment against the privileged housing status of Russians in the capital city. Thus, to protect its flank against a nationalist revolt, the leadership of Kyrgyzstan offered unprecedented concessions to this social movement.

Precipitated by debates over a new language law and by competitive parliamentary elections at the republican and local levels, political participation in Kyrgyzstan grew steadily from the summer of 1989 through the winter of 1990. Among the new informal associations formed in this period were Asaba (Banner), for which the defense of ethnic Kyrgyz interests was the paramount concern, and the United Council of Labor Collectives, an organization of Russian industrial workers designed, like its Baltic counterparts, to block or dilute policies that would diminish Russian cultural and political hegemony in the republic. Perhaps the first explicitly political organization in Kyrgyzstan was the City Voter's Club (Gorodskoi klub izbiratelei), created in Frunze in August 1989. This proto-party, which attracted from 30–100 persons to its meetings, played an active role in contesting republican and local legislative seats in Frunze during the February 1990 elections. These elections produced a small, if vocal, opposition bloc in the Kyrgyz parliament. Having learned from their experience in the 1989 elections, the republican Communist Party used the electoral rules and their superior organizational resources to dominate the electoral campaign. As a result, the party apparatus gained a large and at least temporarily obedient majority in the new supreme soviet. All forty raikom first secretaries, both obkom first secretaries, and the four leading republican secretaries secured seats in the parliament. Much as in the Russian Federation, the conservative composition of this assembly would later complicate relations with a progressive executive in the post-Soviet era.[21]

In 1990, all independent associations together mobilized at most a few thousand of the country's four and a half million persons. Rural areas and even most cities lacked autonomous social movements of any kind. Thus, the most potent pressure for reform continued to come not from below but from Moscow and from the growing number of Moscow's allies within the political establishment of Kyrgyzstan. This small but expanding reformist wing of the Kyrgyzstan Communist Party drew strength in May 1990 from two critical developments in Kyrgyz society. The first was the establishment of the Democratic Movement "Kyrgyzstan" (DMK), which united Ashar, Asaba, and other associations into a national front organization committed to democratic change in the republic. The DMK, whose initial membership totalled approximately 10,000 persons, quickly formed branches throughout the republic. Among its many demands was the removal of Masaliev and the conservative political leadership in Kyrgyzstan.

Less than a week after the founding congress of the DMK, ethnic violence broke out in the Osh region between ethnic Kyrgyz and Uzbeks, shattering once and for all the myth of ethnic and political harmony in the republic. In the first week of June, approximately 250 persons died in savage interethnic fighting. Only the introduction of regular Soviet army troops from outside the republic brought the violence to a halt.[22]

The origins of the Osh violence lay in a volatile mixture of ethnic mobilization from below and ethnic insensitivity by local party officials. In the first months of 1990, ethnic Kyrgyz moving into Osh from rural areas began to create new settlements akin to those being developed by Ashar on the outskirts of Frunze. However, the Kyrgyz organization in Osh, known as Osh aimagy (Osh Region),[23] encountered fierce resistance to its efforts from local Uzbeks, many of whom belonged to their own ethnic-based association, Adolat (Justice).[24] Although the immediate source of the conflict between the rival communities was land, broader issues of cultural and political power were at stake. Leaders of the Uzbek community criticized the disproportionate share of local political posts held by Kyrgyz, and more radical elements advocated the formation of an autonomous area for the Uzbeks within the Osh region. When the local first secretary, an ethnic Kyrgyz, awarded part of an Uzbek collective farm to Kyrgyz settlers, Uzbeks – some from neighboring Uzbekistan – responded with force, further mobilizing both communities.

Although the bloodshed was restricted to the area around Osh, the repercussions of the conflict spread to all areas of the republic. In Frunze, ethnic Kyrgyz held angry demonstrations in front of party headquarters. Repeated personal attempts by Masaliev to quiet the crowd failed, and only the intervention of the head of the newly formed DMK, Tupchubek Turgunaliev, ensured order. Besides a loss of face, the Osh conflict exposed the republic's leadership to investigations by unsympathetic officials in Moscow and to challenges from segments of the nomenklatura that had policy or personal differences with Masaliev. With the Osh events having exposed divisions within the state and society in Kyrgyzstan, a showdown was developing between the republic's traditional elites, who sought to rule over society, and the reformist wing of the political establishment, which envisioned a more active role for society in political life.

The denouement of this intra-elite struggle came in October 1990, when the Kyrgyz parliament – following the example of the Soviet parliament in Moscow – met to elect the first executive president of the republic. But unlike in the all-union case, where Mikhail Gorbachev ascended to the Soviet presidency unopposed, Masaliev faced two rivals for the post. Contrary to expectations, none of the candidates received a majority of the votes in the first round. This result threw the assembly, and the entire political establishment of Kyrgyzstan, into a temporary crisis. The new republican law on the presidency stipulated that, in the event of a hung parliament in the first round of voting, none of the original candidates could proceed to a second round. It was at this point that Moscow seized the opening. In hastily arranged telephone conversations between Moscow and Frunze, reformist Kyrgyz in the center with close ties to Gorbachev, including Chingiz Aitmatov, urged the deputies to back the candidacy of Askar Akaev, a physicist and head of the National Academy of Sciences.[25] In second-round balloting, this meek and politically inexperienced scientist was elected to the presidency of Kyrgyzstan.

This election ushered in an awkward period of cohabitation, or dual power, during which both First Secretary Masaliev and President Akaev claimed political supremacy. For a time, Masaliev – and his successor, Jumgalbek Amanbaev – remained the stronger figures, with the institutional support of the vast party-state bureaucracy. The president's authority rested, by contrast, on the flimsier pillars of parliamentary and public support. The balance of power shifted decisively in Akaev's favor, however, in 1991. In August of that year, with helicopters hovering menacingly overhead and troops marching on the capital of Frunze, Akaev stood defiant against the coup that sought to reverse Gorbachev's reforms.[26] Only Yeltsin among the republican leaders was more vigorous in his resistance to the coup. Two months later, Akaev won direct election to the presidency unopposed.

Barely two years into the reform era in Kyrgyzstan, the breakdown of the old political order was all but complete. It had succumbed to pressures and policies emanating from Moscow and to the elite tactics of Kyrgyz reformers, most notably Askar Akaev. There lay ahead the more difficult and protracted task of constructing democratic institutions.

Constructing a new political order

Within the democratic experience, different strategies of rule are available. At one extreme are cases – such as Thatcherite Britain – where the ruling elite seeks to ignore the opposition between elections. Once a winning coalition, or stable majority, is in place, the leaders implement assiduously the program of the victors. In such a system, the majority rules, no matter how small its margin (and in the case of Thatcher, the electoral rules enabled the Conservative Party to carry out radical reform on the basis of a plurality of popular support). At the other extreme are consociational democracies, which seek to rule with the largest practicable political base. Rather than a minimum winning coalition, consociational democracies construct broad coalitions that include representatives from most, if not all, of the country's major constituencies. In order to avoid alienating minority communities, consociational democracies are willing to sacrifice some efficiency of rule. Such democracies are most likely to be found in smaller countries with diverse ethnic, linguistic, and/or religious communities.

The strategy of rule adopted by President Akaev in Kyrgyzstan was clearly closer to consociational than majoritarian democracy. Given the country's ethnic and regional tensions and the inherent divisiveness of transition-era policies, the political leadership of Kyrgyzstan was intent on creating at least the appearance of a grand ruling coalition that integrated all major social groups. The politics of inclusiveness championed by Akaev led, for example, to the formation of the Assembly of the People of Kyrgyzstan, an extra-parliamentary consultative assembly that drew members from the country's ethnic groups.[27] Such initiatives also served, of course, to coopt political participation before it could develop into open opposition.

The desire to avoid splitting the country into political winners and losers was especially evident in Akaev's decisions on land and language policies. In May 1991, shortly before the collapse of the USSR, nationalist-minded deputies in the republican parliament enacted a land law that designated the country's territory and natural resources as the wealth (*dostoianie*) of the ethnic Kyrgyz. Fearing a backlash among other nationalities, especially Russians and Uzbeks, Akaev quickly vetoed the offending provision.[28] But the president was also sensitive to the exposed position of the traditionally nomadic Kyrgyz to market-oriented land reforms. In order to placate Kyrgyz fears that more economically ambitious ethnic groups would become the dominant landholders in the country, Akaev issued a subsequent decree that set aside one-half of newly privatized land for distribution to ethnic Kyrgyz farmers. Because the newly privatized land was to be taken initially from marginal collective farms, the Kyrgyz land fund represented a symbolic victory for the titular nationality without serious economic costs for other ethnic groups.

In the early 1990s, language reform posed perhaps the most serious threat to ethnic harmony in Kyrgyzstan. The 1989 language law, which called for Kyrgyz to replace Russian as the language of state, subjected the political leadership to intense pressure from three sides. The least Russified segments of the ethnic Kyrgyz population sought the earliest and fullest implementation of the language law. For this group, a Kyrgyz language revival promised to bring greater educational and career opportunities as well as the dignity attached to those fluent in the state language. If the leaders of Kyrgyz nationalist movements viewed the indigenization of language policy as a means of redistributing political, economic and cultural power in the country, so did the Russians. Slavic hostility to the language law was rooted both in great nation chauvinism and in a fear of being marginalized in Kyrgyzstan's political and economic life. In terms of life chances, language had served to mitigate for the Slavs the advantages of family and clan ties among the Kyrgyz. For the Uzbeks, who spoke a Turkic language with broad similarities to Kyrgyz, the prospect of having to master the titular language was less daunting than for the Russians. But they resented, nonetheless, the prospect of a new linguistic hegemony deepening Kyrgyz political dominance.

Taken together with a collapse of the economy, especially its Slavic-dominated industrial sector, the implementation of the language law led to a massive exodus of Russians from Kyrgyzstan (see table 7.4). From 1989 to 1993, the Slavic share of the population of Kyrgyzstan declined from 24 percent to 18 percent, representing a loss of over 200,000 persons. Of the approximately 100,000 Russians who remained in the southern regions of Osh and Jalal-Abad, 60 percent were pensioners.[29] In the same period, half of the country's 100,000 ethnic Germans departed, perhaps less as a result of language reform than out of a desire to return to a newly united Germany. In many ways the most dramatic social movement of the transition period in Kyrgyzstan has been the emigration of peoples who were not indigenous to Central Asia.[30]

For President Akaev, this exodus had potentially perilous political and economic consequences. Those leaving the country depleted the ranks of educated and highly-skilled workers essential for a modern economy. But they also eroded the political base of leaders like Akaev who were committed to governing through a multiethnic alliance. Put starkly, the smaller the share of Europeans in Kyrgyzstan, the more susceptible Akaev was to challenges from ethnic Kyrgyz opponents willing to pursue an aggressive nationalist agenda. The Russian exodus also complicated Kyrgyzstan's relations with the

Table 7.4 *Population change in Kyrgyzstan in the 1990s*

	1990	1991	1992	1993	1994
Population	4,334,500	4,389,500	4,451,800	4,469,300	4,429,900
Growth rate (%)	1.9	1.3	1.4	0.4	-0.9
Migration (net loss)	41,900	33,800	77,500	120,600	51,000
of which:					
Russians	16,300	17,400	48,500	80,900	31,600
Ukrainians	2,400	2,300	6,700	10,600	4,000
Germans	15,200	12,800	12,000	10,600	7,800
Jews	1,000	600	500	600	400

Source: *Kyrgyzskaia Respublika: otchet o chelovecheskom razvitii 1995* (UNDP, May 1995), pp. 12–13.

Russian Federation, which has offered moral and financial support to Russian-language universities and social organizations in Kyrgyzstan.[31] The former foreign minister of Russia, Andrei Kozyrev, publicly called for Akaev to adopt Russian as a second state language alongside Kyrgyz.[32] Recognizing the political and economic costs of an exodus of Europeans, Akaev decided in the spring of 1993 to suspend by decree the implementation of the language law, a decision that appeared to stem the tide of emigration.[33]

On issues of land and language, Akaev was willing to use the full powers of the presidency, including the veto and executive decrees, to overcome parliamentary resistance to his policies. But given the political distance between the president and assembly, such moments of direct confrontation were surprisingly rare in the first two years of Kyrgyz independence. Several factors contributed to the generally cooperative relations between executive and legislature in this period. The first was Akaev's politics of inclusion, which sought to coopt all but the most hostile forces in parliament by making tactical concessions regarding perquisites, patronage, and policies. The second was the president's enormous popularity, both at home and abroad. Akaev's ability to attract generous foreign economic assistance created around the president an aura of indispensability, which for a time discouraged or blunted the criticism of deputies.[34] But perhaps the most effective shield against a parliamentary challenge to presidential authority was the speaker of the assembly, Medetkan Sherimkulov. A former ideology secretary of the Communist Party of Kyrgyzstan, Sherimkulov used his considerable personal and bureaucratic authority to restrain the opposition and to guide much of the presidential program through a fractious parliament. This subtle, discrete, and pragmatic politician joined Akaev in an informal pact, or condominium, that served as a substitute for a permanent parliamentary majority. Although it is tempting to explain Sherimkulov's behavior in terms of interests, and a relationship of "exchange" with Akaev, a more important factor appears to have been his own understanding of how elites should conduct politics. To govern responsibly for Sherimkulov was to minimize the intensity and frequency of open political conflict. For many of Sherimkulov's generation, it was a choice between dignified elite negotiations and the politics of populism and demagoguery.

Even with Sherimkulov's support, however, Akaev's grand coalition was not able to survive a deepening economic crisis (see table 7.5). During 1993 and 1994, the national income of Kyrgyzstan fell by more than 20 percent each year, impoverishing large segments of the population.[35] In interviews with Kyrgyz focus groups in the spring of 1994, three-quarters of the respondents identified the economy as the country's most serious problem.[36] In this climate of economic despair, an unlikely alliance of communists and disaffected democrats began to challenge openly presidential leadership, targeting an issue on which Akaev's administration was immensely sensitive and vulnerable – the rise of official corruption. Initial parliamentary inquiries centered on alleged improprieties in the granting of gold mining rights at Kumtor to a Canadian firm, Cameco.[37] Before signing the original agreement with Cameco in December 1992, the government of Kyrgyzstan had not sought alternative bids, a decision that aroused the ire and suspicion of members of parliament, the press, and the public. Under pressure, the government renegotiated the contract in 1993 to obtain more favorable terms for Kyrgyzstan. But the results of the investigation cast a cloud over the government and led to the resignation in January 1994 of the prime minister, Tursunbek Chyngyshev, an economist with limited political skills.[38]

Moving beyond its original mandate, the parliamentary "gold commission" also uncovered corrupt practices in privatization and foreign trade. Among the subjects of these inquiries were leading executive officials in central as well as regional governments. Even the president's wife aroused suspicion because of her brother's involvement in a large hard currency loan from the National Bank.[39] The torrent of accusations and insinuations engendered by the inquiries into official corruption quickly eroded the civility that had characterized Kyrgyz politics in the initial transition from Communist rule.[40] In the face of a deteriorating political and economic climate, Akaev grew disillusioned with democratic constraints on executive power. Influenced by the examples of presidents in neighboring Central Asian states, Akaev launched an authoritarian offensive in the middle of 1994. He sanctioned the formation of a Committee to Defend the Honor and Dignity of the President, which was designed to intimidate those who criticized the

Table 7.5 *Indicators of economic trends in Kyrgyzstan since 1989*

	1989	1990	1991	1992	1993	1994	1995[a]
GDP	4	3	-5	-25	-16	-27	-6
Industrial output	5.2	-0.6	-0.3	-26.4	-25.3	-29.7	-13
Rate of inflation	n.a.	n.a.	n.a.	954.6	1,308.7	378.1	45
Employed	80.5	80.0	79.2	81.0	74.5	72.6	n.a.
% Workforce in private activity	n.a.	n.a.	n.a.	n.a.	n.a.	n.a.	n.a.
GNP per capita	n.a.	n.a.	n.a.	n.a.	n.a.	1,170	n.a.
% GDP from private sector[b]	n.a.	n.a.	n.a.	n.a.	56.4	58.0	n.a.

Notes: GDP – % change over previous year; industrial output – % change over previous year; rate of inflation – % change in end-year retail/consumer prices (*potrebitel'skie tseny*); employment – as % of labor resources (working age population capable of working plus the working elderly and youth); GNP per capita – in US dollars at PPP exchange rates. [a]Estimate. [b]Non-state sector.

Sources: *Kyrgyzskaia Respublika: otchet o chelovecheskom razvitii 1995* (UNDP, May 1995), pp. 16, 18, 20; European Bank for Reconstruction and Development, *Transition Report 1995: Economic Transition in Eastern Europe and the Former Soviet Union* (London: EBRD, 1995), pp. 30, 185, 199; European Bank for Reconstruction and Development, *Transition Report Update, April 1996: Assessing Progress in Economies in Transition* (London: EBRD, 1996).

president. With the broadcast media already under effective executive control, he began to restrict the freedom of the press, closing down two newspapers in June 1994, including *Svobodnye gory*, a publication registered by the parliament.[41] In the spring of 1995, the president launched a criminal prosecution for defamation against Zamira Sydykova and Tamara Slashcheva, editors of the independent newspaper, *Res Publica*. *Res Publica* had printed an apparently groundless accusation that Akaev owned property overseas.[42] In July 1995, a municipal court in Bishkek sentenced Sydykova and Slashcheva to one-and-a-half year suspended prison sentences. More ominously, it deprived them of the right to work as journalists for the same period. According to one of Akaev's defenders, such actions were essential to stop the nihilist crusade (*bespredel*) in politics and the press, which was led "by democrats and communists, feminists and drug dealers, embezzlers and bribetakers."[43]

Circumventing parliament and the national bureaucracy in Bishkek, Akaev forged a *de facto* ruling alliance with the heads of administration, or *akimy*, of Kyrgyzstan's six regions.[44] The idea was to create an efficient and disciplined executive hierarchy, with the regional *akimy* linking the president to the leaders of local government. In this system, in which the president appointed the regional governors, who in turn appointed officials in towns and villages, executive leaders answered only to their administrative superior and not to local assemblies or the public. According to one political commentator, the idea of popular sovereignty exercised through the parliament was little more than a facade constructed for Western consumption. "The institution of the *akimiaty*," he argued, "is the backbone of authoritarian power."[45]

Although parliament, and even the national bureaucracy, became increasingly irrelevant to the daily governance of the country, opposition-minded deputies in Bishkek retained the potential to erode the image and legislative authority of the president. They were also poised to select new members to the Central Election Commission, which would oversee the parliamentary electoral campaign.[46] Thus, with less than six months before the end of the parliament's term, the *akimy* conspired with the president to disband the assembly. Deputies loyal to Akaev and the regional governors declared a boycott of the parliament, which halted its work in September 1994.[47] The president then called new parliamentary elections designed to return a more cooperative assembly.[48] The results of these elections disappointed both Akaev and the democratic opposition.

The 1995 parliamentary elections and social demobilization in Kyrgyzstan

The second election in a transition regime is often a defining event for the consolidation of democracy. This was not the case in Kyrgyzstan. The Kyrgyz parliamentary elections of 1995 highlighted instead the ways in which traditional politics penetrated and distorted nominally democratic procedures. The country's second contested elections were arguably less open and fair than the first, which were held at the end of the Soviet era. Political and economic elites had learned how to corrupt the electoral process, and many – perhaps most – voters appeared willing to serve as pawns in a political game that they dimly understood.[49] The 1995 elections in Kyrgyzstan marked not the consolidation of democracy but the demobilization of a politically weary and alienated society by corrupt and cynical elites.

In several respects, the institutional design of Kyrgyz politics worked against democratic consolidation in the 1995 parliamentary elections. First, the May 1993 Constitution provided for a dramatic reduction in the size of the unicameral Kyrgyz assembly, from 350 members to 105. Justified as a cost-cutting measure during an economic crisis, this reduction in the number of parliamentary seats served to dilute the representation of ethnic minorities by creating larger districts, where compact non-Kyrgyz settlements were combined with ethnic Kyrgyz areas. A subsequent decision to create two separate chambers without expanding the number of deputies further exacerbated the problem of vote dilution by establishing even larger districts. At the president's insistence, this change was made by referendum in October 1995, on the heels of the closure of parliament. With voters casting ballots in seventy single-member districts for the Chamber of People's Representatives and thirty-five single-member districts for the Legislative Assembly, minority candidates faced structural barriers that would not have been present if Kyrgyzstan had introduced proportional representation or a larger number of single-member seats.

The electoral rules[50] played directly into the hands of the *akimy* and the regional political and economic establishments. The use of single-member districts virtually insured that local issues and loyalties would triumph over attempts to build national parties and national political programs.[51] Furthermore, following the decision to create a bicameral legislature, President Akaev unilaterally lifted the constitutional ban on regional and local executive officials holding office in the larger Chamber of People's Representatives.[52] This vital concession to the *akimy* helped to turn the parliament into an organ of regional power. Although such changes in Kyrgyzstan's institutional design did not by themselves thwart democratization, they clearly reinforced existing social and cultural impediments to democratic reform.

The ability of the *akimy* to influence electoral outcomes was on full display during the 1995 parliamentary campaign. In the Issyk-Kul' region, the regional governor, Jumagul Saadanbekov, mobilized his 200-person akimiat, local state enterprises, the regional procuracy, and young toughs to support the candidacy of the former prime minister, Tursunbek Chyngyshev. Saadanbekov lured one candidate out of the race by promising him an attractive sinecure. He also arranged the firing of the wife of Chyngyshev's main opponent, B. Baikhojoev. Despite these measures, Chyngyshev trailed Baikhojoev in the initial vote tabulation. Only later, with the mysterious appearance of several thousand ballots for Chyngyshev, was the former prime minister able to claim victory. Such scenarios, with varying mixtures of gift-giving, fraud, and intimidation, occurred throughout Kyrgyzstan.[53]

Besides the *akimy*, the other major force in the 1995 parliamentary elections was the new plutocracy, represented by state enterprise directors and private (and nominally private) businessmen. Where the *akimy* exerted bureaucratic power on the campaign, business interests brought financial resources to bear, at times in creative and unorthodox ways. One businessman gave out left-footed boots to the local population, promising to supply the right boot if he won. In most areas, bureaucratic power forged alliances with financial power. In the southern region of Jalal-Abad, E. Uzakbaev, the director of a state agricultural equipment factory, gave out plows to local leaders and vodka and freshly-slaughtered horses to the voters. He also promised to sell flour at reduced prices after the election. On polling day, a district *akim* urged voters to choose Uzakbaev to insure that they would not "lose out" (*propadem*) during spring planting. When asked to explain the population's willingness to succumb to such crude campaign tactics, the losing candidate responded that his fellow southerners remained deferential to the bosses (*nachal'stvu*) and to those who helped them.[54]

The 1995 parliamentary elections also confirmed the continuing strength of tribal and clan ties in Kyrgyz politics. With the backing of Akaev and the local *akim*, a department head in the presidential administration, Tolubek Omuraliev, returned to his native region of Naryn to contest a parliamentary seat. As a member of Naryn's largest tribe, the Tynymseitov, he relied heavily on a network of elders to support his candidacy. Immediately after first-round balloting, leading members of the tribe reportedly gathered to devise a strategy to "destroy" the opponent, from the Sarbagysh tribe, in the second round of the election.[55]

Throughout the country, voting irregularities plagued the elections. In some districts, "campaign vodka flowed like a river."[56] It was not uncommon to see drunken voters sprawled around the voting booths, and in one precinct, an old woman died of overconsumption near the polling station.[57] Furthermore, election officials made little effort to enforce formal voting rules. Thus, older men frequently voted for their wives and families. Some voters cast ballots on the strength of a bus pass, without having to show proper identification. And allegations of ballot stuffing abounded, with mysteriously high turnout in such places as maternity wards and universities.[58] The central and local election commissions, created to insure a fair election, were themselves implicated in favoritism, at times to the point of annulling elections. Yet despite widespread fraud, observers from the CSCE submitted an official report confirming the democratic character of the elections – a document desired by Akaev and by Western governments and financial institutions extending aid to Kyrgyzstan.[59] According to Strobe Talbott, the US deputy secretary of state, "the parliamentary elections will be a decisive test of democracy in Kyrgyzstan, and, we hope, will provide evidence of the sincerity of the assurances given by President Akaev."[60]

Among the biggest losers in the 1995 parliamentary elections were the country's fledgling political parties. The thirty social movements and twelve parties[61] contesting the elections were unable to field a full slate of candidates across the country. Out of a total of 1,021 candidates standing for election, a mere 161 had party affiliations. Only the politically unreconstructed Communist Party, with forty nominees, was able to field more than twenty candidates. Many smaller parties contested elections in fewer than ten

Table 7.6 *Political parties and parliamentary representation in Kyrgyzstan, 1995*

Name of party	Leader	Registration	Parliamentary seats
Democratic Party "Erkin Kyrgyzstan"	Tursunbai Bakir uulu	April 12, 1991	3
Party of National Renewal "Asaba"	Bazarbaev, Ch.	December 30, 1991	4
Communist Party of Kyrgyzstan	Sydykov, Sh.	September 17, 1992	3
"Ata-Meken"	Teekebaev, O.	December 16, 1992	3
Republican Party	Sharshenaliev, J.	December 16, 1992	3
"Democratic Movement of Kyrgyzstan"	Jeksheev, J.	July 16, 1993	1
Social-Democratic Party	Atambaev, A.	December 6, 1994	14
Agrarian Party	Aliev, E.	November 26, 1993	1
"Unity of Kyrgyzstan"	Muraliev, A.	June 8, 1994	4
Democratic Party of Women of Kyrgyzstan	Shailieva, T.	October 14, 1994	1
Democratic Party of Economic Unity	Tashtambekov, A.	October 14, 1994	0
Agrarian-Labor Party of Kyrgyzstan	Sydykov, U.S.	n.a.	1
Unaffiliated			67

Note: All parties had their headquarters in Bishkek.

Sources: A. Elebaeva and N. Omuraliev, "Informatsiia o politicheskikh partiiakh Kyrgyzstana" (unpublished manuscript, September 1995); "List of the Jogorku Kenesh Members," distributed by the Embassy of the Kyrgyz Republic, Washington, DC, November 16, 1995.

of the 105 districts.[62] In general, candidates with national party affiliations found it difficult to blunt the appeal of their locally oriented non-party opponents.[63] As a result, only a third of the newly elected parliamentary deputies had party ties (see table 7.6). And with only 20 of the 350 former deputies finding seats in the new parliament, the organization of factions had to begin anew.[64]

Although eleven parties gained seats in the parliament, only the Social-Democratic Party, a "party of regional power" with a political agenda inspired by reform communism, had more than token representation.[65] The electoral results were especially disappointing for the most prominent offshoot of the DMK, Erkin Kyrgyzstan, which nominated candidates for nineteen seats but emerged victorious in only three districts, and Ata-Meken, a centrist party formed with the implicit blessing of President Akaev. Ata-Meken also gained three seats in the new assembly.[66] Lampooning the new Kyrgyz parliament, a Moscow journalist noted that one must not take the country's party system seriously. "There are many parties, but each has two and a half members."[67]

Compared with the previous assembly, where female deputies held 8 percent of the seats, women also fared poorly, winning only 5 percent of the contests. As expected, ethnic minorities emerged from the elections with low levels of representation. Comprising 42 percent of the population, they won only 18 percent of the parliamentary seats. To Russians and Uzbeks, with six seats respectively, these results were but the latest evidence of a radical indigenization of cadres policy in Kyrgyzstan. Important institutions, such as the *akimiaty* and law enforcement organs, were already functioning as ethnic Kyrgyz preserves. Even the president's own press secretary, the critic-turned-apologist, Kamil Baialinov, noted that: "It is not a secret that responsible officials of the very highest rank come primarily from this or that clan (*rodovogo klana*). That's reality. In our small republic, no matter where you turn, everyone is someone else's man (*kto-to chei-to chelovek*)."[68] And while the president and government issued edicts in mid-1994 outlining specific measures to attract more non-Kyrgyz into government service, they have thus far had little effect on patronage policy.[69] By the end of 1995, even some members of the government, such as the foreign minister, Roza Otunbaeva, were proposing the reintroduction of the social and ethnic quota (*galochka*) system used in the Soviet era.[70] Perhaps the most striking feature of the new parliament was the difference in the composition of the two chambers.[71] In the thirty-five seat Legislative Assembly, the two largest groups were executive officials and members of the intelligentsia (lawyers, journalists, medical workers, and educators), with 33 percent and 25 percent of the seats, respectively. Yet in the seventy-seat Chamber of People's Representatives, business leaders dominated, with over 50 percent of the

Table 7.7 *Social backgrounds of parliamentary deputies in Kyrgyzstan*

	1989 USSR Congress of People's Deputies no.	%	1990 Republican Supreme Soviet no.	%	1995 Kyrgyzstan Jogorku Kenesh no.	%
Deputies	41[a]	100	350	100	105[b]	100
First time elected	n.a.	-	277	81	85	81
Male	34	83	321	92	100	95
Kyrgyz	24	59	277	65	87	83
Russian	12	29	65	19	6	6
Uzbek	2	5	25	7	6	6
German	2	5	5	1	1	1
Other ethnic groups	1	2	28	8	4	4

Notes: [a]Based on backgrounds of 40 deputies. [b]Based on backgrounds of 104 deputies.

Sources: Z. Sorokina, "Demokratiia utverzhdaetsia," *Sovetskaia Kirgiziia*, April 18, 1989, p. 1; V. Tishkov, "An Assembly of Nations or an All-Union Parliament?" *Journal of Soviet Nationalities*, no. 1 (1990), 123; "Doklad Predsedatelia Mandatnoi komissii deputata K.A. Turganova," *Sovetskaia Kirgiziia*, April 11, 1990, pp. 1–2; *Spisok narodnykh deputatov Kirgizskoi SSR (dvenadtsatyi sozyv) na 1 dekabria 1990 goda* (Frunze, 1990); "List of the Jogorku Kenesh Members," distributed by the Embassy of the Kyrgyz Republic, Washington, DC, November 16, 1995.

seats. It appears that many of these business-oriented deputies sought a parliamentary seat in order to acquire immunity from prosecution.[72] The British journalist, Ian Pryde, reported that at the time of the February 1995 elections, "nearly 30 percent of the new deputies were being investigated by the State Prosecutor's Office for illegal financial dealings."[73]

The influence of this new business class in the parliament depends heavily, of course, on the division of labor between the chambers, which remains a subject of intense political struggle almost a year into the life of the new parliament.[74] As students of institutionalism remind us, the creation of new political structures, such as a bicameral assembly, can at times reorient longstanding political attitudes and behavior. There is evidence that this is occurring in Kyrgyzstan, where deputies' defense of the interests of their chamber at times transcends traditional regional and sectoral loyalties.[75] In spite of conflicting loyalties, however, deputies in the parliament voted to extend the tenure of the prime minister, Apas Jumagulov, with only a single dissenting vote, yet another indication of the absence of strong parties and an organized opposition.[76]

If the 1995 parliamentary elections represent a defining moment, it is not in the consolidation of democracy but in the criminalization and regionalization of politics in Kyrgyzstan. The entry of large numbers of corrupt businessmen into the legislature was certain to complicate attempts by Akaev to clean out his administration and to make less likely elite adherence to democratic rules and procedures.[77] To insure its sway over the distribution of such products as tobacco, alcohol, petroleum, and opium, "the mafia already participates in the political processes inside the country."[78] At the end of the election campaign, Almazbek Atambaev, leader of the Social-Democratic Party, observed that the greatest danger facing Kyrgyzstan was not socialism but "sicily-ism."[79] A disillusioned former leader of the party Erkin Kyrgyzstan estimated that approximately two-thirds of the new assembly consisted of corrupt officials and businessmen.[80] In a meeting with the government called in mid-1995 to discuss the fight against corruption, the president completed his remarks with a *cri de coeur* directed at corrupt officials and the country at large. "It's enough . . . Stop it! Stop it! There will be a Judgment Day. Fear God! You see how they drink the blood of the nation and steal, and many of you participate in this. The Spirit of Manas will curse you!"[81] Among the deepening constraints on presidential power and authority was a political elite intent on using public sinecures as a means of private enrichment.

The presidential elections also complicated Akaev's relations with the *akimy*, to whom, he now recognized, he had "given too much freedom."[82] Although the presidential administration worked closely with *akimy* during the election campaign to advance numerous candidates loyal to Akaev, the new parliament had stronger ties to the regions than to the center. And in the regions themselves, the *akimy* generally exercised firm control over local executives and assemblies.[83] During the October 1994 local elections, for example, the vast majority of seats to regional and local parliaments were uncontested. In the Issyk-Kul' region, candidates ran without opposition in 719 of the 888 electoral districts.[84]

Having allied with the president to bring down the parliament in 1994, the regional elites were in a position after the elections of 1995 to play off president and parliament to deepen regional autonomy. Should the president agree to direct elections for regional leaders, which some have demanded, presidential influence over the regions would decline further.[85] Given their support for an extension of the president's term by referendum in late 1995, the *akimy* remain committed, over the short term at least, to a condominium with the president. But this condominium appears designed to accommodate a gradual encroachment of the regions on the prerogatives of the center on issues such as personal and budgetary policy. There is the danger that in the institution of the *akimy*, Akaev created a monster that may one day devour him.[86]

Conclusion

It is tempting to view Kyrgyzstan in the mid-1990s as an example of what Guillermo O'Donnell has called a "delegative democracy." Such democracies, he argues, "rest on the premise that whoever wins election to the presidency is thereby entitled to govern as he or she sees fit, constrained only by the hard facts of existing power relations and by a constitutionally limited term in office."[87] In this tradition, presidents like Akaev seek to retard the development of institutions – such as parliaments, courts, and the press – that can hold executive authority accountable. In the case of the constitutional court, Akaev took numerous steps to delay its installation and limit its authority. Yet the "hard facts" of regional power in Kyrgyzstan impose limits on presidential authority that are unusual in delegative democracies, such as those found in Latin America. The *akimy* may not yet hold the president hostage, but they serve – like the military in many developing countries – as the only reliable source of institutional support for the president. Kyrgyzstan's own military, a fledgling organization of no more than 12,000 army officers and men, has thus far been a symbol of national sovereignty rather than a vital force in defense or politics.[88]

In the Kyrgyz case, the president has exhibited a reluctance to respect the most basic tenet of a democracy, even a "delegative" one – a constitutionally-limited term of office. A year before the expiration of his first five-year term, Akaev launched a campaign to obtain a second term by early referendum. The presidential administration and local *akimiaty* oversaw the collection of signatures on referendum petitions from 1.2 million voters, more than half the electorate. Like the parliamentary campaign, this signature drive relied at times on coercion and fraud. In some areas, the authorities required a signature on a referendum petition before distributing pension or wage payments.[89] The creation of a personality cult around the president was an essential ingredient of the referendum campaign. Villagers wove rugs with Akaev's image to present to the president,[90] and Kyrgyz elders, the *aksakaly*, extolled the virtues of Akaev daily on television and radio. Social organizations and workers' collectives submitted letters of support to the press. Even journalists could not contain their admiration for the president.

For Akaev, a fall 1995 referendum held numerous advantages over competitive presidential elections scheduled for the following October. First, the presidents of Kazakstan, Uzbekistan, and Turkmenistan had all extended their terms in office by referendum. To hold democratic presidential elections in the face of these precedents was to invite a deterioration of relations with

Kyrgyzstan's more powerful and authoritarian neighbors.[91] The timing of the referendum also benefited the president. By staging a referendum in the fall of 1995, Akaev would avoid the erosion of presidential authority that can precede the slow run-up to contested elections, especially in cases where the popularity of the incumbent is declining.[92] Facing a deepening financial crisis, Akaev had every reason to believe that his position would be less secure a year hence.

Finally, the carefully staged celebrations of the 1,000-year anniversary of the Kyrgyz national hero, Manas, in August 1995, placed the president at the center of a moment of immense national pride. The celebrations invited comparisons between the legendary Manas, who led the Kyrgyz at the beginning of their political history, and Askar Akaev, whom history had called to shepherd the country into independence in the modern era. The afterglow of such a moment was not likely to survive the winter.[93]

Akaev's campaign came to an abrupt halt, however, in late September 1995, when the parliament refused to sanction the referendum. It voted instead to reschedule presidential elections for December 1995.[94] Although unconstitutional, the parliamentary decision represented an attractive political compromise by satisfying the president's concern for timing while granting his critics contested elections. Challenged by several prominent opponents, including the former parliamentary speaker, Medetkan Sherimkulov, and the former Communist Party first secretary, Absamat Masaliev,[95] Akaev won the December 24 elections with 71.5 percent of the vote.[96] In the weeks after his landslide victory, Akaev consolidated his position by holding a referendum that expanded presidential powers.[97] New powers were needed, according to Akaev, to overcome the political stalemate that flowed from the election of a bicameral legislature that was divided against itself.[98]

The parliamentary and presidential election campaigns of 1995 illustrate that political culture – or more precisely the interface between elite and mass political cultures – remains one of the most profound barriers to democratization in Kyrgyzstan. Amid the strains of the transition from communism, civic traditions have shown little evidence of taking root in a society dominated by a mixture of family, clan, regional, and ethnic loyalties. The malleability and anomie of the electorate and the cynicism and corruption of political leaders have been mutually reinforcing. "Instead of making the voter proud of being a part of something larger," noted a leading journalist, "[the 1995 elections] reduced him to something inconsequential in a farce."[99]

In the minds of the ruling elite, politics is too important to be left to the vagaries of parliament or people.[100] Kyrgyz political elites, whether "democrats," nationalists, or communists, perceive the public as politically backward and therefore incapable of assuming the full responsibilities of citizenship. Indeed, the most pessimistic leaders in this regard may be the "democrats," who openly lament the "political illiteracy" of the masses.[101] For their part, the citizenry has at best a limited understanding of, and commitment to, democracy. Half of Kyrgyz citizens surveyed in the summer of 1995 believed that "to establish order and discipline, it is necessary to limit the democratic rights and freedoms of citizens."[102]

According to the Issyk-Kul' *akim*, Jumagul Saadanbekov, the political crisis in Kyrgyzstan in the mid-1990s resulted from a disjuncture between the country's cultural conditions and its formal political rules. Young democracies in the West, he noted, protected themselves from insolent populism by numerous methods, including the gradual enfranchisement of the population. In contrast, Kyrgyzstan adopted immediately "the final products of a long [democratic] evolution," such as universal suffrage.[103] During a speech in France in the summer of 1994, President Akaev made similar observations about the democratic potential of Kyrgyzstan. "The misfortune, pain, and weakness of the Kyrgyz through the ages was their tribalism and regionalism, which frequently placed them at the edge of the abyss. The vitality of clan and tribal traditions among the Kyrgyz is amazing [*porazitel'naia*]."[104] Without a fundamental change in rules, leaders, or circumstance, Kyrgyzstan is likely to be caught in the receding tide of democratization's third wave.

NOTES

1 For a short biography of Akaev, see E. Huskey, "Akaev," in *The Gorbachev Encyclopedia*, ed. J. Wieczynski (Gulf Breeze, FL: Academic International Press, 1993), pp. 30–4.

2 L. Lozovskaia, "Den'gi perechisliat MVF, vsemirnyi Bank, Iaponia . . . ," *Biznesmen K* (Bishkek), no. 15 (June 1993), 3, and E. Huskey, "Kyrgyzstan Leaves the Ruble Zone," *RFE/RL Research Report*, 3 September 1993, pp. 38–43.

3 The most authoritative account of the ethnogenesis of the Kyrgyz remains S. M. Abramzon, *Kirgizy i ikh etnogeneticheskie i istoriko-kul'turnye sviazi* (Leningrad: "Nauka," 1971).

4 A. Zhakypov, "Komuz ne dlia frantsuzov," *Sovetskaia Kirgiziia*, 6 September 1991, p. 2.

5 See, for example, Rakhat Achylova, *Political Culture and the Prerequisites of Kyrgyzstan's Foreign Policy*, Russian Littoral Project Occasional Paper no. 83, October 1994, pp. 8–9.

6 In this sense, one might compare Kyrgyzstan to the early American republic, which – as Louis Hartz and others have argued – enjoyed a comparative political advantage over Western Europe because of its lack of a hereditary aristocracy.

7 See, for example, "Akademik Tabyshaliev: 'znaia pravdu istorii, ne pred"iavliat' drug drugu schet za svoikh predkov,'" *Slovo Kyrgyzstana*, 6 April 1991, p. 3; A. Arzymatov, "V sostav Rossii: vkhozhdenie? Prisoedinenie? Zavoevanie?" ibid., 1 June 1991, p. 10; U. Midinova and E. Turaliev, "O 'piknikakh,' dlinnykh

ocherediakh . . . i drugikh malopriiatnykh veshchakh," *Literaturnyi Kirgizstan*, no. 1 (1990), 123–8; and K. Karabekov, "Sotsial'no-ekonomicheskie faktory garmonizatsii mezhnatsional'nykh otnoshenii," *Kommunist Kirgizstana*, no. 2 (1990), 24–9.

8 "Ne sozdadim sebe kumirov," *Res Publica*, 9 May 1995, p. 2. For an argument that Russia was the lesser evil among larger neighbors, see I. Boldzhurova, "Ne zabludit'sia v istorii," *Slovo Kyrgyzstana*, 17 September 1994, p. 7.

9 E. Carrere d'Encausse, "The National Republics Lose Their Independence," in *Central Asia: 120 Years of Russian Rule*, ed. E. Allworth (Durham: Duke University Press, 1989), pp. 256–65; Dzh. Dzhunushaliev, "Politika korenizatsii: opyt i problemy," *Kommunist Kirgizstana*, no. 1 (1990), 69–78.

10 "Idut vstrechi s izbirateliami," *Sovetskaia Kirgiziia*, 9 May 1989, p. 2.

11 For an analysis of the language issue, see Eugene Huskey, "The Politics of Language in Kyrgyzstan," *Nationalities Papers*, no. 3 (1995), 549–72.

12 On the traditional tensions between North and South, exacerbated by the local purges of the 1930s, see Mamat Karataev, "Produkt 30-minutnoi deiatel'nosti nekrupnogo mozga, ili Razgovor s samim soboi po povodu stat'i K. Mambetalieva," *Slovo Kyrgyzstana*, 24 October 1992, p. 7, and "Igra na grani fola, no bez udaleniia s polia," *Slovo Kyrgyzstana*, 23 January 1993, p. 6.

13 There is rising intolerance among Kyrgyz Muslim youth against their ethnic kin who join conservative Protestant sects, such as the Baptists. According to one source, the former are stirred up by "religiously illiterate rural mullahs." ("'No vreden sever dlia menia,' ili nedelia, raspiataia v stranitsakh . . . ," *Slovo Kyrgyzstana*, 5 July 1995, p. 2.) Because of these tensions, in the Naryn region, the local Justice Department has refused to register local Baptist organizations, although their papers are in order. (Ibid.) Intraethnic tensions are also increasingly evident in the armed forces of Kyrgyzstan. According to one source, desertion is on the rise because the contingent from the numerically dominant region in each unit "commands," making life intolerable for Kyrgyz from other regions. See Toktugul Seiitbekov, "Nekotorye mysli o traditsii naroda i politike Prezidenta," *Res Publica*, 14 February 1995, p. 3.

14 For a brief biography of Kulov, who as MVD head was instrumental in protecting Akaev during the 1991 coup, see "Portrety bez ramok," *Literaturnyi Kirgizstan*, no. 5 (1991), 99–103.

15 E. Abildaev, "Rabochii klass Kirgizii: osobennosti razvitiia," *Kommunist Kirgizstana*, nos. 8–9 (1990), 133–8; R. Osmonalieva, "Ob"ektiven li voliuntarizm?" *Kommunist Kirgizstana*, no. 10 (1990), 79–83.

16 Donald Horowitz, *Ethnic Groups in Conflict* (Berkeley: University of California Press, 1985).

17 "Obrashchenie k molodezhi," *Sovetskaia Kirgiziia*, 17 February 1990, p. 3.

18 V. Ponomarev, *Samodeiatel'nye obshchestvennye organizatsii v Kazakhstane i Kirgizii, 1987–1991* (Moscow, 1991), p. 86.

19 On late Soviet-era elections in Kyrgyzstan, see E. Huskey, "The Rise of Contested Politics in Central Asia: Elections in Kyrgyzstan, 1989–1990," *Europe-Asia Studies*, no. 5 (1995), 809–29.

20 E. Denisenko, "'Ashar' deistvyet, i on prav," *Slovo Kyrgyzstana*, 8 May 1991, p. 7.

21 This paragraph draws heavily from Huskey, "The Rise of Contested Politics," pp. 818–22.

22 The best contemporary account of the Osh events is the local KGB report, published in "KGB i oshkaia tragediia [k massovym besporiadkam v oshskoi oblasti (Dokument Upravleniia KGB po Oshskoi oblasti ot 24.06.1990. g.)]," *Literaturnyi Kirgizstan*, no. 11 (1990), 93–100. See also Valery Tishkov, "'Don't Kill Me, I'm a Kyrgyz!': An Anthropological Analysis of Violence in the Osh Ethnic Conflict," *Journal of Peace Research*, no. 2 (1995), 133–49.

23 "Kambaraly Bektemirov: 'Eto byla nechestnaia igra . . . ,'" *Slovo Kyrgyzstana*, 5 December 1990, p. 2.

24 "Rustam Mirakhmedov: 'Mne snitsia chetvertoe iiunia,'" *Rossiiskie vesti*, 7 February 1991, p. 3.

25 Personal interviews by the author with leading Kyrgyz politicians.

26 See A. Barshai, "Diktatura ne proidet," *Slovo Kyrgyzstana*, 23 August 1991, p. 1; V. Rodin, "O chesti i sovesti," ibid., 27 August 1991, p. 2; and A. Galuni-chev, "Tri chernykh dnia avgusta v Bishkeke," ibid., 27 August 1991, p. 3.

27 "Assambleia ne dlia dekoratsii," ibid., 5 May 1994, p. 2. Funded by the state, it contained forty-five persons and an eleven-person presidium.

28 "Veto Prezidenta otvechaiet chaianiiam vsekh liudei dobroi voli," ibid., 28 June 1991, p. 3.

29 V. Uleev, "Chem vymoshchena nasha doroga," *Res Publica*, 22 August 1995, p. 3.

30 For an excellent overview of the emigration, see R. Abdymomunov, "My – ne list'ia na vetru," *Slovo Kyrgyzstana*, 21 March 1995, p. 2. Of those leaving the country, 44 percent were out of work. Sixty percent of the emigrants went to Russia, with more than 10,000 to Western Siberia, 8,000 to the Volga region, 6,000 to the Central Black Earth region, and 5,000 to the Urals. The article also notes that within Kyrgyzstan, a considerable migration occurred into the Chui Valley from the provinces. Ibid.

31 The Russian Federation's Government Commission for the Support of Compatri-ots, headed by Sergei Shakhrai, has purchased newsprint and computers and other equipment for the two leading Russian organizations in Kyrgyzstan, the Slavic Fund and Concord (*Soglasie*). V. Uleev, "Chem vymoshchena nasha doroga," *Res Publica*, 22 August 1995, p. 3.

32 E. Taranova, "Esli druzhat diplomaty – vyigryvaiut strany," *Slovo Kyrgyzstana*, 3–4 October 1995, p. 5.

33 In spite of the indigenization movement in Kyrgyzstan, Russian-language higher education remains the favorite for the country's youth. Whereas there were 3.2 applicants for each place in Kyrgyz State University, whose instruction is primarily in Kyrgyz, the Slavonic University had 7.2 applicants for each seat. Kanybek Imanaliev, "'Iazykom ne spishi, a delom ne lenis,'" ibid., 22 July 1995, p. 6.

34 Eugene Huskey, "Kyrgyzstan Leaves the Ruble Zone," *RFE/RL Research Report*, 3 September 1993, pp. 38–43.

35 *Kyrgyzskaia Respublika. Otchet o chelovecheskom razvitii 1995* (UNDP, 1995), p. 16. Zamira Sydykova argues that the end of the postcommunist euphoria in Kyrgyzstan came on 15 January 1993, when Akaev made his pessimistic report on the economy to the government. Z. Sydykova, "Sygraet li Kyrgyzskoe

pravitel'stvo v russkuiu ruletku, ili kuda dal'she, esli dal'she nekuda," *Res Publica*, 23 January 1993, p. 1.

36 Richard B. Dobson, "Kyrgyzstan in a Time of Change: A Report on Ten Focus Groups in 1994" (Washington, DC: USIA Office of Research, 1994), p. 6.

37 Based in Saskatoon, Cameco is one of the world's largest miners and processors of uranium. It apparently had limited experience in gold mining before the Kumtor venture. See *Principal International Businesses* (Bethlehem, PA: Dun & Bradstreet, 1995), and "Cameco, uranium giant, in Wyoming," *Riverton Ranger* (Wyoming), 21 June 1995. My thanks to David Everett for digging up these sources.

38 V. Niksdorf, "Zhal' tol'ko . . . ," *Slovo Kyrgyzstana*, 7 May 1994, p. 3.

39 V. Niksdorf, "Srochnoe poruchenie Prezidenta prokuroru respubliki," ibid., 27 May 1994, p. 1.

40 An example of the degeneration of political discourse in Kyrgyzstan was accusations by a female collective against the female head of the Constitutional Court, Cholpon Baekova. "Skazhi mne, kto tvoi drug . . .," *Res Publica*, 4 July 1995, p. 1. They linked Baekova's love life and official corruption.

41 *Svobodnye gory* had run a photomontage with Akaev's picture inside a Star of David, surrounded by six Jewish advisors, including Leonid Levitin, perhaps the most influential advisor to the president. Alexander Sabov, "Kirgiziia: spory o fasade?" *Slovo Kyrgyzstana*, 4 March 1995, pp. 6, 14. According to the editor of the newspaper, however, it was not the Jewish issue or impolitic criticism of China that resulted in the closure, but rather the paper's revelations about corruption in the president's entourage. ". . . na menia zh parusami makhnuli," *Slavo Kyrgyzstana*, 12 November 1994, p. 5. *Politika*, the other paper closed down, had distorted a speech of the president. Instead of "the prevention of the exodus of Russians is a condition of democratization," the newspaper reported Akaev's words as "the exodus of Russians is a condition of democratization." "Vot tak 'politika,'" *Slovo Kyrgyzstana*, 24 June 1994, p. 1.

42 In October 1994, the president's specially formed media watchdog agency, the Social Chamber for the Media, had warned Sydykova and *Res Publica* about articles that had "insulted the Kyrgyz people." However, "she had not drawn conclusions from that." "Kogda otkazyvaiut tormoza," *Slovo Kyrgyzstana*, 1 April 1995, p. 3. For the decree establishing the Social Chamber, see "Ob obshchestvennoi palate po voprosam deiatel'nosti sredstv massovoi informatsii," ibid., 20 August 1994, p. 2.

43 Musurkul Kabylbekov, "Krestovyi pokhod protiv Prezidenta," ibid., 29 July 1995, p. 6.

44 According to Kyrgyz observers, this alliance was cemented at a meeting between Akaev and the *akimy* in the town of Kok-Zhaiyke in the summer of 1994. Kusein Isaev, Emil' Niiazov, and Karybek Dzhigitekov, "Esli ne k khramu doroga, to zachem ona?" ibid., 19 November 1994, p. 8. One district *akim* in the Chui Valley, who had served earlier as a district first secretary of the Communist Party, noted that the *akimy* had more autonomy than the first secretaries. Party directives from above had to be obeyed; that was not always the case with decrees from the president. Personal interview with Gennadii Valerevich Davidenko, Head of Administration, Panfilov Raion, and Deputy of the republican Supreme Soviet, 11 June 1993, Kaundy, Kyrgyzstan.

45 Seiit Sasybaev, "Polumery – poluzhizn'," *Slavo Kyrgyzstana*, 25 March 1995, p. 7.
46 "Medetkan Sherimkulov: ia ukhozhu, chtoby vernut'sia," ibid., 4 March 1995, p. 5.
47 For a copy of the "Letter of the 105 Deputies," which prompted the closure, see "Narod dolzhen znat' pravdu!" ibid., 22 July 1994, p. 1.
48 The elections were originally scheduled for 24 December 1994, but the president postponed them until 5 February 1995 to satisfy constitutional requirements about the length of the campaign. "O naznachenii vyborov v Zhogorku Kenesh Kyrgyzskoi Respubliki," ibid., 28 October 1994, p. 1.
49 The elements of continuity in electoral practices in Russia are explored in Michael Urban, "December 1993 as a Replication of Late-Soviet Era Electoral Practices," *Post-Soviet Affairs*, no. 2 (1994), 127–58.
50 For an exhaustive survey of electoral rules and institutions in Kyrgyzstan, see Linda Edgeworth, William Fierman, and Chitra Tiwari, *Pre-Election Assessment: Kyrgyzstan* (Washington, DC: International Foundation for Electoral Studies, 1994), pp. 31–49.
51 Such problems are, of course, not unique to Kyrgyzstan or even to the developing world. In the American South, localism produced "a political process seldom shaped by issues of public policy, but by informal relationships filtered through kin and class at the courthouse, the local cafe, the Masonic lodge, church suppers, and (in the more up-and-coming communities) in the Kiwanis and Rotary clubs." Dan T. Carter, *The Politics of Rage: George Wallace, The Origins of the New Conservatism, and the Transformation of American Politics* (New York: Simon and Schuster, 1995), p. 40.
52 "Pis'mo Prezidenta," *Slovo Kyrgyzstana*, 28 October 1994, p. 2. By forcing national executive officials to respect this prohibition, Akaev weakened the position of the center *vis-à-vis* the regions. "Sprosit' i vyslushat' narod – ne v etom li segodnia real'naia demokratiia v Kyrgyzstane?" ibid., 27 September 1994, p. 1.
53 "Tsena deputatskogo mandata," ibid., 14 March 1995, p. 2; Nadezhda Dobretsova, "Karakol: otstupat' nekuda, pozadi Chyngyshev," *Res Publica*, 14 February 1995, p. 2.; and K. Mambetaliev, "'Mertvye dushi' iz Karakola," *Slovo Kyrgyzstana*, 24 March 1995, p. 2.
54 Nadezhda Dobretsova, "Skol'ko prosish', izbiratel'?" *Res Publica*, 28 February 1995, p. 2.
55 Damir Kalykov, "My prodolzhaem stradat' ot rodoplemennykh rasprei," *Res Publica*, 14 February 1995, p. 2.
56 D. Evlashkov, "Pochem senatorskoe kreslo?" *Slovo Kyrgyzstana*, 18 February 1995, p. 5, and Mar Baidzhiev, "Golos . . . za ukol," ibid., 18 February 1995, p. 6.
57 "Slovo nakanune," ibid., 18 February 1995, p. 4.
58 S. Grigor'ev, "Kak izbirateli Dzhalal-Abad osazhdali," ibid., 25 February 1995, p. 5.
59 To be sure, numerous foreign observers with a knowledge of Russian and familiarity with local conditions noted widespread violations of the electoral rules. See, for example, Ian Praid [Pryde], "Vremia idet, vozmozhnosti ne vostrebovany," *Res Publica*, 14 February 1995, p. 1; M. Sivasheva, "My vybiraem?

Nam byviraiut! Kak eto chasto ne sovpadaet . . . ," *Res Publica*, 14 February 1995, p. 1; D. Evlashkov, "Bylo i takoe," *Slovo Kyrgyzstana*, 14 February 1995, p. 2. The CSCE's "Post-Election Statement of International Observers" (copy in possession of the author) did, however, note "areas for improvement," among which were the discontinuance of family or proxy voting, "more thorough and professionally implemented" counting procedures, and "greater voter education."

60 "'Stavki ochen' vysoki,'" *Slovo Kyrgyzstana*, 24 September 1994, p. 4.

61 A total of 526 social organizations had been registered by the Ministry of Justice in Kyrgyzstan on 1 January 1995. "Information on Political Parties in Kyrgyzstan," compiled by Ainura Elebaeva and Nurbek Omuraliev (typescript in possession of the author).

62 Markil Ibrayev, "Elections Are Crucial for the Future," *Kyrgyzstan Chronicle*, 25–31 January 1995.

63 E. Denisenko, "Askar Akaev: shag po puti demokratii," *Slovo Kyrgyzstana*, 7 February 1995, p. 1.

64 M. Ibraev, "1. Trudnye uroki vyborov," ibid., 28 March 1995, p. 2.

65 For an overview of the party program of the Social-Democrats, see "Rezoliutsiia II s"ezda SKPK," ibid., 4 October 1994, p. 3.

66 Identifying the party affiliation of deputies is difficult because some candidates were nominated by more than one party and some deputies abandoned or changed party affiliation once in the assembly.

67 Alexander Sabov, "Kirgiziia: spory o fasade?" *Slovo Kyrgyzstana*, 4 March 1995, pp. 6, 14. This article appeared originally in *Literaturnaia gazeta*.

68 "Kamil' Baialinov: ia ne igrok v apparatnye igry," *Slovo Kyrgyzstana*, 15 July 1995, p. 3. Before pursuing a journalistic career, Baialinov had worked on a dissertation entitled, "Elements of Tribalism in the Cadres Policy of the Communist Party of Kyrgyzstan."

69 V. Uleev, "Chem vymoshchena nasha doroga," *Res Publica*, 22 August 1995, p. 3. For the specific provisions of the government *postanovlenie*, see "Kak umen'shit' migratsiiu," *Slovo Kyrgyzstana*, 14 September 1994, p. 3.

70 E. Taranova, "Esli druzhat diplomaty – vyigryvaiut strany," *Slovo Kyrgyzstana*, 3–4 October 1995, p. 5. In a concession following the 1995 parliamentary elections, deputies elected a Russian and an Uzbek as deputy speakers in the Chamber of People's Representatives. "Pervaia sessiia Zhogorku Kenesha," ibid., 30 March 1995, p. 1.

71 S. Amanaliev, "Schastlivaia strana 'NKVD,'" ibid., 15 February 1995, p. 2.

72 O. Dziubenko, "Slashche meda, krepche shchita – deputatskii mandat," ibid., 4 April 1995, p. 1. The most serious concern of deputies running businesses is the tax system. They want a less onerous tax schedule and a less intrusive tax inspectorate. A. Gladilov, "Prezidentskii dialog s predprinimateliami," ibid., 31 March 1995, p. 2, and L. Kondrashevskii, "Optimisticheskaia tragediia v inter'ere rynka," ibid., 30 March 1995, p. 5.

73 Ian Pryde, "Kyrgyzstan's Slow Progress to Reform," *The World Today*, June 1995, pp. 115–18.

74 The early practice suggests that the smaller chamber, the Legislative Assembly, will be the more active legislative organ, preparing drafts that will later need the approval of the Chamber of People's Representatives. "Deputy vziali taim-aut," *Slovo Kyrgyzstana*, 4 April 1995, p. 1.

75 According to two Kyrgyz journalists, this "chamber divide" has made old friends into adversaries and old adversaries into friends. O. Dziubenko and D. Kyshtobaev, "Eto sladkoe slovo 'Soglasie,'" ibid., 31 March 1995, p. 1.

76 O. Dziubenko and D. Kyshtobaev, "Vse prokhodit – prem'er ostaetsia," ibid., 1 April 1995, p. 2.

77 In late 1992, Akaev complained that "clans, capital, and connections" in the parliament were halting reform. The 1995 elections seem only to have heightened their importance. ". . . V rezul'tate budushchikh vyborov pridut te, kto segodnia sidit v VS, – byvshaia elita. Vot u kogo fakticheski . . . okazhetsia vlast'. . . ," ibid., 25 November 1992, p. 2.

78 D. Kyshtobaev, "Prezident protiv mafii: kto kogo?" ibid., 8 July 1995, pp. 2–4. For an account of official corruption by the Procurator General, see A. Sharshenaliev, "Ba, znakomye vse famili!" ibid., 17 August 1994, p. 2.

79 "Almazbek Atambaev: nam nuzhno boiat'sia ne sotsializma, a 'sitsilizma,'" ibid., 28 January 1995, p. 3.

80 Topchubek Turgunaly Kozhomberditegin, "Degradatsiia," *Res Publica*, 28 February 1995, p. 1.

81 Kyshtobaev, "Prezident protiv mafii: kto kogo?"

82 "Akayev Fears 'Shouters, Politicians' in New Parliament," INTERFAX in English, 1501 GMT, 22 November 1994, in Foreign Broadcast Information Service, *Daily Report: Central Eurasia*, 23 November 1994, p. 46. Akaev noted that he intended to restrict the power of the regional leaders, in part by strengthening the independence of lower-level officials, who could act as a counterweight. It remains to be seen whether Akaev, operating from Bishkek, can redirect the loyalties of the district governors away from the regional *akimy* and toward the center.

83 The one important exception to this rule is Osh, where the northerner, Jenish Rustenbekov, has been, in the eyes of many local politicians, an unwelcome choice for *akim*. In the fall of 1994, the controversial southern politician, Bekmamat Osmonov, sought to challenge Rustenbekov from a base in the regional assembly, but he failed to be elected speaker by a single vote. Osmonov has now taken his concerns to Bishkek as a newly-elected deputy in the national parliament.

84 "Vybory i referendum sostoialis'!" *Slovo Kyrgyzstana*, 25 October 1994, p. 1.

85 "Rezoliutsiia II s'ezda SKPK," ibid., 4 October 1994, p. 3. Akaev did permit the election of the *akimy*, or mayors, of Bishkek and Osh in 1995. However, he intervened to remove the leading candidate in Bishkek by appointing him to the presidential administration, and at the conclusion of the direct popular election Akaev *appointed* the victor to his post.

86 "Dlia demokratii u nas slishkom tverdaia zemlia," ibid., 22 October 1994, p. 5.

87 Guillermo O'Donnell, "Delegative Democracy," *Journal of Democracy*, no. 1 (1994), 59.

88 Kyrgyzstan's mountainous border with China, for example, is still defended by border troops from the Russian Federation.

89 Personal interviews by the author in Bishkek, 9–15 September 1995.

90 Kanybek Imanaliev, "Litsom k litsu," *Slovo Kyrgyzstana*, 8 July 1995, p. 5.

91 The president's press secretary noted that the referendum was in keeping with the practice of neighbors. It also prevented the assumption of power by an undesirable person. A. Otorbaeva, "Sostoitsia li referendum?" ibid., 4 April 1995, p. 1. To show its displeasure with internal developments in Kyrgyzstan, or with Kyrgyzstan's payment arrears, Uzbekistan had regularly interrupted the flow of national gas into the country.

92 Akaev himself admitted that the uncertain position of the president in a changing climate would make governing difficult. "Askar Akaev: Ia khochu byt' chestnym pered narodom i pered svoei sovest'iu," ibid., 23–24 September 1995, p. 2.

93 Sherimkulov and others criticized Akaev for "tarnishing" the legend of Manas by using it as a cover for the referendum campaign. "Medetkan Sherimkulov: 'ia byl i ostanus' v politike Kyrgyzstane . . . ," Res Publica, 15 August 1995, p. 5.

94 "Vopros postavlen. I khorosho stoit," Slovo Kyrgyzstana, 28–29 September 1995, p. 1.

95 Before formally declaring his candidacy, however, Sherimkulov brought a court case against the early elections, noting their unconstitutionality.

96 Masaliev received 24.4 percent of the vote, Sherimkulov only 1.7 percent. "Bokal shampanskogo: 'S pobedoi,'" Slovo Kyrgyzstana, 28–29 December 1995, p. 1. Three other contenders had been disqualified shortly before the election, when the Supreme Court ruled that some of the signatures required for their nomination were invalid. The candidates responded by staging hunger strikes on the main square in Bishkek.

97 For a text of the extensive changes to the constitution introduced by the referendum of 10 February 1996, see "Zakon Kyrgyzskoi Respubliki 'O vnesenii izmenenii i dopolnenii v Konstitutsiiu Kyrgyzskoi Respubliki,'" ibid., 9–10 January 1996, pp. 2–9.

98 "Obrashchenie Prezidenta Kyrgyzskoi Respubliki k narodu po povodu Referenduma (vsenarodnogo golosovaniia) 10 fevralia 1996 goda," ibid., 4–5 January 1996, p. 3.

99 Viktor Niksdorf, "Dai rvushchimsia k vlasti navlastvovat'sia vslast' . . . ," ibid., 25 February 1995, p. 6.

100 In discussions with members of the Kyrgyz political and intellectual elite, I have found almost universal agreement that the population of the country is culturally and psychologically unprepared for a rapid transition to democracy. This impression of elite attitudes appears to be confirmed by evidence from focus group interviews carried out in Kyrgyzstan in 1994 by the USIA. See Dobson, "Kyrgyzstan in a Time of Change," especially pp. 17–22.

101 "Obzor nedeli," Res Publica, 22 August 1995, p. 1. When I was interviewed for Kyrgyz television in Bishkek on 14 September 1995, the "liberal" correspondent, A. Cheremushkina, viewed as wholly naive my insistence that the people should be given a choice for the presidency.

102 "Key Findings From Kyrgyzstan National Survey" (Washington, DC: International Foundation for Electoral Studies, 1995), p. 2.

103 "'Na tekh, kto ne opasen dlia politicheskikh prostitutok, ne napadaiut,'" Slovo Kyrgyzstana, 15 July 1995, pp. 6–7.

104 K. Bokonbaev, "Pust' traibalizm posluzhit delu," ibid., 14 January 1995, p. 7. The author who cites these words argues that Kyrgyzstan's only hope for stable and democratic development is to accede to the natural inclinations of its people and adopt formal rules that encourage a regionally based political system.

8   Thwarted democratization in Tajikistan

Muriel Atkin

Independent Tajikistan is not a democratic country nor is it in the process of becoming one. Although the Soviet Union no longer exists and the Communist Party of Tajikistan no longer enjoys a monopoly of power, the current political system in Tajikistan bears a fundamental resemblance to the old Soviet order in the sense that a narrow circle of people dominates and uses methods, ranging from control of the mass media to the imprisonment or killing of opponents, that were highly developed in the Soviet era. In some cases the continuity is personal. For example, Rahmon Nabiev, who had been Communist Party first secretary in Tajikistan from 1982 to 1985, became the first president of independent Tajikistan. As under Soviet rule, the outward trappings of a constitutional democracy exist but not the substance. The new regime has written a constitution (1994) but does not respect civil liberties. It has held presidential and legislative elections (November 1994 and February–March 1995, respectively) but these were neither free nor fair.[1] Though no longer all-powerful, the Communist Party is legal in Tajikistan and remains the country's single largest party.

In place of the old communist monopoly, patron–client networks operate the levers of power which are essentially those of the Soviet system. The Soviet concept of nomenklatura, the broad range of positions filled on the basis of the Communist Party's patronage appointments, survived the Soviet Union's demise and the end of the communists' monopoly. The victors of the civil war understand well that patronage, rather than concepts of civil service or meritocracy, is a powerful tool for ensuring loyalty. Other Soviet-era levers of power still available to the new regime include control over the Ministry of Security (the renamed KGB) and police, the mass media, labor unions, and the economy's dominant state sector. Real opposition parties are banned. Several legal parties now exist besides the Communist Party, but they are weak organizations built around personality cliques and thwarted by

Table 8.1 *Indicators of economic trends in Tajikistan since 1989*

	1989	1990	1991	1992	1993	1994	1995[a]
GDP	-2.9	-1.6	-7.1	-28.9	-11.1	-21.4	-12.0
Industrial output	1.9	1.9	-7.4	-35.7	n.a.	-30.0	n.a.
Rate of inflation	n.a.	4	112	1,157	2,195	341	120
GNP per capita	n.a.	n.a.	n.a.	n.a.	1,430	n.a.	n.a.

Notes: GDP – % change over previous year; industrial output – % change over previous year; rate of inflation – % change in end-year retail/consumer prices; GNP per capita – in US dollars at PPP exchange rates. [a]Estimate.

Sources: The World Bank, *Statistical Handbook 1993: States of the Former USSR*; The World Bank, *Statistical Handbook 1994: States of the Former USSR*; European Bank for Reconstruction and Development, *Transition Report 1995: Economic Transition in Eastern Europe and the Former Soviet Union* (London: EBRD, 1995); European Bank for Reconstruction and Development, *Transition Report Update, April 1996: Assessing Progress in Economies in Transition* (London: EBRD, 1996).

the regime to the extent that they attempt to function independently. Thus, this is a system which is qualitatively neo-Soviet.

No significant privatization has yet occurred, though the current regime (like its predecessors since 1990) occasionally promises to bring that about. Whether privatization necessarily leads to democratization is debatable, given the example of China and other countries which have loosened controls over aspects of the economy without loosening the ruling elite's grip on political power. In any event, Tajikistan has not departed far from the Soviet-style command economy. Some joint ventures with Western companies have begun operation but thus far these all involve a partnership with the state, rather than private Tajikistani entrepreneurs. There has not yet developed a powerful new entrepreneurial class, separate from the old ruling elite, which might conceivably press for political changes to favor itself. Whatever the type of economic system, the country remains in dire economic condition, with plummeting industrial and agricultural output and rapid inflation through the end of 1995 (see table 8.1).

Yet the prospects for democratization did not look this bleak at the close of the Soviet period and beginning of independence. There was an attempt to build a civil consensus that was defined by groups and prominent individuals who represented varying combinations of ethnic, political, and religious factors but strove for inclusiveness based on allegiance to the country of Tajikistan and to the belief that the Soviet order had to be reformed. That attempt foundered in a civil war begun by elements determined to preserve the privileges the Soviet system gave to a ruling elite, even if the Soviet

Union itself no longer existed. The war was at its most intense in the second half of 1992; the neo-Soviets took control of the central government in December 1992 and have held power since then, but smaller-scale fighting has continued. The conflict accentuated divisions in the country and at times deliberately exploited them. The result was catastrophic for the people of Tajikistan. Many thousands died (in the absence of a reliable, impartial count, estimates range from an implausibly low 25,000 to 100,000) and some 500,000–600,000 fled their homes;[2] all this in a country which had a population of about 5.1 million on the eve of independence. Reconciliation does not appear imminent.

It has become fashionable to treat the fault lines in Tajikistani society as creating simple opposites: one ideological (secular communists and Islamic radicals) and the other geographic (northern and southern "clans"); sometimes the two pairs are merged. Although ideological and geographic divisions did indeed exist, they were more complex than the polar opposites just mentioned and were not the only ways Tajikistani society was split. There were differences in political and local loyalties within the ideological and regional camps. A different kind of geographic division existed between the educated urban population and the country's peasant majority. Minority ethnic groups also became involved in the power struggle. All of these factors contributed to the fracturing of Tajikistani society but none, taken individually, explains the whole process.

The Tajik people and the Tajikistani state

One important reason for the conflicting pattern of loyalties in contemporary Tajikistan is that the nature of statehood in Central Asia has been transformed in this century. The concept of a state that was at least nominally a Tajik national homeland within some approximation of Tajikistan's current borders began as an artificial product of Soviet nationality policy in the 1920s, yet, over the course of the Soviet era, became credible to a significant number of educated Tajiks. This does not mean that what came to be called Tajik culture was a recent contrivance, for it was not, but that the linkage of culture to political identity owed much to outside influence in this century.

The Tajiks of the former Soviet Union speak Persian as it has evolved in Central Asia.[3] The people and their culture most probably derive from a combination of Eastern Iranian peoples who have inhabited the region since ancient times, the Western Iranian Persians, who had contact with the region in pre-Islamic times and even more so after the Islamic conquest, and some influences from the Turkic and Mongol peoples who began to move into the southern parts of Central Asia some 1,400 years ago.

The linguistic and cultural characteristics of the region have not traditionally been defined by sharp political or ethnic boundaries. The region's traditional high culture and major elements of its popular culture were syntheses of Persian, Turkic, and Arabic, all in an Islamic context. Among the sedentary inhabitants of the main river valleys, Turco-Persian bilingualism was traditionally common; Persian was widely used in government, learning, and literature long after Turkic peoples became numerically and politically dominant in the southern part of Central Asia.

Central Asian states were defined by what dynasties had the power to control, not by a desire to make state borders and ethnicity congruent. There has not been a Central Asian state governed by people whose first language was Persian for 1,000 years. The fact that one had existed a millennium ago has a certain current political relevance. Some educated Tajiks today see in the Samanid realm (875–999), which only partially overlapped contemporary Tajikistan, an independent, culturally vital heritage and counterbalance to the oft-repeated message in this century that Tajiks are a backward people rightly a part of a larger state ruled by others.[4] However, the Samanid era offered no precedent for contemporary democratization. Neither did the states which ruled the future Tajikistan on the eve of the Soviet period – the Russian Empire and its vassal, the oppressive emirate of Bukhara. The impetus for democratic reformism in Tajikistan came, as it did elsewhere in the former Soviet Union, from educated people who looked to contemporary political ideas as they sought to change a system that was manifestly inadequate to the needs of the day, when, for the first time in Soviet history, liberalization seemed an attainable goal.

That an entity called Tajikistan became the main venue for the reformist efforts of Central Asian Persian-speakers is the doing of Soviet officials in Moscow. Through the early twentieth century, sedentary Tajiks and Uzbeks lived in close proximity in cities or in densely populated agricultural areas along the main river valleys and assumed that they had more in common with each other than with Central Asia's nomadic tribesmen, even though the Uzbeks, like the nomads, were Turkic. Given the extent to which Tajiks and Uzbeks had a common culture, understood each other's languages, and intermarried, it was not always clear who was Tajik or Uzbek, which made the Soviet division of Central Asia into ethnically-defined republics even more problematical. Tajiks and Uzbeks were both represented in the small circle of Central Asians who, in the early twentieth century, challenged the status quo. Though they were critical of rule by tsarist officials and the emirs of Bukhara, none of them saw the solution in the form of creating a specifically Uzbek or Tajik state before those were established in 1924 at Moscow's initiative.

Table 8.2 *Educational levels in Tajikistan, 1989*

	No. per 1,000 aged 15 or over
Higher education	
Complete	75
Partial	14
Secondary education	
Complete general	427
Complete specialized	110
Partial	211
Total with at least some secondary education	837

Note: According to the 1926 Soviet census, the literacy rate among the Tajik population of the Soviet Union as a whole was 4 percent for men and 0.1 percent for women. (Institut Etnografii, Akademiia nauk SSSR, *Sotial'no-kul'turnyi oblik sovetskikh natsii* [Moscow: Nauka, 1986], p. 48.)

Source: *The FirstBook of Demographics for the Republics of the Former Soviet Union, 1951-1990* (Shady Side, MD: New World Demographics, L.C., 1992), p. F-3.

Yet caution is warranted when discussing the artificiality of the creation of the Central Asian republics, lest the fact that the present evolves from the past be taken to mean that past attitudes have survived the years unchanged. Over the decades since Tajikistan's creation, the factors which often produce a sense of national identity and association with a nation-state in many countries were at work in Tajikistan. The development of mass literacy and the mass media in a standardized Tajik language, the establishment of a public education system, which taught the Tajik language, literature, and history, the patronage of new performing and visual arts organizations which used Tajik themes, the publication of Tajik literature, and the implementation of personnel policies which took nationality into account in many important positions all contributed significantly to the development of a Tajik national consciousness, especially among the more educated, urban members of society (see table 8.2).[5]

However, the process was far from complete by the time Tajikistan became independent. The reasons for this include the fact that the Soviet central authorities not only created the framework for building national consciousness but also manipulated the process to curtail its impact. The most drastic example of this in the case of Tajikistan was the wholesale purge of Tajiks from the republic's Communist Party in the years between the collectivization of agriculture in the late 1920s and the height of the Terror in the late 1930s. As a result, Tajiks were reduced to a minority within "their" republican Party organization, in which most key positions were occupied by Russians.[6] The central authorities also enforced artificial distinctions between the written Persian of Central Asia – called "Tajik" rather than "Persian" at Moscow's insistence – and literary Persian as used beyond Soviet borders. The Russian language was promoted at the expense of Tajik in many spheres of life. Tajik history and Persian-language literature received short shrift in the curriculum (except for the small number of students who specialized in such subjects in their university education) and were subjected to politically slanted interpretations.[7] Even during the era of the Gorbachev reforms, the Communist leadership still criticized Tajiks in Tajikistan for excessive self-interest.[8]

Despite the considerable difficulties, Tajik intellectuals strove for many years to encourage a sense of national self-awareness and self-worth. For a long time these efforts had a cultural focus (as has been the case with many nationalist movements that operated under conditions which made political participation impossible). The very fact that the processes which can mold a national consciousness were simultaneously encouraged, manipulated, and undercut by Soviet policies gave some intellectuals a sense of grievance which made them all the more nationalist.[9] As political life opened up to a degree in the late 1980s, their sphere of activities expanded to include the interests of the *state* of Tajikistan in dealings with the central authorities on the economy, environment, and general standard of living (in one of the poorest of Soviet republics). Thus, for many Tajik nationalists, their interests as a people were closely linked to the reformist efforts underway in the Soviet Union as a whole, both in the attempts by Russians and members of other nationalities to change the nature of the central authority and by the eponymous nationalities of other republics to assert their own interests as those differed from the center's.

Perestroika

The direct impact of the Gorbachev-era reforms was slight in Tajikistan. This had the unintended result of intensifying the desire for change among reformers, who were aware of the difference between conditions in their own republic and other parts of the Soviet Union. After 1989, the republic's officials took a few cautious steps toward reform, but not enough to satisfy people who sought more than token gestures. In the final years of the Soviet Union's existence, leaders of the Communist Party of Tajikistan, seeing the rising popularity of nationalism within the republic and in the Soviet Union generally, while also seeing the rapid decline of the old certainties of power, adopted elements of nationalism. This leadership's pro-nationalist measures included permitting a lively discussion of nationalist issues in the regime-controlled press, the enactment of a law promoting the use of the Tajik language (rather than Russian) in government affairs, the frequent identification of republican officials by nationality in the mass media, and the assertion that Tajikistan's economy suffered under the Soviet centralized, planned economy.[10] The regime lifted some of its constraints on the practice of Islam in this predominantly Muslim republic. A new head of Islamic institutions (chief *qadi*), Akbar Turajonzoda, was allowed to take office in 1988. Unlike some of the prominent figures of the Soviet-designed Islamic establishment, Turajonzoda's personal piety and religious learning were unimpeachable, though he was by no means the extremist his enemies later accused him of being. In the final years of the Soviet Union's existence, the regime allowed Turajonzoda and others to open some new mosques and religious schools in Tajikistan; this constituted a modest departure from the standing Soviet policy of restricting the faithful's access to either.[11]

These changes were less reforms than tactical maneuvers intended to preserve the Communist Party's hold on power under changing conditions. One example of the continued strength of pre-perestroika politics was the legislative elections of February 1990. At that time, no opposition party had legal status. The regime still controlled the broadcast media and ensured that advocates of change were denied access; its hold over the print media was still strong, though not absolute, as in the past. The capital, Dushanbe, and its environs were still under especially tight control because of a state of emergency which had been imposed following the mid-February riots there (see below). Not surprisingly, Communist Party candidates scored an overwhelming victory, taking 96 percent of the seats in the Supreme Soviet (legislature).[12]

Challenges to the Soviet status quo

By the early 1990s, official nationalism and somewhat increased tolerance of Islam proved insufficient to prevent the emergence of a large, open opposition movement. This was composed of groups with disparate views. What they had in common was the call for popular sovereignty within Tajikistan. All the members of the opposition shared the goal of changing Tajikistan's political system, so that the Communist Party would no longer enjoy a monopoly of power and government policies would reflect the wishes of the governed. Part of the cause of this change lay in developments taking place in the Soviet Union as a whole, notably the calls for democratization and greater scope for private economic initiative, as well as disappointment over the pace of reforms. The dissolution of the Soviet Union in December 1991 made independence for Tajikistan, as opposed to the transformation of the terms of the Union, the frame of reference for politics, even though that had not been pressed by the advocates of change in the republic.

Developments within Tajikistan also helped widen the gap between the regime and sections of the public. Two of the most important were the riots of February 1990 and the local aftermath of the unsuccessful attempt to overthrow Gorbachev in August 1991. These events convinced people who joined the opposition that the republican regime would not negotiate with peaceful demonstrators but would use any means against them, including lethal force, and that the republican regime, which supported the abortive August coup, wanted to reverse the Gorbachev reforms.

In mid-February 1990, false rumors circulated in Dushanbe that thousands of Armenian refugees from the conflict in the Caucasus had been relocated to Dushanbe, where they had been given apartments. That was inflammatory, given the city's acute housing shortage and the fact that various other false rumors had recently increased public anxiety. The precise origin of any of these rumors is difficult to ascertain, but the mere fact of their existence testifies to the public perception that ominous developments were underway. The housing question was part of broader discontent over the republic's low standard of living. Demonstrations began in central Dushanbe, outside the offices of the Central Committee of the Communist Party of Tajikistan, on February 11, 1990. When several thousand demonstrators returned the following day, security forces responded with beatings, then gunfire. What had begun as a peaceful demonstration escalated into rioting which swept the city until February 18. Some of the trouble was the work of criminals who exploited the disorder for their own, non-political ends. While rioters committed arson, looting, and violence against individuals, security forces responded at first ineffectively, then indiscriminately. All told, twenty-five people died and more than 800 were injured; the victims included people who were not involved in the rioting but were shot by police or soldiers nonetheless. The regime launched a propaganda campaign intended to depict the events as an attempted coup by nationalist reformers (belonging to Rastokhez, a popular-front organization) and alleged Islamic extremists. An inquiry later that year by the republic's Supreme Soviet revealed much of the authorities' malfeasance. Therefore the regime tried to block the inquiry and subsequently prevented the publication of its findings within Tajikistan; the report eventually made its way to Moscow where it was published.[13] Subsequent disclosures by officials of the KGB in Tajikistan revealed that the accusation of Islamic radicals' involvement was concocted by authorities in Moscow to help justify a campaign against political Islam in the Soviet Union in general.[14]

To advocates of reform, the February events became a symbol of the regime's implacable resistance to change and its readiness to take the lives of its own citizens.[15] This stimulated the formation of several opposition parties: the Democratic Party of Tajikistan; the Islamic Rebirth Party; and La"li Badakhshon.[16] However the riots also provided a pretext for further repressive measures by the regime, which sentenced more than a score of people, including five Islamic figures, to terms of varying numbers of years, and brought charges against Rastokhez for incitement to riot and being an unregistered political organization.[17] The state of emergency imposed on the Dushanbe area after the riots remained in effect until July 1991.

In the changed climate after the failed coup in Moscow in August 1991, the square which had been the scene of the February 1990 demonstrations was renamed Martyrs' (Shohidon) Square. More fundamentally, the August 1991 events led to an escalating confrontation between the proponents and opponents of reform in Tajikistan. Tajikistan's president and Communist Party first secretary, Qahhor Mahkamov, had supported the coup. When it failed, mass demonstrations in Dushanbe and the maneuvering of rivals within the Party made his position untenable. At first the advocates of change seemed to prevail but defenders of the old order staged a coup of their own on September 23, 1991 and restored to power Rahmon Nabiev, the first secretary whom Gorbachev had fired in 1985. Nabiev and his colleagues took steps to establish a repressive regime of the pre-Gorbachev type.[18] Within weeks of Tajikistan's becoming independent, that would lead to a new wave of demonstrations, and ultimately to civil war (see below).

The emergence of alternative political parties

The early 1990s saw the formation of political organizations[19] determined to end one-party rule in the republic. They had different platforms but all took into account, albeit in different ways, the concepts of popular sovereignty, civil liberties, and nationalism as well as the desire of the country's Muslim majority for religious freedom.[20] These parties strove to build a public base of support – which transcended regional or ethnic differences – for the transformation of the republic's politics. Four groups led the opposition at the beginning of the nineties. They were the Democratic Party of Tajikistan (DPT), Rastokhez ("resurrection"), the Islamic Rebirth Party (IRP), and La"li Badakhshon ("ruby of Badakhshon"). The first two were founded and led by urban intellectuals, many in their forties or younger; some were Communist Party members but were not *apparatchiki* and favored reform. The IRP also included in its leadership younger people who had secular professions in addition to others who were religious figures. Although these parties were composed primarily of Tajiks, the DPT included a few Russians in its leadership circles.[21] La"li Badakhshon drew most of its membership from Eastern Iranian peoples of the Pamirs, who sought reforms which would benefit their province within the context of the democratization of Tajikistan as a whole.

The IRP was the most controversial opposition party because of the widespread tendency to equate any linkage between Islam and politics with extremism and fanaticism. The original idea of establishing an Islamic political party in the Soviet Union began among educated young people of several nationalities, Tajiks included, sometime around 1980, when no such organization could have existed openly. In the heyday of the Gorbachev reforms, the impossible became possible. At a 1990 meeting of Muslims of various nationalities in the old Volga Tatar city of Astrakhan, the Islamic Rebirth Party held its founding meeting. A Tajikistani branch organized as an open, but still illegal, party in October 1990. It eventually separated from its parent party.[22]

The issue of the relationship between Islam and politics in Tajikistan is too complex to be discussed at due length in this paper. Suffice it to say that the IRP repudiated the stereotypical anti-Westernism of Islamic radicals and joined with the secular opposition parties in supporting popular sovereignty, civil liberties, and economic reform. *Qadi* Turajonzoda, who was not a member of the IRP, voiced similar opinions. Both the IRP and the *qadi* held forth an Islamic state as an *ultimate* ideal but consigned it to the indefinite future; the vague description of what it would entail included democratic ideas.[23]

All of these parties remained officially illegal until 1991. The Dushanbe regime permitted each to register as a legal party at one time or another during that year. By the time of the spring 1992 demonstrations, *qadi* Turajonzoda lent the support of his personal prestige and institutional network to the reformist cause.

There is no reliable information on the number of members of these groups or the extent of their public following, in light of the climate of political repression and the absence of free elections in late-Soviet as well as post-Soviet Tajikistan. It is reasonable to speculate that their membership must have been limited, given, among other things, the public's inexperience with multi-party politics, the difficulties opponents of the status quo experienced in trying to disseminate their message via the mass media, and the willingness of regimes to use coercion to maintain their monopoly of power.

Additional political parties proliferated in 1992, many with vaguely defined programs and small followings. For example, the Popular Unity Party[24] favored privatization in general terms but also the preservation of a state sector and promised to address the issue of industrial pollution.[25] This and a few other parties were off-shoots of the DPT. Several parties were associated with one particular area of Tajikistan; apart from La"li

Badakhshon, this included Vodii Hisor (Hisor Valley), linked to the area west of Dushanbe for which it was named, Hamdilon (the likeminded), linked to Leninobod Province in the north, and Zarafshon, linked to the city of Panjakent, in the Zarafshon Valley, in northwestern Tajikitan.[26] None of these parties became powerful actors in Tajikistani politics.

Attempts to mobilize public support for multi-party politics

The opposition groups tried to win the support of the general public by three main methods: the mass media; the presidential election of November 1991; and the use of demonstrations as schools of the new politics. The mass media became useful to dissenting voices once the old system of censorship waned. Beginning in 1989, the regime allowed an increase in the range of opinion which could be voiced in the mass media; the change was substantial relative to the strict censorship of the past, but the media remained far from free. For a few weeks following the failed coup of August 1991, the mass media carried unprecedentedly bold criticism of the old order.[27] That ended soon after defenders of the old order within Tajikistan staged their successful coup in September 1991. The Opposition had more access to the media once again in the second half of 1992, when Tajikistan state television and radio were controlled through the short-lived coalition government. Beginning in the late Soviet-era, the opposition started several newspapers of its own. Some were published in Moscow to escape censorship and were sent to Tajikistan, where the authorities sometimes blocked their distribution. Opposition publications based within Tajikistan appeared irregularly and faced difficulties obtaining publishing materials for distribution as well as official harassment. Therefore, it is not clear how broad an audience they reached, although the intent to reach a wide readership existed. Since the neo-Soviet victory in the civil war (December 1992), tight censorship has prevailed.

The presidential election of November 1991 gave the opposition an opportunity which proved more illusory than real to spread its message to the electorate. The DPT, IRP, and Rastokhez, as well as qadi Turajonzoda, jointly endorsed Davlat Khudonazarov, who headed the then-Soviet Cinematographers' Union. As a member of the Soviet Congress of People's Deputies, he had sided with Andrei Sakharov. He was seen as someone who was not too closely associated with any political group in Tajikistan, which made him acceptable to a broader range of people, and who would support democratization and reform.[28] In the end, the election gave the opposition new grievances instead of victory. The opposition's efforts to publicize its views during the campaign were sharply restricted by the old-guard regime, which still had the power to limit the mass media's coverage of the opposition and prevent opposition campaigners from using the work place as a venue for contacting voters.[29] The election itself was marked by extensive fraud, noted by foreigners as well as supporters of the opposition.[30]

The opposition's most interesting technique for instilling a sense of Tajikistani civil society was the public demonstration. This not only gave the opposition a way to pressure a government that was not democratically elected and was not interested in reflecting the public will, but also provided a school in the streets where the opposition could propound its views to people who gathered, sometimes by the thousands. In a country where there were still major obstacles to bringing word of political alternatives to the general public, demonstrations were not only about confrontation but also about the attempt to create a new attitude toward the political process. The focus of the demonstrations was the capital, Dushanbe, but there were smaller rallies in all the main regions of the country.[31] There were three main waves of demonstrations: the days following the failure to overthrow Gorbachev in August 1991; late September and early October 1991, after hard-line defenders of the old order staged a successful coup in Tajikistan; and from January to May 1992, in protest against the repressive policies of these hard-liners. The demonstrations were peaceful until late in the third phase.

The central message the demonstrations tried to convey was that Tajikistan ought to have a government that represented the governed and that would move away from the old Soviet political and economic order. The most important theme of the demonstrations was the call for democratization and the establishment of a state of laws. Demonstrators objected to having government officials who claimed to speak for them but did not represent their views. They criticized the regime's repression of the opposition.[32] The demonstrations had aspects which invoked Tajik national feeling and Islam but were not exclusively about either of these things.[33] Demonstrators prayed and expressed a favorable attitude toward Islam but no one called for the creation of an Islamic state or advocated intolerance toward non-Muslims. For example, a demonstration in late August 1991, which had as one of its objectives the ouster of those republican officials who had supported the attempted coup against Gorbachev, began with readings from the Koran but proceeded to such topics as criticism of the coup and those in Tajikistan who supported it as well as praise for Boris Yeltsin and those in the Russian legislature who opposed the coup.[34] Russian reformers addressed demonstrators in Dushanbe and commented afterwards that they detected no sign of Islamic exclusiveness or radicalism.[35] The IRP and *qadi* Turajonzoda stated repeatedly, to domestic as well as foreign audiences, that they had no intention of forcing an Islamic state on the people of Tajikistan; if such a state ever came about, they argued, it could only be after a prolonged transition and with the consent of the citizens.[36]

Another important issue raised at the demonstrations was the economic plight of ordinary Tajikistanis. This was a key issue for winning grass-roots support for the organized opposition, with its largely urban, educated leadership. There was a well-established tendency to regard the rural majority as isolated, ignorant, and predisposed to violence in its political interactions with the cities.[37] The presence of peasants at the demonstrations marked a step toward the creation of civil society. Tajikistan's peasants were generally associated with a highly localized sense of identity. They had challenged authority in the past, as when they opposed the collectivization of agriculture or, before Tajikistan existed, the depredations of local officials, the demands of a central government (Tsarist or Central Asian), or the Red Army's conquest of the region. What they had not done before was to act on the assumption that they had the right to pressure the republic's government to give weight to their interests in the state's political institutions. The mere fact that some peasants made the attempt was a significant innovation, even if the issues that brought them to the demonstrations reflected their immediate concerns as peasants, such as the hoped-for dismantling of the collective farms or discontent with bread rationing. Once at the demonstrations they were responsive to broader issues raised by the opposition's leaders.[38]

The opposition tried to make these demonstrations as inclusive as possible and sought to convey the image of inclusiveness to the general public. They portrayed the demonstrators as seeking improved conditions for the country in general and as coming from all parts of Tajikistan, rather than favoring a particular region or ethnic group. Although the demonstrators were highly critical of defenders of the old order, they approved of those Communists who were willing to support change and had been removed from office, even arrested, by the neo-Soviets. There was a particular effort to win the support of Russians. Khudonazarov and a Russian member of the Congress of People's Deputies in Moscow, Andrei Plotnikov, in a joint appearance on Tajikistani television, and *Qadi* Turajonzoda in a separate appearance, all strove to allay Russians' fears. Turajonzoda subsequently claimed that Russians then began to join the demonstrations. The opposition distributed leaflets in Dushanbe's neighborhoods and at the site of the spring 1992 demonstrations to reassure Russians that the opposition did not intend to harm them. Apparently some members of the republic's Uzbek minority joined the demonstrations as well. One of the new opposition newspapers sought to convey the message that the spring 1992 demonstrations in Dushanbe was broadly representative of the country as a whole and acting in the interests of all. Even regime supporters noted the social diversity of the demonstrators.[39]

The destruction of reform

How well the opposition coalition would have lived up to its lofty rhetoric about democracy and inclusiveness remains unproven since it had only a limited voice in government for a few months before being driven from the political arena. The demonstrations in the spring of 1992 became increasingly confrontational as the Nabiev regime resisted all change, escalated its intimidation of the demonstrators, and called forth its own supporters to demonstrate in Dushanbe. By the beginning of May 1992, violence between the two sides had begun in Dushanbe and its environs, resulting in a few fatalities and heightened political tensions. A small-scale clash between demonstrators and security forces on May 10, 1992 near the (renamed) KGB headquarters led to the death of eight demonstrators and wounding of eleven others. Whatever the demonstrators' intent, government forces appear to have fired first. This was the crisis which forced Nabiev to agree to the creation of a coalition government combining a few reformers with neo-Soviets.[40]

The supporters of the old order worked relentlessly to restore their monopoly of power and destroy the opposition through political maneuvering and outright violence. The opposition was unable to find a political solution to either the challenge posed by the neo-Soviets or Tajikistan's problems. Its armed supporters responded to violence with violence of their own. The result was a civil war which delayed the neo-Soviets' victory by several months and drove President Nabiev from power in September 1992 but could not prevent the neo-Soviets' victory by the end of the year. The civil war and the acts of cruelty that occur all too readily when the usual social constraints are shattered eclipsed efforts to create an inclusive, consensual political system in Tajikistan. The concepts of accommodation and modus vivendi between opposing camps in state institutions, so important to democratic systems, were destroyed at their inception by the civil war. The war and the neo-Soviet victory left people on both sides as well as ordinary citizens dead, in prison, in exile, or fighting on in small groups.

The fate of the Communist Party

The political turmoil in the final months of the Soviet era split the Communist Party of Tajikistan, although it remains the single largest party in the country. Here it kept its old name except for a brief interval in late 1992, unlike the case in some other formerly Soviet republics, where Communist Parties took new names which did not bear the stigma of the old regime. In the wake of the August 1991 coup attempt, several prominent party members demonstrated their willingness to work with the groups which advocated change. Prominent among them were the acting head of state, Qadriddin

Aslonov, the mayor of Dushanbe, Maqsud Ikromov, and the minister of internal affairs, Mahmadayoz Navjuvonov. Some of them eventually left the party.

However, the dominant element in the CP of Tajikistan remained unreconciled to the passing of the old order. Perhaps the motivation was at least in part ideological; for example, the hard-liners supported the preservation of as much of the old economic system as possible.[41] A large part of the motivation may have been the desire to preserve the benefits of belonging to the elite that the party's monopoly of power bestowed on its members. They moved against more moderate members of their own party as well as the opposition.

With a membership said to number 18,000 in 1993, the CP was the largest legal party in post-civil-war Tajikistan.[42] It reestablished its organizational network from the workplace to the highest levels of power and strove to reassert its Soviet-era authority over government officials. In the flawed legislative elections held in February and March 1995, it won the largest bloc of seats, 60 out of 181. The head of the CP, Shodi Shabdolov, and other prominent party officials were among those elected.[43] Yet the CP's power was not what it had been in the Soviet era. For example, President Imomali Rahmonov and his circle were linked by their own patron–client relationship, not by the CP hierarchy.

Serious factional rivalries also split the victorious neo-Soviet camp. Eventually, some powerful figures chose to pursue their interests outside the Party organization. For example, Abdumalik Abdullojonov, who was prime minister in the neo-Soviet government which came to power in December 1992, lost a power struggle with his erstwhile ally, the then-speaker of the Supreme Soviet, Imomali Rahmonov, and was forced out of office in December 1993. Abdullojonov was linked to a new party, the Party of Political and Economic Renewal, which, judging by the broad generalizations of the party's self-description, stood for much the same things as the neo-Soviet regime.[44]

Some of the other legal parties of the post-civil-war era were also built around prominent figures in the neo-Soviet camp. For example, the People's Party of Tajikistan was led by neo-Soviets from Kulob who held important political offices in the first post-civil-war government.[45] Other legal parties represented other constituencies, such as small businessmen, but had a small following and no power.[46]

Regional and clique politics

One of the most important characteristics of the power struggle was the way regional and ethnic differences became caught up in it. These kinds of identities pre-dated Tajikistan's civil war; indeed, for indigenous Central Asians, regional identity was a major element of people's perceptions both before and after the creation of nationally-defined republics. By the late-Soviet era, even many educated young people felt stronger ties to their locale of origin than to Tajikistan.[47] What the civil war of 1992 did was to make existing ethnic and regional identities crucial political issues, which they had not been at the outset of the struggle over the future of post-Soviet Tajikistan.

Many accounts of Tajikistan's civil war (both from the formerly Soviet countries and the West) depict the conflict as primarily between regionally-based clans of Tajiks. "Clan" is a misnomer in this context and the provinces were not politically homogeneous. "Clan" is usually understood to refer to groups of people who trace their descent from a common ancestor who lived sometime in the remote past. What were labeled clans in Tajikistan lacked this primordial character. They were patron–client networks linked to extended families. They did not encompass all of the inhabitants of any province but did make alliances with people from other provinces.

For the past half-century, the most powerful of the patron–client networks came from the northern province of Leninobod. This area was Tajikistan's portion of the Farghona Valley, an ethnically mixed area of traditionally prosperous agriculture and, since the Soviet era, some industry. It was also the region of Tajikistan which, since the Russian conquest in the late nineteenth century, had the most contact with Russians and with ideas brought to the region from the European part of Russia or the Soviet Union. Therefore, for decades the Soviet central government tended to favor people from there for important offices in Tajikistan. By one estimate, into 1992, three-quarters of the key positions in the CP of Tajikistan were held by Leninobodis.[48] Those appointees in turn favored their own relatives and clients. However, the Leninobodi clique shared some of the positions in the hierarchy with people from other parts of the republic. According to a former client of Rahmon Nabiev's, Akbarshoh Iskandarov, a veteran party and state official who served as acting president of Tajikistan from September to November 1992, there was a long-standing regional distribution of plum positions. While the Party first secretary was from Leninobod, the prime minister usually came from the southern province of Kulob and the speaker of the legislature came either from Gharm (in the mountains northeast of Dushanbe) or the province of Badakhshon (the Pamir Mountain region in the southeast of the country).[49] Iskandarov himself is a Tajik from Badakhshon who had held various offices in that province and the Dushanbe government before becoming speaker of Tajikistan's legislature, in May 1992. Qadriddin Aslonov, the speaker of the legislature who had had a conventional apparatchik's career until he sided with the opposition after the August 1991 coup, was from Gharm. (He was killed by the neo-Soviets during the civil war.) The Leninobodi clique allegedly learned the utility of sharing the pie with people from other provinces nearly a generation ago, after a personnel decision produced unpleasant results in Kulob Province. The Leninobodis appointed one of their own to head the Communist Party organization in Kulob. On his arrival he was kept out of his office; the next day his body was discovered in his hotel room. From then on, Kulobis were included in the power elite.[50]

Not surprisingly, people who benefited most from the old regime sought to preserve the system of power which had served them so well. However, this applied not only to the favored patronage networks in Leninobod but to others, as well. For example, one of the active defenders of the old order was Narzullo Dustov, vice president under Nabiev until the May 1992 crisis; he is from Darvaz, in Badakhshon, stereotyped as a bastion of opposition support. At the same time, the opposition found support from all parts of Tajikistan. The participation of inhabitants of all Tajikistan's provinces in opposition demonstrations has been noted above. The head of the opposition group Rastokhez, Tohir Abdujabbor, is from Leninobod, as are many of its other members. Even though neither Rastokhez nor the IRP had substantial numbers of followers among Pamiris, members of those two parties joined Pamiris in March 1992 demonstrations in the capital of Badakhshon which called for its elevation from autonomous province to autonomous republic within Tajikistan. The Democratic Party of Tajikistan, Rastokhez, and the Islamic Rebirth Party all had followers in Kulob. There would have been even more open support for the opposition in Leninobod and Kulob but for the ability of the neo-Soviets there to silence dissenters through repression, ranging from the use of bands of toughs to deter demonstrations to murder. Refugees from the repression in Kulob played an active role in the increasingly confrontational demonstrations in Dushanbe during the civil war.[51]

During the spring of 1992, as President Nabiev faced an intensifying challenge on the streets of Dushanbe, he looked to his Kulobi allies for help. He may have been influenced in this decision by the fact that travel between the north and south of the country, which are separated by mountains, would have been even more difficult for large numbers of people than later in the season and by the fact that one of the most determined hard-liners was Safarali Kenjaev, a Kulobi who was speaker of the legislature at that time. Kenjaev drew in particular on unemployed youths, of whom there were many in this province, which was poor and had a high birthrate even by Tajikistani standards. In May 1992, Nabiev had some 1,800 kalashnikov automatics distributed to Kulobis demonstrating for him in Dushanbe; they soon returned to their home province, taking their weapons with them. The Kulobi militia, eventually known as the Popular Front, solidified the neo-Soviets' control over their native province and the province of Qurghonteppa to the west; they subsequently played a major role in the neo-Soviets' drive to capture Dushanbe.[52]

The bloodiest fighting in the civil war took place in the province of Qurghonteppa. Many of the combatants were people whose families had been resettled there from elsewhere during the Soviet era. Massive irrigation works begun there under Stalin created a demand for a larger labor force than had previously lived in these formerly arid lowlands. People from Kulob as well as the mountains, especially the Gharm area, were resettled in the newly irrigated areas from the 1920s to the 1950s. They or their descendants still thought of themselves in terms of their family's region of origin.[53] During the civil war, some inhabitants of Qurghonteppa, especially Gharmis, supported the opposition, perhaps because they were attracted to democratization, some perhaps because they thought the economic privatization would benefit them.[54] Other inhabitants of the province, notably Kulobis and the Laqai tribe supported the neo-Soviets as a way of defending their own privileges and also as a rationale for seizing the property of Gharmis.[55]

Another province where the opposition was perceived to be strong was Badakhshon, the southeastern region of the republic, dominated by the high Pamir Mountains. This remote area had often in the past been under only under loose control by outside powers. Although some Tajiks live there, a majority of the inhabitants belong to several Eastern Iranian peoples, known collectively as Pamiris; Kyrgyzes live in the even more sparsely populated eastern reaches of the province. The Pamiris belong historically to the Ismai'li branch of Shi'ite Islam, as opposed either to the Sunni majority in Tajikistan or the Imami Shi'ite majority in Iran. Although Pamiris are classified as Tajiks by Soviet census takers and are inclined to use that designation themselves outside their own circles, many ordinary Tajiks see them as alien and non-Muslim.[56] Pamiris in their forties or younger, the kinds of people who were politically active in significant numbers during the power struggle in the early 1990s, were likely to speak both Russian and Tajik, especially since none of the Pamiri languages was used in education, the mass media, or written literature. Many Pamiris of these age groups thought in terms of their interests in Tajikistan as a whole, even though some of them were critical of the way the authorities in Dushanbe had treated their province. It is possible that many of them thought that they had so little stake in the status quo that they would do better to side with the advocates of change. They saw themselves as excluded from a voice in decision making and subjected to economic policies that left the province underdeveloped and impoverished.[57] Former presidential candidate Davlat Khudonazarov is a prominent example of a Pamiri who became active in opposition politics.

Two provinces took steps toward secession, without actually seceding, when events in the capital went against them. The repressive policies of the neo-Soviets in Dushanbe combined with the perception that the provincial economy was exploited led Badakhshon to declare its autonomy from the rest of Tajikistan at the start of 1992. The regionally-based political party, La"li Badakhshon, supported this stance, as did Kyrgyzes in the province. However, Badakhshon did not push the idea of secession; La"li Badakhshon remained active in the opposition's political struggle in Dushanbe.[58] After the neo-Soviets' victory in the civil war, thousands of people – many civilians, some combatants – fled to the remote mountains of Badakhshon, where local resources were severely overtaxed and some fighting continued.[59]

Leninobod's officials banned transmission within the province of Dushanbe's radio and television broadcasts after the formation of the coalition government in May 1992. They took a range of institutions in the province out of Dushanbe's control during the 1992 power struggle and created their own provincial militia. They kept provincial representatives from attending meetings of the republic's legislature, thus denying that body a quorum, when it seemed likely to vote to oust President Nabiev in the summer of 1992. Leninobod's obstructionism remained in effect until a rump legislative session dominated by neo-Soviets met in the province in November 1992 to install a new, like-minded government.[60]

The Kulobi neo-Soviets emerged from the civil war more powerful than ever before. The old alliance between Leninobodis and Kulobis continued for a while, albeit with increasing friction, but now the balance between them was reversed. For the first time, the Kulobis were the senior partner. In the first government after the civil war, the prime minister, Abdumalik Abdullojonov, was a Leninobodi but sixteen of the twenty-three top government positions were in Kulobi hands. The head of state,[61] Imomali Rahmonov, was a thirty-eight-year-old who went from collective farm director in Kulob to the highest political office within a few months, not because he was a brilliant politician but because he represented those Kulobis who wanted to preserve the Soviet-style monopoly of power and privilege for their own use. The victors sharply scaled back the practice of allowing compliant Gharmis and Pamiris representation in high office. At the end of the civil war, the Kulobi militia, which fought for the neo-Soviets, conducted a blood purge of people from Badakhshon and Gharm in Dushanbe.[62]

National tensions

Worsening conditions in Tajikistan not only heightened regional divisions within the Tajik population but also increased the alienation of other nationalities living there. According to the last census (1989), Tajiks (including the Eastern Iranian peoples) comprised roughly 62 percent of the republic's total population of 5.1 million. Russians comprised 7.6 percent. In the climate of increased ethnic tensions not only in Tajikistan but also in the other Soviet successor states in the early 1990s, it was common to blur the distinction between Russians and Russian-speakers; the latter category included, in addition to people listed as Russian in their official identity papers, members of other, mostly European, nationalities, who presumably used Russian as their principal language when living in diaspora. This referred, in the case of Tajikistan, to Ukrainians, Belorussians, Germans, Armenians, and Jews, who accounted collectively for less than 4 percent of the republic's population. Russian-speakers lived primarily in the cities, especially Dushanbe and those associated with Soviet-era industrial development projects.

The discontents of the Russian-speakers began to grow even before the political crisis in Tajikistan. These reflected the malaise of the close of the Soviet era and the unsettling effects of decolonization as well as specific problems in Tajikistan. A late Soviet-era survey in Dushanbe of 1,000 non-Tajiks, primarily Russians, reflected these systemic problems. Of the respondents, 29 percent believed that nationality relations in the Soviet Union had deteriorated and 24 percent complained about the waning of internationalism. In the rhetoric of Soviet nationality relations, "internationalism" meant the primacy of the Union and the central authorities, with, *de facto*, a strongly Russian coloration, over minority nationalities.[63] In addition, 42 percent of those surveyed feared interethnic strife. The same proportion expressed the intention of leaving Tajikistan; one-third intended to stay; the remainder was uncertain what to do. Only 13 percent considered nationality relations in Tajikistan better than in the Soviet Union as a whole.[64]

Some of the reasons for the Russian-speakers' worries lay in practical considerations raised by events in late-Soviet and post-Soviet Tajikistan. Other reasons lay in the way many Russian-speakers felt threatened by "uppity" Tajiks. One example of both kinds of concerns was the Tajik language law of 1989. The law gave Tajik primacy in public institutions though it retained Russian as the lingua franca and provided for the use of Russian, Uzbek, and other languages by minority nationalities. Given that the Soviet system had made a fluent knowledge of Russian essential in most areas of higher or technical education and in many of the more desirable jobs, it was not surprising that Russian-speakers generally opposed the new law. However, that was only part of what was at issue. Soviet language policy had not encouraged bilingualism but had favored Russian; the use of Tajik had been circumscribed in many spheres of public life in Tajikistan for years. A knowledge of Russian was required of Tajiks for many jobs; many educated Tajiks were more at home in Russian than Tajik.[65] Few Russians spoke Tajik and many disdained to learn it, something Tajiks resented.[66]

The Dushanbe riots of mid-February 1990, with their killings, injuries, and looting, could readily have frightened inhabitants of the city, regardless of nationality. But some Russian-speakers, both in the republic and in Moscow, interpreted the events as primarily a Tajik offense against Russians. Acts of violence which actually occurred, hostile statements by Tajiks to Russians, and unsubstantiated scare stories left Russian-speakers badly frightened by the riots. For example, claims by *Pravda* that a Russian child was shot and a Russian woman thrown off a bridge during the riots were not substantiated by subsequent investigation.[67] Mikhail Gorbachev, addressing the Supreme Soviet in Moscow towards the end of the Dushanbe riots, likened events there to the anti-Armenian violence in Azerbaijan, stating that "[t]hese people are acting evilly, putting pistols to the heads of women and children."[68] In fact, the women and children who were shot in Dushanbe had been fired on by Soviet security forces.[69] *Literaturnaia gazeta*, despite its reputation for liberalism, reported from Dushanbe that "[t]he overwhelming majority of those injured during the days of terror were Russians; all of those assaulted were Russian."[70] That is not true. Russian-speakers accounted for 56.5 percent of the injured who were treated in Dusahnbe's hospitals and 41.4 percent of those seriously injured; Tajiks accounted for 43.5 percent of the injured and 58.8 percent of those seriously injured. Of the twenty-five people killed during the riots, sixteen were Tajiks and five were Russians. (The other fatalities were two Uzbeks, one Tatar, and one Azerbaijani).[71]

Apart from overt acts of violence, Russian-speakers in Tajikistan became increasingly uneasy over Tajiks' evident lack of deference or outright dislike, which Russian-speakers either experienced directly or heard about by rumor. Thus stories circulated of Tajik sales clerks snubbing Russians or refusing to talk Russian to them and of Tajiks saying (in Russian) within earshot of Russians that the latter ought to leave.[72]

As Soviet authority over Tajikistan declined, many Russian-speakers found the place even more alien and threatening. Russians, even if born in Tajikistan, usually did not think of it as their homeland. They also feared that the growth of Tajik nationalism would make them second-class citizens. Some saw Tajiks as ingrates who had forgotten how much Russians had done to improve Tajikistan. What Russian-speakers probably dreaded the most was that post-Soviet Tajikistan might become an Islamic state.[73]

In 1991 and 1992, as the defenders of the old order faced a serious political challenge in Tajikistan, they worked hard to garner support from Russian-speakers. Their principal technique was to present themselves as the only alternative to a radical Islamic regime. They depicted the coalition of opposition groups as composed in reality of Islamic extremists. They also alleged that the short-lived coalition government of 1992 intended to discriminate against Russian-speakers.[74]

The words and deeds of some Tajiks contributed to the climate of fear. The fact that some Tajik nationalists pointed to Russians as living a privileged existence in the republic while the Tajiks' interests were slighted gave credence to Russian-speakers' worries about reverse discrimination.[75] There were occasional anti-Russian acts during the civil war, although the opposition's leadership did not condone that.[76] Several inflammatory statements made by the head of the Democratic Party of Tajikistan, the quixotic Shodmon Yusuf, during 1992 lent credibility to the warnings about dangers facing Russian-speakers.[77]

The combination of Tajikistan's political turmoil, the transformation of a single Soviet Union into fifteen separate states, and the considerable economic problems of independent Tajikistan drove the Russian-speakers to act. They overwhelmingly supported the neo-Soviets in republican politics. This included voting en masse for Nabiev in the November 1991 presidential election and committing some of the electoral fraud that padded his margin of victory.[78] Another way Russians and most other nationalities living in Tajikistan responded to the upheavals was by voting with their feet. There were roughly 388,000 Russians in Tajikistan in 1989 (a significant date both because that was when the last census was conducted and the controversial language law was enacted). There has been no comprehensive, impartial tally of the number of people who have left Tajikistan since 1989. Various sources have partisan motives for offering high or low counts of Russian emigrants. From 1989 to 1991 (thus before the outbreak of civil war), roughly 100,000 Russian-speakers may have left Tajikistan; this included not only Russians but also Germans and Jews who left the Soviet Union for Germany or Israel.[79] One Russian estimate stated that by 1994, only 70–80,000 Russians were left in Tajikistan, most of them elderly or ill, without the means to relocate.[80] In addition to the way emigration disrupted people's lives, it also had a negative effect on Tajikistan's economic capabilities, given the high concentration of Russians and other Russian-speakers in professional, managerial, and skilled industrial jobs. The problems of Russian-speakers in Tajikistan and as refugees from there also had a significant effect on the policy of Russia towards Tajikistan. (However, that large and important topic lies beyond the scope of this paper.)

The other nationality that was caught up in substantial numbers in the fragmentation of Tajikistani society was the Uzbeks, the largest of Tajikistan's minorities. According to the 1989 census, they comprised fractionally more than 23 percent of the population. (Since that census, Uzbeks have often claimed the figure of 30 percent.) They live in both northern and southern regions of the country, comprising a majority of the population in some districts. Members of the Laqai tribe, which inhabits the southwest, though officially classified as Uzbek by the Soviet system, consider their tribe a distinct entity. Their willingness to fight to preserve their autonomy, long before the 1992 civil war, was reflected in their battles against the establishment of Communist rule in Central Asia during the Russian civil war (until 1926, after fighting had ended elsewhere in Central Asia) and against the collectivization of agriculture.[81]

The very fact that Uzbeks and Tajiks had so much in common for so long contributed to the widening rift between at least some elements in the Tajik and Uzbek communities ever since the Soviet creation of nationally-defined republics in Central Asia. Some Uzbeks saw their nationality, given its precedent of rule over parts of the region and the fact that it was the largest of the region's indigenous nationalities, as the region's natural leader; they saw Tajiks' assertion of a separate identity as divisive. Some Tajiks objected to what they saw as Uzbek efforts to deny the existence of the Tajiks as a people and the oppression of Tajiks in Uzbekistan. However, there was no credible irredentist movement which pressed for the union of Samarqand and Bukhara with Tajikistan. In addition, the states of Uzbekistan and Tajikistan had competing interests in thorny problems of access to resources and repairing damage to the environment.[82] One illustration of the way contemporary animosities played on the historically blurred distinction between the two nationalities was the prevalence of rumors among advocates of change in both republics that unpopular representatives of the old order were really members of the other nationality. This included Uzbekistan's President Karimov and Tajikistan's Presidents Mahkamov and Nabiev. Somehow national origin was supposed to explain the hated policies of the adversary or compound his guilt. One example of both the links between Uzbeks and Tajiks and the perniciousness of the assumption that lineage necessarily determines political loyalty is the fact that the leader of the Tajik rights movement in Uzbekistan, Uktam Bekmuhammedov, is half-Uzbek and was arrested by the government of the "really Tajik" Karimov.

The late-Soviet era regime in Tajikistan made several conciliatory gestures towards the republic's Uzbek minority. Bookstores specifically for Uzbek-language publications opened in three southern cities. A new Uzbek-language weekly was launched; two other Uzbek-language newspapers were already published in the republic. For years, schools which taught in Uzbek had operated in districts with a high concentration of Uzbek inhabitants. Roughly a tenth of the republic's radio broadcasts was in Uzbek.

In the political struggles of 1991 and 1992, the Uzbeks of Tajikistan sided overwhelmingly with the defenders of Soviet institutions of power and privilege. They may have been motivated by the belief that the neo-Soviets would protect their interests better, by fear that the opposition's links to Tajik nationalism would make it anti-Uzbek, by competition with Tajiks from elsewhere in the republic who had been resettled in the southwest in the Soviet era, and by Laqai tribalism. All the while, Uzbekistan's propaganda machinery voiced repeated allegations of Tajik mistreatment of the Uzbek minority.[83] The neo-Soviet forces in southern Tajikistan also played on the fears of Uzbeks living there to obtain their support in the civil war.[84] In the presidential election of November 1991, Uzbeks voted overwhelmingly for Nabiev.[85] When he was ousted in September 1992, officials of the predominantly Uzbek district of Tursunzoda, on the western border of Tajikistan, repudiated the new government in Dushanbe.[86] Uzbeks living in the south of the country also became involved in the civil war, both as combatants and as refugees. (The fighting did not extend to the north of the country.) Laqais as well as non-tribal Uzbeks attacked Tajik-speakers from Gharm and Badakhshon who had settled in the south and who were stereotyped as supporting the political opposition. Uzbeks also joined forces with Tajiks in an area southwest of Dushanbe (Hisor) to attack the capital in concert with the neo-Soviets' militia from Kulob Province.[87]

Uzbek non-combatants sought to escape the conflict in the south by fleeing to the protection of Russian troops stationed there or by leaving the area, heading either northward into Leninobod Province or across the border into Uzbekistan. Some reported having been ordered out or threatened by Tajiks.[88] There is no clear information about who threatened whom first or how many reports of threats were colored by partisanship or were the product of the understandable fears of people caught in a war zone, more than of actual threats. Of course for refugees the answers to those questions offer scant consolation for being uprooted from their homes.

Conflict among the victors

The coalition of patron–client networks which won the civil war did not hold together after victory. Erstwhile allies soon fell to fighting among themselves over the spoils of victory. Rivals used a range of methods against each other, from political maneuvering to armed force. This was not about ideology but about who would benefit from controlling the levers of power. It was different in two ways from the sporadic combat between government forces and remnants of the opposition both in mountainous areas of Tajikistan and across the border with Afghanistan. That conflict was about differing visions of how Tajikistan should be governed as well as who would govern. As warfare, it could not be expected to have the characteristics of democratic politics. In contrast, the government established at the end of 1992 had the outward forms of democracy and described itself as the only secular, democratizing option.[89] Therefore it could legitimately be held accountable for the lack of substance underlying those forms.

Former Prime Minister Abdullojonov, in addition to having been forced out of office by Rahmonov in December 1993, found his attempt to make a comeback through the electoral process frustrated by the dominant faction's manipulation of that process. He was the only candidate who ran against Rahmonov in the presidential election of November 1994, the irregularities of which have been noted above. He tried to present himself as better able than Rahmonov to negotiate a settlement with the opposition and solve the country's economic problems.[90] Abdullojonov's Popular Unity Party (established in 1994) attempted to field candidates in the first round of legislative elections, in February 1995. Ironically, he justified the ruling elite's suppression of other parties, those of the opposition coalition, without linking that intolerance of rivals to the harassment his own party faced.[91] The party encountered various obstacles, such as restrictions on the number of candidates who could run in an electoral district. On the eve of the vote, Abdullojonov pulled his party out of the elections, declaring they could not possibly be fair.[92] In contrast, the head of Tajikistan's electoral commission, Kholmurod Sharifov, hailed the legislative elections, calling them "a vivid sign that popular democracy in Tajikistan is gaining a more stable character" and implying criticism of the Organization for Security and Cooperation in Europe (which had openly faulted the elections) "for violating ethical norms."[93] (According to international observers, defects in the elections included the fact that several opposition parties were still not permitted to function within the country, the regime's censorship of the broadcast and print media remained tight, restrictions on the number of candidates a party was allowed to field, and de facto harrassment of candidates not backed by the regime. Although a majority of the contests had at least two candidates [107 out of 181], most represented a narrow range of political opinion and were either from the Communist Party or members of Rahmonov's patronage network.[94])

Politics under the neo-Soviet regime was plagued by warlordism, in the sense that leaders of armed bands which had supported the victors in the civil war remained in de facto control of those bands and used force in pursuit of their personal goals. This proved a source of recurrent instability in southern and western Tajikistan.

For example, in March 1993, Sangak Safarov, the most important commander in what had been the neo-Soviet militia during the civil war, the Popular Front, quarreled with another major figure in the front, Faizali Saidov, the leader of the Laqais. Safarov, Saidov, and five bodyguards died in a hail of bullets. Although much remains obscure about the incident, the point of contention appears to have been an attempt to subordinate Saidov to Safarov within Tajikistan's new army, which was based on the Popular Front.[95]

One of the neo-Soviet warlords who survived the civil war to become a thorn in the side of his former allies was Ibodullo Boimatov, the mayor of Tursunzoda, the location of Tajikistan's large aluminum smelter, the country's main industry. He led an armed unit of the neo-Soviet forces during the civil war and refused to disarm his men afterwards. That brought him into conflict with the new regime. He was also alleged to have attempted extortion against the manager of the aluminum plant, then shoot at him (but did not kill him.) In any event, he was ousted as mayor in 1994 and fled to Uzbekistan. In January 1996, he returned to Tursunzoda with a band of followers and two armored vehicles from Uzbekistan. He took about ten border guards hostage to press his demand that the regime give him some important government position and then seized control of the city.[96]

His challenge to the new regime became intertwined with the most serious of the warlord conflicts, between the First and Eleventh Brigades of Tajikistan's army. The brigades had been separate units of the Popular Front in 1992 and were transformed into components of the new regime's army. These antagonistic forces were based near each other in Qurghonteppa. In June 1995, their rivalry led to bloodshed, as they fought over control of local economic assets, including cotton, the main crop there. The commander of the Eleventh Brigade died in the fighting. His supporters retaliated by killing the provincial deputy governor. The two battalions fought each other on several subsequent occasions in 1995. An unknown number of civilians caught in the cross fire and a UN cease-fire observer were killed.[97] Early in 1996, the First Brigade, which had emerged as the stronger of the two rose up again. Its commander, Colonel Mahmud Khudoiberdiev, demanded the removal of a number of government officials in Dushanbe, though not of President Rahmonov. The Brigade's public charge against the officials was corruption. This uprising coincided roughly with Boimatov's return to Tursunzoda.

Boimatov and the First Brigade were both placated in February 1996 by substantial government concessions. Prime Minister Jamshed Karimov resigned and was replaced by an obscure factory manager from Khujand Province, Yahyo Azimov. Gone, too, was the deputy prime minister, Mahmadsayid Ubaidulloev, whose powers included jurisdiction over the aluminum plant and cotton, both still state monopolies, as well as the ministries of security and defense. The president had to give up his chief of staff, a Kulobi veteran communist *apparatchik*, Izatullo Hayoev. The head of Tursonzoda's administration was also replaced. Boimatov was named Tajikistan's trade representative to Uzbekistan.[98] He declared after the personnel changes, "Now we shall live better. We want to live better, the way we did under communists in the Soviet Union."[99]

The period after the civil war was also marred by the killing of a number of public figures as well as ordinary citizens. Some of the assassinations may have been apolitical acts, given that violent crimes increased in a country where law enforcement was weak and weapons had become widely available. The Dushanbe government routinely blamed the opposition for all assassinations, though that was not confirmed by independent sources. Even instances when that clearly was not true, such as the shoot-out between Saidov and Safarov, were characterized in those terms.[100] The killing of two men, Deputy Prime Minister Moyonshoh Nazarshoev and the chief Islamic figure, *Mufti* Fathullo Sharifzoda,[101] on the eve of two different rounds of the peace talks (in March 1994 and January 1996) sparked claims that the killings were the work of supporters of the Dushanbe government who did not want the talks to occur; these allegations have not been proven.[102]

Foreign intervention

The brief, tentative movement towards democratization was brought to a halt not only by the domestic conflict but also by foreign intervention to ensure the victory of the neo-Soviets in the civil war and sustain them in power afterwards. Russia and Uzbekistan aided the seizure of Dushanbe by the neo-Soviets in December 1992, the subsequent operations against the remnants of opposition forces, and played a major role in guarding Tajikistan's border with Afghanistan.[103] Symbolic of the new relationship was the minister of defense in the neo-Soviet government established at the end of 1992. Colonel Aleksandr Shishliannikov (later Major-General) was a Russian military officer who was born in Tashkent and had never served in Tajikistan before becoming a member of its government; his previous position was in Uzbekistan's ministry of defense. (He left Tajikistan in 1995.) The deputy minister of internal affairs in the same government was also a Russian, Col. Genadii Blinov. Russian personnel at the embassy in Dushanbe advise the Tajikistani regime.[104] Russia also provided financing desperately needed by the post-civil-war regime. That not only buoyed up the regime in a general sense but also aided the political position of Imomali Rahmonov when he ran for president in November 1994. Weeks before the election, Russia sent the Dushanbe regime 15 billion rubles. That enabled the Rahmonov government to pay salaries which had not been paid for months and in the process undercut rival candidate Abdullojonov's criticism of Rahmonov.[105]

The Russian government hailed Tajikistan's presidential election of November 1994 and the legislative election of February 1995 as proof of Tajikistan's progress toward democracy.[106] In the presidential election, the Russian commanders of the CIS peace keeping force and the border guards openly endorsed the Rahmonov over Abdullojonov.[107] Russia officially supported the so-far inconclusive peace negotiations between the Dushanbe regime and exiled opposition during the series of meetings begun in 1994. Russia's role in the peace process has not been neutral. While its troops in Tajikistan continued to engage in combat operations, it refused to be a party to the cease-fire concluded between the Tajikistani government and opposition in exile.[108] Moscow encouraged the Dushanbe regime to take an unyielding position on all essentials while demanding that the opposition make all the concessions.[109]

Post-civil-war Tajikistan owed a massive foreign debt, including to Russia and Uzbekistan, which it could not repay. Uzbekistan has reacted by cutting off deliveries of natural gas to Tajikistan (which is dependent upon imports.) This seriously disrupted Tajikistan's already troubled economy.[110] Unconfirmed rumors alleged that Uzbekistan had backed the uprisings by former mayor Boimatov and Colonel Khudoiberdiev early in 1996.[111]

Conclusion

No state or nation is primordial and the borders of every state are to some degree arbitrary. States and nations become what people make of them, given the desire and the time, although inhabitants of democratic nation-states established in the past may mistake the manufactured for the intrinsic. In these characteristics, Tajikistan is like other states. It has had some people who intended to build a civil society focused on the nation-state but there has been very little time – and much of that marred by conflict – for those people to achieve their aim. Tajikistan's problems building a nation-state were compounded by its abrupt and unsought transition to what was supposed to be complete independence and has not turned out to be even that, given its dependence on Russia and Uzbekistan. Whether the Soviet Union was an empire in the usual sense of the word may be debated but its collapse threw Tajikistan and some of the other successor states into a particularly acute crisis of decolonization. Even in states which have existed far longer than Tajikistan and have a longer tradition of civil society, accommodating the interests of various groups of inhabitants while maintaining the cohesiveness of the whole is a continual and often contentious process. That problem is compounded when powerful factions have never reconciled themselves to the passing of the old order and have resorted to force to preserve it in substance, if not in name.

NOTES

1 V. Gubarev, "Instability in Tajikistan," *Moscow Times*, 14 November 1994; I. MacWilliam, "Ex-Communist Declared Victor in Disputed Tajik Race," *Los Angeles Times*, 8 November 1994; Deutsche Presse-Agentur, 1 and 4 November 1994, 24 February 1995; Agence France Presse, 26 February 1995; Reuters, 24 February 1995; W. Sloane, "Holding Islam at Bay Ex-Soviet State Votes On Pro-Moscow Slate," *Christian Science Monitor*, 4 November 1994 (all as republished by Nexis).

2 Refugees fled to other parts of Tajikistan, to neighboring Uzbekistan, Kyrgyzstan, and Afghanistan, to Russia, and to more distant countries. Since 1993, some have returned, but there is no reliable count of those who have done so.

3 The name "Tajik" has in the past been used for Persian-speakers over a broader geographic range; in modern times it is normally used only for those living in the formerly Soviet and Chinese parts of Central Asia and some of those in Afghanistan.

4 M. Atkin, "Religious, National, and Other Identities in Central Asia," in *Muslims in Central Asia*, ed. J.-A. Gross (Durham, NC: Duke University Press, 1992), p. 52.

5 Ibid., pp. 53–4.

6 T. Rakowska-Harmstone, *Russia and Nationalism in Central Asia* (Baltimore: The Johns Hopkins University Press, 1970), pp. 39–41; G. Simon, *Nationalism and Policy Toward the Nationalities in the Soviet Union*, trans. K. Forster and O. Forster (Boulder, CO: Westview Press, 1991), p. 32.

7 Atkin, "Tajiks and the Persian World," in *Soviet Central Asia in Historical Perspective*, ed. B. F. Manz (Boulder, CO: Westview Press, 1994), p. 130.

8 Atkin, "Tajikistan: Ancient Heritage, New Politics," in *Nation and Politics in the Soviet Successor States*, ed. I. Bremmer and R. Taras (Cambridge: Cambridge University Press, 1993), p. 363.

9 Atkin, "Religious, National, and Other Identities," pp. 58–62.

10 Atkin, "Tajikistan: Ancient Heritage," pp. 364–7.

11 I. Rotar', "My khotim islamskoi demokratii," *Nezavisimaia gazeta*, 11 September 1992, p. 3; Reuter Library Report, 1 December 1991.

12 P. Pons, "Communists versus Islam," *Manchester Guardian Weekly*, 6 October 1992, p. 14.

13 "Soobshchenie komissii prezidiuma Verkhovnogo Soveta Tadzhikskoi SSR po proverke sobytii 12–14 Fevralia 1990 g. v Dushanbe," *Sogdiana* (Moscow), no. 3, 1990 (October), special issue, pp. 2–8; A. Suord, "Noch' nad Tadzhikistanom," *Moskovskie novosti*, 3 January 1993, p. 3A.

14 Kh. Nazrulloev, "Strasti po Tadzhikistanu," *Nezavisimaia gazeta*, 4 April 1993, p. 4.

15 V. Abdullo, "Roh kujost?" *Javononi Tojikiston* (Dushanbe), 12 October 1991, p. 1; A. Azamova, "Tajikistan Mourns Its Dead," *Moscow News*, 19 February 1992 (as republished by Nexis); Official Kremlin International News Broadcast, 13 February 1992 (as published by Nexis).

16 Comment by Dust Muhammad Dust, deputy chairman of the Democratic Party of Tajikistan, 14 April 1993.

17   Foreign Broadcast Information Service, *Daily Report: Soviet Union* (hereafter *FBIS-SOV*), 4 January 1991, p. 57; TASS, 30 January 1991, as reprinted in ibid., 4 February 1991, p. 86; Moscow domestic radio, 7 July 1990, as translated in ibid., 10 July 1990, p. 72; TASS, 10 September 1990, as reprinted in ibid., 11 September 1990, p. 105.

18   O. Panfilov, "Otechestvo v opasnosti, – skazal Shodmon Iusuf," *Nezavisimaia gazeta*, 23 June 1992, p. 3; R. H. Krieble and S. M. Loui, "'Democracies' Still Precarious," *Christian Science Monitor*, 8 January 1992, p. 19; T. Abdulloev, et al., "Murojiatnoma," *Jumhuriyat* (Dushanbe), 4 October 1991, p. 1; A. Qurbonali, "Oyo Huvaidulloevu Pochomulloev Gdlianu Ivanovi Tojik shuda metavonand?" *Jumhuriyat*, 10 March 1992, p. 3; A. Azamova, "Tajikistan: Duel between Parliament and Opposition," *Moscow News*, 22 April 1992 (as republished by Nexis); *FBIS-SOV*, 10 March 1992, pp. 42–3 and 18 May 1992, p. 49; *Human Rights and Democratization in the Newly Independent States of the Former Soviet Union* (Washington, DC: Commission on Security and Cooperation in Europe, 1993), p. 225; E. Pain, "Internationalization of the Tajik Conflict," *Moscow News*, 4 November 1992 (as republished by Nexis).

19   In the parlance of the late Soviet era, not all of these were officially called parties for much of the period under consideration. In a formal sense, only those organizations which the government consented to register as parties could be called parties. Organizations not classified as parties were usually called "movements."

20   Atkin, "Tajikistan: Ancient Heritage," p. 362.

21   S. Shermatova, "It's Not Koran That Kills," *Moscow News*, 14 April 1993 (as republished by Nexis); Foreign Broadcast Information Service, *Daily Report: Central Eurasia* (hereafter *FBIS-SOV*), 12 May 1992, pp. 59–60; ITAR-TASS, 29 July 1992.

22   A. Lukin and A. Ganelin, "Podpol'nyi obkom deistvuet," *Komsomol'skaia pravda*, 23 March 1991, p. 2; E. Deriabina, "Islamskii faktor, ili spetsluzhby Saudovskoi Aravii v Miniuste RF?" *Stolitsa*, 1992, no. 32 (August), p. 4; *FBIS-SOV*, 18 December 1990, p. 102.

23   I. Rotar', "My khotim islamskoi demokratii," *Nezavisimaia gazeta*, 11 September 1992, p. 3; *Shahodat* (Dushanbe), 1371/1992, no. 9 (Farvardin/April), pp. 1, 2, 3; Atkin, "Islam as Faith, Politics, and Bogeyman in Tajikistan," in *The Politics of Religion in Russia and the New States of Eurasia*, ed. M. Bourdeaux (Armonk, NY and London: M. E. Sharpe, 1995).

24   Not to be confused with the party of the same name established by Abdumalik Abdullojonov, a disaffected neo-Soviet, in 1994.

25   "Zhizn' podskazala programmu etoi partii," *Narodnaia gazeta*, 17 March 1992, p. 2.

26   "Politizirovannye zemliachestva Tadzhikistana," *Moskovskie novosti*, 13 September 1992, p. 6; A. Dubnov, "Katastrofa v Tadzhikistane," *Novoe vremia*, no. 4 (January 1993) (as photocopied in *Russia & CIS Today*, 25 January 1993, p. 37).

27   Representative of this is the denunciation of the Communist Party in J. Said, "Mevae nest beh zi ozodi," *Javononi Tojikiston*, 12 October 1991, p. 1.

28 For example, these reasons for endorsing Khudonazarov were given by *Qadi* Turajonzoda. Reuter Library Report, 23 November 1991; *FBIS-SOV*, 20 July 1992, p. 61.

29 F. Karimzoda, "Rahmon Nabievro tarafdorem!" *Tojikistoni shuravi* (Dushanbe), 14 September 1992, p. 1.

30 Russian Press Digest, 2 and 4 December 1991; Krieble and Loui, "'Democracies' Still Precarious," p. 19; statements made by Mr. Khudonazarov in the author's presence.

31 *FBIS-SOV*, 30 September 1991, p. 97; ibid., 2 October 1991, p. 86.

32 Representative of this are *FBIS-SOV*, 26 September 1991, p. 86; E. Muhammad, "Maromi mo: khudshinosi, bedorii millat," *Tojikistoni shuravi*, 10 September 1991, p. 2; N. Yodgori, "Dar Kulob chi gap?" *Tojikistoni shuravi*, 6 September 1991, p. 3; "Ba mardumi sharifi Khatlonzamin," *Jomi jam* (Dushanbe), 1992, no. 6 (April), p. 3; "Dar Qurghonteppa boz girdihamoi," *Shahodat*, 1371/1992, no. 4 (Bahman/February), p. 1.

33 Atkin, "Tajikistan: Ancient Heritage," p. 366.

34 "Girdihamoi dar maidoni ba nomi Lenin," *Tojikistoni shuravi*, 30 August 1991, p. 2.

35 Official Kremlin International News Broadcast, 1 and 8 October 1991.

36 A. Istad, "Davlati milli chi guna boyad?" *Adabiyot va san"at* (Dushanbe), 4 June 1992, p. 6; Reuter Library Report, 25 September 1991, 1 December 1991, and 9 September 1992; S. Tadjbakhsh, "The Bloody Path of Change: The Case of Post-Soviet Tajikistan," *Harriman Institute Forum* 6, no. 11 (July 1993), p. 6; *FBIS-SOV*, 20 July 1992, p. 61; "Khodzhiakbar Turadzhonzoda," *Moskovskie novosti*, 30 August 1992, p. 11.

37 Atkin, "Religious, National, and Other Identities," pp. 60–2.

38 S. Tadjbakhsh, "Causes and Consequences of the Civil War," *Central Asia Monitor*, no. 1 (1993), 12; N. Yodori, "Dar Kulob chi gap?" *Tojikistoni shuravi*, 6 September 1991, p. 3; "Murojiatnomai muslamononi nohiya," *Shahodat*, 1371/1992, no. 9 (Farvardin/April), p. 1.

39 "Okhirin umedi in umedvoron, zinda bod! . . . ," [sic] *Jumhuriyat*, 5 October 1991, p. 2; *FBIS-SOV*, 26 September 1991, p. 86; "Ba mardumi sharifi Khatlonzamin"; Official Kremlin International News Broadcast, 1 and 8 October 1991; *FBIS-SOV*, 15 April 1992, pp. 55–6; M. Nuriyon, "Tojikistonro digar qismat makun," *Jumhuriyat*, 4 April 1992, p. 4; M Egamzod, "Ruzi boron, zeri khaima, man gurusna . . . ," [sic] ibid., 28 September 1991, p. 1; T. Abdulloev *et al.*, "Murojiatnoma," ibid., 4 October 1991, p. 1; "Shabzinda-dorii demokratho davom dorad," *Tojikistoni shuravi*, 31 August 1991, p. 2.

40 V. Iakov, "Khronika revoliutsii. Ili perevorota?" *Izvestiia*, 18 May 1992, p. 8; U. Babakhanov and A. Ganelin, "Budet li v Dushanbe ploshchad' pobedivshei oppozitsii?" *Komsomol'skaia pravda*, 22 May 1992, p. 1; S. Erlanger, "Tajik Leader Agrees to Coalition With Opponents," *New York Times*, 12 May 1992, p. A5; *FBIS-SOV*, 12 May 1992, pp. 57–8 and 15 May 1992, p. 63; Reuter Library Report, 5 May 1992; "Tajiks Agree to Form Coalition," *Financial Times*, 12 May 1992, p. 3; S. Shihab, "Asie centrale, l'Iran se pose en médiateur," *Le Monde*, 12 May 1992, p. 3.

41 Representative of this are RusData DiaLine-BizEkon News, 14 November 1992; Reuter Library Report, 18 November 1992; *RFE/RL Daily Report*, 21 December 1992, p. 3 and 21 January 1993, p. 3; *FBIS-SOV*, 21 May 1993, p. 63.

42 R. Batyrshin, "Prorok Mukhammad sozdal Koran, kak Lenin – ustav Kompartii," *Nezavisimaia gazeta*, 22 June 1993, p. 3.

43 Russian Press Digest, 22 June 1993 (as republished by Nexis); *Current Digest of the Post-Soviet Press* 47, no. 9 (29 March 1995) (as republished by Nexis); Agence France Presse, 13 March 1995.

44 ITAR-TASS, 2 September 1993.

45 Russian Press Digest, 28 August 1993; ITAR-TASS, 2 September 1993; "Peregovory vozmozhny no ne s prestupnikami," *Pravda*, 15 March 1994, p. 1.

46 Reuter European Business Report, 15 November 1994; Reuters, 24 February 1995.

47 U. Babakhanov and L. Makhkamov, "Nash perekrestok," *Komsomolets Tadzhikistana*, 15 December 1987; A. Tavobov, "Dialog ne poluchilsia," ibid., 21 July 1989, p. 1.; R. Alimov, "V klub ili . . . v molel'nyi dom?" *Sel'skaia zhizn'*, 22 March 1987, p. 3.

48 A. Azamova, "Tadzhikistan: agoniia nezavisimosti," *Moskovskie novosti*, 13 September 1992, p. 6.

49 Agence France Presse, 22 November 1992.

50 I. Rotar', "Voina bez pobeditelei," *Nezavisimaia gazeta*, 10 September 1992, p. 3.

51 T. Akbirsho, "Tazohurot dar Badakhshon," *Javononi Tojikiston*, 14 March 1992, p. 1; Kh. Nazrulloev, "Strasti po Tadzhikistanu," *Nezavisimaia gazeta*, 4 April 1993, p. 4; O. Panfilov, "V Tadzhikistane snova svergaiut prezidenta," ibid., 2 September 1992, p. 1; I. Rotar', "Ob osvobozhdenii Dushanbe my podumaem pozzhe," ibid., 14 November 1992, p. 3; Dubnov, "Katastrofa v Tadzhikistane"; J. Steele, "Aloof Tajiks in North Fear Volatile South," *The Guardian*, 19 May 1992.

52 Nazrulloev, "Strasti po Tadzhikistanu."

53 S. Tadjbakhsh, "The Bloody Path of Change," p. 5; Rotar', "Voina bez pobeditelei."

54 Nazrulloev, "Strasti po Tadzhikistanu."

55 A. Azamova, "Za kogo voiuiut v Tadzhikistane?" *Argumenty i fakty*, 1992, no. 35 (September), p. 4; Rotar', "Voina bez pobeditelei."

56 *Current Digest of the Post-Soviet Press*, 17 February 1993, p. 9.

57 A. Nizom, "Panj soli purtalosh," *Javononi Tojikiston*, 26 March 1992, p. 2; Ia. R. Vinnikov, "Natsional'nye i etnograficheskie gruppy Srednei Azii po dannym etnicheskoi statistiki," *Etnicheskie protsessy u natsional'nykh grupp Srednei azii i Kazakhstana* (Moscow: Nauka, 1980), p. 30; N. Zurobek, "Shoh yo gado?" *Adabiyot va san"at*, 10 August 1989, p. 3; Russian Press Digest, 7 December 1991.

58 *Russian Press Digest*, 7 December 1991; *RFE-RL Daily Report*, 8 January 1993, p. 2; A. Suord, "Noch' nad Tadzhikistanom," *Moskovskie novosti*, 3 January 1993, p. 3A.

59 *FBIS-SOV*, 3 June 1993, p. 53.

60 A. Lugovskaia, "Tadzhikistan: respublika v traure," *Izvestiia*, 8 May 1992, p. 2; I. Rotar', "Kinorezhisser v roli diplomata," *Nezavisimaia gazeta*, 11 July 1992, p. 3; Panfilov, "V Tadzhikistane snova svergaiut prezidenta."

61 The speaker of the republic's legislature became the head of state after the office of president was abolished in November 1992 because of the intense controversy over choosing a new president. The 1994 constitution reestablished the office of president, to which Rahmonov was elected in November of that year.

62 Agence France Presse, 22 November and 16 December 1992; Suord, "Noch' nad Tadzhikistanom"; M. Epstein, "Enfants de Brejnev contre fils d'Allah," *L'Express*, 3 June 1993, p. 23.

63 One example of how "internationalism" exhibited a pro-Russian bias in Tajikistan comes from a 1989 court case. In the town of Konibodom, in Leninobod province, a factory worker in his early twenties who, judging by his name, was either Tajik or Uzbek, was accosted by two "European" men who asked him for a match. He replied that he did not smoke and walked on; the two men then beat him up. Three days later he hung up two signs bearing anti-Russian slogans on the wall of the town park. The provincial KGB tracked the young man down. He was tried and fined 1,000 rubles (a large sum for a factory worker at that time.) An editorial note accompanying an article about the case pointed to the young man's anti-Russian sloganeering as an example of nationalist enmity which illustrated the need for better internationalist education. Neither the account of the trial nor the editorial note criticized the beating of the young man. There was no indication that the two attackers were arrested or prosecuted. *FBIS-SOV*, 18 October 1989, pp. 64–5.

64 R. K. Alimov, Sh. Shoismatulloev, and M. Saidov, "Migratsionnye protsessy i natsional'nyi vopros," *Kommunist Tadzhikistana* (Dushanbe), 1990, no. 5 (May), p. 13.

65 "Dar borai loihai qonuni zaboni RSS Tojikiston," *Tojikistoni soveti*, 23 July 1989, p. 1; "Ma"ruzai ilovagii komissiyahoi mulohizahoi qonunguzori," ibid., 23 July 1989, p. 2; Helsinki Watch, *Conflict in the Soviet Union: Tadzhikistan* (New York and Washington, DC: Human Rights Watch, 1991), p. 11.

66 H. Muhammadiev, "Barodari man boshi, barobari man bosh!" *Adabiyot va san"at*, 7 September 1989, p. 3; Helsinki Watch, *Conflict in the Soviet Union*, pp. 10–11.

67 Helsinki Watch, *Conflict in the Soviet Union*, pp. 5, 52, 53, 62; "Soobshchenie," p. 6.

68 Reuters, 14 February 1990.

69 "Soobshchenie," pp. 3, 4.

70 *FBIS-SOV*, 3 April 1990, p. 100.

71 "Soobshchenie," p. 7.

72 Helsinki Watch, *Conflict in the Soviet Union*, p. 52; *FBIS-SOV*, 16 August 1992, p. 88; Reuter Library Report, 25 September 1991.

73 T. Larsen, "Tadzhikistan: russkoiazychnye trebuiut dvoinoe grazhdanstvo," *Rossiiskie vesti*, 1992, no. 31 (July); Reuter Library Report, 25 September 1991; J. Carley, "Russians return home to Tajikistan," *Financial Times*, 23 May 1991, p. 2.

74 V. Abdullo, "Roh kujost?" *Javononi Tojikiston*, 12 October 1991, p. 1; Reuter Library Report, 25 September 1991; *FBIS-SOV*, 9 July 1992, p. 69, 20 July 1992, p. 60, and 26 October 1992, p. 72.

75 Representative of such statements about the Russians is S. Fathullohzoda, "Iloji voqea pesh as vuqu" boyad kard," *Javononi Tojikiston*, 15 October 1991, p. 1.

76   *FBIS-SOV*, 28 May 1993, p. 19.
77   In particular, he conjured up the threat of reprisals against Russians in Tajikistan for Russian military intervention against the opposition. Nazrulloev, "Strasti po Tadzhikistanu"; Iakov, "Khronika revoliutsii"; E. Gusarenko and V. Esipov, "Esli my poterprim porazhenie, nachavshaiasia zdes' voina dokatitsia do samogo Urala," *Smena*, 7 October 1992 (as photocopied in *Russia & CIS Today*, 31 October 1992, p. 36).
78   Russian Press Digest, 2 and 4 December 1991; *FBIS-SOV*, 28 May 1993, p. 20.
79   Russian Press Digest, 10 December 1991.
80   G. Khasanova, "V Tadzhikistane, kotoryi polnostiu zavisit ot pomoshchi Moskvy, skoro ne ostanetsia ni odnogo russkogo," *Izvestiia*, 6 May 1994, p. 3.
81   H. Carrère d'Encausse, *Réforme et révolution chez les Musulmans de l'Empire russe* (Paris: Librairie Armand Colin, 1966), p. 261; R. Bobojon, "Mughjahoi demokratiya," *Jumhuriyat*, 4 October 1991, p. 2.; TASS, "Novaia obshchestvennaia organizatsiia," *Pravda Vostoka*, 29 March 1991, p. 1; Nazrulloev, "Strasti po Tadzhikistanu."
82   Atkin, "Religious, National, and Other Identities," pp. 50–2; Atkin, "Tajikistan: Ancient Heritage," pp. 371–3.
83   ITAR-TASS, 17 and 23 July 1992; Galimov, "Vlast' u tekh."
84   M. Lipov, "Demokraty i iuzhane: im nikogda ne soitis' . . . ," [sic] *Kommersant*, 29 June–6 July 1992, p. 19.
85   Russian Press Digest, 2 December 1991.
86   I. Rotar', "Moskva pytaetsia pogasit' Tadzhikskuiu mezhdousobitsu," *Nezavisimaia gazeta*, 11 November 1992, p. 3.
87   Nazrulloev, "Strasti po Tadzhikistanu"; I. Rotar' and S. Aiubzod, "Spiker parlamenta ushel v otstavku," *Nezavisimaia gazeta*, 20 November 1992, p. 1.
88   *FBIS-SOV*, 11 September 1992, pp. 42–3; Reuter Library Report, 11 September 1992; Agence France Presse, 26 December 1992.
89   Representative of this are head-of-state Imomali Rahmonov's statement, soon after coming to power, that "We want to build a secular democratic state-of-laws," and his assertion, "We are trying to build a democratic, secular state," in his remarks to the first session of Tajikistan's Supreme Soviet after the civil war. U. Babakhanov, "Kazhetsia, v Tadzhikistane oboidutsia bez 'golubykh kasok,'" *Komsomol'skaia pravda*, 12 January 1993, p. 1; M. Missiri, "Emomali Rakhmonov 'stroit demokratiiu,'" *Segodnia*, 29 June 1993, p. 4.
90   Russian Press Digest, 11 August 1994; Agence France Presse, 16 October 1994.
91   Batyrshin, "Prorok Mukhammad"; Sloan, "Holding Islam at Bay."
92   Reuters, 24 February 1995; Deutsche Presse-Agentur, 24 February 1995.
93   Reuters World Service, 28 February 1995.
94   Reuters, Limited, 24 February 1995; *Current Digest of the Post-Soviet Press* 47, no. 9 (29 March 1995), p. 16; Deutsche Presse-Agentur, 24 February 1995.
95   *FBIS-SOV*, 31 March 1993, p. 73; Reuter Library Report, 30 March 1993 and 26 July 1994.
96   I. Rotar', "Predstaviteli vlastei i oppozitsii vstretiatsia v Moskve," *Nezavisimaia gazeta*, 10 March 1994, p. 3; Deutsche Presse-Agentur, 26 January 1996; ITAR-TASS, 19 February 1996.

97 Reuters World Service, 7 July 1995; Agence France Presse, 18 September 1995; *Current Digest of the Post-Soviet Press* 47, no. 40 (1 November 1995) (as republished by Nexis); B. Pannier, "Tajik Conflict Takes a New Turn," *Jane's Intelligence Review* 7, no. 12 (1 December 1995) (as republished by Nexis).

98 Russian Press Digest, 10 February 1996; G. Tett, "Warlord Rivalry Topples Tajikistan's Reformist Prime Minister," *Financial Times*, 9 February 1996, p. 4; Agence France Presse, 8 February 1996; Reuters, 8 February 1996; ITAR-TASS, 11 and 19 February 1996.

99 Russian Press Digest, 10 February 1996.

100 *FBIS-SOV*, 31 March 1993, pp. 73–4.

101 After *Qadi* Turajonzoda fled the country, his office was abolished and replaced with a newly created office of *mufti*. Sharifzoda, who publicly endorsed the policies of the neo-Soviet government, was the first occupant of that office.

102 Agence France Presse, 11 and 12 March 1994 and 22 January 1996; Russian Press Digest, 23 January 1996; Official Kremlin International News Broadcast, 23 January 1996 (as republished by Nexis).

103 *FBIS-SOV*, 7 December 1992, p. 21; J. Krauze, "L'Armée russe abandonne Douchanbe aux communistes," *Le Monde*, 13–14 December 1992, p. 20; Agence France Presse, 17 December 1992 and 22 April 1995; Reuter Library Report, 14 and 19 December 1992 and 12 April 1995; V. Berezovskii, "Vpravit' mozgi smuti'ianam ili dat' voliu demokratii," *Rossiiskaia gazeta*, 2 December 1992, p. 5; O. Panfilov, "Dushanbe zakhvachen novym ministrom vnutrennikh del," *Nezavisimaia gazeta*, 11 December 1992, p. 3; Dubnov, "Katastrofa," p. 39; R. Allison, "Russian Peacekeeping – Capabilities and Doctrine," *Jane's Intelligence Review* 6, no. 12 (December 1994) (as republished by Nexis); Russian Press Digest, 3 February 1993 (as republished by Nexis); *FBIS-SOV*, 16 December 1992, p. 48, 13 April 1993, p. 15, and 21 May 1993, p. 5; R. Boudreaux, "Russian Copters Attack Tajik Rebels," *Los Angeles Times*, 12 April 1995 (as republished by Nexis).

104 Official Kremlin International News Broadcast, 14 September 1993.

105 S. LeVine, "Tajikistan Swaps Soviet Roubles for Russian Ones," *Financial Times*, 7 January 1994, p. 4; L. Hockstader, "Bloody Central Asian Border War Stirs Afghan Memories in Russia," *Washington Post*, 24 October 1994, p. A13; I. MacWilliam, "Ex-Communist Declared Victor in Disputed Tajik Race," *Los Angeles Times*, 8 November 1994 (as republished by Nexis); Russian Press Digest, 6 May 1994 and 19 April 1995 (as republished by Nexis).

106 Official Kremlin International News Broadcast, 10 November 1994; ibid., 1 March 1995.

107 Official Kremlin International News Broadcast, 10 November 1994; ibid., 1 March 1995; V. Gubarev, "Instability in Tajikistan," *Moscow Times*, 17 November 1994 (as republished by Nexis).

108 Deutsche Presse Agentur, 6 March 1995.

109 Russian Press Digest, 16 March 1994; Reuter Library Report, 6 December 1993; Agence France Presse, 16 March 1994.

110 The Economist Intelligence Unit ViewsWire, 4 October 1995; East European Markets, 1 September 1995; Reuters World Service, 22 August 1995 (as republished by Nexis).

111 Russian Press Digest, 8 February 1996; Agence France Presse, 2 February 1996.

9   Turkmenistan: the quest for stability and control

Michael Ochs

Introduction

The basis of comparison for measuring developments in the Newly Independent States is the pre-Gorbachev (1985) Soviet Union. Domestically, that political system featured top-down rule by the Communist Party, which enjoyed constitutionally mandated monopoly status, strict party control of all branches of government and the mass media, ubiquitous intelligence *apparati*, generalized non-observance of human rights, as well as surveillance and repression of human rights activists and organizations. Ideologically, the state propagated and enforced Marxism–Leninism, and explicitly identified itself with that doctrine. The economy was planned, with institutionalized shortages of consumer goods, and the criminalization of most private, profit-oriented economic activity. Also characteristic of Soviet reality before 1985 was "police-state peace and quiet," that is, relative security and safety from crime, and the absence of open ethnic conflict, let alone large-scale bloodshed and waves of refugees.

Reform, broadly speaking, therefore encompasses decentralization (of institutions of governance and decision-making), democratization (opening the political process by permitting pluralism and instituting fair elections, ending censorship, allowing freedom of speech, association and assembly, and letting non-governmental organizations influence policy), as well as market-oriented economic change. By that standard, Turkmenistan has changed since gaining independence, but is probably the least transformed former Soviet republic.[1] The lack of reform is neither accidental nor due to uncontrollable circumstances; rather, it reflects a deliberate decision by the country's ruling elite to eschew policies initiated in Russia and the other Newly Independent States which, in the regime's view, have generated, or exacerbated, economic hardship, political conflict, civil unrest, ethnic tension, and in some cases, have led to ethnic warfare. Turkmenistan's rulers, by contrast, maintain that a slow, evolutionary approach to reform – which, in principle, they claim not to reject, and to see as inevitable and necessary – will eventually yield the desired results without the attendant dislocation.

In the face of such resolve, and the authorities' harsh suppression of attempts to organize political activity, initiatives from below – limited though they were – to move the political system in more open directions have been unsuccessful. The nationalist, democratic groups that arose in the late 1980s in Turkmenistan, unlike other former Soviet republics, never became mass movements, never came close to taking or even influencing power, and are today isolated and marginalized or exiled. Government repression aside, their fate also reflects the quiescence, compared to other former Soviet republics, of a largely conservative and rural populace that has not been politically mobilized.

The result has been what the regime calls "stability": practically no rallies, meetings, demonstrations, or protests.[2] Turkmenistan has not endured disorder or dislocation, and does not have a refugee problem. The ruling elite, apart from taking credit for the attainment of Turkmenistan's independence, points to the absence of disorder as a great achievement of the regime. Indeed, "stability über alles" has become the mantra, ideology, and self-justification of Turkmenistan's leadership.

Turkmenistan's population has been able to watch television reportage since 1988 of bloody ethnic conflicts in various Soviet, and then formerly Soviet, republics, and undoubtedly is grateful to have been spared such disasters. However, the tacit social compact between state and society depends on the former's provision of basic goods and services gratis or at nominal prices, and this compact is in trouble. Economic hardship and limited prospects for improvement in the near term have significantly diminished living standards, and the public's patience is wearing thin. In July 1995, for the first confirmed time since Turkmenistan became independent, people in Ashgabat marched to protest their conditions, and even made political demands. To maintain itself in power, the regime will have to keep its end of the bargain, change the bargain, consider some kind of reform, or become even more repressive. At the end of 1995, President Saparmurad Niyazov decided to introduce some economic reforms, though he displayed little sign of any intention to open up the political system.

As regards foreign policy, independent Turkmenistan under its present leadership has established diplomatic relations with neighboring and distant states; joined the United Nations, the CSCE and other multilateral organizations; and generally sought to enter the international community, under the proclaimed banner of "positive neutrality." The apparent goals of positive neutrality, which emphasizes bilateral relations, are to avoid becoming involved in disputes among neighbors, and to stay out of alliances with more powerful states, especially Russia, that could threaten Turkmenistan's independence, while maintaining the maximum freedom of maneuverability in a changing and unpredictable regional and global environment. Situated between Russia and Iran,[3] Turkmenistan is trying to navigate well enough to keep the ship of state afloat, and under the command of its own captain and crew, to the extent possible. On December 12, 1995, these efforts bore fruit, when the United Nations General Assembly approved a resolution recognizing Turkmenistan's neutrality.[4]

For Turkmenistan, the nexus between domestic policy and foreign policy (which is not a focus of this study) is critical. The regime's apparent "macro" game plan has been to hold the lid down on any domestic political liberalization or economic reform while working to increase revenues from the sale of natural resources on the world market. This income, in turn, would allow the government to continue large-scale subsidization of basic goods and services provided to a small population, and either substantially alleviate, or possibly even avoid, the discontent and political upheaval that have roiled other former Soviet republics, and cost numerous political leaders their jobs (in some cases, their lives). A failed foreign policy, that is, one which does not produce the desired revenues, threatens the bases of domestic policy.

In sum, the overall strategy of Turkmenistan's leaders seems to be domestic risk avoidance – as they understand and assess "risk" – and maintenance of very tight societal controls while pursuing a consistent campaign for international recognition, legitimacy and income. The consequence of this strategy for systemic liberalization has been what in the Gorbachev era was called "stagnation." Given the weakness of societal forces *vis-à-vis* the regime and its intelligence and law enforcement agencies, change from below seems improbable. Deteriorating economic conditions, however, could spark popular disturbances that lead to some loosening of state controls on society. Another wild card is the overriding systemic emphasis on the image and functions of President Niyazov: were he to leave the scene, it is impossible to predict the course of events.

This chapter examines how Turkmenistan's regime has sought to avoid risk, and how the political institutions and structures, nationality policy, religion, the economy and the human rights situation in this newly independent state reflect the quest for control and stability.

History

Turkmen never had an independent state until 1991. The territory inhabited by tribes that came to be known as Turkmen was frequently invaded throughout the centuries, its conquerors including the Oghuz Turks, the Shahs of Khorezm, the Mongol-Tatar forces of Genghis Khan, and Tamerlane. The Persian Empire subsequently took nominal control of the region. By the eighteenth century, Turkmen tribes, though not united in a state, occupied all of today's Turkmenistan. They often fought among themselves, apart from invading and raiding their more sedentary neighbors in Iran, as well as the Khanates of Khiva and Kokand and the Emirate of Bukhara, for whose leaders they occasionally served as soldiers.

Russians were the region's most recent invaders, and Turkmen tribes mounted the fiercest resistance in Central Asia to their advance. Not until 1881, at the battle of Goek Tepe, did Russia take eastern Turkmenistan, which finalized Russia's conquest of all of Central Asia. Turkmen defiance continued, however, especially in 1916, when a large-scale armed uprising was mounted. During the November 1917 Revolution, the territory of today's Turkmenistan was the battleground of pro- and anti-Bolshevik forces, including British troops. By 1920, the territory fell to the Red Army, and in 1924 Soviet authorities created the Turkmenistan Soviet Socialist Republic.[5]

Soviet rule entailed the collectivization of agriculture in the 1920s and the gradual settling of the still largely nomadic Turkmen. Apart from continuing the growing of cotton, which had been the priority of Imperial Russian administrators, Turkmenistan in the 1930s underwent some industrial development, especially in the energy sectors, and urbanization. According to a Soviet-era official source, Turkmenistan's urban population rose by ten times between 1924 and 1980.[6] Under Soviet central planning, the economy came to feature cotton, gas and oil, most of which was exported to other republics for processing. Turkmenistan's demographic composition was also transformed by the influx of non-Turkmen, among them many Slavs, who came to man the new industries. On the political-national front, during the 1930s, Josef Stalin's country-wide purge decimated Turkmenistan's Communist Party and young national intelligentsia, while Soviet authorities in Moscow and Ashgabat (called "Ashkhabad" at the time) promoted the Russification of Turkmen society.

During Mikhail Gorbachev's perestroika, Turkmenistan had a reputation as one of the most conservative and backward Soviet republics. In August 1990, Turkmenistan declared sovereignty, but like the other heads of the Central Asian Communist Parties, the leadership in Ashgabat did not seek or welcome the breakup of the Soviet Union. Turkmenistan recorded an overwhelming Yes vote in a March 1991 referendum on maintaining the USSR. Nevertheless, the disintegrationist trends and the example of other former republics, including, eventually, the Central Asian states, forced Turkmenistan's hand. When Tajikistan declared independence, Ashgabat had little choice but to follow suit. On October 27, 1991, after a referendum on independence, an extraordinary session of Turkmenistan's Supreme Soviet declared independence.

Tribalism and politics

Turkmen were traditionally a nomadic people, among whose various tribes the Tekke, Yomuts, and Ersary are particularly influential today. Yet there are regional divisions and competition even within individual tribes. For example, the Tekke, numerically the largest tribe, comprise the Tekke of Ahal *velayat* (in the south-central part of the country, including the capital, Ashgabat) and the Tekke of Mary *velayat* (bordering Iran and Afghanistan).[7] Yomuts are concentrated in the (western) Balkan *velayat* (bordering the Caspian Sea), and in the more northern Dashhowuz *velayat*. The Ersary are most closely associated with Lebap *velayat* (bordering Uzbekistan). Smaller groups include the Salyr and Sarik (Mary and Lebap *velayats*) and the Choudour (Dashhowuz and Lebap *velayats*).[8] Obviously, individual members of any of these tribes can be found outside the tribes' traditional areas of habitation and influence, but there is a definite link between tribes and regions.

The significance of tribalism in contemporary Turkmenistan is one of the most difficult subjects of study for outsiders, to whom differences among Tekkes, Yomuts and others are not necessarily obvious, and with whom Turkmen will not necessarily be especially informative about this sensitive issue. Public opinion surveys have been undeveloped in independent Turkmenistan (see below), so researchers must make use of largely anecdotal reportage as well as other sources to draw inferences about tribalism's role in Turkmenistan's politics.

To begin with, while opinions vary about the role of tribal affiliation in self-identification among Turkmen, most Turkmen and resident foreigners[9] concur that tribal consciousness, after seventy years of Soviet rule, migration, urbanization and economic development, has been diluted. Equally widely accepted are the propositions that tribal consciousness is today less pronounced in urban centers than in the countryside, and that young people pay less attention to tribal affiliation than does the older generation. On the other hand, clan consciousness is reportedly maintained by high rates of endogamy, as well as differences in dialect and dress.[10] Beyond these important general points of agreement, however, differences of opinion emerge in a welter of admittedly unscientific, impressionistic accounts. Various sources, for example, claim that women are more conscious of, and attached to, tribal affiliation than are men. Others – especially non-Turkmen – contend that tribal differences had indeed waned under Soviet rule, but are now growing stronger. Thus, some sources told of fights and even stabbings in the army and universities over clan differences, raising questions about the relative indifference of young people to the issue.

The most explicit and important indicator of the significance Turkmenistan's leaders publicly attribute to tribalism are the remarks made by President Niyazov:

Where the people are not prepared, and where there are no prerequisites, any attempt to establish a democratic society may not only be a dangerous adventure but may also bring about the dictatorship of anarchy, civil war and strife between clans and tribes . . . [Furthermore] To have our state united in the future we must completely eradicate the epidemic habit of talking about tribal relationships. No matter what tribes we come from, we remain . . . sons of the one big family of Turkmenistan . . . During the first stage of the transitional period there will be an established control over mass media to prevent any possible conflicts between the ethnic groups and tribes residing here. The experience of neighboring states shows that publications about land disputes would inevitably give birth to nationalistic aspirations, and the feeling of loyalty to one's own tribe, and this eventually caused strifes [sic]. Since the way we have chosen is a democratic one, we fully agree on the issue of a multi-party life. However, within the period of transition we would stay very cautious as far as the multi-party issue is concerned as well as opposition.[11]

These sentiments apparently have influenced meaningfully decisions about symbolism and policy. Though explicitly concerned about recalcitrant tribal consciousness, the country's leadership approved a flag for independent Turkmenistan that features carpet designs associated with various tribes. True, the first emblem (the well-known "gushly gul"), while most closely identified with the Tekke, can be found throughout the country and in the homes of many non-Tekke Turkmen. Still, the choice of flag design is noteworthy for its lack of a single, unifying symbol to represent all the tribes or a non-tribal Turkmenistan.

Moreover, awareness of tribal affiliation colors personnel decisions, an important point in a highly centralized, top-down political system. Turkmenistan's leadership has been careful to ensure tribal representation in the cabinet of ministers and other government institutions, presumably allocating positions according to some sense of equitable treatment. Similar considerations have influenced appointments of the regional governors. A Yomut heads Balkan *velayat*, where Yomuts are concentrated, an Ahal Tekke is *hakim* of Ahal *velayat*, while a Mary Tekke is *hakim* of Mary *velayat*. An Ersary is *hakim* of Lebap *velayat*, populated heavily by Ersary and Uzbeks, and a Yomut is *hakim* of Dashhowuz velayat.[12] A related operating principle seems to apply to particular posts. For example, Turkmenistan's oil and gas minister is usually Yomut, as gas reserves are located in the western parts of the country.[13]

Despite this pattern, there is also a politically significant group of Russified Turkmen, who can barely speak Turkmen and presumably have little attachment to their tribal origins, but who occupy high government positions. Some have close access to President Niyazov and appear to be members of that small circle of individuals who determine policy. Moreover, an ethnic Russian is Minister of Economics and Finance. The prominence of this group testifies to the limits of the tribal principle at the highest levels of government, where presidential familiarity and confidence in associates appear to be more important.

Despite the leadership's apparent recognition of persistent tribalism and the evident care taken to accommodate tribal concerns and to balance tribal aspirations, the topic itself is largely taboo in Turkmenistan's strictly controlled media. In fact, *Izvestiia* reported (May 20, 1994) that President Niyazov had issued unpublished instructions forbidding Tekke government officials to reveal their tribal origin, for fear their purported dominance would offend other tribes.[14] The pat answer of most officials, when asked about this subject, is that the country's wise leadership is cognizant of tribal differences, and has acted so successfully to minimize their significance that there is no problem to speak of.

Nevertheless, President Niyazov's above-cited remarks would lead to the conclusion that the country's leadership sees continuing tribal competition and conflict as a great threat to Turkmenistan's nationhood and statehood, and the state must counter this danger by restricting the citizenry's rights to full freedom of information and political activity. If those expressed convictions really reflect the views of the ruling elite – which, alternatively, could be using them to justify maintaining tight control of Turkmenistan's politics and economy – then the country's tribal disunity has been one of the most influential determinants of the centralized, repressive political system described below.

State and government structure

In the process of state-building after independence, Turkmenistan has adopted a new constitution and created institutions of statehood and governance. Some of these reflect general international practice, some do not. More important, though, is that Turkmenistan's reality does not reflect many provisions of the constitution, another carryover from Soviet practice. This is especially pronounced with respect to political freedom and human rights, observance of which the constitution nominally guarantees.

Turkmenistan, according to the May 1992 constitution, is a democratic, law-governed, secular state in the form of a "Presidential Republic." The constitution also proclaims that the state is based on the principle of division of powers, with executive, legislative and judicial branches balancing each other.

Militating against any genuine balancing, however, are the extremely wide-ranging powers of the president. He heads the Cabinet of Ministers, whose members he appoints without the consent of parliament. The president can dissolve parliament if it does not elect a presidium within six months of its reorganization, or if it votes no-confidence in the government twice during an eighteen-month period. He appoints the *hakims* of all five *velayats*, the judges at every level of the judicial system, and – "with the preliminary agreement with the *Mejlis*" [parliament] – the Chairman of the Supreme Court and the General Procurator. The president is also commander in chief of the armed forces, head of the *Halk Maslakhaty* [People's Council, see below], and he can issue decrees and orders that are binding throughout the country. In addition, the president heads the Council of Defense and National Security, which, as of February 1996, includes fifteen of the country's highest-ranking officials.[15]

Turkmenistan's legislative body is the *Mejlis*. After Mikhail Gorbachev authorized elections to the Supreme Soviets of the Union Republics in 1989, Turkmenistan held elections to a 175-member body in January 1990. The next parliamentary elections took place in December 1994 to a 50-seat legislature, for another five-year tenure. Constitutional provisions empower the *Mejlis* to pass laws, amend the constitution, approve the budget and supervise its implementation. The parliament elected in 1994 is nominally a permanent legislative body composed of full-time, professional lawmakers, whereas previous Supreme Soviets had quotas for workers, peasants, and so forth, and only met several times a year to rubber-stamp decisions already taken.[16] Nevertheless, Turkmenistan's *Mejlis* actually enjoys little independence of action *vis-à-vis* the executive branch, which also determines the basics of legislative initiative.

Officially, the most authoritative and highest representative organ is the *Halk Maslakhaty* [People's Council], to which the president is supposed to report, but whose members he appoints. Composed of the president, parliamentarians, representatives of every *etrap*, the Cabinet of Ministers, Supreme Court judges, the procurator general, *hakims* and local officials, its membership embraces all branches of power. The *Halk Maslakhaty* ratifies treaties, adopts constitutional amendments, can make recommendations on economic, political and social matters, declares war, and can vote no-confidence in the president, if he has violated the constitution or the law. According to Turkmen officials, the *Halk Maslakhaty* has no analogue anywhere in the world: "The idea came to the president [Niyazov] drawing on his own experience."[17] In practice, the *Halk Maslakhaty* gives the president a public forum to present the basic guidelines of domestic and foreign policy, assess the performance of officials, and gain the approval of the country's nominally supreme body for his policy initiatives. The *Halk*

Maslakhaty must meet at least once a year; in 1995, assemblies were held twice, in October and December.

Not mentioned in the constitution is the Council of Elders (*Aksakals*), which was first convened in 1989. The council, which Niyazov chairs, supposedly resurrects a pre-Soviet Turkmen body, and institutionalizes traditional Turkmen respect for elders and clan leaders. Turkmen officials report that President Niyazov chairs council meetings in each of the country's *velayat*s in turn.

Niyazov heads other country-wide institutions, including the National Revival Movement, founded in January 1994. The movement aims to promote the cultural revitalization of Turkmen, and includes virtually all the country's public and political organizations, as well as religious groups.[18] Niyazov is also the head of the Humanitarian Association of Turkmen of the World, an outreach organization to Turkmen abroad, which fosters the revival of Turkmen culture and history.

Culture and practice of elections

The process of state building throughout the former Soviet Union has involved the holding of local, parliamentary and presidential elections, as well as referenda on issues of special importance. These exercises in popular sovereignty aimed to create or enhance the legitimacy of the individual, representative body or issue being voted on, to emphasize the bond between state and society, and to bring the Newly Independent States into accord with democratic principles, which became a political commitment in January 1992 when they joined the Conference on Security and Cooperation in Europe (CSCE).[19]

Turkmenistan has followed suit, but according to its own particular lights. More than any other newly independent state, Turkmenistan has steadfastly maintained the tradition of Soviet-style elections. Even Uzbekistan, for example, has experimented with multiple candidacies, and with pro-government results lower than 90 percent; in the December 1991 presidential election, for instance, Islam Karimov allowed opposition leader Mohammad Solih to run against him, and Karimov won with a margin of "only" 86 percent.[20] In Turkmenistan, by contrast, elections since 1989 have consistently produced pre-Gorbachev-era percentages, with the highest figures reserved for Saparmurad Niyazov himself. For instance, republic leaders reported that about 97 percent of eligible voters had voted to maintain the USSR in a March 1991 referendum organized by Mikhail Gorbachev. In the October 1991 referendum on Turkmenistan's independence, over 94 percent of participants officially voted "for," and almost as high a percentage of voters voiced backing for Niyazov's general program. Niyazov garnered, according to official results, 98 percent of the vote in the October 1990 presidential election, and 99.95 percent in the next election in June 1992, both times running unopposed. According to the announced results of the January 1994 referendum extending his tenure in office until 2002, fully 99.9 percent of the electorate cast ballots, and 99.99 percent voted for the initiative.

This general pattern carried over in the parliamentary election of December 1994, when Turkmenistan's Central Election Commission reported that turnout was 99.8 percent. Moreover, all the races were uncontested,[21] so the winners were known well in advance. Almost all of Turkmenistan's parliamentarians are members of the Democratic Party – formerly the communist party (see below). Apart from the results, the atmosphere of balloting was "Soviet," with "agitators" pressuring people to come to the polling stations, which featured hard to get items, such as food, national costumes and jewelry.[22] Local newspapers reported on candidates' meetings with voters, always praising the nominees' qualifications and stressing the broad-based support they enjoyed among constituents.

Interestingly, Turkmenistan's 1990 parliamentary election did feature alternative candidacies, perhaps because they were in vogue or de rigueur under Gorbachev's electoral perestroika, exemplified by the May 1989 elections to the USSR Supreme Soviet.[23] Nevertheless, about 90 percent of those elected in 1990 were CPSU members. According to a Mejlis member who was reelected in 1994, an average of 2-3 candidates contested all 175 seats in 1990. He said there were no alternative candidacies in 1994 not in order to limit voters' choice, but because people did not seek the post. Many possible candidates, he claimed, did not want to leave their other jobs to become full-time parliamentarians, which the election law demanded, and because deputies' perks and privileges have been eliminated, except for immunity from prosecution.[24]

In fact, notwithstanding the claims of nearly universal turnout and support, there is good, if anecdotal, reason – apart from common sense – to believe that a far smaller percentage of the electorate participates. During voting day in December 1994, for example, the scarcity of people in polling stations was striking.[25] When asked, local election officials explained that most people in the precinct had already voted, would vote later, or were at lunch. But other observers, among them US Embassy officers, also noted the sparse turnout. Asked whether they had already voted or intended to vote, various residents of Ashgabat dismissed the idea, elaborating that their ballot had no meaning, since "the authorities would proclaim a virtual 100 percent turnout anyway. If worst came to worst, they said, an agitator might come to their apartment, and some member of their family might have to go and vote for all of them."[26]

Obviously, elections and referenda in Turkmenistan, which now feature no alternative candidacies and fully controlled nominating processes and media, do not correspond to international norms for free and fair elections. Turkmenistan's elections have become something of a byword for votes in which the results are known in advance, and will reflect full public participation and support for whatever initiative the government is promoting.

One conclusion to be drawn is that the authorities do not insist, though they may exert pressure in this direction, on actual full participation in voting. It appears more important to the regime to publicize the results in a show of unanimity and unity. Though much of the electorate probably does participate, especially in rural areas, where people know each other and local authorities know how to get out the vote, not everyone, at least in cities, so fears the consequences of not voting that they make sure to cast ballots.

It is unclear why the regime continues to place such store in the proclaimed appearance of unanimity through voting culture and practice. After all, 90 percent would serve just as well as 99.8 percent, and given the changes that have swept the communist world since the 1980s, a lower figure might not be deemed as laughable by foreign commentators (or governments). Moreover, the leadership can hardly fail to be aware of the public's cynicism about the endless profession of unified support and the near 100 percent reported turnout at elections and election results.

To some extent, the fact that non-Turkmen constitute 20 to 30 percent of the population, in a post-Soviet environment of generalized ethnic anxiety, if not actual tension and conflict, helps explain the regime's emphasis on unanimity. Official figures in the 90s demonstrate the entire public's backing for independence, President Niyazov, or a carefully picked parliament, regardless of voters' nationality.[27] On the other hand, other former Soviet republics also contain large percentages of national minorities, without producing Turkmenistan-style election results.

The explanation can only be inferred, but it appears that first, the authorities care little what the outside world thinks of Turkmenistan's voting patterns, and are primarily interested in what use elections and referenda offer domestically. Secondly, their approach to voting seems to reflect an underlying belief that Turkmen psychology, history and political culture require such apparent unity: either that Turkmen themselves are reassured by, and demand, ceremonies celebrating consensus and the unity of people and leader, or, that Turkmen will best be ruled by a regime that puts on such a celebration. In fact, the stated official figures for voter turnout and approval of government initiatives have actually risen since 1990.[28] This may indicate growing concern by the regime about insufficient unanimity produced to date, or possibly a stronger sense that even higher results are needed and/or persuasive.[29]

In any case, the tendency towards electoral displays of unanimity is a defining characteristic of the governing style of independent Turkmenistan's rulers. Future elections or referenda yielding results indicating less than total public support would signal a change in the psychology and style of rule and, possibly, greater openness to democratization.

Political parties

Deriving from the conditions described above, political parties are, to put it mildly, undeveloped. Nor is this surprising, considering the leadership's explicit view of "pluralism." Immediately after Turkmenistan's Supreme Soviet declared independence in October 1991, President Niyazov addressed a special session of the legislature and said, *inter alia*, "we don't need formal democracy," and that strong discipline and social togetherness were essential.[30] The then foreign minister, Abdy Kuliev, developed the point in a conversation with the author, saying "we don't intend to play at democracy" [that is, there will be no profusion of political parties], as in the Baltic States, Moscow and Leningrad, where such "playing" had caused chaos. Kuliev added that Turkmenistan had not allowed political groups from the Baltic states and some Russian cities to come and stir up trouble, "and we won't allow them to do so." Political parties, he said, "should not be imported. They should be a natural outgrowth [of the society] and we won't prevent natural parties from becoming established."[31]

In 1992, Niyazov elaborated as follows: "Back at the dawn of perestroika the level of democracy in the republics was determined by the presence of different parties and movements: chaos, all-permissiveness, and thoughtless destruction of the former way of life were served up to us as pluralism and renewal. Anyone who appealed for a gradual process and thoughtfulness was called a conservative."[32] The regime has followed this line consistently. More recently, Foreign Minister Boris Shikmuradov told *Argumenty i fakty*: "We are convinced that it is impossible to create a democracy overnight . . . Whenever we begin to agitate the unpoliticized masses, where does it lead? The politicians remain sitting in their offices and the people on the streets shed blood . . . We are now being accused of not having a multiparty system. No, we will not permit it just so we can be called democrats . . ." But, he added, "I want to emphasize that democracy is our highest goal."[33]

The result of these views is that Turkmenistan is a one-party state, even though the May 1992 constitution guarantees the right to create political parties. At its 25th Congress in December 1991, the Communist Party renamed itself the Democratic Party, which inherited the Communist Party's membership. With President Niyazov as chairman, the Democratic Party is the only registered political party in Turkmenistan. Its leaders reported to the author that membership as of December 1994 was 60,000 and growing. Party structure resembles Communist Party structure, with "primary cells" in factories, enterprises and institutes. The party's program in the December 1994 parliamentary election was vague, calling for a secular, democratic state, political and economic reforms leading to the rule of law and a market economy, humanism, the revitalization of Turkmen traditions, and respect and equal rights for all, regardless of national origin or religion.

Many Turkmen and non-Turkmen observers in Ashgabat, including dissident political activists, describe Turkmen as largely passive and politically indifferent. But the absence of political parties and, generally, a robust civil society in Turkmenistan is primarily due to the relentless determination of a regime that controls all the levers of power not to permit any such development. Turkmenistan's rulers clearly believe that political pluralism, even Uzbekistan-style,[34] has no place in the country. Moreover, they have consistently demonstrated the willingness to act on this conviction. With the economy still largely in state hands, the regime disposes of necessary and sufficient sources of patronage and pressure, not to speak of rougher means of persuasion, to convey this message to society.

Consequently, Turkmenistan did not undergo the critical process that, in other Soviet republics, made possible and fostered the emergence of political activism and organization that led to institutionalized pluralism: what Mikhail Gorbachev and his aide Alexander Yakovlev used to call "freedom from fear." Whereas, for instance, in the Baltic states, various Communist Party leaders in 1988-89 quite actively sponsored Gorbachevian glasnost and perestroika, subsequently shifting flexibly into aborning electoral politics, Turkmenistan's regime, under Niyazov, stifled glasnost and criticized its "excesses" in other Soviet republics. The effect on society was predictable: never having lived through the heady, nervous shedding of entrenched habits and outlooks grounded in fear of repression, never having received signals from the authorities that it would be safe to entertain such fantasies, not many dared to do so. Those relatively few who did, and who even tried to realize their ambitions, soon "were given to understand" that they had seriously miscalculated.

Thus, from 1985 to 1991, Gorbachev's perestroika had an impact on society in Turkmenistan, though not as strong as in other Soviet republics. Speculating on the causes of the relatively weak response, a dissident political activist observed that decades of repression had left a numerically small intelligentsia and a legacy of fear among the populace, which, moreover, was spread over large spaces, as opposed to being concentrated in urban centers.[35] Also relevant, considering how the national intelligentsia in other Soviet republics used perestroika to put forward democratic, nationalist goals, was Turkmenistan's socio-economic structure, in which most Turkmen were agriculturalists in the countryside, whereas non-Turkmen heavily staffed technical and scientific positions in intellectual spheres and the country's weakly developed industrial sector. In addition, Turkmenistan was rather isolated from the rest of the Soviet Union; there are still relatively few televisions and telephones in the country, and newspapers are in short supply.[36]

Nevertheless, those Turkmen who could do so avidly watched Moscow television and read Moscow-based newspapers at that time. Some of Turkmenistan's more daring publications, such as *Edebiyat we sungat* (Literature and Art), *Turkmenistan*, and *Yash Kommunist* (Young Communist) exhibited a corresponding glasnost. Among the topics covered were Russo-Turkmenistan relations, why resource-rich Turkmenistan was so poor, Turkmenistan's pre-Bolshevik history, and the country's ecological problems. Meetings took place, at which students, writers, artists, and scholars called for independence, democratic elections, establishing Turkmen as the state language, and for Turkmen to be heads of the KGB, army, and other government agencies.

This activity led to the creation of organizations dedicated to the goals outlined above. The best known was Agzybirlik (Unity), established in 1989. A representative of the group told the author in October 1991 about several other political groups in Turkmenistan, such as the Popular Front of Turkmenistan (in the city of Mary), and the student organizations Nazaryet (Purpose) and Maksat (Opinion). Some of these organizations formed an independent Helsinki group.

According to dissident political activists, then-Communist Party leader Saparmurad Niyazov occasionally met with them in the late 1980s to discuss their grievances and ideas, and he claimed to be implementing their programs. Moreover, Turkmen officials publicly echoed calls by the intelligentsia to reduce Moscow's control of the country's economy, and the official press published articles about Turkmenistan's having been conquered by Russia, as opposed to "voluntarily joining" the Romanov Empire. But the authorities reacted harshly to organized manifestations of democratic, nationalist strivings. They forbade and shut down meetings, and strengthened censorship, while moving against leading activists. Members of political organizations, according to Agzybirlik spokesmen, suffered repression of various kinds, including harassment at work, dismissals from jobs, fines, and arrest. The most prominent such case was that of the poet and dramatist Shiraly Nurmyradov. He described in *Literaturnaia gazeta* discussions that took place in 1988 among members of the Turkmen intelligentsia about sovereignty, independence, the renaissance of the Turkmen nation, and the 1989 formation of Agzybirlik. Not long afterward, however, the authorities charged Nurmyradov, who had written some anti-Niyazov verses, with

swindling, and he spent almost eighteen months in prison.[37] As for Agzybirlik, there were signs the authorities were initially inclined towards
registration, but Niyazov strongly criticized the group in November 1989. In
January 1990, it was banned, and in May 1990, Niyazov said his early hopes
for what would have been Turkmenistan's only registered "informal"
organization had been disappointed. Nevertheless, the situation in mid-1990
was still sufficiently tolerant that Agzybirlik was able to hold regular
meetings. As late as September 1990, a Turkmen Komosomol publication
printed an interview with an Agzybirlik leader, and in November 1990, a
student expelled from Ashgabat University for Agzybirlik-related activity was
readmitted.[38] But at year's end, Turkmenistan remained the only Soviet
republic with no registered alternative political organization.[39]

In December 1990, democratically oriented political activists founded the
Democratic Party of Turkmenistan. The constituent conference, which a
participant described as having "smashed the last bastion of one-party rule in
the former USSR," took place in secret, as "the authorities have already
accumulated sufficient experience 'working' with local informals, which are
essentially in a semi-legal status."[40] According to a party representative, the
Democratic Party has been in continuous existence since then. In October
1991, the party held its first congress in Moscow. The founders were in
contact with like-minded associates in other Union Republics, and hoped to
establish a USSR-wide Democratic Party.[41] Claiming an estimated 1,400
members, the party applied in Ashgabat for registration in December 1991,
but the authorities returned the documents without any reply. In April 1992,
the party was renamed the Party of Democratic Development, as Turkmenistan's Communist Party had by then taken the name "Democratic Party."
From August 1992 to June 1993, the party published four issues of its
newspaper *Ata Watan* in Azerbaijan, which was then under a supportive
Popular Front government and president.[42]

Turkmenistan's leaders may have felt constrained to act within certain
bounds as long as the USSR – then run by the reformist Gorbachev – existed,
even though their attitude towards unsanctioned, uncontrolled political
organizations was obviously suspicious and hostile. Nevertheless, the
authorities never acknowledged critics or the proponents of alternative views
as an opposition, a stance that only hardened with independence. In May
1992, a Foreign Ministry spokesman told a CSCE Commission delegation
that "there are no opposition parties in Turkmenistan, just people who call
themselves democrats, criticize the government, parliament, and state, but
have no proposals and no support among the people." Turkmenistan's
ambassador to Moscow used essentially the same language in a January 1996
interview.[43]

Moskovskie novosti reported (July 5, 1992) that Niyazov had met with Turkmenistan's intelligence agencies on May 26, 1992, and ordered them to use "their entire arsenal of technical means to struggle with those who try to destabilize the situation."[44] Groups that tried to issue publications found their access to state-run typographs blocked and had to print their materials outside the country. The authorities persecuted their attempts to distribute them in Turkmenistan, confiscating, for example, 24,500 copies of *Dayanch* in early 1992. Law enforcement agencies placed critics under house arrest and refused to let them meet US Secretary of State James Baker and other visiting foreign dignitaries.

In 1993, the authorities took a harder line, arresting and otherwise persecuting opposition activists. The consistently repressive atmosphere in Turkmenistan has chastened political dissidents, who often are too fearful of the consequences to meet foreigners. In December 1994, in fact, the author was unable to arrange a meeting in Ashgabat with representatives of the opposition, who have been harassed into exile, underground, or out of politics. One year later, however, it was possible to find one political activist willing to discuss the state of human rights and the status of the opposition.

The prospects for a multi-party system under the current regime in Turkmenistan are dubious, even though, officially, the idea is accepted as inevitable. Niyazov told *Literaturnaia gazeta* in November 1994: "The time will come when people have matured for a civilized multiparty and opposition system . . . we have no multiparty system or an opposition but we have no political prisoners either."[45] The first secretary of the (ex-communist) Democratic Party predicted to the author in December 1994 that Turkmenistan would eventually have a multiparty system "in five years or fifteen years," but for now, "the people don't want it." A few years earlier, however, he had indicated what role parties have in Turkmenistan, and what purpose any new parties would serve.

We do not see our goals as being separate from the course taken by the president . . . An organizing committee is presently working to establish a peasant party. If this precedent is set, it will not signify the appearance of an ideological rival to the Democratic Party, or establishment of a political force of opposition. For the most part, our objectives are similar – to promote the president's foreign and domestic policy, to support the government in its initiatives, and to help preserve stability in the state and society.[46]

In sum, the regime's approach to political pluralism of any sort has been consistently negative, and there is no reason to expect that Saparmurad Niyazov will allow any serious opposition to develop. The former KGB, renamed in September 1991 the Committee on National Security (KNB), is accountable to Niyazov, and together with the Ministry of Internal Affairs, keeps a close watch on unauthorized political activity. Should political parties emerge under the current leadership, indications are that they will serve regime purposes, rather than reflect the interests of groups or individuals unsanctioned by the authorities. Were parties to arise that criticized President Niyazov or his policies – as opposed to their poor execution by officials – it would mark a major change.

Saparmurad Niyazov

Though not overtly ideological, as was its Marxist–Leninist predecessor, the regime has developed a virtual ideology of Turkmenistani patriotism, perhaps best symbolized by this oath: "Turkmenistan, beloved fatherland, land of my birth, in my thoughts and my heart, I am always with you. For the slightest harm I cause you, may my hand fall off; for the slightest calumny about you, may my tongue become powerless; at the moment of treason to your holy banner, may my breath be cut off." All newspaper mastheads feature the oath, which is recited at public events and, supposedly, every day in schools.[47]

Inextricably interwoven in, and integral to, this virtual ideology is President Niyazov.[48] Though Turkmenistan's constitution characterizes the country as a presidential republic and accords the head of state the very far-reaching powers and prerogatives already described, they do not, in fact, come close to encompassing the actual role and influence of President Niyazov. Indeed, speaking of Turkmenistan's "rulers" or "leadership," as has been done above, requires some qualification, because of Niyazov's public pre-eminence among them. He concentrates in his person all the key institutions of modern governance, as well as positions reflecting historically developed Turkmen symbols of authority, effectively combining state power and national legitimacy. Yet he is more than the sum of his parts.

According to official biographies, Saparmurad Niyazov was born in 1940, in a worker's family. His father was killed in World War II, and his mother and the rest of his family died during the 1948 earthquake in Ashgabat.[49] He grew up in an orphanage and subsequently lived with distant relatives.[50] After training as an engineer at the Leningrad Polytechnical Institute, Niyazov returned to Ashgabat, where he began his impressive rise to head the Communist Party of Ashgabat. In 1984, he went to Moscow for a stint in the Organizational Department of the CPSU Central Committee. Niyazov returned to Ashgabat in 1985, became chairman of the Council of Ministers, and the same year, Mikhail Gorbachev appointed him leader of Turkmenistan's Communist Party. In January 1990, Niyazov acceded, unopposed, to the chairmanship of the republic's Supreme Soviet, and was then elected president in uncontested races in October 1990 and in June 1992. Never having faced an electoral opponent, he is the only leader of a Central Asian country to remain in office throughout Gorbachev's reforms, the disintegration of the USSR and the emergence of the Newly Independent States.

In January 1994, Turkmenistan held a referendum which extended Niyazov's presidency until 2002, canceling the 1997 elections. Why Niyazov chose to hold such a referendum, as opposed to winning another presumably uncontested race by a huge margin in 1997, is unclear. Claims that he feared the emergence of a challenger are not entirely convincing, but it is worth recording that Moscow-based opposition activists with the Turkmenistan Foundation (see below) claim the credit and/or blame. In October 1993, they decided to participate in the scheduled July 1997 presidential election, and nominated former Foreign Minister Abdy Kuliev (see below) as the opposition candidate. The news supposedly made its way to Turkmenistan, whereupon the (ex-communist) Democratic Party proposed canceling the election. This initiative won the support of the *Halk Maslakhaty*, which decided to hold a referendum annulling the vote and extending President Niyazov's term in office until the year 2002.[51]

It is precisely in the exercise, as opposed to the formal institution, of the presidency that Turkmenistan, in many ways reminiscent of the pre-1985 USSR, has taken its most drastic step beyond the post-Stalin Soviet party-state. Even during the Brezhnev-idolatry of the late 1970s to 1982, the CPSU remained officially the vanguard of the Soviet people, their "mind, honor and conscience," with slogans and posters everywhere proclaiming the party's wisdom and unity with the people. Moreover, Brezhnev, despite his prominence, was *primus inter pares;* other Politburo members and CPSU and government officials had influence and could hope for headlines of their own.

By contrast, in independent Turkmenistan, an individual leader has wholly overshadowed and subsumed the party he heads, which is a pale imitation of its powerful forebear.[52] Niyazov's "cult of personality" does not extend to his Democratic Party, which hardly merits graffiti, or to his colleagues in the party or state apparatus.[53] Indeed, newspapers are replete with reports of functionaries' incompetence or misdeeds, and many have been dismissed, with a sound rounding from the president. Criticizing regional leaders in December 1994, for example, he said: "The unconditional implementation of decrees and decisions of the President of Turkmenistan should become law for [them] . . . . And they should not limit themselves to giving instructions to carry out these orders, but should see to their implementation."[54] In fact, according to foreign diplomats in Ashgabat, government officials frequently are fired for failing to carry out their tasks.[55] Many local observers assume they were removed to keep them from becoming entrenched in their positions and/or because they were too corrupt. Few, however, have reportedly been jailed or suffered very serious consequences.[56]

Turkmenistan's president alone is above reproach or even commentary. So thoroughly has Niyazov eclipsed institutions of governance or any other possible individual competitors for power, and come to personify the Turkmen state and nation, that he has a new name to match his virtually mythic status: "Turkmenbashy," or Leader of the Turkmen.[57] This is in itself an innovation and mark of distinction; in no other former Soviet republic has the leader adopted an abstract appellation, which the mass media routinely use. Turkmenbashy's portraits are ubiquitous, including on the new currency (*manat*),[58] and the former city of Krasnovodsk has been renamed Turkmenbashy, as have boulevards, schools, and other entities. *Halk, Watan, Turkmenbashy* (Nation, Homeland, Turkmenbashy) signs are posted all over Ashgabat, and presumably the rest of the country. The mass media constantly feature Niyazov, the symbol of the nation, the father and defender of its independence, its guide, indispensable teacher, elder, and wise leader. In December 1995, the *Halk Maslakhaty* named President Niyazov a Hero of Turkmenistan for the second time.[59]

Niyazov himself and the regime are quite conscious of the cult and how it is perceived in the outside world (if only because interviewers constantly bring it up). Official explanations for the phenomenon – unique in the Newly Independent States for its pervasiveness, intensity and divergence from Western norms – vary from acknowledgment of state sponsorship to coy denials of involvement. In the former case, the cult is described as a deliberate tool of governance, serving specific purposes, as in this assessment by Niyazov: "Such a cult is better than chaos, demonstration mania and calls for the overthrow of everything . . . and this portrait mania will end as soon as the property owner emerges in the state. He will not need Niyazov as an idol."[60] He has further elaborated that the cult of personality is necessary for a people deprived of ideology, faith or any other stable central focus.[61]

Apart from these considerations, Saparmurad Niyazov is an orphan, that is, he lacks the family and clan connections that still play a role in Turkmenistan's society and politics. Though many believe him to be a Tekke, official sources provide no information about his tribal background. Government spokesmen, when asked, usually reply that it is not important, and that Niyazov is President of all Turkmen. His elevation to a supra-clan status that embraces the entire Turkmen people may thus be a mechanism to surmount surviving clan differences. In this sense, Turkmenistan's cult of personality could be seen as a peculiar nation-building enterprise, a device to address concerns about Turkmenistan's unity when people still tend to see other as Tekke or Yomut, as opposed to Turkmen.[62]

Nevertheless, much remains unclear about the nature and functioning of Turkmenistan's political system. During the Soviet era, analysts engaged in Kremlinology and other arcane systems to divine the mechanisms of power-exercise and sharing in the closed, secretive political system headed by the CPSU Politburo and Central Committee. Likewise, in Turkmenistan today, it is virtually impossible for outsiders to know what goes on behind the scenes at the pinnacle of power, or to answer key, if obvious, questions. For example, while the President's closest advisors presumably offer him their views, who, other than Niyazov, has a real influence on policymaking? Is Niyazov in this elite group only one voice who can be outvoted, or are his advisors merely counselors and does he always have the final say? Whose interests – and with what frequency and consistency – must Niyazov accommodate, and whose interests may he slight? Finally, it is difficult to know whether Niyazov managed to impose this system on his elite, or whether they agreed to its imposition, welcomed its imposition, initiated its introduction, or all of the above. To judge by the regime's public face, Niyazov would seem to be a virtual potentate, but perhaps his powers are limited within a collective leadership.[63] Turkmenistan's leaders undoubtedly derive political and economic benefits from their membership in the ruling elite, so barring a falling out among them, it is unlikely that any of these matters will be clarified while Niyazov remains in office.

In at least one respect, the extent of Niyazov's power was illuminated to some extent in March 1996, when he dismissed the *hakim* of Mary province, for failing to provide the population with adequate food supplies.[64] Previously, analysts had wondered whether Niyazov controls these regional governors, whom he appoints, or whether he is somehow beholden to them. Evidently, he can sack at least one of them – indeed, the man often deemed the second most powerful individual in Turkmenistan – without risking any threats to his own position. The fate of the *hakim* of Mary lends credence to the theory that Niyazov runs the show on his own, with all other officials serving at his pleasure.

Psychology and ideology of rule

From the practice of the cult itself, the official statements about it, and the regime's style of rule, it appears that Turkmenistan's rulers regard open conflict – very broadly understood, yet subject to exclusive interpretation by the regime – as a bad thing, and to be avoided. "Conflict" in this sense involves not only public confrontations between/among institutions of government,[65] competing regional, clan, social, religious or ethnic groups, but even any open debate among the leadership about policy choices. The media, for example, convey to society information about decisions taken by the president and other branches of government, and report on the implementation of these policies, but offer no clue to as to how the decision was reached, or what other options were available or discussed.

Underlying this policy appears to be a largely unreconstructed Soviet paternalism *vis-à-vis* Turkmenistan's population, along with a strong distrust of a society not totally controlled. The country's leaders seem to assume that they know better than the people themselves what they need and how best to ensure their safety, security and well being, acting in their name to suppress any public-political initiatives not initiated from above.

To this end, the authorities strictly control the amount and type of information available to the public. There are no independent media in Turkmenistan. The constitution does not explicitly bar censorship, and all media are in fact subject to the stringent regulations of the Committee for the Protection of State Secrets.[66] According to foreign journalists, customs agents search the baggage of people entering the country and confiscate any materials considered seditious. These include Russian newspapers, which have long been unavailable in kiosks, but can still be obtained by subscription, paid for in hard currency or rubles, both of which are extremely difficult to acquire. On July 29, 1995, *Izvestiia* described the closure and seizure of the newspaper's office in Ashgabat on July 20. Turkmenistan's security agents detained Vladimir Kuleshov, *Izvestiia*'s correspondent in Ashgabat since 1985, and accused him of "anti-Turkmenistan propaganda." Kuleshov had filed many stories about the situation in Turkmenistan, most recently on the July 12, 1995 demonstration in Ashgabat [see below], which apparently was the last straw. Interrogators claimed he was not an accredited journalist, but a citizen of Turkmenistan "who lies against his own country."[67]

The official Russian television station Ostankino is seen in Turkmenistan, but residents report that it never broadcasts anything negative about the country. It goes without saying that surveys of public opinion, if they are done at all, are not publicized. Turkmenistan has no analogue, for example, to the All-Russian Center for the Study of Public Opinion in Moscow, which regularly releases information about politicians' popularity ratings.

Well aware of their reputation inside and outside the former Soviet Union, Turkmenistan's leaders make no bones about, or excuses for, their policy choices. President Niyazov has argued, on general terms, that the "East is the East" and applying Western models "is fraught with serious cataclysms."[68] More narrowly, he and other Turkmen officials speak with pride of their "differentness," their refusal to be swayed by policies conceived in other states, and their determination to make policy specifically based on Turkmen history, national tradition, and psychology – as they see, or proclaim, it.[69]

They also contrast the absence of conflict, bloodshed, and ethnic confrontations in Turkmenistan to the sorry state of affairs in neighboring countries as the ultimate vindication of their policy choices. The results, in short, justify the means, which, in turn, cannot fail to be correct since they reflect the nation's mentality and experience. In essence, therefore, the leadership's declared approach to policymaking is nationalist, rejecting rationalist, abstract schemata that claim universal applicability, and explicitly repudiating "experimentation."

It is furthermore reasonable to infer that Turkmenistan's leaders believe the preemption and avoidance of conflict, broadly understood, will not only benefit the population, but will enhance their chances of remaining in power. They have given no sign whatsoever that they are prepared to countenance the possibility of being voted out of office, much less swept out of power.

National minorities

Turkmenistan's authorities carried out a census in January 1995, but did not release the results that year. Pending their publication, various sources cited different estimates of the population.[70] Only in January 1996, at a meeting of the Cabinet of Ministers, did President Niyazov announce that the country's population was 4,483,000,[71] up from the 1989 figure of 3.5 million. The ethnic breakdown also changed significantly: according to the 1989 census, about 72 percent of the general population were Turkmen, about 9 percent Russians, another nine percent Uzbeks, 2.5 percent Kazaks, and the rest (representing, in all, over 100 nationalities) were mixed. In 1994, Foreign Minister Boris Shikmuradov cited 80 percent as the proportion of Turkmen in the country.[72] The figures from the 1995 census supplied by Niyazov in January 1996 indicate that Turkmen are now 77 percent of the population. Russians, previously the second largest group, today comprise only 6.7 percent of the population, while Uzbeks are up to 9.2 percent. Presumably, emigration and low birth rates of non-Turkmen, particularly Russians, and natural increase and immigration of Turkmen since 1989 account for the differences over a six-year period, assuming the 1989 figures were accurate.[73]

About 55 percent of the population is still rural, and 60 percent of the population is twenty-four years old or younger. Turkmen are overwhelmingly predominant in the countryside, with cities more ethnically heterogeneous.[74]

President Niyazov and government officials say Turkmenistan needs ten years of stability and interethnic harmony to effect the country's transformation. With 20 to 30 percent of the population not belonging to the titular nationality, the regime has striven above all to maintain stability, taking particular care to prevent and avoid interethnic violence. A simultaneous goal involves promoting Turkmen national culture, while assuring non-Turkmen of their equality of rights and opportunities. Niyazov has acknowledged that interethnic riots took place in Ashgabat and Nebitdag in 1989, when Turkmen

Table 9.1 *Demographic trends in Turkmenistan since the 1950s*

	1950s	1970s	1980s
Percentage of population	(1951)	(1979)	(1989)
Rural	61.7	52.0	54.6
Urban	38.3	48.0	45.4
Average annual rates of	(1951–61)	(1971–79)	(1990–99)[a]
population growth (%)	2.9	2.7	2.0
Age distribution (%)		(1979)	(1989)
0–14	n.a.	41.6	40.5
15-24	n.a.	21.4	19.7
25-49	n.a.	24.7	27.7
50-59	n.a.	6.0	6.0
Over 60	n.a.	6.3	6.1

Note: [a]Estimate.
Sources: New World Demographics, *FirstBook of Demographics for the Republics of the Former Soviet Union, 1951-1990*; US Department of Commerce, *Statistical Abstracts of the United States*; Paul S. Shoup, *The East European and Soviet Data Handbook*; UNESCO, *Statistical Yearbooks*; United Nations, *Demographic Yearbooks*.

evidently rallied to defend "the exclusive right of the national language."[75] Nevertheless, the campaign to maintain order has been relatively successful. Accommodating Turkmen' hopes and non-Turkmen' concerns has required more juggling.

A May 1990 law declared Turkmen the official language, and, along with Russian, the language of interethnic communication. The law set January 1996 as the deadline for people employed in state agencies, social organizations, law enforcement, health services, education, and other spheres which require "systematic" communication with people of various nationalities to know Turkmen and Russian well enough to carry out their professional duties. In areas compactly inhabited by non-Turkmen nationalities, these officials must also know the native language (Article 5). By July 1999, administration and documentation are supposed to be in Turkmen in state institutions and social organizations (Article 6). Article 23 mandates the study of Turkmen in general secondary schools, vocational schools, specialized secondary schools and higher schools teaching in languages other than Turkmen. Graduates of these schools must take a state examination in the Turkmen language. Moreover, as of 1996, the Turkmen language is scheduled to go over to the Latin alphabet.[76]

These guidelines and deadlines offer leeway to non-Turkmen-speakers, by mandating the use of Russian or other languages in particular circumstances and areas. For example, in areas of compact residence by minority nationalities, education up through secondary school can be in their native language or in Turkmen or Russian (Article 19). The law also guarantees all languages state protection and the right of development (Article 34).

Non-Turkmen have complained about having to learn the language and about their diminished job prospects, due partly to their ignorance of Turkmen[77] and partly to the generally preferential employment of Turkmen. During the October 1991 referendum on independence, a Russian voter in Krasnovodsk told *Turkmenskaia iskra* (October 27) that it was most important to maintain interethnic harmony, adding that many acquaintances had begun studying Turkmen, "not because they're afraid of anything, but just because that's how it should be."

Efforts to teach Turkmen to non-speakers, however, begun in 1990, have been sketchy. A Turkmen-language publication in May 1992 complained about the lack of progress: "The level of teaching Turkmen in these courses is low, there is no curriculum and no textbooks. There is a shortage of specially trained teachers in this field. As a result, these courses have come to a halt in many factories. Under these circumstances it will never be possible to teach the state language to those who do not know it . . . In general, the teaching of Turkmen at higher schools has been allowed to proceed at its own pace . . . by the Ministry of Education and by the commission for implementing the Law on Language . . ."[78]

Since then, the situation has apparently not improved substantially, making non-Turkmen's ignorance of Turkmen a cause for anxiety and, possibly, rancor between the titular nationality and others. Evidently aware of these concerns, President Niyazov has delayed the implementation of problematic language deadlines. Before the December 27, 1995 session of the *Halk Maslakhaty*, he announced that the scheduled transition in 1996 to the Latin alphabet and the implementation of the law making the Turkmen language obligatory did not "correspond to realities and the interests of citizens of all nationalities." He said the process would take place gradually over the next eighteen months, allowing time for the production of educational materials, textbooks and preparing the population.[79]

With respect to formal legal status, non-Turkmen have little cause for complaint. True, the constitution specifies that only a Turkmen can be elected president (Article 55). But a September 1992 law gave citizenship to all residents of Turkmenistan as of the law's adoption. The constitution guarantees the right of all citizens to use their native language and, regardless of citizenship, a person can hold state positions, up to certain level.[80] The constitution forbids discrimination based on ethnic origin or religion, and a separate law made the infringement of anyone's rights on the basis of ethnic origin a serious crime.[81]

The Uzbek minority is situated mostly along the Uzbek-Turkmen border.[82] Uzbekistan's government subsidizes the education of Turkmenistan's Uzbeks in the Uzbek language, supplying textbooks through bilateral agreements (Ashgabat does the same for the Turkmen in Uzbekistan).[83] In January 1996, the two governments signed a treaty on friendship and cooperation, which embraced culture and education. Although personal relations between Presidents Karimov and Niyazov are widely known to be cool, and the two states have had disagreements over water and oil rights in the border territory, Turkmenistan's media portray interstate and interethnic relations as fine.[84]

In 1993, there were about 87,000 Kazaks in Turkmenistan, over half of them in Balkan *velayat*, near the Caspian Sea and Kazakstan. Educational opportunities in the Kazkah language parallel those just described for Uzbeks, and Kazaks in the northwestern parts of the *velayat* could receive television programs from across the border. When President Nazarbaev visited Turkmenistan, President Niyazov said: "Now that an ineradicable bridge of love has been built between neighbor and neighbor, tribe and tribe, nation and nation, there is no place for conflicts such as those which have concerned all of progressive mankind."[85]

The most sensitive national minority issue in many Newly Independent States has been the status and conditions of Russians.[86] Though President Niyazov complains about Russia's tendency not to treat Turkmenistan as an equal, he has carefully limited his criticism of Russia's behavior, present and past, arguing that "Turkmenistan received much from being in the USSR, especially in the educational plane." He points out that "I have a Russian wife, my children are Russian."[87] In Turkmenistan, as elsewhere in Central Asia, Russians have played a particularly important role in the technical, scientific and industrial spheres of the economy, possessing skills and knowledge badly needed by a developing state with a relatively small native intelligentsia.

In fact, Turkmenistan has gone farther than any other former Soviet republic in accommodating concerns about the legal status of representatives of national minorities, first, by introducing in December 1993 dual citizenship with Russia.[88] The accord, *inter alia*, allows Russians in Turkmenistan to educate their children in Russia and to use Russia's health care system not as foreigners, but as Russian citizens.[89] Building on this agreement, Turkmenistan and Russia in May 1995 signed a Treaty of Cooperation for Purposes of Guaranteeing the Rights of the Russian Minority in Turkmenistan and the Turkmen Minority in Russia, and a Treaty on the Legal Status of Citizens of the Russian Federation Who Are Permanently Residing on Territories of the Parties. These documents commit the signatories to safeguard and promote the rights of permanent legal residents, who enjoy all the rights of citizens – including participation in privatization – except for voting or holding high elective office, or serving in executive branch or judicial agencies.

The treaties also obligate Turkmenistan and Russia to create "favorable conditions for implementing the rights of minorities and for preventing attempts to achieve their assimilation by force or to discriminate against citizens on the basis of ethnic criteria." Moreover, both governments are supposed to "create the appropriate opportunities for studying the native language and obtaining an education in the native language in areas densely populated by the minorities." The commitment extends to opening and maintaining "educational institutions financed from funds in the state and local budgets, as well as from other sources; [and creating] opportunities for using, in contact with the official authorities, the language of the minorities in areas densely populated by the minorities."[90]

Having signed these agreements, President Niyazov has gone quite far in meeting the Russian Federation's requests for legal guarantees for Russians and Russian-speakers. That does not necessarily mean, however, that they have been reassured about their status in independent Turkmenistan. Correspondents for Russian newspapers in Ashgabat have chronicled various infringements of the rights of Russians and violations of agreements between Russia and Turkmenistan – such as the 1993 accord on protecting the rights of emigrants, who, reportedly, do not receive permission to sell their apartments. Moreover, Russian correspondents describe the general atmosphere in Turkmenistan as difficult for Russians, who are made to feel unwelcome by officialdom.[91]

To some extent, these tensions and complaints may simply reflect the Russians' indignation over losing their privileged status, but it is equally credible that local officials may well enjoy the opportunity to avenge themselves for past grievances and to feel like "masters in their own home." Under certain circumstances, Turkmen nationalism and Russian resentment about perceived second-class status could lead to conflict, but the regime has given every indication to date of its resolve to keep ethnic anxiety and inter-ethnic tension from breaking out into open confrontation. Still, Niyazov cannot eliminate Russians' (and other non-Turkmens') concerns about living in a country whose official language they do not know, have difficulty learning – or do not care to learn – and about their childrens' prospects as Turkmenistan becomes more Turkmen over time. The US State Department reports on Turkmenistan for 1993, 1994, and 1995 noted general employment practices preferential to Turkmen. Even if the authorities were willing to guarantee employment to non-Turkmen (and today's promises may or may not be valid tomorrow), they would likely feel uneasy and continue to emigrate. President Niyazov told *Turkmenskaya iskra* on December 8, 1994, that about 3,000 people were leaving every month. Their continued, and possibly accelerated, emigration is a far likelier scenario than open ethnic conflict in Turkmenistan.

Islam and the regime

Most Turkmen are Sunni Muslim, but like other nomadic peoples in the former Soviet Union, such as the Kazaks and Kyrgyz, who accepted Islam much later, Turkmen are not primarily defined by religion, especially after seventy years of Soviet rule and enforced atheism. Nevertheless, loosened controls under Mikhail Gorbachev's perestroika and glasnost, and the tolerated awakening of national consciousness and traditions have benefited Islam in Turkmenistan. In July 1989, the first functioning mosque opened in Ashgabat, after years when Turkmenistan was the only Central Asian country without a mosque in its capital. The same month, the Muslim feast of Kurban Bairam, officially long banned, was reinstated.[92] Since 1991, at government initiative, construction of mosques in the country has grown dramatically. Reflecting the renewed emphasis on Islam, a presidential decree in July 1991 reportedly eased taxes on profits from enterprises of religious organizations,[93] and President Saparmurad Niyazov and his entire Cabinet of Ministers made a 1992 pilgrimage to Islam's holy sites. *Turkmenskaya iskra* (December 8, 1995) announced that the first translation into Turkmen of the Koran (begun in 1989) had been completed.

President Niyazov's promotion of Islam, especially given Turkmenistan's proximity to, and good working relations with, Iran, has generated questions about the extent of Turkmenistan's present and potential Islamicization. For example, a correspondent for a Russian publication raised the issue in an interview with Prime Minister Shikmuradov: "According to the Constitution, Turkmenistan is a secular state, but the highest representatives of the Islamic clergy take part in the work of all the most important conferences. [Moreover] the President of Turkmenistan has issued an edict on studying the fundamentals of religion in school."[94] Secular, pro-reform activists, for their part, have accused Niyazov of fostering Islam while crushing the small democratic movement.[95]

In fact, though Islam has benefited from government solicitude,[96] Niyazov has characteristically moved to keep tight reins on religion and to channel its activity into the service of the state and its leader.[97] He has consistently sought to depoliticize religion, legally and in practice; specifically, the May 1992 constitution bans parties based on religion, and the regime has created institutions to maintain strict oversight of Islam while coopting and controlling its official leadership.

The Soviet-era Council on Religious Affairs under the Council of Ministers survived the breakup of the USSR, continuing to carry out its role as the watchdog of religion. In June 1992, Turkmenistan's Ministry of Justice registered the Kaziate Administration of Turkmenistan. Its responsibilities included overseeing the responsibilities, rights and activities of Muslims. The Minister of Justice commented to the press that "We, in our turn, have charged the local law enforcement workers to maintain a working relationship with religious representatives."[98]

In April 1994, Niyazov assembled Turkmenistan's religious officials and warned that "Any attempts to interfere in state affairs will be decisively stopped." He called on them to help secure civic peace, which was indispensable to the fulfillment of his "Ten Years of Prosperity" program.[99] Then, evidently having decided that existing institutions were inadequate to keep state and religion separate and to ensure clerical cooperation in state programs, he announced the creation of a new structure: the *Gengesh* [Council], which apparently absorbed the Council on Religious Affairs and now functions as a sort of ministry of religion. Heading the *Gengesh* is Nasrullo Ibadulla, the former Imam of Dashhowuz and the current Imam of the Kaziate Administration. He was put on the government's payroll at a ministerial level, with the standard ministerial Volvo thrown in for good measure. Father Andrei, the head of the Russian Orthodox Church in Turkmenistan, is one of his deputies.[100] "The clerics then issued a resolution, which, *inter alia*, called upon believers to 'wholly support' and approve the domestic and foreign policy pursued by Most Highly Respected President Saparmurat Turkmenbashy, as well as his policy course in the area of religion . . ."[101]

The Imam, moreover, is an Uzbek, not a Turkmen, who was appointed, not elected locally. In the view of an Imam in Ashgabat, the Turkmen Kaziyat's "leadership is weak and obedient," and the Kazi has "no influence among the believers of the republic. This plays exactly into the hands of those who do not want the appearance of real Islamic leaders."[102] Not content with these measures, the regime has reinforced legislative safeguards against potential Islamic influence in politics by amending in April 1993 and October 1995 the May 1991 law on religion. Two new provisions in Article 5, for example, stipulated that "propaganda against the state order," as well as stirring up religious tension, are to be strictly punished, and strengthened the wording "religious organizations do not carry out state functions" by adding "and do not interfere in state affairs." Furthermore, the 1991 version of Article 13 on the registration of religious organizations by the Ministry of Justice required an application from only ten people; now, no fewer than five hundred individuals must sign the application for registration. The more rigorous requirement evidently seeks to complicate the formation of religious organizations.

Though the regime's policy goal of fostering Islam while controlling it seems clear, its success is more difficult to gauge. Unofficial Imams and mullahs reportedly abounded in Turkmenistan during the Soviet era,[103] and there is little reason to believe they have ceased their activity, though information about this sensitive subject is scarce.[104] Turkmenistan's leadership seems compelled to control virtually all aspects of societal activity, so it is uncertain whether the legal, institutional and exhortative measures undertaken indicate a general reflex or a careful response to a specific perceived threat, current or potential, posed by Islam.

One problem in trying to analyze the influence of religion is the idiosyncratic nature of Islam in Turkmenistan, which scholars describe as a mix of orthodox Islam, Sufi mysticism and shamanism.[105] Indeed, some features of Islam in Turkmenistan, such the practice of making pilgrimages to holy sites, usually tombs of revered individuals, have been criticized by Kazi Ibadulla, on grounds of contravening Koranic precepts.[106] In 1992, the Imam of Ashgabat's largest mosque at the time said "99 percent of young people are indifferent to religion . . ."[107] Turkmen do observe their national traditions in which religion plays a role, regularly visiting their relatives' graves, for example, and births, marriages, and deaths take place in the context of a religious ceremony. But as of late 1995, there is no evidence of a wave of religiosity in Turkmenistan, much less fundamentalism, according to both Turkmen and resident foreigners in Ashgabat. They report that Turkmen eagerly eat pork and drink vodka, and the newly constructed mosques are empty.[108]

In any event, the regime of Saparmurad Niyazov is as unlikely to entertain a challenge from Islam as from secular, democratic forces. The difference, however, is that Islam has more followers, even if only nominal as yet, and would be harder to suppress more seriously, if that became necessary. Second, one neighboring state – Iran – has at least some interest in furthering Islam in Turkmenistan, whereas no neighboring states appear to offer any support to democratic forces.

Economic reform

Nature has blessed Turkmenistan with the fourth largest proven reserves of natural gas in the world, and some seven billion tons of oil reserves.[109] Another vital source of revenue is cotton, which is cultivated on over 45 percent of the available arable land. Agriculture still accounts for about one-third of Gross Domestic Product and roughly 40 percent of total employment.

During the Soviet era, as Turkmenistan's leaders have often groused, the country was a "raw materials appendage," supplying the rest of the USSR with cotton and hydrocarbons. As President Niyazov put it, "we produced oil and gas, and never knew where it went or at what price."[110] Turkmenistan was one of the least industrialized and least developed republics, figuring at or near the bottom of indices measuring health care, and other definitions of standard of living in modern states. For instance, life expectancy was lower in Turkmenistan, while infant mortality was higher, than in any other Soviet republic. Abject poverty was also a feature of life: in 1988, 36.6 percent of the population was below the official subsistence level, compared to 6.3 percent of the Russian Federation.[111] Moreover, presumably because of its proximity to the Soviet-Iranian border, Turkmenistan was also one of the most isolated Soviet republics, visited by few Western tourists or diplomats.

After gaining independence, Turkmenistan's leadership evidently predicated its entire economic policy and aversion to major reforms on the expectation of large revenues from the sale of energy resources. Claiming the overriding priority of maintaining stability through avoiding social hardship, the regime has ever since kept the economy's levers tightly in state hands. In many respects, Turkmenistan maintains a somewhat modified Soviet-style economy, which is only slowly opening up to private enterprise. However, even long-range plans for the transition to the market, which officials call "our own purely Turkmen model," envision continued state control of large sectors of the economy, and promise that the maintenance of subsidies will make the process as painless as possible. "Businessmen" – honest or not, given the context of Russia or the Baltic states – have therefore not had an opportunity to delineate themselves as a social stratum of economic significance, nor have they become overt players in politics.

In repudiating Russian-style reform, Turkmenistan's regime has been consistent. Addressing the Supreme Soviet after the October 1991 declaration of independence, President Niyazov asserted that Turkmenistan would not copy economic initiatives developed anywhere else, and would not hurry to privatize enterprises, land or trade. His December 1992 "Ten Years of Prosperity" program[112] rejected shock therapy as unsuitable to Turkmenistan's social interests and national traditions, and was based on a largely planned economy, including state orders for many industrial products in the early phases of reform.

Though some prices were freed in 1992, regulated prices for basic food products remained in place, with subsidies a key facet of the government's economic program. The regime prides itself on symbolic prices for bread, and especially for providing free water, gas and electricity ever since January 1993, with free salt added in 1994, and some free pharmaceuticals in 1995.

Table 9.2 *Indicators of economic trends in Turkmenistan since 1989*

	1989	1990	1991	1992	1993	1994	1995[a]
GDP	-6.9	2.0	-4.7	-5.3	-10	-20	-5
Industrial output	2.6	3.5	4.8	-14.9	5.3	n.a.	n.a.
Rate of inflation	2.1	4.6	103	493	3,102	2,400	1,800
GNP per capita	n.a.	n.a.	n.a.	3,950	n.a.	n.a.	n.a.

Notes: GDP - % change over previous year; industrial output - % change over previous year; rate of inflation - % change in end-year retail/consumer prices; GNP per capita - in US dollars at PPP exchange rates. [a]Estimate.

Sources: European Bank for Reconstruction and Development, *Transition Report 1995: Economic Transition in Eastern Europe and the Former Soviet Union* (London: EBRD, 1995); European Bank for Reconstruction and Development, *Transition Report Update, April 1996: Assessing Progress in Economies in Transition* (London: EBRD, 1996); The World Bank, *Statistical Handbook 1993: States of the Former USSR* (Washington, DC: The World Bank, 1994); The World Bank, *Statistical Handbook 1994: States of the Former USSR* (Washington, DC: The World Bank, 1995).

As of mid-1995, almost 60 percent of the budget covered health, education, social benefits and subsidies.[113]

Niyazov's economic program envisions transforming Turkmenistan slowly from a supplier of raw materials to a producer of finished output, and he plans to build some 700 processing enterprises, using domestic resources and foreign investment. Meanwhile, gas, oil and cotton form the basis of the economy, with energy exports accounting for about 70 percent of budget receipts.[114]

Turkmenistan introduced its own currency the, "manat," in November 1993, but there has been little market-oriented reform. Niyazov in February 1993 sanctioned privatization of plots of land to private farmers, who may not, however, sell their plots. In May 1994, he authorized the privatization of retail trade and small enterprises.[115] The privatization of small consumer enterprises, especially restaurants and cafes, has begun, and factories that produce autos, construction materials, and refine agricultural produce have also gone to the auction block. In spring 1995, the government simplified taxes on small enterprises, levying 30 percent on net profits, and abolishing all other taxes. Official figures cite almost 7,000 enterprises in the non-state sector.[116]

Nevertheless, the government has focused almost all its support on the state sector of the economy, and trade is little developed. Living standards have fallen victim to inflation, and consumer goods remain in short supply. Newspapers in December 1994 specified thirty-four items which could not be taken out of the country, including cement, bricks, woolen scarfs, toys, furniture, bed linens, suitcases, and mens' and childrens' socks. Moreover, despite the alleged benefits of government subsidies, in summer 1995, residents of Ashgabat complained to Western correspondents about not having had water in their apartments for the second straight year, and about a three-year shortage of milk, flour and cooking oil. Minimum pay has been raised several times over the last few years, but workers often do not receive salaries for months[117] and wage hikes have not kept pace with inflation. In December 1995, there were long lines in Ashgabat for bread, which is rationed, and which reportedly was unavailable in other cities.

On July 12, 1995, a remarkable protest demonstration took place in Ashgabat, which many observers attribute to rising popular discontent.[118] According to an *Izvestiia* account (July 13, 1995), about 1,000 residents of the capital, mostly Turkmen, marched along the city's main street, and made political demands, calling for new presidential and parliamentary elections. Furthermore, they distributed leaflets urging local Russians to ignore rumors that the march was directed against Russian speakers, to whom they appealed not to be so "patient with Niyazov's lies and promises." An examination of one of the leaflets (there were reportedly several) confirmed this *Izvestiia* account of its contents, which combined economic grievances with political demands. The leaflet attacked Niyazov for turning the populace into beggars while building palaces for himself, and for trampling on the human rights of Turkmenistan's citizens of all nationalities. In conclusion, and most provocative, people were urged to demand the removal of Niyazov and the holding of free elections.[119]

Reliable information about the apparently unprecedented outburst on July 12,[120] such as the number of participants, remains sketchy, but it seems clear the demonstration did not last much longer than an hour before the authorities dispersed the participants and arrested an unknown number of them.[121] Law enforcement officials later described the marchers as "drug addicts" on television.[122]

Most striking about the demonstration is that it took place at all, and the authorities felt compelled to acknowledge it on television, instead of trying to hush up the entire affair. This could indicate their recognition that too many people knew about it to pretend it never happened, or – much less likely – it could signal a change in policy towards letting people blow off steam. Residents of the neighborhood in question subsequently told Western correspondents that water and electricity were restored and that local stores were resupplied with goods, which would appear to demonstrate some official responsiveness to the perceived economic causes of public discontent. But it remains to be seen whether the "July events" herald more such outbursts, or whether the authorities will clamp down even harder. In any event, society's patience is obviously not infinite, and economic factors are the most probable spark for any recurrences.

Without serious structural reform of the economy, prospects for gradual change while maintaining subsidies depend on money from external sources. The regime's hope is to sell energy, especially natural gas, to customers who can pay hard currency, as opposed to CIS states, which often do not pay their energy bills in any currency. But Turkmenistan's geography greatly complicates schemes to exploit its natural gifts: existing pipelines run through Russia, which has little interest in letting Turkmenistan develop an independent pipeline grid or become a competing supplier of natural gas, and Moscow has in the past cut Ashgabat's access to pipelines leading to Europe.

Developing new pipelines requires looking south, towards Iran and Afghanistan, where international politics and warfare pose sobering problems. Teheran's involvement in a projected pipeline from Turkmenistan through Iran to Turkey, and thence, to the rest of Europe, has apparently scotched hopes of obtaining financing from international lending institutions, in which the United States exerts substantial influence. This highly touted project, which originated in 1992, now seems dead in the water. As of early 1996, other pipeline deals have drawn more attention. One, involving the US oil company Unocal, braves Afghanistan's instability to build a pipeline through that war-torn country to Pakistan, and farther on to India. Other planned routes envision a pipeline through Uzbekistan and Kazakstan to China and Japan, a project that has enticed Exxon and Mitsubishi, or underneath the Caspian Sea to Azerbaijan. But all these projects face numerous difficulties, and in any case, would probably take years to come to fruition.

Meanwhile, the regime faces a difficult dilemma. President Niyazov evidently has no intention of cutting back subsidies or freeing prices, which would risk popular discontent, yet average citizens have derived little benefit from his large expenditures on grandiose public projects, such as modern hotels, an airport and presidential palaces. Another option is to loosen the state's hold on the economy, but that threatens the loss of control, the leitmotif of Niyazov's rule.

The solution was apparently dictated by worsening economic news: by the end of 1995, the regime's hopes of a pain-free, reform-avoidance route to prosperity had proved illusory. With Moscow controlling Ashgabat's access to international gas markets,[123] pipeline projects running aground or still in the planning stages, inflation at 30 percent per month in the second half of the year, currency devaluation, and international financial institutions urging reform, President Niyazov shifted course. At a December 27, 1995 session of the *Halk Maslakhaty*, he announced economic reforms, which do not open the economy to market forces but at least allow them greater leeway.[124]

Niyazov said that 1,800 enterprises had been privatized in 1994–95, and the pace would now intensify: government agencies will develop a voucher-based plan for mass privatization and 15 percent of enterprises (about 1,600) in all branches of industry will be privatized in 1996. Moreover, state enterprises will no longer receive government financing. Those that remain unprofitable will be reorganized or allowed to go bankrupt. Niyazov also pledged more government help to the private sector, especially those enterprises producing consumer goods. A leasing company will rent equipment to private traders and firms, and supply them with raw materials.[125]

Furthermore, as part of his policy of self-sufficiency in food, Niyazov announced new methods to stimulate agricultural production. Henceforth, family and collective lease holders, after meeting state orders, will be able to sell cotton and wheat at free prices.

To cushion the impact of these reforms, Turkmenistan's safety net will be maintained. Water, gas, electricity and salt will still be free, and the state will continue to set prices for public utilities, oil products, flour, public transport, communications and a variety of goods and services. Niyazov raised minimum salaries and pensions, establishing minimum (6,000 manats), average (20,000 manats) and maximum (34,000 manats) state salaries.[126] Retired and low income people will receive a 50 percent discount on housing fees.

Whatever benefits these reforms might bring, Turkmenistan's hopes still rest on the sale of its energy. In that connection, President Niyazov in November 1995 signed a deal with Russia to sell natural gas through a newly formed company: Turkmenrosgaz. A joint venture among Turkmenistan, Russia's Gazprom and another firm (which nominally is American but is reportedly Russian-controlled), Turkmenrosgaz will buy 10 billion cubic meters of Turkmenistan's gas per year and guarantee Ashgabat payment in hard currency. Turkmen officials, who had cut gas extraction in 1995 because of customers' non-payments, hope the deal will allow them to raise gas extraction and exports significantly.[127]

In short, President Niyazov and his advisors have moved away from some of the basic precepts of Turkmenistan's 1992–95 economic policymaking by liberalizing the domestic economy and tying the sale of natural gas to cooperation with Russia, instead of stressing non-Russian outlets to world markets. The regime's tendency to retain control, however, is clear. The economic reforms are cautious, with the state maintaining a dominant role, and the gas deal with Russia, according to Turkmen officials, is only for one year at a time. Ashgabat (quite sensibly) will not give up the search for alternative pipeline routes while seeking current income through a deal with Moscow.

Nevertheless, these moves involve risks of their own. The liberalization of the economy could worsen the population's living standards before they begin to improve, with the attendant possibility of public expressions of discontent. Turkmenistan, like other repressive states, may find that the most dangerous moment arrives when it begins to reform. Perhaps not coincidentally, foreign residents of Ashgabat report an enhanced police presence on the streets ever since the July 12 demonstration.

Human rights

While Turkmenistan's rulers may be willing to countenance a certain amount of open protest about economic conditions, there is no evidence as yet that they are prepared to tolerate any sort of political opposition. The discussion above on political pluralism provides the backdrop to a brief description of the human rights situation in Turkmenistan.

Despite Turkmenistan's accession to the CSCE (now OSCE), the regime does not observe Helsinki Final Act commitments on political pluralism, freedom of speech, assembly or other fundamental human rights.[128] At the July 1992 CSCE Summit Meeting in Helsinki, President Niyazov said "for us, human rights are inextricably linked with national interests . . . ,"[129] a formulation that emphasizes the needs of the state over the inalienability of human rights. Indeed, Turkmenistan has generally become more repressive over time; in 1992, for instance, the editor of *Dayanch* could still entertain the notion of taking the authorities to court for having confiscated over 20,000 copies of the publication. A representative of an opposition party who met with the author in Ashgabat in December 1995 related that all the other party members were "underground." As in previous years, the US State Department's *Country Report on Human Rights Practices* for 1995 notes that Turkmenistan's authorities have detained and mistreated opposition activists, forbidding any independent political activity. Most political dissidents have had to flee the country.

For many, the first destination was Moscow, where they established in August 1993 the Turkmenistan Foundation, headed by former Foreign Minister Abdy Kuliev.[130] The foundation described itself as the "organized opposition to the current regime," dedicated to the democratization and cultural reform of the country. Specifically, the Foundation's goals included the annulment of the January 15, 1994 referendum extending Niyazov's term until 2002 and the holding of presidential elections in July 1997.[131] In July 1994, the Foundation launched a publication, *Turkmen Ili* (Turkmen Nation), of which several issues were released. Differences of views within the foundation's leadership were apparently one factor in the creation, in January

1995, of the Movement of Democratic Reforms of Turkmenistan, which opened branches in Moscow, St. Petersburg, and Sweden.

The most ominous recent development in regime–opposition relations is the former's reach outside the borders of Turkmenistan to suppress critics. In October 1994, Muhammad Aimuradov and Khoshali Garaev were arrested in Tashkent by the security services of Turkmenistan and Uzbekistan. Extradited to Ashgabat, they faced charges of plotting to assassinate President Niyazov. In November 1994, at the behest of Turkmenistan's government, Russian authorities arrested Murad Esenov and Khalmurad Soyunov, the general director of the Turkmenistan Foundation and a former member of Turkmenistan's parliament, respectively, who also reported on Turkmenistan for Radio Liberty.

On December 21, 1994, Russian authorities released Esenov and Soyunov,[132] but Aimuradov and Garaev were tried in Turkmenistan in June 1995. On June 21, the Supreme Court convicted them of "actively participating in the activities of an anti-state organization which aimed at undermining the constitutional order and seizing power by force, and organizing terrorist acts aimed at the highest-ranking officials."[133] The court sentenced Aimuradov to fifteen years, Garaev to twelve. Garaev's case was particularly problematic, since he has dual Russian-Turkmen citizenship, and Russian authorities consider him a resident of Moscow. Russia's ambassador in Ashgabat filed a complaint about Garaev's trial, which took place *in camera*, with no witnesses, relatives, or journalists present.[134]

More recently, Abdy Kuliev has left Russia for Prague, and Soyunov and Esenov now reside in Sweden.[135] These cases and others demonstrate the long arm of Turkmenistan's authorities, who evidently keep a close eye on critics inside and outside the country, and have proved their readiness to act against them regardless of where they are.

In his December 27, 1995 address to the *Halk Maslakhaty*, President Niyazov made a declaration on human rights. He said that the human rights of everyone in Turkmenistan, regardless of race, nationality, gender, religion, and so on, were inalienable, guaranteed by the state and protected by law. Niyazov announced that an institute of human rights and democratization of society and the state would be established in the parliament. Its mandate will be to "implement programs for socio-economic change," to carry out Turkmenistan's "international commitments consistent with the status of permanent neutrality," to conduct "scientifically applied research on human rights and freedoms, to improve legal provisions for the activities of the highest authorities of the state and administration, and to perfect the legislative system."

What motivated President Niyazov to make these statements on human rights is unclear. Criticism from Western human rights organizations in the past had not had any apparent effect on Turkmenistan's policies, nor is there any particularly credible evidence to indicate any such influence on the December 27 announcements. Perhaps the move represented a belated response to the July 1995 events: the US Embassy in Ashgabat subsequently reported that twenty-seven individuals detained after the July demonstration were tried in secret on December 26 for their participation. The court convicted all of them, but the authorities released twenty on January 12, as part of an amnesty President Niyazov announced on December 27.[136]

Despite Niyazov's statements on behalf of human rights and his proclaimed desire to create institutional guarantees for their observance, Turkmenistan's past practice dictates skepticism. There is little evidence that he will ease up on real or imagined critics or political opponents. With officials denying that there are any political prisoners in the country, they will likely continue to level criminal charges against dissidents.[137]

Conclusion

In the context of the Newly Independent States, Turkmenistan represents a unique case of consciously arrested development,[138] in which a single individual has come to dominate totally the visible political process. President Niyazov has no apparent rivals or credible opposition, having permitted no individual, group or institution to emerge, much less to challenge his authority. In fact, if "politics" assumes the accommodation, resolution and management of competing perspectives and the interests of various groups, Niyazov seems to be denying that politics in general exists in Turkmenistan. To this apparent end, his regime is engaged in large-scale mythologizing, not only about the melding of Turkmenbashy and his people but also about the absence of differences and conflicts in society.

This does not mean, however, that Niyazov's preeminence and continuation in office assure stability. Turkmenistan has obviously been more stable than neighboring CIS states wracked by war (like Tajikístan) and swamped by refugees (like Azerbaijan or Georgia). Saparmurad Niyazov has not faced challenges from parliament (as has Askar Akaev in Kyrgyzstan) or chronic ethnic tension (as has Nursultan Nazarbaev in Kazakstan). But there are no outlets in Turkmenistan for venting societal discontent, which appears to be growing because of economic conditions, and which could, under certain circumstances, erupt into larger-scale disturbances.[139] Moreover, Turkmenistan's campaign against distant dissidents highlights the regime's sense of vulnerability. Various observers in Ashgabat explained the crackdown in November and December 1994 by the need to find scapegoats for a poor economic situation. But those arrests also raise questions about the stability of a regime which maintains extremely tight controls on a mostly quiescent populace yet feels threatened by a small group of dissidents, most of whom live outside the country, and who have little chance of posing a real challenge to the authorities.

Even more fundamentally, any regime in which power and authority are vested in one individual, as opposed to established institutions, is inherently unstable. In Turkmenistan, where institutions are largely powerless, the ruler has become synonymous with state and nation, and the entire political process revolves around him, the instability of the regime is correspondingly greater. Nor is there any vice-presidential post or an obvious successor to a president who has required treatment in Western hospitals for ailments presumed to be cardiological in nature.[140] Article 60 of the constitution specifies that the president can be relieved of his office due to illness, if two-thirds of the *Halk Maslakhaty*'s members so decide. Should the president have to step down or otherwise leave the scene, Article 61 stipulates that the chairman of the Mejlis becomes acting president and elections must take place within two months. What would actually happen, though, is anybody's guess.

In many respects, the analytical tools of Sovietology are more appropriate in Turkmenistan than those applied to systems in transition, yet with a special twist. Officials claim Turkmenistan's political system corresponds to Turkmen traditions of consensus, eschewing open competition for political preeminence, and respect for leaders. They also stress the essentiality of avoiding the turmoil other former Soviet republics have endured, which they blame on political liberalization. Opposition activists, for their part, strongly reject the claim that the country's current political system accords with national traditions. Citing, *inter alia*, the traditional Turkmen Council of Elders, which provided nomadic tribes a forum for discussion and consultation, they claim democracy has deep democratic roots among Turkmen. "In a nation which, for an extended period of time, had a nomadic way of life and waged a cruel struggle for survival with nature and with the invasion of foreigners, elements of 'steppe democracy' have become traditions and customs: equality, justice, honesty, and not rank-worship and the creation of a living god."[141]

In any event, it is improbable that the current regime will substantially modify its psychology or its style of rule, having invested so much time, effort and reputation in its construction and maintenance. True, the virtual monopolization of politics by Turkmenistan's rulers could facilitate even startling shifts in course without evoking open opposition or criticism in the media, leaving them more flexibility than might be apparent. But the best that might be hoped for in a reforming Turkmenistan under Saparmurad Niyazov is probably Uzbek-style pluralism, with Turkmenbashy retaining his special role in the political system.

NOTES

1 Occasionally, journalists and commentators simply describe Turkmenistan as "communist," as, for example, in an Agence France Press report carried in *Sueddeutsche Zeitung*, 19 May 1995.

While Turkmenistan sometimes gets lumped together with Uzbekistan and Tajikistan as the hardline trio of the Commonwealth of Independent States (CIS), those two Central Asian countries differ from Turkmenistan in several important respects. In Uzbekistan, dissident movements, such as Erk and Birlik, arose and were allowed to function from the late 1980s until 1992; in December 1991, Erk leader Mohammad Solih was even able to run against sitting President Islam Karimov in an election; more than one political party is registered and they are currently represented in parliament, even though all are government-controlled, not oppositionist; the races in the December 1994 parliamentary election were nominally multi-candidate; and Karimov's government has introduced market reforms.

Tajikistan is a one-party state and has banned all opposition movements, press, etc. Before the country's devastating civil war, however, the opposition even participated in a coalition government. Tajikistan's rulers, moreover, have been negotiating with the opposition (granted, they have little choice, given the ongoing guerilla war); in summer 1995, the conflicting sides agreed on principles for establishing peace and national accord, and, in fact, the latest rounds of talks have taken place in Ashgabat under Turkmenistan's auspices.

The ruling regimes of Tajikistan and Uzbekistan, in sum, have at times since 1991 at least recognized the existence of opposition forces. This has not happened in Turkmenistan.

2 Turkmenistan has relatively few foreign observers and strictly controlled media. It is possible, as some have supposed, that demonstrations and protests take place outside the capital city, Ashgabat, where foreigners are concentrated, yet few people would learn about them. Spontaneous protests in Turkmenbashy (formerly Krasnovodsk) and Mary about food shortages have, in fact, been reported. However, members of the international diplomatic community told the author in December 1995 that they had not heard of any large demonstrations except for the one that took place in Ashgabat in July 1995, which is discussed in greater detail below.

3 Turkmenistan is the southernmost former Soviet republic. To the south lie Iran and Afghanistan; Kazakstan and Uzbekistan are northern neighbors; to the west is the Caspian Sea. Turkmenistan is approximately 190,000 square miles in area (about 488,000 square kilometers), of which the Kara-Kum desert takes up roughly 80 percent.

4 The resolution recognizes and supports Turkmenistan's declaration of permanent neutrality, and appeals to UN member states to respect and support Turkmenistan's neutral status, independence, sovereignty and territorial integrity. On December 27, 1995, Turkmenistan's constitution was amended to enshrine the country's permanent neutrality, which is "the basis for Turkmenistan's foreign and domestic policy." Turkmenistan "will not participate in military blocs and alliances or in interstate unions with strict obligations or which require collective

responsibility of the participants." December 12 is now a national holiday, "Neutrality Day," in Turkmenistan.

5 David Nissman, "Turkmenistan," *Collier's Encyclopedia*, vol. 22, 1994, p. 549.
6 N. V. Atamamedov, ed., *Turkmenskaya Sovetskaya Sotsialisticheskaya Respublika* (Ashgabat, 1984), p. 66.
7 Pre-independence Turkmenistan was divided into the five oblasts of Ashgabat, Krasnovodsk, Dashhowuz, Mary, and Charjew. In May 1992, simultaneous with the adoption of the country's new constitution, these oblasts became *velayat*s: Ahal, Balkan, Dashhowuz, Mary, and Lebap (the renaming of Ashgabat to Ahal, Krasnovodsk to Balkan and Charjew to Lebap reinstated historical toponyms). The *velayat*s, administered by *hakim*s, are themselves composed of *shakher*s and *etrap*s, which are run by *shakher hakim*s and *etrap hakim*s (or *archin*s), respectively.
8 This breakdown comes from the US Embassy in Ashgabat.
9 The United States established its embassy in Turkmenistan (as in all other former Soviet republics, except for Russia) in 1992. Other countries with embassies in Ashgabat include the United Kingdom, Germany, Russia, Turkey, Iran, China, Pakistan, India, Uzbekistan, and Armenia.
10 Anne Bohr, "Turkmenistan under Perestroika: An Overview," *RFE/RL Report on the USSR*, 23 March 1990, p. 21. See also her "Turkmen Scholar on 1989 Census and Demographic Policy," ibid., 27 January 1989, p. 19.
11 Saparmurat Turkmenbashi, *Address to the Peoples of Turkmenistan* (Ashgabat, 1994), pp. 34-36, 39. The address probably was delivered sometime in 1993.
12 This information comes from the US Embassy in Ashgabat.
13 According to one analyst, the heads of all the force ministries – internal affairs, national security and defense – are Tekkes, but their deputies are Yomuts (*Izvestiia*, 20 May 1994).
14 The article did not provide any source for the information.
15 Foreign Broadcast Information Service, *Daily Report: Central Eurasia*, henceforth, *FBIS-SOV*, 14 February 1996, p. 64. Apart from the usual ministers (Defense, Foreign Affairs, Internal Affairs, Border Troops, etc.), as of February 1996, the *hakim*s of all five *velayat*s were Council members.
16 The Mejlis currently has five standing committees (Legislation, Education and Science, Economy and Social Policy, Foreign Affairs and Inter-Parliamentary Relations, and Legal Affairs). Of the fifty deputies, thirty-five work exclusively in parliament, and the rest continue to hold their other posts as well.
17 Foreign Broadcast Information Service, *Daily Report: Central Eurasia* (hereafter *FBIS-USR*), 7 August 1992, p. 101.
18 *Segodnia*, 21 January 1994.
19 The CSCE was renamed in December 1994 the Organization for Security and Cooperation in Europe, or OSCE.
20 Karimov was the only Central Asian leader not to run unopposed for the presidency. See Commission on Security and Cooperation in Europe, *The Referendum on Independence and Presidential Election in Uzbekistan* (Washington, DC, 1992). Granted, since then, Uzbekistan has recorded virtually 100 percent figures, as when voting in the March 1995 referendum on extending Karimov's tenure in office until the year 2000.

21 The author, who monitored the election, heard in Ashgabat that two individuals tried to run against the approved candidate. Local election authorities refused to register one, and the other withdrew before the voting. See Commission on Security and Cooperation in Europe, *Report on the Parliamentary Election in Turkmenistan* (Washington, DC, 1995).

22 *Vechernii Ashgabat*, 12 December 1994.

23 In late 1989, Turkmenistan's Supreme Soviet elected the Chairman of the Council of Ministers from among three candidates, the first time such a high-ranking official had been elected. Bess Brown, "Democratization in Turkmenistan," *RFE/RL Report on the USSR*, 1 June 1990, p. 13.

24 Conversation with the author, December 1995.

25 The author visited precincts in Ashgabat.

26 *Report on the Parliamentary Election in Turkmenistan*.

27 See Commission on Security and Cooperation in Europe, *Report on Turkmenistan's Referendum on Independence* (Washington, DC, 1991).

28 In the presidential elections that year, the authorities reported that (only) 96.6 percent of voters took part, and 98.3 percent voted for Saparmurad Niyazov. The March 1991 referendum on maintaining the USSR produced the lowest figures: 94 percent turnout, with 94.1 percent voting affirmatively. Since then, however, no election or referendum has drawn fewer than 99 percent of voters.

29 Turkmenistan is, of course, not the only Central Asian state that produces such high percentages of turnout and electoral approval. One government official in an unidentified country in the region, asked why his president had orchestrated a referendum extending his powers rather than fairly win two-thirds of the vote, replied: "Not enough for a convincing victory." (Igor Greenwald, "Being President Isn't Enough For These Ex-Soviet Leaders," *Christian Science Monitor*, 28 March 1996.) In light of this psychology, the experience of Azerbaijan is illuminating: in June 1992, Popular Front Chairman Abulfaz Elchibey won a presidential election with "only" about 60 percent of the vote, reflecting a strikingly Western attitude. When ex-Communist Party leader Heydar Aliev returned to power, he won his October 1993 presidential election with almost Niyazov-like numbers.

30 The author was present in the audience for the speech. See *Report on Turkmenistan's Referendum on Independence*, p. 5.

31 Ibid., p. 11.

32 *FBIS-USR*, 28 October 1992, pp. 94-5.

33 *Argumenty i fakty*, 12 February 1994.

34 See note 1.

35 Interview with the author in Ashgabat in December 1995. See also Bohr, "Turkmenistan under Perestroika," p. 21 and *passim*, for a good discussion of Turkmenistan during perestroika.

36 Ibid.

37 *Literaturnaia gazeta*, 8 July 1992.

38 Charles Colson, "Inching Towards Democratization," *RFE/RL Report on the USSR*, 4 January 1991, p. 35.

39 Ibid., p. 36.

40 *Moskovskie novosti*, no. 2, 13 January 1991. The estimated number of members at the time was 1,200.

41 The party maintained especially close ties with the Democratic Party of Russia, headed by Nikolai Travkin.

42 In June 1993, the newspaper stopped functioning because of lack of funds and support from Azerbaijan's new president, former Communist Party leader Heydar Aliev. Another Turkmen opposition journal, *Dayanch*, began publication in Moscow in January 1991.

43 *Nezavisimaia gazeta*, 10 January 1996.

44 The author did not provide any source for the information.

45 *Literaturnaia gazeta*, 23 November 1994.

46 *FBIS-USR*, 28 October 1992, pp. 98-9.

47 *Turkmenskaia iskra*, 2 December 1995, described the significance of the oath and its relation to President Niyazov, who had instructed that "the oath of loyalty to the homeland become a spiritual tradition," as follows: "God . . . gave Man a homeland for him to love, for the homeland is above everything. It is holy like one's mother, like the Koran . . . If the oath disappears from our life, a vacuum will form and love and respect for the homeland will weaken." On 7 December, *Turkmenskaia iskra* published another article on the oath, in the same vein, indicating a mini-campaign to bolster commitment or to combat flagging dedication, or both.

48 In his *Address to the Peoples of Turkmenistan* (p. 42), President Niyazov said: "Although the term 'ideology' is something that is sending a shock wave, I still use it since there is no state without ideology . . . One of its cornerstones is unity, the other is peace. We were all witnesses of the establishment of yet another support on which our ideology is based – unity of the people with the President."

49 Only six buildings survived the quake, in which over 30,000 of the city's 130,000 inhabitants died.

50 One analyst writing for the Almaty publication *Karavan* has surmised that Niyazov's orphan status made him an attractive recruit to the Communist Party apparatus because Moscow would not have to listen to representatives of aggrieved other clans complain about not having been given such plum positions (*Karavan*, 12 January 1996, p. 9, in *FBIS-SOV*, 9 February 1996, p. 110). It is just as likely Niyazov appealed to CPSU personnel administrators because his lack of Turkmen clan ties would bind him more closely to the Russian-dominated CPSU.

51 Such is the opposition's version of events, as related in *Turkmen Ili*, no. 1, July 1994, p. 7. Perhaps, however, Niyazov simply balked at the idea of having to run for office on a regular basis, or someone thought the idea would please him. In any case, Turkmenistan's decision not to hold elections and to prolong, via referendum, the president's tenure in office began a mini-trend, with Uzbekistan and Kazakstan following suit. Persistent rumors that Kyrgyzstani President Akaev would join the club have yet to materialize.

52 Ondzhik Musaev, first secretary of the Democratic Party, put it this way: "There is a fundamental difference between our party and its precursor . . . It's all simple: We have no functions of power." *FBIS-USR*, 28 October 1992. Two years later, one observer offered this perspective in *Nezavisimaia gazeta*, 16 November 1994: "There are few states in the world with a one-party system. There are even fewer countries where parties are absent altogether."

53 In a December 1994 conversation with the author, Ondzhik Musaev spoke worshipfully about President Niyazov, whom he called "my leader" (*moi vozhd '*). He has also been shown on television kissing Niyazov's hand.

54 *Turkmenskaia iskra*, 13 December 1994. Poor execution of government programs is a chronic problem, despite Niyazov's creation, in November 1994, of a Control Commission to ensure their implementation.

55 In August 1995, for example, President Niyazov dismissed ten of Turkmenistan's fifty local administrative heads for failing to meet grain quotas. *OMRI Daily Digest*, 9 August 1995. In January 1996, he sacked the head of state television and radio, citing "significant shortcomings," specifically, programs that were "dull, monotonous and lacked depth." (*Turkmen Press*, 3 January 1996, in *FBIS-SOV*, 4 January 1996, p. 53). He should take a look at the newspapers.

56 *Karavan*, 12 January 96, p. 9, in *FBIS-SOV*, 9 February 1996, p. 111.

57 Perhaps the inspiration for Niyazov's honorific was "Ataturk" (Father of the Turks), with whom Niyazov would appear to be comparing himself.

58 In spring 1992, the Supreme Soviet's Presidium adopted a Resolution on the Creation and Utilization of the Image of the President, calling for the production and sale of Niyazov's portrait. Christopher Panico, "Turkmenistan Unaffected by Winds of Democratic Change," *RFE/RL Research Report*, 22 January 1993, p. 8.

59 On 30 November 1993, the Moscow-based daily *Segodnia* noted that members of Turkmenistan's Democratic Party had raised the question of making Niyazov "president for life" (*FBIS-SOV*, 2 December 1993, p. 62). Turkmen Press reported on 27 September 1995 that speakers at the Democratic Party's September 1995 plenum proposed the same subject for discussion at the party's second congress, scheduled for the first half of 1996 (*FBIS-SOV*, 29 September 1995, p. 69).

60 *Literaturnaia gazeta*, 23 November 1994.

61 Ibid.

62 Of course, the ego factor should not be discounted. Saparmurad Niyazov may simply enjoy being Turkmenbashy, and the attendant power, honors and perks, including, reportedly, newly constructed presidential residences in all five *velayat*s.

63 This seems unlikely, unless the regime has been putting on a huge smokescreen for outsiders. Diplomatic missions and other foreign representations report that nothing seems to be decided without Niyazov's agreement.

64 *OMRI Daily Digest*, 18 March 1996.

65 In this connection, it is worth noting that Turkmenistan's parliament and government are located in the same building in Ashgabat.

66 On claims of censorship in Turkmenistan, President Niyazov has said: "Nonsense! We print everything, but when anti-Russian or anti-Semitic articles appear, what would you have me do?" *Literaturnaia gazeta*, 23 November 1994.

67 *OMRI Daily Digest*, 2 August 1995.

68 *Literaturnaia gazeta*, 23 November 1994.

69 Niyazov put it this way in *Trud* (28 October 1992): "no abstract formulas or prescription worked out in a prosperous Western country should determine the forms and methods of our transition to the market. We proceed on the basis of our own conditions and the features of our historical development."

70 Since the 1989 Soviet census, the highest figure cited – 4.6 million – comes from *Novoe vremiia*, no. 41, October 1994, pp. 14-16 (see *FBIS-USR*, 8 November 1994, p. 102), and seems too high. The US State Department's *Country Report on Human Rights Practices* for 1995 gives the population of Turkmenistan as "about four million."

71 *Nezavisimaia gazeta*, 14 February 1996. Apart from Turkmen inside the country, the 1895 Anglo-Russian border treaty left an estimated 1 to 2 million Turkmen in northwest Afghanistan, and close to 1 million in northeastern Iran. Nissman, "Turkmenistan," p. 546.

72 *Argumenty i fakty*, 8 February 1994.

73 According to Soviet figures, between 1979 and 1989 the number of Turkmen in the USSR rose by 34 percent, while emigration from Turkmenistan during that decade was six times higher than during the preceding decade. Bohr, "Turkmenistan under Perestroika," pp. 23, 27. The 1995 census statistics should be treated with caution, as the regime might have its own reasons to present the population breakdown as more favorable to Turkmen than to Russians, in light of Ashgabat's sensitive relations with Moscow (see below).

74 In 1989, for example, Russians and Turkmen each constituted 41 percent of the population of the capital city, Ashgabat (ibid., p. 26). Other cities with a significant Russian population include Turkmenbashy (formerly Krasnovodsk) and Charjew.

75 *Rossiiskaia gazeta*, 30 April 1994. See also David Nissman, "Turkmenistan (Un)transformed," *Current History*, April 1994, pp. 183-4. According to Bohr, another cause of the disturbances, in which participants shouted anti-Armenian slogans, were the high prices charged by cooperatives ("Turkmenistan under Perestroika," pp. 29-30).

76 Educational authorities told *Turkmenskaia iskra* (8 December 1995) that new textbooks have already been published for elementary school classes. Turkmen was written in a Latin alphabet from the 1920s to 1940, when Cyrillic became obligatory.

77 According to the 1989 Soviet census, for example, only 3 percent of Russians knew Turkmen.

78 *Turkmenistan*, 14 May 1992, p. 3, in *FBIS-USR*, 3 August 1992, pp. 92-4. Of course, a Turkmen-language publication is more likely to complain about non-Turkmens' poor knowledge of the state language than a Russian-language publication.

79 *Nezavisimaia gazeta*, 21 December 1995.

80 *FBIS-USR*, 12 August 1992, pp. 92-3.

81 See the interview with Boris Shikmuradov in *Argumenty i fakty*, 12 February 1994.

82 They number over 400,000 people, not counting 70,000 mixed Turkmen-Uzbek families. *Pravda vostoka*, 10 February 1996.

83 Nissman, "Turkmenistan (Un)transformed," p. 186.

84 *Turkmenskaia iskra*, 4 December 1995, reported that Uzbek neighbors had greeted December 3, which Ashgabat had designated in 1994 "Good Neighbor Day," with "ecstasy." How, then, "could it be possible not to be proud of such relations, not to treasure them!" For the joint communique issued by Presidents

Niyazov and Karimov after the latter's January 1996 visit to Ashgabat, see BBC *Summary of World Broadcasts*, 21 January 1996 on Lexis-Nexis.

85   *FBIS-USR*, 24 November 1993, p. 105.

86   According to Russia's ambassador in Ashgabat, as of December 1995, there were some 300,000 Russians in Turkmenistan, pending the release of the new census figures.

87   *Literaturnaia gazeta*, 23 November 1994.

88   Boris Yeltsin was the earliest beneficiary of this decision, becoming the first Russian citizen to obtain dual citizenship of Turkmenistan at the December 1993 CIS Summit. On December 12, 1995, *Turkmenskaia iskra* published information about polling stations in Ashgabat, Mary, Charjew, Dashhouwz, Nebitdag and Turkmenbashy (formerly Krasnovodsk), where Russian citizens could vote in Russia's December 17, 1995 parliamentary election. Interfax reported on December 17, that over 3,500 Russian citizens had cast ballots. Of all the other former Soviet republics, only Tajikistan has moved to introduce dual citizenship. According to Tajik parliamentarians, in September 1995 Presidents Yeltsin and Rakhmonov signed an agreement on dual citizenship, which Tajikistan's parliament ratified in November 1995. Russia's Duma, however, has not ratified the accord.

89   The author received a copy of the agreement from the Russian Embassy in Ashgabat. See the interview with Russia's ambassador to Turkmenistan in *Vechernii Ashgabat*, 12 December 1994. According to Russian Embassy figures, during the first seven months of 1994 some 4,000 people in Turkmenistan registered for dual citizenship. In the following months 3,000 registered each month (as of December 1994).

90   *Diplomaticheskii Vestnik*, no. 6 (June 1995), 37-9, as translated in *FBIS-SOV*, 24 August 1995, pp. 14-17.

91   See, for example, *Izvestiia*, 17 May 1995 or 5 August 1995.

92   Bohr, "Turkmenistan under Perestroika," p. 28.

93   *Dayanch*, April 1992.

94   *Argumenty i fakty*, 12 February 1994.

95   *Dayanch*, April 1992.

96   According to Western correspondents, Niyazov has spent as much as $35 million on a single mosque. Steve LeVine and Robert Corzine, "Turkmenistan: A Catalogue of Promises Unfulfilled," *Financial Times*, 22 August 1995.

97   According to former Foreign Minister Abdy Kuliev, the regime turned down Iranian requests to send mullahs to Turkmenistan. Lowell Bezanis, "Some Revival, Much Subordination, More Superstition in Turkmenistan," *Transition*, 29 December 1995, p. 31.

98   *FBIS-USR*, 7 August 1992, p. 110.

99   ITAR-TASS, 19 April 1994, in *FBIS-SOV*, 20 April 1994, p. 72.

100 President Niyazov has supported the construction of a Russian Orthodox cathedral in Ashgabat, which is scheduled to be completed in the year 2000. *Turkmenskaia iskra*, 14 September 1995.

101 ITAR-TASS, 19 April 1994, in *FBIS-SOV*, 20 April 1994, p. 72.

102 *Nezavisimaia gazeta*, 12 August 1992.

103 David Nissman, "Iran and Soviet Islam: The Azerbaijan and Turkmenistan SSRs," *Central Asian Survey* 2, no. 4 (December 1983), 45-59.

104 In July 1993, the Turkmen-language publication *Watan* printed an interview with the chief Imam of Ashgabat, in which he warned against "pseudo-mullahs," whom he described as a "great plague," and whose ignorance of Islam was misleading the faithful. *FBIS-USR*, 3 November 1993, pp. 95-7.

105 Alexandre Bennigsen and S. Enders Wimbush, *Muslims of the Soviet Empire* (Bloomington: Indiana University Press, 1986), pp. 101-4.

106 Bohr, "Turkmenistan under Perestroika," p. 29.

107 He added, in his interview in *Nezavisimaia gazeta*, 12 August 1992, that they were equally indifferent to the party and the state.

108 One resident foreigner said she had never, in over a year, heard a call to prayer. By contrast, in the Baku neighborhood where the author lived from September to December 1995, the muezzin summoned the faithful to service every morning.

109 In an interview with *Rossiiskaia gazeta*, 5 May 1995, President Niyazov said known gas reserves equal 15.5 trillion cubic meters, and oil stocks 6.3 billion tons. At other times, different figures have been cited. For instance, *Rossiiskaia gazeta*, 4 August 1995, reported gas reserves as 21 trillion cubic meters and seven billion tons of oil.

110 *Literaturnaya gazeta,* 23 November 1994.

111 Bohr, "Turkmenistan under Perestroika," pp. 23-5.

112 The program was renamed "Ten Years of Stability" in 1993.

113 *Rossiiskaia gazeta*, 5 May 1995.

114 Ibid.

115 *RFE/RL Daily Report*, 17 May 1994.

116 Turkmen Press, 21 June 1995, in *FBIS-SOV*, 23 June 1995, p. 78.

117 LeVine and Corzine, "Turkmenistan: A Catalogue of Promises Unfulfilled." See also the *Economist*, 22 July 1995, p. 36.

118 *Moskovskie novosti*, 23-30 July 1995, suggested a more conspiratorial explanation: Russia, annoyed at Niyazov's refusal to accept Russian bases and his agreement to deliver eight billion cubic meters of natural gas to Iran, provoked the demonstration. According to still other conspiracy theories heard by the author in Ashgabat in December 1995, the demonstration reflected intra-nomenklatura struggle, and/or was a reminder to Niyazov that lower-level officials can embarrass him and stir up trouble.

119 The author's efforts in December 1995 to obtain an original of the pamphlet(s) were unsuccessful, but a foreign embassy supplied a translation of one of them.

120 *Izvestiia*'s correspondent wrote that nothing like this had happened before in Turkmenistan. According to another source, the largest reported demonstration before July 1995 took place in November 1987, when some 2,000 army veterans protested in Ashgabat against the government's refusal to acknowledge the death of Turkmen soldiers in Afghanistan or to help rehabilitate the wounded. See Ahmed Rashid, *The Resurgence of Central Asia: Islam or Nationalism* (Oxford University Press, 1994), p. 196.

121 According to the US State Department's 1995 *Country Report on Human Rights Practices*, at least eighty people were arrested.

122 Subsequently, the authorities also claimed the participants in the demonstration were certain factory workers who had not been paid. The head of Turkmenistan's KNB (formerly KGB) told the author in December 1995 that the writers of the leaflets were poets whose work was refused for publication, and that the demonstrators were young people who had been intoxicated by the organizers. Even foreign embassies were unable to get any information on those arrested or the status of the investigation.

123 Despite problematic relations with Russia over pipelines, President Niyazov has tried, or felt compelled, to maintain good economic relations with Moscow. In May 1995, he signed an agreement on trade and economic partnership with Russia until the year 2000.

124 As of December 1995, Turkmenistan had not asked the International Monetary Fund for money, so the Fund cannot intervene actively. Nevertheless, the IMF did make strong recommendations about economic reforms.

125 *Nezavisimaia gazeta*, 11 January 1996.

126 Considering inflation and devaluation of the manat, the US Embassy in Ashgabat estimated the average wage to be about five dollars.

127 *Finansovyie Izvestiia*, 27 February 96, p. 2, in *FBIS-SOV*, 4 March 1996, pp. 59-60.

128 For general assessments of human rights in Turkmenistan, see Commission on Security and Cooperation in Europe: *Human Rights and Democratization in the Newly Independent States of the Former Soviet Union* (Washington, DC, 1993); Helsinki Watch, *Human Rights in Turkmenistan*, July 1993; the US State Department's *Country Reports on Human Rights Practices*, issued annually; and a March 1996 report by Amnesty International: "Turkmenistan – Measures of Persuasion."

129 Interfax, 15 July 1992, cited in Panico, "Turkmenistan," p. 8.

130 Kuliev left Turkmenistan in 1992. He told the author in a December 1994 interview in Moscow that he left because President Niyazov made it impossible for him to remain in the country after he unsuccessfully tried to convince Turkmenbashy to permit democratization. Deputy Prime Minister Boris Shikmuradov told *Literaturnaia gazeta*, 23 November 1994, that Kuliev was a blackmailer and linked him to preparations for a terrorist act. He said President Niyazov in November 1994 had instructed law enforcement agencies to investigate Kuliev and others: "People committing criminal offenses and passing themselves off as civil rights advocates and dissidents must be punished."

131 *Turkmen Ili*, no. 1, July 1994.

132 According to Russian Foreign Ministry officials, the Russian Counter-Intelligence Service had arrested the two on the basis of a January 1993 convention on legal aid and legal relations on civil, family, and criminal matters. In fact, it turned out that Turkmenistan had never signed the convention, while Russia had signed it only on December 10, i.e., after the arrests took place. See *Kommersant Daily*, 14 December 1994.

133 *Turkmenskaia iskra*, 23 June 1995.

134 According to the State Department's 1995 *Country Report on Human Rights Practices*, Aimuradov was severely beaten while in detention. The same source states that "The charges against the pair [Aimuradov and Garaev] are widely believed to be fabricated."

135 Esenov and Soyunov received political refugee status and left for Sweden in February 1995. Turkmenistan continues to pursue the case as a criminal matter, although the Swedish authorities have refused to hand over Esenov and Soyunov, *Nezavisimaia gazeta* reported on 15 December 1995. The head of Turkmenistan's KNB (formerly KGB) confirmed to the author in December 1995 that Ashgabat had asked for their extradition.

136 As of January 1996, the government had neither presented any evidence against the seven people still in prison, nor released any information about their identities. They reportedly were charged with narcotics-related crimes.

137 Russia's constitution permits extradition for criminal activity, but not political dissent.

138 This description increasingly reflects the situation of Belarus as well, under President Aleksandr Lukashenko.

139 This seems unlikely, given the strength of the state and the weakness of society in Turkmenistan, but then few people expected the regime of Romania's Nicolae Ceausescu to end as it did.

140 In this connection, *Turkmenskaia iskra*, 12 December 1995, printed the following about a December 11 meeting of the Cabinet of Ministers. "During the past week, Saparmurad Turkmenbashy has been under doctors' observation. At present, he feels better, and has returned to work, but is under medical care." According to residents of Ashgabat, television also reported that Niyazov had been unwell. Nor was this the first such report of Niyazov's illness. But why bother to inform readers in information-starved Turkmenistan of the President's maladies, without offering any details about his condition, diagnosis or prognosis? To elicit sympathy and concern for Niyazov, reinforcing the sense of his indispensability, or to prepare the public for a possible news flash about his departure or demise?

141 *Turkmen Ili*, no. 2, August 1994, p. 15. Former Foreign Minister Kuliev harrumphed, in a December 1994 conversation with the author, about people kissing Niyazov's hand; this, he said, was never done among the Turkmen. Nevertheless, in mid-1992, when Kuliev's relations with Niyazov were better, he said: "The fact that nearly all Turkmen voted for [Niyazov] attests, more convincingly than any theorizing, that strong presidential rule in general and the personality of the president in particular correspond with the mentality of the nation." Cited in Panico, "Turkmenistan," p. 8.

10 Political development in Uzbekistan: democratization?

William Fierman

Introduction

"Democratization" and "political participation" have made no major inroads in Uzbekistan, the most populous of the post-Soviet Central Asian states. Indeed, in some important ways Uzbekistan in the middle of the 1990s is less "democratic" and offers fewer opportunities for "political participation" than Uzbekistan at the end of the 1980s. Perhaps the greatest change in Uzbekistan's politics from a decade ago is the reduced role of a political organization controlled in Moscow. The change in locus of political decision-making may be a prerequisite for the development of a democratic system in Uzbekistan. However, the country is still dominated by an authoritarian political culture, one which its current leader seems determined to preserve.

This study will highlight the lack of fundamental change in political participation and policies toward political participation in Uzbekistan since 1989. It will suggest that the Karimov regime has sought to bolster its legitimacy primarily through policies related to what will be defined as "distribution" and "identity;" by contrast, the government's policies related to "participation" seem to have been devised with little concern about any need to cultivate legitimacy.

In order to remain in power, both authoritarian and democratic regimes must achieve a reasonable level of citizen compliance with their political decisions. Compliance, of course, can be promoted by very different mixtures of coercion and popular legitimacy. Whereas coercion obliges citizens to follow rules because they have no other rational choice, legitimacy fosters voluntary compliance. Regimes may achieve legitimacy in many ways, not all of which require a democratic political order. For example, many Soviet citizens probably viewed their country's very undemocratic political order under the CPSU as legitimate because of the "social contract" that it offered for many years.

360

Because issues of political legitimacy may ultimately be critical in promoting authoritarian erosion, this chapter will relate the recent political history of Uzbekistan to three broad categories of issues related to legitimacy. These broad categories are distribution, participation, and identity. I use "distribution" to refer to problems of economic production and allocation, "participation" for *voluntary* activity by which citizens attempt to affect political decisions, and "identity" for the process of defining the common bonds and boundaries (and thus the characteristics of members) of a particular political community.

Distribution issues are linked to legitimacy because the material conditions affecting citizens' lives depend on economic production and the allocation of wealth. Naturally, citizens who feel that their political system is producing a suitable living standard are more likely to view their government as legitimate. Citizens are also more likely to consider governments legitimate if they believe that appropriate procedures are used to make political decisions in their society. Among the most important decisions are the selection of political leaders (whether based on heredity, charisma, election, or something else). In democratic political systems citizens' perceptions that their own political participation affects outcomes contribute to legitimacy. (This does not, however, mean that an authoritarian regime cannot enjoy legitimacy.) Likewise, citizens are more likely to view their government as legitimate if they perceive it as "their own." Their sense of shared identity with leadership and fellow citizens based on fact and/or myth may draw on such diverse elements as religion, race, language, way of life, perceived history, and geography. Popular perceptions of rulers as "alien" can provide great strength to political movements which bring about change. As we will see, these three sources of legitimacy are not of equal importance in Uzbekistan today.

The first section of the study below will consider the most salient aspects of Uzbekistan's political, economic, social, and cultural life leading up to the June 1989 appointment of Islam Karimov as first secretary of the Communist Party of Uzbekistan (CPUz). This will be followed by an examination of developments under Karimov's leadership, including the CPUz' adoption of the opposition's platforms and efforts to control informal political organizations and emerging parties. After this, the study will examine the brief "thaw" in Uzbekistan's political life following independence, and then the reassertion of authoritarian control. At the end we will reconsider questions of political legitimacy and their relevance to the continuation or weakening of the current authoritarian system.

Because much of the following narrative concerns political participation, it should be noted that new forms of political participation emerged in Uzbekistan beginning in the late 1980s. Not surprisingly, their appearance in

Uzbekistan owed much to developments elsewhere in the USSR. Some, such as multicandidate elections, were to survive well into the post-Soviet era. Others, such as glasnost, independent "informal" organizations, and mass public demonstrations, were viewed by the ruling party as threats, and were practically to disappear by 1992.

Uzbekistan in the pre-Karimov era

General background

One of the most important political facts about Uzbekistan is that it is a Soviet political creation dating from the 1920s. As part of the national delimitation, Uzbekistan was carved from territories formerly belonging to Turkestan, the Bukharan Amirate, and the Khivan Khanate. Initially, Tajikistan was an autonomous republic within Uzbekistan, but in 1929, Tajikistan became a Union republic and it gained a piece of land which had not been part of the autonomous republic. Besides the territorial delimitation, Soviet power also delimited population in a new way, thus producing an "Uzbek people." Soviet rule attempted to reinforce Uzbek identity as part of a greater Soviet identity and as an antidote to pan-Turkic, pan-Islamic, or Turkestan identities. Among other things, this involved the creation of a single standard Uzbek literary language distinct from other Turkic languages and Uzbek historical heroes separate from Tajik and other heroes of the region.

Uzbekistan lacks a single pre-Soviet political tradition, let alone a democratic one. Until after the Bolshevik revolution, both Bukhara and Khiva were controlled by autocratic rulers backed by conservative religious establishments. Likewise, democratic processes had little chance to develop in Russian-ruled Turkestan, a remote outpost of the tsarist empire.

True, in all three political units whose territory eventually became part of Uzbekistan, small groups of Islamic reformers – *jadids* – sought to promote social and political change. The jadids, many from merchant families and/or members of the Tatar ethnic minority, were especially active in areas of education and the press. They developed schools which along with the more traditional religious subjects also taught secular ones; jadids also organized a number of (generally short-lived) newspapers promoting their ideas.

In the weeks immediately following the 1917 Bolshevik Revolution, some of the jadids joined forces with other groups in opposition to the newly established Russian-dominated Tashkent government and participated in the Fourth (Extraordinary) Conference of Central Asian Muslims. This gathering, which met in the Fergana Valley city of Kokand, declared Turkestan to be autonomous and called for election of a constituent assembly; it also organized a provisional government. In January 1918, the plans announced by the Kokand government for popular election of a constituent assembly from all of southern Central Asia provided for up to a third of the seats to represent non-Muslims.[1] Although jadids were active in developing these plans, the Kokand government was neither entirely Muslim, nor did all of its Muslim forces favor jadid reforms. Nevertheless, note should be taken of an early government based on indigenous forces which proclaimed democratic ideals. The Kokand government was very short-lived. In February 1918, Red troops laid siege to the city and crushed the opposition.

Despite their artificiality, the republics and nationality labels molded by the Soviet regime served as meaningful reference points throughout Soviet history and beyond. As elsewhere in the Soviet Union, in Uzbekistan, too, individuals were often hired, admitted into higher education, or promoted based on quotas or slots reserved for members of particular "nationality" groups. This is not to say that under Soviet power "Uzbeks" and members of other nationalities lost their strong sense of regional, clan, or other local identities. Indeed, these remained very important. As Donald Carlisle has demonstrated, geographically based political cliques were a critical instrument which Moscow exploited to exercise its rule of the republic.[2]

Defined in terms of Soviet-created nationality categories, Uzbekistan is predominantly "Uzbek." As of 1989, Uzbeks accounted for 71.4 percent of the republic's population. Russians were the next largest group, with 8.3 percent. Next in proportion were Tajiks and Kazaks, with 4.7 percent and 4.1 percent, respectively. Among others, Tatars and Karakalpaks (each with over 2 percent) were the only groups accounting for over 1 percent. The relative proportions of various nationalities in the republic shifted considerably over the course of Soviet rule. In large part thanks to migration, Russians (who accounted for only 5.2 percent in 1926) constituted 13.1 percent of the population in 1959; by that time Uzbeks were only 62.5 percent. As can be seen from the 1989 statistics, however, this again changed considerably over the next thirty years.

In considering nationality labels, it is important to note that during the Soviet era many individuals apparently claimed "Uzbek" nationality due to pressure, as a matter of convenience, or as a category which promised better opportunities than identification with other groups. This is especially true in Bukhara and Samarkand, where many "Tajiks" allegedly are recorded as "Uzbeks" in their passports. In fact, as reflected in the long tradition of Turkic-Persian bilingualism in many parts of present-day Uzbekistan, the distinction between Uzbeks and Tajiks is an especially problematic one.[3] Most of Uzbekistan's population continues to live in rural areas. This pertains especially to the Muslim nationalities. According to the 1989 census, almost 60 percent of the republic's population was "rural." Among Uzbeks, the proportion was even higher, almost 70 percent. By contrast, Russians and

Table 10.1 *Demographic trends in Uzbekistan since the 1950s*

	1950s	1970s	1980s
Percentage of population	(1951)	(1979)	(1989)
Rural	69.3	59.2	59.4
Urban	30.7	40.8	40.6
Average annual rates	(1951–61)	(1971–79)	(1990–99)[a]
of population growth (%)	3.2	3.0	2.1
Age distribution (%)		(1979)	(1989)
15–24	n.a.	21.7	19.4
25–49	n.a.	24.1	27.2
50–59	n.a.	5.9	6.1
Over 60	n.a.	7.1	6.5

Note: [a]Estimate.
Sources: US Department of Commerce, *Statistical Abstracts of the United States*; Paul S. Shoup, *The East European and Soviet Data Handbook*; UNESCO, *Statistical Yearbooks*; United Nations, *Demographic Yearbooks*.

other Slavs are concentrated in the cities, especially the capital Tashkent. Whereas Russians constituted almost 20 percent of Uzbekistan's urban population in 1989, their share was less than one percent in rural areas.[4]

At least through the 1980s, Uzbekistan continued to have a high birth rate, approximately 2.5 percent annually. Not surprisingly, then, the republic's population is also very young. In 1989, approximately 40 percent of its inhabitants were under age fifteen.

In the Soviet era, Uzbekistan and the other republics of Central Asia were primarily raw materials producers. In the All-Union division of labor Uzbekistan was primarily a source of cotton and importer of manufactured products (including textiles woven from local material). Extensive cotton farming caused horrendous damage to Uzbekistan's environment and its people's health.

Although the Soviet economic record in Central Asia is not without its successes, most economists agree that the standard of living in Uzbekistan was lower than in European parts of the Soviet Union and that the cotton monoculture harmed the republic's development.

During most of the Soviet era the CPSU attempted to encourage integration of Uzbekistan with the rest of the Soviet Union and the "internationalization" of Uzbek culture. Given the Russian dominance of "Soviet" culture, this in effect usually meant the russification of Uzbek culture. As part of this process, the regime encouraged the "enrichment" of many traditional Uzbek art forms with Russian elements, and promoted the study of Soviet (read "Russian") literature and history at the expense of Central Asian counterparts. Islam, the dominant religion of the region, was discouraged not only as a false belief system but as a backward culture which divided Muslims from other Soviet citizens. The Russian language occupied a privileged place in Uzbekistan's central political institutions, higher education, media, and public services (especially in urban areas). Nevertheless, as indicated by the fact that in the 1988–89 academic year, 77 percent of the republic's school children attended class with Uzbek as the medium of instruction, it is obvious that Uzbek held a very strong position in elementary education, especially among Uzbeks.[5]

Although the quality of education in Central Asia generally lagged behind that in other parts of the USSR, the Soviet regime dramatically raised literacy rates in Uzbekistan, achieved universal primary education, and brought secondary and higher education to large segments of the population. Whereas there were under 3,000 students in higher educational institutions in Uzbekistan in 1924–25, by 1940–41 the number had surpassed 16,000, in 1960–61 it had passed 101,000, and by 1990–91 it was almost 341,000.[6]

The dominant figure in Uzbekistan's politics during the Brezhnev era was CPUz First Secretary Sharaf Rashidov. During Rashidov's tenure, which stretched from 1959 until his death in 1983, certain aspects of Moscow's control of the republic began to slip. Uzbekistan continued to report great successes – for example, record cotton harvests, miraculous rises in Russian fluency among Uzbeks, and successes in the struggle against religion. In fact, however, many of the "achievements" existed only on paper.

In the late Brezhnev era, Uzbekistan's politics became less dominated by Russians, especially those from outside the republic. At this time, increasing numbers of better-educated ethnic-Uzbek technical specialists and other cadre born after World War II were making their way into positions of responsibility and power. To be sure, certain slots were reserved for "non-Muslim nationalities." But as an increasing proportion of Uzbeks received secondary and higher education, the groundwork was laid for greater indigenization of the state and party bureaucracies.[7]

Attempting to tighten Moscow's control

The CPSU central leadership made a concerted attempt to reassert Moscow's control over all republics of Central Asia in the middle and late 1980s. This process began almost immediately after Brezhnev's death in 1982 and continued until 1989. All Central Asian republic communist party first secretaries either died (and were subsequently disgraced) or were removed during this period. This, however, was merely the tip of the iceberg that

Moscow attempted to destroy. In Uzbekistan, the new party first secretary Inamjan Usmankhojaev directly linked corruption to his predecessor, the late Rashidov. Rashidov's remains were removed from the place of honor in central Tashkent where he was originally buried. As a result of the unfolding purge, only about one-fourth of the CPUz Central Committee full members elected in 1981 were reelected in 1986. In 1986 the purge went into even higher gear, as many officials at all levels of the CPUz and state hierarchy were accused of incompetence and unreliability. Many were arrested, including the (ethnic Russian) former CPUz second secretary, a former chairman of the republican Council of Ministers and a Russian deputy chairman, and the former first secretaries of five of Uzbekistan's then thirteen oblast party committees. In 1986 alone, eight oblast committee secretaries were removed, along with 100 secretaries of city and raion committees, forty chairmen of city and raion executive committees, and eighteen ministers and other agency heads.[8] Significantly, although Usmankhojaev had worked three years in the All-Union party secretariat in Moscow, he had never served in the secretariat of Uzbekistan.[9]

Moscow's efforts in the Usmankhojaev era to reassert control over personnel matters were accompanied by attempts to rein in other aspects of the republic's life as well, including culture. In 1986, when Moscow was already demonstrating greater flexibility towards religion and cultural heritage in Russia, in Uzbekistan the party was reinforcing anti-religious propaganda, slowing the rehabilitation of nationalist writers, and condemning contemporary writers who "idealized" historical figures.

In the wake of the December 1986 disturbances in neighboring Kazakstan, spring 1987 finally brought "cultural glasnost" to Uzbekistan. Nevertheless, the political purge had still to run much of its course. As part of the continued "clean-up," in January 1988, Moscow removed Usmankhojaev and replaced him with Rafiq Nishanov, a long-time foe of former first secretary Sharaf Rashidov. Significantly, Nishanov had spent much of his career outside of Uzbekistan; moreover, neither he nor Usmankhojaev were part of the Jizzakh-Samarkand political axis which had dominated Uzbekistan under Rashidov. Instead, they represented the Tashkent-Fergana region.

The continuing purge is an important reason that glasnost and the atmosphere of the 19th Party CPSU conference did not have a greater effect on politics in Uzbekistan. Although by mid–1989 the situation would radically change, as of 1988, Moscow (through Nishanov) was still loudly condemning Uzbekistan's corruption and attempting to "correct" it by asserting greater control from above. In such an atmosphere it would have been very difficult for "democrats" inside the CPUz to promote reform.

The emergence of informal organizations

Some of the writers who contributed to the re-evaluation of Uzbek history, culture, and Moscow's policies in the conditions of glasnost became the initial core leadership of Uzbekistan's first important informal group, "Birlik" ("Unity").[10] Birlik was established at the meeting of an initiative group on November 11, 1988.[11] In addition to the writers and other members of the creative intelligentsia, the new organization's leadership also included such scientists as Abdurahim Polatov and Shuhrat Ismatullaev.

One of Birlik's central goals was to improve the position of the Uzbek language, in part by granting it the status of state language; Birlik's program also called for an end to the "unjustified denigration" of great Central Asian historical figures. Much of Birlik's program concerned social, economic, ecological, and health issues. Many of these related to reducing Uzbekistan's role as a producer of raw materials, especially cotton.

In addition, Birlik's agenda also had human rights and other more immediately political dimensions. It called for Uzbekistan to become an independent republic of the USSR determining its fate "on the basis of a leninist nationality policy;" it also proposed inviolability of private communications, individual rights to see and dispute materials in dossiers collected by any organization, and legal protection from slander. The Birlik program supported the CPSU's efforts to "reform the USSR's political system," and noted that petitions, demonstrations, and rallies were appropriate forms of participation.

From its very inception, Birlik had an especially close bond with the Uzbekistan Writers Union. Muhammad Salih, besides being one of Birlik's founders, was also a popular poet.[12] A number of his colleagues in the leadership, some of whom did not join until 1989, were also writers and literary critics; they included Ahmad A"zam, Usman Azim, Zahir A"lam, and Dilaram Ishaqova.

Birlik members and sympathizers were active in organizing demonstrations in Tashkent at the end of 1988 and in 1989. Some of these demonstrations took place without official permission from the authorities. The first one, in Tashkent's university district on December 3, 1988, was in support of the Uzbek language.

Although the organization Birlik formally did not organize the December demonstration, it did seek permission for a rally to be held in early 1989. When over the course of at least two months the authorities refused to grant permission for this gathering, Birlik leaders proceeded without authorization; they called a meeting in support of the Uzbek language which was held March 19 on Tashkent's Lenin Square. At this meeting (which according to one source attracted 12,000 participants), writers and other Birlik leaders were permitted to address a large crowd.[13]

Probably recognizing that they could not prevent gatherings, authorities granted Birlik permission to hold another meeting, on April 9, 1989. This one, however, was not held on a central Tashkent square, but in relatively remote Chuqursay raion.[14] Along with changing directives from Moscow, these demonstrations were likely a factor encouraging the CPUz leadership to make modest concessions on language and other issues on the Birlik agenda in the first half of 1989.

While signalling attention to the problems raised by Birlik, authorities continued to condemn the informal organization's techniques, the character of its leadership, and the chaos it was allegedly creating. For example, a report of a Tashkent city party conference referred to "cliques and an unhealthy moral-psychological climate" and efforts by "self-proclaimed leaders" to create extremist formations and the informal associations "Birlik" and "Free Union of Uzbekistan Youth."[15] At about the same time the republic press carried an especially venomous attack on Muhammad Salih, comparing him to Goebbels.[16]

At the very end of the Nishanov era in spring 1989 the CPUz began to show flexibility in admitting that informal organizations could play a positive role in addressing social and political problems. However, it is clear that the party did not consider Birlik a worthy partner for cooperation. Thus, the report of an April 1989 CPUz *buro* meeting specifically mentioned a high level of harmful activity by "some organizers of the unregistered informal association calling itself 'Birlik' . . ." Moreover, it called upon party committees to assure "high political vigilance" and to "assess in a principled fashion facts of complacency, connivance, and unscrupulousness in relation to extremist actions."[17]

Karimov-era Uzbekistan prior to independence

CPUz adoption of opposition platforms

The CPUz's policy toward the informal opposition forces in Uzbekistan changed when Islam Karimov replaced Rafiq Nishanov as republic party first secretary. The most significant change was Karimov's rapid adoption of much more of the Birlik political agenda on such questions as language, rehabilitation of writers, the environment, and health. These new ideas embraced by the CPUz were part of its bid for greater legitimacy based on issues of identity and distribution.

The shift was facilitated by the weakening of the center's power, which also allowed the new leadership to condemn Moscow's purge of the Uzbek political elite. With Karimov's ascension, the anti-corruption campaign of the Usmankhojaev and Nishanov eras began to be publicly portrayed in Uzbekistan as an action led by central party figures who unfairly singled out Uzbekistan for punishment. Thus, Karimov's ascension also marked the end of an assault on much of the old political guard.

Moscow's key role in the purge had indeed caused widespread resentment among Uzbeks. The perception that "their own" leaders were once again taking charge in 1989 served to enhance the legitimacy of the new first secretary. However, like Karimov and former first secretary Sharaf Rashidov, many of the political forces which the new first secretary rehabilitated were members of the Samarkand-Jizzakh political grouping.

Karimov's appointment also marked a new policy concerning "participation." Karimov opened up new opportunities for informal groups to operate and began to distinguish between those individuals (and wings of organizations) which sought to bring the masses into the streets and those who were satisfied to press for reform through more easily controlled activities. Beginning in fall 1989, the regime granted the "law abiding" leaders positive recognition and permitted them greater freedom to promote their ideas.

In fact, the direction of change in policy toward the opposition was becoming evident even before Nishanov was formally removed. In early June, as riots were rocking the Fergana Valley, Nishanov was formally elected chairman of the USSR Supreme Soviet Council of Nationalities. (Thus, it was already clear that a new CPUz first secretary would soon be elected.) At this point – already in Moscow – Nishanov dispatched Abdurahim Polatov, Muhammad Salih, and Mufti Muhammad Sadiq Muhammad Yusuf (head of the Spiritual Directorate of the Muslims of Central Asia and Kazakstan) to the Fergana Valley in order to attempt to quell the violence. The disturbances in the republic at this time may help explain why Karimov, once elected, was willing to try a new tack.

Over the next few months Islam Karimov began to conduct a dialogue with Birlik and other republic informal organizations, and to recognize that they had a positive role to play in the republic's political life. By early fall, the Tashkent oblast party committee held its first official meeting with leaders of Birlik, as well as the groups Intersoiuz and the Democratic Movement of Uzbekistan. In reporting this development, the republic Komsomol press concluded, "In short, there is hope for fruitful cooperation in the very near future."[18] Even Karimov began to speak of "informal movements" as a "natural [zakonomernyi] and objective" phenomenon in democratic development, and an "indicator of the politicization of our society." He explicitly recognized past CPUz mistakes with regard to "informals" and said that now the party had moved from "total non-recognition to constructive dialogue with them."[19]

As will be discussed in more detail below, the Birlik organization was eventually to split. Although the Birlik leadership was fairly united on long-term goals, they did not agree on questions of strategy. Some leaders, such as M. Salih, apparently believed that positive change could be stimulated without mass public meetings. Others, perhaps inspired by the course of events in the Baltic republics, were less inclined to eschew public demonstrations as an instrument of pressure on the Communist Party. The latter group included Abdurahim Polatov.

The differentiation in CPUz policy towards the two wings of Birlik became clearer in an October 1989 Supreme Soviet resolution "On Measures for the Stabilization of the Social-Political Situation in the Republic." (Not coincidentally, the session which adopted this resolution was the same one which adopted the law making Uzbek the republic's sole state language.) The resolution on stabilization criticized individuals disposed to "extremism" who, while frequently "disguising themselves as human rights champions," called for unsanctioned rallies.[20] It explicitly allowed the MVD to use truncheons, handcuffs, and other unnamed "special devices" needed to keep civil peace, and even set aside special funds for awards to those who would "distinguish themselves in strengthening the public order."[21] Karimov also made it clear that the offer to cooperate did not extend to forces who organized people for "hostile and mean goals" and called them "out onto the public squares."[22]

Even for the less maligned reformers the opportunities to participate in the political process remained quite circumscribed. This became evident in the electoral campaign for the new republic Supreme Soviet which unfolded in the late fall and winter of 1989–90. Before looking at this process, however, it is necessary to describe a couple of other informal groups which appeared in the early Karimov era.

As of late 1989, none of the informal organizations besides Birlik was very large or powerful. Nevertheless, as in other republics, in Uzbekistan, too a group named Intersoiuz arose to protect the interests of the non-indigenous nationalities, especially the Slavs. Uzbekistan's Intersoiuz was created as an initiative group meeting in August 1989.[23] Some Birlik leaders asserted that Intersoiuz was itself an invention of the KGB;[24] in any case it had a natural constituency among Uzbekistan's Slavs, many of whom held fears of the "nationalism" vividly portrayed in the republic press. Another group, the Democratic Movement of Uzbekistan (DMU) also became active in late 1989. This organization, which never gained a large membership, supported political reform; on language and cultural issues it seems to have attempted to balance the interests among various nationalities, taking a middle ground between Birlik and Intersoiuz.

The lines within and between informal groups were quite vague and were constantly changing in Uzbekistan between 1989 and 1992. Some groups seem to have existed more on paper than in fact; others split or joined forces with other organizations. Some individuals were simultaneously members of more than one organization. In the absence of the documents themselves, it is difficult to determine specific informal groups' platforms. The problem is even more difficult because at times unauthorized individuals claimed to represent a group's ideas; the CPUz propaganda organs often attempted to misrepresent their opponents' ideas, and it is quite possible that some of the most extreme positions "advocated" by supposed members of individual groups were really concoctions of police disinformation specialists.

In any case, Birlik and DMU encountered numerous obstacles as they attempted to participate in the nomination process for the new (often multi-candidate) February elections to the Supreme Soviet. Thus, for example, a request from Birlik leaders to hold a December 17 mass rally was rejected by the Tashkent city executive committee.[25] Likewise, authorities often blocked nomination meetings and discredited their organizers.[26] According to writer Timur Polatov, authorities decided in advance who was supposed to be nominated in each district, and did what they could to prevent meetings to nominate other candidates. Polatov also maintains that 200 of the candidates who secured nomination – mostly in districts with no contest – were workers of the communist party apparat.[27] No reliable data are available on the election success of candidates supported by informals; one source reports that the 500 deputies elected to the Supreme Soviet included fifty whom Birlik had supported (ten of whom were actually members of that organization); however, another source says that these "Birlik members" were all moderates in fact supported by the authorities.[28] In any case, though these elections were a bit more democratic than the familiar Soviet variety, they left very little room for opposition forces to organize and promote their candidates.

Just prior to the elections the UzSSR Supreme Soviet issued a decree "On Reinforcing Responsibility for Actions Directed Against Public Order and the Security of Citizens." It specified penalties for preparing and distributing materials that created a threat "to the public order or people's safety"; the sanctions, which applied to communications in oral, manuscript, printed, or audiovisual form, could be invoked even for "storage [*khranenie*]" of such items "with intent to distribute."[29]

On the very day of the Supreme Soviet election, February 18, *Pravda Vostoka* published a full page of letters and telegrams from citizens expressing approval of the recent action to reinforce public order.[30] Recent days had given the Karimov leadership good reason to be worried about keeping things calm. Tensions had been rising in Uzbekistan's densely populated Fergana Valley.

Against this background, just three days after the Supreme Soviet election, that body's presidium decreed that "temporarily, until the stabilization of the social-political situation in the republic," there would be no "public processions and demonstrations;" moreover, sanctioned public rallies and meetings would be allowed only if conducted "in prescribed fashion and only in enclosed locations."[31] Within days the press carried additional letters from citizens calling for strict enforcement of these measures rather than, as they implied, lax attitudes which were responsible for illegal release of law breakers.[32]

Given the CPUz's persecution of the "bad" groups and the genuine philosophical disagreement about utility of confrontational tactics, it is not surprising that Salih's wing of Birlik decided to distance itself from those led by Aburahim Polatov. Consequently, on February 20, 1990, Salih became head of a new smaller "Erk Public Organization." ("Erk" translates into English as "Freedom" or "Will.")[33]

A separate and smaller organization had the advantage of permitting better control over membership. According to some sources in Tashkent, the authorities had been infiltrating Birlik with provocateur "extremists" in order to discredit it.[34] In establishing this separate organization, Salih criticized Birlik for having become carried away with public demonstrations.[35]

Within days, the regime was once again to condemn Polatov's Birlik. At the end of February, leaflets had been distributed in the town of Parkent calling on people to attend a Birlik meeting scheduled for March 3. Militia units and MVD troops, which had gathered at the appointed meeting site, clashed with the crowd, leaving four people dead and seventy wounded.[36] *Pravda Vostoka*'s lengthy unsigned article about the event placed the blame for the violence directly on the "not unknown Polatov;" besides allegedly summoning the people to "non-compliance with decisions of state organs," he had supposedly attempted to convince them that the government would not resolve the social and economic problems.[37]

As its treatment of Birlik and Erk demonstrates, the Karimov regime showed a willingness to allow informal organizations to exist and carry out activities, but only within very narrow lines. Many interlocutors interviewed in Tashkent in 1989 and 1990 felt that Muhammad Salih had been "bought off" by the regime. Some were certain that Islam Karimov had even urged Salih to break off from Birlik and form his own organization. Erk members, of course, disagreed; they maintained that Salih remained true to his goals and was acting sensibly, not in weak fashion; in fact, they suspected that the authorities were spreading rumors about Salih's "selling out" merely to discredit him, and to detract from what these members claimed was high popularity.[38] It is impossible, of course, to know Salih's motives for choosing less confrontational tactics and creating a new party. Nevertheless, there is evidence that in 1990 Islam Karimov facilitated the creation of Salih's moderate group.[39]

Given the very poor personal relations between Abdurahim Polatov and Muhammad Salih, it was very difficult for Birlik and Erk to cooperate in Tashkent. Aside from personal factors, there was a widespread feeling among Erk members that Birlik was too radical, whereas the Birlik leadership tended to view Erk as a "pocket" party. Despite this tension at the top, numerous reports from around the country attest to cooperation by local branches of Erk and Birlik.[40]

Birlik apparently remained a much larger organization than Erk. Shortly after the split, it claimed to have over 300,000 members. It had already held founding *qurultays* (congresses) in six oblasts and dozens of raions. In April 1990, some members held a preparatory meeting to organize the "Uzbekistan Democratic Party." This organization held a founding qurultay in June 1990, but it appears to have remained much less important than the "parent" Birlik organization.[41] Given the differentiation of CPUz policy toward Birlik and Erk, it is remarkable that the authorities allowed Birlik to continue to operate and hold congresses. In particular, on May 26–27, approximately 600 members were allowed to gather for the popular movement's third qurultay in Tashkent.[42]

For its part Erk transformed itself from a movement into a political party. Perhaps with Karimov's blessing, on April 30, 1990, its founding qurultay elected a thirty-five-member central committee headed by Muhammad Salih.[43] Erk was permitted to continue to use the Writers Union building for its headquarters until fall 1991, when it moved to the building of the Kuibyshev Raion executive committee. Although in early 1990 Birlik was able to acquire a building (a music studio which belonged to one of its leaders, Zahid Haqnazarov), the authorities closed it down in spring 1991 claiming that it was a health hazard.[44]

The tightening up which would soon begin was undoubtedly closely related to the greater autonomy which Uzbekistan was gaining from Moscow; ironically, this had been one of the primary goals of the Birlik organizers from both wings. In spring 1990, Gorbachev announced that he would be using his office to negotiate a new union treaty, and work on the new treaty began in June. That same month Karimov supported and the republic's Supreme Soviet adopted a declaration of sovereignty.[45]

The more that Uzbekistan could "run its own show," the more Karimov could dictate the terms of political participation in his republic. As early as July, Karimov used an international news conference to stress that public movements and informal organizations appeared not in places like Uzbekistan, but in those where a vacuum of authority existed. After thus implying that there was little need for groups outside the party, he insisted that in

Uzbekistan "[a]ll rights and possibilities have been provided wherever there are *serious* movements (emphasis added)." He continued, "In the very near future all of these organizations will be registered in order for them to have equal rights and opportunities to promote their ideas and for popularizing their policies."[46]

A number of violent outbreaks in spring 1990 also must have encouraged Karimov to pursue a more restrictive policy toward independent political groups, and especially their involvement in public demonstrations. Violence broke out in May in the Fergana Valley city of Andijan, and in early June in nearby Osh oblast (Kirgiz [Kyrgyz] SSR). The latter was especially serious, and developed as a conflict between Uzbeks and Kyrgyz. In tracing the roots of that conflict, many Central Asians have seen the hidden hand of Moscow. Whoever was at fault, the strife demonstrated once again that violence could easily get out of hand. The corollary for Karimov was that everything had to be done to keep politics out of the streets.

Restricting the opposition at the end of the Soviet era

The last months of 1990 and early months of 1991 marked the appearance of new forces challenging the Karimov regime. With the exception of Erk, which continued to enjoy favored treatment, the response of the regime was to increase repression. As we will see, the clampdown became much more severe in 1992. The Karimov regime's policy in this and subsequent periods suggests that it feared threats to its power that might accompany any erosion of the authoritarian system. In this calculation, the regime appears to have given little weight to the possible costs to its legitimacy which might accrue from blocking broader political participation.

The most threatening new group to appear in Uzbekistan in 1990–91 was the Islamic Renaissance Party (IRP). The IRP's membership included Muslims spread out in the Caucasus and Central Asia, as well as in European parts of the USSR. In Central Asia, it was strongest in Tajikistan, where it was active in fall 1990.

Appreciating the political benefits of associating himself with Islam, Karimov had created new opportunities for worship and religious practice. But he had no reason to want to see Islam used as a political banner or weapon by forces he did not control. Regardless of any disagreements he may have had with the head of the official Islamic establishment, Karimov could hardly have been pleased to learn of a demonstration in Namangan with up to 15,000 clergy and other faithful in late summer 1990.[47] The possible use of Islam for political purposes was brought home again in December 1990 when members of the IRP requested permission to hold a founding conference in Tashkent the following month. Authorities denied permission for the meeting and warned the organizers of serious consequences if they proceeded with their plans. The IRP organizers' invitation to Abdurahim Polatov to speak at their meeting must have been especially threatening to the CPUz leadership. Not surprisingly, when over 300 delegates gathered in January 1991 for the unsanctioned IRP conference, authorities quickly forced them to disperse.[48]

It is especially difficult to gather information about this party in Uzbekistan because it was repressed throughout its visible existence in the republic, and because the official media consistently portrayed it in the most threatening and sinister terms. No accurate membership data are available, but one source claims that after the dispersal of the founding conference over 20,000 applications for admission were received.[49]

The publicly proclaimed program of the All-Union IRP was hardly a recipe for violence. In fact, the organization claimed it would operate by constitutional methods and it openly condemned the practice of terrorism, extremism, and all forms of discrimination. It also advocated equality between believers and non-believers. Its "Islamic" inclination manifested itself in such proposals as support for religious education and scholarship, introduction of "the economic principles of Islam," and reinforcement of women's roles as mothers and preservers of "the home and hearth."[50]

New legal foundations were laid which provided a basis for Karimov to increase pressure on such "uncooperative" groups as Birlik and the IRP. One was a new February 1991 law on protecting the honor and dignity of the UzSSR president and other top officials. The law specified the punishments for insulting various officials, with heavier penalties for repeat offenders and those using the mass media. The use of mass media publicly to insult the republic's highest officials could lead to imprisonment for up to six years. According to the law, repeated infractions by a particular mass media institution became grounds for authorities to close it.[51]

In assessing the importance of this law as a weapon to control the opposition, it is critical to note Karimov's masterful use in 1990 of the memory of the late Sharaf Rashidov and the "Uzbek affair," and Birlik's reaction to this. Throughout 1990 Karimov had overseen the rehabilitation of the late first secretary's reputation. After the Moscow-inspired campaign of the 1980s to drag Rashidov through the mud, it was a very effective way to enhance Karimov's own legitimacy (as one who restored Uzbekistan's honor), allow him quietly to restore an aura around his own position, and to justify authoritarian rule.[52]

Birlik leaders were opposed to the authoritarian drift and were not afraid to point out how Karimov was using the "Rashidov" weapon. Because it was impossible to publish such views in Uzbekistan, however, Karimov's opponents turned to outlets in Moscow. Thus, for example, in January 1991,

Izvestiia carried an article by Birlik co-chairmen assessing the glorification of Rashidov as part of "an attempt to bring back totalitarian rule in all its links."[53] Following February 1991, the Moscow press still remained accessible to Karimov's opponents, but the consequences of activities such as portraying the president in an unfavorable light carried more serious legal consequences.

Another early 1991 legal measure to cripple the opposition was the February 15 "Law on Public Associations in the Uzbek SSR."[54] In very vague language, Art. 3 of this law prohibited the creation of associations whose activity was "directed towards the destruction of moral foundations of society, universal humanistic values, and likewise whose goal was the illegal change of the constitutional structure or the destruction of the unity of the territory of the USSR, the Uzbek SSR and the Karakalpak ASSR"; also prohibited were associations seeking to "propagandize war, violence and cruelty, or inflame social hatred (including hatred of a class, or racial, national, or religious [character]), leading to the division of society." Unlike the All-Union law, Uzbekistan's law specifically outlawed religious political parties; it also prohibited the use of "antidemocratic coercive pressure by public associations" on the official organs of power and administration. Art. 22 stipulated that associations which violated these provisions would be dissolved, as would those that failed to heed repeating warnings that they were engaged in activities not included in their charter.

These very vague rules which in effect provided a legal basis to harass or close any organization were accompanied by other rules which made it more difficult for organizations pursuing political goals to finance their work. Art. 18 explicitly prohibited such organizations from receiving any financial or other material help from foreign governments, organizations, or citizens, as well as from religious organizations.

Some provisions of the republic law "On the Mass Media" adopted in June 1991 also restricted the opposition's ability to gather support.[55] For example, although the law prohibited censorship (Art. 2), other provisions were vague enough to provide for prosecution of a very broad range of offenses. Thus, Art. 4 prohibited "use of the mass media . . . to propagandize war, violence, cruelty, or racial, national, or religious exclusivity, to disseminate pornography, or for the purposes of committing other criminally punishable actions." The law provided for suspending an institution's activity for repeated violations of requirements as stipulated by law (Art. 10). It guaranteed the right for a wide variety of organizations to receive permission to establish mass media – including *registered* political parties, public associations, and religious associations (Art. 5). Significantly, in contrast to the analogous All-Union law adopted in 1990, Uzbekistan's did not give individuals the right to establish mass media.

The "Law on Freedom of Conscience and Religious Organizations," adopted simultaneously with the law on mass media, made even more remote the possibility that the IRP could legally become a political force.[56] As provided for in the law on public associations, the new law affirmed that the "creation of activity of any party of a religious nature is not permitted in the Uzbek SSR, nor are branches, departments, or divisions of religious parties created outside the republic" (Art. 7). Likewise, it listed vague categories of activities in which religious organizations could not engage (Art. 5). As all other groups, religious organizations were obliged to receive registration by local authorities, which could in turn revoke the same (Arts. 11–15).

One other organization with political goals should be mentioned in the period prior to August 1991, the Samarkand Society. This association, apparently created in 1989, promoted the cultural interests of the Tajik population in Samarkand. This was an especially sensitive problem because of the competing cultural – if not for the time being political – claims about whether the population of the city is really of Persian or Turkic origin. Little information is available about this group. One source claims that, like Birlik, it was split among those willing to work with Uzbekistan authorities and more radical ones, in this case demanding some form of "independence."[57]

The resources of the opposition political organizations at this time were quite meager. During 1989 and into early 1990, thanks to the collaboration of a few administrators with access to state resources, informal groups had occasionally enjoyed use of public meeting facilities, transport, equipment, and so forth. But by 1991, except for Erk, most of these resources appear to have dried up. The ban on public demonstrations had eliminated one of the best opportunities for political communications that had existed in the early days of Karimov's tenure. Erk and even Birlik were allowed to publish their own newspapers, but the editions were very small, probably no larger than a few thousand copies each.[58] Despite charges by the official press which suggest the contrary, there is no evidence that the leadership of Birlik, Erk, or the IRP advocated or even suggested the use of violence as a political weapon at this time.

The post-coup "thaw"

Although Karimov's ambition to achieve greater control over affairs in Uzbekistan undoubtedly inclined him to seek greater autonomy from Moscow, he was unprepared and probably did not desire the sudden collapse of the center. In any case, the failure of the August 1991 coup in Moscow brought in its wake Uzbekistan's independence, which was declared August 31, 1991. These events put on the new country's political agenda the legitimization of independence and the confirmation of Karimov's place as president through a popular vote. The confirmation of independence itself was not a problem since there does not appear to have been serious organized opposition to it, least of all among Uzbeks, who accounted for over 70 percent of the population.[59] On the other hand, Karimov had not yet achieved an unchallenged position *vis-à-vis* other prominent former communists who wielded considerable support in the Supreme Soviet. This became evident at a Supreme Soviet session about one month after Uzbekistan's proclamation of independence when about 200 deputies, with the support of Vice President Shukrulla Mirsaidov, signed a letter to the legislature's deputies critical of Karimov's increasingly dictatorial position. The details are not clear, but evidence suggests that the vice president may have been attempting to enlist the support of powerful forces in Moscow in opposition to Karimov. Indeed, according to Karimov's press service, the Moscow media reported a distorted version of the expression of dissatisfaction even before the fact – on September 26 – and then repeated it on October 2. At the time, the president's press service admitted that Karimov was criticized at the Supreme Soviet session; however, it claimed that this was nothing "unnatural," and that no attempt had been made to suppress criticism.[60]

During the summer and fall, the Moscow press provided a convenient and accessible forum for the opposition to Karimov, and it was a constant thorn in his side. For its part, the Karimov regime attempted to discredit the Moscow press and to blame it for meddling in the affairs of independent Uzbekistan.[61]

Although only indirectly related to Mirsaidov and the Moscow press, fall 1991 brought something of a political thaw in Uzbekistan. During this time the country prepared for its first presidential elections. The most visible element of the thaw was that Karimov allowed a presidential race in which he permitted his rival to appeal openly for support. Just as important, and perhaps a more positive sign of authoritarian erosion, other political forces such as Birlik and even the IRP were not persecuted as they had been in the preceding months. Birlik even achieved formal registration.

Despite these optimistic signs, Karimov was determined to block any serious challenge to his personal rule. Although he permitted an opposition candidate to face him in the presidential election, he manipulated the rules to make sure that no serious contest took place.

The limits to Karimov's willingness to democratize were evident in the election rules and the deadlines for registration. Although the election was scheduled for December 29, 1991, the rules governing its conduct were not published until November 23; even worse, the rules for collecting signatures – which non-party organizations had to submit to the Central Election Commission by December 3 – was not promulgated until November 26. Due to weekends (that is, non-working days) and the three days required to call a nomination meeting, groups other than registered parties were in effect given only one day to gather the necessary signatures![62]

Because registered political parties were not subject to these regulations, differential treatment of Birlik and Erk registration in fall 1991 was of critical importance. The political party Erk received registration on September 4, 1991. This was the very day of its application and less than a week after Uzbekistan's declaration of independence.[63] Birlik did not have such good fortune. Over a year earlier it had created the "Uzbekistan Democratic Party"; in October 1991, Birlik called another meeting at which it replaced or renamed its older party with one called "Birlik."[64] At about the same time, the Birlik Popular Movement applied to the Ministry of Justice for registration. This was granted on November 12, 1991. This development provided a moment for a rare expression of optimism by co-chairman Abdurahim Polatov, who saw the registration as "Uzbekistan's first step on the road of truly democratic reforms."[65] However, the Birlik *Party*'s application for registration was rejected on the grounds that parties could not be registered with the same name as popular movements.[66]

The Birlik *Party*'s failure to achieve registration meant that it had no right to nominate a presidential candidate without gathering signatures. The Birlik Popular Movement did attempt to do the impossible – that is, to gather the required 60,000 of signatures in the course of one day. Indeed, it claims to have gathered more than the minimum, 63,000. However, because 25,000 of these were rejected by the authorities, the movement was not permitted to register Abdurahim Polatov, its chosen representative, as a candidate for president.[67]

In response to what its leaders claimed was turning the presidential elections into a "farce," the presidium of the Birlik Popular Movement sent a letter to Islam Karimov and Muhammad Salih in which they asked the candidates to refuse to participate in the process. They called for new elections to be scheduled on a "democratic basis," but their appeal was ignored.[68]

Throughout the fall, authorities continued to keep Birlik-organized mass activities under close control. The organization's attempt to hold a mass meeting on September 6 in support of democrats in Russia was dispersed, with 100 participants – including almost the entire Birlik leadership – arrested and fined. Within days Birlik attempted to hold another meeting, which led to even more arrests. According to what Birlik co-chairman Shuhrat Ismatullaev called "entirely reliable sources," the regime mobilized 12,000 militia to prevent the meeting, and prepared a huge quantity of weapons at the stadium where the gathering was supposed to take place.[69]

Despite these problems, the registration of the Birlik Popular Movement was accompanied by greater opportunities for the group leaders to organize, present their views to the population of Uzbekistan, and demonstrate support for various platforms.[70] One striking example of this was a long article by Shuhrat Ismatullaev published in November 1991 in *Pravda Vostoka*. In this article Birlik's co-chair argued for major changes in the proposed law "On the Elections of the President of Uzbekistan." Among other things, Ismatullaev called for popular movements (in addition to political parties) to have the right to nominate candidates for president. He also argued for reducing the required number of signatures from 60,000 to 30,000 or 40,000, and stipulating that international observers be present to assure observance of the election law.[71] One other newspaper, the literary weekly *Ozbekistan adabiyati va san"ati*, published an appeal from the tenth congress of Uzbekistan Writers to President Karimov, expressing the hope that the Birlik Party would be registered.[72] (Such public appeals on behalf of the organization would disappear within weeks, if not days.)

As noted above, Erk's candidate, Muhammad Salih, was not required to gather signatures because he was nominated by a registered party.[73] Nevertheless, the presidential race was hardly played on a level field. One of the greatest advantages was that Karimov as president could directly or indirectly mobilize resources – among them the press, transportation, meeting space, and supplies – in his support. These advantages frequently manifested themselves in subtle ways. For example, the pictures which accompanied the notices of registration of the two candidates for president were of very uneven quality: In contrast to Karimov's, which was quite crisp, Salih's was somewhat blurred.[74]

Moreover, Karimov was the candidate of a large political organization, the People's Democratic Party (PDP). This party had emerged when in September a CPUz extraordinary congress adopted a declaration calling for the PDP's creation.[75] Not all CPUz members joined its successor, but as of December 1, 1991, the PDP had 351,000 members.[76] In contrast, Erk had 3,000 members, while Birlik claimed 500,000 supporters.[77]

In accordance with the election law, all campaign financing for both Salih and Karimov was paid by the government. Given that Karimov was much better known than Salih, this naturally worked to the president's advantage. Likewise, the election rules specified that candidates should have equal access to the mass media. This was clearly violated, as the press devoted much more attention to the incumbent. Karimov's speeches were regularly broadcast on television. Salih was granted only fifteen minutes of air time, and this only after Birlik and Erk supporters demonstrated with demands that this time be provided; in the end, however, two minutes of Salih's speech were cut by censors.[78]

Erk alleged that there were numerous violations of the election law, including the failure to include its representatives in electoral commissions at all levels. Erk also charged that the official republic media refused to print any information about the election law or criticism of the government, that extra ballots were delivered to polling stations, and that artificial obstacles were created to hinder Erk's election observers.[79]

Although in fall 1991 the official Uzbekistan press was more favorable towards Birlik than at any time in the previous year, this policy was not reflected in leniency towards Birlik's own publications. Indeed, at some point in fall 1991, Birlik's newspaper was shut down.[80] For the time being, Erk had better luck. The party, which had been publishing its paper erratically and distributing it informally, gained permission in fall 1991 which theoretically made it possible for readers to subscribe to the paper through official subscription channels.[81]

Although other registered and unregistered public associations and embryonic parties came into existence in fall 1991, none of them were a significant force on a national scale. One of these was the "Free Peasants' Party" which was organized at some point in 1991 but did not hold its founding qurultay until December. It claimed to have 3,000 members. The heart of its program was the distribution of land as private property to peasants, along with reduction of cotton planting, and provision of equipment and technology to allow peasants to shift from cotton to other crops, as well as dairy farming and livestock herding. Although it favored the development of individual and cooperative farms, it did not seek the immediate dissolution of collective and state farms. In the political sphere, the party's program supported a multiparty system with a separation of the legislative, executive, and judicial powers. At least initially, the party's application for registration was rejected because of invalid signatures on its petition.[82]

Another group which registered as a public association at the end of 1991 was the Uzbekistan Writers Union's "Committee to Save the Aral" led by author Pirmat Shermuhamedov. The next year, in 1992, it was transformed into the "Green Party." Its platforms were primarily related to environmental issues. It is unclear whether it ever received registration as a political party; in any case, it was of minimal political importance.[83]

Among the other groups with political aspirations in Uzbekistan in 1991 was the "Turkestan People's Movement." This organization shared many of the ideals of Birlik and Erk, but its orientation went beyond Uzbekistan and extended to the whole of Turkestan. According to some sources, this organization sought to unite the republics of Central Asia into a federation or confederation. Like both Birlik and Erk (and unlike the IRP) this group was secular. An initiative group that gathered in Tashkent in July 1991 to create this organization chose Uzbek poet Bahram Ghayib as chairman. It does not appear that the Turkestan People's Movement ever achieved registration or grew very large.[84] Among other short-lived and minor organizations was the

Homeland National Independence Front (Vatan milliy istiqlal jahbhasi) formed in September 1991 by poet Dadahan Hasan. This organization described itself as a social-political and literary-educational movement.[85]

Of much greater importance, though probably only for a short time, were two religious-based organizations which sprang up in Namangan oblast of the Fergana Valley in fall 1991 – Islam lashkari ("Islamic Forces" or "Islamic Army") and Adalat (Justice). These apparently continued to operate until about March 1992. Adalat, which appeared in October, is said to have cooperated with local authorities in law enforcement operations, organizing neighborhood patrols to combat the rising crime rate. The suspects it arrested were tried by informal courts.[86] Adalat's membership was said to be around 8,000.

In November 1991, Karimov made a scheduled trip to Namangan where he met with local party and government leaders. Informal groups, primarily religious ones, had been promised that four of their representatives would be permitted to meet with Karimov and present their ideas to him. In fact, however, the informal group representatives were not permitted to meet with Karimov, who returned the same evening to Tashkent. Dissatisfaction mounted as word spread around Namangan about this snub. Thousands of people gathered, seizing the former oblast party committee headquarters and demanding that Karimov return to Namangan. When on the next day Karimov met with the demonstrators, he was presented with a list of fifteen demands, said to include the transformation of the former party building into an Islamic center, the establishment of an Islamic republic in Uzbekistan, and legalization of the IRP. Although Karimov consented to the conversion of the building, neither of the latter demands were met.[87]

Before closing this section, a few words should be said about the respective platforms of Muhammad Salih and Islam Karimov in the presidential elections. Karimov's official campaign appeal was vague, referring to such general themes as the importance of Uzbekistan's independence, the spiritual rebirth of society, principles of relations with foreign countries, and the destruction of Uzbekistan's economy under Soviet power. He also spoke in very general terms about economic reform, such as extending privileges and greater freedom to peasants, and the need for a social safety net. Karimov's platform did not contain any specifics about political reform or guarantees of political rights.[88]

In contrast to Karimov, Salih's appeal stressed economic change more than stability. He also emphasized changes in political structures, such as the separation of legislative, executive, and judicial branches of power, and guarantees of such freedoms as speech, press, and assembly. Salih also placed an "absolute priority" on the protection of personal freedoms, including the privacy of communication. In the economic sphere, Salih expressed strong support for the introduction of a market economy and privatization "on a priority basis" of the service and household sectors, as well as the trade system, housing, and unprofitable and low-profit enterprises and farms.[89]

Official election results purported to show that 94 percent of eligible voters took part in the election. In these same tallies, 86 percent of the votes cast for president went to Karimov, and 12 percent to Salih.[90]

Reassertion of authoritarian control

The crackdown of January–July 1992

It is impossible to determine with any certainty what factors encouraged Karimov to allow a "thaw" at the end of 1991. In any case, the early months of 1992 marked its end; indeed, the next three and a half years would bring no significant relaxation of Uzbekistan's authoritarian system. By July 1992, Karimov's regime had suppressed even Erk to such an extent that M. Salih would withdraw from the official political process and soon flee the country.

The first signs of Karimov's harsher policy appeared during a January 16, 1992 student demonstration in Tashkent organized to express economic grievances. Despite rapidly escalating food costs, students had failed to receive ration coupons allowing them to purchase food at reduced prices. When the demonstrating students refused militia orders to disperse, shots were fired into the crowd, killing at least one student and seriously wounding others. The next day students gathered from early morning to protest militia actions. Eventually, the militia shot into the air and used truncheons to force the students to disperse. Authorities then declared a "winter vacation." Students were sent home, despite the fact that it was the middle of the exam session.

Curiously, the demonstrations brought a rare moment of apparent harmony among such diverse forces as Birlik and the Karimov regime. On the second day of the protest, Tashkent Mayor Adham Fazylbekov, Abdumannob Polatov, and Muhammad Salih attempted to urge calm on the crowd. In commenting later on the crisis, Karimov acknowledged the positive role played by some of the opposition groups. According to some accounts, the president even publicly promised that the Birlik Party and the IRP would soon be registered. He also stated that unlike certain individuals who were invested with power, Birlik did not engage in filthy provocation.[91] The latter was almost certainly a reference to Shukrulla Mirsaidov, whom, as we will see briefly, Karimov had recently demoted.

Karimov's fears of losing control were undoubtedly aggravated by events in neighboring Tajikistan, where in November 1991 the former communist leader Nabiev had won election as president in a much more closely contested election than Uzbekistan's. Moreover, the strong showing by the coalition opposition was followed by demands – eventually agreed to – for a coalition government; throughout most of 1992, fighting among heavily armed factions was to take place in much of Tajikistan. The Tajik case showed how Islam could be used successfully to rally political support in opposition to the old communist apparat.

In early 1992, two government structural changes in Uzbekistan reinforced Karimov's position. One was the introduction of the institution of "hakim" (governor), approved at a special session of the Supreme Soviet on January 4. Much in the spirit of the old communist system, the new law stipulated that hakims were to be appointed and removed by the president, with decisions confirmed by the oblast level councils. In similar fashion, raion level hakims were to be appointed and removed by oblast hakims, with confirmation by the raion council.[92] Within a few more days, President Karimov issued a decree eliminating the post of vice president. Karimov's rival who had occupied that post, Shukrulla Mirsaidov, was appointed "state secretary"; the newly created post of prime minister was filled by Abdul-hashim Mutalov. (A week later Mirsaidov resigned from his new post in protest.)[93]

Another institutional move followed in March 1992, with the creation of the presidential committee for state control. This body, the "highest control organ serving the executive branch," was given responsibility for investigating activities of public officials in implementing laws and decrees adopted by the Supreme Soviet, and the executive orders of the President. The new Commission was to "investigate the work of and send 'mandatory instructions' to, ministries, agencies, financial and tax services, local organs of executive authority and all enterprises, both state and privately owned."[94]

As the regime was severely limiting the possibilities for dissident voices to organize within the legislative and executive branches, it also took measures to limit opportunities for foes to find support in other quarters. On April 3, the Supreme Soviet presidium adopted a resolution "On Measures to Prevent the Illegal Financing of Public Associations of the Uzbekistan Republic." This measure prohibited political parties and mass movements that pursued political goals from financing their publications with funds from religious organizations, or from foreign states, organizations or citizens. It also entrusted the Ministry of Finance to review declarations on sources of funding for all associations seeking registration in the republic, and to "strictly adhere" to the relevant regulations in the February 15, 1991 Law on Public Associations.[95]

These and other regulations provided a basis for some of the growing harassment of forces that Islam Karimov did not control in spring 1992. As it became ever clearer that Uzbekistan's legal institutions would not provide protection of rights that are essential to a civil society, dissident forces sought to create bodies outside the official ones. One such effort was the Uzbekistan Human Rights Society, organized under the leadership of Abdumannob Polatov, Abdurahim Polatov's brother. Refusing to register this organization, the Karimov regime instead created and quickly registered a rival state-controlled "National Committee for the Protection of Human Rights." Contrary to the rules on registration, this latter organization was approved even though it had not yet adopted its statutes.[96]

Another attempt to circumvent official institutions and organizations was *Milliy Majlis*, founded in May 1992 by a political dissident of the Soviet-era, Babur Shakirov. Preliminary drafts of the organization's charter indicated that its leaders intended to coordinate a broad grouping of opposition organizations and serve as an alternate "parliament."

The growing repression convinced a wide range of the opposition – including Muhammad Salih – that a change in the dynamics of republic politics would come only with the election of a new Supreme Soviet. Consequently, as the preparations were made for the early July convening of the Supreme Soviet, leaders of Birlik and Erk held an unprecedented joint news conference where they announced plans for a demonstration on Tashkent's Independence (formerly Lenin) Square and in other cities to demand dissolution of the Supreme Soviet and new parliamentary elections.

On May 28, just two days before the planned protest, a group of plain-clothes men attacked and severely injured Abdurahim Polatov with metal rods as he emerged from an interrogation at the procuracy building in Tashkent.[97] The regime dispatched the militia in great force to prevent the planned demonstrations. In Tashkent during the day of July 2, authorities even closed down the subway stop nearest Independence Square "for technical reasons."[98]

The Karimov regime's increasingly crude tactics made Muhammad Salih lose any hope that change could be achieved from within the system. In a journal article that went to press in May 1992 he is quoted as saying that Erk favored "cooperation with the official powers on the basis of mutual respect, pluralism of opinions, and political freedom;"[99] in July, however, he walked out of the Supreme Soviet session that his party claimed was illegal, and he resigned from his seat.[100] Karimov, for his part, justified the continuing crackdown. In his speech on the day that Salih left the Supreme Soviet the president stated, "It is necessary to straighten out the brains of one hundred people in order to preserve the lives of thousands."[101]

Consolidating and "legalizing" the crackdown

Although beginning with the July 1992 session of the Supreme Soviet both Erk and Birlik were marginalized, they would remain legal forces into 1993. In the meantime, the Karimov regime intensified repression against both organizations and created a new "opposition." It also increasingly sought to isolate Uzbekistan from external "interference" in Uzbekistan's politics, and to give the changes a sheen of legitimacy through the adoption of the new constitution. Not coincidentally, this process went hand-in-hand with Uzbekistan's participation in bringing "order" to neighboring Tajikistan.

In late July, just weeks after Salih's departure from the Supreme Soviet, a new law took effect which provided a basis for that now even more compliant body to remove independent members. According to this law, in "exceptional cases" the parliament could "curtail the powers of deputies prior to the expiration of their terms of office." Among the conduct which qualified for such treatment was anything that "besmirch[ed] or discredit[ed] the high calling of people's deputy" or "unconstitutional acts directed . . . at destabilizing the sociopolitical situation, or calling for such acts. . ."[102] Against this background, in August, another major opposition figure with a parliamentary seat, former Vice President Mirsaidov, also resigned in protest.[103] In the coming months various techniques would be used to force out other non-compliant Supreme Soviet deputies as well.[104]

The regime had been tightening censorship and other control of information ever since early 1992. This process intensified in the summer of that year. *Erk* newspaper editors found it increasingly difficult to publish materials critical of the regime and to distribute their publication. Paper, largely under government control, was in critically short supply. This forced *Erk* to cut its print run, which meant that it was no longer available through kiosks, only through subscription.[105] By January 1993, the paper was shut down entirely.

The Birlik publication *Mustaqil haftalik*, which was never available by subscription to anyone, was also subjected to new interference. By fall 1992, entire editions of the publication (published in Moscow) were being confiscated by the Tashkent MVD.[106] Local authorities throughout Uzbekistan were usually able to prevent publication in their jurisdictions even without citing political reasons. Most printing facilities in Uzbekistan are controlled by oblast administrations, which can charge prohibitively high prices or simply make excuses such as inadequate capacity.[107] By the end of 1992, the risks increased for anyone who might try to issue publications without official sanction. Uzbekistan's criminal code was supplemented with an article threatening violators with heavy fines and confiscation of equipment.[108]

A new "Law on Protection of State Secrets" signed in May 1993 placed additional restrictions on the dissemination of information, and even its disclosure. In accordance with this law, individuals could be held responsible (and, presumably, punished) for revealing information that would "entail grave consequences . . . for the economic and political interests" of Uzbekistan, as well as information in areas of science, technology, and production and management, "the disclosure of which would inflict damage" on the interests of Uzbekistan.[109]

Against the background of these changes, the new party Progress of the Homeland (PH, Vatan taraqqiyati) was created to replace Erk. Not coincidentally, its founding on May 26, 1992 preceded by only one month the Abdurahim Polatov beating and Muhammad Salih's departure from the Supreme Soviet.[110]

The squeeze on local media was accompanied by greater controls on access to media from Russia. In fall 1992, authorities clashed with *Izvestiia* when the latter complained that editions printed in Tashkent had failed to carry an article criticizing Uzbekistan censorship. This eventually led to Uzbekistan's refusal to print *Izvestiia* editions in Tashkent, which had been running at 160,000 copies. Similarly, in fall 1992, Uzbekistan prohibited the importation of *Komsomol'skaia pravda*.[111] Republic authorities also began to take steps toward insulating the population from unwanted "interference" in electronic media. In January 1993, Karimov's press secretary sent a letter to the chairman of Russia's state-run television and radio broadcasting company threatening to discontinue transmitting Ostankino broadcasts on the territory of Uzbekistan unless Ostankino condemned and halted the broadcast of what the press secretary called slanderous information about Uzbekistan.[112]

Although a great number of arrests, beatings, and other forms of intimidation and pressure were used by the regime in the months after the Supreme Soviet session, it will suffice here to point to a few to note the variety and the wide range of opponents against whom they were directed. In August 1993, former Vice President Mirsaidov was charged with embezzlement, abuse of position, and sentenced to three years in prison.[113] The wife of Abdulla Otaev, head of the illegal IRP, reported that her husband was abducted from his home in December 1992 by six men armed with submachine guns and never heard from again.[114] In September 1992, a mysterious fire destroyed the apartment of Birlik activist and journalist Anvar Usmanov, who at the time was away in Turkey.[115] One of the most bizarre incidents involved the December 1992 kidnapping of Abdumannob Polatov from Bishkek. Upon repatriation, the human rights activist was sentenced to three years in a corrective labor colony. (He was soon released, however, under a presidential amnesty.[116])

Polatov's abduction occurred on the very same December day as the ratification of Uzbekistan's new constitution. Although this document contained many democratic-sounding provisions, some others left individual citizens' rights unprotected. For example, Art. 10 gave the Aliy Majlis (the new parliament) and the President of the Republic the "exclusive right to act on behalf of the people." It explicitly denied this right to any section of society, political party, public association, movement, or individual. Art. 20 of the constitution mandated that citizens' exercise of rights "shall not encroach on the lawful interests, rights, and freedoms of other citizens, the state or society." And although Art. 29 guaranteed citizens the right to seek, obtain, and disseminate any information, this did not apply to cases of information "directed against the existing constitutional structure and in some other instances specified by law."

The new party system and the state

In March 1993, the Karimov regime removed the legal foundation of operations for Birlik and Erk through a Cabinet of Ministers resolution requiring the re-registration of all public associations in the republic by October.[117] In the case of Birlik, the writing on the wall had appeared already in December 1992, when by a vote of 383 to 7 the Supreme Soviet called for an investigation of the organization to determine if it had violated any provisions of the Law on Public Associations.[118] In January 1993, a legal collegium of the Supreme Court suspended the movement's activity for three months; in supporting this action the Ministry of Justice claimed that Birlik activists had "spoken out with words and conversations offending the authority, honor, and dignity of the President and other leaders of the republic on the pages of the official and unofficial mass media."[119] Probably feeling that it would be a useless exercise, the Erk leadership did not seek to renew its registration. In September 1993, Birlik submitted registration documents by mail to the Ministry of Justice, but the Ministry claimed never to have received them.[120]

Given the increasing danger to individuals involved in Erk and Birlik activity, fewer and fewer people were willing to publicly associate themselves with the organizations, and some former members of Erk publicly denounced the organization and its leaders, saying that they had been misled or that the organization had changed for the worse.[121] It is important to note that even at its peak Erk membership remained quite modest. As of mid-1992, when the organization was still operating legally, the party headquarters in Tashkent had only four full-time paid workers on its staff. In the early months of 1992, in the wake of the presidential election, Muhammad Salih claimed that Erk's membership had mushroomed from 18,000 to 45,000. In any case, other reports indicate that by the end of the year membership was only 5,000.[122] A few other small parties appeared in 1992 and 1993, but it became increasingly clear that the only politically significant ones were Karimov's People's Democratic Party and the pocket party Progress of the Homeland (PH).[123]

As noted above, PH had been founded at the end of May 1992. Its leader was former Birlik activist and poet Usman Azim, who since his departure from Birlik had made his peace with the regime and become Karimov's adviser on youth problems. PH held its founding congress in Tashkent in August 1992, and by the end of that year had held meetings to establish its presence in almost all oblasts of the country. By January 1993 it claimed 15,000 members, and by fall 1994, approximately 35,000. The party proclaims that it represents "practitioners," including businessmen in areas of banking, joint enterprises, and trade.

Given the persecution of true opposition groups, PH's growth could only have occurred with Karimov's blessing. Indeed, PH's existence allowed Karimov to declare that he allowed more than one party, but it did not pose any challenge. According to PH's own press service, the party's primary goal is not "the struggle for power" but rather cooperation with the government for the country's well being. The party maintains that "the authority of the president means the authority of all of Uzbekistan," and it has expressed thanks to the "boldness and selflessness of our Yurtbashi [President Karimov]," that "the sun of independence is shining."[124] In all of the available information about Progress of the Homeland, there is no indication that it has ever criticized any policies of Karimov or his party.

The PDP, of course, with over 300,000 members and 12,000 primary party organizations, is much more powerful than any other political party in Uzbekistan. But such figures reveal only part of the organization's strength. Indeed, Karimov's power today is based less on the PDP itself than on the close integration of the PDP and the state, other semi-official institutions, and their ability to command resources. The shift to reliance on state rather than party began in the Soviet era, and the phenomenon was one that affected the All-Union as well as the republic parties. Today Karimov's post as chairman (*rais*) of the PDP has become far less important than his post as president.

It is clear that the state is not neutral in the sense of all parties having equal access to it. The Uzbekistan Foreign Ministry, for example, illustrated the partiality to the PDP – or at least to Karimov – in predicting in 1995 that if presidential elections were held in 1997, "without any doubt" the president would be re-elected due to his "supreme authority and popularity among the people."[125] Just as the Communist Party before it, the PDP also has close ties with many other semi-official organizations, such as the Youth Union. In recent elections, leaders of the Council of Federations of Trade Councils, the Women's Committee, and the Society of Invalids all agreed to support PDP candidates.[126]

The strong executive office which underpins Karimov's authority was reinforced by May and September 1993 laws "On the Republic Cabinet of Ministers" and "On State Power," respectively. The former reaffirmed the president's power to appoint and dismiss the prime minister, deputy prime ministers, and members of the Cabinet of Ministers (with confirmation by the parliament), and the latter reaffirmed the president's power to appoint and remove oblast hakims (with confirmation by the oblast soviet). This law gives powers to the oblast hakims *vis-à-vis* raions which are analogous to the president's *vis-à-vis* the oblast. Moreover, it gives great powers to the oblast and lower level hakims by putting them in charge of both the legislative and executive structures at their respective levels.[127]

Elections to a new parliament and the aftermath

With authoritarian culture firmly reestablished at least for the short term, Uzbekistan prepared to create the structure of its new Aliy Majlis and to elect it. In December 1993, it adopted a law "On the Election to the Aliy Majlis of the Republic of Uzbekistan," and in May 1994, an analogous law on elections to oblast, raion, and city and town councils. Only in September 1994 were elections announced for December and a law adopted "On the Aliy Majlis of the Republic of Uzbekistan." Although Art. 77 of the constitution provided for 150 seats in the legislature, the September 1994 law changed this to 250.[128]

To judge from the law setting out its powers, the Aliy Majlis is potentially a very powerful body. It can amend the constitution with a two-thirds majority. It also has the right to ratify presidential decrees concerning the prime minister and deputy prime ministers, and elects the supreme and constitutional courts.[129]

Uzbekistan's government structure and election law, however, especially in combination with the current political atmosphere, militate against the legislature becoming an independent force. One major reason is that only two kinds of organizations can nominate candidates. One type is oblast councils, which – because oblast hakims are selected by the president – are controlled directly from above.[130] In an environment where voting is still not secret, few citizens are willing to vote against local political bosses.[131] Although political parties may nominate candidates, this right is given only to parties which have been registered for at least six months with the Ministry of Justice. In the case of the December 1994 election, parties would have had to have been registered even prior to adoption of the September law with this provision.[132]

In one sense, the December 1994 balloting did offer voters of Uzbekistan a great choice. Of the 250 seats, only 5 were uncontested; 106 districts had 2 candidates and 139 districts had 3.[133] But it would be next to impossible for a candidate opposed to government policy to gain a place on the ballot. At least one candidate from Progress of the Homeland, however, was more outspoken than authorities wished: a meeting of the Central Electoral Commission removed Rustam Usmanov as a candidate from his district because he was said to be "preparing and distributing leaflets which denigrated citizens' constitutional rights and freedoms."[134]

According to official statistics, 93.4 percent of the eligible electorate took part in Uzbekistan's December 1994 parliamentary elections. After subsequent runoffs were held early in the new year, 69 seats (28 percent) of the Aliy Majlis had been won by PDP-nominated candidates, 167 (67 percent) by candidates nominated by oblast councils, and 14 (6 percent) nominated by PH. This was not, however, a rout for the PDP. According to a local human rights organization estimate, 90 percent of the 205 deputies elected in the first round of voting – including the vast majority of the oblast soviet-nominated – actually represented the president's party. Moreover, the PDP nominees were more successful at the oblast level, where they won 37 percent of the seats, and still better at the raion and city levels, where they garnered 54.5 percent.[135]

In 1995 there were a few subtle signs which might be interpreted as a willingness by President Karimov to relax political controls and open opportunities for meaningful political participation by opposition forces. In January, for example, Karimov dispatched his minister of justice to the US for a meeting with many of the opposition leaders, including Muhammad Salih, Abdurahim and Abdumannob Polatov, and even his ex-minister of justice (who also served as ambassador to the US before requesting and receiving political asylum).

Karimov's speech to the new Aliy Majlis also seemed to suggest that he intended to take a more modest role. After calling for a whole system of laws to expand the rights of public associations, foundations and unions, Karimov reacted to a deputy who had cited him ten times in a single speech with a lecture about the need to maintain the separation of powers.[136]

The regime has also tried to create the image of more debate within the Aliy Majlis itself. Subsequent to the elections, a new organization called the Adalat Social Democratic Party was created under the leadership of deputy Anvar Jorabayev, who was also editor of the government newspaper *Khalq sozi*. Forty-seven deputies were said to belong to this party's fraction in the parliament.[137] This is very puzzling on two counts. Presumably many of the new party's members were, at the time of their election, members of the PDP, even if they were not nominated by that organization. Moreover, the name "Adalat" has a special significance in that, as described above, it had also been used by Islamic groups in the Fergana Valley. More recently, however, in late 1994 or early 1995, former Vice President Mirsaidov had himself organized a party named "Adalat" with himself as co-chairman![138]

The creation of the Adalat Social Democratic Party has been followed by still another party, the National Revival Democratic Party (Milliy tiklanish). Its spring 1995 congress elected a presidium consisting largely of writers, scholars, and educators. This is clearly not an opposition party; in fact, some of its leaders also head committees in the parliament chosen in the recent elections.[139]

At about the same time that Milliy tiklanish appeared, a new mass organization with the name "Birlik" also made its debut. To judge from the composition of its forty-nine-member central council, it appears unlikely to pursue an independent course. The council includes many of the chairmen of Uzbekistan's officially sanctioned ethnic minority cultural centers, newspaper editors and deputy editors, and Aliy Majlis deputies elected in late 1994 and early 1995.[140] Although the new "Birlik" ostensibly has no connection to the informal mass organization which was active between 1989 and 1992, it is remarkable that the regime has decided to recycle the name.

The creation of these organizations has been accompanied by other signs that Karimov is going through the motions of democratic process without permitting (let alone creating) favorable conditions for a civic culture: The first session of the Aliy Majlis decided to hold a referendum in March 1995 to extend Karimov's presidential term – due to expire in 1997 – until the year 2000. (The reason given for this was to coordinate the president's and legislature's terms.)[141] Preparations were quickly made for the vote, in which – in true authoritarian fashion – 99.6 percent of the electorate was said to have participated, with an overwhelming 99.4 percent approving.

Despite these negative signs, recent political events provide some basis for optimism concerning authoritarian erosion. One is that a new generation of politicians is emerging. For all its compliance, the Aliy Majlis nevertheless contains a high proportion of new faces. Most of them are hakims of oblasts and raions, and economic leaders and party functionaries who have advanced in recent years. This is not a group of radicals, but it is very significant that only 67 of the 636 *candidates* for the Aliy Majlis had served in the previous Supreme Soviet. Moreover, over 95 percent of the candidates had a higher education.[142] Likewise, chairman of the Aliy Majlis Erkin Khalilov is a fairly young politician who had been appointed acting speaker of the parliament in December 1983 at age 38; his career had included a stint as a department head at the Academy of Science's Institute of Philosophy.[143] None of this, however, is convincing evidence that the new Aliy Majlis members seek to overhaul or destroy an autocratic system.

The legitimacy crisis and political reform

Most of the discussion in this chapter has dealt less with "legitimacy issues" than with the "coercive" side of Karimov's policies, that is, his efforts to restrict mass political participation and participation by his political opponents. This does not mean, however, that Karimov has been blind to the need to cultivate legitimacy. Indeed, Karimov's adoption of the Birlik and Erk platforms in 1989–90 can be viewed as efforts to undermine the opposition's legitimacy and to enhance his own. In practice Karimov went much further in adopting the informal opposition's policies related to identity than those concerning participation or distribution. But even in the latter two areas – and especially since the end of the Soviet era – Karimov has demonstrated a keen appreciation of the relation between legitimacy and political compliance.

In the case of identity, the country's post-Soviet leadership has presided over the glorification of Uzbekistan, with the Uzbek people as the country's *primus inter pares*. Attempting to reassure nervous minorities, Karimov has pointedly and repeatedly remarked that Uzbekistan is the home of all of nationalities inhabiting its territory (and not just the Uzbeks). In many ways, however, independent Uzbekistan's policy on this score is reminiscent of the Soviet era, when official statements about equality of nationalities were nevertheless qualified about a special role for Russia, the Russian people, and Russian culture. Although Slavs and other non-Uzbeks often perceive "Uzbek first" policies as irritating and demeaning, it appears that many Uzbeks approve of them as a way to redress perceived and real denigration suffered under Soviet rule. This, in turn, may contribute substantially to the president's legitimacy among the Uzbek population.[144]

"Nationality," of course, is just one of the relevant categories concerning identity in Uzbekistan today. As noted above, regional identities are still very strong and politically important. To date, Islam Karimov seems to be following a Soviet-era pattern of balancing regional interests yet promoting cadres from his own political homeland (in Karimov's case the Samarkand-Jizzakh region).

Without the controlling hand from Moscow, competing regional interests in Uzbekistan might eventually contribute to a breakdown of authoritarianism in society. The correlation of forces in the republic may eventually force Karimov or his successor to build regional coalitions, and thus promote this process. As evident, however, in Karimov's reaction to the challenge from former Vice President Mirsaidov, at least in their early stages these challenges do not necessarily encourage the use of democratic procedures in dealing with opponents.

Karimov's reaction to the IRP suggests that he fears an opposition movement could exploit Islam for political purposes. The president has been careful to show great deference to Islam (for example, performing the *haj* and taking his oath of office with his hand on a Koran) and in his speeches he has identified Islam as an integral part of Uzbek culture. At the same time, Karimov has insisted that Uzbekistan is a secular state. To date this approach has not evoked mass dissatisfaction among Uzbekistan's Muslims. Moreover, it appears unlikely that such dissatisfaction alone would unite Uzbekistan's people in a movement to promote change, let alone overthrow the government. Islam, after all, means very different things to different segments of Uzbekistan's population, and it would likely be difficult for such diverse groups to agree upon a common definition, and certainly a common leadership. Nevertheless, under certain economic and social conditions, Islam could become the symbolic standard for opposition; in this capacity it has the potential to bring closer together a broad spectrum of opposition forces which would otherwise be divided along regional, nationality, and linguistic lines. Perhaps over time, mass (or even elite) political organizations based on perceived regional, ethnic, linguistic and/or even class interests will evolve in Uzbekistan. To date, however, such bodies do not exist. They have been precluded by the severe limitations on all political activity in Uzbekistan.

Throughout his tenure, and especially since independence, Karimov has faced very complex economic problems. As other leaders of the post-Soviet states, he has had to attempt to increase or at least maintain economic production while assuring that economic stratification does not create social unrest. Many of the most important factors affecting Uzbekistan's economy – above all developments in Russia and the disruptions and barriers in the former single Soviet economic space – are largely beyond his control. Moreover, as elsewhere, the most obvious solutions to some of Uzbekistan's economic difficulties threaten to exacerbate others.

Although it is impossible to fix an accurate dollar amount on the country's economic output, Uzbekistan appears to have been more successful than most other post-Soviet states in minimizing the drop from the agricultural and industrial production levels of the late Soviet era. According to EBRD data, the worst annual drop in GDP was in 1992 (11.1 percent), the same year as the greatest drop in industrial output (12.3 percent).

The apparently modest drops in these indicators, however, are more a sign of the regime's reluctance to begin the painful process of economic reform than one of successful economic innovation. Indeed, in some major ways efforts to maintain production and preserve the social safety net have worked against economic reform. This approach has meant that many inefficient factories have continued to operate, and that it has remained unattractive for private suppliers to offer goods or services which might otherwise leave state

Table 10.2 *Indicators of economic trends in Uzbekistan since 1989*

	1989	1990	1991	1992	1993	1994	1995[a]
GDP	3.7	1.6	-0.5	-11.1	-2.3	-3.5	-2
Industrial output	3.6	1.8	1.8	-12.3	-8.3	n.a.	n.a.
Rate of inflation	0.7	3.1	82.2	645	534	1,568	315
Rate of unemployment	0	0	0	0.1	0.2	0.4	n.a.
GNP per capita	n.a.	n.a.	n.a.	n.a.	n.a.	2,390	n.a.
% Workforce in private activity[b]	n.a.	n.a.	n.a.	42.2	48.7	59.7	n.a.
% GDP from private sector[b]	n.a.	n.a.	n.a.	38.8	46.7	54.2	n.a.

Notes: GDP – % change over previous year; industrial output – % change over previous year; rate of inflation – % change in end-year retail/consumer prices; rate of unemployment, annual average as of end of year; GNP per capita – in US dollars at PPP exchange rates. [a]Estimate. [b]Non-state sector.

Sources: European Bank for Reconstruction and Development, *Transition Report 1995: Economic Transition in Eastern Europe and the Former Soviet Union* (London: EBRD, 1995); European Bank for Reconstruction and Development, *Transition Report Update, April 1996: Assessing Progress in Economies in Transition* (London: EBRD, 1996).

management. A new class of "businessmen" has appeared in Uzbekistan, but by and large they seem to be former Komsomol or party activists who have used their skills, positions, and contacts to generate new profit-making ventures. A recent *Economist Intelligence Unit* report characterized privatization in Uzbekistan as "simply the appropriation of state property by the *nomenklatura*, communist bosses turning into businessmen."[145] To the extent that this "private sector" is flourishing, it probably owes more to monopolies and special government favors than market forces. For this reason, the EBRD data on percent of workforce in "private activity" and percent of GDP from the "private sector" should not be taken at face value. In time, business people may organize in independent fashion in order to promote their own independent economic interests. (Indeed, the PH party is supposedly one of "businessmen.") To date, however, there has been little evidence of independent political activity by such individuals.

There is no evidence that workers' or other unions in Uzbekistan have served at all as centers for potential political organization. The trade unions, for example, are very closely tied to the current regime. This is demonstrated in a very brief account of their recent congress which heralds the "high awards" that the president has granted a group of union activists; the same account reports Karimov's greetings to the congress, notes the support for his policies as a "program of action for the future," and announces that the parliament's decision to hold a referendum on extending Karimov's term of office as president until the year 2000 has received "the enthusiastic approval and support of the entire population of our country." (This was, incidentally, more than a week *in advance of* the referendum.)[146]

Popular fear of disorder and of even greater economic deterioration may well be among the major reasons that Uzbekistan's population has been reluctant to press their leaders for more economic or political change. In a recent survey in Uzbekistan, about 90 percent of respondents said that they considered "establishing government control over prices" and the need to "strengthen social order and discipline" to be among the "most important" problems in their country.[147] Karimov's awareness of such sentiments is reflected in Uzbekistan's press, which prominently carries articles purporting to show that Uzbekistan's citizens are faring well compared to inhabitants of other post-Soviet states. The worst-case scenario – which occupies a special place in Uzbekistan's media – is war-torn Tajikistan. Reports of instability there and elsewhere undoubtedly aggravate fears of change and for the time being foster patience with a political order that supports a tolerable – even if deteriorating – standard of living.

Ultimately, of course, in order to satisfy the demands of Uzbekistan's population, the government will need to encourage economic growth. Fortunately, Uzbekistan possesses considerable natural wealth, including gold, oil, and gas. There is reason to hope that such factors will help Uzbekistan raise its GDP and become less dependent on other countries for energy. It remains to be seen, however, whether the masses will benefit from the wealth which will in the first place end up in the hands of a small elite. Inflation has certainly taken a toll on the buying power of many of Uzbekistan's citizens. Despite increases, wages are not keeping up with the high annual rates of inflation. Today, many inhabitants of Uzbekistan whose standard of living is stagnant or dropping are nevertheless aware that a better life is possible, and that a select few of their fellow citizens are enjoying it. This is, perhaps, not such a big change, for great discrepancies in wealth were present in Soviet-era Uzbekistan as well. But today the masses are confronted with fancy shop windows, kiosks, and mass media advertising that bring home the message that only a few can afford many of the goods that are becoming increasingly "available." Over time, this could erode much-needed legitimacy.

Closely related to this is the impact of widespread crime and corruption. Many citizens of Uzbekistan – both "haves" and "have-nots" – may share the view that crime *does* pay. It should be noted in this regard, however, that the regime has undertaken a broadly publicized campaign to combat crime and corruption. In a recent USIA-commissioned survey, 88 percent of respondents in Uzbekistan identified the fight against crime as a "very important" task for their country's leaders; and 83 percent said the same about fighting corruption.[148] To the extent that Karimov's efforts in this area are effective (or, perhaps more important, broadly perceived as effective), they may contribute to enhanced legitimacy. If they are viewed as a sham, however, they could have the opposite effect.

Despite the limits on political participation and Uzbekistan's at best negligible progress toward democratization, Karimov has also attempted to enhance legitimacy by encouraging the perception that Uzbekistan's citizens now have a genuine voice in their country's political affairs. In important ways Karimov's policies – as when he claims that over 99 percent of the population voted in favor of the referendum to extend his presidential term to the year 2000 – maintain well established Soviet traditions. The Soviet legacy – in particular the "voluntary" political participation which was in fact obligatory – also helps to explain the population's willingness to accept such practices. The high rates of voting and "approval" in recent balloting in Uzbekistan tell more about coercion than legitimacy; it is also unlikely that the 1994 and 1995 election and referendum enhanced Karimov's legitimacy any more than similar practices legitimized the communist regime during the Soviet era.

As described above, opposition movements have had very little success in mobilizing the masses against Uzbekistan's former communist leaders. In addition to the Soviet heritage, cultural factors may also play a very important role. In Uzbek society, figures of authority, especially the elderly, enjoy great reverence. It is very difficult for young people to create groups of political opposition in rural areas, where veteran farm chairmen and other Soviet-era local elites still have great authority, and where would-be organizers face tremendous logistical problems of communication and transportation.

As noted above, Karimov's regime seems to see fear rather than legitimacy as the most important way to achieve mass compliance with its rules. However, even to the extent that it depends *on legitimacy*, this appears only remotely related to participation. Karimov seems to believe that at present the masses will *not* judge his regime primarily by whether it creates conditions for uninhibited voluntary political activity from below; for the time being he has likely written off political participation as a source of legitimacy.

Survey data suggest that Karimov's calculation on this issue are well-founded. In one recent study, fewer than half of the respondents in Uzbekistan claimed to believe that securing a free press and free speech were important problems. Moreover, only one-eighth said they felt that a "Western style democracy" was the best political system to promote resolution of their country's problems. And even among that small group, just one fourth stated that a politician should be "democratic" in order to win votes.[149]

Another study presents a picture of similar beliefs. Only 32 percent of respondents in its sample said they felt it was "very important" for Uzbekistan's media to be independent, and only 16 percent expressed "strong agreement" with a statement that political opposition is necessary in a democracy. (Another 25 percent said that they "somewhat agreed" with this statement.) Indeed, the study submits that politics are far removed from the day-to-day concerns of most of Uzbekistan's citizens: only a third could name *any* political party in the country, even the ruling People's Democratic Party.[150]

Uzbekistan's propaganda apparatus credits the current leadership with a key role in restoring Uzbeks to a respected place in history. Much more so than the Soviet-style elections, this has probably paid significant political dividends. Broad segments of the Uzbek population are undoubtedly gratified by the government's policies in this area.

Even though the policies concerning participation may not foster legitimacy, they also do not appear to evoke mass dissatisfaction among Uzbekistan's population. Thus, for the foreseeable future, the greatest threat to the regime's legitimacy probably concerns distribution: if the government can produce a satisfactory level of perceived economic well-being, citizens may be quite willing to forego personal participation in the process. If not, the picture could radically change. This tendency is suggested in the above-cited USIA survey, in which 56 percent of the respondents either "strongly" or "somewhat" agreed with a statement that it was appropriate to limit political rights and freedoms in order to solve the country's economic problems.[151]

Though economic stability and progress appear critical for the regime's survival, it is much less clear whether Uzbekistan's leaders will come to favor privatization or other steps that decentralize economic decision-making. Even if undertaken to preserve the current regime, genuine privatization (and other forms of decentralization) seem likely to reduce the current political leaders' power, and could contribute to a deterioration of authoritarian culture.

If the Karimov regime discovers a path to economic growth without decentralizing economic decision making, it might be able to "buy off" popular demand for political change and thus maintain the current constellation of power relations. Even this scenario, however, would require that the leaders convince diverse geographical, class, and ethnic groups that they are also among the beneficiaries of the economic gains. In time, perhaps this scenario would also lead to a civil society and the emergence of democratic political institutions.

On the other hand, if basic economic demands are not met, the regime will not be able to preserve its legitimacy. In such case, it might be undermined and quietly go from the scene. Given the record to date, however, it seems much more likely that the leaders would attempt to maintain power through greater reliance on coercion.

Despite the current leadership's efforts, various processes may be contributing to authoritarian erosion. Perhaps the most important is the new opportunities for competing groups to accumulate economic wealth, and thus to make important economic (and ultimately political) decisions. Even though the Karimov leadership is attempting to hold the critical economic levers in its hands, its control is far from complete. Another process, related to the first, is that Uzbekistan engages in a much expanded volume of communication with the outside world. In the case of most citizens, this may only be the greater availability of usually unaffordable foreign consumer goods and entertainment; however, for a much smaller number of individuals (who are more important in terms of political leadership), this involves access to alternative sources of information, business contacts, and personal travel abroad. Moreover, a new generation is coming of age in Uzbekistan; thanks in part to the first two factors the attitudes of this cohort may dispose them to behave very differently from their parents.

On numerous occasions Karimov has justified his reluctance to discard elements of the Soviet political and economic systems with the logic that no new structures have been created to replace the old. As he put it in an interview in early 1993, "One should not destroy one's old house before building a new one."[152] Haste in destroying the old system does involve risks. But the same logic also serves as a perfect excuse for efforts to preserve the current political configuration, in particular the power of the president and his allies. To the extent that work on Uzbekistan's political house has begun, it does not appear to be a fundamentally new kind of structure. In fact, rather than construction of a new house, the activity has tell-tale signs of being more an effort to hammer boards of the old house back into place and cover them with a new coat of paint. This may indeed serve the leadership's aims for the immediate future. However, if democratic construction is to take place, the house owners will need to rethink the blueprints and will be obliged to plan for more doors through which competing interests will be able to enter and participate in Uzbekistan's politics.

Postscript

It is worth noting several developments in Uzbekistan that have occurred since the above analysis was written. One is President Islam Karimov's June

1996 departure from "his" political party, the PDP. Upon taking this action, Karimov justified his move, saying that only a non-partisan head of state could act as a genuine guarantor of the country's constitution and respect for human rights.[153] Just prior to this, the Uzbekistan government granted a prisoner amnesty which included the release of a number Erk activists, among them the brother of Muhammad Salih (Safar Bekjan).[154] Another set of political dissidents were released in accordance with an August amnesty. Fall 1996 brought new positive omens that greater rights might be accorded to independent political groups in Uzbekistan. Most notable were a Tashkent human rights conference sponsored by the Organization for Security and Cooperation in Europe and the return to Uzbekistan by Abdumannob Polatov for meetings of the Uzbekistan Human Rights Society.

Unfortunately, there is substantial evidence that although Uzbekistan has gone through the motions of democratic development in order to gain more favorable treatment from Western countries, it has not allowed or encouraged any substantial change. It hardly seems coincidental that the above-cited June developments immediately preceded Karimov's official visit to the United States. Moreover, it was during his stay in the US that Karimov extended the invitation to Polatov to return from several years of self-imposed exile.

Uzbekistan's press in the second half of 1996 shows no signs of relaxed controls. Moreover, Karimov continues to deal with his political opponents in a threatening fashion. In early November 1996, thugs kidnapped the son of former vice president Sh. Mirsaidov at gunpoint; several weeks later a court order threatened Mirsaidov and his sons with forcible eviction if they did not vacate their homes voluntarily within a week. These and other recent events do not inspire hope that the blueprints for Uzbekistan's new house have yet undergone any major alteration.

Acronyms

CPUz	Communist Party of Uzbekistan (Russian: Kommunisticheskaia partiia Uzbekistana)
IRP	Islamic Renaissance Party (Russian: Islamskaia partiia vozrozhdeniia)
DMU	Democratic Movement of Uzbekistan (Russian: Demokraticheskoe dvizhenie Uzbekistana)
PDP	People's Democratic Party (Uzbek: Khalq demokratik partiyasi)
PH	Progress of the Homeland (Uzbek: Vatan taraqqiyati)

NOTES

I would especially like to express my gratitude for comments provided by two important players in Uzbekistan's political life, Muhammad Salih and Abdumannob Polatov. Given their often adversarial roles in the events described here, it is not surprising that many of the changes suggested by one of these gentlemen contradicted those offered by the other. I have attempted to sort through conflicting accounts and reconstruct historical developments in an objective fashion. Naturally, this is a risky undertaking. I would also like to thank Professors Karen Dawisha, Bruce Parrott, and especially Muriel Atkin for their comments on an earlier draft of my manuscript. Of course, the interpretation in this chapter is my own and I take full responsibility for it.

1   Richard Lorenz, "Economic Bases of the Basmachi Movement in the Farghana Valley," in *Muslim Communities Reemerge*, ed. Edward Allworth (Durham, NC: Duke University Press, 1994), p. 289; Hélène Carrère d'Encausse, "Civil War and New Governments," in *Central Asia. A Century of Russian Rule*, ed. Edward Allworth (New York: Columbia University Press, 1967), pp. 224-8.
2   Donald Carlisle, "The Uzbek Power Elite: Politburo and Secretariat (1938-83)," *Central Asian Survey* 5, nos. 3-4 (1986), 91-132.
3   On the question of dividing territory and assigning nationality labels at the time of the national delimitation, see chapter 12 in Edward Allworth, *The Modern Uzbeks* (Stanford, CA: Hoover Institution Press, 1990).
4   *Statisticheskii komitet sodruzhestva nezavisimykh gosudarstv. Itogi Vsesoiuznoi perepisi naseleniia 1989 goda*, vol. 7, pt. 2 (Minneapolis: Eastview Publishers, 1993), pp. 192, 196, 198, 199.
5   Statistics provided to the author by the Uzbekistan Ministry of Education in summer 1992.
6   William K. Medlin, William M. Cave, and Finley Carpenter, *Education and Development in Central Asia* (Leiden: E. J. Brill, 1971), p. 115; and *Narodnoe khoziaistvo Uzbekskoi SSR 1990* (Tashkent: Uzbekistan, 1991), p. 118.
7   For a description of this process at work throughout the former USSR, see Gerhard Simon, *Nationalism and Policy Toward the Nationalities in the Soviet Union* (Boulder, CO: Westview, 1991), chapter 9. With regard to Uzbekistan, see Michael Rywkin, "Power and Ethnicity: Regional and District Staffing in Uzbekistan," *Central Asian Survey* 4, no. 1 (1985), 41-73, and "Cadre Competition in Uzbekistan: The Ethnic Aspect," *Central Asian Survey* 5, nos. 3-4 (1986), 183-94.
8   James Critchlow, "Prelude to Independence," in *Soviet Central Asia: The Failed Transformation*, ed. William Fierman (Boulder, CO: Westview, 1991), pp. 135-6.
9   Donald S. Carlisle, "Power and Politics in Soviet Uzbekistan," in ibid., p. 113.
10 For a discussion of these issues, see William Fierman, "*Glasnost'* in Practice: The Uzbek Experience," *Central Asian Survey* 8, no. 2 (1989). The analysis of political developments in the rest of this study focuses on Tashkent. This is not to imply that the rest of the republic is unimportant. Unfortunately, however, much less reliable information is available on it.

11   Aleksandr Verkhovskii, *Sredniaia Aziia i Kazkhstan. Politicheskii spektr* (Moscow: n.p., 1992), p. 33.

12   Abdumannob Polatov claims that although Salih was active in Birlik's embryonic stage and in the fall of 1989, in December 1988, Salih declared that he was a not a Birlik member, only a sympathizer (personal communication from Abdumannob Polatov).

13   Timur Kocaoglu, "Demonstrations by Uzbek Popular Front," *Report on the USSR* (28 April 1989), pp. 13–14.

14   Although some sources indicate that this meeting was much larger than the one held in March (Kocaoglu, "Demonstrations," p. 14), Abdumannob Polatov maintains that it attracted no more than 5,000 participants.

15   *Pravda Vostoka* (hereafter, *PV*), 11 December 1988.

16   *PV*, 15 December 1989. Despite this attack on Salih, it is a remarkable testimony to the relatively free press of the times that just a week afterwards, the literary weekly *Ozbekistan adabiyati va san"ati* published a favorable review of his poetry (23 December 1988), and in another two weeks Salih was permitted to publish a response to the December attack (*PV*, 7 January 1989).

17   *PV*, 6 May 1989. First Secretary Nishanov distinguished between "good" and "bad" groups in a speech given about a month before he would be replaced (*PV*, 20 May 1989).

18   *Kommunist Uzbekistana* (hereafter, *KU*), 4 October 1989.

19   *Ozbekistan adabiyati va san"ati* (hereafter, *Ozas*), 22 September 1989; *PV*, 1 December 1989.

20   *PV*, 24 October 1989.

21   Ibid., 24 October 1989.

22   Ibid., 26 October 1989.

23   Verkhovskii, *Sredniaia Aziia*, p. 38.

24   *Kuranty*, 23 November 1991.

25   *PV*, 10 December 1989.

26   For an example of an effort to discredit the techniques of DMU to gather people for a nomination meeting see *PV*, 1 December 1989. See also Vladimir Zolotukhin, "Democracy at a Crossroads," *Ogonek*, no. 3, 13-20 January 1990, pp. 7-8, translated in JPRS-UPA, 12 March 1990, p. 16.

27   *Moskovskie novosti*, 21 January 1990.

28   The statistics are cited by Verkhovskii, *Sredniaia Aziia*, p. 33; Abdumannob Polatov claims all of these candidates enjoyed official support.

29   *PV*, 11 February 1990. The decree noted that it was adopted in accordance with the Uzbek SSR Supreme Soviet resolution of 21 October.

30   *PV*, 18 February 1990.

31   Ibid., 22 February 1990.

32   See, for example, ibid., 23 February 1991.

33   *KU*, 24 February 1990. Tensions between the two wings of Birlik were apparent at a tumultuous November meeting that organizers hoped would reconcile the groups ("Nachalo: Kruglyi stol redaktsii," *Zvezda Vostoka*, no. 5 (1990), p. 76).

34   Personal communications from Birlik members.

35   *KU*, 30 March 1990.

36   Yaacov Ro'i, "Central Asian Riots and Disturbances, 1989-1990: Causes and Context," *Central Asian Survey* 10, no. 3 (1991), 37-8.

37   *PV*, 10 March 1990.
38   Personal communications from Birlik and Erk members.
39   In a recent interview with a correspondent of *Novoe russkoe slovo*, President Karimov was asked about the prospects for improving relations with the Uzbek opposition. Before describing alleged terrorist activities planned by Salih, Karimov told the correspondent, "Incidentally, if you should have an opportunity to communicate with 'Erk' leader Muhammad Salih, remind him that it was I who helped him in the creation of this party, and he cannot deny it. For him all the conditions were created for the normal functioning of the party; moreover, they were present in the parliament" (21–22 October 1995, p. 16).
40   For a report on cooperation, see US Commission on Security and Cooperation in Europe, *The Referendum on Independence and Presidential Election in Uzbekistan* (Washington, DC, 1992), p. 6.
41   Abdumanob Pulatov, "Uzbekistan posle vyborov prezidenta," *Novoe russkoe slovo*, 27 March 1992; "Nachalo: Kruglyi stol redaktsii," p. 74, *Ozas*, 1 June 1990. (In this citation and others the English transliteration of Mr. Pulatov's name differs from the version I have adopted.)
42   *Ozas*, 1 June 1990.
43   *Yash leninchi*, 5 May 1990.
44   US Commission on Security and Cooperation in Europe, *Human Rights and Democratization in the Newly Independent States of the Soviet Union* (Washington, DC, 1993), p. 211. In the spring of 1990, Birlik activist and Tashkent Conservatory professor Zahid Haqnazarov was granted permission to use a building as a studio which (certainly with the authorities' knowledge) served as a kind of headquarters for Birlik. Often parts or all of the building were not usable due to the poor state of repair, lack of electricity, etc. In any case, in the spring of 1991, Birlik was forced to relinquish these quarters (personal communication from Abdumannob Polatov).
45   By December 1990 the "sovereignization" already had extended to the CPUz, which adopted a new charter stressing its independence from the CPSU central apparatus (*PV*, 27 December 1990, in JPRS-UPA, 23 May 1991, pp. 42–53). According to Abdumannob Polatov, the first draft of Uzbekistan's declaration of sovereignty had been presented by Birlik already in October 1989.
46   *PV*, 18 July 1990.
47   *RFE/RL Daily Report*, 10 September 1990, p. 7.
48   Verkhovskii, *Sredniaia Aziia*, p. 35 and *Sovet Ozbekistani* (hereafter, *SOz*), 30 January 1991.
49   Verkhovskii, *Sredniaia Aziia*, p. 35.
50   *Kosomolets Tadzhikistana*, 21 November 1990.
51   *KU*, 23 February 1991. The creation of the presidential post in March 1990 and its subsequent enhancement would over time facilitate the process of anchoring Karimov's authority more firmly in the *state* (rather than party) structures.
52   As will be noted below in the context of consolidation of Karimov's rule, his rise had begun the return to power of the Samarkand-Jizzakh political axis.
53   *PV*, 11 January 1991, including reprint from *Izvestiia*, 7 January 1991.
54   *PV*, 26 February 1991. The vagueness of rules which could be used against public associations reflects the analogous All-Union law. Article 3 of that

document, for example, prohibits organizations which promote the inflaming of national and religious discord (*Pravda*, 16 October 1990, p. 3).

55   *PV*, 29 June 91, in Foreign Broadcast Information Service, *Daily Report: Central Eurasia* (hereafter *FBIS-USR*), 10 September 1991, p. 86.

56   Ibid., 2 July 1991, in *FBIS-USR*, pp. 91–6.

57   Bess Brown, "Tajik Civil War Prompts Crackdown in Uzbekistan," *RFE/RL Research Report*, 12 March 1993, p. 5 and Verkhovskii, *Sredniaia Aziia*, p. 37.

58   Verkhovskii, *Sredniaia Aziia*, p. 34.

59   Although no one in Birlik or Erk openly opposed independence, not all were enthusiastic about it. Abdurahim Polatov and his wing of Birlik had not pressed for greater immediate independence from Moscow, at least partly because they saw Russia's democrats and the press of Russia as allies in their struggle. Salih, however, had advocated sovereignty in the summer of 1990 and, he claims, won Karimov over in favor of the sovereignty declaration, thus securing its passage in the republic Supreme Soviet (personal communication).

60   *PV*, 4 October 1991 and *Nezavisimaia gazeta*, 16 January 1992. Perhaps Mirsaidov had used a trip he made to Moscow earlier in September to help gather support (Moscow Radio Rossii 8 September 1991, in Foreign Broadcast Information Service, *Daily Report: Central Eurasia* (hereafter *FBIS-SOV*), 10 September 1991, p. 101.

61   See, for example, *Izvestiia*, 14 September 1991; Moscow Radio Rossii 8 September 1991, in *FBIS-SOV*, 10 September 1991, p. 101; *PV*, 21 and 24 September 1991, 4 October 1991.

62   *Referendum*, p. 10.

63   Pulatov, "Uzbekistan posle vyborov."

64   Even members of the movement seem to have been confused about the party and popular movement. According to *PV*, some of the delegates to the congress thought they were coming to a meeting of the popular movement rather than a congress of the party. Co-chairman of the Birlik Movement, Abdurahim Polatov, was elected chairman of the Party (29 October 1991).

65   Interfax, 12 November 1991, in *FBIS-SOV*, 14 November 1991, p. 83.

66   Interfax, 25 November 1991, in *FBIS-SOV*, 26 November 1991, p. 90.

67   *Referendum*, pp. 8-10 and Pulatov, "Uzbekistan posle vyborov."

68   "To Presidential Candidates of the Republic of Uzbekistan I. A. Karimov and M. Salih," personal copy of letter dated 4 December 1991.

69   *Kuranty*, 23 November 1991.

70   Birlik was allowed, apparently without any interference, to participate in creating a small and very short-lived "Movement of Democratic Reforms of Uzbekistan." Perhaps as surprising as Birlik's participation in this undertaking was *Pravda Vostoka*'s upbeat reporting of the organizational committee meeting (*KU*, 21 September 1991, in *FBIS-USR*, 11 February 1992, p. 130; *PV*, 16 November 1991; Verkhovskii, *Sredniaia Aziia*, p. 35; and Abdumannob Pulatov, "Prezident i ego 'karmannye' partii," *Ekspress-khronika*, 30 June-6 July 1992, pp. 6-7).

71   *PV*, 16 November 1991.

72   The appeal was dated 28 November 1991, only five days after the publication of the election law in the press; however, the appeal was not published until 13 December. This was just a little more than two weeks before the elections scheduled for 29 December.

73 For the announcement of his nomination by Erk, see *PV*, 22 November 1991.
74 See, for example, *KU*, 3 December 1991.
75 *PV*, 18 September 1991.
76 Ibid., 14 December 1991.
77 *Izvestiia*, 18 September 1991, in *FBIS-SOV*, 25 September 1991, p. 90.
78 *Referendum*, pp. 9–11 and Bess Brown, "The Presidential Election in Uzbekistan," *RFE/RL Research Report*, 24 January 1992.
79 *Referendum*, p. 11.
80 Helsinki Watch, *Human Rights in Uzbekistan* (May 1993), p. 16.
81 *KU*, 16 November 1991. Abdumannob Polatov claims that Erk's newspaper appeared in weekly editions of 60,000 to 100,000.
82 Abdumannob Pulatov, "Prezident i ego 'karmannye' partii"; *Altin vadiy*, 9–10 June 1992; Mirza Ali Muhammadjanov, "Dehqanlar partiyasi," *Gulistan*, nos. 3–4 (1992), 26.
83 Abdumannob Pulatov, "Prezident i ego 'karmannye' partii" and Verkhovskii, *Sredniaia Aziia*, p. 36.
84 *Vatan*, 27 April–4 May 1994 and Verkhovskii, *Sredniaia Aziia*, p. 37.
85 *Human Rights in Uzbekistan*, p. 5.
86 The reports of size of membership of this organization vary greatly, with one source (Abdumannob Polatov "Prezident i ego 'karmannye' partii") claiming membership of over 15,000, and an *Izvestiia* correspondent claiming 2,500 (*Izvestiia*, 6 December 1991, in *FBIS-USR*, 24 December 1991, p. 101). See also Brown, "Tajik Civil War," p. 3.
87 Much of the description here is based on a personal communication from Abdumannob Polatov. For reports of the mosque seizure (somewhat at odds with Polatov's), see *PV*, 13 December 1991 and *Moskovskii komsomolets*, 30 July 1992.
88 *PV*, 3 December 1991.
89 *PV*, 10 December 1991 and *Referendum*, p. 7.
90 *Referendum*, p. 15.
91 *Moskovskie novosti* no. 4, 25 January–1 February 1992; *Moscow News*, no. 5, 2–9 February 1992, in *FBIS-USR*, 8 April 1992, pp. 85–86; Russian Television Network, 20 January 1992, in *FBIS-SOV*, 21 January 1992, p. 88. Abdumannob Polatov claims that some details of the reports of events published in Moscow are inaccurate.
92 *PV*, 9 January 1992.
93 TASS, 8 January 1992, in *FBIS-SOV*, 9 January 1992, p. 67; *Nezavisimaia gazeta*, 16 January 1992, in *FBIS-USR*, 18 February 1992, p. 118.
94 *Human Rights and Democratization*, p. 219.
95 *PV*, 14 April 1992. The resolution was a temporary measure until the law on public associations was formally amended in July (*PV*, 11 July 1992). This, presumably, provided the basis for authorities to confiscate Erk's bank account (Brown, "Tajik Civil War," p. 4).
96 Abdumannob Pulatov, "Prezident i ego 'karmannye' partii."
97 *Human Rights in Uzbekistan*, p. 41.
98 Personal observation. See also *Izvestiia*, 3 July 1992.

99 "Vybor po ubezhdeniiu," *Narod i demokratiia*, nos. 7–8, 1992, 27. In the same interview Salih indicated that it was possible and necessary to cooperate with "other political forces . . . in the interests of civil peace and a stable society."

100 *Nezavisimaia gazeta*, 22 August 1992, in *FBIS-USR*, 13 September 1992, p. 117.

101 "'Straightening Out the Brains of One Hundred': Discriminatory Political Dismissals in Uzbekistan," *Helsinki Watch* 5, no. 7 (April 1993), 2. At the same time, however, the regime consistently denied responsibility for any beatings. See, for example, *PV*, 18 July 1992.

102 Helsinki Watch, *Human Rights in Uzbekistan* (May 1993), p. 220.

103 *Nezavisimaia gazeta*, 22 August 1992, in *FBIS-USR*, 13 September 1992, p. 117. In an open letter Mirsaidov claimed that because he and other deputies were not allowed to speak out in opposition, there was "no sense in remaining a deputy any longer" (personal copy of Mirsaidov "Open Letter" dated 19 August 1992.)

104 Brown, "Tajik Civil War," pp. 4–5; *Moskovskie novosti*, 16 May 1993.

105 *Ozas*, 24 July 1992.

106 *Human Rights and Democratization*, p. 216.

107 Eric Johnson with Martha Olcott and Robert Horvitz, "The Media in Central Asia: Kazakhstan, Kyrgyzstan, Uzbekistan" (analysis conducted by Internews for AID) (April 1994), pp. 32–3.

108 Interfax, 22 December 1992, in *FBIS-SOV*, 23 December 92, p. 75.

109 *Tashkentskaia pravda*, 18 May 1993, in *FBIS-USR*, 21 July 1993, p. 93.

110 Interfax, 26 September 1994, in *FBIS-SOV*, 27 September 1994, p. 71.

111 *Human Rights and Democratization*, p. 216; Brown, "Tajik Civil War," p. 4; *Izvestiia*, 11 December 1992, in *FBIS-SOV*, 17 December 1992, pp. 59–60. By the time that Internews produced a study of Uzbekistan media in early 1994, the only newspapers from Russia regularly available in Uzbekistan at kiosks or by subscription were *Trud*, *Sovetskii sport*, and *Rabochaia tribuna* (Johnson, "The Media," p. 31).

112 *Human Rights in Uzbekistan*, p. 16.

113 Mirsaidov was amnestied, but forced to live in virtual house arrest.

114 Abdumannob Polat, "Uzbekistan: What Dialogue?" *Uncaptive Minds* (Fall–Winter 1994), 53–60.

115 *Komsomol'skaia pravda*, 8 September 1992.

116 *Human Rights in Uzbekistan*, p. 13; Brown, "Tajik Civil War," p. 4.

117 *Khalq sozi*, 29 December 1993.

118 *Human Rights and Democratization*, p. 218.

119 *Human Rights in Uzbekistan*, p. 24. For the announcement of the suspension, see *PV*, 23 January 1993.

120 "Political Prisoners in Uzbekistan: Five Pardoned, Eight on Trial. Statement of Abdumannob Polat," *Central Asia Monitor*, no. 6 (17 November 1994), 35. Uzbekistan's Ministry of Justice formally revoked Uzbekistan's registration on 12 November 1993. (I am grateful to Pauline Jones for providing the document with this information.)

121 See, for example, *Khalq sozi*, 29 December 1993 and 10 August 1994.

122 "Vybor po ubezhdeniiu," p. 26 and Brown, "The Presidential Election."

123 In the spring of 1992 a "Party of Social Progress" was reportedly being organized with an agenda of "political reform," including the separation of the legislative, executive, and judicial branches of government (*PV*, 19 May 1992).

A Workers' Communist Party was being organized late in the same year. A spokesman for this group said they did not consider themselves "opponents" of the PDP, but rather favored "constructive collaboration" with it. It claimed to be opposed primarily to "right wing bourgeois parties of an extreme nationalistic bent" and forces of extreme reaction primarily among the "Islamic fundamentalists" (*Glasnost* [Moscow], 19–25 November 1992, in *FBIS-SOV*, 27 January 93, pp. 114–15). Likewise, in July 1992, a party named *Ijtimayi taraqqiyat* appeared headed by historian Fayzulla Ishaqov (*Human Rights in Uzbekistan*, p. 5).

124 *Turkistan*, 26 January 1993; *Vatan*, 27 April–4 May 1994; Interfax, 26 September 1994, in *FBIS-SOV*, 27 September 1994, p. 71; *Segodnia*, 15 July 1994; *Human Rights and Democratization*, p. 220.

125 Uzbekistan Foreign Ministry Press Service, 15 March 1995, in *FBIS-SOV*, 17 March 1995, p. 82.

126 *Ozbekistan avazi* (hereafter, *Ozavaz*), 29 October 1994.

127 *Tashkentskaia pravda*, 15 May 1993, in *FBIS-USR*, 21 July 1993, p. 85; *PV*, 18 September 1993.

128 At least in Karimov's view, not all of the 250 members need to work as professionals. Rather, only a certain proportion needs to do this, while the rest of the members "should combine their previous work with parliamentary work" (Radio Tashkent, 23 February 1995, in *FBIS-SOV*, 24 February 1995, p. 66).

129 *Narodnoe slovo*, 5 October 1994, in *FBIS-SOV*, 14 October 1994, pp. 48–53.

130 Art. 20 of election law, *Ozavaz*, 12 November 1994.

131 For a description of the December 1994 Aliy Majlis elections in Uzbekistan, see *Project Activity Report: Republic of Uzbekistan Election of Deputies to the Oliy Majlis and Regional and Local Councils of Peoples' Deputies* [sic] (Washington: International Foundation for Electoral Systems, 1995). An analogous situation pertains to lower levels, where, for example, raion councils have the right to nominate candidates to oblast councils.

132 Interfax, 13 January 94, in *FBIS-SOV*, 14 January 1994, p. 88.

133 *Khalq sozi*, 30 December 1994.

134 *Ozavaz*, 17 December 1994.

135 *Khalq sozi*, 30 December 1994; Informatsionnyi tsentr po pravam cheloveka v Tsentral'noi Azii and Obshchestvo sodeistviia sobliudeniiu prav cheloveka v Tsentral'noi Azii, *Informatsionnyi biulleten'*, no. 1 (29) (January 1995), 3; *Ozavaz*, 1 March 1995, in *FBIS-SOV*, 6 March 1995, p. 90.

136 *Narodnoe slovo*, 24 February 1995, in *FBIS-SOV*, 7 March 1995, p. 82; Tashkent Radio Mashal, 24 February 1995, in *FBIS-SOV*, 27 February 1995, p. 79.

137 Tashkent Radio Mashal, 24 February 1995, in *FBIS-SOV*, 27 February 95, p. 79.

138 Mirsaidov claimed that his new party had 15,000 members (*Lidove Noviny* [Prague], 16 March 1995, in *FBIS-SOV*, 22 March 1995, p. 68). The party's goals are said to include democracy, freedom of the press, private enterprise, tax reform, and greater involvement in public life by religious leaders (Interfax, 18 January 1995, in *FBIS-SOV*, 19 January 1995, p. 48).

139 "The National Revival Democratic Party's Presidium," *Milliy tiklanish*, 10 June 1995, p. 1, in *FBIS-SOV*, 12 June 1995, pp. 85–6.

140 "Composition of the Central Council of the People's Unity Movement," *Birlik/Edinstvo*, 10 June 1995, p. 7, in *FBIS-SOV*, 12 June 1995, pp. 86–8.
141 Uzbekistan Foreign Ministry Press Service, 15 March 1995, in *FBIS-SOV*, 17 March 1995, p. 82.
142 *Rossiiskaia gazeta*, 18 January 1995, in *FBIS-SOV*, 20 January 1995, p. 59; *PV*, 13 December 1994.
143 Moscow Mayak Radio, 28 December 1993, in *FBIS-SOV*, 28 December 1993, p. 43.
144 It is worth emphasizing that the popular "Uzbek first" sentiment is probably no less offensive or threatening to local Muslim minorities than it is to Slavs, Armenians, Jews, or Koreans.
145 *Economist Intelligence Unit Country Report*, Fourth Quarter 1994, p. 70.
146 *Pravda Vostoka*, 18 March 1995.
147 Nancy Lubin, *Central Asians Take Stock: Reform, Corruption, and Identity* (Washington, DC: United States Institute of Peace, 1995), pp. 4–6. The political climate in Uzbekistan makes it impossible to view this survey and those cited below as precise measures of public opinion. The data are cited here as possibly supporting this chapter's hypotheses, not proof of their validity.
148 "Uzbekistanis Broadly Back Karimov" (Office of Research and Media Reaction, United States Information Agency, 27 December 1994).
149 Half of all respondents said they were willing to support "any system, as long as there is order" (Lubin, *Central Asians Take Stock*, p. 4).
150 "Uzbekistanis Broadly Back Karimov" and "In Uzbekistan, Checkered Views of Democracy," (Office of Research and Media Reaction, United States Information Agency, 15 June 1995).
151 "In Uzbekistan, Checkered Views of Democracy."
152 *Komsomol'skaia pravda*, 12 February 1993.
153 "Presidential Bulletin," Interfax in English, 21 June 1996, in *FBIS-SOV*, 26 June 1996, p. 56.
154 *OMRI Daily Digest*, 17 June 1996.

Appendix

Research guidelines for country-studies

Factors influencing the formation of political groups and parties

1. What are the key elements of the precommunist historical legacy of each country? Did the country have any precommunist experience of democracy, and have any elements of the postcommunist polity, such as particular government structures, intermediary associations, and political parties, been modeled on precommunist patterns?

2. What are the key elements of the legacy of the communist era? How has the political and social evolution of each country in the late communist era (e.g., the emergence or nonemergence of a significant dissent movement) affected the postcommunist formation of societal interest groups and parties?

3. How did the nature of the transition from communism (e.g., gradual versus abrupt; peaceful versus violent; internally – versus externally – precipitated) affect the formation of intermediary associations and parties in the early postcommunist period?

4. In the postcommunist selection of government leaders, what has been the importance of competitive elections and other forms of citizen political participation compared with threats of violence and the use of violence? Have military officers or the political police played a significant role in the selection process?

5. What political forces and calculations shaped the late-communist and especially the postcommunist electoral legislation and the timing of elections?

6. In brief, what are the main social and ethnic cleavages in postcommunist society?

7. In brief, what have been the pattern and pace of postcommunist economic change, and which social groups have been the winners and losers?

8. How has the presence or absence of violent conflict inside the country or with other states affected the inclination and ability of political parties or other organizations with political agendas to mobilize social groups in support of internal democratization?

The political evolution of society

9. Which types of political associations or actors have become most prominent in each country's political life? (For example, political parties, state sector managerial lobbies, trade unions, business organizations, professional associations, religious organizations, clans, paramilitary units, criminal groups, etc.) How has the public perception of political parties and what they claim to represent affected citizens' attitudes toward the political system? What is the relative importance of parties as vehicles for new elites intent on accumulating political power and wealth? What alternative vehicles have been used or preferred?

10. How have attempted marketization and privatization affected the political strength and behavior of business and managerial groups? Have labor groups formed or formally affiliated themselves with political parties, and what role have they assumed in the financing of elections and the control of the media?

11. How have attempted marketization and privatization affected the political strength and behavior of agricultural groups? Have these groups formed or formally affiliated themselves with political parties, and what role have they played in elections?

12. How have attempted marketization and privatization affected the political strength and behavior of organized industrial labor? Have labor unions sponsored or become affiliated with political parties? In their political programs and behavior (e.g., strikes), what is the relative importance of preserving democracy versus improving economic welfare?

13. What has been the political impact of organized criminal groups? Are associations or political parties linked with organized crime? How has the public perception of the role of organized crime affected citizens' attitudes toward the political system?

14. What do existing survey data show about the level of public support within the country for democratization? Do attitudes toward democratic governmental institutions, political compromise, participation in elections, and membership in

political parties and intermediary associations differ significantly between younger and older citizens? Do attitudes on these matters differ substantially between major ethnic groups? Similarly, are there significant attitudinal differences between men and women over democracy and the various forms of political participation? How has the performance of the postcommunist economy affected public attitudes toward democracy?

15. Have the media become a channel for the expression of a range of societal interests independent of the preferences of the government? How has control of the media affected the conduct of elections and other forms of political participation?

Political parties and the party system

16. How strong are the country's political parties and party system? Since the end of communism, has the country's party system been characterized only by the creation of ephemeral parties, or do patterns of leadership, electoral results, and survey data indicate that some stable parties have emerged?

17. How have the structure and durability of political parties been affected by the electoral law(s) and by laws – if any – on campaign finance? How have parties been affected by the timing of elections – including regional versus countrywide elections?

18. How have the cohesion and durability of political parties been affected by the structure of government – in particular, the existence of a parliamentary versus a presidential system, of a unitary versus a federal state, and the amount of discretionary power in the hands of a state bureaucracy independent of the top governmental authorities?

19. To what extent have the renamed communist parties actually changed (a) their attitudes toward liberal democracy (b) their political leadership, and (c) the interests that they represent? What role has been played by electoral competition in any changes that have occurred?

20. Apart from communist successor-parties, have anti-democratic parties or social movements based on clericalism, fascist traditions, or radical nationalism developed?

21. Among the major parties, what proportion consists of parties that are: a) disloyal or loyal to democratic procedures b) ethnically or religiously based c) based primarily in one geographic region d) willing to endorse political violence, and e) linked with paramilitary forces?

22. Has the party system facilitated or obstructed the creation of governments able to formulate and carry through reasonably coherent policies? How has the capacity of postcommunist regimes to formulate and implement policies affected citizen support of democratization and marketization processes?

Index

418   Index